WOMEN'S AMERICA

WOMEN'S AMERICA

Refocusing the Past

SECOND EDITION

EDITED BY

Linda K. Kerber
University of Iowa

Jane De Hart-Mathews
*University of North Carolina
at Chapel Hill*

New York   Oxford
OXFORD UNIVERSITY PRESS
1987

Oxford University Press

Oxford   New York   Toronto
Delhi   Bombay   Calcutta   Madras   Karachi
Petaling Jaya   Singapore   Hong Kong   Tokyo
Nairobi   Dar es Salaam   Cape Town
Melbourne   Auckland

and associated companies in
Beirut   Berlin   Ibadan   Nicosia

Published by Oxford University Press, Inc.,
200 Madison Avenue, New York, New York 10016

Oxford is a registered trademark of Oxford University Press

Library of Congress Cataloging-in-Publication Data

Women's America.

Bibliography: p.
Includes index.
1. Women—United States—History—Sources.
2. Women—Employment—United States—History—
Sources. 3. Women in politics—United States—
History—Sources. 4. Women—Health and hygiene—
United States—History—Sources. 5. Feminism—
United States—History—Sources. I. Kerber, Linda K.
II. De Hart-Mathews, Jane.
HQ1426.W663   1986   305.4'0973   86–12876
ISBN 0-19-504202-6 (alk. paper)
ISBN 0-19-504203-4 (pbk.: alk. paper)

Printing (last digit): 9 8 7 6 5 4 3 2 1

Printed in the United States of America
on acid-free paper

To our nieces
Carol Anne Coulter and Jane De Hart Coulter
Meredith Harper Epstein, Lauren Elizabeth Epstein,
Elyse Marin Kerber, Erica Beth Kerber

Acknowledgments

It is only five years since we prepared the first edition of *Women's America*, but in that time an extraordinary amount of new scholarship has appeared, changing the way in which professional historians address the major issues in the field and, indeed, redefining many of these issues. "What do you think you're doing, biochemistry?" complained a colleague recently when we pointed out that an article dated 1980 had been superseded by new work. The pace of scholarly development is so rapid that comparisons can appropriately be made to scientific fields, which are expected to change overnight, rather than to the leisured pace of traditional history. When we began our work on this revised edition we had not anticipated quite how extensive the newest scholarship would be, how much we would have to choose from, and how difficult would be our decisions on what to reprint. The new research is not only quantitatively extensive but qualitatively impressive.

Although the idea is rarely articulated, it seems to us that work in women's history has been kept vital by its connection with pressing matters of public policy and discourse. Underneath much investigation into the nature of women's work, the economic status of women, the ideologies by which women made sense out of their lives, lies a faith that those who understand history may not be doomed to repeat it; if we can solve some of the puzzles of what has been women's distinctive reality in the past, perhaps we will be in a better position to understand women's lives in our own time. The term *gender* as an analytical device, introduced into the discourse of historians by Joan Kelly in 1979, was available to us when this book went to press in 1981, but the possibilities of its use had only begun to be explored. In preparing this edition, we find historians even more willing than they had been to specify the distinctive experiences of men and women and to argue—either implicitly or explicitly—that changing relationships between the sexes are as important to understand as relations of class and of race. This principle has served not only as a torch guiding historians of women but also as a device that has had far-reaching consequences for "traditional" fields of history—social history, labor history, legal history, architectural history, even diplomatic history. It is a trend that we anticipate will continue in full vigor; by the end of the decade, we dare to predict, a history that does not take account of gender relationships, whatever its subject, will be felt by readers to be "old-fashioned."

One of the most rewarding aspects of working in women's history is sharing the extraordinary collegiality and mutual support provided by others working in this field. There is now a network of historians that spans generations and geographical distance, bonding together those who seek to recapture women's historical experience. We are beneficiaries of that network, and we are deeply grateful to many people who have generously shared their time, energy, and knowledge.

In preparing this second edition, we are particularly indebted to Martha Chamallas of the University of Iowa College of Law, who offered generous counsel on the legal documents. Helpful advice was offered by Catherine Clinton, Harvard University; Blanche Wiesen Cook, John Jay College of Criminal Justice; Andrew Federer, University of Iowa; Estelle Freedman, Stanford University; Jean Gordon, University of North Carolina at Greensboro; Susan Hartmann, Ohio State University; Mary Kelley, Dartmouth College; Theda Perdue, University of Georgia; Elisabeth Perry, Vanderbilt University; Barbara Bennett Peterson, University of Hawaii; Anne Firor Scott, Duke University; Barbara Sicherman, Trinity College; H. Shelton Stromquist, University of Iowa; and Judith Walkowitz, Rutgers—the State University.

We continue to be grateful to those who assisted us when the manuscript was in its formative stages: William Chafe, Duke University; Myra Dinnerstein, University of Arizona; Jacquelyn Dowd Hall, University of North Carolina at Chapel Hill; Gerda Lerner, University of Wisconsin; Donald G. Mathews, University of North Carolina at Chapel Hill; Julia Mears, University of Iowa; Dorothy Ross, University of Virginia; Joan Wallach Scott, Institute for Advanced Study, Princeton; and Virginia Yans, Douglass College, Rutgers—The State University.

Many colleagues have been kind enough to comment on the manuscript and on its usefulness for general readers. We are particularly grateful to Laura Becker, Clemson University; G. Cullom Davis, Sangamon State University; Michael D'Innocenzo, Hofstra University; Sylvia Frey, Newcomb College, Tulane University; Shirley Jackson, Boston College; Carmela A. Karnoutsos, Jersey City State College; and Ellen Widiss of Iowa City. As research assistants, Gary Eblen at the University of North Carolina at Greensboro; Harlan Gradin, Kristina Groover, and Barbara Ladd at the University of North Carolina at Chapel Hill; and JoAnn Castagna, Cynthia Hamilton, Jill Harsin, Kimberly James, David Manderscheid, Kathryn Penningroth, Jane Roules, and Roseanne Sizer at the University of Iowa have transformed what were routine chores into labors of love.

From the beginning of this enterprise Nancy Lane of Oxford University Press has played an important role. She encouraged us to write this book, and she monitored every stage of its development, blending patience and impatience in proper proportion. We feel ourselves extraordinarily fortunate to have worked with an editor whose commitment to excellence and whose personal friendship have enriched our lives. We are also deeply indebted to Ann Hofstra Grogg, who copyedited both editions with skill, shrewdness, and a clear sense of proportion. We can hardly imagine this complex book, which includes so many voices, without her orchestration.

Linda K. Kerber
May Brodbeck Professor
 in the Liberal Arts
Professor of History
University of Iowa

Jane De Hart-Mathews
Professor of History
 and American Studies
Director of Women's Studies
University of North Carolina
 at Chapel Hill

Contents

               Ritual: Relations between Women in Nineteenth-Century
               America, 167

(*Biology*)   James C. Mohr, Abortion in America, 190

(*Politics*)   Lois W. Banner, Elizabeth Cady Stanton: Early Marriage
               and Feminist Rebellion, 201

               Documents: Political Oratory, 213

               Sojourner Truth, "And a'n't I a woman?" 213

               Mary C. Vaughan, "We would act as well as endure," 215

               Susan B. Anthony, "Guaranteed to us and our daughters
               forever," 216

II B INDUSTRIALIZING AMERICA, 1880–1920

(*Economics*) Documents: Working for Wages, 226

               David M. Katzman, Seven Days a Week: Domestic
               Work, 226

               Elizabeth Beardsley Butler, Women and the Trades, 228

               Pauline Newman, The Triangle Shirtwaist Factory, 234

               Alice Kessler-Harris, Where Are the Organized Women
               Workers?, 237

(*Ideology*)   Documents: Struggling for Educational Opportunities, 254

               Zitkala-Ša, The School Days of an Indian Girl, 254

               Mary Antin, The School Days of an Immigrant Girl, 258

               M. Carey Thomas, "The passionate desire of women . . .
               for higher education," 263

               Mary McLeod Bethune, "How the Bethune-Cookman
               college campus started," 266

(*Politics*)   Documents: Reforming America, 269

               Florence Kelley, The Women at Hull House, 269

               Blanche Wiesen Cook, Female Support Networks and
               Political Activism: Lillian Wald, Crystal Eastman,
               Emma Goldman, 273

               Dolores Hayden, The Grand Domestic Revolution:
               The Feminist Paradise Palace, 294

               Anne F. Scott and Andrew M. Scott, One Half the People:
               The Fight for Woman Suffrage, 298

WOMEN'S AMERICA

Introduction

Fifty years ago the historian Mary Beard published an anthology called *America through Women's Eyes.* In it she argued that an accurate understanding of the past required women's experience to be analyzed with as much care as historians had normally devoted to the experience of men. Our perspective and our goals in this book are similar to hers.

From ancient Greece to our own day it has been easy for men to write about human experience from their own perspective. *Mankind* is the noun used as synonymous with humanity; women are the specific exceptions to the general experience. "When we speak of mankind," complained one historian, "we mean men and women collectively, but when we speak of womenkind, we mean the ladies, God bless them."[1] This is an easy habit, but it is a lazy one, and its effect is to distort our understanding of the past. It does not take into account the possibility that the characteristics of men and the characteristics of women may differ, or that the experiences of men and women may differ because their gender is different, even if they are of the same race, class, and ethnic group.

Two decades ago the historian David Potter offered a useful, commonsensical rule that echoed Mary Beard's work of a generation before. "When one meets with a social generalization it is frequently worthwhile to ask concretely: Does it apply to women, or only to the masculine component in the population?"[2] Historical phenomena, when viewed through women's eyes and evaluated for the impact they have had on women, often appear to be very different than when evaluated for their impact on men.

In the last fifteen years historians seeking to test old generalizations have refreshed and often changed our understanding of general trends in American history by what they have learned about women's history. Things we thought we "knew" about American history turn out to be more complex than we had suspected. For example, most textbooks suggest that the frontier meant opportunity for Americans, "a gate of escape from the bondage of the past." But it was men who more readily found on the frontier compensation for their hard work; many women found only drudgery. Other generalizations turn out to be equally suspect. We have often assumed that American slaves were provided with at least adequate diets, but the generalization holds better for male slaves than for pregnant women and nursing mothers who found that the slaves' diet meant semistarvation. Differences in experience often worked to women's disadvantage, but they did not always do so. In a success-oriented society, for example, men have been expected to meet the pressures of competition directly; women, however, have been in some measure shielded from these pressures. Upper-middle-class women, freed from the demands of the marketplace, could pursue their own private interests—in the arts, in philanthropy, in horticulture—at their leisure, for the benefit not only of themselves but also of society.

Whether the differences seem advantageous to one sex or the other, the point remains that to consider one sex while ignoring the other is like looking at an old family photograph in which the male members occupy the foreground as distinct figures, while the female members are an undifferentiated blur in the background. Women's history enables us to see the women in that photograph more clearly. It enables us to set women in the context of their distinctive past, deriving from their different biological, economic, and political situation. Women's history enlarges our vision. And with that wider sight, we can hope to readjust generalizations so that our understanding of the whole now takes into account experiences special to each sex.[3]

The final, authoritative history will never be written. We can only approach the reality of the past, constantly refocusing our vision and refining our understanding. "Probably every historian," observes a recent writer, "has at one time or the other day-dreamed about finding a lost trunk of letters which, when opened, would almost automatically revolutionize our historical understanding. What most of us did not know is that we have had that trunk in our intellectual attics for a long time and never thought to look inside. Women's historians, having pried open the lid, invite us now to think in new terms, leading to a new perspective and therefore to a new past."[4]

This anthology will introduce you to that trunk of materials and to the interpretations historians have been making of what they have found there. Like all anthologists, we are enthusiasts. We reprint here essays and documents that we have enjoyed reading and rereading. We think they deserve a wider audience.

Perhaps the most striking conclusion forced upon us by these materials is that public experience and private experience cannot be sharply separated. For example, instead of being at opposite poles, one private and the other public, the home and factory have strongly interacted in the American economic system. In the early stages of industrialization women working in their homes sold carded wool that was spun by factory machinery. As the consumer society developed, women, as part of their role as homemakers, became the chief buyers of manufactured goods. As mothers they have long inculcated in their children those traits of obedience, honesty, and industry that employers expect of their workers. Private activities that women engaged in for their families in their homes had— and continue to have—significant public implications.

Women's history suggests a more complex understanding of traditional categories of historical interpretation. Conventional periodization has used presidential administrations or wars as major guideposts in organizing our description of the past: the Revolutionary Era, the Age of Jackson, the Civil War, the Eisenhower Years. Conventional interpretations have tended to emphasize the accomplishments of men, whether they be presidents, generals, farmers, or ranch hands. But all men had women for contemporaries, and women experienced the same great social phenomena that men did. Certainly women felt the terrible trauma of war. Even in periods when they did not vote, women were citizens who offered allegiance to government and were affected by its policies. If men and women both felt the force of social change, each did so in distinctive ways. Thus, in trying to include most of the major traditional themes of American history from colonial times to the present, we have also tried to show the distinctiveness of their impact on women and the distinctiveness of women's response to them.

This book is divided into three major chronological sections. Because dates that mark major turning points in traditional historical accounts do not automatically coincide with those dates that mark significant changes in the lives of American women, women's history challenges us to reexamine conventional periodization. Our sections are generally congruent with familiar periodization; they also reflect changing realities in women's experience. The dividing date between traditional and industrial America is 1820, by which time forces were in motion that would erode the domestic economy of an agrarian society, slowly transforming women's lives in the process. The long period of industrialization that followed 1820 may conveniently be broken at 1880, by which time large-scale industries in which women were employed were firmly established. By this time, too, women's rights leaders had come to recognize that suffrage would not be granted by the courts on the basis of a fresh interpretation of the Constitution, and they demanded a specific constitutional amendment. The second major period ends at 1920, when the necessary ingredients for emancipation were present. The historian Gerda Lerner has identified these as "urbanization; industrialization with technology permitting society to remove food preparation and care of the sick from the home; the mechanization of heating and laundry;

spread of health and medical care sufficient to lower infant mortality and protect maternal health; birth control; . . . and availability of education on all levels to all children."[5] These conditions existed in varying measure by 1920, which was also the year of the passage of the Equal Suffrage Amendment, the first year in which women attended large state universities in numbers comparable to men, and the first year in which more women were working in factories and white-collar jobs than in domestic service.

The study of women's history not only challenges us to reconsider conventional periodization but it also changes traditional history by emphasizing the interrelationship among fields that have often been treated separately. To look at the past through women's eyes is to see the complex interaction of biology (reproduction), economics, politics, and ideology. These essential categories appear and reappear throughout the book. Taken by themselves they are simple divisions that capture part of women's historical experience. Taken as parts of an interacting whole, these categories underscore the peculiarity of women's experience. The key to the interaction is the way in which biology affects the other three categories. An example of this interaction can help explain what this book is about. The mistress of a plantation in pre–Civil War South Carolina could not vote; her dependent political status was dictated by her dependent economic status, which in turn was dictated by law and custom (ideology). She had no property of her own; whatever she had received from inheritance had been vested in her husband when she married. The *economic* facts of her position could have been that she had brought more wealth to the marriage than had her husband; the *political* facts were that only her husband could manage her property and participate in the community by voting and holding office—these were facts that changed the economic "facts" of life for her. The reason for one set of facts altering another set of facts was rooted in biology and the ideological explanation that accompanied the undeniable fact that women gave birth. The economic and political implications of this biological fact need not have dictated women's political role—this we know from the passage of married women's property acts and the Equal Suffrage Amendment (1920). In the nineteenth century, however, the role of women was defined by the ideological expectation that all women bear and care for children; if some did not, they were deviant. Our plantation mistress could best understand herself—in terms of the prevailing ideology—as appropriately deferential to her husband while strict and demanding to her slaves, nurturing and caring to her children. These were the attitudes assigned to her by her "place" in society and that, expressed as the ideology of "true womanhood" (discussed below), celebrated the economic and political dependence of women not because biology actually dictated such dependence but because most people *believed* that it did. Biology, economics, politics, and ideology combined to describe reality. Historical reality, however, is characterized by change. Our antebellum lady's granddaughters would find their reality to be different from hers; changes in each of the four categories would make their world different. Because the complex interaction of these four categories over time is so crucial to understanding women's differing historical experience, each merits fuller discussion.

BIOLOGY

Exploring the past through women, we become aware that history embraces the private sphere of reproduction and domesticity as well as the public sphere of battlefield, court, and legislature. Indeed, changing patterns of reproduction are the key to understanding women's experience; during most of human history, anatomy has been destiny. Without reliable methods of contraception women spent their entire adult lives bearing, rearing, and often burying children, undergoing pregnancy as often as every two years until finally liberated by menopause. So fundamentally has biology defined the stages of women's lives that historians increasingly use the concept of the life cycle—a concept that makes it possible to analyze female behavior by separating women into age and marital groupings (daughters, single women, wives, mothers, grandmothers, widows). Although these stages of the cycle remain constant, the number of years women have spent in each stage has shifted. For example, while women have tended to marry around the age of twenty throughout most of American history, the child-bearing stage of life has changed dramatically. Quaker women in the eighteenth century who could expect to bear children regularly until nearly forty contrast sharply to their mid-twentieth-century counterparts who completed their families by the age of thirty. Since women in the 1950s could expect to live much longer than their colonial forebears and to devote less time to the care of small children, they enjoyed a vastly wider range of choices and were freed, if they chose, to move out of the domestic sphere. Changing degrees of biological constraints have made women's lives—and therefore their history—significantly different from those of men.

Biological differences have also contributed to different assumptions about sexuality. Women have traditionally been regarded as sexual beings. Reference to woman as Eve, the temptress, can be found in much of Western literature. During the nineteenth century, however, assumptions about female sexuality shifted drastically. "Respectable" women came to be seen as passionless creatures whose duty it was to repel the advances of men (who were thought to be more highly sexed by nature) until wifely duty required their submission in the marriage bed. Some historians argue that the Victorian Lady's effort to deny her husband his conjugal "rights" should be seen as an effort to improve women's lot at a time when periodic or even permanent abstinence was often the only reliable form of birth control.[6] (Periodic abstinence in the form of the rhythm method was not effective as a birth control measure in the nineteenth century; only in the 1920s was the ovulation cycle correctly understood and plotted.) Not until the twentieth century and the widespread use of dependable contraceptive devices such as the diaphragm were most Americans able to separate sex from reproduction, to recognize that sexual relations are a valuable and pleasurable part of life for both men and women, and to acknowledge the full dimensions of female sexuality. As historians examine the sermons, marriage manuals, and other writings that told how women were *supposed* to behave and those records that offer evidence as to how they *actually did behave*, we are fast discovering that sexuality has its own history. In that history, too, gender has made a difference.

ECONOMICS

DOMESTIC ECONOMY

To view work through women's eyes provides a new appreciation of the economic function of the home. Homes were—and to an appreciable extent still are—restaurants, nurseries, schools, hospitals, and lodging places. The colonial housewife, for example, was expected not merely to prepare and serve meals but to provide much of the food she brought to the table. The curing of meat and the pickling and preserving of vegetables and fruits were her responsibility, as were the garden, dairy, and poultry yard. Clothing the family was another of her tasks. In the northern colonies and on the frontier this meant not only cutting and sewing various garments but also spinning the thread and weaving and dyeing the cloth that went into clothes, household linens, and quilts. Rag rugs, too, were of her making. While more affluent households might include servants to lighten the physical burdens of the mistress of the house, she had to oversee their training and work, often exercising in the process considerable managerial skills of her own. Wives of poorer men lived simply, but they, too, were responsible for feeding and clothing their families and—in the case of illness, childbirth, or death—for serving as nurse, pharmacist, midwife, and undertaker who dressed the body for burial.

As the nation developed, women in cities were gradually relieved of some of these tasks. Even in the twentieth century, however, women in rural areas were expected to do arduous household chores, preserve many dozen quarts of food, and also take their turn in the fields as necessity dictated. Because their homes lacked the plumbing and electricity required for use of an electric washing machine, women in 90 percent of the rural households in the United States were still doing laundry by hand as late as 1930. In the tobacco-growing country of the Carolinas and Virginia young girls not only learned household skills but they, along with their brothers, were taught the basics of crop production: how to drop tobacco plants into carefully prepared soil; how to remove worms from the growing plants; how to bind harvested tobacco leaves for curing; and, afterwards, how to tie them into bundles for the trip to market. Although it was usually the man in the family who took the fruits of the harvest to market, whatever the crop, many a prudent farmwife in the eighteenth century as well as the twentieth gathered up her surplus eggs or other foodstuffs to sell or barter. The domestic economy blended unobtrusively into the market economy.

This subtle blending occurred in other ways as well. In hard times women, especially young unmarried daughters, sold their labor, using their pay to sustain the household. Domestic service attracted many women because it involved traditional women's work and, for live-in servants, room and board as well as wages. Those seeking jobs in towns and cities enjoyed a wider range of options: work in a shop often seemed to offer greater independence and dignity. Census takers and many historians perceived these women to be part of the public market economy because they were working for wages. But the women usually thought of themselves as serving the domestic economy. Most regarded wage work as a temporary necessity undertaken in order to help their families in a time of financial stress.

The change in the status of women's work from that of belonging to the family to that of belonging to women themselves was a significant step in their emancipation. Because of economic necessity the change is not yet complete, even in advanced industrialized countries such as the United States. Emancipation is not achieved until the work itself is seen as liberating or until women can spend their income as they wish. It was not until the middle of the nineteenth century that the earnings of a married woman were hers to dispose of as she chose. Although in reality many women did indeed regard their "egg money" as their own, English tradition and colonial practice dictated that when a woman married, control of her earnings automatically passed to her husband. Indeed, all that had been hers was at the wedding transferred to him. Except for certain technical exceptions utilized by the wealthy, everything a woman owned at the time of her marriage and anything she might earn or inherit in the future were her husband's to dispose of as he saw fit, even on the draw of a card or a throw of the dice. The desire of married women to retain or gain control over property that would have been theirs had they been men was an important force in sustaining women's struggle for political rights in the nineteenth century.

MARKET ECONOMY

The location of white women's work in early America was predominantly in the home, as was the case in most preindustrial, rural societies. But even in the colonial period there were many women whose work was performed directly for the market, most notably slave women, who worked on crops destined for sale. Indeed, black women's work has always been part of the market economy in America. For white northern women, however, the pre–Civil War process of industrialization did much to transform work. The spinning of thread, weaving of cloth, sewing of clothes, preserving of foods—all tasks formerly done in the homes as part of a domestic economy—were now done in mills and factories as part of the market economy. Poorer women followed these traditional tasks into the public sector as the economy modernized. They became part of a paid labor force, as did their children, since low wages made it impossible for many families to subsist on the income of one adult worker. Yet, surprisingly, women's work patterns changed less than we once assumed. Work in the public sector, as in the private sector, continued to conform in large measure to family pressure and to traditional role expectations about what women could and should do, to the great financial detriment of women wage earners.

The extent to which female employment patterns in industry were shaped by family needs is apparent in a study of a New England textile factory that employed an average of fourteen thousand workers in the years before World War I. Women were very much a part of that work force. As young girls, they went into the mill to supplement family income, often allowing brothers to improve their job prospects by staying in school; as wives, they withdrew when children were born and returned as mothers of small children when the perilous state of family finances required them to do so; as mothers of grown children, they returned to stay.[7] Thus family responsibilities were a crucial factor not only in determining at what stage in their life cycle women were gainfully employed but also in explaining why their employment patterns differed from those of male workers. (Indeed, it was not until after World War II that the number of working mothers with small children increased dramatically.)

Family responsibilities did much to determine *when* women worked; they also affected *where* women worked. Since employers shared the popular belief that women's primary obligations were familial and their basic talents domestic, female wage earners were persistently channeled into jobs that corresponded with the kind of work done in the domestic sphere or with characteristics long associated with women. Even in colonial times most women who performed services for pay worked as housekeepers, cooks, nurses, or widwives. In the nineteenth century women seeking new avenues through which to gain economic independence laid claim to the teaching and nursing professions by emphasizing that the attributes required for such work were precisely those considered unique to the female sex. Thus nursing, considered in pre–Civil War years an occupation no respectable woman would enter, was eventually touted as a profession eminently suited to women. Providence, after all, had endowed the fairer sex with that "compassion which penetrate[s] the heart, that instinct which divines and anticipates the wants of the sick, and the patience which pliantly bends to all their caprices."[8] As the economy grew more complex, middle-class women infiltrated the ranks of librarians and secretaries. These occupations had been primarily male, but, like teaching and nursing, were redefined so as to emphasize the nurturing, service-oriented qualities ascribed to women—with a corresponding decrease in pay. Newer industries provided new job titles but old work categories. Receptionists, social workers, and stewardesses were hired by employers still convinced that the tasks required in these jobs were consistent with the attributes and skills traditionally associated with women. Because gender rather than individual talent or capability has been the primary consideration, the result of this kind of stereotyping has been to segregate women into certain kinds of work, whether in the professions or in industry. Occupations and professions that for one generation constituted a lifeline have become a chain to the next; once a form of work has been defined as female, it has invariably become associated with low pay and minimal prestige. Pay and prestige have been reserved for those professions remaining overwhelmingly male. It is not surprising that until very recently women in significant numbers have been effectively barred from wielding scalpels, addressing juries, passing laws, or designing buildings.

Working-class women, especially, have been victims of discrimination. Low pay, long hours, and difficult—often dangerous—working conditions have characterized industrial work for both male and female employees during much of our history. Southern mills, where discrimination was based on race as well as sex, afford a classic example of occupational segregation and the inferior position of white and particularly black women. In a typical southern textile mill in the 1930s management positions were reserved for college-educated white males. Men from working-class backgrounds monopolized supervisory and skilled positions. Semiskilled operative positions were divided among white men and women, with men predominating in better-paying jobs in the card room and dye houses. Women predictably took their place in the spinning and sewing rooms. Black men and women divided the manual labor. Opportunities to work up to a better position were confined to a few white males. For factory and mill women, already bearing the brunt of housework and child care, wage labor frequently meant—and still means—insecure employment in hazardous, low-paying, dead-end jobs.

While unionization enabled many working men to better their lot, it has not provided the same benefit for women. Male members, fearing women would work for lower pay and threaten their jobs, often barred women workers from union membership during the early years of organizing. Even in unions that included women, labor leaders sought only limited economic gains for female workers. They, too, thought of the public economy as an essentially male preserve, and they failed to confront the problem of occupational segregation. The basic inequities built into the system have gone unchallenged until very recently, when pressure from the federal government has helped to produce changes.

Thus segregated into jobs associated with low status and low pay, denied equal pay for equal work, burdened doubly as the parent primarily responsible for home and child care, women have experienced work in the public sector differently from men. Viewed through women's eyes, work in the public sector is different. While it has given women a small measure of economic independence, it has not provided the monetary rewards and the avenues to power and autonomy open to some men. The history of women's participation in the labor force is, therefore, a history of marginality.

POLITICS

Most Americans, for much of their history, were convinced that God and nature had decreed that the two sexes inhabit different spheres and have different roles. Men's roles were public and political, women's domestic. Men's activities were defined as distinct from women's activities even when goals were shared, the place of work the same, and the physical effort equally taxing (as John Mack Faragher shows in his description of work on a family farm). To be sure, such distinctions might be temporarily suspended in emergency situations. Women worked together with men in the fields to harvest hay before the crop was destroyed by rain; they worked to replace men in factories, on railroads, and at construction sites during World Wars I and II. When the emergency subsided, however, conventional patterns again prevailed. Given the tenacity of these assumptions about separate roles and spheres, it is not surprising that women seeking to enter the public world were inhibited by a formidable set of expectations about where men and women belonged and how they should behave.

In Anglo-American tradition the right to participate in political activities— jury duty, officeholding, voting—was conditioned on the holding of property. Since married women could not direct the use of their property, it seemed to follow that they could be neither jurors, nor voters, nor officeholders. That politics was considered a male domain, that women were simply not political beings, is an understanding as old as Western civilization. Aristotle, whose classic work provided the basic terms by which Westerners have understood politics, said that men alone realized themselves as citizens. It is no accident that the civic *virtue* he extolled derives from the same root as the word *virile*. Women, Aristotle maintained, realized themselves only within the confines of the household. Their relationship to the world of politics, like their social status, was derivative—through fathers, husbands, and sons.

Colonists brought this understanding with them to the New World. Even the Revolution, in the course of which the relationship of men to the state was radically redefined, did little to reorient the relationship of women to the state. It was left for women of the post-Revolutionary generations to reassess the promise of republicanism and to devise political strategies by which they would demand full inclusion in the republic.

The political history of American women has been out of phase with that of American men. In the early nineteenth century propertyless white men were successful in demanding the vote; following the Civil War black men were enfranchised. After 1880 one of the major political challenges facing men was to mobilize successful coalitions in support of particular candidates and programs. The political tasks that women faced after 1880, however, remained those that men had already accomplished; women still needed to move from petitioners to voters to electable candidates. Only recently have women in increasing numbers begun to run for office and to mobilize political coalitions in support of candidates and programs. Thus the political experience of men and women in America has diverged widely.

The political activities of American women have generally fallen into two categories. The first might be called the Politics of Inclusion. It involves all efforts to become part of the political system: suffrage, jury service, officeholding, and the shaping of policies and statutes. A major goal of the Politics of Inclusion has been and still is to secure equal treatment under the law, to change the many statutes that treat men and women differently. Not until 1975, for example, did the Supreme Court require that women be assigned to juries on the same terms as men.

The second category might be called the Politics of Reform. It proposes to achieve a more just and orderly society. Among these goals have been the abolition of slavery, protective legislation for women workers, and racial justice. Also involved have been radical attempts to restructure society along various socialist lines.

Women gave their loyalty sometimes to the Politics of Inclusion, sometimes to the Politics of Reform, sometimes to both. For example, Carrie Chapman Catt, who was president of the National American Woman Suffrage Association from 1914 to 1920, placed inclusionary politics first on her own agenda; only after suffrage was achieved did she work primarily in the peace movement. On the other hand, Emma Goldman distrusted the system so much that she felt the vote was inconsequential for the reformed society of which she dreamed. An example of someone who combined the Politics of Reform with the Politics of Inclusion was the temperance advocate Frances Willard, who supported suffrage as a vehicle by which the social reform she was primarily committed to might be achieved.

A distinctive feature of women's reformist politics has been the way in which women have made their *domestic* experience into a *public* issue and, through this transformation, enhanced both their domestic and public roles. Sometimes women justified moving into the political arena by arguing that public involvement would permit them to fulfill their domestic responsibilities more competently. Jane Addams made this appeal when she argued that women should have the vote so that they could elect city officials who would see to it that rotting garbage was removed from homes, decaying meat taken out of markets, and polluted water purified; otherwise, the best efforts of mothers to assure their children clean homes and wholesome food were to no avail. Other women supported the Sheppard-Towner Maternity Act of 1921 on the grounds that women had a special interest in maternal health and infant care. In these and similar cases women worked in the public sphere to protect and improve the domestic one. But once they moved into the public life of politics, no matter how much they justified their presence there in traditionalist terms—arguing that they were acting only as partisans of domestic virtue, health, and safety—the fact of the matter was that they had done something quite untraditional.

Women who crusaded for legislation to prohibit the manufacture and sale of alcoholic beverages were a case in point. The women themselves may have *said* in traditionalist phrases that their only concern was with home and children— homes destroyed and children abused by alcoholic fathers—but what they *did* on behalf of liquor-free homes involved public speeches, parades, demonstrations, and even lobbying of public officials. These actions were certainly not traditionalist—at least not for women in the nineteenth century. Nevertheless, traditionalist words, when added to the innovation of widespread and effective political action, were part of a process. Changes within this process were not always anticipated but came as women in the nineteenth century created for themselves a public life not necessarily at odds with domestic life but as an extension of it. By looking at reformist crusades as an opportunity for women to establish a public role, we begin to understand that, whether or not their goals were feminist, the process itself was a liberating one.

IDEOLOGY

Finally, to examine the past with a new sensitivity to women's experience is to discover how profoundly women's lives have been shaped by ideologies that have developed out of their distinctive biological, economic, and political histories. Implicit in the concept of ideology is the emphasis on the fact that ideas are cradled in social experience and, when used to explain that experience, form interworking networks of meaning that have a compelling attractiveness to those who believe them. The word *ideology* can be used in a negative way—to convey the idea that ideologies distort reality—or in a neutral way. We use it in a neutral way, in part because we do not believe that ideas based upon social experience and explaining that experience *necessarily* distort reality. (Historical "reality" is itself often a matter of social consciousness, i.e., defined by the groups explaining it.) Thus by ideology we mean the terms and assumptions by which Americans think about women, the notions they have about what is appropriate demeanor for women, and the ideas they have about the kind of roles it is normal for women to assume and the kind of goals they should have for their lives.[9]

For example, since the early nineteenth century one of the most pervasive ideologies has been what one historian has called the "Cult of True Womanhood," which extolled the virtues of piety, sexual purity, submissiveness, and domesticity. In the sermons they heard and the books they read, women were instructed to internalize these virtues and to dedicate themselves to the private sphere, nurturing and serving their families and transforming their homes into a "Haven in a Heartless World."[10] "Woman's sphere," declared a newspaper in 1850, "is about the domestic altar and within the tranquil precincts of the social circle. When she transgresses that sphere and mingles in the miserable brawlings and insane agitations of the day, she descends from her lofty elevation and becomes an object of disgust and contempt."[11]

Educational theory and practice reflected and perpetuated many of these same assumptions about women's nature, capacities, and proper place. The belief that women's brains and nervous systems simply were not capable of the sustained intellectual effort expected of men and, more important, that women's place was in the home led to the founding of special female academies that emphasized religion and the domestic arts rather than the classical training provided for young men. Too much study of Greek, Latin, philosophy, and logic, it was feared, might make young females unfit for their primary role as wives and mothers. Given women's inferior mental capacity and their delicate emotional system, intense intellectual debate was also considered inappropriate. School texts often disseminated ideas about correct attitudes and proper demeanor.

Dress, too, reflected ideology insofar as it mirrored what people believe themselves to be and what they wanted others to believe them to be. In the nineteenth century, when women of affluence were expected to be both home centered and leisured, their clothing announced that expectation. They wore boned, tightly laced corsets, which inhibited breathing, and hoops or multiple layers of long, heavy petticoats, which made vigorous walking difficult. Fashion seemed to conspire to keep the lady hobbled to her home—to the dismay of radicals who believed that an uncorseted, loose, shorter dress supplemented by bloomers rather than petticoats would improve women's physical and emotional health by making it easier for them to exercise and to move about more freely in the public world.

An ideology that sought to impose on all women a pattern of life only marginally appropriate for middle-class women could also serve to insulate women from a clear understanding of political and economic relationships. Social divisions made it difficult for women to perceive the subordination they shared. The shopkeeper's wife whose divorce from an alcoholic husband deprived her of custody of her children might underpay the immigrant seamstress who made her clothes. Women's perception of themselves as an oppressed group was further masked by the fact that, unlike other minority groups, they lived on intimate terms with their oppressors, deriving their status from fathers and husbands and, in the case of the more fortunate, benefiting from social and economic advantages that distinguished them from other women. (The respect and privileges accorded a married woman often depended—and in some respects still do—on the position of her husband in the community, not on her own accomplishments.) So completely did many women internalize conventional wisdom about women's proper place that they rejected any attempt to change it.

Women did, however, devise methods of coping with the more constraining aspects of their culture. They struggled to gain some measure of reproductive control not only through abstinence from sexual intercourse but also through widespread use of dangerous abortive devices. They subverted legal constraints on their economic independence by recourse to trusteeships and premarital contracts to protect their own property. They sought and found solace and emotional sustenance in the churches, which welcomed them as communicants, offered them the companionship of fellow believers, and lauded their piety. Indeed, women were considered by nature to be more pious than men, a belief that women could exploit to enlarge their sphere of public activity. Religion, for example, confirmed a sense of mission that found expression in the church-related but increasingly secular female reform societies so prevalent in the nineteenth century—organizations such as the Female Missionary Society for the Poor of the City of New York. Out of common needs, experiences, and associations women created what might be called a female culture, characterized by strong affectionate ties among women of the same class and family networks. Although historians have only begun to explore this subculture, the essay by Carroll Smith-Rosenberg is an important introduction to this "female world of love and ritual." Moreover, as women began moving beyond the home, they brought with them these strong emotional ties to other women, thus creating female networks. These networks provided crucial encouragement and support for individuals whose public activities made them out of step with conventional society, whether in battle on behalf of birth control or against "demon rum" or child labor.

While ideology is reflected in newspapers, books, sermons, and even dress, the real test of its power is how we live our lives, what options we believe are open to us, and what choices we make. For poorer women who could not financially afford to devote themselves exclusively to the domestic sphere and the rearing of their children, the Cult of True Womanhood bore little resemblance to the reality of their everyday lives. For many middle-class women who could afford financially *and* emotionally to live their lives in accordance with these ideological dictates, prescription and practice were one. For some women, however, the emotional cost was too high because the constraints seemed too great. Inherent in the nineteenth-century Cult of True Womanhood and in its twentieth-century counterpart, the Feminine Mystique, is the premise that women's lives are determined by their biology and by the gratification that they might find in self-abnegating service to others rather than in the more abstract exercise of the mind or the pursuit of a career in a traditionally male profession. While these beliefs have served in varying measure to limit all women, they have proved particularly burdensome to those individuals endowed with special talents or creativity that they sought to develop fully.

Women who wished to be artists or intellectuals have encountered difficulties not usually experienced by men of equal talent. They discovered that they lived in a society which assumed that women's family obligations must take precedence over all other activities. As late as 1935 Margaret Mead, whose own career in anthropology was one of great productivity and distinction, observed wryly that a woman might identify herself as "a woman and therefore less an achieving individual, or an achieving individual and therefore less a woman." If she chose the first option, the one presumably consistent with her biological destiny, she was more likely to be "a loved object, the kind of girl whom men will woo and boast of, toast and marry." If she opted for the second, however, she lost "as a woman, her chance for the kind of love she wants."[12] The ideological message delivered was quite clear. Although it is impossible to measure precisely how such messages affected behavior, there are various indications suggesting that they did indeed affect women's perceptions of the options open to them.

CHALLENGES TO PREVAILING VIEWS

We also know that women who challenged the piety, submissiveness, and sexual purity associated with "true womanhood" were punished. Women in Puritan

Massachusetts could, as Anne Hutchinson learned, be privately pious but not publicly prophetic. While Hutchinson's remarkable personality attracted to her cause men as well as women who believed in her religious vision, she suffered banishment. In nineteenth-century America women whose sexuality was celebrated, like those in the Oneida community, or whose marital patterns were unusual, like those among the Mormons, were able to withstand social disapproval of their deviance only by living in relatively isolated communities. Even those women who assumed for themselves moral responsibilities which were the logical extension of women's piety found that, if they pursued those responsibilities with greater independence and public activism than society deemed appropriate, they, too, could be condemned as unwomanly. Accordingly, southern ladies who openly agitated against lynching in the early twentieth century discovered that one could be opposed to legal violence in theory but not in practice. The much-vaunted protection that the South bestowed upon the fairer sex existed only so long as the ladies obeyed the "rules." To deviate from the norm was to be labeled unfeminine. "Tomboys" might be acceptable; "mannish" women were not. The accusation of "mannishness" was tinged with intimations of being "unnatural"—sexually deviant—or, if one were not too threatening, merely eccentric.

Despite pressures to conform, there have always been individuals who dissented from prevailing beliefs about women's proper role. For some, frustration, doubts, and questions developed slowly, sometimes requiring years before culminating in outright revolt. Ironic as it may seem, those very doubts and questions could be nourished by precisely those institutions that encouraged women to conform to accepted standards of behavior. Religion and education were two-edged swords. Schools conveyed the expectations of society. But inasmuch as people were encouraged to think, the result might be a questioning of those very expectations.

Similarly, organized religion, while reinforcing traditional values, contributed to the very process by which they were slowly eroded. For example, Protestant evangelicalism, in its emphasis on the Christian home and the place of women within it, stressed—as did nineteenth-century society generally—piety, domesticity, and a self-denying submissiveness. However, the evangelical woman, whether she was Baptist, Methodist, Presbyterian, or even Episcopalian, was encouraged to be "useful." Although the initial intent was to discourage frivolity, a woman who was encouraged to be self-disciplined, sober, and reflective— "the mistress of herself and her actions"—could also become a woman who thought for herself.[13] As she participated in church-related activities and the many reform societies that were an extension of the religious impulse, she could discover an institutional framework within which to meet other women in networks of associates as well as develop leadership skills and become competent in dealing with the public. Efforts to improve the plight of others could lead some women to the conclusion that their own condition needed improving. Thus women active in the antislavery crusade of the 1840s and women active in the civil rights movement of the 1960s learned in those movements not only how to be effective organizers and dissenters but how easily those dedicated to achieving the rights of one group could perpetuate the assumptions and practices that denied the very same rights to another. For some women the result, in the mid-twentieth century as in the mid-nineteenth, was to transform reformers into feminists; advocacy of racial justice developed into commitment to sexual equality.

By whatever process women came to question prevailing assumptions about women's place, they expressed their frustrations in many different ways. Those who were unwilling or unable to confront the real source of their distress sometimes found release from conflicting feelings in psychosomatic illnesses or that most common affliction of nineteenth-century women, hysteria. Those who were able to recognize the conflict between society's expectations and their own needs sometimes expressed their dissent privately, thereby escaping the censure society directs toward those who challenge the status quo. Others expressed their dissent more openly, turning to groups sharing their views. Incorporating equality for women into the party's public statements, socialists enlisted thousands of female members in the first decades of this century. Other women gravitated toward explicitly feminist groups that, although initially quite small, were active in the North before the Civil War and grew dramatically in the decades before World War I. But while organized movements for women's rights have flourished intermittently, it was not until the development of the contemporary women's movement of the 1960s and 1970s that women in significant numbers embraced an ideology that radically challenges traditional values and assumptions, an ideology that incorporates not only family and service but ambition and achievement.

FEMINIST AND TRADITIONALIST

Contemporary feminists reject traditional views about women's role and place because they see these views as supporting attitudes and practices that deny women equality. Women, they believe, should be able to define themselves as individuals, choosing work that at least provides economic independence and at best brings personal and professional fulfillment. Women should also be able to express freely their sexuality and sexual preferences; to decide whether and when to marry; to choose whether and when to have children. As today's feminists have injected these concerns into the public consciousness, they have criticized values that define women primarily as reproductive beings who, simply because they bear children, must automatically lead domestic, mothering lives. It is not surprising that feminists also reject the notion that the most significant goal of women's lives is to make themselves attractive to the men who will provide for them. (Nineteenth-century critics were also scornful of the dependent women who exchanged sexual favors for economic support, whether within marriage or outside of it.)

Because feminists value independence and equality, they see as absolutely basic the right of all women to control their own bodies through access to birth control measures and, when necessary, safe, legal abortions. Believing that financial independence is also essential to full freedom and autonomy, contemporary feminists are very concerned with economic status. They have explored ways in which women working solely within the home might receive economic recognition for their labor. They have criticized those factors that account for the inferior position of women who work outside the home. Because such women now constitute a majority of all American women, and because they average in earnings only 64 percent of those received by men, it would be fair to say that a majority of American women as a class are directly discriminated against in the economic system. Therefore feminists attack discriminatory practices on the part of employers who do not pay men and women equal wages for equal work. They point out the occupational segregation evidenced in the fact that 80 percent of all working women are concentrated in 20 of 411 occupations, the vast majority working as nurses, teachers, saleswomen, and secretaries. The socialization that channels many men into high-paying professions and trades and many women into low-paying, "pink-collar" work is especially deplored. This socialization is epitomized by parents who give young daughters nurses' kits and young sons doctors' bags, guidance counselors who urge mathematically talented girls to become bookkeepers and boys to become engineers.

To escape this double bind, feminists use books, toys, and parental example to demonstrate to young girls that they need not limit their aspirations. They also recognize, however, that the young woman who aspires to a high-level business or professional career will in reality have two full-time jobs if she chooses to have a family in a society in which women are still seen as primarily responsible for home and child care.

The effort of contemporary feminists to redistribute the burdens of the domestic economy makes them part of a tradition. A few feminists in the nineteenth century and a few more early in the twentieth, wrestling with precisely this problem, advocated public schemes, such as kitchenless apartment buildings, while urging a new set of private decisions within the family as to who would do various chores.[14] Contemporary feminists call for institutional measures such as low-cost, quality child care facilities, maternity leaves, and flexible work schedules. They also propose changes in attitudes and life styles, believing that couples working in the public sector can reassess responsibilities so that men and women share equally the burdens and pleasures associated with earning a living, maintaining a household, and rearing a family.

Private action, however, is no substitute for the broad institutional changes that many feminists believe will come when women, historically powerless, have the political power necessary to change a society in which sexual inequality has for centuries been a pervasive and persistent reality. In order to become part of the political power structure women, they believe, must no longer be confined— or confine themselves—to housekeeping chores within the political parties. Instead they must seek and hold elective and appointive office at every level commensurate with their numbers. Having women in positions of political power is a dubious gain, however, unless those women are willing to support the kind of changes feminists believe are necessary if all women are to achieve greater reproductive, economic, and political control of their lives. They are convinced that women and men alike must examine existing values and assumptions about what is appropriate for men and especially women to be and do, ultimately putting together and acting upon a set of new values that liberate rather than constrain and oppress. The end result, many feminists believe, must be the restructuring of both persons and institutions—in short, a feminist transformation.

Challenges to long-standing beliefs and behavior, whether issued now or in the past, have been criticized by traditionalists. They perceive feminists' demands for equality not as an effort to remove discrimination based solely on gender and to expand options for men and women alike but rather as a rejection of cherished norms and values. Men who possess power and privileges they do not wish to share understandably see in feminism a threat. Moreover, many women who believe they have lived useful and admirable lives by traditional rules see feminist attacks on traditional sex roles as an attack on a way of life they have perfected—and hence an attack on them personally. Thus feminist insistence that women should be able to seek fulfillment in the public world of work and power as well as in the private world of home and family is viewed by traditionalists as an egocentric demand that places personal gratification above familial duty. By the same token, the demand that women themselves be the ultimate judge of whether and when to bear children is seen by some not as a legitimate desire to control one's own body but as an escape from maternal obligations that threatens the future of the family and ultimately, therefore, society itself.

To suggest that some women find feminism a route to personal fulfillment while other women find that route in traditionalism is not to suggest that the ideological history of women is bipolar. It embraces many variants. Traditionalist women may be as suspicious of male-controlled institutions as feminists; feminist women may be as "feminine" as traditionalists. Traditional women may be as publicly active on behalf of their goals as feminists; feminists may be as concerned with family as traditionalists. Both groups identify with a sisterhood and see "women's issues" as special ones, although they do not consistently agree as to what they are. Partisans of the two groups may unite or divide along class, occupational, or political lines. But no matter what the issue and the proposed solution, wherever women are on the ideological spectrum they are part of women's history.

"Woman has always been acting and thinking . . . at the center of life," wrote Mary Beard a half century ago; but the significance of women's activities has, until recent years, often been discounted and rarely been understood. The scholarship of the past decades has spotlighted much that had lain in the shadows of history, unnoticed and unappreciated. As we have examined that scholarship, we find ourselves less impressed by sex role constraints—which were very real—than by the vigor and subtlety with which women have defined the terms of their existence. These creative experiences show how the private lives of historical persons can help us understand the rich complexities of change. To study women's history, then, is to take part in a bold enterprise that can eventually lead us to a new history, one that, by taking into account both sexes, should tell us more about each other and, therefore, our collective selves.

NOTES

1. David M. Potter, "American Women and the American Character" (1962), in *History and American Society: Essays of David M. Potter*, ed. Don E. Fehrenbacher (New York, 1979), p. 279.

2. Potter, "American Women and the American Character," p. 280.

3. These issues have been thoughtfully explored by Joan Kelly. See "The Doubled Vision of Feminist Theory," *Feminist Studies* 5 (1979):216–27; and Joan Kelly-Gadol, "The Social Relation of the Sexes: Methodological Implications of Women's History," *Signs: Journal of Women in Culture and Society* 1 (1976):809–24.

4. Donald G. Mathews, "Women's History/Everyone's History," in *Women in New Worlds*, ed. Hilah F. Thomas and Rosemary Skinner Keller (Nashville, 1981), p. 30.

5. Gerda Lerner, *The Majority Finds Its Past: Placing Women in History* (New York, 1979), pp. 49–50. Lerner's essays in this collection include not only her pioneering contributions to women's history but also her important effort to set the history of women in the general historical context. Her explorations, both narrative and theoretical, of the possibilities inherent in feminist scholarship have done much to shape our own thinking. See also her collection of documents, *The Female Experience: An American Documentary* (Indianapolis, 1977).

6. Nancy F. Cott, "Passionlessness: An Interpretation of Victorian Sexual Ideology, 1790–1850," *Signs: Journal of Women in Culture and Society* 4 (1978):219–36.

7. Tamara Hareven and Randolph Langenbach, *Amoskeag: Life and Work in an American Factory-City* (New York, 1978).

8. *Raleigh* (N.C.) *News and Observer*, November 24, 1904.

9. For discussion of the concept of ideology, see Clifford Geertz, "Ideology as a Cultural System," in *Ideology and Discontent*, ed. David Apter (New York, 1964), pp. 47–76.

10. Barbara Welter, "The Cult of True Womanhood: 1820–1860," *American Quarterly* 18 (1966):151–74; Christopher Lasch, *Haven in a Heartless World* (New York, 1977).

11. *Raleigh* (N.C.) *Register*, 1850, quoted in Albert Coates, *By Her Own Bootstraps: A Saga of Women in North Carolina* (n.p., 1975), pp. 142–43.

12. Margaret Mead, "Sex and Achievement," *Forum* 94 (1935):303.

13. Mary McGehee to John W. F. Burruss, May 29, 1836, in John C. Burruss Papers, Louisiana State University Library, Baton Rouge.

14. See Dolores Hayden, *The Grand Domestic Revolution: A History of Feminist Designs for American Homes, Neighborhoods, and Cities* (Cambridge, Mass., 1981).

Obstetrical Instruments Case, ca. 1780
The case includes forceps, a double lever, two double blunt hooks, and a perforator. Perhaps no technological invention in traditional America had more direct connection to women's lives than these. Hooks were used to dismember and remove a fetus that had died during delivery. Skillfully employed, forceps could be lifesaving. Professional training in the use of instruments was monopolized by male physicians, to whom the urban middle class turned in the late eighteenth and early nineteenth centuries. Advances in medical technology were accompanied by the exclusion of midwives from advanced training and, increasingly, from the birthing room itself. Division of Medical Sciences, National Museum of American History, Smithsonian Institution

I

Traditional America
1600–1820

Most American histories treat the colonial period as a time when government and order were imposed upon a wilderness. The important subjects tend to be Indian wars, international trade, the establishment of legislatures, and rivalries between British colonies and those of other nations. The first woman mentioned is usually Pocahontas, the innocent Indian princess who allegedly saved the life of the hero of Jamestown, Captain John Smith. The second woman who appears is often Anne Hutchinson, who was banished from Massachusetts Bay Colony for heresy. Both met premature and unpleasant deaths. Unaccustomed to the climate of England, where she had been taken to be shown to Queen Anne, Pocahontas died of pneumonia. Hutchinson was massacred by Indians during a raid on her lonely dwelling in what is now Westchester County, New York. The reader who concludes from these examples that women were not very important in colonial America, and that the few women whom we remember are likely to have been troublesome and to have come to a bad end, may be pardoned.

But if we pose Mary Beard's question and ask, What did colonial America look like, seen through women's eyes? the picture changes. More constructive than troublesome, women were among the founders of virtually every colony. Indeed, a settlement counted itself as having passed the stage of a temporary camp only after it had attracted a reasonable complement of women. A sex ratio approaching 100 (that is, 100 women to every 100 men) was taken to be evidence that the settlement was here to stay. Once founded, communities were maintained in large part by women's labor. The productivity of housekeepers is not easily measured, but nearly fifty years ago Julia Cherry Spruill established the complexity of the tasks performed in fronter households.[1] Housekeeping, after all, provided the context of the employment of nearly half the adult population, both slave and free.

It may be that America seemed to women less radical a change from the Old World than it did to men. The terrors of the ocean crossing and of the wilderness were, of course, shared by all. In the farming communities Europeans planted along the eastern seaboard daily tasks proceeded in the manner of England, whether the agricultural laborer were farmer or farmer's wife. As Catherine M. Scholten's description shows, the rituals of childbirth were transmitted intact from Old World to New, although it may well have been that the rate of survival of mother and infant was better in the American countryside, where the dangers of infection were far fewer than in the towns and cities of Europe. By contrast, the innovations that made the colonies most distinctive from the Old World—especially governmental institutions like town meetings and provincial legislatures—were settings from which women were barred.

One institution in which women were welcome was the church, but despite repeated quotation of St. Paul's rule that "in Christ there is neither man nor woman," believers of every faith were very conscious of gender distinctions. As Lyle Koehler's account of Anne Hutchinson's trials demonstrates, Hutchinson's heresy was compounded by the fact that it was formulated by a woman. Many of the questions in her trial were grounded in the objection that she had stepped out of her proper place. For women, Puritans had special expectations and understood there to be special punishments. When dissenting women like Mary Dyer were delivered of malformed infants, John Winthrop saw no reason to be surprised at the divine punishment. Witchcraft, too, was a religious heresy; it, too, was gender specific, a woman's crime. Although witchcraft accusations normally arose in places where the entire community was troubled, the accusers were usually teen-aged girls, and the "witches" usually women.

English colonists brought with them a system of property rights which assumed that any property held by a woman normally passed to her husband's control when she married. Marylynn Salmon describes the ways in which women nevertheless might continue to control their property after marriage, through prenuptial agreements or marriage settlements. The right to participate in the political system—to vote and to hold office—was conditioned on holding property. It therefore seemed logical to colonists that political rights be granted only to men. Since girls could not grow up to be legislators, or ministers, or lawyers, little care was taken to provide them with any but the most elementary forms of schooling. "How many female minds, rich with native genius and noble sentiment, have been lost to the world, and all their mental treasures buried in oblivion?" mourned one writer.[2]

Like it or not, women were part of the community. What they chose to do or not to do set constraints on men's options. The Revolutionary army, lacking an effective quartermaster corps, was dependent on women for nursing, cooking, and cleaning. The army, in turn, could not march as quickly as Washington would have liked because provision had to be made for the "woemin of the army." The task of the recruiting officer was eased when men could rely on their female relatives to keep family farms and mills in operation, fend off squatters, and protect family property by their heavy labor, often at grave physical risk. We have no simple calculus for measuring the extent to which women's services made it possible for men to act in certain ways during the Revolution, but it is clear that women's work provided the civilian context in which the war was carried on.

When the war was over and the political structure of the new nation was being reshaped in federal and state constitutions, little attention was given to the political role women might directly play. Yet women did have distinctive political interests. For example, if women had had the vote in 1789, they might well have used it to establish pensions for widows of veterans. Women's distinctive needs tended to be discounted as trivial. It was left to women of succeeding generations to accomplish for themselves what the Revolution had not.

Notes

1. Julia Cherry Spruill, *Women's Life and Work in the Southern Colonies* (Chapel Hill, 1938).
2. Clio [pseud.], "Thoughts on Female Education," *Royal American Magazine*, January 1774, pp. 9–10.

LAUREL THATCHER ULRICH
The Ways of Her Household

One of the greatest barriers to an accurate assessment of women's role in the community has been the habit of assuming that what women did was not very important. Housekeeping has long been women's work, and housework has long been regarded as trivial. Laurel Thatcher Ulrich shows, however, that housekeeping can be a complex task and that real skill and intelligence might be exercised in performing it. The services housekeepers perform, in traditional as well as contemporary America, are an important part of the economic arrangements that sustain the family and need to be taken into account when describing any community or society. Note the differences Ulrich finds between rural and urban women, and between middle-class and impoverished women.

By English tradition, a woman's environment was the family dwelling and the yard or yards surrounding it. Though the exact composition of her setting obviously depended upon the occupation and economic status of her husband, its general outlines were surprisingly similar regardless of where it was located. The difference between an urban "houselot" and a rural "homelot" was not as dramatic as one might suppose.

If we were to draw a line around the housewife's domain, it would extend from the kitchen and its appendages, the cellars, pantries, brewhouses, milkhouses, washhouses, and butteries which appear in various combinations in household inventories, to the exterior of the house, where, even in the city, a mélange of animal and vegetable life flourished among the straw, husks, clutter, and muck. Encircling the pigpen, such a line would surround the garden, the milkyard, the well, the henhouse, and perhaps the orchard itself—though husbands pruned and planted trees and eventually supervised the making of cider, good housewives strung their wash between the trees and in season harvested fruit for pies and conserves.

The line demarking the housewife's realm would not cross the fences which defined outlying fields of Indian corn or barley, nor would it stretch to fishing stages, mills, or wharves, but in berry or mushroom season it would extend into nearby woods or marsh and in spells of dearth or leisure reach to the shore. Of necessity, the boundaries of each woman's world would also extend into the houses of neighbors and into the cartways of a village or town. Housewives commanded a limited domain. But they were neither isolated nor self-sufficient. Even in farming settlements, families found it essential to bargain for needed goods and services. For prosperous and socially prominent women, interdependence took on another meaning as well. Prosperity meant charity, and in early New England charity meant personal responsibility for nearby neighbors. . . .

. . . For most historians, as for almost all antiquarians, the quintessential early American woman has been a churner of cream and a spinner of wool. Because home manufacturing has all but disappeared from modern housekeeping, many scholars have assumed that the key change in female economic life has been a shift from "production" to "consumption," a shift precipitated by the industrial revolution.[1] This is far too simple, obscuring the variety which existed even in the pre-industrial world. . . .

. . . Beatrice Plummer, Hannah Grafton, and Magdalen Wear lived and died in New England in the years before 1750. One of them lived on the frontier, another on a farm, and a third in town. Because they were real women, however, and not hypothetical examples, the ways of their households were shaped by personal as well as geographic factors. A careful examination of the contents of their kitchens and chambers suggests the varied complexity as well as the underlying unity in the lives of early American women.

Let us begin with Beatrice Plummer of Newbury, Massachusetts.[2] Forgetting that death brought her neighbors into the house on January 24, 1672, we can use the probate inventory which they prepared to reconstruct the normal pattern of her work. With a clear estate of £343, Francis Plummer had belonged to the "middling sort" who were the church members and freeholders of the Puritan settlement of Newbury. As an immigrant of 1653, he had listed himself as a "linnen weaver," but he soon became a farmer as well.[3] At his death, his loom and tackling stood in the "shop" with his pitchforks, his hoes, and his tools for smithing and carpentry. Plummer had integrated four smaller plots to form one continuous sixteen-acre farm. An additional twenty acres of salt marsh

and meadow provided hay and forage for his small herd of cows and sheep. His farm provided a comfortable living for his family, which at this stage of his life included only his second wife, Beatrice, and her grandchild by a previous marriage. . . .

The house over which Beatrice presided must have looked much like surviving dwellings from seventeenth-century New England, with its "Hall" and "Parlor" on the ground floor and two "chambers" above. A space designated in the inventory only as "another Roome" held the family's collection of pots, kettles, dripping pans, trays, buckets, and earthenware. . . . The upstairs chambers were not bedrooms but storage rooms for foodstuffs and out-of-season equipment. The best bed with its bolster, pillows, blanket, and coverlet stood in the parlor; a second bed occupied one corner of the kitchen, while a cupboard, a "great chest," a table, and a backless bench called a "form" furnished the hall. More food was found in the "cellar" and in the "dairy house," a room which may have stood at the coolest end of the kitchen lean-to.[4]

The Plummer house was devoid of ornament, but its contents bespeak such comforts as conscientious yeomanry and good huswifery afforded. On this winter morning the dairy house held four and a half "flitches" or sides of bacon, a quarter of a barrel of salt pork, twenty-eight pounds of cheese, and four pounds of butter. Upstairs in a chamber were more than twenty-five bushels of "English" grain—barley, oats, wheat, and rye. (The Plummers apparently reserved their Indian corn, stored in another location, for their animals.) When made into malt by a village specialist, barley would become the basis for beer. Two bushels of malt were already stored in the house. The oats might appear in a variety of dishes, from plain breakfast porridge to "flummery," a gelatinous dish flavored with spices and dried fruit.[5] But the wheat and rye were almost certainly reserved for bread and pies. The fine hair sieves stored with the grain in the hall chamber suggest that Beatrice Plummer was particular about her baking, preferring a finer flour than came directly from the miller. A "bushell of pease & beans" found near the grain and a full barrel of cider in the cellar are the only vegetables and fruits listed in the inventory, though small quantities of pickles, preserves, or dried herbs might have escaped notice. Perhaps the Plummers added variety to their diet by trading some of their abundant supply of grain for cabbages, turnips, sugar, molasses, and spices. . . .

Since wives were involved with early-morning milking, breakfast of necessity featured prepared foods or leftovers—toasted bread, cheese, and perhaps meat and turnips kept from the day before, any of this washed down with cider or beer in winter, with milk in summer. Only on special occasions would there be pie or doughnuts. Dinner was the main meal of the day. Here a housewife with culinary aspirations and an ample larder could display her specialties. After harvest Beatrice Plummer might have served roast pork or goose with apples, in spring an eel pie flavored with parsley and winter savory, and in summer a leek soup or gooseberry cream; but for ordinary days the most common menu was boiled meat with whatever "sauce" the season provided—dried peas or beans, parsnips, turnips, onions, cabbage, or garden greens. A heavy pudding stuffed into a cloth bag could steam atop the vegetables and meat. The broth from this boiled dinner might reappear at supper as "pottage" with the addition of minced herbs and some oatmeal or barley for thickening. Supper, like breakfast, was a simple meal. Bread, cheese, and beer were as welcome at the end of a winter day as at the beginning. . . .

Preparing the simplest of these meals required both judgment and skill. . . . The most basic of the housewife's skills was building and regulating fires—a task so fundamental that it must have appeared more as habit than craft. Summer and winter, day and night, she kept a few brands smoldering, ready to stir into flame as needed. The cavernous fireplaces of early New England were but a century removed from the open fires of medieval houses, and they retained some of the characteristics of the latter. Standing inside one of these huge openings today, a person can see the sky above. Seventeenth-century housewives *did* stand in their fireplaces, which were conceived less as enclosed spaces for a single blaze than as accessible working surfaces upon which a number of small fires might be built. Preparing several dishes simultaneously, a cook could move from one fire to another, turning a spit, checking the state of the embers under a skillet, adjusting the height of a pot hung from the lugpole by its adjustable trammel. The complexity of fire-tending, as much as anything else, encouraged the one-pot meal.[6]

The contents of her inventory suggest that Beatrice Plummer was adept not only at roasting, frying, and boiling but also at baking, the most difficult branch of cookery. Judging from the grain in the upstairs chamber, the bread which she baked was "maslin," a common type made from a mixture of wheat and other grains, usually rye. She began with the sieves stored nearby, carefully sifting out the coarser pieces of grain and bran. Soon after supper she could have mixed the "sponge," a thin dough made from warm water, yeast, and flour. Her yeast might have come from the foamy "barm" found on top of fermenting ale or beer, from a piece of dough saved from an earlier baking, or even from the crevices in an unwashed kneading trough. Like fire-building, bread-making was based upon a self-perpetuating chain, an organic sequence which if once interrupted was difficult to begin again. Warmth from the banked fire would raise the sponge by morning, when Beatrice could work in more flour, knead the finished dough, and shape the loaves, leaving them to rise again.

Even in twentieth-century kitchens with standardized yeast and thermostatically controlled temperatures, bread dough is subject to wide variations in consistency and behavior. In a drafty house with an uncertain supply of yeast, bread-making was indeed "an art, craft, and mystery." Not the least of the problem was regulating the fire so that the oven was ready at the same time as the risen loaves. Small cakes or biscuits could be baked in a skillet or directly on the hearth under an upside-down pot covered with coals. But to produce bread in any quantity required an oven. Before 1650 these were frequently constructed in dooryards, but in the last decades of the century they were built into the rear of the kitchen fireplace, as Beatrice Plummer's must have been. Since her oven would have had no flue, she would have left the door open once she kindled a fire inside, allowing the smoke to escape through the fireplace chimney. Moving about her kitchen, she would have kept an eye on this fire, occasionally raking the coals to distribute the heat evenly, testing periodically with her hand to see if the oven had reached the right temperature. When she determined that it had, she would have scraped out the coals and inserted the bread—assuming that it had risen enough by this time or had not risen too much and collapsed waiting for the oven to heat.[7]

Cooking and baking were year-round tasks. Inserted into these day-by-day routines were seasonal specialties which allowed a housewife to bridge the dearth of one period with the bounty of another. In the preservation calendar, dairying came first, beginning with the first calves of early spring. In colonial New England cows were all-purpose creatures, raised for meat as well as for milk. Even in new settlements they could survive by browsing on rough land; their meat was a hedge against famine. But only in areas with abundant meadow (and even there only in certain months) would they produce milk with sufficient butterfat for serious dairying.[8] Newbury was such a place.

We can imagine Beatrice Plummer some morning in early summer processing the milk which would appear as cheese in a January breakfast. Slowly she heated several gallons with rennet dried and saved from the autumn's slaughtering. Within an hour or two the curd had formed. She broke it, drained off the whey, then worked in a little of her own fresh butter. Packing this rich mixture into a mold, she turned it in her wooden press for an hour or more, changing and washing the cheesecloth frequently as the whey dripped out. Repacking it in dry cloth, she left it in the press for another thirty to forty hours before washing it once more with whey, drying it, and placing it in the cellar or dairy house to age. As a young girl she would have learned from her mother or a mistress the importance of thorough pressing and the virtues of cleanliness. . . .

The Plummer inventory gives little evidence of the second stage of preservation in the housewife's year, the season of gardening and gathering which followed quickly upon the dairy months. But there is ample evidence of the autumn slaughtering. Beatrice could well have killed the smaller pigs herself, holding their "hinder parts between her legs," as one observer described the process, "and taking the snout in her left hand" while she stuck the animal through the heart with a long knife. Once the bleeding stopped, she would have submerged the pig in boiling water for a few minutes, then rubbed it with rosin, stripped off the hair, and disemboweled it. Nothing was lost. She reserved the organ meats for immediate use, then cleaned the intestines for later service as sausage casings. Stuffed with meat scraps and herbs and smoked, these "links" were a treasured delicacy. The larger cuts could be roasted at once or preserved in several ways.[9] . . .

Fall was also the season for cider-making. The mildly alcoholic beverage produced by natural fermentation of apple juice was a staple of the New England diet and was practically the only method of preserving the fruit harvest. With the addition of sugar, the alcoholic content could be raised from five to about seven percent, as it usually was in taverns and for export. . . .

Prosaic beer was even more important to the Plummer diet. Although some housewives brewed a winter's supply of strong beer in October, storing it in the cellar, Beatrice seems to have been content with "small beer," a mild beverage usually brewed weekly or bi-weekly and used almost at once. Malting—the process of sprouting and drying barley to increase its sugar content—was wisely left to the village expert. Beatrice started with cracked malt or grist, processing her beer in three stages. "Mashing" required slow steeping at just below the boiling point, a sensitive and smelly process which largely determined the success of the beverage. Experienced brewers knew by taste whether the enzymes were working. If it was too hot, acetic acid developed which would sour the finished product. The next stage, "brewing," was relatively simple. Herbs and hops were boiled with the malted liquid. In the final step this liquor was cooled and mixed with yeast saved from last week's beer or bread. Within twenty-four hours—if all had gone well—the beer was bubbling actively.[10]

. . . A wife who knew how to manage the ticklish chemical processes which changed milk into cheese, meal into bread, malt into beer, and flesh into bacon was a valuable asset, though some men were too churlish to admit it. After her husband's death, Beatrice married a man who not only refused to provide her with provisions, but insisted on doing his own cooking. He took his meat "out of ye pickle" and broiled it directly on the coals, and when she offered him "a cup of my owne Sugar & Bear," he refused it. When the neighbors testified that she had been a dutiful wife, the Quarterly Court fined him for "abusive carriages and speeches." Even the unhappy marriage that thrust Beatrice Plummer into court helps to document the central position of huswifery in her life.[11] . . .

Beatrice Plummer represents one type of early American housewife. Hannah Grafton represents another.[12] Chronology, geography, and personal biography created differences between the household inventories of the two women, but there are obvious similarities as well. Like Beatrice Plummer, Hannah Grafton lived in a house with two major rooms on the ground floor and two chambers above. At various locations near the ground-floor rooms were service areas—a washhouse with its own loft or chamber, a shop, a lean-to, and two cellars. The central rooms in the Grafton house were the "parlour," with the expected featherbed, and the "kitchen," which included much the same collection of utensils and iron pots which appeared in the Plummer house. Standing in the corner of the kitchen were a spade and a hoe, two implements useful only for chipping away ice and snow on the December day on which the inventory was taken, though apparently destined for another purpose come spring. With a garden, a cow, and three pigs, Hannah Grafton clearly had agricultural responsibilities, but these were performed in a strikingly different context than on the Plummer farm. The Grafton homelot was a single acre of land standing just a few feet from shoreline in the urban center of Salem.[13]

Joshua Grafton was a mariner like his father before him. His estate of £236 was modest, but he was still a young man and he had firm connections with the seafaring elite who were transforming the economy of Salem. When he died late in 1699, Hannah had three living children—Hannah, eight; Joshua, six; and Priscilla, who was just ten months.[14] This young family used their space quite differently than had the Plummers. The upstairs chambers which served as storage areas in the New-bury farmhouse were sleeping quarters here. In addition to the bed in the parlor and the cradle in the kitchen, there were two beds in each of the upstairs rooms. One of these, designated as "smaller," may have been used by young Joshua. It would be interesting to know whether the mother carried the two chamber pots kept in the parlor upstairs to the bedrooms at night or whether the children found their way in the dark to their parents' sides as necessity demanded. But adults were prob-ably never far away. Because there are more bedsteads in the Grafton house than members of the immediate family, they may have shared their living quarters with unmarried relatives or servants.

Ten chairs and two stools furnished the kitchen, while no fewer than fifteen chairs, in two separate sets, crowded the parlor with its curtained bed. The pres-ence of a punch bowl on a square table in the parlor reinforces the notion that so-ciability was an important value in this Salem household. Thirteen ounces of plate, a pair of gold buttons, and a silver-headed cane suggest a measure of luxury as well—all of this in stark contrast to the Plummers, who had only two chairs and a backless bench and no discernible ornamentation at all. Yet the Grafton house was only slightly more specialized than the Newbury farmhouse. It had no servants' quarters, no sharp segregation of public and private spaces, no real sepa-ration of sleeping, eating, and work. A cradle in the kitchen and a go-cart kept with the spinning wheels in the upstairs chamber show that little Priscilla was very much a part of this workaday world.

How then might the pattern of Hannah Grafton's work have differed from that of Beatrice Plummer? Certainly cooking re-mained central. Hannah's menus probably varied only slightly from those prepared in the Plummer kitchen, and her cooking techniques must have been identical. But one dramatic difference is apparent in the two inventories. The Grafton house con-tained no provisions worth listing on that December day when Isaac Foot and Sam-uel Willard appeared to take inventory. Hannah had brewing vessels, but no malt; sieves and a meal trough, but no grain; and a cow, but no cheese. What little milk her cow gave in winter probably went di-rectly into the children's mugs. Perhaps she would continue to breast-feed Priscilla until spring brought a more secure sup-ply. . . . Trade, rather than manufactur-ing or agriculture, was the dominant motif in her meal preparations.

In colonial New England most food went directly from processer or producer to consumer. Joshua may have purchased grain or flour from the mill near the ship-building center called Knocker's Hole, about a mile away from their house. Or Hannah may have eschewed bread-mak-ing altogether, walking or sending a ser-vant the half-mile to Elizabeth Haskett's bakery near the North River. Fresh meat for the spits in her washhouse may have come from John Cromwell's slaughter-house on Main Street near the Congrega-tional meetinghouse, and soap for her washtubs from the soap-boiler farther up the street near the Quaker meetinghouse.[15] Salem, like other colonial towns, was laid out helter-skelter, with the residences of the wealthy interspersed with the small houses of carpenters or fishermen. Because there was no center of retail trade, assem-bling the ingredients of a dinner involved many transactions. Sugar, wine, and spices came by sea; fresh lamb, veal, eggs, but-ter, gooseberries, and parsnips came by land. Merchants retailed their goods in shops or warehouses near their wharves and houses. Farmers or their wives often hawked their produce door to door.[16] . . .

In such a setting, trading for food might require as much energy and skill as manufacturing or growing it. One key to success was simply knowing where to go. Keeping abreast of the arrival of ships in the harbor or establishing personal contact with just the right farmwife from nearby Salem village required time and attention. Equally important was the ability to evaluate the variety of unstandardized goods offered. An apparently sound cheese might teem with maggots when cut.[17] Since cash was scarce, a third necessity was the establishment of credit, a problem which ultimately devolved upon husbands. But petty haggling over direct exchanges was also a feature of this barter economy.

Hannah Grafton was involved in trade on more than one level. The "shop" attached to her house was not the all-purpose storage shed and workroom it seems to have been for Francis Plummer. It was a retail store, offering door locks, nails, hammers, gimlets, and other hardware as well as English cloth, pins, needles, and thread. As a mariner, Joshua Grafton may well have sailed the ship which brought these goods to Salem. In his absence, Hannah was not only a mother and a housewife but, like many other Salem women, a shopkeeper as well.

There is another highly visible activity in the Grafton inventory which was not immediately apparent in the Plummers'—care of clothing. Presumably, Beatrice Plummer washed occasionally, but she did not have a "washhouse." Hannah did. The arrangement of this unusual room is far from clear. On December 2, 1699, it contained two spits, two "bouldishes," a gridiron, and "other things." Whether those other things included washtubs, soap, or a beating staff is impossible to determine. . . .

But on any morning in December the washhouse could . . . have been hung with the family wash. Dark woolen jackets and petticoats went from year to year without seeing a kettle of suds, but linen shifts, aprons, shirts, and handkerchiefs required washing. Laundering might not have been a weekly affair in most colonial households, but it was a well-defined if infrequent necessity even for transient seamen and laborers. One can only speculate on its frequency in a house with a child under a year. When her baby was only a few months old, Hannah may have learned to hold little Priscilla over the chamber pot at frequent intervals, but in early infancy, tightly wrapped in her cradle, the baby could easily have used five dozen "clouts" and almost as many "belly bands" from one washing to another. Even with the use of a "pilch," a thick square of flannel securely bound over the diaper, blankets and coverlets occasionally needed sudsing as well.[18]

Joshua's shirts and Hannah's own aprons and shifts would require careful ironing. Hannah's "smoothing irons" fitted into their own heaters, which she filled with coals from the fire. As the embers waned and the irons cooled, she would have made frequent trips from her table to the hearth to the fire and back to the table again. At least two of these heavy instruments were essential. A dampened apron could dry and wrinkle while a single flatiron replenished its heat.

As frequent a task as washing was sewing. Joshua's coats and breeches went to a tailor, but his shirts were probably made at home. Certainly Hannah stitched and unstitched the tucks which altered Priscilla's simple gowns and petticoats as she grew. The little dresses which the baby trailed in her go-cart had once clothed her brother. Gender identity in childhood was less important in this society than economy of effort. It was not that boys were seen as identical to girls, only that all-purpose garments could be handed from one child to another regardless of sex, and dresses were more easily altered than breeches and more adaptable to diapering and toileting. At eight years of age little Hannah had probably begun to imitate her mother's even stitches, helping with the continual mending, altering, and knitting which kept this growing family clothed.[19]

In some ways the most interesting items in the Grafton inventory are the two spinning wheels kept in the upstairs chamber. Beatrice Plummer's wheel and reel had been key components in an intricate production chain. The Plummers had twenty-five sheep in the fold and a loom in the shed. The Graftons had neither. Children—not sheep—put wheels in Hannah's house. The mechanical nature of spinnnng made it a perfect occupation for women whose attention was engrossed by young children. This is one reason why the ownership of wheels in both York and Essex counties had a constancy over time unrelated to the ownership of sheep or looms. In the dozen inventories taken in urban Salem about the time of Joshua Grafton's death, the six non-spinners averaged one minor child each, the six spinners had almost four. Instruction at the wheel was part of the almost ritualistic preparation mothers offered their daughters.[20] Spinning was a useful craft, easily picked up, easily put down, and even small quantities of yarn could be knitted into caps, stockings, dishcloths, and mittens.

. . . a cluster of objects in the chamber over Hannah Grafton's kitchen suggests a fanciful but by no means improbable vignette. Imagine her gathered with her two daughters in this upstairs room on a New England winter's day. Little Priscilla navigates around the end of the bedstead in her go-cart while her mother sits at one spinning wheel and her sister at the other. Young Hannah is spinning "oakum," the coarsest and least expensive part of the flax. As her mother leans over to help her wind the uneven thread on the bobbin, she catches a troublesome scent from downstairs. Have the turnips caught on the bottom of the pot? Has the maid scorched Joshua's best shirt? Or has a family servant returned from the wharf and spread his wet clothes by the fire?

Hastening down the narrow stairs to the kitchen, Hannah hears the shop bell ring. Just then little Priscilla, left upstairs with her sister, begins to cry. In such pivotal but unrecorded moments much of the history of women lies hidden.

The third inventory can be more quickly described.[21] Elias Wear of York, Maine, left an estate totaling £92, of which less than £7 was in household goods—including some old pewter, a pot, two bedsteads, bedding, one chest, and a box. Wear also owned a saddle, three guns, and a river craft called a gundalow. But his wealth, such as it was, consisted of land (£40) and livestock (£36). It is not just relative poverty which distinguished Elias Wear's inventory from that of Joshua Grafton or Francis Plummer. Every settlement in northern New England had men who owned only a pot, a bed, and a chest. Their children crowded in with them or slept on straw. These men and their sons provided some of the labor which harvested barley for farmers like Francis Plummer or stepped masts for mariners like Joshua Grafton. Their wives and their daughters carded wool or kneaded bread in other women's kitchens. No, Elias Wear was distinguished by a special sort of frontier poverty.

His father had come to northern New England in the 1640s, exploring and trading for furs as far inland in New Hampshire as Lake Winnipesaukee. By 1650 he had settled in York, a then hopeful site for establishing a patrimony. Forty years later he died in the York Massacre, an assault by French and Indians which virtually destroyed the town, bringing death or captivity to fully half of the inhabitants. Almost continuous warfare between 1689 and 1713 created prosperity for the merchant community of Portsmouth and Kittery, but it kept most of the inhabitants of outlying settlements in a state of impecunious insecurity.[22]

In 1696, established on a small homestead in the same neighborhood in which his father had been killed, Elias Wear married a young widow with the fitting name of Magdalen. When their first child was born "too soon," the couple found themselves in York County Court owning a presentment for fornication. Although New England courts were still sentencing couples in similar circumstances to "nine stripes a piece upon the Naked back," most of the defendants, like the Wears, managed to pay the not inconsequential fine. The fifty-nine shillings which Elias and Magdalen pledged the court amounted to almost half of the total value of two steers. A presentment for fornication was expensive as well as inconvenient, but it did not carry a permanent onus. Within seven years of their conviction Elias was himself serving on the "Jury of Tryalls" for the county, while Magdalen had proved herself a dutiful and productive wife.[23]

Every other winter she gave birth, producing four sons—Elias, Jeremiah, John, and Joseph—in addition to the untimely Ruth. A sixth child, Mary, was just five months old when her father met his own death by Indians in August of 1707 while traveling between their Cape Neddick home and the more densely settled York village. Without the benefits of a cradle, a go-cart, a spinning wheel, or even a secure supply of grain, Magdalen raised these six children. Unfortunately, there is little in her inventory and nothing in any other record to document the specific strategies which she used, though the general circumstances of her life can be imagined.

Chopping and hauling for a local timber merchant, Elias could have filled Magdalen's porridge pot with grain shipped from the port of Salem or Boston. During the spring corn famine, an almost yearly occurrence on the Maine frontier, she might have gone herself with other wives of her settlement to dig on the clam flats, hedging against the day when relief would come by sea.[24] Like Beatrice Plummer and

Hannah Grafton, she would have spent some hours cooking, washing, hoeing cabbages, bargaining with neighbors, and, in season, herding and milking a cow. But poverty, short summers, and rough land also made gathering an essential part of her work. We may imagine her cutting pine splinters for light and "cattails" and "silkgrass" for beds. Long before her small garden began to produce, she would have searched out a wild "sallet" in the nearby woods, in summer turning to streams and barrens for other delicacies congenial to English taste—eels, salmon, berries, and plums. She would have embarked on such excursions with caution, however, remembering the wives of nearby Exeter who took their children into the woods for strawberries "without any Guard" and narrowly avoided capture.[25] . . .

. . . The Wears probably lived in a single-story cottage which may or may not have been subdivided into more than one room. A loft above provided extra space for storage or sleeping. With the addition of a lean-to, this house could have sheltered animals as well as humans, especially in harsh weather or in periods of Indian alarm. Housing a pig or a calf in the next room would have simplified Magdalen's chores in the winter. If she managed to raise a few chickens, these too would have thrived better near the kitchen fire.[26]

Thus, penury erased the elaborate demarcation of "houses" and "yards" evident in yeoman inventories. It also blurred distinctions between the work of a husbandman and the work of his wife. At planting time and at harvest Magdalen Wear undoubtedly went into the fields to help Elias, taking her babies wtih her or leaving Ruth to watch them as best she could.[27] A century later an elderly Maine woman bragged that she "had dropped corn many a day with two governors: a judge in her arms and a general on her back."[28] None of the Wear children grew up to such prominence, but all six of them survived to adulthood and four married and founded families of their own. Six children did not prevent Magdalen Wear from remarrying within two years of her husband's death. Whatever her assets—a pleasant face, a strong back, or lifetime possession of £40 in land—she was soon wed to the unmarried son of a neighboring millowner.[29]

Magdalen Wear, Hannah Grafton, and Beatrice Plummer were all "typical" New England housewives of the period 1650–1750. Magdalen's iron pot represents the housekeeping minimum which often characterized frontier life. Hannah's punch bowl and her hardware shop exemplify both the commerce and the self-conscious civilization of coastal towns. Beatrice's brewing tubs and churn epitomize home manufacturing and agrarian self-sufficiency as they existed in established villages. Each type of housekeeping could be found somewhere in northern New England in any decade of the century. Yet these three women should not be placed in rigidly separate categories. Wealth, geography, occupation, and age determined that some women in any decade would be more heavily involved in one aspect of housekeeping than another, yet all three women shared a common vocation. Each understood the rhythms of the seasons, the technology of fire-building, the persistence of the daily demands of cooking, the complexity of home production, and the dexterity demanded from the often conflicting roles of housekeeper, mother, and wife.

The thing which distinguished these women from their counterparts in modern America was not, as some historians have suggested, that their work was essential to survival. "Survival," after all, is a minimal concept. Individual men and women have never needed each other for mere survival but for far more complex reasons, and women were *essential* in the seventeenth century for the very same reasons

they are essential today—for the perpetuation of the race. . . . Nor was it the monotony of these women's lives or the narrowness of their choices which really set them apart. Women in industrial cities have lived monotonous and confining lives, and they may have worked even harder than early American women. The really striking differences are social.

. . . the lives of early American housewives were distinguished less by the tasks they performed than by forms of social organization which linked economic responsibilities to family responsibilities and which tied each woman's household to the larger world of her village or town.

For centuries the industrious Bathsheba has been pictured sitting at a spinning wheel—"She layeth her hands to the spindle, and her hands hold the distaff." Perhaps it is time to suggest a new icon for women's history. Certainly spinning was an important female craft in northern New England, linked not only to housework but to mothering, but it was one enterprise among many. Spinning wheels are such intriguing and picturesque objects, so resonant with antiquity, that they tend to obscure rather than clarify the nature of female economic life, making home production the essential element in early American huswifery and the era of industrialization the period of crucial change. Challenging the symbolism of the wheel not only undermines the popular stereotype, it questions a prevailing emphasis in women's history.

An alternate symbol might be the pocket. In early America a woman's pocket was not attached to her clothing, but tied around her waist with a string or tape. (When "Lucy Locket lost her pocket, Kitty Fisher found it.") Much better than a spinning wheel, this homely object symbolizes the obscurity, the versatility, and the personal nature of the housekeeping role. A woman sat at a wheel, but she carried her pocket with her from room to room, from house to yard, from yard to street. The items which it contained would shift from day to day and from year to year, but they would of necessity be small, easily lost, yet precious. A pocket could be a mended and patched pouch of plain homespun or a rich personal ornament boldly embroidered in crewel. It reflected the status as well as the skills of its owner. Whether it contained cellar keys or a paper of pins, a packet of seeds or a baby's bib, a hank of yarn or a Testament, it characterized the social complexity as well as the demanding diversity of women's work.

NOTES

1. William H. Chafe, *Women and Equality: Changing Patterns in American Culture* (New York: Oxford University Press, 1977), p. 17; Mary P. Ryan, *Womanhood in America from Colonial Times to the Present* (New York: New Viewpoints, 1975), p. 30; Ann Douglas, *The Feminization of American Culture* (New York: Alfred A. Knopf, 1977), pp. 53–54; and Nancy F. Cott, *The Bonds of Womanhood* (New Haven and London: Yale University Press, 1977), p. 21.

2. Unless otherwise noted, the information which follows comes from the Francis Plummer will and inventory, *The Probate Records of Essex County* (hereafter EPR) (Salem, Mass.: Essex Institute, 1916–1920), II, 319–322.

3. Joshua Coffin, *A Sketch of the History of Newbury, Newburyport, and West Newbury* (Boston, 1845; Hampton, N.H.: Peter E. Randall, 1977), p. 315.

4. Abbott Lowell Cummings, *The Framed Houses of Massachusetts Bay, 1625–1725* (Cambridge, Mass., and London: Harvard University Press, 1979), pp. 29–32.

5. Darrett B. Rutman, *Husbandmen of Plymouth* (Boston: Beacon Press, 1967), pp. 10–11. Other Newbury families did use corn, including the local miller, who ate "samp"; *Records and Files of the Quarterly Courts of Essex County, Massachusetts* (hereafter ECR) (Salem, Mass.: Essex Institute, 1911–1975), III, 50, and Coffin, *Newbury*, p. 43. On oats, see Massachusetts Historical Society (hereafter MHS) *Collections*, 5th Ser., I, 97, and Jay Allen Anderson, "A Solid Sufficiency: An Ethnography of Yeoman Foodways in Stuart England" (Ph.D. Dissertation, University of Pennsylvania, 1971), pp. 171, 203–204, 265, 267, 268.

6. Cummings, *Framed Houses*, pp. 4, 120–122; Anderson, "Solid Sufficiency," p. 157; Jane Carson, *Colonial Virginia Cookery* (Charlottesville: University Press of Virginia, 1968), p. 104; Frances Phipps, *Colonial Kitchens: Their Furnishings and Their Gardens* (New York: Hawthorn Books, 1972), p. 94 ff.

7. Carson, *Colonial Virginia Cookery*, pp. 104–106.

8. Anderson, "Solid Sufficiency," pp. 63, 65, 118; Howard S. Russell, *A Long, Deep Furrow: Three Centuries of Farming in New England* (Hanover, N.H.: University Press of New England, 1976), p. 160; New Hampshire Historical Society (hereafter NHHS) *Collections*, V (1837), 225.

9. Anderson, "Solid Sufficiency," pp. 99–108, 120–132.

10. Sanborn C. Brown, *Wines and Beers of Old New England* (Hanover, N.H.: University Press of New England, 1978), pp. 50–97; Anderson, "Solid Sufficiency," pp. 89–98.

11. ECR, IV, 194–195, 297–298.

12. Unless otherwise noted, the information which follows comes from the Joshua Grafton will and inventory, Manuscript Probate Records, Essex County Probate Court, Salem, Mass. (hereafter Essex Probate), CCCVII, 58–59.

13. "Part of Salem in 1700," pocket map in James Duncan Phillips, *Salem in the Seventeenth Century* (Boston: Houghton Mifflin, 1933), H-6.

14. Sidney Perley, *The History of Salem, Massachusetts* (Salem, 1924), I, 435, 441.

15. Phillips, *Salem in the Seventeenth Century*, pp. 328, 314, 318, 317, and James Duncan Phillips, *Salem in the Eighteenth Century* (Boston: Houghton Mifflin, 1937), pp. 20–21.

16. The nature of petty trade in colonial America is largely unstudied. I have relied on Karen Friedman, "Victualling Colonial Boston," *Agricultural History*, XLVII (July 1973), 189–205, and suggestive glimpses in Benjamin Coleman, *Some Reasons and Arguments Offered to the Good People of Boston and Adjacent Places, for the Setting Up Markets in Boston* (Boston, 1719), pp. 5–9.

17. One of the accusations against Mary Bradbury was that she sold maggoty cheese. *The Salem Witchcraft Papers*, ed. Paul Boyer and Stephen Nissenbaum (New York: Da Capo Press, 1977), I, 117–129.

18. "Washing and diet" are often grouped in charges for boarders; e.g., *Province and Court Records of Maine* (hereafter *MPCR*) (Portland, Me.: Maine Historical Society, 1928–1975), IV, 205–206. A maid in one New Hampshire house testified to having made a pair of linen sleeves in April which were stolen from the washline in May; Manuscript Court Records, New Hampshire State Archives, Concord, N.H. (hereafter NH Court), IV, 237. For infant's clothing, see Claire Elizabeth Fox, "Pregnancy, Childbirth and Early Infancy in Anglo-American Culture: 1675–1830" (Ph.D. Dissertation, University of Pennsylvania, 1966), pp. 240–245, and Essex Probate, CCCXXI, 96, which lists infant's linen: 57 clouts, 27 caps, 2 headbands, 1 swather, 50 belly bands and bibs, and 6 shirts.

19. Susan Burrows Swan, *Plain and Fancy: American Women and Their Needlework, 1700–1850* (New York: Holt, Rinehart and Winston, 1977), pp. 18–19, 34–38.

20. "Letter-Book of Samuel Sewall," *MHS Collections*, 6th Ser., I, 19. Spinning wheels were staple equipment in traditional dame schools, as a number of engravings show. Lucy Larcom, *A New England Girlhood* (repr. Gloucester: Peter Smith, 1973), p. 43, recalls "Aunt Hannah" spinning at her flax wheel and singing hymns for the children.

21. Unless otherwise noted, the information which follows comes from the Elias Wear will and inventory, Manuscript Probate Records, York County Probate Court, Alfred, Me. (hereafter York Probate), II, 26.

22. Charles Clark, *The Eastern Frontier* (New York: Alfred A. Knopf, 1970), pp. 67–72.

23. *MPCR*, IV, 91–92, 175, 176, 206, 263, 307, 310.

24. Maine Historical Society (hereafter MeHS) *Collections*, IX, 58–59, 457, 466; MHS *Collections*, 6th Ser., I, 126–165, 182–184, 186–189; *Journals of the Rev. Thomas Smith . . .* , ed. William Willis (Portland, Me., 1849), pp. 85–86, 87, 88, 96.

25. Cotton Mather, *Decennium Luctuosum* (Boston, 1699), repr. Charles H. Lincoln, ed., *Narratives of the Indian Wars* (New York: Charles Scribner's Sons, 1913), pp. 266–267.

26. Richard M. Candee, "Wooden Buildings in Early Maine and New Hampshire: A Technological and Cultural History, 1600–1720" (Ph.D. Dissertation, University of Pennsylvania, 1976), pp. 18, 42–48. Secondary accounts have not discussed the sharing of shelter with animals, but there are some tantalizing hints in John Josselyn, *An Account of Two Voyages Made during the Years 1638, 1663* (Boston, 1865), p. 193, on chickens fed under the table in rainy weather; *ECR*, IV, 159, on "goeing into the other roome to give my piggs corne"; and *The Saltonstall Papers, 1607–1814*, ed. Robert E. Moody (Boston: Massachusetts Historical Society, 1972), I, 219, on being "billeted" with "ould Jersey" during Indian troubles.

27. The Rev. John Pike noted that "The Indians killed Henry Barns, Edward Hammonds & his wife, as they were at work in a field at Spruce-Creek" in Kittery. MHS *Proceedings* (1876), p. 129. Also see *ECR*, II, 372–373, 22, 442; *The Diary of Matthew Patten* (Concord, N.H., 1903), pp. 6, 11, 19, 68, 84, 129, 141; and G. E. and K. R. Fussell, *The English Countrywoman* (New York: Benjamin Blom, 1971), pp. 95–96.

28. Sarah Orne Jewett, *The Old Town of Berwick* (Berwick, Me.: Old Berwick Historical Society, 1967), n.p., quoting a local story about Margery Sullivan, whose son John became governor of New Hampshire and whose son James became governor of Massachusetts.

29. Sybil Noyes, Charles Thornton Libby, and Walter Goodwin Davis, *A Genealogical Dictionary of Maine and New Hampshire* (Portland, Me.: Southworth-Anthoensen Press, 1928), pp. 726, 729.

MARYLYNN SALMON
Women and Property in South Carolina: The Evidence from Marriage Settlements, 1730–1830

Marriage is a personal and private relationship. But it is also a public and economic one. This was especially true in traditional America, when, according to British common law, husbands assumed control of their wives' property. Beatrice Plummer and Hannah Grafton, whom we met in the previous essay, could not buy or sell family property unless their husbands specifically agreed to each transaction; Hannah Grafton traded on her husband's account and had no legal right to the money she earned in her shop; neither she nor Plummer could make a will, since they had no property to convey. Magdalen Wear was in the same situation, except during the years of her widowhood.

But as Marylynn Salmon shows, women who were reasonably knowledgeable about the legal system could establish some control over the property they brought into a marriage by the device of a "marriage settlement"; a contract signed before marriage specifying the rights the wife could continue to exercise. In recent years, marriage contracts spelling out the obligations of both parties have once again become popular.

What forms of property were normally protected in eighteenth-century marriage settlements? What forms were not? In what ways were provisions chosen by women facing their second marriage likely to differ from settlements drawn up by women about to be married for the first time? How does Salmon account for these differences? In what ways do eighteenth-century marriage relationships differ from marriage relationships in the twentieth century? In what ways are they similar?

During the eighteenth and early nineteenth centuries two distinct sets of legal principles—those of the common law and equity law—governed the status of women in the British-American colonies and the American states. Complications arose when the rules contradicted each other, as they did, for example, with regard to property ownership. Under the common law, a married woman (feme co-

Excerpted from "Women and Property in South Carolina: The Evidence from Marriage Settlements, 1730–1830" by Marylynn Salmon, in *William and Mary Quarterly*, 3d ser., 39 (1982):655–85. Copyright © 1982 by Marylynn Salmon. Reprinted by permission of Marylynn Salmon. Notes have been renumbered, tables omitted, and cross-references adjusted.

vert) could not own property, either real or personal. All personalty a woman brought to marriage became her husband's. He could spend her money, sell her stocks or slaves, and appropriate her clothing and jewelry. He gained managerial rights to her lands, houses, and tenements and decided if land was to be farmed by the family or leased.[1] He also controlled the rents and profits from all real estate. With regard to conveyances, however, women held a single note of power. No husband could sell real property without the consent of his wife. The common law sanctioned conveyances only when wives freely agreed to them, although "free" consent was sometimes quite difficult to determine in court.[2]

Since women could not own property under the common law, they could not exercise legal controls over it. A feme covert could not make a legally binding contract. She could not sell or mortgage property that she brought to the marriage or that she and her husband acquired. She possessed no power to execute a deed of gift or write a will unless her husband consented, and even then her power was restricted to personal property. During widowhood, the law allowed women dower in one-third of her husband's real property. Hers was a life interest only, and she gained no right to sell or mortgage the land. With regard to personal property, widows could claim absolute ownership of one-third, but only if the estate were free of debts. If a husband died heavily indebted or insolvent, his wife lost all her personal property (and in some jurisdictions her real property as well), even though she had exercised no control over the accumulation of her husband's debts. Regarding property, then, women were virtually powerless under the common law.[3]

Equity law as administered by the British and American courts of chancery was not similarly harsh. Through formal contracts called marriage settlements, femes covert owned and controlled property.[4] In their various forms, marriage settlements allowed women full or partial managerial rights over property. Separate clauses gave women the right to sell or mortgage property, give it away, or write wills. Some marriage settlements stated explicitly the traditional rights that men relinquished by signing them. Many settlements barred husbands from "intermeddling" with their wives' estates in any way and, perhaps most important, stated that settlement property could not be taken by creditors to pay a husband's debts. Separate estates for women also frequently included clauses guaranteeing the inheritances of children. Once women or their relations protected property from the possible business misfortunes of a husband, it could safely be passed through the maternal line.

Marriage settlements were designed, then, to serve several functions. They gave women a measure of financial security during marriage and widowhood. They protected a portion of family property from creditors. They provided grandparents with the assurance that family fortunes would not be spent before grandchildren came of age. Historians of aristocratic society in seventeenth- and eighteenth-century England have tended to emphasize this last function of marriage settlements. They have found that beginning in the late sixteenth century, fathers created trust estates for their daughters in an effort to prevent sons-in-law from controlling, and perhaps squandering, family fortunes. For a man who wanted to guarantee the inheritances of his grandchildren, a trust presented an alternative to turning property over to an outsider— his daughter's husband. According to this interpretation, the primary purpose of English marriage settlements was to create and preserve large family estates.[5] . . .

. . . Historical understanding of equity law and the use of marriage settlements has been based on scant research and impressionistic evidence. . . . We must learn who used marriage settlements, how often they were used, and for what purposes. Such information should reveal the degree to which settlements provided women with financial security and whether they were written to benefit women, or children and grandchildren, or all three groups.

Before the role of equity law in America can be understood, many separate studies of settlements must be conducted, because each colony and state handled principles of equity law differently.[6] . . . This article reports findings for South Carolina, for which a wealth of information is available. The extent of the documentation makes South Carolina a good place to begin an investigation into the nature of equity law. The legal record reveals remarkably liberal attitudes toward women's property rights—quite possibly the most liberal of all the colonies and states, although that supposition must be tested by comparative study.

In 1720 the colony established a court of chancery that handled cases concerning marriage settlements in a sophisticated manner, imitating the English Chancery Court in style and decisions. The court kept good records and remained active throughout the colonial and early national periods. The legislature did not require registration of marriage settlements until 1785, but before that date prudent persons frequently recorded their settlements with the secretary of state in Charleston. After 1785, all settlements had to be recorded within three months of their creation to be considered valid. Altogether some 2000 settlements have survived from the colonial and early national periods.[7] For this study, an attempt was made to discover and analyze all recorded marriage settlements for the colonial and Revolutionary periods. For the period 1785–1830, when the law required settlements to be recorded and the number increased accordingly, a sample consisting of all deeds registered in Charleston in every fifth

year has been analyzed, for a total of 638. Each settlement gives the names of the parties, the dates of creation and recording, the type of property settled, and the terms of the settlement. Also frequently noted are the occupations of the parties, their residence, their marital status, the name of the owner(s) of the property, and the location and amount of the property.

Proper marriage settlements were complicated documents, usually made in the form of trusts. . . .

To create a trust estate in the normal fashion, the man, woman, and trustee(s) all joined in the execution of an "indenture tripartite," a contract stipulating the terms of the settlement. This form guaranteed the knowledge and consent of the parties, as required by law. In cases involving separate estates, equity standards demanded that men be fully apprised of the terms of their wives' settlements. Judges refused to support a woman who deceived her fiancé or husband into expecting property at marriage, only to secure it to herself through a trustee. They viewed such action as a fraud against the husband's marital rights and held that "he [or she] that hath committed Iniquity, shall not have Equity."[8]

Settlements granting women separate estates could be written either before or after marriage, but most couples executed them prior to marriage. For the period under study, 87 percent (552) of the settlements were prenuptial. There was no significant change in this pattern over time, indicating the constancy of women's desire to secure separate property at the point when they exercised the greatest bargaining power over men.[9] Postnuptial settlements usually resulted when a wife inherited property unexpectedly, or when her husband encountered financial difficulties that made it necessary to secure some family property against creditors.

For understandable reasons, creditors disliked trust estates, particularly those made after marriage. They resented the ability of a feme covert to deny them access to her separate estate and argued that husbands as well as wives could find protection under the terms of marriage settlements. A man who lost his own estate through business misfortunes or extravagant living, they claimed, could fall back on the income from his wife's trust property. Indebted or insolvent husbands might even attempt to preserve a portion of their own fortunes by fraudulently settling property on their wives.

Evidence from South Carolina undermines the argument that settlements commonly benefited husbands rather than wives. Women who wrote marriage settlements usually wanted to control the property they brought to their marriages, not their husbands' property. Eighty-two percent (523) of the settlements studied included only the wife's estate; 11 percent (68), only the estate of the husband; and 5 percent (35), property from both the husband and wife. (In 12 cases, 2 percent, it is unknown who owned the property.) No man put his entire estate into a trust for his wife. These figures demonstrate no general attempt by men to protect their property through marriage settlements. . . .

. . . Through marriage settlements, families possessed a source of income that was free from obligations of the male head, either business or, if the estate were so designed, personal. Since separate estates could prove so beneficial, it is important to know how many women actually employed them. In this regard the documentation for colonial South Carolina is sadly limited. . . . For the period 1785–1810, however, when virtually all marriage settlements were recorded in Charleston and when accurate census records are available for the state, it is possible to arrive at a rough estimate of the number of couples with settlements. During those years, approximately 1–2 percent of marrying couples created separate estates.[10] Settlements apparently were far from the

common occurrence that some historians have believed, at least in South Carolina. Few women had either means or reason to utilize them.

Who, then, did create marriage settlements? Perhaps the small number of deeds indicates use of settlements only among the wealthy, landed families of South Carolina in the manner of the English aristocracy. Fortunately, the detailed information available in the deeds allows us to discover something about the status of couples who employed trust estates and marriage settlements. This can be done by analyzing the value of settled property and by noting the occupations of husbands. (We cannot consider the occupations of wives, because few identified themselves by occupation.) The following discussion investigates property values first, and then turns to male occupations. . . .

The upper ranks of South Carolina society relied on settlements more often than people of middling status. It appears that 69 percent (316/456) of the estates that specified types of property included property worth more than £500 sterling, or more than five slaves, or more than one town lot with appurtenances, or a plantation of more than three hundred acres.[11] Settlements of more than ten slaves and hundreds of pounds sterling were common. . . .

Although the elite employed marriage settlements most often, persons with small amounts of property also used them. Settlements sometimes included only one or two slaves, a few articles of household furniture, or the woman's clothing and household goods. Approximately 9 percent (41/456) of the settlements included property estimated to be worth less than £150 sterling, or included only one slave, or a part of a house. Another 22 percent (99) included property estimated at £151–500 sterling, or contained two to five slaves, or one house, or 100 to 299 acres of land. The settlement of John Darrell and Elizabeth Legeaux is typical of contracts made by persons from the middling ranks of society:

> This is to certify to all whom it may concern that I John Smith Darrell of the city of Charleston and State aforesaid Mariner being now about to be joined in the holy Bond of Wedlock to Miss Elizabeth Browne Legeaux conceiving it just and right that she should continue after marriage to hold what property she might have at that time I do therefore by this Instrument Secure to her and the heirs of her body for ever all right and title to Two Negroes left to her by her Father (Vizt.) the Woman Named Constant and her son Caesar together with any other Issue that the said Constant may have. I do also secure to her her Bed Bedding and the household furniture that she now possesses reserving to myself the Services of the said Negroes during my Natural life.[12]

. . . Although the desire to protect family property for future generations may have motivated some of the wealthy couples with settlements, the preservation of family status was not the dominant consideration for all. Given the wide range of individuals with separate estates—from a woman with one slave, to an heiress with one hundred—we cannot rely on the traditional English interpretation of settlements.

Most women who made settlements owned personal rather than real property. Very few of the settlements included real estate to the exclusion of personalty (10/456), and only one-third (147) included some real estate. The other two-thirds (301) involved only personal property. In South Carolina, women's marriage settlements most often included slaves, money, cattle, and household goods, but not land. Such a pattern may indicate that fathers gave their land to sons, while daughters received slaves or money. . . . Given the fact that under the common law men acquired absolute ownership of their wives' personal estates at marriage, while they exercised only managerial rights over real property, this is not surprising. Settle-

ments were more useful to women who owned personal property.

This consideration may explain why a substantial number of settlements involved slaves. Eighty-two percent (372) of the deeds that specify the nature of the property included at least some slaves, and 28 percent (129) included only slaves. No other type of property appears so frequently in the settlements. Moreover, settlements including only a few slaves appeared in the sample as often as those with many slaves. When settlements including only slaves are singled out, we learn that fully 32 percent (41/129) contained five slaves or fewer, and that an additional 19 percent contained six to ten slaves. Women with slaves appreciated the importance of protecting their property.

More may be learned about the function of settlements by studying the occupational status of the men who made them. Of of whole number of deeds analyzed, 68 percent (434) noted the husband's occupation. Over half of these (228) involved planters (30 percent, N = 131) or gentlemen (22 percent, N = 97). From the settlements, we can learn no more about the status of these men than the words they used to describe themselves. We do not know, for example, how many of the planters were large landowners and therefore considered members of the social elite. The word planter stood for all farmers and landowners in South Carolina, large and small. The fact that 22 percent of the sample referred to themselves as "gentlemen," however, reveals the high social standing of a significant proportion of settlement holders.

Merchants composed the next largest group of men with settlements, 13 percent (58/434). Perhaps the volatile fortunes of merchant families gave them special incentives to protect their property from creditors. Indentures tripartite involving merchants frequently alluded to the financial risks of trade. The settlement of William Edwards and Elizabeth Moore in 1774, for example, gave the couple joint control over her property—seven slaves and a £6000 current money bond—"unless it shall happen that the said William Edwards shall become Bankrupt or meet with losses or misfortunes in Trade or Business so as to be unable to support himself and family."[13] In that case, Elizabeth Edwards would have full managerial rights, free from "interference" by her husband. . . . The overseas expeditions of merchants could place wives and children in precarious financial situations. Before Josiah Smith left on a "sea voyage," he took out the 1789 equivalent of flight insurance. He settled six slaves on his wife for her sole and separate use, free from his debts, if he never returned.[14] . . .

Almost as many artisans, innkeepers, and mariners made marriage settlements as gentlemen—20 percent (86/434). Although we cannot learn the economic standing of these men from the settlements (and some of them may have owned considerable amounts of property), the fact that they identified themselves by trade rather than by status indicates that they were not a part of the South Carolina elite. Even persons at the lowest social level could make use of equity law, as demonstrated by the appearance of a free black man in the sample. On the basis of male occupations, then, it is possible to state that marriage settlements were not made exclusively by the South Carolina aristocracy. Couples from the middling and even the lower ranks of society also sometimes took the precaution of establishing separate estates for wives. . . .

Each marriage settlement contained various clauses for delineating control over settlement property. Couples could place property under the management of trustees, or they could give trustees no managerial powers at all, reducing them to figureheads. Some husbands retained control over their wives' estates, and in many cases, as will be shown below, femes covert managed their own property. The powers retained by women became sig-

nificant for determining their level of independence. Some trusts gave women extensive authority over their own property, while others gave them none at all but instead directed trustees to pay them the rents and profits of their estates. Some settlements gave women one privilege of control while denying others. For example, if a deed granted a feme covert the right to devise, she could not also sell or mortgage her estate; those powers had to be granted in a separate clause. . . .

. . . Over the entire period studied, 40 percent (254) of the women administered their estates alone. In 28 percent (180) of the deeds, husbands and wives managed settlement property together, and in 25 percent (157), men possessed exclusive managerial rights.

Some change in this division of authority occurred over time. There was a small but steady decline in the number of women who managed their own estates, offset by an increase in the number of husbands and wives who shared control. With the exception of a slight rise between 1780 and 1800, the number of men who managed settlement property alone remained fairly constant, at about 22 percent. What we see then, is a shifting pattern, away from exclusive privileges for women and toward joint privileges for couples.

A plausible explanation for this pattern may be found in Mary Beth Norton's study of marital relationships in the eighteenth and early nineteenth centuries.[15] Norton discovered that before the Revolution wives rarely played an active role in family business beyond their sphere of domestic concerns. They deferred to their husbands on most questions and relied on men to manage family finances. By the end of the century, however, this deferential relationship was changing. Marriages became more egalitarian, as wives abandoned passivity to participate in broader decisions concerning family affairs. The need for female autonomy in regulating separate estates would decrease as relationships between spouses became more equal over time. Femes covert might no longer desire total independence in managing their own estates precisely because they exercised more authority over the general fund of family property. . . .

Unfortunately, some individuals did not understand the importance of precision. They wrote loose documents, failing to delineate specific powers of control. Occasionally, friends or relatives failed to clarify the fact that they were creating a separate estate for a feme covert through a deed of gift or a devise. They gave a woman property, meant for her separate use, but failed to say so explicitly. In South Carolina, when settlements were vague and disputes brought couples into court, judges in equity did everything in their power to protect women. The intent of settlements, gifts, or wills, however haphazardly designed, governed judicial decisions.

Court records indicate that by the early nineteenth century, South Carolina jurists interpreted unclear words in a deed of gift or marriage settlement consistently for the benefit of women. For example, following the English Chancery case of *Tyrrel* v. *Hope* (1743), the South Carolina court ceased requiring the specific words "to her sole and separate use" for the creation of a separate estate.[16] Instead, chancellors began to assume that any conveyance to a married woman was meant for her own use, whether the donor said so explicitly or not. . . .

South Carolina chancellors also interpreted unclear words in settlements for the benefit of married women. When coercion was not an issue, judges assumed that the absence of restrictive clauses meant freedom to exercise control. In *Lowndes' Trustee* v. *Champneys' Executors* (1821), the chancellor declared that it was "immaterial in what form or phrase a trust of this nature creating a seperate [sic] estate for the Wife is described— technical language is not necessary—All that is requisite is that the intention of the gift should appear manifestly to be for the wife's seperate enjoyment."[17] . . .

. . . Settlements became so respectable, and chancellors supported them so wholeheartedly, that by the mid-eighteenth century in England and by 1762 in South Carolina, equity courts regarded them as a positive right for all married women. Under certain circumstances, chancellors ordered men to give their wives separate estates. . . .

Chancellors ordered the creation of a separate estate when the financial situation of a husband caused them concern for his wife's well being. Men of good standing in the community were not usually handled as harshly as Thomas Lloyd. When William Henry Drayton, a prosperous planter, member of the Governor's Council, and subsequently chief justice of South Carolina, won a chancery suit against his father-in-law's executors, he did not have to place the property into a trust.[18] Undoubtedly the court believed that his respectable position, added to the fact that his wife already possessed a settlement, made the order unnecessary. . . .

On one point South Carolina chancellors were not willing to make liberal interpretations. Unless a settlement explicitly gave a feme covert power to write a will, she could not do so.[19] Women and their benefactors were careful, therefore, to include this right as a clause in settlements. It appeared frequently, particularly during the first two decades under study, when 62 percent (36/58) of the women specified the power to make a will. The figure rises to 71 percent if we include those women who possessed the right to bequeath in the event they outlived their husbands. Over the course of the eighteenth century, this figure fell, but until 1800 more than half of the women with settlements possessed testamentary powers. After the turn of the century the figure declined until fewer than one-third of all femes covert could write wills under the stated terms of their settlements. From 1801 to 1830, 26 percent (45/172) of the settlements sampled gave women this privilege, while 29 percent (50/170) gave it to either the feme covert or the survivor of the marriage. As the number of settlements allowing women to write wills declined, those arranging for automatic descent to children increased.

The reasons for this decline are not clear. . . . as marriages became less patriarchal over the period, women may have regarded the right to make wills as less vital to their financial autonomy. The desire to exert control after death dwindled as more women possessed authority during life. Most mothers undoubtedly divided their estates equally among children, even when they did write wills. . . .

Some mothers were fully aware of the potential power of testamentary rights. Mary Ladson, marrying for the first time in 1760, included a clause in her settlement allowing her to write a will. She wanted her estate to be divided among her children "in such shares and proportions and at such times as the said Mary by her last Will and Testament shall give Limit." The widow Jane Wilkie was equally explicit about her desire to decide what property should go to her children. In 1774 she wrote in her settlement, "All such Child or Children shall possess & enjoy all such part & proportion in the manner & form as she the said Jane Wilkie shall point out & direct." Even after the turn of the century, when fewer women possessed the legal ability to write wills, some women still realized the power they held. Elizabeth Legare wrote in 1825 that she intended to use her estate during her lifetime for the provision of her children "at her own discretion," and not otherwise.[20]

Women who had already experienced married life, such as Jane Wilkie and Elizabeth Legare, took special care to protect their property rights in marriage settlements. Most single women were not so careful. Comparison of settlements made by widows and single women proves valuable for understanding some individuals' needs for separate estates. A woman's marital status frequently acted as a motivating force for the creation of a settlement and for the inclusion of female managerial and testamentary powers.[21]

Of the 638 settlements sampled, 532 recorded a marital status for the woman. During the period 1730 to 1780, widows appeared in over half of the settlements giving status, 56 percent (159/286), while single women constituted 44 percent (127) of the sample. Even if we take into account the high mortality rate in colonial South Carolina and the use of the state as a Revolutionary battlefield, the high percentage of widows is surprising. After 1780, the number of widows declined, but they still made settlements in 40 percent (98/246) of the sample.

When we compare the powers of control exercised by widows with those held by single women, it becomes clear that experienced matrons were more emphatic about managing their own property than were women marrying for the first time. Widows held complete managerial powers and specified the right to make wills at more than double the rate of first brides. Rather than directing settlement property by themselves, most single women divided between giving their husbands authority and arranging for coadministration. They also provided for automatic descent of settlement property in fully two thirds of their deeds, whereas widows did so less than one-third of the time. The settlements of first brides thus demonstrate a less protective attitude than those of experienced matrons. Moreover, after 1740 there was remarkably little change in this pattern either for control or descent.

Clearly, the experience of marriage affected the attitudes of women toward property control and management. Before entering a second union, many women demanded the right to administer their own property. Widows' desire for active control may have reflected the fact that their estates were no longer simply gifts from parents and friends but property they had worked for themselves, either alone or with their former husbands. Parents who initiated the settlements of new brides concerned themselves primarily with protecting property from husbands' creditors. They did not seek to provide daughters with the power to control and devise property as much as they created a fund for family income. Widows, however, frequently demanded the right to manage the property that they had obtained themselves. Elizabeth Meshaw's settlement in 1736 observed, "The said Elizabeth Meshaw since the Death of her said Husband hath by her great pains care Labour and Industry acquired a considerable addition to the Estate and Interest so left her. . . . [P]articularly [she] hath purchased a Tract of Land containing Two hundred and Fifty Acres." Elizabeth retained the right to devise her estate as she saw fit, without the interference of her new husband. When Christiana Hoff purchased a slave through her own labor, she wrote a settlement in 1772 explicitly denying her husband any rights to it. The case of Elizabeth Baxter may be most revealing. Before Elizabeth, a "merchant," consented to marry Thomas Robinson, a "mariner," in 1771, she executed a settlement of all her personal estate and business property. She reserved absolute control over the property for herself "in order the better to enable her to support & maintain her & her children & which the said Thomas Robinson is at present rendered incapable of doing."[22] Elizabeth was taking no chances. If Thomas could not support her, she would arrange to do so herself. Women such as Elizabeth, who knew the dangers of marriage and widowhood, took special care for their own and their children's futures.

Although the number of widows who provided for children in their settlements increased throughout the period, widows remained less likely than young brides to arrange for automatic descent. Widows

such as Elizabeth Baxter had the responsibility of caring for the children of their previous marriages and undoubtedly felt pressure to include protective clauses for children in their settlements, yet did so at half the rate of single women. Thus Mrs. Baxter retained the right to devise her estate. Although she clearly was concerned with providing for her children, she did not think is necessary to arrange for their inheritances when she wrote her settlement. Such dispositions could be made later, when she was closer to death. For the moment she worried primarily about living in a male-dominated world with a new husband who could not support her. The failure to arrange for automatic descent implies that many widows did not view settlements primarily as a means of guaranteeing the inheritances of their children. More than anything else, they wanted absolute control over management decisions and the right to bequeath to whomever they pleased. When they chose to remarry, they did so with strings attached.

Although the comparative powers of widows and single women remained largely the same throughout the eighteenth and early nineteenth centuries, one development in the settlements of single women may indicate an increasing desire on their part to exercise authority. There was a gradual but steady increase in the number of settlements allowing couples joint powers of administration. Single women did not feel the need to exercise sole control to the same degree as widows, but they did become less willing to give husbands absolute managerial rights. From 1730 to 1780, only 32 percent (41/127) of their settlements gave couples joint powers of administration, whereas 45 percent (66/148) did so from 1781 to 1830. The number of men with sole powers fell from 39 percent (49/127) to 28 percent (41/148). With regard to the management of property, therefore, the settlements of widows and single women became slightly more uniform over time, with both groups favoring partnerships in managing separate estates.

Widows, heiresses, merchants' wives, the wives of debtors, and women whose parents warned them about the dangers of married life—these were the South Carolina matrons with trust estates. They were frequently women of wealth with a great deal to lose if their husbands proved wasteful or unfortunate in business. Sometimes they were women of small fortunes intent on protecting what little they had. They were intelligent, or experienced, or protected by concerned parents. Above all, given the legal status of women under the common law, they were fortunate.

Courts of chancery in South Carolina offered liberal support for marriage settlements. Judges regarded separate estates as the right of every feme covert, necessary for women's security in many cases and helpful to society in providing some families with economic support. Judges consistently ruled in favor of the creation of separate estates and enforced liberal precedents for administering them. Realizing the delicate position of married women under the common law, chancellors acted to mitigate legal hardships by wholeheartedly supporting women's rights to separate estates. Judicial acceptance of settlements increased in the period studied, demonstrating expansion of women's property rights under equity law. . . . Women with separate estates in eighteenth- and early nineteenth-century South Carolina enjoyed many of the legal rights of men. It remains to be seen if other jurisdictions duplicated this pattern.

Although chancellors supported the use of separate estates, settlements were rare, used either by wealthy women with valuable family interests to protect or by women with an uncommon perspective on their legal status. Equity proved invaluable to women such as the widow Elizabeth Holson, who wanted to enjoy her own estate without "the Least or Smallest Controul or intermeddling" of her husband, but Elizabeth was one of only a small number of women with marriage settlements.[23] We still do not know why so few women relied on separate estates. Either they were satisfied with their common law status, or they did not regard equity law as a viable alternative. In South Carolina, it may be important that settlements were not necessary to confer feme sole trader status. Independent businesswomen functioned under the common law as long as their husbands demonstrated tacit consent to their activities. But more important, the majority of women apparently regarded equity law protections as superfluous to their needs. For women without much property or for women who perceived their legal status as secure, separate estates served no purpose.

We must learn more about the application of common law principles before we will fully understand the meaning of equity law. Perhaps the harshness of common law rules was mitigated in practice, making separate estates largely unnecessary. If most women did not feel a need to use equity law, then we must reevaluate the effect of common law restrictions on women's lives. We must also consider an alternative possibility: that social custom so oppressed women, they did not consider the possibility of employing separate estates. Community scorn or family opposition may have prevented women from acting on their desire for separate estates. There is some evidence to show that the fear and distrust women exhibited by creating settlements antagonized men. The wording of settlements, for example, occasionally reveals attempts to appease men's feelings. Some women wrote that their desire for separate estates arose from a fear of the system, not the individual. Such public statements relieved men of responsibility for the anxiety experienced by women and thus saved them face in the community. Otherwise, the mere existence of a settlement attested to the insecurity of a particular woman.

At this point it is impossible to be sure

whether male antipathy to settlements prevented most women from making them. Final conclusions await further research on the social customs of families in the South and on the use of common law rules pertaining to the rights of women. Perhaps the words of Sarah Ann Baxter demonstrate, as well as anything we now have, the attitude of women who wrote settlements. Sarah's settlement stated that its object was to protect her separate interests so that she would not be "defeated or defrauded" out of her property "by the collusive act or device" of her husband. The job of Sarah's trustees was to sue her husband in case he "bargained, sold, or inveigled away" her lands and to demand damages from the court "for any waste which he may commit upon the said lands or injury he may commit upon the said personal or any of the said personal property."[24] There can be no doubt that Sarah did not trust her husband-to-be. It is unlikely that most couples began married life with such distrust. Undoubtedly women as well as men preferred to demonstrate hope, rather than fear, on the day of their marriage. But if experience proved women naive, then we can understand why so many widows insisted on the creation of settlements, and we can also comprehend why they carefully reserved managerial rights for themselves.

NOTES

Ms. Salmon wishes to thank Mary Maples Dunn, Mary Beth Norton, and the members of the 1979–1980 seminar of the Philadelphia Center for Early American Studies for their critical comments on this and an earlier version of the article. The invaluable technical assistance of Joseph O'Rourke is also gratefully acknowledged.

1. William Blackstone, *Commentaries on the Laws of England . . .* , 4 vols. (Oxford, 1765–1769), II, 132, 136, 255, 293, 355; . . . William Holdsworth, *A History of English Law*, 16 vols. (London, 1903–1966), III (5th ed.), 193, 195–196, 249; *An Essay on the Nature and Operation of Fines and Recoveries* (London, 1728), 68–69; *The Laws Respecting Women . . .* (Dobbs Ferry, N.Y., 1974 [orig. publ. London, 1777]), 181; James Kent, *Commentaries on American Law*, 4 vols. (New York, 1826–1830), II, 151–154. . . .

2. Tapping Reeve, *The Law of Baron and Femme, of Parent and Child, of Guardian and Ward, of Master and Servant, and of the Powers of Courts of Chancery . . .* (New Haven, Conn., 1816), 98; *Laws Respecting Women*, 70–72; Marylynn Salmon, "The Property Rights of Women in Early America: A Comparative Study" (Ph.D. diss., Bryn Mawr College, 1980), 27–84.

3. See Marylynn Salmon, *Women and the Law of Property in Early America* (Chapel Hill: University of North Carolina Press, 1986).

4. Holdsworth cited *Avenant v. Kitchen* (1581) as the first case in which an equity court supported the right of a woman to hold property separately from her husband by the force of a prenuptial contract. Within a short period of time, the Chancery Court permitted women to exert active control over settlements. Decisions recognized the right of women to enter into binding contracts (1582), write wills (1594), make presents to their husbands (1614), and convey to strangers (1619). Holdsworth, *History of English Law*, I (7th rev. ed.), 494, V, 303, 310–315; Richard Francis, *Maxims of Equity . . .* (London, 1728), 5; Reeve, *Baron and Femme*, 222–223, 238; *Laws Respecting Women*, 179; Zephaniah Swift, *A System of the Laws of the State of Connecticut: In Six Books*, 2 vols. (New Haven, Conn., 1795–1796), I, 200–201.

5. Christopher Clay, "Marriage, Inheritance, and the Rise of Large Estates in England, 1660–1815," *Economic History Review*, 2d Ser., XXI (1968), 503–518; H. J. Habakkuk, "Marriage Settlements in the Eighteenth Century," Royal Historical Society, *Transactions*, 4th Ser., XXXII (1950), 15–31; Lawrence Stone, *The Crisis of the Aristocracy, 1558–1641* (Oxford, 1965).

6. Some colonies, such as Massachusetts, Connecticut, and Pennsylvania, did not have separate courts of equity in the English fashion.

7. Anne King Gregorie, ed., *Records of the Court of Chancery of South Carolina, 1671–1779* (Washington, D.C., 1950), 5–7;

. . . Marriage Settlements, Vols. 1–10 (1785–1830); Records of the Register of the Secretary of the Province, Vols. A–I (1721–1733); Miscellaneous Records of the Secretary of State, Charleston Series, Vols. AB, BB–XX (1735–1789). All manuscripts cited are located in the South Carolina State Archives, Columbia, unless noted otherwise.

8. Francis, *Maxims of Equity*, 5.

9. Reeve noted the significant role of parents and guardians in bargaining with the suitors of young women (see *Baron and Femme*, 174).

10. There are no accurate marriage rates for South Carolina in the period under study. Population figures are available, however, and by applying the earliest available marriage rate, that of 1860 (1/115), we can arrive at a rough percentage of marrying couples with settlements. Thus in 1790 when the white population was 140,000 the estimated number of marriages was 1610. Twenty-two settlements were written in that year and therefore the percentage of marrying couples with settlements was 1.4. The next federal census (1800) revealed a population figure of 196,000, making the estimated number of marriages 2254. Since 28 settlements were written in 1800, the percentage of marrying couples with settlements was 1.2. *The Statistical History of the United States: From Colonial Times to the Present* (New York, 1976), 1168; *Population of the United States in 1860* (Washington, D.C., 1869), xxxvi.

11. For the purpose of making comparative statements concerning settlement property, I assigned estimated values to certain types of property, based on information provided in Alice Hanson Jones, *American Colonial Wealth: Documents and Methods*, 2d ed. (New York, 1977), III. A slave was valued at £85, one acre of improved land at £1, one head of cattle at £10, one riding horse at £75, one town lot with appurtenances at less than £500, and more than one town lot with appurtenances at more than £500. Settlements with a single slave were all classified as containing property of a value less than £150, as were settlements containing only part of a house. Settlements including only slaves, numbering two to five, were all classified in the £150–500 range. All pounds are pounds sterling. Although estimated valuations such as these are extremely unreliable for determining absolute wealth, they enable us to distinguish between individuals of great and middling wealth.

12. Marriage Settlement between Eliza-beth Legeaux and John Smith Darrell (1809), Marriage Settlements, 5, 522–523.

13. Marriage Settlement between Elizabeth Moore and William Edwards (1744), Miscellaneous Records, RR, 212–213.

14. Marriage Settlement between Mary Smith and Josiah Smith (1789), Marriage Settlements, I, 446–447.

15. Mary Beth Norton, *Liberty's Daughters: The Revolutionary Experience of American Women, 1750–1800* (Boston, 1980).

16. *Tyrrel v. Hope*, 2 Atkyns 561 (1743); Reeve, *Baron and Femme*, 164; *Lowndes' Trustee v. Champneys' Executors* (1821), Charleston District Equity Decrees, 3, 354.

17. *Lowndes' Trustees v. Champneys' Executors* (1821), Charleston District Equity Decrees, 3, 354.

18. Marriage Settlement between Dorothy Golightly and William Henry Drayton (1764), Marriage Settlements, 2, 185–192.

19. Women without the right to make wills through marriage settlements could bequeath personal property if their husbands consented. See *Grimke v. Grimke*, 1 S.C. Eq. (1 Des.) 366–382 (1794), and *Smelie v. Smelie*, 2 S.C. Eq. (2 Des.) 66–79 (1802). The law on this point is discussed in Blackstone, *Commentaries*, II, 498, and *Laws Respecting Women*, 178–179. Without valid marriage settlements, however, women could never devise real property. . . .

20. Marriage Settlements between Mary Ladson and Thomas Poole (1760), Miscellaneous Records, MM, 41–44; Jane Wilkie and Charles Cogdell (1774), Miscellaneous Records, RR, 314–316; Elizabeth Legare and William B. Legare (1825), Marriage Settlements, 9, 185–187.

21. For a discussion of one enterprising widow's experience, see Mary Beth Norton, "A Cherished Spirit of Independence: The Life of an Eighteenth-Century Boston Businesswoman," in Carol Ruth Berkin and Mary Beth Norton, eds., *Women of America: A History* (Boston, 1979), 48–67.

22. Marriage Settlements between Elizabeth Meshaw and Thomas Snipes (1736), HH, 27–28; Christiana Hoff and John Hoff (1772), PP, 254; Elizabeth Baxter and Thomas Robinson (1771), PP, 6–8, Miscellaneous Records.

23. Marriage Settlement between Elizabeth Holson and John Harth (1779), Marriage Settlements, 1, 152.

24. Marriage Settlement between Sarah Ann Baxter and Joseph Binnikes (1825), Marriage Settlements, 9, 159.

LYLE KOEHLER
The Case of the American Jezebels:
Anne Hutchinson and Female Agitation during the
Years of Antinomian Turmoil, 1636–1640

The Antinomian heresy threw the colony of Massachusetts Bay into turmoil for years and forced its leaders to reconsider the nature of their experiment. Antinomians placed greater emphasis on religious feeling than did orthodox Puritans. They tended to be suspicious (*anti*) of law (*nomos*) or formal rules and came close to asserting that individuals had access to direct revelation from the Holy Spirit. Historians usually study Antinomianism as a serious religious upheaval in an important colony. In this essay Lyle Koehler reports that the fact that Anne Hutchinson, the leader of the dissenters, was a woman made an important difference in the way courts treated her and in the sort of people who followed her. This information has always been available in the trial records, but until recently historians tended to pay little attention to it. Koehler emphasizes that many other women were attracted to Hutchinson's cause, so that Antinomianism became the occasion for the expression of widely shared dissatisfaction and uneasiness. When Hutchinson was held up to public ridicule and exiled, explicit dissent by women was firmly squelched in the Puritan community. The accusation that dissenting or independent women were witches, voiced in the Hutchinson case, would reverberate through the rest of the century until the massive witchcraft trials in Salem in 1692.

Between 1636 and 1638 Massachusetts boiled with controversy, and for more than three centuries scholars have attempted to define and redefine the nature, causes, and implications of that controversy. Commentators have described the rebellious Antinomians as "heretics of the worst and most dangerous sort" who were guilty of holding "absurd, licentious, and destructive" opinions, as "a mob scrambling after God, and like all mobs quickly dispersed once their leaders were dealt with," and as the innocent victims of "inexcusable severity and unnecessary virulence."[1] Other narrators have called the most famous Antinomian, Anne Hutchinson, a "charismatic healer, with the gift of fluent and inspired speech," another St. Joan of Arc, a rebel with a confused, bewildered mind, and a woman

Excerpted from "The Case of the American Jezebels: Anne Hutchinson and Female Agitation during the Years of Antinomian Turmoil, 1636–1640" by Lyle Koehler, in *William and Mary Quarterly*, 3d ser., 31 (1974):55–78. Copyright © 1974 by Lyle Koehler. Reprinted by permission of the author. Notes have been renumbered.

"whose stern and masculine mind . . . triumphed over the tender affections of a wife and mother."[2]

Almost without exception, these critics and defenders of Hutchinson and the Antinomians have dealt specifically with Antinomianism as a religious movement and too little with it as a social movement. . . .

That Anne Hutchinson and many other Puritan women should at stressful times rebel, either by explicit statement or by implicit example, against the role they were expected to fulfill in society is readily understandable, since that role, in both old and New England, was extremely limiting. The model English woman was weak, submissive, charitable, virtuous, and modest. Her mental and physical activity was limited to keeping the home in order, cooking, and bearing and rearing children, although she might occasionally serve the community as a nurse or midwife. She was urged to avoid books and intellectual exercise, for such activity might overtax her weak mind, and to serve her husband willingly, since she was by nature his inferior. In accordance with the Apostle Paul's doctrine, she was to hold her tongue in church and be careful not "to teach, nor to usurp authority over the man, but to be in silence."[3]

In their letters, lectures, and historical accounts many of the Bay Colony men and some of the women showed approval of modest, obedient, and submissive females. Governor John Winthrop's wife Margaret was careful to leave such important domestic matters as place of residence to her husband's discretion, even when she had a preference of her own. She was ashamed because she felt that she had "no thinge with in or with out" worthy of him and signed her letters to him "your faythfull and obedient wife" or "your lovinge and obedient wife." Lucy Downing, Winthrop's sister, signed her chatty letters to her brother, "Your sister to commaund." Elizabeth, the wife of Winthrop's son John, described herself in a letter to her husband as "thy eaver loveing and kinde wife to comande in whatsoeaver thou plesest so long as the Lord shall bee plesed to geve me life and strenge."[4]

Winthrop himself was harshly critical of female intellect. In 1645 he wrote that Ann Hopkins, wife of the governor of Connecticut, had lost her understanding and reason by giving herself solely to reading and writing. The Massachusetts statesman commented that if she "had attended her household affairs, and such things as belong to women, and not gone out of her way and calling to meddle in such things as are proper for men, whose minds are stronger, etc. she had kept her wits, and might have improved them usefully and honorably in the place God had set her." Earlier he had denounced Anne Hutchinson as "a woman of a haughty and fierce carriage, of a nimble wit and active spirit, and a very voluble tongue, more bold than a man, though in understanding and judgement, inferiour to many women."[5]

. . . Reverend John Cotton arrived in Boston in 1633 and soon requested that women desiring church membership be examined in private since a public confession was "against the apostle's rule and not fit for a woman's modesty." At a public lecture less than a year later Cotton explained that the apostle directed women to wear veils in church only when "the custom of the place" considered veils "a sign of the woman's subjection." Cambridge minister Thomas Shepard, one of Anne Hutchinson's most severe critics, commended his own wife for her "incomparable meekness of spirit, toward myself especially," while Hugh Peter, a Salem pastor and another of Hutchinson's accusers, urged his daughter to respect her feminine meekness as "Womans Ornament."[6]

The female role definition that the Massachusetts ministers and magistrates perpetuated severely limited the assertiveness, the accomplishment, the independence, and the intellectual activity of Puritan women. Bay Colony women who might resent such a role definition before 1636 had no ideological rationale around which they could organize the expression of their frustration—whatever their consciousness of the causes of that frustration. With the marked increase of Antinomian sentiment in Boston and Anne Hutchinson's powerful example of resistance, the distressed females were able—as this article will attempt to demonstrate—to channel their frustration into a viable theological form and to rebel openly against the perpetuators of the spiritual and secular status quo. Paradoxically enough, the values that Antinomians embraced minimized the importance of individual action, for they believed that salvation could be demonstrated only by the individual feeling God's grace within.

The process of salvation and the role of the individual in that process was, for the Puritan divines, a matter less well defined. The question of the relative importance of good works (i.e., individual effort) and grace (i.e., God's effort) in preparing man for salvation had concerned English Puritans from their earliest origins, and clergymen of old and New England attempted to walk a broad, although unsure, middle ground between the extremes of Antinomianism and Arminianism. But in 1636 Anne Hutchinson's former mentor and the new teacher of the Boston church, John Cotton, disrupted the fragile theological balance and led the young colony into controversy when he "warned his listeners away from the specious comfort of preparation and re-emphasized the covenant of grace as something in which God acted alone and unassisted."[7] Cotton further explained that a person could become conscious of the dwelling of the Holy Spirit within his soul and directed the Boston congregation "not to be afraid of the word *Revelation*."[8] The church elders, fearing that Cotton's "Revelation" might be dangerously construed to invalidate biblical law, requested a clarification of his position.

While the elders debated with Cotton the religious issues arising out of his pronouncements, members of Cotton's congregation responded more practically and enthusiastically to the notion of personal revelation by ardently soliciting converts to an emerging, loosely-knit ideology which the divines called pejoratively Antinomianism, Opinionism, or Familism.[9] According to Thomas Weld, fledgling Antinomians visited new migrants to Boston, "especially, men of note, worth, and activity, fit instruments to advance their designe." Antinomian principles were defended at military trainings, in town meetings, and before the court judges. Winthrop charged the Opinionists with causing great disturbance in the church, the state, and the family, and wailed, "All things are turned upside down among us."[10]

The individual hungry for power could, as long as he perceived his deep inner feeling of God's grace to be authentic, use that feeling to consecrate his personal rebellion against the contemporary authorities. Some Boston merchants used it to attack the accretion of political power in the hands of a rural-dominated General Court based on land instead of capital. Some "ignorant and unlettered" men used it to express contempt for the arrogance of "black-coates that have been at the Ninneversity."[11] Some women, as we will see, used it to castigate the authority of the magistrates as guardians of the state, the ministers as guardians of the church, and their husbands as guardians of the home. As the most outspoken of these women, Anne Hutchinson diffused her opinions among all social classes by means of contacts made in the course of her profession of midwifery and in the biweekly teaching sessions she held at her home. Weld believed that Hutchinson's lectures were responsible for distributing "the venome of these [Antinomian] opinions into the very veines and vitalls of the People in the Country."[12]

Many women identified with Hutchinson's rebellious intellectual stance and her aggressive spirit. Edward Johnson wrote that "the weaker Sex" set her up as "a Priest" and "thronged" after her. John Underhill reported he daily heard a "clamor" that "New England men usurp over their wives, and keep them in servile subjection." Winthrop blamed her for causing "divisions between husband and wife . . . till the weaker give place to the stronger, otherwise it turnes to open contention," and Weld charged the Antinomians with using the yielding, flexible, and tender women as "an Eve, to catch their husbands also."[13] . . .

From late 1636 through early 1637 female resistance in the Boston church reached its highest pitch. At one point, when pastor John Wilson rose to preach, Hutchinson left the congregation and many women followed her out of the meetinghouse. These women "pretended many excuses for their going out," an action which made it impossible for the authorities to convict them of contempt for Wilson. Other rebels did, however, challenge Wilson's words as he spoke them, causing Weld to comment, "Now the faithfull Ministers of Christ must have dung cast on their faces, and be no better than Legall Preachers, Baals Priests, Popish Factors, Scribes, Pharisees, and Opposers of Christ himselfe."[14]

Included among these church rebels were two particularly active women, Jane Hawkins and milliner William Dyer's wife Mary, both of whom Winthrop found obnoxious. The governor considered the youthful Mary Dyer to be "of a very proud spirit," "much addicted to revelations," and "notoriously infected with Mrs. Hutchinson's errors." Dyer weathered Winthrop's wrath and followed Hutchinson to Rhode Island, but her "addictions" were not without serious conse-quence. Twenty-two years later she would return to Boston and be hanged as a Quaker.[15] The other of Hutchinson's close female associates, Jane Hawkins, dispensed fertility potions to barren women and occasionally fell into a trance-like state in which she spoke Latin. Winthrop therefore denounced her as "notorious for familiarity with the devill," and the General Court, sharing his apprehension, on March 12, 1638, forbade her to question "matters of religion" or "to meddle" in "surgery, or phisick, drinks, plaisters, or oyles." Hawkins apparently disobeyed this order, for three years later the Court banished her from the colony under the penalty of a severe whipping or such other punishment as the judges thought fit.[16]

Other women, both rich and poor, involved themselves in the Antinomian struggle. William Coddington's spouse, like her merchant husband, was "taken with the familistical opinions." Mary Dummer, the wife of wealthy landowner and Assistant Richard Dummer, convinced her husband to move from Newbury to Boston so that she might be closer to Hutchinson. Mary Oliver, a poor Salem calenderer's wife, reportedly exceeded Anne "for ability of speech, and appearance of zeal and devotion" and, according to Winthrop, might "have done hurt, but that she was poor and had little acquaintance [with theology]." Oliver held the "dangerous" opinions that the church was managed by the "heads of the people, both magistrates and ministers, met together," instead of the people themselves, and that anyone professing faith in Christ ought to be admitted to the church and the sacraments. Between 1638 and 1650 she appeared before the magistrates six times for remarks contemptuous of ministerial and magisterial authority and experienced the stocks, the lash, the placement of a cleft stick on her tongue, and imprisonment. One of the Salem magistrates became so frustrated with Oliver's refusal to respect his authority that he seized her and put her in the stocks without a trial. She sued him for false arrest and collected a minimal ten shillings in damages. Her victory was short-lived, however, and before she left Massachusetts in 1650 she had managed to secure herself some reputation as a witch.[17]

Mary Oliver and the other female rebels could easily identify with the Antinomian ideology because its theological emphasis on the inability of the individual to achieve salvation echoed the inability of women to achieve recognition on a sociopolitical level. As the woman realized that she could receive wealth, power, and status only through the man, her father or her husband, so the Antinomian realized that he or she could receive grace only through God's beneficence. Thus, women could have found it appealing that in Antinomianism *both* men and women were relegated vis-à-vis God to the status that women occupied in Puritan society vis-à-vis men, that is, to the status of malleable inferiors in the hands of a higher being. All power, then, emanated from God, raw and pure, respecting no sex, rather than from male authority figures striving to interpret the Divine Word. Fortified by a consciousness of the Holy Spirit's inward dwelling, the Antinomians could rest secure and self-confident in the belief that they were mystic participants in the transcendent power of the Almighty, a power far beyond anything mere magistrates and ministers might muster. Antinomianism could not secure for women such practical earthly powers as sizable estates, professional success, and participation in the church and civil government, but it provided compensation by reducing the significance of these powers for the men. Viewed from this perspective, Antinomianism extended the feminine experience of humility to both sexes, which in turn paradoxically created the possibility of feminine pride, as Anne Hutchinson's dynamic example in her examinations and trials amply demonstrated.

Anne Hutchinson's example caused the divines much frustration. They were chagrined to find that she was not content simply to repeat to the "simple Weomen"[18] the sermons of John Wilson, but that she also chose to interpret and even question the content of those sermons. When she charged that the Bay Colony ministers did not teach a covenant of grace as "clearly" as Cotton and her brother-in-law, John Wheelwright, she was summoned in 1636 to appear before a convocation of the clergy. At this convocation and in succeeding examinations, the ministers found particularly galling her implicit assertion that she had the intellectual ability necessary to judge the truth of their theology. Such an assertion threatened their self-image as the intellectual leaders of the community and the spokesmen for a male-dominated society. The ministers and magistrates therefore sharply criticized Hutchinson for not fulfilling her ordained womanly role. In September 1637 a synod of elders resolved that women might meet "to pray and edify one another," but when one woman "in a prophetical way" resolved questions of doctrine and expounded Scripture, then the meeting was "disorderly." At Hutchinson's examination on November 7 and 8, Winthrop began the interrogation by charging that she criticized the ministers and maintained a "meeting and an assembly in your house that hath been condemned by the general assembly as a thing not tolerable nor comely in the sight of God nor fitting for your sex." Later in the interrogation, Winthrop accused her of disobeying her "parents," the magistrates, in violation of the Fifth Commandment, and paternalistically told her, "We do not mean to discourse with those of your sex." Hugh Peter also indicated that he felt Hutchinson was not fulfilling the properly submissive, nonintellectual feminine role. He ridiculed her choice of a female preacher of the Isle of Ely as a model for her own behavior and told her to reconsider "that you have stept out of your place, *you have rather bine a Husband than a Wife and a preacher than a Hearer; and a Magistrate than a Subject.*"[19]

When attacked for behavior inappropriate to her sex, Hutchinson did not hesitate to demonstrate that she was the intellectual equal of her accusers. She tried to trap Winthrop when he charged her with dishonoring her "parents": "But put the case Sir that I do fear the Lord and my parents, may not I entertain them that fear the Lord because my parents will not give me leave?" To provide a biblical justification for her teaching activities, she cited Titus's rule (2:3–4) "that the elder women should instruct the younger." Winthrop ordered her to take that rule "in the sense that elder women must instruct the younger about their business, and to love their husbands." But Anne disagreed with this interpretation, saying, "I do not conceive but that it is meant for some publick times." Winthrop rejoined, "We must . . . restrain you from maintaining this course," and she qualified, "If you have a rule for it from God's word you may." Her resistance infuriated the governor, who exclaimed, "We are your judges, and not you ours." When Winthrop tried to lure her into admitting that she taught men, in violation of Paul's proscription, Anne replied that she thought herself justified in teaching a man who asked her for instruction, and added sarcastically, "Do you think it not lawful for me to teach women and why do you call me to teach the court?"[20]

Anne soon realized that sarcastic remarks would not persuade the court of the legitimacy of her theological claims. Alternatively, therefore, she affected a kind of modesty to cozen the authorities at the same time that she expressed a kind of primitive feminism through double-entendre statements and attacked the legitimacy of Paul's idea of the nonspeaking, nonintellectual female churchmember. When the Court charged her with "proph-esying," she responded, "The men of *Berea* are commended for examining *Pauls* Doctrine; wee do no more [in our meetings] but read the notes of our teachers Sermons, and then reason of them by searching the Scriptures."[21] Such a statement was on one level an "innocent" plea to the divines that the women were only following biblical prescription. On another level it was an attack on the ministers for presuming to have the final word on biblical interpretation. On yet a third level, since she focused on "Pauls Doctrine" and reminded men that they should take another look at that teaching, her statement was a suggestion that ministerial attitudes toward women ought to be reexamined.

At another point Anne responded to Winthrop's criticism with a similar statement having meaning on three levels. The governor had accused her of traducing the ministers and magistrates and, when summoned to answer this charge, of saying that "the fear of man was a snare and therefore she would not be affeared of them." She replied, "They say I said the fear of man is a snare, why should I be afraid. When I came unto them, they urging many things unto me and I being backward to answer at first, at length this scripture came into my mind 29th Prov. 15. The fear of man bringeth a snare, but who putteth his trust in the Lord shall be safe."[22] Once again, her response was phrased as an "innocent" plea to God to assuage her fears, while at the same time it implied that God was on her side in opposition to the ministers and magistrates. Her statement also told women that if they trusted in God they need not fear men, for such fear trapped them into being "backward" about reacting in situations of confrontation with men.

Anne, although aware of the "backwardness" of women as a group, did not look to intensified group activity as a remedy for woman's downtrodden status. Her feminism consisted essentially of the subjective recognition of her own strength and gifts and the apparent belief that other women could come to the same recognition. A strong, heroic example of female self-assertiveness was necessary to the development of this recognition of one's own personal strength. Anne chose the woman preacher of the Isle of Ely as her particular heroic model; she did, Hugh Peter chided, "exceedingly magnifie" that woman "to be a Womane of 1000 hardly any like to her." Anne could thus dissociate herself from the "divers worthy and godly Weomen" of Massachusetts and confidently deride them as being no better than "soe many Jewes," unconverted by the light of Christ.[23] Other Bay Colony women who wished to reach beyond the conventional, stereotypic behavior of "worthy and godly Weomen" attached themselves to the emphatic example of Anne and to God's ultimate power in order to resist the constraints which they felt as Puritan women.

Fearful that Hutchinson's example might be imitated by other women, the divines wished to catch her in a major theological error and subject her to public punishment. Their efforts were not immediately successful. Throughout her 1637 examination Anne managed to parry the verbal thrusts of the ministers and magistrates by replying to their many questions with questions of her own, forcing them to justify their positions from the Bible, pointing out their logical inconsistencies, and using innuendo to cast aspersions upon their authoritarianism. With crucial assistance from a sympathetic John Cotton, she left the ministers with no charge to pin upon her. She was winning the debate when, in an apparently incautious moment, she gave the authorities the kind of declaration for which they had been hoping. Raising herself to the position of judge over her accusers, she asserted, "I know that for this you goe about to doe to me, God will ruine you and your posterity, and this whole State." Asked how she knew this, she explained, "By an immedi-

ate revelation."[24] With this statement Anne proved her heresy to the ministers and they then took steps to expose her in excommunication proceedings conducted before the Boston church. The divines hoped to expel a heretic from their midst, to reestablish support for the Puritan way, to prevent unrest in the state and the family, and to shore up their own anxious egos in the process.

The predisposition of the ministers to defame Hutchinson before the congregation caused them to ignore what she was actually saying in her excommunication trial. Although she did describe a relationship with Christ closer than anything Cotton had envisioned, she did not believe that she had experienced Christ's Second Coming in her own life. Such a claim would have denied the resurrection of the body at the Last Judgment and would have clearly stamped her as a Familist. Hutchinson's accusers, ignoring Thomas Leverett's reminder that she had expressed belief in the resurrection, argued that if the resurrection did not exist, biblical law would have no validity nor the marriage covenant any legal or utilitarian value. The result would be a kind of world no Puritan could tolerate, a world where the basest desires would be fulfilled and "foule, groce, filthye and abominable" sexual promiscuity would be rampant. Cotton, smarting from a psychological slap Anne had given him earlier in the excommunication proceedings and in danger of losing the respect of the other ministers, admonished her with the words "though I have not herd, nayther do I thinke, you have bine unfaythful to your Husband in his Marriage Covenant, yet that will follow upon it." By referring to "his" marriage covenant Cotton did not even accord Anne equal participation in the making of that covenant. The Boston teacher concluded his admonition with a criticism of Anne's pride: "I have often feared the highth of your Spirit and being puft up with your owne parts."[25]

Both the introduction of the sexual issue into the trial and Cotton's denunciation of Hutchinson must have had the effect of curbing dissent from the congregation. Few Puritans would want to defend Anne in public when such a defense could be construed as supporting promiscuity. Since Cotton had earlier been sympathetic to the Antinomian cause and had tried to save Anne at her 1637 examination, his vigorous condemnation of her must have confused her following. Cotton even went so far as to exempt the male Antinomians from any real blame for the controversy when he characterized Antinomianism as a woman's delusion. He urged that women, like children, ought to be watched, reproved Hutchinson's sons for not controlling her theological ventures, and called those sons "Vipers . . . [who] *Eate through the very Bowells of your Mother*, to her Ruine." Cotton warned the Boston women "to looke to your selves and to take heed that you reaceve nothinge for Truth which hath not the stamp of the Word of God [as interpreted by the ministers] . . . for you see she [Anne] is but a Woman and *many unsound and dayngerous principles are held by her*." Thomas Shepard agreed that intellectual activity did not suit women and warned the congregation that Anne was likely "to seduce and draw away man, Espetially simple Weomen of her owne sex."[26]

The female churchmembers, who would have had good reason to resent the clergy's approach, could not legitimately object to the excommunication proceedings because of Paul's injunction against women speaking in church. Lacking a clearly-defined feminist consciousness and filled with "backward" fear, the women could not refuse to respect that injunction, even though, or perhaps because, Anne had been presented to the congregation as the epitome of despicableness, as a woman of simple intellect, and as a liar, puffed up with pride and verging on sexual promiscuity. This caricature of Anne did not, however, prevent five men, including her brother-in-law Richard Scott and Mary Oliver's husband Thomas, from objecting to her admonition and excommunication. Cotton refused to consider the points these men raised and dismissed their objections as rising out of their own self-interest or their natural affection for Hutchinson.[27]

In Anne's excommunication proceedings the ministers demonstrated that they had found the means necessary to deal effectively with this rebellious woman and a somewhat hostile congregation. At her examination and her excommunication trial Anne attempted to place the ministers on the defensive by questioning them and forcing them to justify their positions while she explained little. She achieved some success in the 1637 trial, but before her fellow churchmembers she found it difficult to undercut the misrepresentation of her beliefs and the attack on her character. Perhaps fearing the banishment which had been so quickly imposed on her associate, John Wheelwright, she recanted, but even in her recantation she would not totally compromise her position. She expressed sorrow for her errors of expression but admitted no errors in judgment and assumed no appearance of humiliation. When Wilson commanded her "*as a Leper to withdraw your selfe out of the Congregation*," Anne rose, walked to the meetinghouse door, accepted Mary Dyer's offered hand, and turned to impugn her accusers' power: "The Lord judgeth not as man judgeth, better to be cast out of the Church then to deny Christ."[28]

During the year and a half following Hutchinson's excommunication, the Massachusetts ministers and magistrates prosecuted several other female rebels. In April 1638 the Boston church cast out Judith Smith, the maidservant of Anne's brother-in-law, Edward Hutchinson, for her "obstinate persisting" in "sundry Errors." On October 10 of the same year the Assistants ordered Katherine Finch to be whipped for "speaking against the magistrates, against the Churches, and against the Elders." Less than a year later Finch again appeared before the Assistants, this time for not carrying herself "dutifully to her husband," and was released upon promise of reformation. In September 1639 the Boston church excommunicated Phillip(a?) Hammond "as a slaunderer and revyler both of the Church and Common Weale." Hammond, after her husband's death, had resumed her maiden name, operated a business in Boston, and argued in her shop and at public meetings "that Mrs. Hutchinson neyther deserved the Censure which was putt upon her in the Church, nor in the Common Weale." The Boston church also excommunicated two other women for partially imitating Anne Hutchinson's example: Sarah Keayne was found guilty in 1646 of "irregular prophesying in mixed assemblies," and Joan Hogg nine years later was punished "for her disorderly singing and her idleness, and for saying she is commanded of Christ so to do."[29] . . .

The magistrates not only used the threat of a humiliating courtroom appearance and possible punishment to keep female rebels quiet but also levied very stringent penalities on male Antinomian offenders. Anne Hutchinson's son-in-law William Collins was sentenced to pay a £100 fine for charging the Massachusetts churches and ministers with being anti-Christian and calling the king of England the king of Babylon. Anne's son Francis, who had accompanied Collins to Boston in 1641, objected to the popular rumor that he would not sit at the same table with his excommunicated mother and, feeling that the Boston church was responsible, called that church "a strumpet." The church excommunicated Francis and the Assistants fined him £40, but neither he nor Collins would pay the stipulated amounts (even when those fines were reduced to £40 and £20) and therefore spent some time in jail.[30] . . .

. . . Bay Colony leaders popularized the idea that the intellectual woman was influenced by Satan and was therefore unable to perform the necessary functions of womanhood. Weld described Mary Dyer's abortive birth as "a woman child, a fish, a beast, and a fowle, all woven together in one, and without an head," and wrote of Anne Hutchinson's probable hydatidiform mole as "30. monstrous births . . . none at all of them (as farre as I could ever learne) of humane shape." According to Winthrop's even more garish account of Mary Dyer's child, the stillborn baby had a face and ears growing upon the shoulders, a breast and back full of sharp prickles, female sex organs on the rear and buttocks in front, three clawed feet, no forehead, four horns above the eyes, and two great holes upon the back.[31] . . .

. . . Weld's opinion that "as she had vented mishapen opinions, so she must bring forth deformed monsters" impressed the people of the Bay Colony, a people who believed that catastrophic occurrences were evidence of God's displeasure. Some Massachusetts residents viewed the births as the products of both the women's "mishapen opinions" and their supposed promiscuity. . . . A rumor reached England that Henry Vane had crossed the Atlantic in 1637 with Dyer and Hutchinson and had "debauched both, and both were delivered of monsters." It was also widely rumored that three of the Antinomian women, Anne Hutchinson, Jane Hawkins and Mary Oliver, had sold their souls to Satan and become witches. Anne in particular "gave cause of suspicion of witchcraft" after she easily converted to Antinomianism one new male arrival in Rhode Island.[32]

The promotion of the belief that the Antinomian female leaders were witches filled with aberrant lusts and unable to live as proper women was accompanied by an attack on the masculinity of some of the Antinomian men. Although Anne's husband, William, had been a prosperous landowner, a merchant, a deputy to the General Court, and a Boston selectman, Winthrop described him as a "man of very mild temper and weak parts, and wholly guided by his wife." Roger Clap also felt that William Hutchinson and the other Antinomian men were deficient in intellect and judgment. He expressed surprise that any of the men in the movement had "strong parts."[33]

While Massachusetts gossip focused on disordered Antinomian births, lusty Antinomian women, and weak Antinomian men, Winthrop and Cotton tried to convince their English and New England readers that public opinion had been solidly behind Hutchinson's excommunication. Winthrop contended that "diverse women" objected to this rebel's example and would have borne witness against her "if their modesty had not restrained them." Cotton supported the governor's claim by construing the relative silence at Anne's church trial to mean that the "whole body of the Church (except her own son) consented with one accord, to the publick censure of her, by admonition first, and excommunication after." By asserting this falsehood and ignoring Leverett's admission that many churchmembers wished to stay Anne's excommunication, Cotton made it appear that any person who complained about her censure was contradicting the near-unanimous opinion of the congregation.[34]

The effort to discredit the Antinomians and Antinomian sentiment in the Bay Colony was quite successful. By the late 1640s Antinomianism, in a practical sense, was no longer threatening; the ministers and magistrates had managed to preserve a theological system they found congenial. "*Sanctification* came to be in some Request again; and there were *Notes* and *Marks* given of a good Estate."[35] The position of Massachusetts women within the religious system remained essentially unchanged, while in Rhode Island and nearby Providence Plantations the status of women was somewhat improved. In Providence and Portsmouth the men listened to the wishes of the women and protected the "liberty" of women to teach,

preach, and attend services of their choosing. . . .

After Anne Hutchinson's arrival and throughout the remainder of the century, women taught and preached in public in Rhode Island. Johnson wrote that in 1638 "there were some of the female sexe who (deeming the Apostle Paul to be too strict in not permitting a room [woman] to preach in the publique Congregation) taught notwithstanding . . . having their call to this office from an ardent desire of being famous." According to Johnson, Anne Hutchinson, "the grand Mistresse of them all, . . . ordinarily prated every Sabbath day, till others, who thirsted after honour in the same way with her selfe, drew away her Auditors." This prating was more purposive than Johnson might have been willing to admit, for Anne soon involved herself in a new controversy, this one springing out of the resentment of many of the poorer inhabitants of the settlement toward Judge (Governor) William Coddington's autocratic rule, his land allotment policy, and his efforts to establish a church resembling closely the Massachusetts example.[36] Allying herself with Samuel Gorton, a religious freethinker and a defender of justice for all men, "rich or poore, ignorant or learned," Anne began to attack the legitimacy of *any* magistracy. Together, she and Gorton managed to foment the rebellion of April 28, 1639, in which the Portsmouth inhabitants formed a new body politic, ejected Coddington from power, and chose William Hutchinson to replace him. William, however, also did not believe in magistracy and soon refused to occupy the office of judge. Coddington, who had fled south with his followers to found Newport, then claimed the judgeship by default, was recognized by the Massachusetts authorities, and proceeded to administer the affairs of Rhode Island.[37] Gorton and at least eleven others responded to Coddington's resumption of power by plotting armed rebellion against him and were ultimately banished from the colony. Anne broke with the Gortonists over that issue, and she and William joined the Newport settlement.[38]

William Hutchinson died at Newport in 1640, and for much of that year Anne was silent. By 1641, however, she had come out of mourning and, according to Winthrop, turned anabaptist. She and "divers" others supported passive resistance to authority, "denied all magistracy among Christians, and maintained that there were no churches since those founded by the apostles and evangelists, nor could any be." Such opinions achieved enough popularity in Rhode Island to contribute to the dissolution of the church at Newport, although not enough to remove Coddington from power. Disgruntled and fearing that Massachusetts would seize the Rhode Island settlements, Anne sought refuge in the colony of New Netherland in 1642, but her stay there was not long. In August 1643 she, William Collins, two of her sons, and three of her daughters were killed by Indians who had quarreled with her Dutch neighbors.[39]

The Massachusetts clergy rejoiced. Not only had God destroyed the "American Jesabel," but the Lord's vengeance had descended upon her sons and daughters, the poisoned seed. Peter Bulkeley spoke for all the Massachusetts ministers when he concluded, "Let her damned heresies shee fell into . . . and the just vengeance of God, by which shee perished, terrifie all her seduced followers from having any more to doe with her leaven."[40] But her "seduced followers" were horrified only at the reaction of the Puritan clergy. Anne's sister, Katherine Scott, commented that the Bay Colony authorities "are drunke with the blod of the saints," and Anne's former Portsmouth neighbor, Randall Holden, blamed those same authorities for forcing Anne first to Rhode Island and ultimately to her death. He reminded them of her partially successful struggle against authority: "you know . . . your great and terrible word magistrate is no more in its original, than masterly or mas-

terless which hath no great lustre in our ordinary acceptation."[41]

Impervious to such protests, the Bay Colony divines considered Anne Hutchinson's death to be the symbolic death of Antinomianism. To these divines she had been the incarnation of the Antinomian evil, and their accounts of the Antinomian stress in Boston accented *her* beliefs, *her* activities, and *her* rebelliousness. The ministers were not as concerned with the important roles played by Coddington, Wheelwright, Vane, and the other male Antinomian leaders because none of these men threatened the power and status structure of society in the concrete way that Anne Hutchinson did. Anne was clearly not, as the ministers might have wished, a submissive quiet dove, content to labor simply in the kitchen and the childbed. She was witty, aggressive, and intellectual. She had no qualms about castigating in public the men who occupied the most authoritative positions. She claimed the right to define rational, theological matters for herself and by her example spurred other women to express a similar demand. Far from bewildered, she thwarted her accusers with her intellectual ability. Perceiving her as a threat to the family, the state, the religion, and the status hierarchy, the Puritan authorities directed their antagonism against Anne's character and her sex. By doing so, they managed to salve the psychological wounds inflicted by this woman who trod so sharply upon their male status and their ministerial and magisterial authority. Their method had a practical aspect as well; it helped restore respect for the ministry and curb potential dissent.

Anne's ability to attract large numbers of women as supporters caused the ministers and magistrates some worry but little surprise, since they believed that women were easily deluded. They chided Anne for choosing a female preacher as a role model and refused to attribute any merit to her at times subtle, at times caustic intellectual ability. They could see only the work of Satan in Anne's aggressiveness and not the more human desire for equal opportunity and treatment which this rebel never hesitated to assert by example in the intellectual skirmishes she had with her accusers throughout her trials. The double oppression of life in a male-dominated society, combined with biological bondage to her own amazing fertility, could not destroy her self-respect. Because of the theologically based society in which she lived, it was easy for her to ally herself with God and to express her self-confidence in religious debates with the leading intellectual authorities. Neither Anne's rebellion nor the rebellion of her female followers was directed self-consciously against their collective female situation or toward its improvement. Specific feminist campaigns for the franchise, divorce reform, female property ownership after marriage, and the like would be developments of a much later era. For Anne Hutchinson and her female associates Antinomianism was simply an ideology through which the resentment they intuitively felt could be focused and actively expressed.

NOTES

1. John A. Albro, ed., *The Works of Thomas Shepard*, I (New York, 1967 [orig. publ. n.p., 1853]), cxvi–cxvii; Darrett B. Rutman, *Winthrop's Boston: Portrait of a Puritan Town, 1630–1649* (Chapel Hill, N.C., 1965), 121; John Stetson Barry, *The History of Massachusetts: The Colonial Period* (Boston, 1855), 261.

2. Andrew Sinclair, *The Emancipation of the American Woman* (New York, 1966), 23; Edith Curtis, *Anne Hutchinson: A Biography* (Cambridge, Mass., 1930), 72–73; Emery Battis, *Saints and Sectaries: Anne Hutchinson and the Antinomian Controversy in the Massachusetts Bay Colony* (Chapel Hill, N.C., 1962), 9, 50–56, 90; . . . Peter Oliver, *The Puritan Commonwealth. An Historical Review of the Puritan Government in Massachusetts in its Civil and Ecclesiastical Relations* . . . (Boston, 1856), 181.

3. 1 Tim. 2:11–12. St. Paul told the Corinthians: "Let your women keep silence in the churches; for it is not permitted unto them to speak; but they are commanded to be under obedience, as also saith the law. And if they will learn any thing, let them ask their husbands at home; for it is a shame for women to speak in the church" (1 Cor. 14:34–35).

4. Margaret Winthrop to John Winthrop, 1624–1630, *The Winthrop Papers* (Boston, 1929–1944), I, 354–355; II, 165, 199; Lucy Downing to John Winthrop, 1636–1640, Massachusetts Historical Society, *Collections*, 5th Ser., I (Boston, 1871), 20, 25, 27; Elizabeth Winthrop to John Winthrop, ca. June 1636, *Winthrop Papers*, III, 267.

5. James Kendall Hosmer, ed., *Winthrop's Journal: "History of New England," 1630–1649*, Original Narratives of Early American History (New York, 1908), II, 225; John Winthrop, *A Short Story of the Rise, reign, and ruine of the Antinomians, Familists and Libertines*, in David D. Hall, ed., *The Antinomian Controversy, 1636–1638: A Documentary History* (Middletown, Conn., 1968), 263.

6. William Wood, *New Englands Prospect* . . . (London, 1634), 121–122; Hosmer, ed., *Winthrop's Journal*, I, 107, 120; Michael McGiffert, ed., *God's Plot: The Paradoxes of Puritan Piety, Being the Autobiography and Journal of Thomas Shepard* (Amherst, Mass., 1972), 70; Hugh Peter, *A Dying Fathers Last Legacy to An Only Child: Or, Mr. Hugh Peter's Advice to His Daughter* . . . (Boston, 1717), 22.

7. Edmund S. Morgan, *The Puritan Dilemma: The Story of John Winthrop* (Boston, 1958), 137. . . . Puritan attitudes toward the preparation process are treated comprehensively and perceptively in Norman Pettit, *The Heart Prepared: Grace and Conversion in Puritan Spiritual Life* (New Haven, Conn., 1966).

8. John Cotton, *A Treatise of the Covenant of Grace, as it is despensed to the Elect Seed, effectually unto Salvation* (London, 1671), 177. Cotton's subsequent debate with the other ministers appears in Hall, ed., *Antinomian Controversy*, 24–151.

9. The Familists or Family of Love, a sect which originated in Holland about 1540 and spread to England, gained a largely undeserved reputation for practicing promiscuity.

Antinomianism was associated in the Puritan mind with the licentious orgies that accompanied the enthusiasm of John Agricola in sixteenth-century Germany. Opinionism was a term often used for any theology that the divines disliked. James Hastings, ed., *Encyclopaedia of Religion and Ethics* (New York, 1908–1926), I, 581–582; V, 319; IX, 102.

10. Thomas Weld, "The Preface," to Winthrop, *Short Story*, in Hall, ed., *Antinomian Controversy*, 204, 208–209; Winthrop, *Short Story*, ibid., 253.

11. J. Franklin Jameson, ed., *Johnson's Wonder-Working Providence, 1628–1651*, Original Narratives of Early American History (New York, 1910), 127.

12. Weld, "Preface," to Winthrop, *Short Story*, in Hall, ed., *Antinomian Controversy*, 207.

13. Jameson, ed., *Johnson's Wonder-Working Providence*, 132; John Underhill, *Newes from America; or A New and Experimentall Discoverie of New England . . .* (London, 1638), reprinted in Mass. Hist. Soc., *Colls.*, 3d Ser., VI (Boston, 1837), 5; Winthrop, *Short Story*, in Hall, ed., *Antinomian Controversy*, 253; Weld, "Preface," to Winthrop, *Short Story*, ibid., 205–206. . . .

14. John Cotton, *The Way of Congregational Churches Cleared*, in Hall, ed., *Antinomian Controversy*, 423, and Weld, "Preface," to Winthrop, *Short Story*, ibid., 209.

15. Hosmer, ed., *Winthrop's Journal*, I, 266; Winthrop, *Short Story*, in Hall, ed., *Antinomian Controversy*, 281; Horatio Rogers, "Mary Dyer Did Hang Like a Flag," in Jessamyn West, ed., *The Quaker Reader* (New York, 1962), 168–175.

16. Jameson, ed., *Johnson's Wonder-Working Providence*, 132; Winthrop, *Short Story*, in Hall, ed., *Antinomian Controversy*, 281; Nathaniel B. Shurtleff, ed., *Records of the Governor and Company of the Massachusetts Bay in New England, 1628–1641* (Boston, 1853), I, 224, 329.

17. Hosmer, ed., *Winthrop's Journal*, I, 270; "The Rev. John Eliot's Record of Church Members, Roxbury, Massachusetts," in *A Report of the Boston Commissioners, Containing the Roxbury Land and Church Records* (Boston, 1881), 77; Hosmer, ed., *Winthrop's Journal*, I, 285–286; George Francis Dow, ed., *Records and Files of the Quarterly Courts of Essex County, Massachusetts, 1636–1656*, I (Salem, Mass., 1911), 12, 138, 180, 182–183, 186; John Noble, ed., *Records of the Court of Assistants of the Colony of the Massachusetts Bay, 1630–1644*, II (Boston, 1904), 80, hereafter cited as *Assistants*

Records; Sidney Perley, *History of Salem, Massachusetts, 1638–1670*, II (Salem, Mass., 1926), 50; Thomas Hutchinson, *The Witchcraft Delusion of 1692* (Boston, 1870), 6.

18. "A Report of the Trial of Mrs. Anne Hutchinson before the Church in Boston," in Hall, ed., *Antinomian Controversy*, 365.

19. Hosmer, ed., *Winthrop's Journal*, I, 234; "The Examination of Mrs. Anne Hutchinson at the Court at Newtown," in Hall, ed., *Antinomian Controversy*, 312–314, 318; "Trial of Anne Hutchinson before Boston church," ibid., 380, 382–383.

20. "Examination of Mrs. Hutchinson at Newtown," in Hall, ed., *Antinomian Controversy*, 313–316.

21. Winthrop, *Short Story*, ibid., 268.

22. "Examination of Mrs. Hutchinson at Newtown," ibid., 330.

23. "Trial of Anne Hutchinson before church," ibid., 380. . . . Little is known about Anne Hutchinson's role-model, the woman of Ely. Thomas Edwards, a contemporary Puritan divine, remarked that "there are also some women preachers in our times, who keep constant lectures, preaching weekly to many men and women. In Lincolnshire, in Holland and those parts [i.e., the parts about Holland in Lincolnshire] there is a woman preacher who preaches (it's certain), and 'tis reported also she baptizeth, but that's not so certain. *In the Isle of Ely (that land of errors and sectaries) is a woman preacher also.*" See his *Gangraena . . .* (London, 1646), Pt. ii, 29, quoted in Battis, *Saints and Sectaries*, 43n.

24. Winthrop, *Short Story*, in Hall, ed., *Antinomian Controversy*, 273, and "Examination of Mrs. Hutchinson at Newtown," ibid., 337.

25. Hutchinson had responded to an argument of Cotton's with the rejoinder, "I desire to hear God speak this and not man." "Trial of Anne Hutchinson before Boston church," in Hall, ed., *Antinomian Controversy*, 358, 362, 355, 372. See Battis, *Saints and Sectaries*, 52n.

26. "Trial of Anne Hutchinson before Boston church," in Hall, ed., *Antinomian Controversy*, 369, 370, 365.

27. Ibid., 385–87, 366–368.

28. Ibid., 378, 388, and Winthrop, *Short Story*, ibid., 307.

29. Richard D. Pierce, ed., *The Records of the First Church in Boston, 1630–1868*, I, in Colonial Society of Massachusetts, *Publications*, XXXIX (Boston, 1961), 22, 25; *Assistants Records*, II, 78, 82; Emil Oberholzer, Jr., *Delinquent Saints: Disciplinary Action in*

the Early Congregational Churches of Massachusetts (New York, 1956), 85; "The Diaries of John Hull," American Antiquarian Society, Archaelogia Americana, III (Worcester, Mass., 1857), 192n.

30. Assistants Records, III, 109; Hosmer, ed., Winthrop's Journal, II, 38–40; John Cotton to Francis Hutchinson, Mass. Hist. Soc., Colls., 2d Ser., X (1823), 186. . . .

31. Weld, "Preface," to Winthrop, Short Story, in Hall, ed., Antinomian Controversy, 214, 280–281. Dr. Paul A. Younge's diagnosis of Hutchinson's "30. monstrous births" as an hydatidiform mole, a uterine growth which frequently accompanies menopause, is adopted in Battis, Saints and Sectaries, 346.

32. Weld, "Preface," to Winthrop, Short Story, in Hall, ed., Antinomian Controversy, 214; "From Majr. Scott's mouth," Mass. Hist. Soc., Proceedings, 1st Ser., XIII (1873–1875), 132; Hosmer, ed., Winthrop's Journal, II, 8.

33. Hosmer, ed., Winthrop's Journal, I, 299, and "Roger Clap's Memoirs," in Alexander Young, ed., Chronicles of the First Planters of Massachusetts Bay, from 1623–1636 (Boston, 1846), 360.

34. Winthrop, Short Story, in Hall, ed., Antinomian Controversy, 307, and Cotton, Congregational Churches Cleared, ibid., 420.

35. George H. Moore, "Giles Firmin and His Various Writings," Historical Magazine, 2d Ser., III (1868), 150, quoting Giles Firmin, Πανουργια, a brief review of Mr. Davis's Vindication: giving no satisfaction . . . (London, 1693).

36. Jameson, ed., Johnson's Wonder-Working Providence, 186, and Howard M. Chapin, Documentary History of Rhode Island, II (Providence, R.I., 1916), 68, 84. . . .

37. Edward Winslow, Hypocrisie Unmasked: A true Relation of the Proceedings of the Governour and Company of the Massachusetts against Samuel Gorton . . . (London, 1646), 44, 54–55, 67; Hosmer, ed., Winthrop's Journal, I, 297, 299; Chapin, History of Rhode Island, II, 56–57; William Coddington to John Winthrop, Dec. 9, 1639, Winthrop Papers, IV, 160–161; Robert Baylie, A Dissuasive from the Errours of the Time . . . (London, 1645), 150.

38. Chapin, History of Rhode Island, II, 68, and Winslow, Hypocrisie Unmasked, 53, 83.

39. Hosmer, ed., Winthrop's Journal, II, 39; . . . "Letter of Randall Holden, Sept. 15th, 1643," in Mass. Hist. Soc., Colls., 3d Ser., I (1825), 13; Samuel Niles, "A Summary Historical Narrative of the Wars in New-England with the French and Indians, in the several Parts of the Country," ibid., VI (1837), 201.

40. Winthrop, Short Story, in Hall, ed., Antinomian Controversy, 310, and Perry Miller, The New England Mind: The Seventeenth Century (New York, 1939), 391. Increase Mather saw the hand of God at work again when Anne's son Edward died from Indian wounds in 1675. "It seems to be an observable providence," Mather observed, "that so many of that family die by the hands of the uncircumcised." "Diary of Increase Mather, 1674–87," Mass. Hist. Soc., Procs., 2d Ser., XIII (1900), 400.

41. Katherine Scott to John Winthrop, Jr., 1658, Mass. Hist. Soc., Colls., 5th Ser., I (1871), 96–97, and "Letter of Randall Holden, Sept. 15th, 1643," ibid., 3d Ser., I (1825), 13–15.

CATHERINE M. SCHOLTEN

"On the Importance of the Obstetrick Art": Changing Customs of Childbirth in America, 1760–1825

Anthropologists have long known that the rituals of daily life can provide important insights into the life of a community. "Common sense" changes from

Excerpted from " 'On the Importance of the Obstetrick Art': Changing Customs of Childbirth place to place, and from time to time. Catherine M. Scholten's report on the way Americans handled childbirth shows that in the early eighteenth century the "common sense" of the matter seemed to be that women would assist in the birth process. By the early nineteenth century it had become "common sense" that male physicians would be called to the bedside. Scholten suggests that this change is a symptom of an important shift in attitudes toward women as patients and as professionals. Despite a few unenthusiastic efforts to teach improved obstetric techniques to midwives, women were usually denied access to training in the newest medical skills. As medicine became more professional, it also became more strictly segregated by gender. Ironically, scientific developments that had the result of making childbirth less risky also increased the dependence of women on male physicians. A similar result accompanied the spread of "twilight sleep" anesthesia in the twentieth century.

In October 1799, as Sally Downing of Philadelphia labored to give birth to her sixth child, her mother, Elizabeth Drinker, watched her suffer "in great distress." Finally, on the third day of fruitless labor, Sally's physician, William Shippen, Jr., announced that "the child must be brought forward." Elizabeth Drinker wrote in her diary that, happily Sally delivered naturally, although Dr. Shippen had said that "he thought he should have had occasion for instruments" and clapped his hand on his side, so that the forceps rattled in his pocket.[1]

Elizabeth Drinker's account of her daughter's delivery is one of the few descriptions by an eighteenth-century American woman of a commonplace aspect of women's lives—childbirth.[2] It is of special interest to social historians because it records the participation of a man in the capacity of physician. Shippen was a prominent member of the first generation of American doctors trained in obstetrics and commencing in 1763, the first to maintain a regular practice attending women in childbirth.[3] Until that time midwives managed almost all deliveries,

but with Shippen male physicians began to supplant the midwives.

The changing social customs and medical management of childbirth from 1760 to 1825 are the subjects of this article. By analyzing the rituals of childbirth it will describe the emergence of new patterns in private and professional life. It shows that, beginning among well-to-do women in Philadelphia, New York, and Boston, childbirth became less a communal experience and more a private event confined within the intimate family. In consequence of new perceptions of urban life and of women, as well as of the development of medical science, birth became increasingly regarded as a medical problem to be managed by physicians. For when Shippen, fresh from medical studies in London, announced his intention to practice midwifery in Philadelphia in 1763, he was proposing to enter a field considered the legitimate province of women.[4] Childbearing had been viewed as the inevitable, even the divinely ordained, occasion of suffering for women; childbirth was an event shared by the female community; and was supervised by a midwife.

in America, 1760 to 1825" by Catherine M. Scholten, in *William and Mary Quarterly*, 3d ser., 34 (1977):426–45. Copyright © 1977 by the Estate of Catherine M. Scholten. Reprinted by permission of the Estate of Catherine M. Scholten; Pauline Scholten, Executor. Notes have been renumbered.

During the colonial period childbearing occupied a central portion of the lives of women between their twentieth and fortieth years. Six to eight pregnancies were typical, and pregnant women were commonly described as "breeding" and "teeming."[5] Such was women's natural lot; though theologians attributed dignity to carrying the "living soul" of a child and saluted mothers in their congregations with "Blessed are you among women," they also depicted the pains of childbirth as the appropriate special curse of "the Travailing Daughters of Eve."[6] Two American tracts written specifically for lying-in women dwelt on the divinely ordained hazards of childbirth and advised a hearty course of meditation on death, "such as their pregnant condition must reasonably awaken them to."[7]

Cotton Mather's pamphlet, *Elizabeth in Her Holy Retirement*, which he distributed to midwives to give to the women they cared for, described pregnancy as a virtually lethal condition. "For ought you know," it warned, "your Death has entered into you, you may have conceived that which determines but about Nine Months more at the most, for you to live in the World." Pregnancy was thus intended to inspire piety.[8] . . .

Surely women did not need to be reminded of the risks of childbirth. The fears of Mary Clap, wife of Thomas Clap, president of Yale College, surface even through the ritual phrases of the elegy written by her husband after her death in childbirth at the age of twenty-four. Thomas remembered that before each of her six lyings-in his wife had asked him to pray with her that God would continue their lives together.[9] Elizabeth Drinker probably echoed the sentiments of most women when she reflected, "I have often thought that women who live to get over the time of Child-bareing, if other things are favourable to them, experience more comfort and satisfaction than at any other period of their lives."[10]

Facing the hazards of childbirth, women depended on the community of their sex for companionship and medical assistance. Women who had moved away at marriage frequently returned to their parents' home for the delivery, either because they had no neighbors or because they preferred the care of their mothers to that of their in-laws. Other women summoned mothers, aunts, and sisters on both sides of the family, as well as female friends, when birth was imminent.[11] Above all, they relied on the experience of midwives to guide them through labor.

Women monopolized the practice of midwifery in America, as in Europe, through the middle of the eighteenth century. As the recognized experts in the conduct of childbirth, they advised the mother-to-be if troubles arose during pregnancy, supervised the activities of lying-in, and used their skills to assure safe delivery. Until educated male physicians began to practice obstetrics, midwives enjoyed some status in the medical profession, enhanced by their legal responsibilities in the communities they served.

English civil authorities required midwives to take oaths in order to be licensed but imposed no official test of their skills. The oaths indicate that midwives had responsibilities which were serious enough to warrant supervision. They swore not to allow any infant to be baptized outside the Church of England, and promised to help both rich and poor, to report the true parentage of a child, and to abstain from performing abortions. Oath-breaking midwives could be excommunicated or fined.[12]

Some American midwives learned their art in Europe, where midwifery was almost exclusively the professional province of women. Though barber surgeons and physicians increasingly asserted their interest in midwifery during the seventeenth century, midwives and patients resisted the intruders.[13] The midwives' levels of skill varied. Some acquired their medical education in the same way as many surgeons and physicians, by apprenticeship; some read manuals by more learned midwives and physicians; and after 1739, when the first British lying-in hospital was founded, a few were taught by the physicians who directed such hospitals.[14] But more often than not, women undertook midwifery equipped only with folk knowledge and the experience of their own pregnancies.[15]

Disparity of skills also existed among American midwives. Experienced midwives practiced alongside women who were, one physician observed, "as ignorant of their business as the women they deliver."[16] By the end of the eighteenth century physicians thought that the "greater part" of the midwives in America took up the occupation by accident, "having first been *catched*, as they express it, with a woman in labour."[17] The more diligent sought help from books, probably popular medical manuals such as *Aristotle's Master Piece*.[18]

American midwives conducted their practice free, on the whole, from governmental supervision and control. Only two colonies appear to have enacted regulatory statutes, and it does not seem that these were rigorously enforced. In the seventeenth century Massachusetts and New York required midwives, together with surgeons and physicians, not to act contrary to the accepted rules of their art. More specifically, in 1716 the common council of New York City prescribed a licensing oath for midwives, which was similar to the oaths of England though without the provision on baptism. The oath included an injunction—significant for the theme of this article—that midwives not "open any matter Appertaining to your Office in the presence of any Man unless Necessity or Great Urgent Cause do Constrain you to do so."[19] This oath, which was regularly re-enacted until 1763, suggests the common restriction of midwifery to women, excluding male physicians or barber surgeons, who, in any case, were few and usually ill trained. There are records of male midwives in New York,

Philadelphia, Charleston, and Annapolis after 1740, but only one, a Dr. Spencer of Philadelphia, had London training in midwifery, and it was said of another that "he attended very few natural labors."[20]

Though their duties were not as well defined by law, American midwives served the community in ways similar to those of their British counterparts. In addition to assisting at childbed, they testified in court in cases of bastardy, verified birthdates, and examined female prisoners who pleaded pregnancy to escape punishment.[21] Some colonials also observed the English custom of having the midwife attend the baptism and burial of infants. Samuel Sewall reported that Elizabeth Weeden brought his son John to church for christening in 1677, and at the funeral of little Henry in 1685 "Midwife Weeden and Nurse Hill carried the Corps by turns."[22]

The inclusion of the midwife in these ceremonies of birth and death shows how women's relationships with their midwives went beyond mere respect for the latters' skill. Women with gynecologic problems would freely tell a midwife things "that they had rather die than discover to the Doctor."[23] Grateful patients eulogized midwives.[24] The acknowledgment of the services of one Boston midwife, recorded on her tombstone, has inspired comment since 1761. The stone informs the curious that Mrs. Phillips was "born in Westminster in Great Britain, and Commission'd by John Laud, Bishop of London in ye Year 1718 to ye Office of a Midwife," came to "this Country" in 1719, and "by ye Blessing of God has brought into this world above 3000 Children."[25]

We may picture Mrs. Phillips's professional milieu as a small room, lit and warmed by a large fire, and crowded by a gathering of family and friends. In daytime, during the early stages of labor, children might be present, and while labor proceeded female friends dropped in to offer encouragement and help; securing refreshments for such visitors was a part of the preparation for childbirth, especially among the well-to-do families with which we are concerned. Men did not usually remain at the bedside. They might be summoned in to pray, but as delivery approached they waited elsewhere with the children and with women who were "not able to endure" the tension in the room.[26]

During the final stages of labor the midwife took full charge, assisted by other women. As much as possible, midwives managed deliveries by letting nature do the work; they caught the child, tied the umbilical cord, and if necessary fetched the afterbirth. In complicated cases they might turn the child and deliver it feet first, but if this failed, the fetus had to be destroyed. In all circumstances the midwife's chief duty was to comfort the woman in labor while they both waited on nature, and this task she could, as a woman, fulfill with social ease. Under the midwife's direction the woman in labor was liberally fortified with hard liquor or mulled wine. From time to time the midwife examined her cervix to gauge the progress of labor and encouraged her to walk about until the pains became too strong. There was no standard posture for giving birth, but apparently few women lay flat in bed. Some squatted on a midwife's stool, a low chair with an open seat. Others knelt on a pallet, sat on another woman's lap, or stood supported by two friends.[27]

Friends were "welcome companions," according to one manual for midwives, because they enabled the woman in labor "to bear her pains to more advantage," and "their cheerful conversation supports her spirits and inspires her with confidence."[28] Elizabeth Drinker endeavored to talk her daughter into better spirits by telling her that as she was thirty-nine "this might possibly be the last trial of this sort."[29] Some women attempted to cheer the mother-to-be by assuring her that her labor was easy compared to others they had seen, or provoked laughter by making bawdy jokes.[30]

For some attendants, a delivery could be a wrenching experience. Elizabeth Drinker relived her own difficult deliveries when her daughters suffered their labors, and on one such occasion she noted with irony, "This day is 38 years since I was in agonies bringing her into this world of troubles: she told me with tears that this was her birthday."[31] For others the experience of assisting the labors of friends was a reminder of their sex. Sarah Eve, an unmarried twenty-two-year-old, attended the labor of a friend in 1772 and carried the tidings of birth to the waiting father. "None but those that were like anxious could be sensible of a joy like theirs," she wrote in her journal that night. "Oh! Eve! Adam's wife I mean—who could forget her today?"[32]

After delivery, the mother was covered up snugly and confined to her bed, ideally for three to four weeks. For fear of catching cold she was not allowed to put her feet on the floor and was constantly supplied with hot drinks. Family members relieved her of household duties. Restless women, and those who could not afford weeks of idleness, got up in a week or less, but not without occasioning censure.[33]

The social and medical hold of midwives on childbirth loosened during the half century after 1770, as male physicians assumed the practice of midwifery among urban women of social rank. Initially, physicians entered the field as trained practitioners who could help women in difficult labors through the use of instruments, but ultimately they presided over normal deliveries as well. The presence of male physicians in the lying-in chamber signaled a general change in attitudes toward childbirth, including a modification of the dictum that women had to suffer. At the same time, because medical training was restricted to men, women lost their position as assistants at childbirth, and an event traditionally managed by a community of women became an experience shared primarily by a woman and her doctor.

William Shippen, the first American physician to establish a steady practice of midwifery, quietly overcame resistance to the presence of a man in the lying-in room. Casper Wistar's *Eulogies on Dr. Shippen*, published in 1809, states that when Shippen began in 1763, male practitioners were resorted to only in a crisis. "This was altogether the effect of prejudice," Wistar remarked, adding that "by Shippen this prejudice was so done away, that in the course of ten years he became very fully employed."[34] A few figures testify to the trend. The Philadelphia city directory in 1815 listed twenty-one women as midwives, and twenty-three men as practitioners of midwifery. In 1819 it listed only thirteen female midwives, while the number of men had risen to forty-two; and by 1824 only six female midwives remained in the directory.[35] "Prejudice" similarly dissolved in Boston, where in 1781 the physicians advertised that they expected immediate payment for their services in midwifery; by 1820 midwifery in Boston was almost "entirely confined" to physicians.[36] By 1826 Dr. William Dewees, professor of midwifery at the University of Pennsylvania and the outstanding American obstetrician of the early nineteenth century, could preface his textbook on midwifery with an injunction to every American medical student to study the subject because "everyone almost" must practice it. He wrote that "a change of manners within a few years" had "resulted in almost exclusive employment of the male practitioner."[37] . . .

On one level the change was a direct consequence of the fact that after 1750 growing numbers of American men traveled to Europe for medical education. Young men with paternal means, like Shippen, spent three to four years studying medicine, including midwifery, with leading physicians in the hospitals of London and the classrooms of Edinburgh. When they returned to the colonies they brought back not only a superior set of skills but also British ideas about hospitals, medical schools, and professional standards.[38]

In the latter part of the eighteenth century advanced medical training became available in North America. At the time of Shippen's return in 1762 there was only one hospital in the colonies, the Pennsylvania Hospital, built ten years earlier to care for the sick poor. Shippen and his London-educated colleagues saw that the hospital could be used for the clinical training of physicians, as in Europe. Within three years the Philadelphia doctors, led by John Morgan, established formal, systematic instruction at a school of medicine, supplemented by clinical work in the hospital.[39] Morgan maintained that the growth of the colonies "called aloud" for a medical school "to increase the number of those who exercise the profession of medicine and surgery."[40] Dr. Samuel Bard successfully addressed the same argument to the citizens of New York in 1768.[41]

In addition to promoting medical schools, Morgan and Bard defined the proper practitioner of medicine as a man learned in a science. To languages and liberal arts their ideal physician added anatomy, material medicine, botany, chemistry, and clinical exprience. He was highly conscious not only of his duty to preserve "the life and health of mankind,"[42] but also of his professional status, and this new emphasis on professionalism extended to midwifery.

The trustees of the first American medical schools recognized midwifery as a branch of medical science. From its founding in 1768, Kings College in New York devoted one professorship solely to midwifery, and the University of Pennsylvania elected Shippen professor of anatomy, surgery, and midwifery in 1791. By 1807 five reputable American medical schools provided courses in midwifery.[43] In the early years of the nineteenth century some professors of midwifery began to call themselves obstetricians or professors of obstetrics, a scientific-sounding title free of the feminine connotations of the word midwife.[44] Though not compulsory for all medical students, the new field was considered worthy of detailed study along the paths pioneered by English physicians.

Dr. William Smellie contributed more to the development of obstetrics than any other eighteenth-century physician. His influence was established by his teaching career in London, from 1741 to 1758, and by his treatise on midwifery, first published in 1752.[45] Through precise measurement and observation Smellie discovered the mechanics of parturition. He found that the child's head turned throughout delivery, adapting the widest part to the widest diameter of the pelvic canal. Accordingly, he defined maneuvers for manipulating an improperly presented child. He also recognized that obstetrical forceps, generally known for only twenty years when he wrote in 1754, should be used to rectify the position of an infant wedged in the mouth of the cervix, in preference to the "common method" of simply jerking the child out. He perfected the design of the forceps and taught its proper use, so that physicians could save both mother and child in difficult deliveries, instead of being forced to dismember the infant with hooks.[46]

To Smellie and the men who learned from him, the time seemed ripe to apply science to a field hitherto built on ignorance and supported by prejudice. Smellie commented on the novelty of scientific interest in midwifery. "We ought to be ashamed of ourselves," he admonished the readers of his *Treatise*, "for the little improvement we have made in so many centuries." Only recently have "we established a better method of delivering in laborious and preternatural cases."[47] Smellie's countryman Dr. Charles White reflected in his text on midwifery in 1793 that "the bringing of the art of midwifery

to perfection upon scientific and medical principles seems to have been reserved for the present generation."[48]

Some American physicians shared this sense of the new "Importance of the Obstetrick Art." Midwifery was not a "trifling" matter to be left to the uneducated, Thomas Jones of the College of Medicine of Maryland wrote in 1812. Broadly defined as the care of "all the indispositions incident to women from the commencement of pregnancy to the termination of lactation," it ranked among the most important branches of medicine. "With the cultivation of this branch of science," women could now "reasonably look to men for safety in the perilous conditions" of childbirth.[49] . . .

. . . Social as well as medical reasons account for the innovations in the practice of midwifery in such cities as Boston, Philadelphia, and New York. Physicians received their medical education in cities, and cities offered the best opportunities to acquire patients and live comfortably. Urban families of some means could afford the $12 to $15 minimum fee which Boston physicians demanded for midwife services in 1806.[50] Obstetrics was found to be a good way to establish a successful general practice. The man who conducted himself well in the lying-in room won the gratitude and confidence of his patient and her family, and they naturally called him to serve in other medical emergencies. It was midwifery, concluded Dr. Walter Channing of Boston, that ensured doctors "the permanency and security of all their other business."[51]

The possibility of summoning a physician, who could perhaps insure a safer and faster delivery, opened first to urban women. The dramatic rescue of one mother and child given up by a midwife could be enough to convince a neighborhood of women of a physician's value and secure him their practice.[52] Doctors asserted that women increasingly hired physicians because they became convinced "that the well instructed physician is best calculated to avert danger and surmount difficulties."[53] Certainly by 1795 the women of the Drinker family believed that none but a physician should order medicine for a woman in childbed, and had no doubts that Dr. Shippen or his colleague Dr. Nicholas Way was the best help that they could summon.[54]

Although she accepted a male physician as midwife, Elizabeth Drinker still had reservations about the use of instruments to facilitate childbirth and was relieved when Shippen did not have to use forceps on her daughter. Other women feared to call a physician because they assumed that any instruments he used would destroy the child.[55] However, once the capabilities of obstetrical forceps became known, some women may have turned to them by choice in hope of faster deliveries. Such hope stimulated a medical fashion. By about 1820 Dewees and Bard felt it necessary to condemn nervous young doctors for resorting unnecessarily to forceps.[56]

The formal education of American physicians and the development of midwifery as a science, the desire of women for the best help in childbirth, the utility of midwifery as a means of building a physician's practice, and, ultimately, the gigantic social changes labeled urbanization explain why physicians assumed the ordinary practice of midwifery among well-to-do urban women in the late eighteenth and early nineteenth centuries. This development provides insight into the changing condition of women in American society.

The development of obstetrics signified a partial rejection of the assumption that women had to suffer in childbirth and implied a new social appreciation of women, as admonitions to women for forbearance under the pain of labor turned to the desire to relieve their pain. . . . In his doctoral dissertation in 1812 one American medical student drew a distinction between childbirth in primitive societies

and his own. In the former, "women are generally looked on by their rugged lords as unworthy of any particular attention," and death or injury in childbirth is "not deemed a matter of any importance." Well-instructed assistants to women in childbirth were one sign of the value placed on women in civilized societies.[57]

The desire to relieve women in childbirth also signified a more liberal interpretation of scripture. At the University of Pennsylvania in 1804, Peter Miller, a medical student, modified the theological dictum that women must bear in sorrow. The anxieties of pregnancy and the anguish caused by the death of so many infants constituted sorrow enough for women, argued Miller. They did not need to be subjected to bodily pain as well.[58] Reiterating this argument, Dewees bluntly asked, "Why should the female alone incur the penalty of God?"[59] To relieve the pain of labor Dewees and his fellows analyzed the anatomy and physiology of childbirth and defined techniques for the use of instruments.

If the development of obstetrics suggests the rise of a "special tenderness for women" on the part of men, it also meant that women's participation in medical practice was diminished and disparaged. A few American physicians instructed midwives or wrote manuals for them, but these efforts were private and sporadic, and had ceased by 1820. The increasing professionalization of medicine, in the minds of the physicians who formed medical associations that set the standards of the field, left little room for female midwives, who lacked the prescribed measure of scientific training and professional identity.[60]

William Shippen initially invited midwives as well as medical students to attend his private courses in midwifery. His advertisement in the *Pennsylvania Gazette* in January 1765 related his experience assisting women in the country in difficult labors, "most of which was made so by the unskillful old women about them," and announced that he "thought it his duty to immediately begin" courses in midwifery "in order to instruct those women who have virtue enough to own their ignorance and apply for instructions, as well as those young gentlemen now engaged in the study of that useful and necessary branch of surgery." Shippen taught these private lessons until after the Revolution, when he lectured only to the students at the University of Pennsylvania, who, of course, were male.[61]

At the turn of the century Dr. Valentine Seaman conducted the only other known formal instruction of midwives. He was distressed by the ignorance of many midwives, yet convinced that midwives ought to manage childbirth because, unlike physicians, they had time to wait out lingering labors, and, as women, they could deal easily with female patients. Seaman offered his private lectures and demonstrations at the New York Almshouse lying-in ward, and in 1800 published them as the *Midwives Monitor and Mothers Mirror*.[62] A handful of other men wrote texts at least nominally directed to midwives between 1800 and 1810; some of these, like Seaman's, discussed the use of instruments.[63] In 1817 Dr. Thomas Ewell proposed that midwives be trained at a national school of midwifery in Washington, D.C., to be supported by a collection taken up by ministers. There is no evidence that Ewell's scheme, presented in his medical manual, *Letters to Ladies*, ever gained a hearing.[64]

Seaman and Ewell, and other authors of midwives' manuals, presumed that if women mastered some of the fundamentals of obstetrics they would be desirable assistants in ordinary midwifery cases. In 1820 Dr. Channing of Boston went further in his pamphlet, *Remarks on the Employment of Females as Practitioners of Midwifery*, in which he maintained that no one could thoroughly understand the management of labor who did not understand "thoroughly the profession of medicine as a whole." Channing's principle would have totally excluded women from midwifery, because no one favored professional medical education for women. It was generally assumed that they could not easily master the necessary languages, mathematics, and chemistry, or withstand the trials of dissecting room and hospital. Channing added that women's moral character disqualified them for medical practice: "Their feelings of sympathy are too powerful for the cool exercise of judgement" in medical emergencies, he wrote; "they do not have the power of action, nor the active power of mind which is essential to the practice of the surgeon."[65]

Denied formal medical training, midwives of the early nineteenth century could not claim any other professional or legal status. Unlike Great Britain, the United States had no extensive record of licensing laws or oaths defining the practice of midwifery. Nor were there any vocal groups of midwives who, conscious of their tradition of practice or associated with lying-in hospitals, were able to defend themselves against competition from physicians.[66] American midwives ceased practice among women of social rank with few words uttered in their defense.

The victory of the physicians produced its own problems. The doctor's sex affected the relationships between women and their attendants in childbirth, and transformed the atmosphere of the lying-in room. In his advice to his male students Dewees acknowledged that summoning a man to assist at childbed "cost females a severe struggle."[67] Other doctors knew that even the ordinary gynecologic services of a physician occasioned embarrassment and violated woman's "natural delicacy of feeling," and that every sensitive woman felt "deeply humiliated" at the least bodily exposure.[68] Doctors recognized an almost universal repugnance on the part of women to male assistance in time of labor.[69] Because of "whim or false delicacy" women often refused to call a man until their condition had become critical.[70] It is unlikely that physicians exaggerated these observations, although there is little testimony from women themselves about their child-bed experience in the early nineteenth century.

The uneasiness of women who were treated by men was sometimes shared by their husbands. In 1772 the *Virginia Gazette* printed a denunciation of male midwifery as immoral. The author, probably an Englishman, attributed many cases of adultery in England to the custom of employing men at deliveries. Even in labor a woman had intervals of ease, and these, he thought, were the moments when the doctor infringed on the privileges of the husband. It would be a matter of utmost indifference to him "whether my wife had spent the night in a bagnio, or an hour of the forenoon locked up with a man midwife in her dressing room."[71] Such arguments were frequently and seriously raised in England during the eighteeth century.[72] They may seem ludicrous, but at least one American man of Dr. Ewell's acquaintance suffered emotional conflict over hiring a male midwife. He sent for a physician to help his wife in her labor, yet "very solemnly he declared to the doctor, he would demolish him if he touched or looked at his wife."[73]

Physicians dealt with the embarrassment of patients and the suspicion of husbands by observing the drawing-room behavior of "well-bred gentlemen." Dewees told his students to "endeavor, by well chosen conversation, to divert your patient's mind from the purpose of your visit."[74] All questions of a delicate nature were to be communicated through a third party, perhaps the only other person in the room, either a nurse or an elderly friend or relative. The professional man was advised "never to seem to know anything about the parts of generation, further than that there is an orifice near the rectum leading to an os."[75]

Physicians did not perform vaginal examinations unless it was absolutely important to do so, and they often had to cajole women into permitting an examination at all. Nothing could be more shocking to a woman, Shippen lectured his students, "than for a young man the moment he enters the Chamber to ask for Pomatum and proceed to examine the uterus."[76] Doctors waited until a labor pain clutched their patients and then suggested an examination by calling it "taking a pain." During examination and delivery the patient lay completely covered in her bed, a posture more modest, if less comfortable, than squatting on a pallet or a birth stool. The light in the room was dimmed by closing the shutters during the day and covering the lamps at night. If a physician used forceps, he had to manipulate them under the covers, using his free hand as a guide.[77] On this point doctors who read Thomas Denman's *Obstetrical Remembrancer* were reminded that "Degorges, one of the best obstetricians of his time, was blind."[78]

The crowd of supportive friends and family disappeared with the arrival of the doctor. The physician guarded against "too many attendants; where there are women, they must talk."[79] The presence of other women might increase the doctor's nervousness, and they certainly did not help the woman in labor. Medical men interpreted women's talk of other experiences with childbirth as mere gossip "of all the dangerous and difficult labours they ever heard any story about in their lives," which ought to be stopped lest it disturb the patient.[80] Especially distracting were the bawdy stories visitors told, expecting the physician to laugh, too. Medical professors recommended "grave deportment," warning that levity would "hurt your patient or yourself in her esteem."[81] Far from providing the consolation of a friend, the physician was often a stranger who needed to "get a little acquainted" with his patient. One medical text went so far as to coach him in a series of conversational ice breakers about children and the weather.[82]

Etiquette and prudery in the lying-in chamber affected medical care. Physicians were frustrated by their inability to examine their patients thoroughly, for they knew full well that learning midwifery from a book was "like learning shipbuilding without touching timber."[83] Examinations were inadequate, and the dangers of manipulating instruments without benefit of sight were tremendous. Dewees cautioned his students to take great care before pulling the forceps that "no part of the mother is included in the locking of the blades. This accident is frequent."[84] Accidental mutilation of infants was also reported, as the navel string had to be cut under the covers. Lecturers passed on the story of the incautious doctor who included the penis of an infant within the blades of his scissors.[85]

In view of such dangers, the conflict between social values and medical practice is striking. The expansion of medical knowledge brought men and women face to face with social taboos in family life. They had to ask themselves the question, Who should watch a woman give birth? For centuries the answer had unhesitatingly been female relatives and friends, and the midwife. The science of obstetrics, developing in the eighteenth century, changed the answer. Though women might socially be the most acceptable assistants at a delivery, men were potentially more useful.

In consequence of the attendance of male physicians, by 1825, for some American women, childbirth was ceasing to be an open ceremony. Though birth still took place at home, and though friends and relatives still lent a helping hand, visiting women no longer dominated the activities in the lying-in room. Birth became increasingly a private affair conducted in a quiet, darkened room. The physician limited visitors because they hindered proper medical care, but the process of birth was also concealed because it embarrassed both patient and physician.

Between 1760 and 1825 childbirth was thus transformed from an open affair to a restricted one. As one consequence of the development of obstetrics as a legitimate branch of medicine, male physicians began replacing midwives. They began to reduce childbirth to a scientifically managed event and deprived it of its folk aspects. Strengthened by the professionalization of their field, these physicians also responded to the hopes of women in Philadelphia, New York, and Boston for safe delivery. Although they helped some pregnant women, they hurt midwives, who were shut out of an area of medicine that had been traditionally their domain. All these innovations took place in the large urban centers in response to distinctly urban phenomena. They reflected the increasing privatization of family life, and they foreshadowed mid-nineteenth-century attitudes toward childbirth, mother, and woman.

Notes

1. Cecil K. Drinker, *Not So Long Ago: A Chronicle of Medicine and Doctors in Colonial Philadelphia* (New York, 1937), 59–61.

2. Although births are noted frequently in diaries and letters of the seventeenth, eighteenth, and early nineteenth centuries, the event itself is rarely described. For the most part, information on the medical procedures and social customs of birth analyzed in this article is derived from midwives' manuals, medical textbooks, and lecture notes of medical students. This literature mingles plain observation with partisan advocacy of medical reform. It seems reasonable to accept the physician's evaluations of midwifery as evidence of their desire for change, and their case histories as documents of the actual circumstances of birth. Despite ambiguities, the material provides a glimpse of social change not directly reflected in many conventional sources.

3. Betsy Copping Corner, *William Shippen, Jr.: Pioneer in American Medical Education* (Philadelphia, 1951), 103; Irving S. Cut-

ter and Henry R. Viets, *A Short History of Midwifery* (Philadelphia, 1964), 150.

4. Cutter and Viets, *Short History*, 148–149.

5. For a discussion of childbearing patterns see Wilson H. Gabill, Clyde V. Kiser, and Pascal K. Whelpton, "A Long View," in Michael Gordon, ed., *The American Family in Social-Historical Perspective* (New York, 1973), 392; J. Potter, "The Growth of Population in America, 1700–1860," in D. V. Glass and D. E. C. Eversley, eds., *Population in History: Essays in Historical Demography* (Chicago, 1965), 644, 647, 663, 679; Robert V. Wells, "Demographic Change and the Life Cycle of American Families," in Theodore K. Rabb and Robert I. Rotberg, eds., *The Family in History: Interdisciplinary Essays* (New York, 1971), 85, 88.

When William Byrd II wrote in his diary in 1712, "my wife was often indisposed with breeding and very cross," he used a term common until the nineteenth century. Louis B. Wright and Marion Tinling, eds., *The Secret Diary of William Byrd of Westover, 1709–1712* (Richmond, Va., 1941), 548. "Breeding" was used colloquially and in popular medical literature. The use of the term to describe the hatching or birth of animals parallels its application to humans. The word lingered longest in speech in the American South, where fertile or pregnant black slaves were called "breeding women," an indication of the animality implied in the word. *The Oxford English Dictionary*, s.v. "breeding"; Mitford M. Mathews, ed., *A Dictionary of Americanisms on Historical Principles* (Chicago, 1951), s.v. "breeding." "Teeming," also considered archaic dialect by the *OED*, applied to women from the sixteenth through eighteenth centuries.

6. Benjamin Colman, *Some of the Honours that Religion Does unto the Fruitful Mothers in Israel* . . . (Boston, 1715), 8; Cotton Mather, *Elizabeth in Her Holy Retirement. An Essay to Prepare a Pious Woman for her Lying-in. Or Maxims and Methods of Piety, to Direct and Support an Hand Maid of the Lord, Who Expects a Time of Travail* (Boston, 1710), 3; Cotton Mather, *Ornaments for the Daughters of Zion, or the Character and Happiness of a Woman: in a Discourse*, 3d ed. (Boston, 1741), 2–3. Even a secular medical manual affirmed the curse of Eve: American edition of *Aristotle's Master Piece*, 1766, discussed in Otho T. Beall, Jr., "*Aristotle's Master Piece* in America: A Landmark in the Folklore of Medi-

cine," *William and Mary Quarterly*, 3d Ser., XX (1963), 216.

7. Mather, *Elizabeth in Her Retirement*, 1.

8. *The Diary of Cotton Mather* (Massachusetts Historical Society, *Collections*, 7th Ser., Pt. II [1912]), VIII, 618, 700; Mather, *Elizabeth in Her Retirement*, 2, 6, 7.

9. [Thomas Clap], "Memoirs of a College President: Womanhood in Early America," ed. Edwin Stanley Wells, *The Connecticut Magazine*, XII (1908), 233–239, esp. 235.

10. Drinker, *Not So Long Ago*, 48.

11. Stewart Mitchell, ed., *New Letters of Abigail Adams, 1788–1801* (Boston, 1947), 3–5, 56; Clayton Harding Chapman, "Benjamin Colman's Daughters," *New England Quarterly*, XXVI (1953), 182; Malcolm R. Lowell, ed., *Two Quaker Sisters, from the Original Diaries of Elizabeth Buffum Chace and Lucy Buffum Lovell* (New York, 1937), 1, 12; Drinker, *Not So Long Ago*, 51–60; Mary Vial Holyoke's diary, in George Francis Dow, ed., *The Holyoke Diaries, 1709–1856* (Salem, Mass., 1911), 70, 73, 75, 83, 95, 100, 101, 107; *Diary of Samuel Sewall* (Mass. Hist. Soc., *Colls.*, 5th Ser. V–VII [1878–1882]), I, 11, 40, 110, 166, 222–223, 351, 394, 426, II, 49, hereafter cited as *Diary of Sewall*; Ethel Armes, ed., *Nancy Shippen: Her Journal Book* (Philadelphia, 1935), 122–124.

12. James Hobson Aveling, *English Midwives: Their History and Prospects* (London, 1967 [orig. publ. 1872]), 3–4, 7, 10; E. H. Carter, *The Norwich Subscription Books: A Study of the Subscription Books of the Diocese of Norwich, 1637–1800* (London, 1937), 17–18, 134; facsimile oath of 1661, in Thomas Forbes, *The Midwife and the Witch* (New Haven, Conn., 1966), 145.

13. Cutter and Viets, *Short History*, 5–55; Isaac Flack, *Eternal Eve* (London, 1950), 218–219; Alfred McClintock, ed., *Smellie's Treatise on the Theory and Practice of Midwifery* (London, 1876–1878), II, 248–250, III, 26–27, 298, 317–319; Percival Willughby, *Observations in Midwifery*, ed. Henry Blenkinsop (Wakefield, Eng., 1972 [orig. publ. 1803]), 37, 155.

Save for midwifery, medical practice in England was divided among three guilds of physicians, surgeons, and apothecaries. Physicians, titled "doctor" and usually possessing university degrees, theoretically as gentlemen did not work with their hands. Surgeons, trained by apprenticeship and rarely holding degrees, dealt with structural emergencies. Apothecaries, also apprenticed, sold drugs. These distinctions disappeared in the rural areas and small towns of England, as well as in colonial America, where medical men, usually without formal training and indiscriminately called doctor, engaged in general practice. Even after 1765, the American men who were by strict definition physicians practiced general medicine. Richard Harrison Shryock, *Medicine and Society in America, 1660–1860* (Ithaca, N.Y., 1960), 2–3, 7, 10.

14. Aveling, *English Midwives*, 138–144; Alice Clark, *Working Life of Women in the Seventeenth Century* (London, 1919), 265, 269, 270–275; *The Compleat Midwifes Practice, in the Most Weighty and High Concernments of the Birth of Man* . . . (London, 1656), 119–124; John Memis, *The Midwive's Pocket Companion: or a Practical Treatise on Midwifery* (London, 1765), v–vii; Jane Sharp, *The Compleat Midwife's Companion: or, the art of midwifery improved* . . . , 4th ed. (London, 1725), x–xii; Willughby, *Observations in Midwifery*, ed. Blenkinsop, 73.

15. John Kobler, *The Reluctant Surgeon: A Biography of John Hunter* (New York, 1960), 31; Sharp, *Compleat Midwife's Companion*, introduction; Willughby, *Observations in Midwifery*, ed. Blenkinsop, 102.

16. Valentine Seaman, *The Midwives Monitor, and Mothers Mirror; Being Three Concluding Lectures of a Course of Instruction of Midwifery* (New York, 1800), viii.

17. Ibid. See also Joseph Brevitt, *The Female Medical Repository* . . . (Baltimore, 1810), 6.

18. Beall, *"Aristotle's Master Piece,"* WMQ, 3d Ser., XX (1963), 209–210; Seaman, *Midwives Monitor*, ix. Beall's article is the best study of the popular manuals of "Aristotle." The *Master Piece*, which was the creation of an English physician, "W. S.," and a succession of hack writers, first appeared in England in 1684. The numerous later editions were the only works on sex and gynecology widely available to eighteenth-century Americans.

19. Jane B. Donegan, "Midwifery in America, 1760–1860: A Study in Medicine and Morality" (Ph.D. diss., Syracuse University, 1972), 9–10, 12; "A Law for Regulating Mid Wives Within the City of New York," Minutes of the Common Council of New York, 1716, Appendix I, in Claire E. Fox, "Pregnancy, Childbirth and Early Infancy in Anglo-American Culture, 1675–1830" (Ph.D. diss., University of Pennsylvania, 1966), 442–445; Richard Harrison Shryock, *Medical Licensing in America, 1650–1965* (Baltimore, 1967), 3, 16; James J. Walsh, *History of Medi-*

cine in New York: Three Centuries of Medical Progress, II (New York, 1919), 22, 25.

20. Cutter and Viets, *Short History*, 145, 150; *Maryland Gazette* (Annapolis), Sept. 30, 1747; Francis R. Packard, *History of Medicine in the United States*, I (New York, 1931), 52–53; Shryock, *Medicine and Society*, 11–12; J. Whitridge Williams, *A Sketch of the History of Obstetrics in the United States up to 1860* (Baltimore, 1903), 1.

21. Wyndham B. Blanton, *Medicine in Virginia in the Seventeenth Century* (Richmond, 1930), 166; Packard, *History of Medicine*, I, 52; Julia C. Spruill, *Women's Life and Work in the Southern Colonies* (Chapel Hill, N.C., 1938), 272; Herbert Thoms, *Chapters in American Obstetrics* (Springfield, Ill., 1961), 10.

22. *Diary of Sewall*, I, 40, 114; Sharp, *Compleat Midwife's Companion*, frontispiece of midwife at christening.

23. Aristotle (pseud.), *Aristotle's Compleat and Experienc'd Midwife, in two Parts. I. Guide for Childbearing Women. II. Proper and Safe Remedies for the Curing of all those Distempers that are incident to the Female Sex* . . . , 9th ed. (London, [1700?]), iii.

24. Broadside of elegy to Mary Broadwell, in Francisco Guerra, *American Medical Bibliography, 1639–1783* (New York, 1962), 69.

25. Packard, *History of Medicine*, I, 49.

26. Drinker, *Not So Long Ago*, 51, 52, 54, 59; Dow, ed., *Holyoke Diaries*, 70, 73, 75, 81, 83, 95, 101, 107; *Diary of Sewall*, V, 40, 222–223, 394, VI, 49; Charles White, *A Treatise on the Management of Pregnant and Lying-in Women* (Worcester, Mass., 1793), 19–20.

27. Aristotle (pseud.), *Compleat and Experienc'd Midwife*, 50–51, 56, 57; Nicholas Culpeper, *A Directory for Midwives: or, a Guide for Women in Their Conception, Bearing, and Suckling their Children* (London, 1651), 167; Drinker, *Not So Long Ago*, 60; *Diary of Sewall*, V, 40; Sharp, *Compleat Midwife's Companion*, 81, 82, 124, 125, 128; White, *Treatise on Pregnant Women*, 20, 74; Willughby, *Observations in Midwifery*, ed. Blenkinsop, 4, 11, 13, 19.

28. Seaman, *Midwives Monitor*, 90–91.

29. Drinker, *No So Long Ago*, 59.

30. William Buchan, *Advice to Mothers on the Subject of Their Own Health* (Charleston, S.C., 1807), 28; *The London Practice of Midwifery by an American Practitioner* (Concord, N.H., 1826), 129; Thomas Chalkey James, "Notes from Drs. Osborne's and Clark's Lectures on Midwifery taken by T. C. James,

London, 1790–1791," MS, Historical Collections, College of Physicians of Philadelphia.

31. Drinker, *Not So Long Ago*, 53, 59.

32. Mrs. Eva Eve Jones, ed., "Extracts from the Journal of Miss Sarah Eve," *Pennsylvania Magazine of History and Biography*, V (1881), 195.

33. Mitchell, ed., *New Letters of Adams*, 4–5; Jack P. Greene, ed., *The Diary of Colonel Landon Carter of Sabine Hall, 1752–1788*, II (Charlottesville, Va., 1965), 86; Dow, ed., *Holyoke Diaries*, 49, 56, 58, 62, 63, 65, 67, 73, 77, 78, 82, 95, 100, 107; *Diary of Seawall*, II, 51; Sharp, *Compleat Midwife's Companion*, frontispiece drawing of lying-in; McClintock, ed., *Smellie's Treatise*, I, 380.

34. Corner, *William Shippen*, 124; Cutter and Viets, *Short History*, 150.

35. *Kite's Philadelphia Directory for 1815* (Philadelphia, 1815), xi–xii; John Paxton, *The Philadelphia Directory and Register for 1819* (Philadelphia, 1819), n.p.; Robert Desilver, *The Philadelphia Directory and Register for 1824* (Philadelphia, 1824), n.p.

36. Walter Channing (John Ware?), *Remarks on the Employment of Females as Practitioners in Midwifery* (Boston, 1820), 1; *Independent Chronicle and the Universal Advertiser* (Boston), Nov. 8, 1781.

37. William Potts Dewees, *A Compendious System of Midwifery, Chiefly Designed to Facilitate the Inquiries of Those Who may be Pursuing This Branch of Study* (Philadelphia, 1826), xiv.

38. Charles M. Andrews, *Colonial Folkways: A Chronicle of American Life in the Reign of the Georges* (New Haven, Conn., 1919), 147; Maurice Bear Gordon, *Aesculapius Comes to the Colonies: The Story of the Early Days of Medicine in the Thirteen Original Colonies* (Ventnor, N.J., 1949), 156–157, 460–465; Francis Packard, "How London and Edinburgh Influenced Medicine in Philadelphia in the Eighteenth Century," College of Physicians of Philadelphia, *Transactions*, 3d Ser., LIII (1931), 167.

39. Gordon, *Aesculapius*, 465; Packard, *History of Medicine*, I, 181–230; Packard, "How London and Edinburgh Influenced Medicine," College of Psyicians of Philadelphia, *Trans.*, 3d Ser., LIII (1931), 163, 166.

40. John Morgan, *A Discourse Upon the Institution of Medical Schools in America* (Baltimore, 1937 [orig. publ. 1765]), 33.

41. Samuel Bard, *Two Discourses Dealing with Medical Education in Early New York* (New York, 1921), 1.

42. Ibid., 10, 16, 19; Morgan, *Discourse Upon the Institution of Medical Schools*, 14–17.

43. Packard, *History of Medicine*, II, 1125–1127; Williams, *Sketch of the History of Obstetrics*, 5–7.

44. *OED*, s.v. "obstetrics"; Packard, *History of Medicine*, II, 1125–1126.

45. Cutter and Viets, *Short History*, 26–28.

46. Ibid., 44–59; John Glaister, *Dr. William Smellie and His Contemporaries* (Glasgow, 1894), 170, 174, 178–179, 187; McClintock, ed., *Smellie's Treatise*, II, 250–251, 339.

47. McClintock ed., *Smellie's Treatise*, II, 339.

48. White, *Treatise on Pregnant Women*, viii, 70–71.

49. Thomas Dashiell Jones, *An Essay on the Importance of the Obstetrick Art; Submitted to the Examination of Charles Alexander Warfield, M.D., President of the Medical Faculty of the College of Medicine of Maryland . . .* (Baltimore, 1812), 5, 11, 21, 23.

50. Boston Medical Association, *Rules and Regulations of the Boston Medical Association* (Boston, 1806), 4–5. The minimum fee escalated to $15/day case, $20/night by 1819. Boston Med. Assoc., *Rules and Regulations* (1819 ed.).

51. Channing, *Remarks on Employment of Females*, 19; Edward Warren, *The Life of John Collins Warren, M.D., Compiled Chiefly from his Autobiography and Journals*, I (Boston, 1860), 219.

52. Dewees, *Compendious System of Midwifery* (Philadelphia, 1824), 307.

53. Ibid. (1826), xiv.

54. Drinker, *Not So Long Ago*, 51, 54–56, 59.

55. Dewees, *Compendious System of Midwifery* (1824), 307; Drinker, *Not So Long Ago*, 60.

56. Samuel Bard, *A Compendium of the Theory and Practice of Midwifery*, 5th ed. (New York, 1819), v, 176, 289; Dewees, *Compendious System of Midwifery* (1826) xv.

57. Jones, *Essay on Obstetrick Art*, 8.

58. Peter Miller, *An Essay on the Means of Lessening the Pains of Parturition* (Philadelphia, 1804), 340.

59. William Potts Dewees, *Essays on Various Subjects Connected with Midwifery* (Philadelphia, 1823), 24.

60. Channing, *Remarks on Employment of Females*, 6–12; Jones, *Essay on Obstetrick Art*, 20; Joseph F. Kett, *The Formation of the American Medical Profession: The Role of Institutions, 1780–1860* (New Haven, Conn., 1968), 10–30.

61. *Pennsylvania Gazette* (Philadelphia), Jan. 31, 1765.

62. Williams, *Sketch of the History of Obstetrics*, 13; Seaman, *Midwives Monitor*, iii–vii.

63. Bard, *Compendium of Theory and Practice of Midwifery*, iv, 289; Brevitt, *Female Medical Repository*, 149–155; William Buchan, *A Compend of Domestic Midwifery for the Use of Female Practitioners, Being an Appendix to Buchan's Domestic Medicine* (Charleston, S.C., 1815); Samuel Jennings, *Married Lady's Companion, or Poor Man's Friend* . . . (New York, 1808), 135; Seaman, *Midwives Monitor*, 31–32. All of these works were directed entirely or in part to midwives.

64. Thomas Ewell, *Letters to Ladies, Detailing Important Information Concerning Themselves and Infants* (Philadelphia, 1817), vii–viii.

65. Channing, *Remarks on Employment of Females*, 4–7.

66. Aveling, *English Midwives*, 138–144, 153–159; Cutter and Viets, *Short History*, 43; Glaister, *William Smellie*, 32–36.

67. Dewees, *Compendious System of Midwifery* (1826), xv.

68. Channing, *Remarks on Employment of Females*, 16, 17; Ewell, *Letters to Ladies*, 27.

69. Jones, *Essay on Obstetrick Art*, 11.

70. Seaman, *Midwives Monitor*, iv.

71. *Virginia Gazette* (Purdie and Dixon), Oct. 1, 1772; reprinted in *New-London Gazette* (Conn.), Jan. 29, 1773.

72. Elizabeth Nihill, *A Treatise on the Art of Midwifery, Setting Forth Various Abuses Therein, Especially as to the Practice With Instruments* (London, 1760), and S. W. Fores, *Man-Midwifery Dissected* (London,

1793), are outstanding examples of arguments made about the supposed immorality of man midwives. Glaister, *William Smellie*, discusses other examples of such literature.

73. Ewell, *Letters to Ladies*, 27.

74. Dewees, *Compendious System of Midwifery* (1826), 189; Daniel B. Smith, "Notes on lectures of Thomas Chalkley James and William Potts Dewees, University of Pennsylvania, 1826," MS, Hist. Colls., College of Physicians of Philadelphia.

75. *London Practice of Midwifery*, 109.

76. Bard, *Compendium of Theory and Practice of Midwifery*, 181; lecture notes from lectures of William Shippen, Jr., University of Pennsylvania, n.d., MS, Hist. Colls., College of Physicians of Philadelphia.

77. Bard, *Compendium of Theory and Practice of Midwifery*, 181; Dewees, *Compendious System of Midwifery* (1826), 189–190; *London Practice of Midwifery*, 108–109.

78. Thomas Denman, *The Obstetrical Remembrancer, or Denman's Aphorisms on Natural and Difficult Parturition* (New York, 1848 [orig. U.S. publ. 1803]), 46.

79. *London Practice of Midwifery*, 129.

80. Ibid., 129–130.

81. James, "Notes from Osborne's and Clark's Lectures," Hist. Colls., College of Physicians of Philadelphia; notes on Shippen lectures, ibid.

82. Notes on Shippen lectures, ibid.; *London Practice of Midwifery*, 127.

83. Bard, *Compendium of Theory and Practice of Midwifery*, 220; Seaman, *Midwives Monitor*, ix.

84. Dewees, *Compendious System of Midwifery* (1826), 313.

85. Kobler, *Reluctant Surgeon*, 32; *London Practice of Midwifery*, 132–133.

DOCUMENTS: Fund Raising for the Revolution

The Sentiments of an American Woman

This broadside of 1780 announced a women's campaign to raise contributions for patriot soldiers. Organized and led by Esther DeBerdt Reed, wife of the president of Pennsylvania, and Benjamin Franklin's daughter Sarah Franklin Bache, the campaign was large and effective. "Instead of waiting for the Donations being sent the ladys of each Ward go from dore to dore and collect them," wrote one participant. Collecting contributions this way invited confrontation. One loyalist wrote to her sister, "Of all absurdities, the ladies going about for money exceeded everything; they were so extremely importunate that people were obliged to give them something to get rid of them."* The campaign raised $300,000 paper dollars in inflated war currency. Rather than let George Washington merge it with the general fund, the women insisted on using it to buy materials for making shirts so that each soldier might know he had received an extraordinary contribution from the women of Philadelphia. The broadside itself is an unusually explicit justification for women's intrusion into politics.

On the commencement of actual war, the Women of America manifested a firm resolution to contribute . . . to the deliverance of their country. Animated by the purest patriotism, they are sensible of sorrow at this day, in not offering more than barren wishes for the success of so glorious a Revolution. They aspire to render themselves more really useful; and this sentiment is universal from the north to the south of the Thirteen United States. Our ambition is kindled by the fame of those heroines of antiquity, who have rendered their sex illustrious, and have proved to the universe, that, if the weakness of our Constitution, if opinion and manners did not forbid us to march to glory by the same paths as the Men, we should at least equal, and sometimes surpass them in our love for the public good. I glory in all that which my sex has done great and commendable. I call to mind with enthusiasm and with admiration, all those acts of courage, of constancy and patriotism, which history has transmitted to us: The people favoured by Heaven, preserved

* Mary Morris to Catharine Livingston, June 10 [1780], Ridley Family Papers, Massachusetts Historical Society, Boston; Anna Rawle to Rebecca Rawle Shoemaker, June 30, 1780, in *Pennsylvania Magazine of History and Biography* 35 (1911): 398.

Excerpted from *The Sentiments of an American Woman* ([Philadelphia]: John Dunlap, 1780).

from destruction by the virtues, the zeal and the resolution of Deborah, of Judith, of Esther! The fortitude of the mother of the Macchabees, in giving up her sons to die before her eyes: Rome saved from the fury of a victorious enemy by the efforts of Volumnia, and other Roman Ladies: So many famous sieges where the Women have been seen forgetting the weakness of their sex, building new walls, digging trenches with their feeble hands, furnishing arms to their defenders, they themselves darting the missile weapons on the enemy, resigning the ornaments of their apparel, and their fortune, to fill the public treasury, and to hasten the deliverance of their country; burying themselves under its ruins; throwing themselves into the flames rather than submit to the disgrace of humiliation before a proud enemy.

Born for liberty, disdaining to bear the irons of a tyrannic Government, we associate ourselves to the grandeur of those Sovereigns, cherished and revered, who have held with so much splendour the scepter of the greatest States, The Batildas, the Elizabeths, the Maries, the Catharines, who have extended the empire of liberty, and contented to reign by sweetness and justice, have broken the chains of slavery, forged by tyrants in times of ignorance and barbarity. . . .

We know that at a distance from the theatre of war, if we enjoy any tranquility, it is the fruit of your watchings, your labours, your dangers. . . . Who, amongst us, will not renounce with the highest pleasure, those vain ornaments, when she shall consider that the valiant defenders of America will be able to draw some advantage from the money which she may have laid out in these. . . . The time is arrived to display the same sentiments which animated us at the beginning of the Revolution, when we renounced the use of teas, however agreeable to our taste, rather than receive them from our persecutors; when we made it appear to them that we placed former necessaries in the rank of superfluities, when our liberty was interested; when our republican and laborious hands spun the flax, prepared the linen intended for the use of our soldiers; when [as] exiles and fugitives we supported with courage all the evils which are the concomitants of war. . . .

RACHEL WELLS
Petition to Congress

Rachel Wells was probably sixty-five years old when she wrote the following words. She had bought loan office certificates from the state of New Jersey during the Revolution: subsequently she had moved to Philadelphia, but returned to Bordentown, New Jersey, after the war. In an effort to curb speculation, the New Jersey legislature decided that only state residents had a claim on interest

Rachel Wells, Petition to Congress, May 18, 1786, Microfilm Papers of the Continental Congress, National Archives, Washington, D.C., microfilm M247, roll 56, item 42, vol. 8, pp. 354–55.

payments; Rachel Wells's claim on her money was turned down because she had not been in the state at the war's end in 1783. She appealed directly to the Continental Congress. Although her petition was tabled, it remains—despite its bad spelling—as perhaps the most moving witness to the Revolution left to us by a woman. What did Rachel Wells think had been her contribution to the Revolution? What did she think the government owed to her?

To the Honnorabell Congress I rachel do make this Complaint Who am a Widow far advanced in years & Dearly have ocasion of ye Interst for that Cash I Lent the States. I was a Sitisen in ye jersey when I Lent ye State a considerable Sum of Moneys & had I justice dun me it mite be Suficant to suporte me in ye Contrey whear I am now, near burdentown. I Leved hear then . . . but Being . . . so Robd by the Britans & others i went to Phila to try to get a Living . . . & was There in the year 1783 when our assembley was pleasd to pas a Law that No one Should have aney Interest that Livd out of jearsey Stats . . .

Now gentlemen is this Liberty, had it bin advertised that he or She that Moved out of the Stat should Louse his or her Interest you mite have sum plea against me. But I am Innocent Suspected no Trick. I have Don as much to Carrey on the Warr as maney that Sett now at ye healm of goverment. . . . your asembly Borrowed

£300 in gould of me jest as the Warr Comencd & Now I Can Nither git Intrust nor principall Nor Even Security. . . . My dr Sister . . . wrote to me to be thankfull that I had it in my Power to help on the Warr which is well enough but then this is to be Considerd that others gits their Intrust & why then a poor old widow to be put of[f]. . . . I hartely pity others that ar in my Case that Cant Speak for themselves. . . .

god has Spred a plentifull table for us & you gentlemen are ye Carvers for us pray forgit Not the Poor weaklings at the foot of the Tabel ye poor Sogers has got Sum Crumbs That fall from their masters tabel. . . . Why Not Rachel Wells have a Littel intrust?

if She did not fight She threw in all her mite which bought ye Sogers food & Clothing & Let Them have Blankets & Since that She has bin obligd to Lay upon Straw & glad of that. . . .

LINDA K. KERBER
The Republican Mother

The years of the early republic (1776–1820) were a time of profound social and political change. Rebellion against England meant that throughout America there was a major reconsideration of political relationships, culminating in the Declaration of Independence, new state constitutions, and the federal Constitution. Male political leaders redefined the relationship of the individual to the state. They rarely explored what the new relationship of women to the state might be, though they left some important questions open: women were citizens and alien women could become naturalized citizens; the qualifications for suffrage were framed in terms of "persons." But full political identity was also based on a willingness to take up arms for the republic, and for this role women were thought biologically unfit. Even more important, full political autonomy was assumed to involve control of enough property so that one was not vulnerable to economic pressure by a master or employer, yet married women could not control property. They were denied suffrage in large part because it was thought that to give women a vote was, in practice, to give a double vote to their husbands. (On the other hand, a substantial minority of adult women at any given moment were single or widowed and *did* control their own property; political theorists ignored their presence.)

Those who articulated the ideology of Republican Motherhood sought to draw together the political, biological, and economic reality experienced by free white women and to redefine the role of women in the new post-Revolutionary era in a way that reflected realistically the constraints of their lives but also emphasized that women, too, were part of a deeply radical republican experiment. What features of this ideology were conservative? What features were radical? What elements of the ideology of Republican Motherhood persist into our own time?

When women looked back to the years of the Revolution, what did they remember? Several themes were repeated with great frequency. The war had been a nightmare. It had frightened people and disrupted lives. It had been a time when women

A revised version of " 'Why Should Girls Be Learnd or Wise?' Education and Intellect in the Early Republic" and "The Republican Mother: Female Political Imagination in the Early Republic," chaps. 7 and 9 of *Women of the Republic: Intellect and Ideology in Revolutionary America* (Chapel Hill: University of North Carolina Press, for the Institute of Early American History and Culture, 1980; paperback ed., New York: W. W. Norton, 1986).

had chosen political identities, prided themselves on their loyalism or on their patriotism, and performed services for the government of their choice. Women who had survived the war had been strong and courageous, but the republic had offered only the most grudging response to their sacrifices, as Rachel Wells had discovered.

Americans did not choose to explore with much rigor the socially radical implications of their republican ideology. For example, only haltingly did a few develop the obvious antislavery implications of egalitarian rhetoric. Nor did they explore very deeply the implications of female citizenship; the Revolution and the republic that followed were thought to be men's work. "To be an adept in the art of Government," Abigail Adams observed to her husband, "is a prerogative to which your Sex lay almost an exclusive claim."[1] Women were left to invent their own political character. They devised their own interpretation of what the Revolution had meant to them as women, and they began to invent an ideology of citizenship that merged the domestic domain of the preindustrial woman with the new public ideology of individual responsibility and civic virtue. They did this in the face of severe ridicule, responding both to the anti-intellectual complaint that educating women served no practical purpose and to the conservative complaint that women had no political significance.

Memories of the Revolution, as they appear in postwar fiction, suggest some of the lessons women drew from the wartime experience. An early exploration of women's political options appears in Mercy Otis Warren's verse play The Ladies of Castile, written shortly after the close of the war. The play concerns two women of contrasting temperaments caught up in a civil war in Spain that, Warren makes clear in her introduction, is meant to be a metaphor for the Revolutionary War in America. The soft and delicate Louisa introduces herself with the words, "I wan-

der wilder'd and alone / Like some poor banish'd fugitive . . . I yield to grief"; while the determined Maria, wife of the leader of the rebellion, announces in her opening scene, "Maria has a bolder part to act— / I scorn to live upon ignoble terms." The message of The Ladies of Castile is simple and obvious. Even in the exigencies of war, women must control themselves and their options. The Louisas of the world do not survive revolutions; the Marias—who take political positions, make their own judgment of the contending sides, and risk their lives—emerge stronger and in control. "A soul, inspir'd by freedom's genial warmth," says Maria, "expands,—grows firm—and by resistance, strong."[2]

The experience of war had given words like independence and self-reliance personal as well as political overtones. As the song played at Yorktown had it, the world could turn upside down: the rich could quickly become poor, wives might suddenly have to manage the family economy, women might even shoulder a gun. Revolutionary experience taught that it was useful to be prepared for a wide range of unusual possibilities; political theory taught that republics rested on the virtue and intelligence of their citizens. The stability and competence on which republican government relied required a highly literate and politically sophisticated constituency. Maintaining the republic was an educational as well as a political challenge.

Warren was joined in her demand for self-reliance by Judith Sargent Murray, of Salem, Massachusetts, whose essays provide the most fully developed articulation of the idea that political independence should be the catalyst for female autonomy. When the Revolution ended, she published a prescient argument calling for the strengthening of what she called "Self-Complacency in Female Bosoms." She decried the tradition of educating middle-class girls for an upwardly mobile marriage by encouraging fashion, flirtatiousness, and charm. Lacking a strong and positive sense of their own identity, Murray complained, young women had no personal resources to give them confidence, and so they rushed into marriages to establish their social status.[3] Eight years later, widowed and remarried, she developed this theme at great length in a series of newspaper essays in which she emphasized the need for an education for competence. "I would give my daughters every accomplishment which I thought proper," she wrote,

> and, to crown all, I would early accustom them to habits of industry and order. They should be taught with precision the art economical; they should be enabled to procure for themselves the necessaries of life; independence should be placed within their grasp. . . . THE SEX should be taught to depend on their own efforts, for the procurement of an establishment in life.[4]

The model republican woman was competent and confident. She could resist the vagaries of fashion; she was rational, benevolent, independent, self-reliant. Nearly every writer who described this paragon prepared a list of role models, echoing the pantheon of heroines admired by the fundraising women of Philadelphia in 1780. There were women of the ancient world, like Cornelia, the mother of the Gracchi; rulers like Elizabeth of England and the Empress Catherine the Great of Russia; and a long list of British intellectuals: Lady Mary Wortley Montagu, Hannah More, Mary Wollstonecraft, and the historian Catharine Macaulay. Those who believed in these republican models demanded that their presence be recognized and endorsed and that a new generation of young women be urged to find in them patterns for their own behavior. "I expect to see our young women forming a new era in female history," Murray wrote.[5]

Other Americans made demands for the direct participation of women in public affairs. There is the well-known comment by Abigail Adams, which her husband jokingly turned away, that women ought to have the right to participate in the new system of government, for "all men would be tyrants if they could." All her life Abigail Adams was a shrewd commentator on the political scene, assuming as active an obligation to judge good and evil as if she were called upon annually to vote. But she was known, of course, only in a circle that, though relatively large, remained private. In *Alcuin*, the Philadelphia novelist Charles Brockden Brown sneered at the "charming system of equality and independence" that denied women a part in the choice of the governors, but the circulation of his novel was small. The distinguished Virginia jurist St. George Tucker admitted that laws neither respected nor favored females, but he made the concession in a single footnote in a three-volume work.[6]

Expressions of women's desire to play a frankly political role were regularly camouflaged in satire, a device that typically makes new ideas and social criticism seem less threatening and more palatable. In 1791, for example, a New Jersey newspaper published a pair of semiserious satires in which women discuss the politics of excise taxes and national defense. "Roxana" expresses a feminist impatience:

> In fifty quarto volumes of ancient and modern history, you will not find fifty illustrious female names; heroes, statesmen, divines, philosophers, artists, are all of masculine gender. And pray what have they done during this long period of usurpation? . . . They have written ten thousand unintelligible books. . . . They have been cutting each other's throats all over the globe.[7]

Some years later, the students at Sarah Pierce's famous school for girls in Litchfield, Connecticut, prepared a "Ladies Declaration of Independence" for July Fourth. Alongside the frivolous phrasing is some earnest comment on the unfilled promises of the republic. Less than ten years after that Elizabeth Cady Stanton would use the same technique. "When in the Course of Human Events," the Litchfield declaration begins,

> it becomes necessary for the Ladies to dissolve those bonds by which they have been subjected to others, and to assume among the self styled Lords of Creation that separate and equal station to which the laws of nature and their *own talents* entitle them, a decent respect to the opinions of mankind requires, that they should declare the causes which impel them to the separation.
>
> We hold these truths to be self evident. That all *mankind* are created equal.

The Litchfield women wished to change "social relations." They complained about men who "have undervalued our talents, and disparaged our attainments; they have combined with each other, for the purpose of excluding us from all participation in Legislation and in the administration of Justice; . . . [they have declared] themselves invested with power to act & legislate for us in all cases whatsoever."[8]

To accept an openly acknowledged role for women in the public sector was to invite extraordinary hostility and ridicule. Although neither political party took a consistent position on the matter, hostility to the political participation of women seems to have been particularly acute in Federalist circles. It is no accident that it was a Republican periodical that first reprinted Mary Wollstonecraft's *Vindication of the Rights of Woman*. "It is said by one of the federalist papers," remarked the Republican *Register* of Salem, Massachusetts, that

> "Women have no business to speak about politicks and that a woman meddling in politicks is like a monkey in a china ware shop, where he can't do any good but may do a great deal of mischief." On our part we are of a contrary opinion, we can see no reason why, with the same evidence before them, they cannot judge on

politicks or any other subject equally with men—On many subjects they certainly are better judges.[9]

Some counterarguments developed a life of their own, appearing and reappearing under different disguises. Among these the most persistent was that linking female intellectual activity and political autonomy to an unflattering masculinity. "From all we read, and all we observe, we are authorized in supposing that there is a *sex of soul*," announced the Boston minister John Gardiner. "Women of masculine minds, have generally masculine manners. . . . Queen Elizabeth understood Latin and Greek, swore with the fluency of a sailor, and boxed the ears of her courtiers. . . . Mrs. Macaulay, the author of a dull democratic history, at a tolerably advanced age, married a boy." A "mild, dove-like temper is so necessary to Female beauty, is so natural a part of the sex," reflected Parson Mason Locke Weems wistfully. "A masculine air in a woman frightens us."[10]

When women addressed political issues, the attacks were similar. A good example of this response appears in a newspaper letter written in 1790 by a Marylander who signed as "Philanthropos." Warning against literal interpretations of the phrase "All mankind are born equal," "Philanthropos" thought the principle of equality could be "taken in too extensive a sense, and might tend to destroy those degrees of subordination which nature seems to point out," including the subordination of women to men. "However flattering the path of glory and ambition may be, a woman will have more commendation in being the mother of heroes, than in setting up, Amazon-like, for a heroine herself." The reasons he offered in support of the continued exclusion of women from "political bustle and anxiety" were of three sorts. Women, involved as they were with domestic cares, had no time for politics. Women were inept at politics; behind every queen lurked male advisers and guiding the well-known political vigor of Quaker women was a peculiar and distasteful view of the nature of the universe. But if women were inept, they were also somehow too effective.

> A Female Orator, in haranguing an Assembly, might like many crafty politicians, keep her *best argument* for last, and would then be sure of the victory— Men would be exposed to temptations too great for their strength, and those who could resist a bribe, offered in the common way, might reasonably yield to what it would be hardly possible for a *man* to refuse.

Although the political woman was thus thought to be sexually aggressive, "famous" women of the past were, however, "generally deficient in those charms which it is the peculiar lot of the fair sex to excel in." "Philanthropos" ended with the familiar argument that so long as virtuous women had private opportunity to influence men and to "mould our minds," they ought not regret "their exclusion from the perplexity and tumult of a political life."[11]

Mary Wollstonecraft had borne one illegitimate daughter (Fanny Imlay) and lived with William Godwin before marrying him; after marriage she maintained lodgings in another house so that she could be free to write. Once her life history became generally known, it could be used to link political feminism to aggressive sexuality, as the Federalist Timothy Dwight did in his bitter "Morpheus" essays, which ran in a Boston newspaper in 1802. In an early dream sequence in "Morpheus," Wollstonecraft has arrived in America and sets out to teach its inhabitants wisdom.

> Women . . . are entitled to all the rights, and are capable of all the energies, of men. I do not mean merely mental energies. If any dispute remained on this subject, I have removed it entirely by displaying, in my immortal writings, all the mental energy of LOCKE and BACON. I in-

tend bodily energies. They can naturally run as fast, leap as high, and as far, and wrestle, scuffle, and box with as much success, as any of the . . . other sex.

> That is a mistake (said an old man just before her.)

> It is no mistake, (said the Female Philosopher.)

> . . . Why then, (said the senior again) are women always feebler than men?

> Because (said MARY) they are educated to be feeble; and by indulgence . . . are made poor, puny, baby-faced dolls; instead of the *manly women*, they ought to be.

> *Manly women!* (cried the wag). Wheu! a manly woman is a hoyden, a non descript.

> Am I a hoyden? (interrupted MARY, with spirit.)

> You used to be a strumpet.

Wollstonecraft tells him that she was not a strumpet but a sentimental lover, "too free to brook the restraints of marriage." Her interlocutor responds, "We call them strumpets here, Madam—no offense, I hope," and then argues that when a woman claims the rights of men and the character of a manly woman, she necessarily forgoes what he calls women's "own rights" to "refined consideration." The implication is that Wollstonecraft can be insulted with impunity. "Still, (said the senior) you ought to remember that she is a woman. *She* ought to remember it (said the young man.)" Thus political behavior, like abstract thought, continued to be specifically proscribed as a threat to sensual attractiveness. "*Cupid* is a timid, playful child, and is frightened at the helmet of Minerva," observed Maria Edgeworth.[12]

Only the Republican Mother was spared this hostility. The concept was a variant of the argument for the improved education of women that republicans like Judith Sargent Murray and Wollstonecraft herself had demanded. It defended education for women not only for their autonomy and self-realization but also so that they could be better wives and better mothers for the next generation of virtuous republican citizens—especially sons. In a widely reprinted speech, "Thoughts upon Female Education," originally given at the new Young Ladies Academy of Philadelphia, the physician and politician Benjamin Rush addressed the issue directly: "The equal share that every citizen has in the liberty and the possible share he may have in the government of our country make it necessary that our ladies should be qualified to a certain degree, by a peculiar and suitable education, *to concur in instructing their sons in the principles of liberty and government.*"[13] The Republican Mother was an educated woman who could be spared the criticism normally directed at the intellectually competent woman because she placed her learning at her family's service.

The Republican Mother's life was dedicated to the service of civic virtue. She educated her sons for it; she condemned and corrected her husband's lapses from it. It was commonly believed that republican government was fragile and rested on the presence of virtuous citizens. The creation of those virtuous citizens required wives and mothers who were well informed, "properly methodical," and free of "invidious and rancorous passions." It was perhaps more than mere coincidence that the word *virtue* was derived from the Latin word for *man*, with its connotations of virility. Political action seemed somehow inherently masculine. Virtue in a woman seemed to require another theater for its display. To that end theorists created a mother who had a political purpose and argued that her domestic behavior had a direct political function in the republic.

This constellation of ideas and the republican rhetoric that made it convincing appear at great length in the Columbia College commencement oration of 1795 entitled "Female Influence." Behind the flowery language lurks a social and political message.

> Let us then figure to ourselves the accomplished woman, surrounded by a sprightly band, from the babe that imbibes the nutritive fluid, to the generous youth just ripening into manhood. . . . Let us contemplate the mother distributing the mental nourishment to the fond smiling circle, by means proportionate to their different powers of reception, watching the gradual openings of their minds, and studying their various turns of temper; see, under her cultivating hand, reason assuming the reins of government, and knowledge increasing gradually to her beloved pupils. . . . the Genius of Liberty hovers triumphant over the glorious scene. . . . Yes, ye fair, the reformation of a world is in your power. . . . Contemplate the rising glory of confederated America. Consider that your exertions can best secure, increase, and perpetuate it. The solidity and stability of the liberties of your country rest with you; since Liberty is never sure, 'till Virtue reigns triumphant. . . . Already may we see the lovely daughters of Columbia asserting the importance and the honour of their sex. "Let us" . . . say they . . . "assiduously employ our influence over the men, in promoting their happiness and the best interests of society." . . . Begin then, ye fair! . . . It rests with you to make this retreat [from the corruptions of Europe] doubly peaceful, doubly happy, by banishing from it those crimes and corruptions, which have never yet failed of giving rise to tyranny, or anarchy. While you thus keep our country virtuous, you maintain its independence.[14]

Defined this way, the educated woman ceased to threaten the sanctity of marriage; the intellectual woman need not be masculine. In this awkward and, in the 1790s, still only vaguely expressed fashion, the traditional womanly virtues were endowed with a political purpose. "Let the ladies of a country be educated properly,"

Rush said, "and they will not only make and administer its laws, but form its manners and character."[15]

The ideology of Republican Motherhood was deeply ambivalent. Those who opposed women in politics were challenged by the proposal that women could—and should—play a political role through influencing their husbands and raising patriotic children. The Republican Mother was to encourage in her sons civic interest and participation. She was to educate both sons and daughters and guide them in the paths of morality and virtue. She was to take advantage of the "authority" invested in her by love and courtship to "mould the taste, the manners, and the conduct" of her admirers and her husband. But she was not to tell her male friends and relatives for whom to vote. She was a citizen but not really a constituent.

On the one hand, Republican Motherhood was a progressive ideology. Women were redefined as more than "helpmates" to their husbands. Within the dynamic relationships of the private family—between husbands and wives, mothers and children—it allocated an assertive role to women. In the past Western political theory had rarely contemplated the role of women in the civic culture. A political community that now accepted women as political actors would have to eliminate the assumption that the world of women is separate from the empire of men. The ideology of Republican Motherhood seemed to accomplish what the Enlightenment had not by identifying the intersection of the woman's private domain and the public order.

The notion that a mother can perform a political function represents the recognition that a citizen's political socialization takes place at an early age, that the family is a basic part of the system of political communication, and that patterns of family authority influence the general political culture. Most premodern political societies—and even some fairly modern democracies—maintained unarticulated, but nevertheless very firm, social restrictions that isolated the family's domestic world from politics. The willingness of the American woman to overcome this ancient separation brought her into the all-male political community.[16] In this sense Republican Motherhood was a very important, even revolutionary invention. It altered the female domain in which most women had always lived out their lives; it justified women's absorption and participation in the civic culture. Women had the major role in developing this formulation, women who had learned from the exigencies of the Revolution that the country needed Marias, not Louisas. Those who shared the vision of the Republican Mother usually insisted upon better education, clearer recognition of women's economic contributions, and a strong political identification with the republic. The ideology was strong enough to rout "Philanthropos" and "Morpheus" by redefining female political behavior as valuable rather than abnormal, as a source of strength to the republic rather than an embarrassment. The ideology would be revived as a rallying point for many twentieth-century women reformers of the progressive era who saw their commitment to honest politics, efficient urban sanitation, and pure food and drug laws as an extension of their responsibilities as mothers.

But Republican Motherhood legitimized only a minimum of political sophistication and interest. Women were expected to be content to perform their narrow political role permanently and were not expected to wish for fuller participation. Just as planters claimed that democracy in the antebellum South rested on the economic base of slavery, so egalitarian society was said to rest on the moral base of deference among a class of people—women—who would devote their efforts to service by raising sons and disciplining husbands to be virtuous citizens of the republic. The learned woman, who might very well wish to make choices as well as to influence attitudes, was a visible threat to this arrangement. Women were to contain their political judgments within their homes and families; they were not to bridge the world outside and the world within.

In this sense restricting women's politicization was one of a series of conservative choices that Americans made in the postwar years as they avoided the full implications of their own Revolutionary radicalism. In America responsibility for maintaining public virtue was channeled into domestic life. By these decisions Americans may well have been spared the agony of the French cycle of revolution and counterrevolution, which spilled more blood and produced a political system more retrogressive than had the American war. Nevertheless the impact of this choice was to delay the resolution of matters of particular concern to women—the continuation of coverture, for example, the inability of married women to control their own earnings, the right to judgment by a jury of their peers.

When the war was over, Judith Sargent Murray predicted "a new era in female history."[17] That new era remained to be created by women, fortified by their memories and myths of female strength during the trials of war, politicized by their resentment of male legislators slighting issues of greatest significance to women. But it could not be created until the inherent paradox of Republican Motherhood was resolved, until the world was not separated into a woman's realm of domesticity and nurture and a man's world of politics and intellect. The promises of the republic had yet to be fulfilled; remembering the Revolution helped to keep confidence alive. "Yes, gentlemen," said Elizabeth Cady Stanton to the New York legislature in 1854, "in republican America . . . we, the daughters of the revolutionary heroes of '76 demand at your hands the redress of our grievances—a revision of your State constitution—a new code of laws."[18] Stanton would wrestle throughout her own career with the contradictory demands of domesticity and civic activism. The ambivalent relationship between motherhood and citizenship would be one of the most lasting, and most paradoxical, legacies of the Revolutionary generation.

NOTES

1. Abigail Adams to John Adams, May 9, 1776, *Adams Family Correspondence*, ed. L. H. Butterfield (Cambridge, Mass., 1963), 1:404.

2. Mercy Otis Warren, *The Ladies of Castile*, in her *Poems, Dramatic and Miscellaneous* (Boston, 1790), pp. 100, 125–26, 144, 162–64.

3. Judith Sargent Murray, "Self-Complacency in Female Bosoms," *Gentlemen and Ladies Town and Country Magazine* (October 1784), pp. 251–52.

4. Murray's essays were reprinted in a collected edition entitled *The Gleaner* (Boston, 1798). These comments appear in 1:167, 168.

5. Ibid., 3:189.

6. Abigail Adams to John Adams, March 31, 1776, *Adams Family Correspondence*, 1: 370; Charles Brockden Brown, *Alcuin: A Dialogue* (1798), ed. Lee R. Edwards (New York, 1971), p. 33; St. George Tucker, ed., *Blackstone's Commentaries, With Notes of Reference, to the Constitution and Laws, of the Federal Government of the United States, and of the Commonwealth of Virginia* (Philadelphia, 1803), vol. 1.

7. *Burlington* (N.J.) *Advertiser*, February 1, 1791.

8. Miss Pierce's School Papers, 1839, Litchfield Historical Society, Litchfield, Conn.

9. *Register* (Salem, Mass.), October 4, 1802.

10. *New-England Palladium*, September 18, 1801; Mason Locke Weems, *Hymen's Re-

cruiting *Serjeant; or, The New Matrimonial Tatoo, for Old Bachelors* (Philadelphia, 1800).

11. *Virginia Gazette and Alexandria Advertiser,* April 22, 1790.

12. *Mercury & New-England Palladium,* March 1, 1802; Maria Edgeworth, *Letters for Literary Ladies* (Georgetown, D.C., 1810), p. 22.

13. Benjamin Rush, "Thoughts upon Female Education . . ." (1787), in *Essays on Education in the Early Republic,* ed. Frederick Rudolph (Cambridge, Mass., 1965), pp. 25–40.

14. *New York Magazine,* May 1795, pp. 301–5.

15. Rush, "Thoughts upon Female Education," p. 36.

16. See Gabriel Almond and Sidney Verba, *The Civic Culture* (Princeton, 1963), pp. 377–401.

17. Murray, *Gleaner,* 3:189.

18. Elizabeth Cady Stanton, Susan B. Anthony, and Matilda Joslyn Gage, eds., *History of Woman Suffrage,* vol. 1 (New York, 1881), p. 595.

Sojourner Truth (ca. 1797–1883)
Sojourner Truth was born a slave in New York; she escaped only a year before mandatory emancipation came into effect in 1828. Two daughters were sold away from her; she was successful in retrieving a son who had been sold illegally. A religious mystic and an enthusiastic abolitionist, Sojourner Truth developed a wide reputation as a public speaker well before, at the age of fifty-four, she appeared at the women's rights meeting in Akron, Ohio, to deliver the speech that permanently established her reputation and association with its refrain, "And a'n't I a woman?" The Schomburg Center for Research in Black Culture, The New York Public Library, Astor, Lenox and Tilden Foundations

II A

Industrializing America
1820-80

To Americans who lived through it, the Civil War was the most traumatic experience of the nineteenth century. The years from 1830 to 1860 have come to be called the *antebellum* period, as though their importance derives from what they preceded rather than what they encompassed. Other familiar labels—the Jacksonian era, the Rise of the Common Man, Freedom's Ferment—suggest the difficulty historians have had in characterizing the period.

In these years the American economy was transformed by the industrial revolution. Railroads and steamboats linked distant parts of the country and simplified economic interaction; during the Civil War the control of transportation networks would be an important ingredient in the North's success. The cotton gin ensured the profitability of the crop and reinforced the system of slave labor in the South. Steam-powered spinning and weaving equipment was placed in northern factories and tended by a new class of wage workers. The distinctive economies of North and South fostered a political dialogue that became increasingly acerbic over the years. The position of legislators on issues as disparate as tariffs or free speech could be linked to the economic interests of their sections and to the distinctive regional cultures. By 1860 institutions that had helped connect the two cultures—political parties, churches, economic networks—had broken down completely.

It has been relatively easy for historians to see that economic and political developments affected men's lives. The right to vote and hold office was extended to virtually every white man, whether or not he held property; after the Civil War it was extended to black men as well. Congress was a national forum for debate among male political leaders; by the 1850s speeches made there were rapidly diffused to the public by cheap newspapers, printed by newly efficient presses and distributed by railroads throughout the nation. A host of new careers opened to men as politicians, journalists, teachers, capitalists, physicians, and reformers. The expansion of the physical boundaries of the country, by treaty and by war, opened new frontiers and created new opportunities for farmers, merchants, civic promoters, and land speculators.

When we look at these developments through women's eyes, we find that women's lives also changed markedly. The transportation revolution, for example, had special significance for women. Single women rarely traveled in the colonial period; long trips meant nights in unfamiliar taverns and lodging houses where accommodations were uncertain and safety could not be assured. The railroad changed that. The women who traveled to raise funds for abolition societies and women's seminaries could not have played that role a century before. After the Civil War Elizabeth Cady Stanton and Susan B. Anthony traveled a regular lyceum circuit throughout the North and Midwest, speaking on behalf of women's rights.

Improvements in the printing technology and distribution of newspapers meant that women as well as men were no longer dependent on local sources of information and political guidance. Even if one's town lacked a temperance society or an abolitionist organization, one could still subscribe to a temperance or abolitionist newspaper. A person who did so was reaching out, past the local notables—ministers, politicians, lawyers—who had shaped opinion in the colonial period, to make contact with a larger political community. Abolition newspapers like the *National Anti-Slavery Standard* (which was, for a time, edited by a woman, Lydia Maria Child) and women's rights newspapers like *Una* or *The Revolution* could come straight to a woman's mailbox, enlarging her political world.

Although women could travel more freely and read more widely, in other ways the new industrial economy constrained their lives. As Gerda Lerner has pointed out, many of the new opportunities for men came in a form that closed options for women. When additional men were granted suffrage, for example, "women's political status, while legally unchanged, . . . deteriorated relative to the advances made by men."[1] When new medical schools offered formal training only to men, "the process of professionalization . . . proceeded in such a way as to institutionalize an exclusion of women. . . . The status differential between male and female practitioners was more obviously disadvantageous and underscored women's marginality."[2]

If we recall David Potter's rule and ask whether established generalizations about the nineteenth century apply to women as accurately as they apply to men, we find that they do not. Several traditional pictures must be refocused.

For example, the great religious revival of the early part of the century is often described as though it affected both men and women with equal force. But careful examination of church records has suggested that women were already church members when the revival began; the new recruits were most likely to be sons and husbands of women who had long since been "saved." Seen in this light, the Second Great Awakening may be better understood as an occasion on which women acted as a catalyst for church recruitment.[3]

Although the experience of slavery has received fresh attention from historians, the distinctive experience of female slaves has been little examined. Deborah Gray White's work makes it clear that work roles on the plantation were defined by gender as well as by race. Women were especially vulnerable to sexual exploitation and to debilitating chronic ailments incidental to childbearing. The research of Michael P. Johnson has shown that excessive labor requirements affected not only the slave women but their unborn children.[4]

In free households female work—including taking in boarders, washing their clothes, and cooking for them—might account for as much income as working-class husbands gained from their own employment. If the husband's work was seasonal or erratic, the steady income from taking in boarders could be crucial to the family's survival. The story of the work done by women who took in boarders ought not to be relegated to the obligatory chapters on "home and family life"; it is central to the history of American labor.

Traditional interpretations of industrialization require refinement. Familiar accounts are likely to ignore the dependence of early mills on women for their labor force, yet even Alexander Hamilton recognized that a crucial factor in the development of new factories was that their owners could count on a steady supply of female workers at low rates of pay. As Barbara Mayer Wertheimer shows, women were among the first self-conscious laborers in America. They were also among the poorest. Christine Stansell's study of New York working women and children shows that the "feminization of poverty" long predated the twentieth century.

Viewed through women's eyes, antebellum America looks different. The common school movement looms even larger than in traditional accounts. As Kathryn Kish Sklar's essay suggests, the story of the building of public schools does not begin and end with Horace Mann and Henry Barnard. The work of Emma Willard and Catharine Beecher also requires attention. A history of education in antebellum America needs to explain how the great gap in literacy between men and women was closed during those years, and it must also find room for the large number of women who worked, even briefly, as schoolteachers at wage rates so low that planners could think it feasible to construct enough classrooms to educate every child in America.

The frontier has traditionally been treated as a metaphor for unbounded opportunity. But the experience of married women in the trans-Mississippi West was likely to be one of hardship encountered at the urging of their husbands, not out of their own initiative and choice.

Finally, in the middle years of the nineteenth century women pressed at the limits of the ways in which nonvoting citizens could influence the political order. In antislavery petition campaigns, in efforts to persuade legislatures to reform laws dealing with married women's property rights and child custody, in responding to the crisis of the Civil War, in volunteering as teachers for freedmen's schools after the war, women expressed political opinions and sought to shape political events. Some, like Catharine Beecher and Sarah Josepha Hale, began to formulate an interpretation of the republican community which suggested that women could play an important part in it without voting; others, like Elizabeth Cady Stanton, insisted that women's political rights ought to be the same as those of men. But whatever particular solutions they proposed, whether suffragist or not, the way in which women's citizenship was displayed was a significant element on the American political scene.

Notes

1. Gerda Lerner, *The Majority Finds Its Past: Placing Women in History* (New York, 1979), p. 18.

2. Ibid., p. 20.

3. Mary P. Ryan, "A Woman's Awakening: Evangelical Religion and the Families of Utica, New York, 1800–1840," *American Quarterly* 30 (1978):602–23. See also her *Cradle of the Middle Class: The Family in Oneida County, New York, 1790–1865* (Cambridge, 1981).

4. Michael P. Johnson, "Smothered Slave Infants: Were Slave Mothers at Fault?" *Journal of Southern History* 47 (1981):493–520.

DOCUMENTS: *The Testimony of Slave Women*

MARIA PERKINS
"I am quite heartsick"

Because masters understood the connection between literacy and rebelliousness, slaves were rarely taught to read and write. This anguished letter from Maria Perkins is unusual because it was written by an enslaved woman. We do not know whether Perkins's husband Richard managed to persuade his master to buy her and keep the family together. If a trader did buy Maria Perkins or her child, the likelihood of permanent separation was great. Scottsville, mentioned in the letter, is a small town near Charlottesville; Staunton is some forty miles away.

Charlottesville, Oct. 8th, 1852

Dear Husband I write you a letter to let you know my distress my master has sold albert to a trader on Monday court day and myself and other child is for sale also and I want you to let [me] hear from you very soon before next cort if you can I don't know when I don't want you to wait till Christmas I want you to tell dr Hamelton and your master if either will buy me they can attend to it know and then I can go afterwards. I don't want a trader to get me they asked me if I had got any person to buy me and I told them no they took me to the court houste too they never put me up a man buy the name of brady bought albert and is gone I don't know where they say he lives in Scottesville my things is in several places some is in staunton and if I should be sold I don't know what will become of them I don't expect to meet with the luck to get that way till I am quite heartsick nothing more I am and ever will be your kind wife Maria Perkins.

To Richard Perkins

Maria Perkins to Richard Perkins, October 8, 1852, Ulrich B. Phillips Collection, Yale University Library, New Haven.

ROSE

"Look for some others for to 'plenish de earth"

Letters like Maria Perkins's are very rare. Most firsthand evidence of the experience of being a slave comes from narratives prepared by ex-slaves after they were free. Some accounts were published by abolitionist societies before the Civil War; some people were interviewed by agents of the Freedmen's Bureau after the war. A large group of elderly ex-slaves was interviewed in the 1930s as part of the Federal Writers' Project. One of these speakers we know only as Rose.

Abolitionists shrilly accused masters of breeding slaves as they did cattle. Masters denied these charges and claimed that high birth rates among slave women should be taken as evidence of high levels of nutrition and of good treatment. In Brazil, for example, where the treatment of slaves was much more brutal, fewer children survived. There was some truth in this defense. But slave women lacked the normal legal protections against rape, and, as Rose's moving narrative shows, the line between "forced breeding" and "strong encouragement" could be a very thin one.

What I say am de facts. If I's one day old, I's way over 90, and I's born in Bell County, right here in Texas, and am owned by Massa William Black. He owns mammy and pappy, too. Massa Black has a big plantation but he has more niggers dan he need for work on dat place, 'cause he am a nigger trader. He trade and buy an sell all de time.

Massa Black am awful cruel and he whip de cullud folks and works 'em hard and feed dem poorly. We'uns have for rations de cornmeal and milk and 'lasses and some beans and peas and meat once a week. We'uns have to work in de field every day from daylight till dark and on Sunday we'uns do us washin'. Church? Shucks, we'uns don't know what dat mean.

I has de correct mem'randum of when de war start. Massa Black sold we'uns right den. Mammy and pappy powerful glad to git sold, and dey and I is put on de block with 'bout ten other niggers. When we'uns gits te de tradin' block, dere lots of white folks dere what come to look us over. One man shows de intres' in pappy. Him named Hawkins. He talk to pappy and pappy talk to him and say, "Dem my woman and chiles. Please buy all of us and have mercy on we'uns." Massa Hawkins say, "Dat gal am a likely lookin' nigger, she am portly and strong, but three am more dan I wants, I guesses."

De sale start and 'fore long pappy a put on de block. Massa Hawkins wins de bid for pappy and when mammy am put on de block, he wins de bid for her. Den dere am three or four other niggers sold befo' my time comes. Den massa Black calls me

Manuscript Slave Narrative Collection, Federal Writers' Project, 1941, vol. 17, Texas Narratives, part 4, pp. 174–78, Library of Congress, Washington, D.C.

to de block and de auction man say, "What am I offer for dis portly, strong young wench. She's never been 'bused and will make de good breeder."

I wants to hear Massa Hawkins bid, but him say nothin'. Two other men am biddin' 'gainst each other and I sho' has de worryment. Dere am tears comin' down my cheeks 'cause I's bein' sold to some man dat would make sep'ration from my mammy. One man bids $500 and de auction man ask, "Do I hear more? She am gwine at $500.00." Den someone say, $525.00 and de auction man say, "She am sold for $525.00 to Massa Hawkins." Am I glad and 'cited! Why, I's quiverin' all over.

Massa Hawkins takes we'uns to his place and it am a nice plantation. Lots better am dat place dan Massa Black's. Dere is 'bout 50 niggers what is growed and lots of chillen. De first thing massa de when we'uns gits home am give we'uns rations and a cabin. You mus' believe dis nigger when I says dem rations a feast for us. Dere plenty meat and tea and coffee and white flour. I's never tasted white flour and coffee and mammy fix some biscuits and coffee. Well, de biscuits was yum, yum, yum to me, but de coffee I doesn't like.

De quarters am purty good. Dere am twelve cabins all made from logs and a table and some benches and bunks for sleepin' and a fireplace for cookin' and de heat. Dere am no floor, jus' de ground.

Massa Hawkins am good to he niggers and not force 'em work too hard. Dere am as much diff'ence 'tween him and old Massa Black in de way of treatment as 'twixt de Lawd and de devil. Massa Hawkins 'lows he niggers have reason'ble parties and go fishin', but we'uns am never tooken to church and has no books for larnin'. Dere am no edumcation for de niggers.

Dere am one thing Massa Hawkins does to me what I can't shunt from my mind. I knows he don't do it for mean-ness, but I allus holds it 'gainst him. What he done am force me to live with dat nigger, Rufus, 'gainst my wants.

After I been at he place 'bout a year, de massa come to me and say, "You gwine live with Rufus in dat cabin over yonder. Go fix it for livin'." I's 'bout six-teen year old and has no larnin', and I's jus' igno'mus chile. I's thought dat him mean for me to tend de cabin for Rufus and some other niggers. Well, dat am start de pestigation for me.

I's took charge of de cabin after work am done and fixes supper. Now, I don't like dat Rufus, 'cause he a bully. He am big and 'cause he so, he think everybody do what him say. We'uns has supper, den I goes here and dere talkin', till I's ready for sleep and den I gits in de bunk. After I's in, dat nigger come and crawl in de bunk with me 'fore I knows it. I says, "What you mean, you fool nigger?" He say for me to hush de mouth. "Dis am my bunk, too," he say.

"You's teched in de head. Git out," I's told him, and I puts de feet 'gainst him and give him a shove and out he go on de floor 'fore he knows what I's doin'. Dat nigger jump up and he mad. He look like de wild bear. He starts for de bunk and I jumps quick for de poker. It am 'bout three feet long and when he comes at me I let him have it over de head. Did dat nigger stop in he tracks? I's say he did. He looks at me steady for a minute and you's could tell he thinkin' hard. Den he go and set on de bench and say, "Jus' wait. You thinks it am smart, but you's am foolish in de head. Dey's gwine larn you somethin'."

"Hush yous big mouth and stay 'way from dis nigger, dat all I wants," I say, and jus' sets and hold dat poker in de hand. He jus' sets, lookin' like de bull. Dere we'uns sets and sets for 'bout an hour and den he go out and I bars de door.

De nex' day I goes to de missy and tells her what Rufus wants and missy say dat am de massa's wishes. She say, "Yous am de portly gal and Rufus am de portly man. De massa wants you-uns for to bring forth portly chillen."

I's thinkin' 'bout what de missy say, but say to myse'f, "I's not gwine live with dat Rufus." Dat night when him come in de cabin, I grabs de poker and sits on de bench and says, "Git 'way from me, nigger, 'fore I busts yous brains out and stomp on dem." He say nothin' and git out.

De nex' day de massa call me and tell me, "Woman, I's pay big money for you and I's done dat for de cause I wants you to raise me chillens. I's put yous to live with Rufus for dat purpose. Now, if you doesn't want whippin' at de stake, yous do what I wants."

I thinks 'bout massa buyin' me offen de block and savin' me from bein' sep'-rated from my folks and 'bout bein' whipped at de stake. Dere it am. What am I's to do? So I 'cides to do as de massa wish and so I yields.

When we'uns am given freedom, Massa Hawkins tells us we can stay and work for wages or share crop de land. Some stays and some goes. My folks and me stays. We works de land on shares for three years, den moved to other land near by. I stay with my folks till they dies.

If my mem'radum am correct, it am 'bout thirty year since I come to Fort Worth. Here I cooks for white folks till I goes blind 'bout ten year ago.

I never marries, 'cause one 'sperience am 'nough for dis nigger. After what I does for de massa, I's never wants no truck with any man. De Lawd forgive dis cullud woman, but he have to 'scuse me and look for some others for to 'plenish de earth.

DEBORAH GRAY WHITE
The Nature of Female Slavery

There was much in the slave experience that men and women shared. Denied any legal ability to control the conditions of their lives, both men and women labored according to their masters' demands. Both women and men were vulnerable to brutal punishment and to the separation of families; both men and women had no choice but to accept marginal food and clothing. They were part of the productive system of the master's economy (usually, but not always, an agricultural one).

But women also did reproductive work. By this we mean not only the actual bearing and nurturing of children but the domestic work within slave quarters

Excerpted from "The Nature of Female Slavery," chap. 2 of *Ar'n't I a Woman? Female Slaves in the Plantation South* by Deborah Gray White (New York: W. W. Norton, 1985). Copyright © 1985 by Deborah Gray White. Reprinted by permission of the author and the publisher. Notes have been renumbered.

that fed husbands, fathers, and children and gave them the strength to persevere at the productive work of the plantation. As childbearing women they were physically vulnerable in ways that men were not; indeed as the work of Michael P. Johnson (to which Deborah White refers) has shown, slaves suffered a heavy proportion of deaths due to Sudden Infant Death Syndrome because of the malnutrition and overwork of mothers. In the lives of slave women, economics and biology intersected in complex and sorrowful ways.

Considering both physical and psychological factors, in what ways was the experience of enslaved women different from that of enslaved men?

The images of African-American women that grew out of the slavery era reflect the fact that black males and females did not experience slavery the same way. For both sexes the broad outline of racial oppression was similar, as was the general way in which the race resisted and survived. However, within the institution of racial slavery there were two systems, one for women, the other for men. This was due, in part, to the different expectations that slave owners had of male and female slaves. Different expectations gave rise to different responsibilities, and these responsibilities often defined the life chances of the male or female slave. . . .

Male and female slavery was different from the very beginning. . . . women did not generally travel the middle passage in the holds of slave ships but took the dreaded journey on the quarter deck. According to the 1789 Report of the Committee of the Privy Council the female passage was further distinguished from that of males in that women and girls were not shackled. The slave trader William Snelgrave mentioned the same policy: "We couple the sturdy Men together with Irons; but we suffer the Women and children to go freely about."[2]

This policy had at least two significant consequences for black women. First, they were more easily accessible to the criminal whims and sexual desires of seamen, and few attempts were made to keep the crew members of slave ships from molesting African women. As one slaver reported, officers were permitted to indulge their passions at pleasure and were "sometimes guilty of such brutal excesses as disgrace human nature."[3]

Conversely, African women were occasionally able to incite and/or assist slave insurrections that occurred at sea. For instance, in 1721 the crew on board the *Robert* was stunned when they were attacked by a woman and two men intent on gaining their freedom. Before they were subdued by the captain and other crew members, the slaves, including the woman, had killed several sailors and wounded many others. In his investigation into the mutiny, Captain Harding reflected on the near success of the slaves and found that they had been assisted by the woman "who being more at large, was to watch the proper Opportunity." The woman had served as a lookout and alerted the leader as to the number of sailors on deck. She had also stolen all the weapons used in the mutiny. For her exceptional participation she paid dearly: "The Woman he hoisted up by the Thumbs, whipp'd, and slashed her with Knives before the other Slaves till she died."[4]

In another incident, in 1785, the captain of a Bristol slaver was attacked by a group of women who tried to throw him overboard. When he was rescued by his

Slavery is terrible for men: but it is far more terrible for women. Superadded to the burden common to all, *they* have wrongs, and sufferings, and mortifications peculiarly their own.[1]

crew the women threw themselves down the hatchway. Some died from the injuries incurred in their desperate plunge. Others starved themselves to death. Nine years earlier a similar incident had occurred aboard the Rhode Island vessel the *Thames*. As reported by Dr. Bell, the physician on board, two women aided thirty-two men and two boys in their attempt at mutiny. In a letter to his employer, John Fletcher of London, Bell indicated that the women played a limited role only because the revolt had been so spontaneous that the men did not have time to consult and plan with the women. "Had the women assisted them, in all probability your property here at this time would have been small."[5]

It would seem that a primary reason for allowing women to go without irons was the natural assumption that women could be overpowered. However, since seventeenth- and eighteenth-century merchants and captains were convinced that "prime male slaves generally sell best in any market," slavers crammed the holds full of men and brought women almost as an afterthought. . . .

Therefore, for most of the seventeenth century and for at least the first third of the eighteenth, the system of slavery relied mostly upon black males. This was the case in both the Chesapeake and Carolina regions. For the period from 1658 to 1730 black men in colonial Maryland outnumbered women by roughly one and one half to one. Indeed, the entire Chesapeake area had many more slave men than women. In Surry County, Virginia, the ratio was about 145 men to 100 women in the 1670s and 1680s, and rose to over two to one in the 1690s and 1700s. In South Carolina, too, men outnumbered women. In 1720 in St. George's Parish the sex ratio was 129 to 100. A sample of slaves taken from inventories in 1730 and 1731 revealed that on sizable plantations throughout the colony slave men outnumbered slave women 180 to 100.[6]

The uneven sex ratio clearly made colonial slavery different for black men and women; it was much harder for a man to find a wife than for a woman to find a husband. Until about 1730 a significant number of men could expect to die without ever having had a spouse, and because plantations were small it was likely that many of those with wives had had to seek them in other plantations and therefore did not live with them. On colonial plantations both married and unmarried men lived together in small groups. In short, the emphasis that white colonialists put on muscle and brawn in the development of their plantation systems made early colonial slavery very lonely and desolate for men.

The situation was different for the bonded woman. Few went without husbands and even though plantations were small the preponderance of men made it likely that a woman would be able to live with her spouse. Nevertheless, many women had husbands on plantations other than their own, and these women lived with their children and raised them without the daily company of their husbands.[7]

These sex-segregated living arrangements did have some imperfect analogs in the African experience. Like their American counterparts, seventeenth- and eighteenth-century West African women usually did not raise small children with the help of their husbands, but raised them alone or with the assistance of other women. While West African men lived with their spouses in the same compound, and couples were free to come together at will, they did not share the same hut or area of the compound. But in Africa segregated living arrangements flowed from the corporate nature of the family and from a belief in the inherent differences of the sexes. The Africans' definition of family extended far beyond parents and children, or the nuclear family, to aunts, uncles, and grandparents. Since a husband and wife did not alone compose a family there was no reason for them to reside alone together. A woman's duty was to bear and raise small children, a duty that was hers alone. In colonial North America the African woman was separated from the cultural foundations and environment that had lent meaning to sex-segregated living and independent child rearing in Africa, but the demographics of slave settlement caused such living and rearing patterns to persist in a not too dissimilar form.

Slavers separated the black woman from most of what had lent meaning to her life. In Africa, her primary role had been motherhood, yet in the early years of plantation settlement she figured in some plantation building as a means of keeping male slaves content. Between 1763 and 1783 Britain attempted to establish a plantation colony in East Florida modeled after that of South Carolina. The slaves involved in this endeavor were mostly men. Correspondence among the governor, his overseer, and those assisting in the undertaking reveals a concern that women be purchased and transported forthwith lest the men become dissatisfied and run away. Thus, the Earl of Egmont wrote that the slaves could not be happy and content without each having a wife. This, he wrote, "will greatly tend to keep them at home and to make them Regular."[8]

The use of black female labor in the fields tended to make farming profitable for seventeenth-century Virginia planters. Although some Virginia white women did field work, this was generally assumed to be a temporary state of affairs and therefore no taxes were levied on their labor. No such assumption was made about the field labor of black women. In fact, in 1629, in colonial Virginia, a tax was levied on any person who worked in the ground, and subsequent laws defined those subject to taxation as black and white male servants and "negro women at age of sixteen years." Because the cost of a female slave was less than that of a male slave, female slave labor was cheaper than male slave labor, particularly when planters applied to black women the same tax-exempt status that applied to white female servants. Naturally, Virginia planters did just that, necessitating another series of laws, passed between 1662 and 1672, reiterating that tithes were to be paid on all field workers including black women.[9]

Surprisingly, slaveholders were slow to appreciate the economic value of the slave woman's procreative ability, but by the middle of the eighteenth century most slave owners, especially those with twenty or more slaves, had come to realize the potential benefits. Thomas Nairne, an eighteenth-century South Carolina planter, expected bondwomen to do the same work as his male slaves. They would, he thought, clear, plant and hoe three acres of land in six months. Besides doing field work he expected them to have children, and thus, by natural means increase the slave population. In 1732, Nairne estimated that the yearly advantage from this increase would be 540 British pounds.[10]

Although many planters made similar calculations, they did not move to increase the number of female slaves through importation. In the years prior to the American Revolution, the female slave population grew more as a result of natural increase than by importation. It was not until sometime between 1730 and 1750 that the sex ratio evened out. The first African-American women began childbearing earlier than their African mothers, and thus had more children, including more females, than their mothers. The second generation also had more children than the first, and on, and on until the ratio was even.[11]

Although a one to one sex ratio was achieved slowly, the consequences were astounding. First, the presence of an even slave sex ratio made American slavery unique in the Western Hemisphere. Everywhere else that slavery reared its ugly head, black men composed the overwhelming majority of the labor force. A related consequence was the creation by North American slaves of monogamous families. In Latin America and the Caribbean black men lived in barracklike environments and had far fewer opportunities to establish long-lasting emotional relationships with black women.[12] Taken together, these two facts suggest that North American male slaves had a more balanced life than their Caribbean or South American counterparts. However, the Earl of Egmont's request for wives to make men more "regular" suggests that powerless North American male slaves were more easily manipulated, because their spouses and children could be held hostage and compelled to answer for their transgressions. Black women, unfortunately, proved to be mirrors for black men. Each time the former was abused, the latter's own helplessness was reflected.[13]

For black women the consequences of the even sex ratio were also severe. Once slaveholders realized that the reproductive function of the female slave could yield a profit, the manipulation of procreative sexual relations became an integral part of the sexual exploitation of female slaves. Few of the calculations made by masters and overseers failed to take a slave woman's childbearing capacity into account. This was particularly true after Congress outlawed the overseas slave trade in 1807. The slave woman's "marital" status, her work load, her diet all became investment concerns of slaveholders, who could maximize their profits if their slave women had many children.

It was little consolation for slave women; in fact, they may not have even realized that when slaveholders put a premium on female slave childbearing, slaveholders unwittingly supplied another thread of continuity between Africa and North America. As noted, in the seventeenth and eighteenth centuries many first-generation African slave women raised their children without a lot of male assistance, much as they had done in Africa. In all likelihood this helped preserve that part of African culture that put emphasis on motherhood, and the African mother probably passed it on to her daughters. When mid-eighteenth-century slaveholders made female slave childbearing their desired goal and acted on that goal, they reinforced a cultural attitude which for African-American women now had roots in both Africa and North America. The nature and conditions of black motherhood in Africa and the North American South obviously differed because the motivations of Africans, African-Americans, and slaveholders were different. But for the purpose of our current discussion it is important to note the continuity. . . .

In the one hundred years after 1750 the American black population, 90 percent of which was enslaved, was notable for, among other things, its fertility. In the pre–Civil War period black women were very prolific. According to demographers the crude birthrate exceeded fifty per one thousand, meaning that each year more than one fifth of the black women in the 15–44 age cohort bore a child.[14] This statistic indicates a major functional difference between male and female bondage. Male slavery centered mostly around the work that black men did for whites. Female slavery had much to do with work, but much of it was concerned with bearing, nourishing, and rearing children whom slaveholders needed for the continual replenishment of their labor force. This does not mean that work and childbearing were always kept in perfect balance. The extent to which the slaveowner consciously emphasized one or the other ultimately depended on his needs. In antebellum America, these were often determined by the region of the country in which he was settled. The lower black fertility rates in the lower and newer regions of the south (Alabama, Mississippi, Louisiana, and Texas) may be an indication that female labor in the fields superseded childbearing in importance. In both the upper and lower South, however, slave owners attended to the proverbial bottom line by striving to maximize profits. Few ignored the important role that natural increase played in the realization of that goal.

Meanwhile, the responsibilities of childbearing and child care seriously circumscribed the female slave's life. The limits were reflected in patterns of female resistance. Studies of fugitive slaves reveal that their ranks were not swelled with women. Seventy-seven percent of the runaways advertised in colonial South Carolina during the 1730s were men. This pattern persisted throughout the century. South Carolina was by no means unique. The 1,500 newspaper advertisements published in Williamsburg, Richmond, and Fredricksburg, Virginia, from 1736 to 1801 evince much the same pattern. Of the runaways whose sex could be discerned 1,138 were men, while only 142 were women. The same pattern existed in antebellum Huntsville, Alabama, where, between 1820 and 1860, of the 562 fugitives advertised, 473 were listed as male and only 87 as female. In North Carolina from 1850 to 1860, only 19 percent of the runaway ads described women. In 1850, 31.7 percent of the runaways advertised for in New Orleans newspapers were women.[15]

Some of the reasons why women were underrepresented in the fugitive population had to do with childbearing. Most runaways were between sixteen and thirty-five years old.[16] A woman of this age was either pregnant, nursing an infant, or had at least one small child to care for. While all that men between sixteen and thirty-five could count on was hard work and severe punishment if they angered the master or overseer, it was during these years that many slave women got their best care. Slave owners were less likely to insist on a full day's heavy workload when the laborer involved was a pregnant woman.

Also important in understanding why females ran away less frequently than men is the fact that women tended to be more concerned with the welfare of their children, and this limited their mobility. Fugitive men loved their offspring, but unlike the runaway male, the slave woman who left her children behind could not be certain that they would be given the best possible care. A father could not provide for a suckling infant because "in dem days no bottle was given to no baby under a year old." Moreover, since women and small children were often sold as a group, a father was more likely to be sold away from his children. Sometimes the children of runaway mothers were lucky enough to have an aunt or grandmother on the same or nearby plantation, and sometimes a father or uncle cared for the child. But, for those fugitive women who left children in slavery, the physical relief which freedom brought was limited compensation for the anguish they suffered. Of the same one hundred fifty-one fugitive women advertised for in the 1850 New Orleans newspapers, none was listed as having run away without her children.[17]

This, of course, was no secret to slaveholders and probably accounts for the casual attitude many masters and overseers had about female runaways. For years the Flint family's hold upon Linda Brent's children kept her from fleeing. In her narrative Brent explained: "I was certain my children were to be put in their power, in order to give them a stronger hold on me." Similarly, in 1838 a slave named Clarissa was sent to Philadelphia even though there was some concern about her running away once she reached free territory. Mrs. Trigg, her mistress, had few qualms because Clarissa's husband and children remained in Kentucky.[18]

Women could probably have escaped more often if they could have done so with their husbands and offspring, but children, in particular, made the journey more difficult than it already was and increased the chances of capture. For instance, although Josiah Henson successfully reached Cincinnati with his wife and children he had to carry his two stout toddlers most of the way and listen to their cries of hunger and exhaustion at night. Henry Bibb also tried to escape with his family but was unsuccessful. With his wife, Malinda, and small child, he started on his journey north, but a pack of bloodthirsty canines and patrollers put a stop to his quest for freedom. For Bibb, the difficulties of escaping with a wife and child proved insurmountable, and although he regretted his capture he was actually relieved. Some time later he escaped, but without Malinda or his child.[19] . . .

If women in the company of men encountered insurmountable difficulties, imagine the problems encountered by women and children escaping alone. For conductors and directors of the Underground Railroad, fugitive women with children were a tremendous source of anxiety. William Still, the chairman of the Vigilance Committee of the Philadelphia Underground Railroad, was always nervous about transporting women with children since they stood a greater chance of being caught. "Females," he wrote, "undertook three times the risk of failure that males are liable to." William Penn, who worked with the Underground Railroad, also expressed apprehension. Speaking of two women, both of whom had two children, he noted: "none of these can walk so far or so fast as scores of *men* that are constantly leaving.[20] . . .

The few women who ran away did so for a variety of reasons. Some escaped with men and many left for the same reasons as men—cruel treatment or the fear of it, fear of sale or sale of a loved one, or just the desire to be free. Not surprisingly, for many women it was the children, or more properly, the fear of losing them, that provided the incentive to flee. The desperation of some slave mothers was captured in Harriet Beecher Stowe's

fictionalized account of the escape to freedom by Eliza Harris and her son across the ice floes of the Ohio River. Many took the heart-rending tale of Eliza's flight as evidence of Stowe's vivid imagination, but actually Stowe described in fiction what was a real life episode for a few women. One such woman was a Kentucky slave who feared that her two little girls were to be sold away from her. Surviving only on fruits and green corn she managed to cross the river. The odds were formidable even when there was no river to cross. For instance, there was the Maryland slave named Maria who with the help of the Underground Railroad escaped in 1859 with all *seven* of her children.[21]

Many female fugitives were much less fortunate than Maria and had to leave some of their children behind. . . .

. . . A Maryland slave woman named Vina was forced to choose which of her children would be free and which would remain enslaved. She fled to New Jersey to meet her husband with her two daughters after having consigned her two small sons "into the hands of God." The journey still proved to be too much for her; she left one of them on a lonely road to be retrieved by her husband. The story of Mary Montgomery is especially heartbreaking. Although sickly, Mary had a nursing infant at her breast. According to Christopher Nichols, a successful fugitive, Mary had been given conflicting work orders by the overseer and master. Unable to satisfy both she "took to the woods" and disappeared. "It was said that she got to the North, but nobody knew." Mary Montgomery did what few other bondwomen did; she left her suckling infant behind to die for lack of nourishment.[22]

Such desperate decisions inevitably induced emotional trauma and psychological torment. At age twenty-seven, when she fled to Pennsylvania to escape the sexual overtures of her master, Linda Brent made a decision similar to Mary Montgomery's. She knew her grandmother would keep a watchful eye on her son and daughter. However, she feared her mistress's vengeance would put them in danger of severe punishment, even sale. The advice she sought and was given served only to confuse her and increase her anxiety. From her friend and accomplice, Betty, she received encouragement to escape: "Lors, chile! What's you crying 'bout? Dem young uns vil kill you dead. Don't be so chick'n hearted! If you does, you vil nebber git thro' dis world." But, her grandmother, who, unlike childless Betty, had helped raise three generations of black children, admonished: "Stand by your own children, and suffer with them till death. Nobody respects a mother who forsakes her children; and if you leave them, you will never have a happy moment."[23]

Truancy seems to have been the way many slave women reconciled their desire to flee and their need to stay. Studies of female runaways demonstrate that females made the most likely truants because they were more concerned about breaking family ties. Benjamin Johnson of Georgia remembered that "sometimes de women wouldn't take it an' would run away an' hide in de woods. Sometimes dey would come back after a short stay an' den again dey would have to put de hounds on dere trail to bring dem back home." Short-term absences of this sort were not mere flights of fancy. Truants were often no less angry, resentful, and frightened than their fugitive brethren who chose to flee to the North. If anything they were more frightened of the unknown to the North than of the certainties they left behind. However, this frightful ambivalence did not keep them from shouldering substantial risk. Thus we find cases such as that of a St. Simon's woman who, after being severely beaten by her master, found the rattlesnakes of the South Carolina rice swamps more comforting than her own cabin. Sickness induced by hunger finally forced her back to her plantation.[24] . . .

Such behavior was not unique to the nineteenth century. As early as 1710 Virginian William Byrd recorded a case of truancy that had a tragic ending. One of his slave women ran away on June 25, 1710, and was found on June 28, only to disappear again two days later. She was recovered again on July 8, but ran away again on the fifteenth. Three weeks later she turned up again, but in November she disappeared and was soon found dead.[25]

Motherhood structured the slave woman's behavior, but so too did the female slave work experience. The division of labor on most plantations conferred greater mobility on male than on female slaves. Few of the chores performed by bondwomen took them off the plantation. Usually masters chose their male slaves to assist in the transportation of crops to market, and the transport of supplies and other materials to the plantation. More male than female slaves were artisans and craftsmen, and this made it more difficult to hire a female slave than a male slave. Fewer bondwomen therefore had a chance to vary their work experience. As a consequence, more men than women were able to test their survival skills under different circumstances.

Another factor affecting slave mobility was the "abroad marriage," a marriage between slaves who resided at different locations. When "abroad" spouses visited each other, usually once a week, it was most often the husband who traveled to the wife. All in all, it was female bondage, more than male bondage, that meant being tied to the immediate environment of the plantation or farm. This was a liability when it came to running away. The would-be female fugitive, including the domestic who conceivably had more polished verbal and language skills than the field slave, had to consider her unfamiliarity with the surrounding countryside before fleeing. She also had to consider how conspicuous a lone black woman or group of black women would be in a countryside infrequently traveled by such humanity.

Some female fugitives overcame this last impediment by disguising themselves as males.[26] However, the small number of female runaways indicates that more bondwomen than bondmen just "stayed put."

This does not mean that they did not resist enslavement or sexual exploitation. As historians have been quick to point out, the dearth of large-scale slave revolts suggests that in the United States slave resistance often manifested itself in intransigent behavior. If resistance in the United States was seldom politically oriented, consciously collective, or violently revolutionary, it was generally individualistic and aimed at maintaining what the slaves, master, and overseer had, in the course of their relationships, perceived as an acceptable level of work, shelter, food, punishment, and free time. Slaves may have thought about overthrowing the system of slavery but the odds against them were so overwhelming that the best most could hope for was survival with a modicum of dignity. Slave resistance was aimed at maintaining what seemed to all concerned to be the status quo.

Bondwomen, like bondmen, were adept in inventing schemes and excuses to get their own way. After her mistress died, Alcey, the cook on the Burleigh plantation in Virginia, decided she no longer wanted to work in the kitchen. When her request to be transferred to the field was ignored, she found another way to make her desire known. "She systematically disobeyed orders and stole or destroyed the greater part of the provisions given to her for the table." When that failed "she resolved to show more plainly that she was tired of the kitchen": "Instead of getting chickens for dinner from the coop, as usual, she unearthed from some corner an old hen that had been sitting for six weeks and served her up as a fricassee!" Alcey achieved her objective and was sent to the field the following day without even so much as a reprimand.[27] . . .

Some bondwomen were more direct in their resistance. Some murdered their masters, some were arsonists, and still others refused to be whipped. Overseers and masters learned which black women and men they could whip, and which would not be whipped. Sometimes they found out the hard way. Equipped with a whip and two healthy dogs, an Alabama overseer tied a woman named Crecie to a stump with intentions of beating her. To his pain and embarrassment she jerked the stump out of the ground, grabbed the whip, and sent the overseer running. Women fought back despite severe consequences. An Arkansas overseer decided to make an example of a slave woman named Lucy "to show the slaves that he was impartial." Lucy, however, was not to be made an example of. According to her son, "she jumped on him and like to tore him up." Word got around that Lucy would not be beaten. She was sold, but she was never again whipped.[28]

Slave women also sometimes violently resisted sexual exploitation. Since Southern laws did not recognize the rape of a black woman as a crime, often the only recourse slave women had was to fight off their assailants. When Jermain Loguen's mother was attacked she picked up a stick and dealt her would-be rapist a blow that sent him staggering. She stood her ground even as he rebounded with a knife, and finally she knocked him out cold.[29] . . .

Bondwomen used dissembling tactics and force much as bondmen did. It was probably safe to assume that women chose violent resistance, particularly that which involved fisticuffs, less often than did men. However, it should also be remembered that such resistance was not really a viable option for bondmen, either. A bullet through the head, a jail cell, a merciless whipping, and/or sale was the likely fate of any slave, male or female, who demonstrated aggressive behavior, even in self-defense.

A less overt form of resistance involved

the use of poison and this suited women because they officiated as cooks and nurses on the plantation. As early as 1755 a Charleston slave woman was burned at the stake for poisoning her master, and in 1769 a special issue of the *South Carolina Gazette* carried the story of a slave woman who had poisoned her master's infant child. No one will ever know how many slave owners and members of their families were poisoned. The slave's objective was not to get caught because punishment was sure and swift. A case in point was recorded by Mary Chesnut in her diary. A friend of hers told her the story of a man named Dr. Keitt who was chronically ill. Dr. Keitt's friend suggested to him that his slaves were perhaps trying to kill him: Dr. Keitt promised to be prudent and to come the next day. As soon as his friend left, a Negro woman brought him a cup of tea. As he stirred it, a white powder became evident, settled in the bottom of the cup. In a moment he believed what his friend had suspected. He dashed the tea in her face. "You ungrateful beast, I believe you are trying to poison me." Next morning, he was found with his throat cut from ear to ear. It was found that the woman, in league with two male slaves, was putting a poison in Dr. Keitt's coffee every morning and when discovered they murdered him outright. Interestingly enough, and consistent with female runaway statistics, the men successfully escaped but the woman was caught and hanged.[30]

Perhaps the most important difference between male and female slave resistance was the greater propensity of women to feign illness in order to gain a respite from their work or to change the nature of their work altogether. This strategy was feasible precisely because childbearing was the primary expectation that slave owners had of slave women. The perpetuation of the institution of slavery, as nineteenth-century Southerners knew it, rested on the slave woman's reproductive capacity.

In an age when women's diseases were still shrouded in mystery, getting the maximum amount of work from women of childbearing age while remaining confident that no damage was done to their reproductive organs was a guessing game that few white slave owners wanted to play or could afford to lose. A Virginia planter summed up the "problem" when he complained of the "liability of women, especially to disorders and irregularities which cannot be detected by exterior symptoms, but which may be easily aggravated into serious complaints." He further explained that women were rendered "nearly valueless" for work because of the ease with which they could impose upon their owners. His frustration was obvious as he told Frederick Olmsted that "they don't come to the field and you go to the quarters and ask the old nurse what's the matter and she says, 'Oh, she's not . . . fit to work sir'; and . . . you have to take her word for it that something or other is the matter with her, and you dare not set her to work; and so she will lay up till she feels like taking the air again, and plays the lady at your expense."[31] Although few slave women were given as much latitude as this planter suggested, they did sometimes "play the lady" and get away with it.

By the time Olmsted heard this complaint slave women had been engaging in such behavior for some time. On Landon Carter's eighteenth-century Virginia plantation, this form of resistance was raised to an art. Although Carter was certain that Mary faked her fits, her violent and uncontrollable howls always got the better of him, and she spent a good deal of time away from the fields. Another woman, named Sarah, laid up for *eleven* months before delivering her infant. She, no doubt, "played the lady" at Carter's expense, and even tried to do it again during her next pregnancy. To her chagrin she met a wiser Landon Carter who was determined not to let her get away with it. Sarah was determined, too, and proved to be as good at truancy as she was at feigning illness. Although "big with child" she took to the woods and stayed over a week.[32] . . .

The case of Maria, one of President James Polk's slaves, is particularly revealing. Since Polk spent a good deal of time away from his plantations, they were run by overseers with the aid of a few of his close friends. With the exception of Eophraim Beanland, all of Polk's overseers had trouble with Maria, who was always complaining of some malady. Maria began pleading illness in May 1839, significantly, after the strict Beanland was replaced by the more indulgent George Bratton. At that time, Bratton wrote to Polk that "she had bin in bad helth since the first of march and is likely not to be able to do any sirvice." Bratton died that year and was replaced by John Garner who also had difficulty making Maria work. In June 1840, Garner informed Polk that Maria "has spels onste a month very bad." A week later he explained in greater detail that "she is in a very bad condishon every thre or fore weks, so very bad onst this spring she was thone into fits of spasms." Maria's health continued to keep her from the fields and finally she was reassigned to the house where she was taught to weave. She was particularly good at weaving and Garner soon reported that "Marier aperes to enjoy as good helth at present as any person." In fact, Maria had such a miraculous recovery, and became so good at weaving that she informed Polk that she had increased her worth by at least thirty dollars.[33]

Maria was "fortunate" because many slave masters refused to accept even obvious illness as an excuse to lay off work. James Mercer, for instance, had a strict formula for judging illness: "No woman was allowed to 'lay up' unless her illness was accompanied by a fever." Some masters insisted on giving the "patient" a thorough examination before excusing her from work. After sending his slave, Caroline, to the fields in spite of her protestations, a Mississippi Valley planter claimed: "We have to be sharp with them; if we were not, every negro on the estate would be abed."[34]

The subject of feigning illness is as difficult for the historian as it was for the planter. Was Maria actually ill, or was she deceiving the overseers? The description of her complaint suggests a menstrual disorder but she could also have been quite an actress. Whatever we conclude we must not overlook the important point that Maria's behavior, feigned or otherwise, is what landed her the easier weaver's job. This case, and the many like it, suggest that while slaveowners had a vested interest in keeping pregnant women healthy, the relatively better care expectant mothers received was as much a result of the pressure slave women exerted as of self-serving benevolence extended by slave owners and overseers. If slave women frequently "played the lady," as the Virginia planter argued, it was only after they risked a lot to be treated humanely.

Data on slave illness on Southern plantations reveal that plantations were havens for disease, and that slaves were indeed plagued by sickness. Slaves suffered and often died from pneumonia, diarrhea, cholera, and smallpox. The slave diet was high in calories but suffered from dangerously low levels of protein and other nutrients. Lean meats, poultry, eggs, milk, and grain products other than corn—foods needed to help the human immune system produce antibodies to fight off infections—were only sporadically seen on most slave's plates. In addition, most slaves did not get nearly enough fruits and vegetables. Blindness, sore eyes, skin irritations, rickets, toothaches, pellagra, beriberi, and scurvy were among the many afflictions that resulted from vitamin deficiencies caused by the monotonous daily servings of rice, fat-back, corn meal, and salt pork.[35]

Slave women suffered from these illnesses as well as from those associated with the menstrual cycle and childbirth. According to Todd Savitt, Virginia bondwomen probably lost more time from work for menstrual pain, discomfort, and disorders than for any other cause. Among the menstrual maladies were amenorrhea (lack of menstrual flow), abnormal bleeding between cycles (sometimes caused by benign and malignant tumors), and abnormal discharges (resulting from such conditions as gonorrhea, tumors, and prolapsed uterus). Although the 1850 mortality statistics for Virginia indicate that slave women were slightly less likely than white women to die from complications of pregnancy, bondwomen suffered during childbirth. Convulsions, retention of placenta, ectopic pregnancy, breech presentation, premature labor, and uterine rigidity were among the difficulties they faced. Birthing was complicated further by the unsanitary practices of midwives and physicians who delivered a series of children in the course of a day without washing their hands, thereby triggering outbreaks of puerperal (child bed) fever. These infections of the reproductive organs were often fatal.[36]

Still it is difficult to ascertain whether bondwomen who claimed to be ill were actually sick or whether they were practicing a kind of passive resistance. They certainly had more leverage in the realm of feigning illness than men, but they also perhaps had more reason than men to be ill. This does not mean that women were more disadvantaged than black men in this regard. It does suggest, however, that their health experiences were radically different. Although women may have had a less healthy day-to-day existence they could generally expect to outlive their male counterparts, probably because men were engaged usually in heavier and more dangerous work. On the average, antebellum black women out-lived their men by two years. This average varied depending on the state. In Louisiana in 1850, for instance, at birth a black male could expect

to live about twenty-nine years, while a black female had a life expectancy of about thirty-four years. At age thirty the life expectancy of a Louisiana black male was approximately another twenty-seven years. The thirty-year-old black woman could expect to live for another thirty-one years.[37]

If it is hard to differentiate real sickness from passive resistance it is almost impossible to determine whether slave women practiced birth control and abortion. These matters were virtually exclusive to the female world of the quarters, and when they arose they were attended to in secret and were intended to remain secret. Some Southern whites were certain that slave women knew how to avoid pregnancy as well as how to deliberately abort a pregnancy. When Daph, a woman on the Ferry Hill plantation in Virginia, miscarried twins in 1838 the overseer reported that Daph took some sort of abortifact to bring about the miscarriage. Suspicions about slave abortions ran high enough to spur public comment. In an essay entitled "On the Susceptibility of the Caucasian and African Races to the Different Classes of Disease," Dr. E. M. Pendleton claimed that planters regularly complained of whole families of women who failed to have any children. A Tennessee physician, Dr. John H. Morgan said of slave women that "often they will attempt to bring all the aids into requisition that they can ascertain that will increase the parturient effort, either by medicine, violent exercise, or by external and internal manipulations." Morgan was relatively certain that black females declined the use of mechanical implements to effect miscarriage but he was convinced they used abortifacts. Among those he listed were the herbs of tansy and rue, the roots and seed of the cotton plant, pennyroyal, cedar berries, and camphor, either in gum or spirits.[38]

The suspicions of planters on this account were not without foundation. For example, an 1869 South Carolina court case revealed that a slave woman sold as "unsound" and barren in 1857 had three children *after* emancipation. In another instance, a bondwoman refused to have children because her master forced her to marry someone she did not like. After she was sold and found someone of her own choosing, she had ten children. Sarah Shaw of Missouri remembered that when her father was sold away, her master compelled her mother to take a new husband. Her mother complied but she was determined not to have any more children. "Mama said she would never marry a man and have children so she married my step-father Trattle Barber, because she knew he had a disease and could not be a father."[39]

The record on self-imposed sterility and self-induced miscarriages is ambiguous. Strenuous work might have been the culprit in many cases involving barrenness or abortion. For example, on the Ball rice plantations in South Carolina, from 1760 to 1865, the months of greatest hoeing and weeding activity—May, June, and July—produced the smallest number of conceptions resulting in a birth.[40] Several physicians, including Doctors Morgan and Pendleton, made the connection between the bonded woman's work regimen and sterility and miscarriages. Dr. Morgan thought that slave fertility would be higher if, among other things, female field hands were not so "exposed" during menstruation and pregnancy: "When by proper care and attention during these periods, in the way of moderate labor, good clothing etc., they are much more thrifty and fruitful."[41]

The jury will have to remain out on whether slave women were guilty of practicing birth control and abortion, but some reasons why they might have been guilty as accused should be considered. Certainly, they had reason not to want to bear and nurture children who could be sold from them at a slave master's whim. They had ample cause to want to deny whites the satisfaction of realizing a profit on the birth of their children. But they also had as much reason as any antebellum woman, white or free black, to shun pregnancy and childbirth. As long as obstetrics had not yet evolved into a science, childbirth was dangerous. We would also be remiss if we did not at least suppose that a few abortions were motivated by attempts to hide teenage pregnancy or marital infidelity. Black women were slaves but they were also human.

The entire subject of feigned illness, sterility, deliberate and nondeliberate miscarriages illustrates some of the ways in which female slavery was different from male slavery; at the same time it raises interesting points of comparison between antebellum black and white women. Although black women did considerably more heavy labor than white women, on a diet with less nutritional value, their fertility rates were usually similar to or higher than that of Southern white women. One explanation offered for the symmetry revolves around the natural immunity blacks have to malaria, or more specifically, the greater susceptibility of whites to this disease, which destroys male sperm by elevating male scrotal temperature. It has been argued that had not malaria been so devastating to whites, black fertility would not have compared so favorably, given the deprivation under which slave women functioned.[42] Historians have also observed that some white women of this period, particularly of the middle and upper classes, feigned illness or pretended to be very delicate in order to avoid sexual intercourse that could result in an unwanted pregnancy. There seems to be no evidence to confirm or deny that slave women did the same. It is truly ironic, though, that while slave women probably shared with white women a natural fear of childbirth, slave women had to feign illness to ease the burden of work in order to make bearing a child easier. Some female slaves even got pregnant in order to avoid backbreaking field labor. The plight of both groups of women was unenviable but on the average white women were much more successful in avoiding pregnancies than black women. The white birthrate declined throughout the nineteenth century and continued to do so well into the twentieth century. The black birthrate did not begin to show a significant decline until the very end of the nineteenth century.[43] Throughout the antebellum period especially, the incentives to have children were greater for black than for white women. Although they showed much concern, planters had little to worry about when it came to the rate of slave reproduction.

Did slave infanticide pose a serious threat? Probably not. There were some cases where mothers were accused of murdering their children, and a few women may have done so. In 1830 a North Carolina slave woman was convicted of murdering her own child. A year later a Missouri slave was accused of poisoning and smothering her infant, and in 1834, Elizabeth, one of James Polk's slaves, was said to have smothered her newborn. No one will ever know what drove these women to kill their infants, if they did. Some whites thought slave women lacked maternal feelings, yet a few women who killed their children claimed to have done so because of their intense concern for their offspring. Thus, an Alabama woman killed her child because her mistress continually abused it. In confessing her guilt, she claimed that her master was the father of the child, and that her mistress knew it and treated it so cruelly that she had to kill it to save it from further suffering. Another woman killed her newborn because she knew that the master had plans to sell the baby, the same way he had sold her three older children. Years later Lou Smith recalled the incident: "When her fourth baby was born and was about two months old, she just studied all the time about how she would have

to give it up, and one day she said, 'I just decided I'm not going to let Old Master sell this baby; he just ain't going to do it.' She got up and give it something out of a bottle, and pretty soon it was dead."[44]

These cases represent atypical behavior on the part of slave mothers. Runaway and truancy data suggest mothers cared dearly for their children, and recent historical and medical research suggests that many children who supposedly were suffocated by a mother were actually victims of what today is known as Sudden Infant Death Syndrome (SIDS) or "crib death." According to Michael P. Johnson the 1850 census showed that of the victims of suffocation 82 percent were slaves. The 1860 census showed a similar high percentage of slave deaths due to suffocation. Johnson estimates that between 1790 and 1860 smothering was reported to be responsible for the deaths of over sixty thousand slave infants. Most white Southerners attributed these deaths to the carelessness of slave mothers who rolled onto them while sleeping, deliberately murdered them, or otherwise provided insufficient care. Johnson and Savitt, however, argue that recent medical discoveries suggest that "crib death"—the sudden death of any infant or young child who does not have a history of illness and whose postmortem examination fails to demonstrate an identifiable cause of death—was probably responsible for the majority of such slave infant deaths. Statistics compiled by Johnson show that most "smothered" slave infants died in the winter months, and a significant number were between two and four months old. Modern day physicians have pinpointed the peak age period for "crib death" victims to be between two and four months, and have found that more infants succumb between October and March than in any other time period. In addition, a disproportionately high number of today's victims come from low socioeconomic groups, infants of women who are not likely to get good prenatal care.[45] Therefore, we can suppose that some of the infant deaths that planters attributed to infanticide and some that whites blamed on maternal carelessness were actually due to causes which even today baffle medical experts. We might also suppose that it was easier and cheaper for planters to malign slave women than to thoroughly investigate infant slave deaths and that, based on findings linking prenatal care and nutrition to SIDS, it was the planters who fed pregnant women too little and worked them too hard who were more responsible for "smothered infants" than the women who subsequently bore the guilt and blame.

Female slave bondage was not better or worse, or more or less severe, than male bondage, but it was different. From the very beginning of a woman's enslavement she had to cope with sexual abuse, abuse made legitimate by the conventional wisdom that black women were promiscuous Jezebels. Work assignments also structured female slave life so that women were more confined to the boundaries of the plantation than were men. The most important reason for the difference between male and female bondage, however, was the slave woman's childbearing and child care responsibilities. These affected the female slave's pattern of resistance and figured prominently in her general health.

NOTES

1. Linda Brent, *Incidents in the Life of a Slave Girl*, Lydia Maria Child, ed. (New York: Harcourt Brace Jovanovich, 1973 [1860]), p. 79.

2. Elizabeth Donnan, ed., *Documents Illustrative of the History of the Slave Trade to America*, 4 vols. (Washington, D.C.: Carnegie Institute of Washington, 1930), 2:595, 353.

3. Charles H. Nichols, *Many Thousand Gone, The Ex-Slaves' Account of Their Bondage and Their Freedom* (Bloomington: Indiana University Press, 1963), p. 9; George Francis Dow, *Slave Ships and Slaving* (Salem, Mass.: Marine Research Society, 1927), p. 145.

4. Donnan, ed., *Slave Trade*, 2:266.

5. Helen T. Catterall, ed., *Judicial Cases Concerning American Slavery and the Negro*, 5 vols. (Washington, D.C.: Carnegie Institute of Washington, 1936), 1:19; Donnan, ed., *Slave Trade*, 3:323.

6. Russell R. Menard, "The Maryland Slave Population, 1658 to 1730: A Demographic Profile of Blacks in Four Countries," *William and Mary Quarterly* (January 1975), 32:33; Allan Kulikoff, "The Beginnings of the Afro-American Family in Maryland," in *The American Family in Social-Historical Perspective*, Michael Gordon, ed., 2nd ed. (New York: St. Martin's, 1978), p. 446; Peter H. Wood, *Black Majority, Negroes in Colonial South Carolina from 1670 through the Stono Rebellion* (New York: Norton, 1974), p. 160. . . .

7. See Kulikoff, "The Beginnings of the Afro-American Family," pp. 446–448; Menard, "The Maryland Slave Population," p. 354. . . .

8. Daniel C. Littlefield, *Rice and Slaves, Ethnicity and the Slave Trade in Colonial South Carolina* (Baton Rouge: Louisiana State University Press, 1981), pp. 63–65.

9. William Waller Hening, ed., *The Statutes at Large, Being a Collection of all the Laws of Virginia* (Richmond: Samuel Pleasants, 1823), 1:144, 242, 292, 454; ibid., 2:170, 187, 296.

10. Thomas Nairne, *A Letter from South Carolina Giving an Account of the Soil, Air, Products, Trade, Government, Laws, Religion, People, Military Strength, etc. of that Province* (London: J. Clarke, 1732), pp. 50–60.

11. Edmund S. Morgan, *American Slavery, American Freedom, The Ordeal of Colonial Virginia* (New York: Norton, 1975), pp. 295–315; . . . Allan Kulikoff, "A 'Prolifick' People: Black Population Growth in the Chesapeake Colonies, 1700–1790," *Southern Studies* (Winter 1977), 16(4):398–414.

12. See the discussion presented in Carl N. Degler, *Neither Black Nor White, Slavery and Race Relations in Brazil and the United States* (New York: Macmillan, 1971), pp. 61–67. . . .

13. See Henry Bibb, *Narrative of the Life and Adventures of Henry Bibb, An American Slave*, in *Puttin' On Ole Massa*, Gilbert Osofsky, ed. (New York: Harper & Row, 1969), pp. 74, 80, 81 (hereafter cited as Bibb in Osofsky, ed., *Ole Massa*); William Wells

Brown, *A Fugitive Slave*, in Osofsky, ed., *Ole Massa*, pp. 180, 213. . . .

14. Reynolds Farley, *Growth of the Black Population, A Study of Demographic Trends* (Chicago: Markham, 1970), pp. 21, 34. . . .

15. Wood, *Black Majority*, p. 244; . . . Gerald W. Mullin, *Flight and Rebellion, Slave Resistance in Eighteenth-Century Virginia* (London: Oxford University Press, 1972), p. 40. James Sellers, *Slavery in Alabama* (University, Ala.: University of Alabama Press, 1950), p. 292; Eugene Genovese, *Roll, Jordan, Roll, The World The Slaves Made* (New York: Random House, 1974), p. 798; Judith Kelleher Schafer, "New Orleans Slavery in 1850 as Seen in Advertisements," *Journal of Southern History* (February 1981), 46: 43. . . .

16. Kenneth Stampp, *The Peculiar Institution, Slavery in the Ante-Bellum South* (New York: Random House, 1956), p. 110; Genovese, *Roll, Jordan, Roll*, p. 648. . . .

17. . . . See Kenneth F. Kipple and Virginia Himmelstieb King, *Another Dimension to the Black Diaspora. Diet, Disease, and Racism* (Cambridge: Cambridge University Press, 1981), p. 97; . . . Schafer, "New Orleans Slavery," p. 47.

18. Brent, *Incidents in the Life of a Slave Girl*, p. 97; Catterall, ed., *Judicial Cases*, 1: 411.

19. Josiah Henson, *Autobiography of the Reverend Josiah Henson*, in *Four Fugitive Slave Narratives* (Reading, Mass.: Addison Wesley, 1969), p. 60; Bibb, in Osofsky, ed., *Ole Massa*, pp. 126–128.

20. William Still, *The Underground Railroad, A Record of Facts, Authentic Narratives, Letters, etc.* (Philadelphia: Porter and Coates, 1872), pp. 50, 188.

21. Harriet Beecher Stowe, *Uncle Tom's Cabin* (New York: Washington Square Press, 1962 [1852]), p. 74; Levi Coffin, *Reminiscences of Levi Coffin* (Cincinnati: Robert Clarke, 1898), pp. 147–149, 114; Marion Gleason McDougall, *Fugitive Slaves* [1619–1865] (New York: Bergman, 1967 [1891]), p. 47; Still, *Underground Railroad*, pp. 68, 264. . . .

22. Still, *Underground Railroad*, p. 158; Benjamin Drew, *The Refugee: A North-Side View of Slavery*, in *Four Fugitive Slave Narratives*, p. 49.

23. Brent, *Slave Girl*, pp. 93, 104. . . .

24. Mullin, *Flight and Rebellion*, pp. 103–104, 187; Wood, *Black Majority*, p. 241; Catterall, ed., *Judicial Cases*, 5:220; . . . Frances Anne Kemble, *Journal of a Residence on a Georgian Plantation*, John A. Scott, ed. (New York: Knopf, 1961), pp. 215–216.

25. William Byrd, *The Secret Diary of William Byrd of Westover, 1709–1712*, Louis B. Wright and Marion Tinling, eds. (Richmond, Va.: Dietz, 1941), pp. 196, 197, 199, 202, 205, 206, 215, 257. . . .

26. . . . See Still, *Underground Railroad*, p. 182; Coffin, *Reminiscences*, p. 347; Brent, *Slave Girl*, p. 114. . . .

27. Susan Dabney Smedes, *Memorials of a Southern Planter*, Fletcher M. Greene, ed. (New York: Knopf, 1965), p. 180. . . .

28. Frederick Law Olmsted, *The Cotton Kingdom*, David Freeman Hawke, ed. (New York: Bobbs-Merrill, 1971), p. 153; Olmsted, *A Journey in the Seaboard Slave States* (New York: Dix and Edwards, 1856), p. 194; B. A. Botkin, ed., *Lay My Burden Down, A Folk History of Slavery* (Chicago: University of Chicago Press, 1945), pp. 174, 175. . . .

29. Rev. J. W. Loguen, *The Rev. J. W. Loguen as a Slave and as a Free Man* (Syracuse, N.Y.: by the author, 1859), pp. 20–21.

30. Joshua Coffin, ed., *An Account of Some of the Principal Slave Insurrections . . .* (New York: American Anti-Slavery Society, 1860), reprinted in *Slave Insurrections: Selected Documents* (Westport, Conn.: Negro Universities Press), p. 15; *South Carolina Gazette*, August 1, 1769; C. Vann Woodward, ed., *Mary Chesnut's Civil War* (New Haven: Yale University Press, 1981), pp. 218–219.

31. Olmsted, *Seaboard Slave States*, p. 190.

32. Landon Carter, *The Diary of Colonel Landon Carter of Sabine Hall, 1752–1778*, Jack P. Greene, ed., 2 vols. (Charlottesville: Virginia Historical Society, 1965), 2:604, 610, and 1:371–372.

33. John Spencer Bassett, ed., *The Southern Plantation Overseer as Revealed in His Letters* (Northampton, Mass.: Southworth, 1925), pp. 35, 59, 77, 119, 139, 142, 144, 150, 151, 156, 157.

34. See Mullin, *Flight and Rebellion*, p. 55; Frederick Law Olmsted, *A Journey through the Back Country, 1853–1854* (New York: Putnam's Sons, 1907), p. 79.

35. Leslie Howard Owens, *This Species of Property, Slave Life and Culture in the Old South* (Oxford: Oxford University Press, 1976), pp. 50–69. . . .

36. Todd L. Savitt, *Medicine and Slavery: The Diseases and Health Care of Blacks in Antebellum Virginia* (Urbana: University of Illinois Press, 1978), pp. 115, 119–20.

37. Farley, *Growth of the Black Population*, p. 33; The Seventh Census, *Report of the Superintendent of the Census* (Washington, D.C.: Robert Armstrong, 1853), p. 13. . . .

38. Fletcher M. Greene, ed., *Ferry Hill Plantation Journal*, in *The James Sprunt Studies in History and Political Science* (Chapel Hill: University of North Carolina Press, 1961), pp. 25–56; E. M. Pendleton, "On the Susceptibility of the Caucasian and African Races to the Different Classes of Diseases," *Southern Medical Reports* (1949 [1856]), 2:338; John H. Morgan, "An Essay on the Production of Abortion among Our Negro Population," *Nashville Journal of Medicine and Surgery* (August 1860), 19: 117–118. . . .

39. Catterall, ed., *Judicial Cases*, 2:475; Botkin, ed., *Lay My Burden Down*, pp. 130–131; George P. Rawick, ed., *The American Slave: A Composite Autobiography*, 19 vols. (Westport, Conn.: Greenwood Press, 1972), Mo., 10(7):135.

40. Cheryll Ann Cody, "Slave Demography and Family Formation. A Community Study of the Ball Family Plantation, 1720–1896" (Ph.D. dissertation, University of Minnesota, 1982), pp. 122–123.

41. Morgan, "Essay on the Production of Abortion," pp. 117, 122.

42. Kipple and King, *Diet, Disease, and Racism*, p. 65. . . .

43. Farley, *Growth of the Black Population*, p. 57; Linda Gordon, *Woman's Body, Woman's Right, A Social History of Birth Control in America* (New York: Penguin, 1976), p. 48.

44. Catterall, ed., *Judicial Cases*, 2:59, 5: 139; Bassett, ed., *Plantation Overseer*, p. 59; Olmsted, *Seaboard Slave States*, p. 601; Rawick, ed., *American Slave*, Ok., 6:302.

45. Michael P. Johnson, "Smothered Slave Infants: Were Slave Mothers at Fault?" *Journal of Southern History* (November 1981), 47(4):495–509; Savitt, *Medicine and Slavery*, pp. 122–127. . . .

JOHN MACK FARAGHER
The Midwestern Farming Family, 1850

The folklore of rural America suggests that farm people understood intuitively that female work was central to the domestic economy even if the full extent of women's labors were little appreciated. Male farmers spoke of the need to marry a "good strong woman," and folk songs expressed the same understanding. "There was an old man who lived in the woods," runs one song, who wagers that

> he could do more work in one day
> Than his wife could do in three.

She leaves him with a list of her tasks and goes off to do his plowing. When the farmer tries to do her work, he comes to grief; even milking presents unforeseen difficulties:

> But Tiny hitched, and Tiny switched,
> And Tiny she cocked her nose,

* Jean Ritchie, *The Swapping Song Book* (Oxford, 1952), pp. 54–55. © 1952 Jean Ritchie, Geordie Music Publishing Co. Suggested by Laura Becker, Clemson University.

Excerpted from "The Midwestern Farming Family, 1850," chap. 2 of *Women and Men on the Overland Trail* by John Mack Faragher (New Haven: Yale University Press, 1979). Copyright © 1979 by Yale University Press. Reprinted by permission of the author and the publisher. Notes have been renumbered, tables omitted, and cross-references adjusted.

And Tiny she gave the old man such a kick
That the blood ran down to his toes.

By the time the song ends the old man is swearing

by all of the stars in heaven
That his wife could do more work in one day
Than he could do in seven.*

As long as anyone could remember, farmers had ordered their lives by work patterns strictly defined by gender. Historians and anthropologists can now see that both sorts of tasks were central to the maintenance of the economic health of the family farm. As John Mack Faragher shows, what was missing was a convenient set of measures for female productivity; in the absence of these, women's work tended to be undervalued.

The dominant paradigm of farm life was the cycle: the recurrence of the days and seasons, the process of growth and reproduction.[1] Hand-power technology did not deceive men into thinking they could overcome nature; their goal was to harmonize man's needs with natural forces as best they could. The length of the working day, for example, was largely determined by the hours of sunlight. Candles and grease lamps were common but expensive, and the hearth's flickering light was too dim for more than a little work after dark.[2] So most work was largely confined to daylight: up and at work by dawn, nights for sleeping. And in keeping with this daily round, midwesterners told time by the movements of the sun, not the clock. There was a variety of time phrases so rich they nearly matched the clock in refinement; the hours before sunrise, for example, were distinguished thus: long before day, just before day, just comin' day, just about daylight, good light, before sunup, about sunup, and finally, sunup. Each period of the day was similarly divided.[3]

The seasons imposed the same kind of rule as the sun. The farm's work demands were primarily shaped by the seasons, each quarter calling upon husbandman and housewife to perform appointed tasks. The farming year opened in mid-March when thaws called the tenants outside. Land had to be cleared, drained, manured, and plowed, fields sown, gardens planted. Sheep, grown woolly, needed washing and shearing, geese plucking. In the hardwood stands farmers might spend a few days collecting and rendering maple sap, or searching out and hiving bees.

As the sun approached summer solstice, the work load increased with the day's length. The corn needed cultivation and hilling until it was strong enough to compete successfully with the weeds and "laid by" till harvest. There was hay to make, garden crops to nurture, gather, and replant, and often a winter wheat crop to harvest and thresh. In August, with the corn laid by and harvest coming, men took the opportunity for a respite; there were the dog days when "onery" farmers took long naps and "progressive" farmers mended fences. But August was soon overwhelmed by the frantic pace of September's harvest. Summer grain had to be cut, bound, and shocked within a critically short period, the corn picked, the last round of garden vegetables safely packed away in cold storage while still fresh.

Days continued to shorten, but after harvest the pace of work slowed as well. Still the grain needed threshing, the corn husking and cribbing, there was perhaps fruit to pick, dry, or preserve in a variety of ways, possibly pickles and kraut to make. These and other activities prepared the way for the winter: sowing the winter wheat, making firewood, daubing the cracks in old cabins, barns, and outbuildings, banking dirt around foundations to keep out some of the cold, and butchering enough hogs for salted and smoked meat until the spring again provided a larder of milk, eggs, and poultry.

Summer's activity was counterbalanced by winter's leisure. The daily chores of the farm—tending livestock, hauling wood and water, the domestic routine—continued. There were also numerous tasks to keep an industrious farmer busy: fences to mend, manure to haul and spread, trees to girdle and later fell, roads to maintain. But there was comparatively little opportunity for productive activity in the winter, aside from work in the woodlot. So winter months were occupied with general farm repair and improvement, visiting neighbors, trading the surpluses that summer's labor had produced. In late winter farmers would begin to plan the plantings of the next season, setting out planting dates in traditional fashion by carefully determining with the farm almanac the timing of the phases of the moon and the rising and falling of astrological signs.

Encouraged by their subordination to the natural world, the people of the Midwest held to a traditional animistic conception of the universe: the inanimate world was infused with will, feeling, and spirit. "The world was a huge kaleidoscope, whose bewildering pieces fell by the twist of analogy or contrast into beautifully logical patterns of form, direction, texture, quality, process—patterns to cover everything that might happen, from evening to evening and from spring to spring." As William Oliver, an English visitor and resident of Illinois in the 1840s, wrote, "There is a good deal of superstition or belief in witchcraft, omens, lucky times, etc." The world could be best understood by analogy (if an animal disturbed the afterbirth, that baby would take on some trait of the beast) or contrast (cold hands, warm heart) or the rule of "firsts" (if a woman cries on her wedding day she will cry throughout her married life). Many of the beliefs were employed in a half-embarrassed way, perhaps pulled out only in times of emergencies like sickness, death, disaster; others were the stock-in-trade of midwestern life.[4]

The cycle of the seasons encouraged a traditional view of work as well. Work was the expenditure of human energy to meet given tasks. When wheat was ready for harvesting, for example, men would readily work fifteen-hour days to bring it in before the precious grain was shed on the ground. On the other hand, when seasonal demands slackened, as in winter, a man might quit early without qualms, and few worried when a winter storm closed in the family for a few days. The persistent pace of modern labor, measured not by natural cycles but by the clock, was almost unknown to midwesterners. By the same token, work was understood not as the opposite of leisure but as life's requirement for all creatures, regardless of sex or age. Men, women, and children would share life's burdens. "The rule was," William Howells remembered of his farm life, "that whoever had the strength to work, took hold and helped."[5]

The common work of the farm was, then, divided among family members, but the principal division of work was by sex. Men and women worked in different areas, skilled at different tasks, prepared and trained for their work in different ways. In an economy based on the family unit, women and men in midwestern society achieved common goals by doing different jobs.

Sex and gender is a foundation of individual and social identity in all human societies. As Michael Banton puts it, gender roles "are related so closely to the performance of most other roles that the sex of a party can be concealed only in the most restricted situations."[6] The differences of sex are the starting place for gender roles: each person is given a polar label, either man or woman. Sex implies general natural potentials and limitations, to be sure, but the biological distinctions alone have never been sufficient social determinants of distinctive gender roles; sex differences have always had to be elaborated by patterned cultural forms. "Natural features are never translated directly into social ones. They are always dressed in cultural clothing."[7]

If gender roles are essentially cultural constructions, it follows that the notion of what constitutes the masculine and the feminine will vary greatly from one culture to another and from one time to another. Men and women play their gender roles according to a cultural script outlining the appropriate activities and tasks (the sexual division of labor) as well as the attitudes and personality (the character) of the two sexes. People appear most obviously in society and history as players of their gender roles.[8]

For historians (as well as other social scientists), the proper place to begin an understanding of gender roles is by reconstructing and examining the customary ways in which men and women divided the work of society among themselves.[9] This priority makes methodological sense if for no other reason than because outward behavior is what historians can best determine, and broad areas of behavioral uniformity suggest the presence of roles. These patterns then establish a context of human action for the evaluation of what men and women thought.[10] Such an approach employs an active, concrete concept of gender roles: gender roles are social regularities observed in what men and women do and the ways they think and feel about what they do, as well as how and why they do what they do. In this study both behavioral and attitudinal facts must be derived from the same subjective sources—the diaries and recollections. But even with such documents of personal experience the behavioral regularities are readily exposed and pieced together to form a whole pattern.

The functional principles of the general divisions of work by sex on the midwestern farm were quite clear and quite strict in application. In only a few areas did the work of men and women overlap. Most clearly, men were occupied with the heaviest work. First, they had responsibility for work with the broadax. If the family was taking up new wooded ground—as many Oregon emigrants would be doing, for example—the land had to be cleared. Frequently a farmer would gird the trees with his ax the first season to kill foliage, felling trees and removing stumps in the following winters. Logrolling, when the men of the neighborhood joined together to clear a field belonging to one of them, was a common late-winter social event for men. Construction, including making fences, was also a male job, as was the ongoing work in the family woodlot. Wood was chopped, hauled and stacked, or dumped near the house.

Men also controlled work with the plow. For new land a breaking plow, drawn by several yoke of oxen, was often needed, especially in prairie sod. Working improved acres was easier, but still hard, heavy work. And within the limitations of available labor and marketability, men were usually itching to put new land to the plow, so the plow was associated with work of the heaviest sort and understood to be male. Work in the cleared and plowed fields, where grain or corn grew, also fell to male control and supervision. Men plowed in spring or winter, sowed their wheat broadcast (until the 1850s), and planted their corn in hills. Men and boys harrowed and weeded until harvest, when they picked the corn together and cooperated in bringing in the wheat, men cradling and boys binding. Fieldwork kept men extremely busy. Two mature men on fifty acres of corn and wheat land spent three-quarters of the whole growing season plowing, planting, and harvesting, exclusive of any other work.[11]

There was plenty of other work to do. Men were responsible for upkeep and repair of tools, implements, and wagons and care of the draft animals, the oxen, mules, or horses. Hogs and sheep, both pretty much allowed to roam, were herded, fed, and tended by men and boys. Finally, men were responsible for cleanup and maintenance of the barn, barnyard, fields, and woodlot. This meant ditching and trenching, innumerable repairs on all the things that could—and did—break, laying down straw and hay, and hauling manure.[12]

Less important in fact, but work which nonetheless played an important role in male thinking, was hunting. For the early pioneers game provided most of the protein in the family diet. By mid-century those pioneer days had passed in the Midwest. But the rifle remained in its central place over the door or mantle long after the emergencies that might call it out had gone the way of the forests. Hunting remained, if only as an autumn sport or shooting match, a central aspect of male identity. "Even farmers," says Buley, "at certain seasons felt a peculiar restlessness."[13] The hunting legacy had one practical consequence for male work loads: men had primary responsibility for slaughtering and butchering large farm animals. Indeed, when hogs ran wild, they were sometimes picked off by rifle shot. Hunting was the male activity that most embodied men's self-conceived role—keystone of the hearth, defender of the household, and main provider.

In fact, women were more centrally involved in providing subsistence for the farm family than men. Nearly all the kinds of food consumed by farm families were direct products of women's work in growing, collecting, and butchering. An acre or so of improved land near the house was set aside for the domestic garden. After husbands had plowed the plot, farm women planted their gardens. Housewives began by setting out onions and potatoes in early April, following up later that month by planting lettuce, beets, parsnips, turnips, and carrots in the garden, tomatoes and cabbages in window boxes indoors. When danger of late frosts had passed, the seedlings were moved outside and set out along with May plantings of cucumbers, melons, pumpkins, and beans. Women also frequently laid down a patch of buckwheat and a garden of kitchen and medicinal herbs—sage, peppers, thyme, mint, mustard, horseradish, tansy, and others.[14]

The garden required daily attention. At first the seedlings needed hand watering. Then crops required cultivation, and the everlasting battle against weeds began. Garden harvesting could commence in late April and was a daily chore throughout the summer, supplying fresh vegetables for the family table.

Wives and daughters were also traditionally responsible for the care of henhouse and dairy. After a dormant winter poultry came alive in the spring. The farm-wise woman carefully kept enough chickens to produce both eggs for the kitchen and to set hens for a new flock of spring roasters. From late spring to late fall the family feasted regularly on fresh-killed rooster, selected and usually butchered by the housewife. Daughters and young boys gathered the eggs that were another mainstay of the summer diet. Women's responsibility for the henhouse extended even to cleaning out the manure by the bucket load.[15]

Cows were sheltered in whatever served as a barn, and men's general supervision there relieved women of having to shovel the stalls. But women milked, tended, and fed the animals. The milking and the man-ufacture of butter and cheese was one of their central tasks. Cows were milked first thing in the morning and the last thing at night; housewives supervised the milking but parceled the job out to children as soon as they were able. Boys, however, with their father's sanction would rebel from milking; "the western people of the early days entertained a supreme con-tempt for a man who attended to the milking."[16] Making good butter was a matter of pride among farm women. The churn had to be operated with patience and persistence if the butter was to come.

> Come butter, come;
> Come butter, come;
> Little Johnny's at the gate,
> Waiting for his buttered cake.
> Come butter, come.[17]

The meter marked the up and down of the churn. When it had come, the butter was packed into homemade, hand-decorated molds, and pounds of it consumed each week. Cheesemaking was less general, ripened cheeses were the product of a mi-nority. Nearly all women, however, were trained in the manufacture of cottage cheese and farmer's cheese. Dairy produc-tion was especially important to the house-hold and central to the definition of wom-en's work. In 1839 a Springfield, Illinois, newspaper reprinted with horror a report that New England women were pressur-ing their husbands to take over the milk-ing.[18]

There were some areas of food produc-tion where women's and men's operations overlapped, but these were the exceptions. When hogs were butchered in fall, men from several farms might work together; it was mainly when it became necessary to supplement the meat supply that women helped men to slaughter and dress the ani-mal. In any event, women were always a part of the butchering, there to chop the scraps and odd pieces into sausage, pre-pare the hams for curing, and cook the ribs immediately. At other social and al-most ritual occasions of food prepara-tion—making cider or apple butter, ren-dering maple sugar—men and women regularly worked side by side. All of the work of the orchard was often a joint project.

The sexes also sometimes combined their energies during planting. If not pre-occupied with field planting, men might help to set out garden seed. More likely, however, field planting would fall behind the schedule set by zodiac or moon, and men called their womenfolk out to help. Women most often assisted in the corn-field. "Tarpley made a furrow with a sin-gle-shovel plow drawn by one horse," Iowa farm woman Elmira Taylor remem-bered of the 1860s. "I followed with a bag of seed corn and dropped two grains of seed each step forward." A farmer with no sons worked his daughters in the fields at planting time without a second thought.[19]

Food preparation was, of course, wom-en's work, and by all reports midwestern men kept women busy by consuming great quantities at mealtime.[20] Wives were re-sponsible for preparing three heavy meals a day; most farm wives spent their entire mornings cooking and tried to save after-noons for other work. Included in the daily midwestern diet were two kinds of meat, eggs, cheese, butter, cream (espe-cially in gravies), corn in one or more forms, two kinds of bread, three or four different vegetables from the garden or from storage, several kinds of jellies, pre-serves, and relishes, cake or pie, and milk, coffee, and tea. Making butter and cheese were only two of the innumerable femi-nine skills needed to set the farm ta-ble. . . .

Women cooked on the open hearth, directly over the coals; it was low, back-breaking work that went on forever; a pot of corn mush took from two to six hours with nearly constant stirring.[21] Cast-iron, wood-burning cook stoves were available in Illinois in the mid-1840s, and by 1860 most midwestern women had been given the opportunity to stand and cook.[22] The next great improvement in domestic technology was the general introduction of running water in close proximity to the kitchen. But throughout the antebellum Midwest, water had to be carried to the house, sometimes from quite a distance, and that invariably was women's work. Domestic work—housecleaning, care of the bedding, all the kitchen work, in addition to responsibility for decorating and adding a "woman's touch"—was a demanding task under the best of circumstances, and farms offered far from the best. The yard between the kitchen and barn was always covered with enough dung to attract hordes of summer houseflies. In those days before screen doors kitchens were infested; men and women alike ignored the pests. In wet months the yard was a mess of mud, dung, and cast-off water, constantly tracked into the house. A cleanly wife had to be a constant worker.

A farmer was said to be a jack-of-all-trades. But women's work outdistanced men's in the sheer variety of tasks performed. In addition to their production of food, women had complete responsibility for all manufacture, care, and repair of family clothing. During the first half of the nineteenth century, domestic manufacture gave way to industrial production of thread and cloth, but in the Midwest, from 1840 to 1860, while home manufactures declined, they remained an important activity for women. On the Taylor homestead in southeastern Iowa, for example, the assessed valuation of household manufactures declined from $73 in 1850 to $50 in 1860, but this marked a decline, not an end to the use of the wheel and loom: in 1861 Elmira Taylor spun her own wool, took it to a mill to be carded, and wove it into cloth throughout the winter on her mother-in-law's loom.[23] Midwestern homespun was mostly of

flax and wool, supplemented by a little homegrown cotton or purchased cotton thread. A few sheep and a quarter-acre of flax were enough to supply the largest family. Farm wives sowed flax in March, harvested it in June (replanting immediately with a sterile-soil crop like potatoes), and prepared it that summer by soaking and sun-drying it to rot the outer coating.[24] Men lent a hand by crushing the flax on the flax break to remove the inner fibers and washing and shearing the sheep, but from that point it was a woman's operation. Spinning wheels were in universal use; each household required separate wheels for wool and flax. Wheels were precision tools, but families could get them rather cheaply from the wheelwright, and according to William Oliver, "spinning wheels and a loom are very general items in a farmer's establishment."[25] Wool had first to be carded into lean bunches, then spun on the great wheel; the spinner paced back and forth, whirling the wheel with her right hand, manipulating the wool and guiding the yarn on the spindle with her left. Two miles of yarn, enough for two to four yards of woven wool, required pacing over four miles, a full day's work. An excellent spinner, sitting at the smaller flax wheel, could spin a mile of linen thread in a day.[26]

The yarn was woven into wool and linen cloth or more commonly combined into durable linsey-woolsey on homemade looms. If cotton was available it was woven with wool warp to make jean. The giant loom dominated cramped living quarters when in use; it was knocked down and put away when weaving was completed.[27] The cloth still had to be shrunk and sized (fulled)—a job usually put out to the fulling mill if one were nearby—and dyed, sometimes from home dyes, but increasingly with commercial dyes bought at local stores. Nearly all farm clothing was cut from this cloth. Coarser tow cloth, made from the short-fiber, darker parts of the flax, was used for toweling, bandage, menstrual cloth, rags, or rough field clothing. Pillows and mattresses were made of tow and stuffed with the down women collected from the geese and ducks in their charge. The finest homespun, the pure linen bleached scores of times till it reached its characteristic color, was reserved for coverlets, tablecloths, appliqué, and stitchery. For their annual clothing a family of four would require a minimum of forty yards of cloth, or at least two full weeks at the wheel and loom for an experienced housewife. This work was, of course, spread throughout the available time, and one could expect to find women spinning or weaving at almost any time of the day, at every season of the year.[28]

Itinerant weavers first made their appearance in the Midwest during the 1840s, their Jacquard looms offering what seemed incredible detail in patterns. For most farm families, however, everyday cloth remained home-produced until the general availability of low-cost factory-produced dry goods. It was during the commercial shift in midwestern agriculture that family looms and then wheels gave way to cheap commercial cloth. Until the Civil War, however, a good deal of all midwestern clothing, and most clothing on emigrant backs, was homespun.

Every wife was a tailor, fitting and cutting cloth for her own slip-on dresses and those of her daughter, her son's and husband's blouses and pantaloons, and the tow shirts of the younger ones. If there was "boughten" cloth available—cotton or woolen broadcloth, gingham or calico—it was used for dress-up clothing, home-tailored of course. Socks, mittens, and caps were knit for winter wear, but every adult went sockless and children barefoot in summer. Underclothes were not manufactured or worn, for they were considered an unnecessary extravagance.[29]

Women were personally involved in clothing manufacture, from sowing the flax seed to sewing the garment. Homespun "could not be lightly cast aside after so much toil and patience, on account of being slightly or considerably worn."[30] So worn pants and shirts were continually mended, garments too worn to be used saved for patches, and every scrap of every kind of cloth that passed through the house was saved for that special purpose it would one day find. As an old Kentucky woman remembered,

> You see you start out with just so much caliker; you don't go to the store and pick it out and buy it, but the neighbors will give you a piece here and a piece there, and you will have a piece left every time you cut out a dress, and you take what happens to come and that's predestination. But when it comes to cuttin' out why you're free to choose your patterns. You can give the same kind o' pieces to two persons, and one will be a *Nine Patch* and one'll make a *Wild Goose Chase* and there'll be two quilts made out o' the same kind of pieces, and jest as different as they can be, and that is just the way with livin'. The Lord sends in the pieces, but we can cut 'em out and put 'em together pretty much to suit ourselves.[31]

Sewing was the consummate feminine skill, a domestic necessity but one practiced and refined until in the hands of many it achieved the status of an art form. Girls were taught to sew before they were taught to read, and started on a four- or nine-patch quilt cover as soon as they could hold a needle. Coverlets, counterpanes, crocheted samplers, and most especially the elaborate patchwork or appliqué front pieces for quilts were the highest expression of the material culture of women. With patchwork, appliqué, and quilt stitchery, utility was a secondary consideration; these were primarily modes of creative artistry for women. One farm woman testified to the importance of this avenue for her: "I would have lost my mind if I had not had my quilts to do."[32]

On a more mundane level, clothes had to be washed, and women made their own soap for both the clothes and the family who wore them. Women loaded hardwood ashes into the ash hopper, poured water over, and collected the lye in the trough below. They boiled kitchen fats and grease, added the lye, and if everything was going well the soap would "come" after long, hot hours of stirring. They poured the hot soap into molds or tubs and stored it. Soapmaking was a big, all-day job, done only two or three times a year.[33] Monday, by all accounts, was the universal washday. Rainwater was used for washing, or alternately a little lye was added to soften well water. The water was heated in the washtub over hearth or stove, soap added, and clothes were pounded against a washboard, then rinsed, wrung out by hand, and hung. The lye, harsh soap, and hot water chapped and cracked the skin; women's hands would often break open and bleed into the tub. In the winter, the clothes were hung outside where sore, wet hands would freeze painfully, or inside, draped over chairs or lines, steaming up the windows and turning the whole place clammy. Ironing and mending were also allocated one day each week.

To women fell a final task. Women bore the children and nursed them for at least the first few months, and in this they worked completely alone. Even after weaning, farm women remained solely responsible for the supervision of young children; both boys and girls were under their mother's supervision until the boys were old enough to help with the fieldwork, at about ten years, at which time they came under their father's guidance. Girls, of course, remained apprenticed to the housewife's craft. Farm mothers put their charges to work "almost as soon as they could walk," and although they could not contribute materially until they were five or six, the correct work attitude had by then been instilled.[34] There was plenty that children could do around the garden, dairy, and henhouse; they watered, fed the animals, collected eggs,

milked, hauled water, weeded, and performed innumerable other chores that housewives could never have finished but for the work of their children.

Midwestern farm mothers had relatively large families. The mean family size in the Midwest in 1850 was 5.7.[35] Mean family size of the overland emigrants in this study was a little less, 5.0, mainly because there were so many newlyweds; otherwise the size of emigrant families was very typical of the population at large. The mean size of emigrating families in their full childbearing phase was 7.6. In her lifetime, then, a farm woman could expect to raise five or six children of her own. These children helped significantly with the burden of farm work, but not without the expenditure of a great deal of physical and emotional energy by their mothers.

To determine the full occupations of women, their total work load, we must consider the social effects of childbearing as well as childrearing. Miscarriages, stillbirths, birth accidents, and infant mortality took a terrible toll on the energies and spirit of women. Counting infant deaths alone, one in five children died before its fifth birthday, and prenatal losses were at least as high.[36] Childbirth certainly was a central experience for farm women. It was no occasional or unique event but occurred with demanding regularity. To assess women's reproductive burdens fairly we can measure women's fertility. The mean age of marriage for emigrant men and women was 25.1 and 20.5, respectively. Some women, of course, married earlier than the average and were pregnant before their twentieth birthdays. The peak childbearing years were from age twenty to thirty-five, during which time emigrant women bore over four out of five of their children. Fertility declined precipitously after thirty-five as a combined effect of lowered male and female fecundity, although some mothers continued to bear children into their late forties.

Let us translate abstract fertility into

the real terms of farm women's lives: childbearing had to be a dominant fact. Over half the emigrant women gave birth to their first child within their first year of marriage, another quarter the second year, and fully 98 percent by the end of the third. Thereafter a mean of 29.0 months intervened between births throughout a woman's twenties and thirties. For their most vital years farm women lived under the dictatorial rule of yet another cycle, a two-and-a-half-year cycle of childbirth, of which nineteen or twenty months were spent in advanced pregnancy, infant care, and nursing. Until her late thirties, a woman could expect little respite from the physical and emotional wear and tear of nearly constant pregnancy or suckling.

Given the already burdensome tasks of women's work, the additional responsibilities of the children were next to intolerable. Women must have searched for some way of limiting the burden. It is possible that mothers introduced their babies to supplemental feeding quite early and encouraged children's independence in order to free themselves from the restrictions of nursing, which had to seriously limit their capacity to work.[37] There is almost no mention of child-feeding practices in the literature, but there are some indirect indications that babies were soon consuming "bread, corn, biscuits and pot-likker" right along with their parents. On the other hand, there was a prevalent old wives' notion that prolonged nursing was a protection against conception. To achieve a twenty-nine-month cycle without practicing some form of self-conscious family limitation, women would have had to nurse for at least a year.[38]

Short of family planning there was no easy choice for women in the attempt to reduce the burden of child care. Other groups had practiced family limitation before this time, but the need for labor may have been a mitigating factor here. It comes as no surprise, then, that as soon as it was possible, children were pretty much allowed and encouraged to shift for

themselves, to grow as they might, with relatively little parental or maternal involvement in the process. We will find children little mentioned in overland diaries and reminiscences.

By no means were men the "breadwinners" of this economy. Both women and men actively participated in the production of family subsistence. Indeed, women were engaged in from one-third to one-half of all the food production of the farm, the proportions varying with regional and individual differences.[39] Of the farm staples—meat, milk, corn, pumpkins, beans, and potatoes—women produced the greater number as a product of their portion of the division of labor. Women were also likely to be found helping men with their portion at peak planting time. To this must be added the extremely important work of clothing manufacture, all the household work, and the care of the children. To be sure, men and women alike worked hard to make their farms produce. But one cannot avoid being struck by the enormousness of women's work load.

In 1862, in its first annual report, the Department of Agriculture published a study by Dr. W. W. Hall on the condition of farm women. "In plain language," Hall proclaimed, "in the civilization of the latter half of the nineteenth century, a farmer's wife, as a general rule, is a laboring drudge. . . . It is safe to say, that on three farms out of four the wife works harder, endures more, than any other on the place; more than the husband, more than the 'farm hand,' more than the 'hired help' of the kitchen."[40] In his recommendations for improvements in women's condition, Hall's report supplements our view of farm work. The practice of many farmers of letting their wives cut the firewood and haul the water, especially in the cold of winter, needed correction. Men should be responsible for providing a root cellar for potatoes and other vegetables, otherwise wives were compelled to go out in the cold "once or twice every day, to leave a heated kitchen, and most likely with thin shoes, go to the garden with a tin pan and a hoe, to dig them out of the wet ground and bring them home in slosh or rain." Equally perilous for women were the extremes of heat and cold encountered in washing and hanging the winter laundry; men were stronger and should take that job." The truth is, it perils the life of the hardiest persons, while working over the fire in cooking or washing, to step outside the door of the kitchen for an instant, a damp, raw wind may be blowing, which coming upon an inner garment throws a chill or the clamminess of the grave over the whole body in an instant of time." . . .

Hall lamented the lack of attention to women's needs and recommended to men that they adopt a more sympathetic attitude. "There are 'seasons' in the life of women which, as to some of them, so affect the general system, and the mind also, as to commend them to our warmest sympathies. . . . Some women, at such times, are literally insane. . . ." Husbands had to be patient and affectionate or risk driving their wives to a "lunatic's cell." In addition, a man should realize that his wife loved finery and beauty and should supply her "according to his ability, with the means of making her family and home neat, tasteful and tidy." Hall reminded the farmer that "his wife is a social being; that she is not a machine, and therefore needs rest, and recreation, and change." If hands were to be hired perhaps help in the kitchen was worth considering. Women should be allowed to get out of the house once in a while to do a little visiting with other people; in fact, it was a good idea for both husband and wife to dress up and step out for the day now and then. . . .

Hall's report was a mixture of constructive suggestions and temporizing platitudes; it is unlikely that many farmers or farm women ever saw, let alone heeded, its advice.[41] In the end it is more impor-

tant for what it suggests concerning the working relations of husbands and wives than for its proposed reforms. Hall implicitly leveled a harsh indictment against farmers: that they were insensitive to the work load of their wives and drove women past reasonable limits; that they did not comprehend the natural or psychological needs of their wives; that they refused to give women the respect and authority that was their due. Hall attributed the problem to calculations of profit and loss which ignored social and emotional needs (although he made his appeal to men on the very same basis: "no man will ever lose in the long run").

The report adds depth to what we have thus far seen and suggests that the division of labor was structured in favor of men, that it exploited women, and that it was perpetuated, in part, by a masculine attitude of superiority. Daniel Drake, who visited the Midwest in the late 1830s, concluded that the farmer's wife was one who "surrounded by difficulties or vexed with hardships at home, provided with no compensation for what she has left behind, pines away, and wonders that her husband can be so happy when she is so miserable."[42] The true inequity in the division of labor was clearly expressed in the aphorism, "A man may work from sun to sun, but a woman's work is never done." The phrase has a hollow ring to us today, but it was no joke to farm women, who by all accounts worked two or three hours more each day than the men, often spinning, weaving, or knitting late into the dark evening hours.

There are some areas of women's participation in farm life that suggest a higher status. Cross-cultural studies indicate that the responsibility for exchanging goods and services with persons outside the family tends to confer family power and prestige. "The relative power of women is increased if women both contribute to subsistence *and also* have opportunities for extra domestic distribution and exchange of valued goods and services."[43] In the Midwest, the products of dairy, henhouse, garden, and loom were often the only commodities successfully exchanged for other family necessities. Powder, glass, dyes, crockery, coffee, tea, store cloth, metal utensils, and sugar were bought on credit from the local merchant; butter, cheese, eggs, vegetables, home-spun, and whiskey were the main items offered in trade to pay the tab.[44]

However, while it was true that women traded, the proceeds were not credited to them individually, but to the family in general. Commodity exchange in corn and grain surpluses, on the other hand, was most frequently used for male economic pursuits: paying off the farm mortgage, speculating in new lands, and as innovations in technology became available, experimenting with new farm equipment. Men's product was for male use; women's product was for the family. It has been claimed that "there was no doubt of her equality in those days because she showed herself equally capable in all the tasks of their life together, and she was proud to know that this was true. Her position and dignity and age-old strength was that of the real help-mate in everything that touched the welfare of the family and the home." From a modern perspective equal work may seem a first step toward sexual equality, but the question of power is not only a question of what people do but also of the recognition they are granted for what they do and the authority that recognition confers. There is little evidence to suggest that men, for their part, gave women's work a second thought. That it was a woman's lot to work that hard was simply taken for granted.[45]

Indeed, one theme of midwestern folksongs was the lament of the husband wronged by the wife who refused to perform her appointed tasks.

Come all you wary bachelors,
Come listen unto me
Come all you wary bachelors,
Who married once would be.

Before my wife was married
She was a dainty dame.
She could do all kinds of cunjer work,
Like butter, cheese an' cream.

She'd weed her father's oats an' flax,
And milk the cows I know;
And when she would return at night
She could spin a pound of tow.

But since my wife got married,
Quite worthless she's become.
An' all that I can say of her
She will not stay at home.

She will wash herself, an' dress herself,
An' a-visiting she will go;
An' that's the thing she'd rather do
In place of spinning tow.[46]

One looks in vain for evidence of songs that sang the praises of women's diligence. Even the woman accomplished at all of her duties was likely to fall short in male estimation.

She could wash and she could brew,
She could cut and she could sew,
But alas and alas! she was dumb,
    dumb, dumb.

.   .   .   .

She could card and she could spin,
She could do most anything,
But alas and alas! she was dumb,
    dumb, dumb.

She was pretty, she was smart,
An' she stole away my heart,
But alas, in the door she was dumb,
    dumb, dumb.[47]

Men and women were locked into productive harmony. The farm could not exist without the cooperative labor of both sexes. Yet men gave women minimal recognition for their work. Women, fully equal in production, were not granted the status of equality.

Despite its interdependence, the character of men's and women's work was essentially different. Woman's work was dominated by the omnipresent awareness of the immediate usefulness of her product, be it milk, cabbage, eggs, or flax. Whatever processing was required she herself performed. Her view was inward, to her household and family. For them she was not simply to provide food and clothing and keep up the house, but to do these things with imagination and care: by gardening industriously, by preserving, drying, and storing to overcome the limitations of nature, by preparing the season's fare with distinction, by dyeing, bleaching, and cutting clothes in ways to please, and by keeping not only a clean but a well-appointed house. The joys of women's work lay in the satisfactions of accomplishment—of bread well made, butter nicely molded, quilts intended for heirlooms—and in the variety of skills each woman had to master. Women who worked up to this standard were good wives; those who failed on these counts were cast in male folklore as improvident slatterns.[48]

Men, for their part, worked long, monotonous, solitary hours at a single pursuit in the fields, plowing row after row, hoeing hill after hill. Hamilton remembered work in the cornfield: "Usually you cultivated the corn with a hired man or two. But you each had your own 'land,' maybe two dozen rows each was working on, a row at a time. So you did not pass close as the two or three crossed and recrossed the fields, stopping, uncovering corn, pulling cockleburrs."[49] Such work would produce, it was hoped, quantities of staple grain great enough to sustain the family and provide a surplus, but there was little satisfaction in the immediate labor. The flavor of male work was quantitative: acres, fields, bushels—all measured a man's work. Neither the corn nor the grain was immediately consumable but required processing; the connections between production and consumption—the full cycle of work—was not embodied in a man's own activity. The cyclical nature of farm women's work might allow her to see in a flowering field of blue flax the linen for next summer's chemise. For men the fields would yield not usable, tangible articles—bread or hominy—but bushels; quantities, not things.

On the self-sufficient farm, or farms approaching self-sufficiency, the character of men's work was a powerful link between the field and the house. The housewife converted the corn to hominy, the grain to bread, while the farmer looked on: only woman could realize the product of man. But the somewhat abstract nature of men's work enabled them to envision another mode within which they were not dependent upon their wives to fulfill their labor. The market could connect men's work to a larger social process and renumerate them in the tokens of commerce. In order to qualify as social labor, work had to have this characteristic: to be able to reach out and connect the family to the larger social world. Women's work, always cyclical, always looking inward, did not qualify; it was hidden by domestic draperies. Men's work, even in the precommercial Midwest, encouraged a kind of economic vision women could not ordinarily achieve.

NOTES

1. The following section is based on numerous sources, but see especially Logan Esarey, *The Indiana Home* (Crawfordsville, Ind.: R. E. Banta, 1943); Rodney Loehr, "Minnesota Farmers' Diaries," *Minnesota History* 18 (1937):284–97; Eric Sloane, *Seasons of America Past* (New York: Wilfred Funk, 1958); Henry C. Taylor, *Tarpleywick:* *A Century of Iowa Farming* (Ames: Iowa State University Press, 1970); and Carl Hamilton, *In No Time at All* (Ames: Iowa State University Press, 1975).

2. Kerosene lamps came into wide use during the early 1860s; Evadene Burris, "Keeping House on the Minnesota Frontier," *Minnesota History* 14 (1933):265–67.

3. W. O. Rice, "The Pioneer Dialect of Southern Illinois," *Dialect Notes* 2 (1902): 233.

4. Frank R. Kramer, *Voices in the Valley: Mythmaking and Folk Belief in the Shaping of the Middle West* (Madison: University of Wisconsin Press, 1964), p. 107; . . . William Oliver, *Eight Months in Illinois* (Chicago: W. M. Hill, 1924; original ed. 1843), p. 71; Kramer, *Voices in the Valley*, p. 70. "Animistic" is used here in its general sense—the belief in spirits—and is not meant to imply more specific forms like ancestor worship, object worship, and so on.

5. William Cooper Howells, *Recollections of Life in Ohio from 1813–1840* (Cincinnati: Robert Clarke, 1895), p. 157.

6. Michael P. Banton, *Roles: An Introduction to the Study of Social Relations* (London: Tavistock Publications, 1965), p. 71. I distinguish between the terms *sex* and *gender* by limiting sex to the biological status of a person, either male or female; gender is the culturally assigned status of a person in regard to what is deemed masculine or feminine behavior or belief. Gender roles, then, consist of attributes, beliefs, and behaviors appropriate for masculine men and feminine women. See Resca M. Vaughter, "Review Essay: Psychology," *Signs* 2 (1976): 122 n.

7. Banton, *Roles*, p. 19. Is there any longer any need to cite references for the assertion that biology is *not* destiny? See Eleanor Emmons Maccoby, ed., *The Development of Sex Differences* (Stanford: Stanford University Press, 1965), and Maccoby and Carol Nagy Jacklin, *The Psychology of Sex Differences* (Stanford: Stanford University Press, 1974), for both text and bibliography. . . .

8. . . . See Thomas C. Cochran, "The Historian's Use of Social Role," in Louis Gottschalk, ed., *Generalization in the Writing of History* (Chicago: University of Chicago Press, 1963), pp. 103–4.

9. . . . The best work on gender roles continues to be done in anthropology, where field observation of behavior determines the focus; this tradition runs from Margaret Mead, *Male and Female: A Study of the Sexes in a Changing World* (New York: William Morrow, 1949), to Ernestine Friedl, *Women and Men: An Anthropologist's View* (New York: Holt, Rinehart, and Winston, 1975). For an excellent symposium of recent work, see Reyna R. Reiter, ed., *Toward an Anthropology of Women* (New York: Monthly Review Press, 1975).

10. . . . Historically, the definition of masculinity and femininity itself has often acted as a fetter on (or less frequently, a stimulus to) what men and women could do, and thus culture has become the active force in the formation and change of the division of labor. I proceed here on the assumption that to begin by examining the organization of sex-specific behavior provides a reasonable context for the evaluation of evidence about attitudes and feelings. By following this methodological convention, however, I do not wish to imply judgments about a specific genesis and development of the sexual division of labor to 1850, or judgments concerning the historical play of cultural and behavioral forces in the development of relations between the sexes in the century since. These are matters calling not for assumptions but for specific historical investigation.

For a historical and structural discussion of the origins of men's and women's work, I have found the following most helpful and influential: M. Kay Martin and Barbara Voorhies, *Female of the Species* (New York: Columbia University Press, 1975); . . . Reiter, ed., *Toward an Anthropology of Women*; and . . . Heidi Hartmann, "Capitalism, Patriarchy, and Job Segregation by Sex," *Signs* 1, no. 3, pt. 2 (1976): 137–69. . . .

11. Calculated from figures in R. C. Buley, *The Old Northwest Pioneer Period, 1815–1840* (Indianapolis, 1950), I:182.

12. Men were responsible for cleaning the privy. Most farms had outhouses used by women and children but disdained by men as effeminate. Ibid., 1:223.

13. Ibid., 1:153, 319.

14. Ibid., 1:217–18; Marjorie Caroline Taylor, "Domestic Arts and Crafts in Illinois (1800–1860)," *Journal of the Illinois State Historical Society* 33 (1940): 294. Jo Ann Carrigan, "Nineteenth Century Rural Self-sufficiency," *Arkansas Historical Quarterly* 21 (1962): 132–45, reprints from an antebellum manuscript many kitchen, garden, washday, and medicinal formulas and recipes, most from women's experience.

15. Oliver, *Eight Months*, pp. 109–10; Hamilton, *In No Time*, p. 163.

16. M. G. Wadsworth, in *History of Sangamon County, Illinois* (Chicago: Inter-State Publishing Company, 1881), p. 176; Everett N. Dick, *The Dixie Frontier* (New York: Knopf, 1948), p. 104; Buley, *Old Northwest*, 1:216–17.

17. For American variations of this traditional English chant, see Chuck Perdue, "Come Butter Come: A Collection of Churning Chants from Georgia," *Foxfire* 3 (1966): 20–24, 65–72.

18. Buley, *Old Northwest*, 1:392.

19. Loehr, "Diaries," p. 296; Taylor, *Tarpleywick*, p. 15; Howells, *Recollections*, pp. 156–57.

20. For this discussion of diet I have relied on Buley, *Old Northwest*, 1:218–21; Evadene A. Burris, "Frontier Food," *Minnesota History* 14 (1933):378–92; Burris, "Keeping House"; Edward Everett Dale, "The Food of the Frontier," *Journal of the Illinois State Historical Society* 40 (1947):38–61; Hamilton, *In No Time*, pp. 143–45.

21. Taylor, "Domestic Arts," p. 287; Charles Beneulyn Johnson, *Illinois in the Fifties* (Champaign, Ill.: Flanigan-Pearson, 1918), pp. 18 ff.; Ocie Lybarger, "Every Day Life on the Southern Illinois Frontier" (Master's thesis, Southern Illinois University, 1951), pp. 47 ff.

22. Samuel Willard, "Personal Reminiscences of Life in Illinois, 1830–1850," *Transactions of the Illinois State Historical Society* 11 (1906):80; Evadene A. Burris, "Furnishing the Frontier Home," *Minnesota History* 15 (1934):192; Richard Lyle Power, *Planting Corn Belt Culture* (Indianapolis: Indiana Historical Society, 1953), pp. 109–10.

23. Taylor, *Tarpleywick*, pp. 9, 13. For general studies, see Rolla Milton Tryon, *Household Manufactures in the United States, 1640–1860* (Chicago: University of Chicago Press, 1917); Luther Hooper, "The Loom and Spindle: Past, Present and Future," in Smithsonian Institution, *Annual Report* (Washington, D.C., 1914), pp. 629–78. . . .

24. Howells, *Recollections*, p. 123.

25. Oliver, *Eight Months*, pp. 89–90. "Inventories of the property of estates all through the period mention wheels"; Hubert Schmidt, "Farming in Illinois . . . ," *Journal of the Illinois State Historical Society* 31 (1938): 144.

26. Jared Van Wagenen, Jr., *The Golden Age of Homespun* (Ithaca: Cornell University Press, 1953), pp. 264–65; Sloane, *Seasons of America*, p. 118.

27. Johnson, *Illinois*, p. 16.

28. Van Wagenen, *Golden Age of Homespun*, pp. 264–65; Sloane, *Seasons of America*, p. 118; Buley, *Old Northwest*, 1:205.

29. Buley, *Old Northwest*, 1:201–10; Margaret Gilbert Mackey and Louise Pickney Sooy, *Early California Costumes, 1769–1847* (Stanford: Stanford University Press, 1932), pp. 101–10.

30. Wiley Britton, *Pioneer Life in Southwestern Missouri* (Kansas City: Smith-Grieves Company, 1929), p. 130.

31. Aunt Jane (of Kentucky), quoted in Elizabeth Wells Robertson, *American Quilts* (New York: Studio Publications, 1948), pp. 59–60.

32. Taylor, "Domestic Arts," p. 303; Patricia Mainardi, "Quilts: The Great American Art," *Radical America* 7 (1973):39–40; quote in Mainardi, "Quilts," p. 40.

33. Soapmaking, Buley reports, was the last domestic manufacture to pass from the farm household; *Old Northwest*, 1:223. Soapmaking was still a common activity among Kansas farm women in the 1920s; Edgar Schmiedler, *The Industrial Revolution and the Home: A Comparative Study of Family Life in Country, Town, and City* (Washington, D.C., 1927), pp. 4–6.

34. Vance Randolph, *The Ozarks: An American Survival of Primitive Society* (New York: Vanguard Press, 1931), p. 59.

35. *Compendium of the Eleventh Census; 1890: Part I—Population* (Washington, D.C.: Government Printing Office, 1893), p. 866.

36. Grabill estimates an age-specific infant (0–5) mortality of 220 out of 1,000 live births for the nineteenth century as a whole; W. H. Grabill, C. V. Kiser, and P. K. Whelpton, *The Fertility of American Women* (New York: John Wiley, 1958), p. 379.

37. S. B. Nerlove, "Women's Workload and Infant Feeding Practices: A Relationship with Demographic Implications," *Ethnology* 13 (1974):207–14; establishes that in societies where women contribute significantly to the production of subsistence, mothers tend to introduce their babies to supplemental food earlier than mothers in other societies. . . .

38. Buley, *Old Northwest*, 1:310. Lactation does indeed have the effect of prolonging postpartum amenorrhea and delaying ovulation. Lactation beyond a year, however, by which time the infant must be receiving its essential protein from supplemental sources, has little continued effect in delaying the menses. . . .

39. Using the scale employed by Nerlove, "Women's Workload," pp. 208–10. The several variables can be only approximated—the dependence of the midwestern economy on hunting, husbandry, and agriculture, respectively, and the determination of women's participation in the various subsistence activities listed. Scaling at the lowest range for women (that is, giving high relative importance to hunting, or estimating women's participation at low levels) and at the maximum (giving husbandry relative importance; or estimating women's participation at high levels) provides the range of 32 to 46 percent.

40. Dr. W. W. Hall, "Health of Farmer's Families," in *Report of the Commissioner of Agriculture for the Year 1862* (Washington, D.C.: Government Printing Office, 1863), pp. 462–63. All subsequent quotations from ibid., pp. 462–70, passim.

41. The following all document the same situation for farm women in the first quarter of the twentieth century: Randolph, *The Ozarks*, pp. 41–43; Schmiedler, *Industrial Revolution and the Home*; Edward B. Mitchell, "The American Farm Woman As She Sees Herself," in U.S. Department of Agriculture, *Yearbook of Agriculture, 1914* (Washington, D.C.: Government Printing Office, 1915), pp. 311–18; U.S. Department of Agriculture, "The Needs of Farm Women," Reports nos. 103–106 (Washington, D.C.: Government Printing Office, 1905).

42. Daniel Drake, quoted in Harriet Martineau, *Retrospect of Western Travel* (London: Saunders and Otley, 1838), 3:224.

43. Friedl, *Women and Men*, pp. 8, 135.

44. Of these, only whiskey was a male product. Buley, *Old Northwest*, 1:235; Taylor, *Tarpleywick*, p. 14; Hamilton, *In No Time*, pp. 46, 168.

45. Mitchell, "American Farm Woman," p. 314; Mary Meek Atkeson, *The Woman on the Farm* (New York: Century, 1924), pp. 4–5.

46. "The Wife Who Wouldn't Spin Tow," Vance Randolph, *Ozark Folksongs*, 4 vols. (Columbia: State Historical Society of Missouri, 1946–1950), 1:123–24.

47. "The Scolding Wife," Paul G. Brewster, "Some Folk Songs from Indiana," *Journal of American Folk Lore* 57 (1944):282–83; Mary O. Eddy, *Ballads and Songs from Ohio* (New York: J. J. Augustin, 1939), p. 214; last verse supplied in another version, "The Dumb Wife Cured," Randolph, *Ozark Folksongs*, 3:119.

48. Randolph, *The Ozarks*, p. 42.

49. Hamilton, *In No Time*, p. 73.

CHRISTINE STANSELL

Women, Children, and the Uses of the Streets: Class and Gender Conflict in New York City, 1850–1860

As John Mack Faragher shows, rural life involved hard work and insecurities—not only the unpredictability of the weather but the difficulties of paying debts and the loneliness that came with being far from friends and neighbors. The insecurities of urban life for working people could be even more severe. By the 1830s, the conditions of the urban poor had begun to command attention: in Philadelphia, Mathew Carey published a landmark investigation of the lives of working women. In many cities groups of middle-class reformers tried to help with food, clothing, and religious consolation. But as Christine Stansell shows, this "help" could involve intrusion into the patterns of family relationships.

How did middle-class women define the role of the mother? In what ways was this definition different from the way working-class mothers understood

Excerpted from "Women, Children, and the Uses of the Streets: Class and Gender Conflict in New York City, 1850–1860" by Christine Stansell, in *Feminist Studies*, 8 (1982):309–35. Copyright © 1982 by Feminist Studies, Inc. Reprinted by permission of the publisher, Feminist Studies, Inc., c/o Women's Studies Program, University of Maryland, College Park, Maryland 20742. Notes have been renumbered.

their role? What parallels does Stansell draw between conditions in New York City in the 1850s and today?

On a winter day in 1856, an agent for the Children's Aid Society (CAS) of New York encountered two children out on the street with market baskets. Like hundreds he might have seen, they were desperately poor—thinly dressed and barefoot in the cold—but their cheerful countenances struck the gentleman, and he stopped to inquire into their circumstances. They explained that they were out gathering bits of wood and coal their mother could burn for fuel and agreed to take him home to meet her. In a bare tenement room, bereft of heat, furniture, or any other comforts, he met a "stout, hearty woman" who, even more than her children, testified to the power of hardihood and motherly love in the most miserable circumstances. A widow, she supported her family as best she could by street peddling; their room was bare because she had been forced to sell her clothes, furniture, and bedding to supplement her earnings. As she spoke, she sat on a pallet on the floor and rubbed the hands of the two younger siblings of the pair from the street. "They were tidy, sweet children," noted the agent, "and it was very sad to see their chilled faces and tearful eyes." Here was a scene that would have touched the heart of Dickens, and seemingly many a chillier mid-Victorian soul. Yet in concluding his report, the agent's perceptions took a curiously harsh turn.

> Though for her pure young children too much could hardly be done, in such a woman there is little confidence to be put . . . it is probably, some cursed vice has thus reduced her, and that, if her children be not separated from her, she will drag them down, too.[1]

Such expeditions of charity agents and reformers into the households of the poor were common in New York between 1850 and 1860. So were such harsh and unsupported judgments of working-class mothers, judgments which either implicitly or explicitly converged in the new category of the "dangerous classes." In this decade, philanthropists, municipal authorities, and a second generation of Christian evangelicals, male and female, came to see the presence of poor children in New York's streets as a central element of the problem of urban poverty. They initiated an ambitious campaign to clear the streets, to change the character of the laboring poor by altering their family lives, and, in the process, to eradicate poverty itself. They focused their efforts on transforming two elements of laboring-class family life, the place of children and the role of women.

There was, in fact, nothing new about the presence of poor children in the streets, nor was it new that women of the urban poor should countenance that presence. For centuries, poor people in Europe had freely used urban public areas—streets, squares, courts, and marketplaces—for their leisure and work. For the working poor, street life was bound up not only with economic exigency, but also with childrearing, family morality, sociability, and neighborhood ties. In the nineteenth century, the crowded conditions of the tenements and the poverty of great numbers of metropolitan laboring people made the streets as crucial an arena as ever for their social and economic lives. As one New York social investigator observed, "In the poorer portions of the city, people live much and sell mostly out of doors."[2]

How, then, do we account for this sudden flurry of concern? For reformers like the agent from the CAS, street life was antagonistic to ardently held beliefs about childhood, womanhood and, ultimately, the nature of civilized urban society. The middle class of which the reformers were a part was only emerging, an economically ill-defined group, neither rich nor poor, just beginning in the antebellum years to assert a distinct cultural identity. Central to its self-conception was the ideology of domesticity, a set of sharp ideas and pronounced opinions about the nature of a moral family life. The sources of this ideology were historically complex and involved several decades of struggles by women of this group for social recognition, esteem, and power in the family. Nonetheless, by midcentury, ideas initially developed and promoted by women and their clerical allies had found general acceptance, and an ideology of gender had become firmly embedded in an ideology of class. Both women and men valued the home, an institution which they perceived as sacred, presided over by women, inhabited by children, frequented by men. The home preserved those social virtues endangered by the public world of trade, industry, and politics; a public world which they saw as even more corrupting and dangerous in a great city like New York.[3]

Enclosed, protected, and privatized, the home and the patterns of family life on which it was based thus represented to middle-class women and men a crucial institution of civilization. From this perspective, a particular geography of social life— the engagement of the poor in street life rather than in the enclave of the home— became in itself evidence of parental neglect, family disintegration, and a pervasive urban social pathology. Thus in his condemnation of the impoverished widow, the CAS agent distilled an entire analysis of poverty and a critique of poor families: the presence of her children on the streets was synonymous with a corrupt family life, no matter how disguised it might be. In the crusade of such mid-Victorian reformers to save poor children from their parents and their class lie the roots of a long history of middle-class intervention

in working-class families, a history which played a central part in the making of the female American working class.

Many historians have shown the importance of antebellum urban reform to the changing texture of class relations in America, its role in the cultural transformations of urbanization and industrialization.[4] Confronted with overcrowding, unemployment, and poverty on a scale theretofore unknown in America, evangelical reformers forged programs to control and mitigate these pressing urban problems, programs which would shape municipal policies for years to come. Yet their responses were not simply practical solutions, the most intelligent possible reactions to difficult circumstances; as the most sensitive historians of reform have argued, they were shaped by the world view, cultural affinities, conceptions of gender, class prejudices, and imperatives of the reformers themselves. Urban reform was an interaction in which, over time, both philanthropists and their beneficiaries changed. In their experience with the reformers, the laboring poor learned— and were forced—to accommodate themselves to an alien conception of family and city life. Through their work with the poor, the reformers discovered many of the elements from which they would forge their own class and seuxal identity, still ill-defined and diffuse in 1850; women, particularly, strengthened their role as dictators of domestic and familial standards for all classes of Americans. The reformers' eventual triumph in New York brought no solutions to the problem of poverty, but it did bring about the evisceration of a way of urban life and the legitimation of their own cultural power as a class.

The conflict over the streets resonated on many levels. Ostensibly the reformers aimed to rescue children from the corruptions and dangers of the city streets; indeed the conscious motives of many, if not all, of these well-meaning altruists went no further. There were many unquestioned assumptions, however, on which their benevolent motives rested, and it is in examining these assumptions that we begin to see the challenge which these middle-class people unwittingly posed to common practices of the poor. In their cultural offensive, reformers sought to impose on the poor conceptions of childhood and motherhood drawn from their own ideas of domesticity. In effect, reformers tried to implement their domestic beliefs through reorganizing social space, through creating a new geography of the city. Women were especially active; while male reformers experimented, through a rural foster home program, with more dramatic means of clearing the streets, middle-class ladies worked to found new working-class homes, modeled on their own, which would establish a viable alternative to the thoroughly nondomesticated streets. Insofar as the women reformers succeeded, their victory contributed to both the dominance of a class and of a specific conception of gender. It was, moreover, a victory which had enduring and contradictory consequences for urban women of all classes. In our contemporary city streets, vacated, for the most part, of domestic life yet dangerous for women and children, we see something of the legacy of their labors.

CHILDREN'S USES OF THE STREETS

Unlike today, the teeming milieu of the New York streets in the mid-nineteenth century was in large part a children's world. A complex web of economic imperatives and social mores accounted for their presence there, a presence which reformers so ardently decried. Public life, with its panoply of choices, its rich and varied texture, its motley society, played as central a role in the upbringing of poor children as did private, domestic life in that of their more affluent peers. While

middle-class mothers spent a great deal of time with their children (albeit with the help of servants), women of the laboring classes condoned for their offspring an early independence—within bounds—on the streets. Through peddling, scavenging, and the shadier arts of theft and prostitution, the streets offered children a way to earn their keep, crucial to making ends meet in their households. Street life also provided a home for children without families—the orphaned and abandoned—and an alternative to living at home for the especially independent and those in strained family circumstances.

Such uses of the streets were dictated by exigency, but they were also intertwined with patterns of motherhood, parenthood, and childhood. In contrast to their middle- and upper-class contemporaries, the working poor did not think of childhood as a separate stage of life in which girls and boys were free from adult burdens, nor did poor women consider mothering to be a fulltime task of supervision. They expected their children to work from an early age, to "earn their keep" or to "get a living," a view much closer to the early modern conceptions which Philippe Ariès describes in *Centuries of Childhood*.[5] Children were little adults, unable as yet to take up all the duties of their elders, but nonetheless bound to do as much as they could. To put it another way, the lives of children, like those of adults, were circumscribed by economic and familial obligations. In this context, the poor expressed their care for children differently than did the propertied classes. Raising one's children properly did not mean protecting them from the world of work; on the contrary, it involved teaching them to shoulder those heavy burdens of labor which were the common lot of their class, to be hardworking and dutiful to kin and neighbors. By the same token, laboring children gained an early autonomy from their parents, an autonomy alien to the experience of more privileged children. But there were certainly generational tensions embedded in these practices: although children learned independence within the bounds of family obligation, their self-sufficiency also led them in directions that parents could not always control. When parents sent children out to the streets, they could only partially set the terms of what the young ones learned there.

Street selling, or huckstering, was one of the most common ways for children to turn the streets to good use. Through the nineteenth century, this ancient form of trade still flourished in New York alongside such new institutions of mass marketing as A. T. Stewart's department store. Hucksters, both adults and children, sold all manner of necessities and delicacies. In the downtown business and shopping district, passers-by could buy treats at every corner: hot sweet potatoes, bake-pears, teacakes, fruit, candy, and hot corn. In residential neighborhoods, hucksters sold household supplies door to door: fruits and vegetables in season, matchsticks, scrub brushes, sponges, strings, and pins. Children assisted adult hucksters, went peddling on their own, and worked in several low-paying trades which were their special province: crossing-sweeping for girls; errandrunning, bootblacking, horseholding and newspaperselling for boys.[6] . . .

Younger children, too, could earn part of their keep on the streets. Scavenging, the art of gathering useful and salable trash, was the customary chore for those too small to go out streetselling. Not all scavengers were children; there were also adults who engaged in scavenging full-time, ragpickers who made their entire livelihoods from "all the odds and ends of a great city."[7] More generally, however, scavenging was children's work. Six- or seven-year-olds were not too young to set out with friends and siblings to gather fuel for their mothers. Small platoons of these children scoured neighborhood streets, ship and lumber yards, building lots, demolished houses, and the precincts of artisan shops and factories for chips, ashes, wood, and coal to take home or peddle to neighbors. . . .

The economy of rubbish was intricate. As children grew more skilled, they learned how to turn up other serviceable cast-offs. "These gatherers of things lost on earth," a journal had called them in 1831. "These makers of something out of nothing."[8] Besides taking trash home or selling it to neighbors, children could peddle it to junk dealers, who in turn vended it to manufacturers and artisans for use in industrial processes. Rags, old rope, metal, nails, bottles, paper, kitchen grease, bones, spoiled vegetables, and bad meat all had their place in this commercial network. The waterfront was especially fruitful territory: there, children foraged for loot which had washed up on the banks, snagged in piers, or spilled out on the docks. . . . Old rope was shredded and sold as oakum, a fiber used to caulk ships. Whole pieces of hardware—nails, cogs, and screws—could be resold: broken bits went to iron- and brass-founders and coopersmiths to be melted down; bottles and bits of broken glass, to glassmakers.[9] . . . The waterfront also yielded trash which could be used at home rather than vended: tea, coffee, sugar, and flour spilled from sacks and barrels, and from the wagons which carried cargo to nearby warehouses.[10]

By the 1850s, huckstering and scavenging were the only means by which increasing numbers of children could earn their keep. A decline in boys' positions as artisans' apprentices and girls' positions as domestic servants meant that the streets became the most accessible employer of children. Through the 1840s, many artisan masters entirely rearranged work in their shops to take advantage of a labor market glutted with impoverished adults, and to survive within the increasingly cutthroat exigencies of New York commerce and manufacturing. As a result, apprenticeship in many trades had disappeared by 1850. Where it did survive, the old perquisites, steady work and room and board, were often gone: boys' work, like that of the adults they served, was irregular and intermittent.[11]

There were analogous changes in domestic service. Until the 1840s, girls of the laboring classes had easily found work as servants, but in that decade, older female immigrants, whom employers preferred for their superior strength, crowded them out of those positions. By the early 1850s, domestic service was work for Irish and German teenagers and young women. In other industrial centers, towns like Manchester and Lowell, children moved from older employments into the factories; New York, however, because of high ground rents and the absence of sufficient water power, lacked the large establishments which gave work to the young in other cities.[12] Consequently, children and adolescents, who two generations earlier would have worked in more constrained situations, now flooded the streets.

The growth of the street trades meant that increasing numbers of children worked on their own, away from adult supervision. This situation magnified the opportunities for illicit gain, the centuries-old pilfering and finagling of apprentices and serving-girls. When respectable parents sent their children out to scavenge and peddle, the consequences were not always what they intended: these trades were an avenue to theft and prostitution as well as to an honest living. Child peddlers habituated household entryways, with their hats and umbrellas and odd knickknacks, and roamed by shops where goods were often still, in the old fashion, displayed outside on the sidewalks.[13] And scavenging was only one step removed from petty theft. The distinction between gathering spilled flour and spilling flour oneself was one which small scavengers did not always observe. Indeed, children skilled in detecting value in random objects strewn about the streets, the seemingly inconsequential, could as easily spot value in other people's property. . . . Thefts against persons, pickpocketing and mugging, belonged to another province, that of the professional child criminal.

Not all parents were concerned about their children's breaches of the law. Reformers were not always wrong when they charged that by sending children to the streets, laboring-class parents implicitly encouraged them to a life of crime. The unrespectable poor did not care to discriminate between stolen and scavenged goods, and the destitute could not afford to. . . .

As scavenging shaded into theft, so it also edged into another street trade, prostitution. The same art of creating commodities underlay both. In the intricate economy of the streets, old rope, stray coal, rags, and sex all held the promise of cash, a promise apparent to children who from an early age learned to be "makers of something out of nothing." For girls who knew how to turn things with no value into things with exchange value, the prostitute's act of bartering sex into money would have perhaps seemed daunting, but nonetheless comprehensible. These were not professional child prostitutes; rather, they turned to the lively trade in casual prostitution on occasion or at intervals to supplement other earnings. One encounter with a gentleman, easy to come by in the hotel and business district, could bring the equivalent of a month's wages in domestic service, a week's wages seamstressing, or several weeks' earnings huckstering. Such windfalls went to pay a girl's way at home or, more typically, to purchase covertly some luxury—pastries, a bonnet, cheap jewelry, a fancy gown—otherwise out of her reach.

Prostitution was quite public in antebellum New York. It was not yet a statutory offense, and although the police harassed streetwalkers and arrested them for vagrancy, they had little effect on the trade. Consequently, offers from men and inducements from other girls were common on the streets, and often came a girl's way when she was out working. This is the reason a German father tried to prevent his fourteen-year-old daughter from going out scavenging when she lost her place in domestic service. "He said, 'I don't want you to be a rag-picker. You are not a child now—people will look at you—you will come to harm,'" as the girl recounted the tale.[14] The "harm" he feared was the course taken by a teenage habitue of the waterfront in whom William Bell, police inspector of second-hand shops, took a special interest in 1851. After she rejected his offer of a place in service, he learned from a junk shop proprietor that, along with scavenging around the docks, she was "in the habit of going aboard the Coal Boats in that vicinity and prostituting herself."[15] Charles Loring Brace, founder of the CAS, claimed that "the life of a swill-gatherer, or coal-picker, or chiffonier [ragpicker] in the streets soon wears off a girl's modesty and prepares her for worse occupation," while Police Chief George Matsell accused huckster-girls of soliciting the clerks and employees they met on their rounds of counting houses.[16]

While not all girls in the street trades were as open to advances as Brace and Matsell implied, their habituation to male advances must have contributed to the brazenness with which some of them could engage in sexual bartering. Groups of girls roamed about the city, sometimes on chores and errands, sometimes only with an eye for flirtations, or being "impudent and saucy to men," as the parents of one offender put it.[17] In the early 1830s, John R. McDowall, leader of the militant Magdalen Society, had observed on fashionable Broadway "females of thirteen and fourteen walking the streets without a protector, until some pretended gentleman gives them a nod, and takes their arm and escorts them to houses of assignation."[18] McDowall was sure to exaggerate, but later witnesses lent credence to his description. In 1854, a journalist saw nearly fifty girls soliciting one evening as he walked a mile up Broadway, while diarist George Templeton Strong referred to juvenile prostitution as a permanent feature of the promenade in the early 1850s: "no one can walk the length of Broadway without meeting some hideous troop of ragged girls."[19] But despite the entrepreneurial attitude with which young girls ventured into prostitution, theirs was a grim choice, with hazards which, young as they were, they could not always foresee. Nowhere can we see more clearly the complexities of poor children's lives in the public city. The life of the streets taught them self-reliance and the arts of survival, but this education could also be a bitter one.

The autonomy and independence which the streets fostered through petty crime also extended to living arrangements. Abandoned children, orphans, runaways, and particularly independent boys made the streets their home: sleeping out with companions in household areas, wagons, marketplace stalls, and saloons. In June 1850, the *Tribune* noted that the police regularly scared up thirty or forty boys sleeping along Nassau and Ann streets; they included boys with homes as well as genuine vagabonds.[20] . . .

Reformers like Matsell and the members of the CAS tended to see such children as either orphaned or abandoned, symbols of the misery and depravity of the poor. Their perception, incarnated by writers like Horatio Alger in the fictional waifs of sentimental novels, gained wide credibility in nineteenth-century social theory and popular thought. Street children were essentially "friendless and homeless," declared Brace. "No one cares for them, and they care for no one."[21] His judgment, if characteristically harsh, was not without truth. If children without parents had no kin or friendly neighbors to whom to turn, they were left to fend for themselves. . . . But the testimony garnered by reformers about the "friendless and homeless" young should also be taken with a grain of salt. The CAS, a major source of these tales, was most sympathetic to children who appeared before the agents as victims of orphanage, desertion, of familial cruelty; accordingly, young applicants for aid sometimes presented themselves in ways which would gain them the most favor from philanthropists. . . .

Not surprisingly, orphanage among the poor was a far more complex matter than reformers perceived. As Carol Groneman has shown, poor families did not disintegrate under the most severe difficulties of immigration and urbanization.[22] In the worst New York slums, families managed to keep together and to take in those kin and friends who lacked households of their own. Orphaned children as well as those who were temporarily parentless— whose parents, for instance, had found employment elsewhere—typically found homes with older siblings, grandparents, and aunts. The solidarity of the laboring-class family, however, was not as idyllic as it might seem in retrospect. Interdependence also bred tensions which weighed heavily on children, and in response, the young sometimes chose—or were forced— to strike out on their own. Step-relations, so common in this period, were a particular source of bad feelings. . . . If natural parents died, step-parents might be particularly forceful about sending children "on their own hook." . . .

Moreover, the difficulties for all, children and adults, of finding work in these years of endemic underemployment created a kind of half-way orphanage. Parents emigrating from New York could place their boys in apprenticeships which subsequently collapsed and cast the children on their own for a living. . . . Similarly, adolescents whose parents had left them in unpleasant or intolerable situations simply struck out on their own. . . . Thus a variety of circumstances could be concealed in the category of the street "orphan."

All these customs of childhood and work among the laboring poor were reasons for the presence of children, girls and boys, in the public life of the city, a presence which reformers passionately denounced. Children and parents alike had their uses for the streets. For adults, the streets allowed their dependents to contribute to their keep, crucial to making ends meet in the houeshold economy. For girls and boys, street life provided a way to meet deeply ingrained family obligations. This is not to romanticize their lives. If the streets provided a way to meet responsibilities, it was a hard and bitter, even a cruel one. Still, children of the laboring classes lived and labored in a complex geography, which reformers of the poor perceived only as a stark tableau of pathology and vice.

To what degree did their judgments of children redound on women? Although reformers included both sexes in their indictments, women were by implication more involved. First, poverty was especially likely to afflict women.[23] To be the widow, deserted wife, or orphaned daughter of a laboring man, even a prosperous artisan, was to be poor; female self-support was synonymous with indigence. The number of self-supporting women, including those with children, was high in midcentury New York: in the 1855 census report for two neighborhoods, nearly 60 percent of six hundred working women sampled had no adult male in the household. New York's largest charity reported in 1858 that it aided 27 percent more women than men.[24] For women in such straits, children's contributions to the family income were mandatory. As a New York magistrate had written in 1830: "of the children brought before me for pilfering, nine out of ten are those whose fathers are dead, and who live with their mothers."[25] Second, women were more responsible than men for children, both from the perspective of reformers and within the reality of the laboring family. Mothering, as the middle class saw it, was an expression of female identity, rather than a construction derived from present and past social conditions. Thus the supposedly neglectful ways of laboring mothers reflected badly not only on their character as parents, but also on their very identity as women. When not depicted as timid or victimized, poor women appeared as unsavory characters in the annals of reformers: drunken, abusive, or, in one of the most memorable descriptions, "sickly-looking, deformed by over work . . . weak and sad-faced."[26] Like prostitutes, mothers of street children became a kind of half-sex in the eyes of reformers, outside the bounds of humanity by virtue of their inability or unwillingness to replicate the innate abilities of true womanhood.

REFORMERS AND FAMILY LIFE

In the 1850s, the street activities of the poor, especially those of children, became the focus of a distinct reform politics in New York. The campaign against the streets, one element in a general cultural offensive against the laboring classes which evangelical groups had carried on since the 1830s, was opened in 1849 by Police Chief Matsell's report to the public on juvenile delinquency. In the most hyperbolic rhetoric, he described a "deplorable and growing evil" spreading through the streets. "I allude to the constantly increasing number of vagrants, idle and vicious children of both sexes, who infest our public thoroughfares."[27] Besides alerting New York's already existing charities to the presence of the dangerous classes, Matsell's exposé affected a young Yale seminarian, Charles Loring Brace, just returned from a European tour and immersed in his new vocation of city missionary. Matsell's alarmed observations coalesced with what Brace had learned from his own experiences working with

boys in the city mission. Moved to act, Brace in 1853 founded the CAS, a charity which concerned itself with all poor children, but especially with street "orphans." Throughout the 1850s, the CAS carried on the work Matsell had begun, documenting and publicizing the plight of street children.[28] In large measure because of its efforts, the "evil" of the streets became a central element in the reform analysis of poverty and a focus of broad concern in New York.

Matsell, Brace, and the New York philanthropists with whom they associated formed—like their peers in other Northeastern cities—a closely connected network of secular and moral reformers. By and large, these women and men were not born into New York's elite, as were those of the generation who founded the city's philanthropic movement in the first decades of the century. Rather, they were part of an emerging middle class, typically outsiders to the ruling class, either by birthplace or social status.[29] Although much of the ideology which influenced reformers' dealings with the poor is well known, scholars have generally not explored the extent to which their interactions with the laboring classes were shaped by developing ideas of gentility: ideas, in turn, based upon conceptions of domestic life. Through their attempts to recast working-class life within these conceptions, this still-inchoate class sharpened its own vision of urban culture and its ideology of class relations. Unlike philanthropists in the early nineteenth century, who partook of an older attitude of tolerance to the poor and of the providential inevitability of poverty, mid-Victorians were optimistic that poverty could be abolished by altering the character of their almoners as workers, citizens, and family members. The reformers of the streets were directly concerned with the latter. In their efforts to teach the working poor the virtues of the middle-class home as a means of self-help, they laid the ideological and programmatic groundwork for a sustained intervention in working-class family life.

What explains the sudden alarm about the streets at midcentury? The emergence of street life as a target of organized reform was partly due to the massive immigrations of those years, which created crises of housing, unemployment, and crime. The influx of Irish and German immigrants in the 1840s greatly increased the presence of the poor in public areas. Thousands of those who arrived after 1846 wandered through the streets looking for housing, kin, work, or, at the least, a spot to shelter them from the elements. A news item from 1850 reported a common occurrence.

> Six poor women with their children, were discovered Tuesday night by some police officers, sleeping in the alleyway, in Avenue B, between 10th and 11th streets. When interrogated they said they had been compelled to spend their nights wherever they could obtain any shelter. They were in a starving condition, and without the slightest means of support.[30]

Indeed, severe overcrowding in the tenements meant that more of the poor strayed outside, particularly in hot weather. . . .

The existence of the new police force, organized in 1845, also aggravated the reformers' sense of crisis by broadening their notions of criminal behavior. The presence of these new agents of mediation between the poor and the propertied shed light on a milieu which theretofore had been closed to the genteel. Indeed, the popularization of the idea of the dangerous classes after 1850 was partly due to publicized police reports and to accounts written by journalists who accompanied the police on their rounds. The "vicious" activities of the laboring classes were elaborated in such reports as Matsell's, published in pamphlet form for philanthropic consumption, and novelists' and journalists' exposés like those of Ned Buntline and Charles Dickens's description of Five Points in his *American Notes.*

The police also seem to have enforced prohibitions on street life with their own definitions of juvenile crime. Because conceptions of vagrancy depended on whether the police considered the child's presence in the streets to be legitimate, it is possible that some of the high number of juvenile commitments—about two thousand a year[31]—can be attributed to conflicting notions of the proper sphere of children. Brace was struck by the drama of children, police, and mothers in Corlear's Hook (now the Lower East Side). The streets teemed with

> wild ragged little girls who were flitting about . . . some with baskets and poker gathering rags, some apparently seeking chances of stealing. . . . The police were constantly arresting them as "vagrants," when the mothers would beg them off from the good-natured justices, and promise to train them better in the future.[32]

As for petty larceny, that at least some of the arrests were due to an ambiguity about what constituted private property was testified to by one New York journalist. The city jail, he wrote, was filled, along with other malefactors, "with young boys and girls who have been caught asleep on cellar doors or are suspected of the horrible crime of stealing junk bottles and old iron!"[33] As children's presence in the public realm became inherently criminal, so did the gleaning of its resources. The distinction between things belonging to no one and things belonging to someone blurred in the minds of propertied adults as well as propertyless children.

There were, then, greater numbers of children in the New York streets after 1845, and their activities were publicized as never before. Faced with an unprecedented crisis of poverty in the city, reformers fastened on their presence as a cause rather than a symptom of impoverishment. The reformers' idea that the curse of poor children lay in the child-rearing methods of their parents moved toward the center of their analysis of the etiology of poverty, replacing older notions of divine will.[34] In the web of images of blight and disease which not only reflected but also shaped the midcentury understanding of poverty, the tenement house was the "parent of constant disorders, and the nursery of increasing vices," but real parents were the actual agents of crime.[35] In opposition to the ever more articulate and pressing claims of New York's organized working men, this first generation of "experts" on urban poverty averred that familial relations rather than industrial capitalism were responsible for the misery which any clear-headed New Yorker could see was no transient state of affairs. One of the principal pieces of evidence of "the ungoverned appetites, bad habits, and vices"[36] of laboring-class parents was the fact that they sent their offspring out to the streets to earn their keep.

The importance of domesticity to the reformers' own class identity fostered this shift of attention from individual moral shortcomings to the family structure of a class. For these middle-class city dwellers, the home was not simply a place of residence; it was a focus of social life and a central element of class-consciousness, based on specific conceptions of femininity and childrearing. There, secluded from the stress of public life, women could devote themselves to directing the moral and ethical development of their families. There, protected from the evils of the outside world, the young could live out their childhoods in innocence, freed from the necessity of labor, cultivating their moral and intellectual faculties.[37]

From this vantage point, the laboring classes appeared gravely deficient. When charity visitors, often ladies themselves, entered the households of working people, they saw a domestic sparseness which contradicted their deepest beliefs about what constituted a morally sustaining family life.[38] "[Their] ideas of domestic comfort and standard of morals, are far below our own," wrote the Association for Improving the Condition of the Poor (AICP).[39] The urban poor had intricately interwoven family lives, but they had no *homes*. Middle-class people valued family privacy and intimacy: among the poor, they saw a promiscuous sociability, an "almost fabulous gregariousness."[40] They believed that the moral training of children depended on protecting them within the home; in poor neighborhoods, they saw children encouraged to labor in the streets. The harshness and intolerance with which midcentury reformers viewed the laboring classes can be partly explained by the disparity between these two ways of family life. . . . The AICP scoffed at even using the word: "Homes . . . if it is not a mockery to give that hallowed name to the dark, filthy hovels where many of them dwell."[41] To these middle-class women and men, the absence of home life was not simply due to the uncongenial physical circumstances of the tenements, nor did it indicate the poor depended upon another way of organizing their family lives. Rather, the homelessness of this "multitude of half-naked, dirty, and leering children"[42] signified an absence of parental love, a neglect of proper childrearing which was entwined in the habits and values of the laboring classes.

THE CHILDREN'S AID SOCIETY

Although Brace shared the alarm and revulsion of reformers like Matsell at the "homelessness" of the poor, he also brought to the situation an optimistic liberalism, based upon his own curious and ambiguous uses of domesticity. In his memoirs of 1872, looking back on two decades of work with the New York laboring classes, Brace took heart from the observation that the absence of family life so deplored by his contemporaries actually operated to stabilize American society. Immigration and continual mobility disrupted the process by which one generation of laboring people taught the next a cultural identity, "that continuity of influence which bad parents and grandparents exert." . . . "The mill of American life, which grinds up so many delicate and fragile things, has its uses, when it is turned on the vicious fragments of the lower strata of society."[43]

It was through the famed placing-out system that the CAS turned the "mill of American life" to the uses of urban reform. The placing-out program sent poor city children to foster homes in rural areas where labor was scarce. With the wages-fund theory, a common Anglo-American liberal reform scheme of midcentury which proposed to solve the problem of metropolitan unemployment by dispersing the surplus of labor, the society defended itself against critics' charges that "foster parents" were simply farmers in need of cheap help, and placing-out, a cover for the exploitation of child labor.[44] At first, children went to farms in the nearby countryside, as did those the city bound out from the Almshouse, but in 1854 the society conceived the more ambitious scheme of sending parties of children by railroads to the far Midwest: Illinois, Michigan, and Iowa. By 1860, 5,074 children had been placed out.[45]

At its most extreme, the CAS only parenthetically recognized the social and legal claims of working-class parenthood. The organization considered the separation of parents and children a positive good, the liberation of innocent, if tarnished, children from the tyranny of unredeemable adults. Here, as in so many aspects of nineteenth-century reform, the legacy of the Enlightenment was ambiguous: the idea of childhood innocence it had bequeathed, socially liberating in many respects, also provided one element of the ideology of middle-class domination.[46] Since the CAS viewed children as innocents to be rescued and parents as

corrupters to be displaced, its methods depended in large measure on convincing children themselves to leave New York, with or without parental knowledge or acquiescence. Street children were malleable innocents in the eyes of the charity, but they were also little consenting adults, capable of breaking all ties to their class milieu and families. To be sure, many parents did bring their children to be placed-out, but nonetheless, the society also seems to have worked directly through the children.[47] . . .

Placing-out was based on the thoroughly middle-class idea of the redeeming influence of the Protestant home in the countryside.[48] There, the morally strengthening effects of labor, mixed with the salutary influences of domesticity and female supervision, could remold the child's character. Thus domestic ideology gave liberals like Brace the theoretical basis for constructing a program to resocialize the poor in which force was unnecessary. Standards of desirable behavior could be internalized by children rather than beaten into them, as had been the eighteenth-century practice. With home influence, not only childrearing but the resocialization of a class could take the form of subliminal persuasion rather than conscious coercion.[49]

Earlier New York reformers had taken a different tack with troublesome children. In 1824, the Society for the Reformation of Juvenile Delinquents had established an asylum, the House of Refuge, to deal with juvenile offenders. As in all the new institutions for deviants, solitary confinement and corporal punishment were used to force the recalcitrant into compliance with the forces of reason.[50] But Brace thought the asylum, so prized by his predecessors, was impractical and ineffectual. Asylums could not possibly hold enough children to remedy the problem of the New York streets in the 1850s; moreover, the crowding together of the children who were incarcerated only reinforced the hab-

its of their class.[51] The foster home, however, with its all-encompassing moral influence, could be a more effective house of
refuge. "We have wished to make every
kind of religious family, who desired the
responsibility, an Asylum or a Reforma-
tory Institution . . . by throwing about
the wild, neglected little outcast of the
streets, the love and gentleness of home.[52]
The home was an asylum, but it was
woman's influence rather than an institutional regimen that accomplished its cor-
rections.

This is an overview of the work of the
CAS, but on closer examination, there was
also a division by sex in the organization,
and domesticity played different roles in
the girls' and boys' programs. The emigrants to the West seem to have been
mostly boys: they seem to have been more
allured by emigration than were girls, and
parents were less resistant to placing out
sons than daughters. "Even as a beggar
or pilferer, a little girl is of vastly more
use to a wretched mother than her son,"
the society commented. "The wages of a
young girl are much more sure to go to
the pockets of the family than those of a
boy."[53] Brace's own imagination was more
caught up with boys than girls; his most
inventive efforts were directed at them.
Unlike most of his contemporaries, he appreciated the vitality and tenacity of the
street boys; his fascination with the Western scheme came partly from the hope
that emigration would redirect their tough-
ness and resourcefulness, "their sturdy independence,"[54] into hearty frontier individualism.[55] Similarly, the agents over-
seeing the foster home program were men,
as were the staff members of the society's
much-touted Newsboys' Lodging-House,
a boardinghouse where, for a few pennies,
news boys could sleep and eat. The
Lodging-House, was, in fact, a kind of
early boys' camp, where athletics and
physical fitness, lessons in entrepreneur-
ship (one of its salient features was a savings bank), and moral education knit poor

boys and gentlemen into a high-spirited
but respectable masculine camaraderie.[56]

Women were less visible in the society's literature, their work less well-
advertised, since it was separate from
Brace's most innovative programs. The
women of the CAS were not paid agents
like the men, but volunteers who staffed
the girls' programs: a Lodging-House and
several industrial schools. The work of
the women reformers was, moreover, less
novel than that of the men. Rather than
encouraging girls to break away from
their families, the ladies sought the opposite: to create among the urban laboring
classes a domestic life of their own. They
aimed to mold future wives and mothers
of a reformed working class: women who
would be imbued with a belief in the importance of domesticity and capable of
patterning their homes and family lives
on middle-class standards.

Yet it was this strategy of change,
rather than Brace's policy of fragmentation, which would eventually dominate attempts to reform working-class children.
The ladies envisioned homes which would
reorganize the promiscuously sociable lives
of the poor under the aegis of a new,
"womanly" working-class woman. In the
CAS industrial schools and Lodging-
House, girls recruited off the streets
learned the arts of plain sewing, cooking,
and housecleaning, guided by the precept
celebrated by champions of women's domestic mission that "nothing was so honorable as industrious *house-work*."[57] These
were skills which both prepared them for
waged employment in seamstressing and
domestic service and outfitted them for
homes of their own: as the ladies proudly
attested after several years of work, their
students entered respectable married life
as well as honest employment. "Living in
homes reformed through their influence,"[58]
the married women carried on their female mission, reformers by proxy.

Similarly, the women reformers instituted meetings to convert the mothers of

their students to a new relationship to household and children. Classes taught the importance of sobriety, neat appearance, and sanitary housekeeping: the material basis for virtuous motherhood and a proper home. Most important, the ladies stressed the importance of keeping children off the streets and sending them to school. Here, they found their pupils particularly recalcitrant. Mothers persisted in keeping children home to work and cited economic reasons when their benefactresses upbraided them. The CAS women, however, considered the economic rationale a pretense for the exploitation of children and the neglect of their moral character. "The larger ones were needed to 'mind' the baby," lady volunteers sardonically reported, "or go out begging for clothes . . . and the little ones, scarcely bigger than the baskets on their arms, must be sent out for food, or chips, or cinders."[59] The Mothers' Meetings, tried, however unsuccessfully, to wean away laboring women from such customary practices to what the ladies believed to be a more nurturant and moral mode of family life: men at work, women at home, children inside.

In contrast to the male reformers, the women of the society tried to create an intensified private life within New York itself, to enclose children within tenements and schools rather than to send them away or incarcerate them in asylums. There is a new, optimistic vision of city life implied in their work. With the establishment of the home across class lines, a renewed city could emerge, its streets free for trade and respectable promenades, and emancipated from the inconveniences of pickpockets and thieves, the affronts of prostitutes and hucksters, the myriad offenses of working-class mores and poverty. The "respectable" would control and dominate public space as they had never before. The city would itself become an asylum on a grand scale, an environment which embodied the

eighteenth-century virtues of reason and progress, the nineteenth-century virtues of industry and domesticity. And as would befit a city for the middle class, boundaries between public and private life would be clear: the public space of the metropolis would be the precinct of men, the private space of the home, that of women and children.

In the work of the CAS female volunteers lie the roots of the Americanization campaign which, half a century later, reshaped the lives of so many working-class immigrants. The settlement houses of turn-of-the-century New York would expand the mothers' classes and girls' housekeeping lessons into a vast program of nativist assimilation. Female settlement workers would assure immigrant mothers and daughters that the key to decent lives lay in creating American homes within the immigrant ghettoes: homes that were built on a particular middle-class configuration of possessions and housekeeping practices and a particular structure of family relations. And, as in the 1850s, the effort to domesticate the plebeian household would be linked to a campaign to clear the streets of an ubiquitous, aggressive, and assertive working-class culture.

Neither the clearing of the streets nor the making of the working-class home were accomplished at any one point in time. Indeed, these conflicts still break out in Manhattan's poor and working-class neighborhoods. Today, in the Hispanic *barrios* of the Upper West and Lower East sides and in black Harlem, scavenging and street huckstering still flourish. In prosperous quarters as well, where affluent customers are there for the shrewd, the battle continues between police on the one hand, hucksters and prostitutes on the other. Indeed, the struggle over the streets has been so ubiquitous in New York and other cities in the last 150 years that we can see it as a structural element of urban life in industrial capitalist societies. As high unemployment and casualized work have persisted in the great cities, the streets have continued to contain some of the few resources for the poor to make ends meet. At the same time, the social imagination of the poor, intensified by urban life, has worked to increase those resources. All the quick scams—the skills of the con men, street musicians, beggars, prostitutes, peddlers, drug dealers, and pickpockets—are arts of the urban working poor, bred from ethnic and class traditions and the necessities of poverty.

Neither is the conflict today, however, identical to the one which emerged in the 1850s. The struggle over the streets in modern New York takes place in a far different context, one defined by past victories of reformers and municipal authorities. Vagrancy counts against children are now strengthened by compulsory school legislation; child labor laws prohibit most kinds of child huckstering; anti-peddling laws threaten heavy fines for the unwary. Most important, perhaps, the mechanisms for "placing out" wandering children away from "negligent" mothers are all in place (although the wholesale breakdown of social services in New York has made these provisions increasingly ineffectual, creating a new problem in its wake). The street life of the working poor survives in pockets, but immeasurably weakened, continually under duress.

In more and more New York neighborhoods, the rich and the middle class can walk untroubled by importunate prosti-tutes, beggars, and hucksters. The women gossiping on front stoops, the mothers shouting orders from upstairs windows, and the housewife habitués of neighborhood taverns have similarly disappeared, shut away behind heavily locked doors with their children and television sets. New York increasingly becomes a city where a variant of the nineteenth-century bourgeois vision of respectable urban life is realized. "No LOITERING/PLAYING BALL/ SITTING/PLAYING MUSIC ON SIDEWALKS IN FRONT OF BUILDINGS," placards on the great middle-class apartment houses warn potential lingerers. The sidewalks are, indeed, often free of people, except for passers-by and the doormen paid to guard them. But as Jane Jacobs predicted so forcefully two decades ago, streets cleared for the respectable have become free fields for predators. The inhabitants of modern-day New York, particularly women and children, live in a climate of urban violence and fear historically unprecedented save in wartime. In the destruction of the street life of the laboring poor, a critical means of creating urban communities and organizing urban space has disappeared. As the streets are emptied of laboring women and children, as the working-class home has become an ideal, if not a reality, for ever-widening sectors of the population, the city of middle-class hopes becomes ever more bereft of those ways of public life which once mitigated the effects of urban capitalism.

NOTES

Many colleagues commented on drafts of this essay. My thanks especially to the participants in the Bard College Faculty Seminar at which the paper was originally presented, and to my friends Ellen Ross, Judith Walkowitz, and Sean Wilentz.

1. Children's Aid Society (hereafter referred to as CAS), *Third Annual Report* (New York, 1856), pp. 26–27.

2. Virginia Penny, *The Employments of Women* (Boston, 1863), p. 317.

3. For the class character of the New York reformers, see Carroll Smith-Rosenberg, *Religion and the Rise of the American City: The New York City Mission Movement, 1812–1870* (Ithaca, N.Y.: Cornell University Press, 1971), p. 6. For a more recent and ambitious analysis of the class base of the evangelical reform movement, see Mary Ryan, *Cradle of the Middle Class* (Cambridge: Cambridge University Press, 1981).

4. The literature on antebellum reform is voluminous. Two of the most helpful books

specifically treating New York are Thomas Bender, *Toward an Urban Vision: Ideas and Institutions in Nineteenth-Century America* (Lexington, Ky.: University Press of Kentucky, 1975); and Paul Boyer, *Urban Masses and Moral Order in America, 1820–1920* (Cambridge, Mass.: Harvard University Press, 1978).

5. Philippe Ariès, *Centuries of Childhood: A Social History of Family Life* (New York: Random House, 1965).

6. Penny, *Employments of Women*, pp. 133–34, 143–44, 150–52, 168, 421, 473, 484; William Burns, *Life in New York: In Doors and Out of Doors* (New York, 1851); Phillip Wallys, *About New York: An Account of What a Boy Saw on a Visit to the City* (New York, 1857), p. 50; CAS, *First Annual Report* (1854), pp. 23–24, *Seventh Annual Report* (1860), p. 16.

7. Charles L. Brace, *The Dangerous Classes of New York and Twenty Years' Work among Them* (New York, 1872), pp. 152–53.

8. *New York Mirror* 9 (1831):119, quoted in the I.N.P. Stokes Collection, New York Public Library, New York, p. 461.

9. Brace, *Dangerous Classes*, pp. 152–53; Penny, *Employments of Women*, pp. 122, 435, 444, 467, 484–85; Solon Robinson, *Hot Corn: Life Scenes in New York Illustrated* (New York, 1854), p. 207; CAS, *Second Annual Report* (1855), p. 36. See also Sean Wilentz, "Crime, Poverty and the Streets of New York City: The Diary of William H. Bell 1850–51," *History Workshop* 7 (Spring 1979):126–55.

10. See also *New York Daily Tribune*, 16 March 1850.

11. Sean Wilentz, *Chants Democratic: New York City and the Rise of the American Working Class* (New York: Oxford University Press, 1983). In this respect as in many others, I am deeply indebted to Wilentz for my understanding of New York history.

12. Victor S. Clark, *History of Manufactures in the United States*, 3 vols. (New York: McGraw-Hill Book Company, 1929), 1:351. For the lack of children's factory employment, see CAS, *Seventh Annual Report* (1860), p. 7.

13. The aggressive character of juveniles on the streets and the prevalence of juvenile petty theft are discussed in David R. Johnson, "Crime Patterns in Philadelphia, 1840–70," in *The Peoples of Philadelphia: A History of Ethnic Groups and Lower Class Life, 1790–1940*, ed. Allen F. Davis and Mark H. Haller (Philadelphia, 1973).

14. Brace, *Dangerous Classes*, p. 120.

15. Bell Diary, 10 June 1851, in Wilentz, "Crime, Poverty, and the Streets of New York City," p. 147.

16. Brace, *Dangerous Classes*, p. 154; "Semi-Annual Report of the Chief of Police," *Documents of the Board of Aldermen*, vol. 17, part 1 (1850), p. 63.

17. House of Refuge Papers, Case Histories, New York State Library, Albany, vol. 1, case no. 61.

18. John R. McDowall, *Magdalen Facts* (New York, 1832), p. 53.

19. Allan Nevins and Milton Halsey Thomas, eds., *The Diary of George Templeton Strong*, 2 vols. (New York: The Macmillan Company, 1952), 2:57 (entry for 7 July 1851).

20. *New York Daily Tribune*, 3 June 1850.

21. Brace, *Dangerous Classes*, p. 91.

22. Carol Groneman (Pernicone), "The 'Bloudy Ould Sixth': A Social Analysis of a New York City Working-Class Community in the Mid-Nineteenth Century" (Ph.D. dissertation, University of Rochester, 1973).

23. See my essay "Origins of the Sweatshop," in *Working-Class America: Essays in the New Labor History*, ed. Michael Frish and Daniel Walkowitz (Urbana: University of Illinois Press, 1982), for an extended treatment of this point.

24. New York State Census, 1855, Population Schedules, Ward 4, Electoral district 2, and Ward 17, Electoral district 3, MSS at County Clerk's Office, New York City; Association for Improving the Condition of the Poor, *Fifteenth Annual Report* (New York, 1858), p. 38.

25. Letter reprinted in Mathew Carey, "Essays on the Public Charities of Philadelphia," *Miscellaneous Essays* (Philadelphia, 1830), p. 161.

26. CAS, *Third Annual Report* (1856), p. 27.

27. "Semi-Annual Report," p. 58.

28. Miriam Z. Langsam, *Children West: A History of the Placing-Out System in the New York Children's Aid Society* (Madison, Wis., 1964).

29. Boyer, *Urban Masses*, stresses the role of charity work in providing status and fellowship for newcomers to the city. Brace was from a family of declining Connecticut gentry; Matsell was born into an artisan family, became a dyer by trade, and rose to prominence and fortune in the city through Tammany Hall politics. See Emma Brace, ed., *The Life of Charles Loring Brace . . . Edited by His Daughter* (New York, 1894); "George W. Matsell," *Palimpsest* 5 (July 1924):237–48.

30. *New York Daily Tribune*, 4 July 1850.

31. From "Reports of Commitments to First District Prison published in Commissioners of the Almshouse," *Annual Reports* (1850–60).

32. Brace, *Dangerous Classes*, p. 145.

33. George C. Foster, *New York in Slices; By an Experienced Carver* (New York, 1849), p. 20.

34. Smith-Rosenberg, *Religion and the Rise of the American City*, pp. 3, 29.

35. New York Assembly, *Report of the Select Committee Appointed to Examine into the Condition of Tenant Houses in New-York and Brooklyn*, Assembly doc. 205, 80th sess., 1857, p. 12.

36. CAS, *Third Annual Report* (1856), p. 29.

37. The best works on nineteenth-century domesticity are Nancy F. Cott, *The Bonds of Womanhood: 'Woman's Sphere' in New England, 1780–1835* (New Haven: Yale University Press, 1977); Ann Douglas, *The Feminization of American Culture* (New York: Avon, 1978); Kathryn Kish Sklar, *Catharine Beecher: A Study in American Domesticity* (New Haven: Yale University Press, 1973).

38. Here I strongly disagree with the view of the sisterly relations between women charity workers and their almoners presented in Barbara Berg, *The Remembered Gate: Origins of American Feminism—the Women and the City, 1800–1860* (New York: Oxford University Press, 1975).

39. Association for Improving the Condition of the Poor, *Thirteenth Annual Report* (1856), p. 23.

40. New York Assembly, *Report of the Select Committee*, p. 20.

41. Association for Improving the Condition of the Poor, *Fourteenth Annual Report* (1857), p. 21.

42. CAS, *Third Annual Report* (1856), p. 4.

43. Brace, *Dangerous Classes*, pp. 46–47.

44. CAS, *Sixth Annual Report* (1859), p. 9.

45. Figures are from Langsam, *Children West*, p. 64.

46. Michel Foucault has most forcefully analyzed this ambiguity. See *Madness and Civilization: A History of Insanity in the Age of Reason* (New York: Random House, 1973).

47. See the appendices in CAS, *Annual Reports* (1854–60).

48. CAS, *Third Annual Report* (1856), p. 8.

49. This is similar to the shift in criminal law from corporal punishment to the more enlightened environmental techniques of the penitentiary. See Michael Ignatieff, *A Just Measure of Pain: The Penitentiary in the Industrial Revolution, 1750–1850* (New York: Pantheon, 1978).

50. Ibid.

51. CAS, *First Annual Report* (1854), p. 7; *Second Annual Report* (1855), p. 5. See also Boyer, *Urban Masses*, pp. 94–95.

52. CAS, *Second Annual Report* (1855), p. 5.

53. CAS, *Fifth Annual Report* (1858), p. 17.

54. Brace, *Dangerous Classes*, p. 100.

55. See Boyer, *Urban Masses*, pp. 94–107; and Brace, *Dangerous Classes*, pp. 98–99.

56. Brace, *Dangerous Classes*, pp. 99–105.

57. CAS, *Ninth Annual Report* (1862), p. 13. See also *First Annual Report* (1854), pp. 7, 9.

58. CAS, *Tenth Annual Report* (1863), p. 23; *Seventh Annual Report* (1860), p. 8.

59. CAS, *Eleventh Annual Report* (1864), p. 28.

BARBARA MAYER WERTHEIMER
The Factory Bell

Traditional histories are apt to discuss industrialization in technical and economic terms, then pause for a colorful description of the Lowell mill girls. These views require refocusing. To put it simply, the textile factories of the first wave of industrialization might not have been built at all had their owners not believed they could count on a steady supply of cheap female labor. The history of industrialization as it affected both men and women needs to be understood in the context of the segmented labor market that women entered. Women formed the first new work force that was shaped into "modern" work patterns: long, uninterrupted hours of labor in a mechanized factory with little or no room for individual initiative. As the strikes at Lowell described in the following selection show, women were among the earliest workers to use modern forms of labor protest such as work stoppages, strikes, and unions.

> Despite of toil we all agree
> Or out of the mills, or in,
> Dependent on others we ne'er will be
> So long as we're able to spin.
> —"Song of the Spinners," *The Lowell
> Offering*, 1842

THE BOARDINGHOUSES

The Merrimack River races through New Hampshire and Massachusetts and tumbles over six waterfalls on its way to the sea. Each of these falls provided a site for ambitious nineteenth-century industrialists to develop what soon became New England's leading industry: textiles.

Lowell, Massachusetts, was one such site, a sleepy village of 200 farm families in 1820. By 1826, just three years after the first cloth was produced there by the Merrimack Manufacturing Company, it had mushroomed into a bustling town of 2,000. Its six textile mills employed 1,200 persons, 90 percent of them women.[1]

Who were these women and how were they recruited to millwork? Factory owners knew how angry agricultural interests would be if men were drawn away from farming, yet in the immediate vicinity of the mills the female labor supply was most inadequate. The young women they needed as workers would have to be recruited from miles away and housed "respectably" in town if family permission was to be obtained for their coming to work in the mills.

Thus it was that the boardinghouse plan, known later as the Waltham or Lowell system, evolved. Morally acceptable to farmers, since their daughters would be supervised by matrons (often widows with children to bring up), it was socially enticing to young farm women. Relishing the chance to get out on their own, they flocked to the mills in response to company advertisements and recruiters. They met women with similar backgrounds from different New England towns, tasted independence, earned their own money, and enjoyed the excitement of what must have seemed "the big city." For unmarried women forced to live with relatives, millwork opened the door to self-support. Nor has anyone counted the numbers of brothers these mill women put through college, the farm mortgages they helped to pay off, or the sweethearts they supported while they built their new homes in the West.

This is only part of the story however. Farm families could no longer count on the "putting out" system, the home weaving of yarn supplied by contractors, for extra income. Wives were still needed on the farms to raise the children and cook, but daughters could be spared for the mills, work that young women found vastly preferable to the other option open to most of them: domestic service. In any event, they viewed millwork as merely an interlude before marriage and family responsibilities. The farm was always there to come home to in case of illness, homesickness, job loss, or—as they would learn—blacklisting.

Each boardinghouse became a close-knit community, a sisterhood, for the mill women seldom were alone. They spent thirteen or more hours a day together at work, their evenings together in the boardinghouse sewing, talking, reading, and singing, and their Sundays together at church and walking by the river. This boardinghouse community became a surrogate family. If a woman did not fit into her particular rooming house, she felt the group pressure and moved. This same pressure, plus the ability to return home whenever they wished, gave these spirited young women the freedom to "turn out," or strike, against company wage cuts that

threatened their livelihood and company rules that offended their dignity.

As prices skyrocketed during the 1830s, the matrons could no longer maintain the dormitory atmosphere of the boardinghouses. The $1.25 a week they received for board and room, deducted by the company from the pay of each millworker, proved most inadequate. The mill women soon found themselves crowded six and eight to a room, often three to a bed. The quality and quantity of their food declined; after a long day in the mill, bread and gravy might be their only supper. As their anger and militancy grew, the women came to regard the housemothers as spies who reported their activities and church attendance (or nonattendance) to the company, and evicted them, on company orders, when they went on strike. The regulations that surrounded their lives in and out of the mills rankled. These rules, from one of the earliest boardinghouses, that of the Poignaud and Plant mill at Lancaster, seem typical:

Rules and Regulations to be attended to and followed by the Young Persons who come to Board in this House:

Rule first: Each one to enter the house without unnecessary noise or confusion, and hang up their bonnet, shawl, coat, etc., etc., in the entry.

Rule second: Each one to have their place at the table during meals, the two which have worked the greatest length of time in the Factory to sit on each side of the head of the table, so that all new hands will of course take their seats lower down, according to the length of time they have been here. . . .

Rule seventh: As a lamp will be lighted every night upstairs and placed in a lant-horn, it is expected that no boarder will take a light into the chambers.

Rule eighth: The doors will be closed at ten o'clock at night, winter and summer, at which time each boarder will be expected to retire to bed.

Rule ninth: Sunday being appointed by our Creator as a Day of Rest and Religious Exercises, it is expected that all boarders will have sufficient discretion as to pay suitable attention to the day, and if they cannot attend to some place of Public Worship they will keep within doors and improve their time in reading, writing, and in other valuable and harmless employment.[2]

BEHIND THE FAÇADE

The New England mills of the 1820s and 1830s usually fronted on a river, tall, imposing buildings five, six, or even seven stories high. They were also low-ceilinged, poorly lit, and badly ventilated. Overseers insisted on closed windows, often nailing them shut to preserve the humidity they thought kept the threads from breaking. Weaving rooms, unbearably hot in summer, were even more unhealthy in winter, the "lighting up" season. Then workers started up their looms before daylight and worked until after dark, their only light from whale-oil "petticoat" lamps that hung on each loom, mingling their smoky fumes with the thick cotton dust in the air.

From Hannah Borden, reported to be the best weaver of her day, comes our first account of millwork, and we begin to sense the role of the factory bell in the lives of the women. Borden had learned handloom weaving at the age of eight and was quick to adapt her skill to the early power looms of Fall River, Massachusetts, when, in 1817, she became one of its first three weavers.

The factory bell woke her at 4:00 in the morning. Taking her breakfast along, she readied her looms by 5:00, when the bell signaled the start of work. At 7:30 it announced the breakfast break, and called workers back afterward. At noon it rang the half-hour lunch period, and at 12:30 summoned them back. It dismissed them at 7:30 each evening, unless they worked overtime. When they got back to their boardinghouses at night, they were often too tired to eat. At 10:00 the bell rang for

bed and lights out. Sundays it called them to church.[3]

Early mill songs reflect the workers' resentment of the bells that ruled their lives.

> The factory bell begins to ring
> And we must all obey,
> And to our old employment go
> Or else be turned away.[4]

Later, another millworker would write:

> It was morning, and the factory bell
> Had sent forth its early call,
> And many a weary one was there,
> Within the dull factory wall.
>
> And amidst the clashing noise and din
> Of the ever beating loom,
> Stood a fair young girl with throbbing brow
> Working her way to the tomb.[5]

Poetry from mill women? Yes, indeed. Not only were the New England women from the farms literate, but many of them could trace their independent spirit directly to parents and grandparents who had fought in the Revolution. They read the protest journals of the day and followed accounts of strikes on the docks and in the cities, and of the political activities of working men's associations in their campaigns for the ten-hour day and for Andrew Jackson's election.

It was the mill women who made Lowell one of the cultural centers of its day. Many of these women, 80 to 85 percent of whom were under thirty, found the energy at the end of a long workday to organize and attend lectures, forums, and language classes, sewing groups, and literary "improvement circles." Out of one of these circles grew the Lowell Offering, the first journal ever written by and for mill women. From the start it seems to have been influenced by the considerable though quiet financial support it received from the owners, who saw in it a useful vehicle for counteracting community prejudice against millwork and for recruiting new workers. The women who wrote for the *Offering,* however, found it an outlet for their talents and a vindication of their role as millworkers; they portrayed themselves in a dignified light, and this gave status to their work.[6]

But mill life was changing. Tourists to Lowell saw only the bright red factories with their white cupolas, wide flowered lawns, and mill windows lit up prettily at night. They did not see the growing impersonality of industrialization. As absentee owners took over the mills, they left overseers in charge who had total power over their workers. Factory rules became increasingly severe. So little time was allowed for meals—one half-hour at noon for dinner—that the women raced from the hot, humid weaving rooms several blocks to their boardinghouses, gulped down their main meal of the day, and ran back to the mill in terror of being fined if they were late. In winter they dared not stop to button their coats and often ate without taking them off. This was pneumonia season; in summer, spoiled food and poor sanitation led to dysentery. Tuberculosis was with them in every season.

To combat the high turnover in the mills, overseers sought to stabilize the work force and limit worker protest. They fired women for the smallest offense, or for none at all, and imposed mill rules requiring two weeks' notice plus one year's employment at the mill to earn an honorable discharge. Workers who left without this discharge were blacklisted in every mill village. . . .

MILL WOMEN STRIKE

Inflation! Depression! No matter which, wages lagged behind prices, and factory owners sought to increase stockholder profits by cutting costs—in particular, the monthly paycheck. Throughout the late 1820s and 1830s workers struck in protest. Mill women took part in these "turnouts" from the start.

The first record we have of women turning out is that of the 202 women who joined the men in walking out of a Pawtucket, Rhode Island, mill in 1824, and held their own meetings. Women struck on their own for the first time, however, not in the New England mills, but in New York City, when the United Tailoresses formed their own union in 1825 and demanded higher wages.

Dover, New Hampshire, can lay claim to the first strike of mill women on their own. In 1828, several hundred young women shocked the community by parading with banners and flags, shooting off gunpowder, and protesting the company's attempt to enforce new factory rules. They objected to the company's locking the yard gate after the bell had rung and then charging a 12½-cent fine to open it for latecomers; forbidding any talking on the job; giving "disgraceful" discharges for undefined "debaucheries"; requiring church attendance; and specifying fourteen days' notice in order to leave the mill "honorably."[7] The fine for lateness and the threat of blacklisting for dishonorable discharge provoked the most bitterness.

Newspapers from Maine to Georgia carried the strike story. A Philadelphia journal reported that the walkout exhibited "the Yankee sex in a new and unexpected light."[8] Dover millowners advertised for several hundred "better behaved women" to replace the strikers, while some papers made sport of the women for objecting to the ban on talking during work. The strike was soon over, with nothing gained, and the women returned to the mill—minus their leaders, who undoubtedly received "disgraceful dismissals" and were blacklisted. . . .

. . . When a wage cut was announced at the Lowell mills in February 1834, the women met and laid careful plans. To avoid the blacklist, they gave the required two weeks' notice of intent to leave the mill, then trooped down to the Lowell banks en masse to withdraw their savings. The company-owned banks, unprepared for this "run," were embarrassed (as the women hoped they would be) and had to send to Boston for funds to pay the accounts. Meanwhile the company, not unexpectedly, called in the woman they spotted as the leader and fired her. As she left the mill office, she waved her calash in the air, a prearranged signal to the women watching from the windows, and out they poured, eight hundred strong, to march bravely around the town. One of the women "mounted a stump and made a flaming Mary Wollstonecraft speech on the rights of women and the iniquities of the 'monied aristocracy.'" The strikers vowed they would "have their own way, if they died for it."[9]

On Saturday, the second day of the strike, they issued a proclamation, their words such a touching mixture of ladylike dignity and revolutionary zeal that they are reprinted here in full:

> Issued by the ladies who were lately employed in the factories at Lowell to their associates, they having left their former employment in consequence of the proposed reduction in their wages from 12 to 25 per cent, to take effect on the first of March.
>
> UNION IS POWER.—Our present object is to have union and exertion, and we remain in possession of our own unquestionable rights. We circulate this paper, wishing to obtain the names of all who imbibe the spirit of our patriotic ancestors, who preferred privation to bondage and parted with all that renders life desirable—and even life itself—to produce independence for their children. The oppressing hand of avarice would enslave us, and to gain their object they very gravely tell us of the pressure of the times; this we are already sensible of and deplore it. If any are in want of assistance, the ladies will be compassionate and assist them, but we prefer to have the disposing of our charities in our own hands, and, as we are free, we would remain in possession of what kind Providence has bestowed upon us, and remain daughters of freemen still.
>
> All who patronize this effort we wish to have discontinue their labor until terms of reconciliation are made.
>
> Resolved, That we will not go back into the mills to work unless our wages are continued to us as they have been.
>
> Resolved, That none of us will go back unless they receive us all as one.
>
> Resolved, That if any have not money enough to carry them home that they shall be supplied.
>
> Let oppression shrug her shoulders,
>   And a haughty tyrant frown,
> And little upstart Ignorance
>   In mockery look down.
> Yet I value not the feeble threats
>   Of Tories in disguise,
> While the flag of Independence
>   O'er our noble nation flies.[10]

Each woman pledged to forfeit five dollars (close to a month's pay) if she went back to work before they all went back together. But the company did not stand idly by. Sunday brought church sermons against the strike by company-supported ministers, and on Monday, at a meeting which it seems likely the company arranged, a Methodist preacher exhorted the women to return in gratitude that they had jobs at all. Meanwhile the company publicized its attempts to recruit women from nearby farms to fill the jobs of those who did not return to work. This threat, combined with criticism from the local press and clergy, brought the women back at reduced wages. Only strike leaders were refused entrance. . . .

. . . the Lowell women, wiser after the disastrous strike of 1834, organized the Factory Girls' Association. By the time dissatisfaction in the mills erupted again in 1836, it had 2,500 members. This time mill women struck over an increase in their board charges. Although rising prices certainly made the increase from $1.25 a week to $1.50 necessary, and only half the increase would have come from the paychecks of the women, still it amounted to a 12.5 percent pay cut for them.

Close to 1,500 women walked out in protest. Young Harriet Hanson, only eleven at the time, recalled years later her impressions of that strike:

> I worked in a lower room where I had heard the proposed strike fully, if not vehemently, discussed; I had been an ardent listener to what was said against this attempt at "oppression" on the part of the corporation, and naturally I took sides with the strikers. When the day came on which the girls were to turn out, those in the upper rooms started first, and so many of them left that our mill was at once shut down. Then, when the girls in my room stood irresolute, uncertain what to do . . . I, who began to think they would not go out, after all their talk, became impatient, and started on ahead, saying, with childish bravado, "I don't care what you do, *I* am going to turn out, whether anyone else does or not;" and I marched out, and was followed by the others.
>
> As I looked back at the long line that followed me, I was more proud than I have ever been since at any success I may have achieved, and more proud than I shall ever be again until my own beloved State gives to its women citizens the right of suffrage.[11]

The strikers, twice as strong in number as in the turnout two years earlier, marched through the Lowell streets singing parodies of popular songs of the day. The best known, to the tune of "I Won't Be a Nun," is:

> Oh! Isn't it a pity that such a pretty girl as I
> Should be sent to the factory to pine away and die?
> Oh! I cannot be a slave,
> I will not be a slave,
> For I'm so fond of liberty
> That I cannot be a slave.[12]

Resolving that millowners would have to communicate with them through the officers of the Factory Girls' Association, and that they would accept no discrimination against strike leaders, they stated:

> As our fathers resisted unto blood the lordly avarice of the British ministry, so we, their daughters, never will wear the yoke which has been prepared for us.[13]

By the end of the month their money ran out. Evicted from their boarding-houses and with no funds, many straggled back to their jobs, although the 250 skilled weavers who went home instead caused considerable havoc to mill production for a while afterward. Strike leaders were fired, and revenge was taken even on young Harriet Hanson's mother, a widowed boardinghouse matron. "Mrs. Hanson," a factory agent told her, "you could not prevent the older girls from turning out, but your daughter is a child, and *her* you could control." Mrs. Hanson was removed from her post.[14]

Perhaps with more help the women might have held out. The National Trades' Union Convention* voted moral support, but more clearly revealed its attitude toward working women by passing resolutions that millwork was physically and morally injurious to women and that hiring them caused unnecessary competition for the men. When it proposed protective laws and equal pay for women, it declared that these would successfully restrict women's jobs, since employers would have to pay women equally and would therefore prefer to hire men. For women who remained in the work force, however, the National Trades' Union recommended that unions take them in and set up all-female locals.

Some unionists saw farther into the future. Seth Luther, New England's leading labor organizer, urged unions to admit women. "It is quite certain," he stated,

* The National Trades' Union was a loose federation of local craft unions and city trades assemblies which met in 1834 and 1835. By 1837, it seems to have vanished.

"that unless we have the female sex on our side, we cannot hope to accomplish any object we have in view."[15] Luther discovered and publicized the fact that mill women often were locked in during the day, with serious consequences when fires broke out, and that mill windows were nailed shut and ventilation nonexistent.

THE 1840s; THE FEMALE LABOR REFORM ASSOCIATION AND THE TEN-HOUR DAY

But, if I still must wend my way,
Uncheered by hope's sweet song,
God grant that, in the mills, a day
May be but "ten hours" long.[16]

All labor organization came to a standstill with the depression of 1837. The mills, particularly hard hit in the early 1840s, did not begin to recover until after 1843. At the same time the farm was no longer a refuge for the mill women. Mortgages were being foreclosed, and families depended on every penny the women could send home.

Millwork was different now. The premium system of production bonuses to the overseers added new pressures. Heavier, faster, noisier machines were installed and regularly speeded up, while workers were assigned extra looms to tend and piece rates were cut. Take-home pay for mill women remained at the same level as when the mills first opened in 1823, while the amount each worker was required to produce increased all the time. Some skilled workers had already won the ten-hour day, but mill women still worked a seventy-five-hour week. With jobs scarce, overseers easily forced workers into competing with each other for their favor. Women feared staying out even when they were ill because it affected production and angered the bonus-hungry overseer. Independent, spirited mill women lost their jobs for reading publications the overseer thought radical, or for taking part in the ten-hour movement.

When the long recession shattered their unions, workers turned to organizing politically, focusing on the shorter workday. Although voteless, the mill women had as great a stake in the ten-hour day as the men and eagerly took part in the movement.

One of the most remarkable women of her day surfaced during this campaign. Agitator, labor organizer, journalist, public speaker, adult educator, abolitionist, and political activist, Sarah Bagley appeared on the scene about 1836, coming to Lowell from her native New Hampshire to work in the mills. We know little about her except during the period between that date and 1846, when she slips from view. She believed all women workers should belong to labor unions and was the first to pressure a state legislature into holding public hearings on working conditions, as well as the first to initiate a political campaign by women.

During the first four years of the 1840s, Bagley conducted free classes at night for her sister millworkers and was an early contributor to the *Lowell Offering*, until articles of hers pointing out flaws in the Lowell system were rejected for publication. Late in December 1844, she began meeting with eleven fellow workers to plan an organization to work for the ten-hour day. In January 1845, the Female Labor Reform Association was born. The idea caught on. Within six months 500 women had joined. Bagley was elected president and her friend and close associate, Huldah Stone, secretary.

A fiery, persuasive speaker, Bagley was as skilled and effective in a small committee meeting as she was addressing a crowd of two thousand, without the aid of microphones, at a Fourth of July rally. She also possessed boundless energy, and knew how to organize and what was important to women in the mill. She had watched the mills grow and change, and had seen overseers speed up the machines and post ever harsher rules, including the hated blacklist. She lived in a boarding-house and knew how it had deteriorated. After a full day in the mill, she devoted her evenings to the Female Labor Reform Association and to organizing the Industrial Reform Lyceum to give a platform to liberal lecturers not invited to Lowell's company-dominated forums. Somehow she found time to initiate fairs and socials to keep her organization together and raise money for its campaigns. Contributing regularly to *Voices of Industry*, the labor paper of the New England Workingmen's Association, she served also as one of its three-member publications committee.

Under her leadership, the Lowell Female Labor Reform Association adopted as its slogan "Try Again," and affiliated with the New England Workingmen's Association, where Bagley and her co-workers represented the mill women at numerous conventions. She knew the lonely path she would have to travel as she violated society's sanctions on women's proper place, but as she said in a speech to the first convention of the Workingmen's Association:

For the last half a century, it has been deemed a violation of woman's sphere to appear before the public as a speaker; but when our rights are trampled upon and we appeal in vain to legislators, what shall we do but appeal to the people?[17]

By 1845, mill women were eager for a new kind of campaign. They had the Female Labor Reform Association, and a newspaper to publicize their views—the association bought *Voices of Industry* and moved it to Lowell. They had a goal: the ten-hour day; and they had allies in the New England Workingmen's Association. The campaign they evolved was political, and began with petitions to the Massachusetts legislature.

Launched in Fall River in 1842, the petition drives to the state legislature rapidly gathered momentum. In 1843, 1,600 signed a ten-hour-day petition in Lowell.

In 1844, 1,000 signed another on hours and against wage cuts. They submitted still another with 2,000 names, until finally the legislature was forced to hold public hearings on working conditions in the mills—the first such investigation ever held by an American governmental body. Six mill women and two men were invited to testify before the legislative committee, and unladylike or not, all six women appeared, including Sarah Bagley.

Like experts, they documented their statements. Eliza Hemingway told of the poor ventilation in the room where she worked with 150 others, of the thick smoke that filled the air from 293 small and 61 large oil lamps that burned morning and night during the "lighting season." Judith Payne reported on her own illnesses due to millwork. Other witnesses told of low wages, rushed mealtimes, and long hours. The testimony brought out the fact that newly arrived immigrant workers, illiterate and uninformed, were paid 18 percent less than the New England mill women.[18]

So keen was the pressure on the legislative committee that it decided to visit Lowell to see conditions for itself. But, with ample warning, the company made sure the mills were clean and sparkling when the committee arrived. The committee's report echoed industry's concern about placing Massachusetts at a competitive disadvantage with textile mills elsewhere, and found nothing unhealthy about the long hours the women worked. It spoke of grassy lawns and fine flowers, and found "everything in and about the mills and boardinghouses . . . to have for its end, health and comfort. . . . Your committee returned fully satisfied that the order, decorum, and general appearance of things in and around the mills could not be improved by any suggestion of theirs or by any act of the legislature."[19] It was small comfort that the committee also stated that it would be nice if shorter hours prevailed, ventilation were improved, and mealtimes extended, for it disclaimed any responsibility for legislating to make these improvements possible.

"Shame, shame," cried the Female Labor Reform Association, and passed unanimously a resolution chastising the committee:

> . . . the Female Labor Reform Association deeply deplore the lack of independence, honesty, and humanity in the committee to whom were referred sundry petitions relative to the hours of labor, especially in the chairman of that committee; and as he is merely a corporation machine, or tool, we will use our best endeavors and influence to keep him in the "City of Spindles" where he belongs, and not trouble Boston folks with him.[20]

A political campaign began such as Lowell had never before witnessed, spearheaded by voteless females determined to punish Colonel William Schouler, chairman of the hearings committee and Lowell's representative to the state legislature. After his defeat, the Female Labor Reform Association publicly thanked the voters of Lowell for "consigning William Schouler to the obscurity he so justly deserves."[21]

Schouler, however, retaliated promptly, digging up damaging information, not about Bagley, but about one of the men with whom she had worked during the election campaign, and damning her by association. She and her beloved Female Labor Reform Association suffered, and not long afterward she withdrew from her leadership role. But not before she had helped organize a new petition for the ten-hour day and against the year-employment rule of the mills. This petition, 130 feet long, with 4,500 signatures, was submitted along with the names of 10,000 workers from other parts of the state who signed similar petitions. But the special legislative committee that resulted from this effort reported even less satisfactorily than the first. Nothing was changed, except that after 1846, the Lowell mills

extended the dinner hour by fifteen minutes in the summer, while in 1847 the New Hampshire mills did the same.[22]

We see Bagley's spirit best in the constitution she drafted for the Female Labor Reform Association, the model for similar reform associations that she and her core of organizers helped to establish in Manchester, Nashua, and Dover, New Hampshire, as well as in Waltham and Fall River, Massachusetts. Article 8 states: "Any person signing this constitution shall literally pledge herself to labor actively for reform in the present system of labor." Article 9 continues:

> The members of this association disapprove of all hostile measures, strikes, and turn-outs until all pacific measures prove abortive, and then that it is the imperious duty of everyone to assert and maintain that independence which our brave ancestors bequeathed us and sealed with their blood.[23]

The preamble to the constitution reveals not only the influence of the Associationists and Utopians, reform groups allied with labor organizations at that time, but also the struggle, as leaders of the Female Labor Reform Association saw it, of worker against owner. Their need to maintain their dignity and self-esteem as factory workers is clear. . . .

At its convention in 1846, probably in recognition of the role of the mill women in the organization, the New England Workingmen's Association changed its name to the New England Labor Reform League. Three of its eight board members were women: Huldah Stone, recording secretary (with a man to assist her), Mary Emerson, and Mrs. C. N. M. Quimby. The Female Labor Reform Association held equal status with other affiliates in the League from the start.

Sadly, this first convention of the New England Labor Reform League in Nashua, New Hampshire, was also its last. . . .

In the late 1840s, the exodus of the

militant New England farm women from the mills began. Some went home to marry, some to teach in other New England towns or in the West; some sought work as missionaries or in occupations that were opening to women in offices or stores. As they left—and strikes in 1848 and 1853 contributed to the exodus—their places were taken by increasing numbers of immigrants, particularly the Irish fleeing the potato famine in their homeland.

The steady flow of immigrants to America had become a flood. The fifty-year period between 1776 and 1825 had seen the arrival of 1 million immigrants. But in the single decade of 1840–1850, close to 2 million came, and in the ten years between 1850 and 1860, the number rose to over 2.5 million.[24] The Irish who arrived in America during the twenty years preceding the Civil War totaled 1.7 million, equal to almost one-quarter of the population of Ireland at the time the famine began in 1845.[25] They came in family groups, huddled into the poorest slum tenements in town, and accepted less pay than the New England mill women had received. They knew little about unions and did not contribute to organizing efforts at this point. By the 1860s, the permanent mill population of textile towns formerly on the Lowell plan could hardly be distinguished from those which from the start had operated on the family system and employed men, women, and children as workers.

Notes

1. *Encyclopaedia Britannica*, 14th ed. (1929), vol. 14, p. 443; Edith Abbott, *Women in Industry* (New York, 1910), p. 90.

2. Abbott, *Women in Industry*, pp. 374–5.

3. Ibid., pp. 94–95, 125–7.

4. "The Lowell Factory Girl," *Southern Exposure*, vol. 2, no. 1 (spring-summer 1974), p. 42.

5. Helen L. Sumner, *History of Women in Industry in the United States* (Washington, D.C.: Government Printing Office, 1910), p. 102, from *Voice of Industry*, May 7, 1847.

6. Caroline F. Ware, *The Early New England Cotton Manufacture* (Boston: Houghton Mifflin Co., 1931), pp. 214, 221. The Hamilton Company's agent is quoted by Ware as having written in 1845: "I should have mentioned to you yesterday that the proprietors of the *Lowell Offering* have recently made a request to the agents of the mills here for some aid to relieve them from the embarrassment they find themselves in. . . . It has been thought advisable to aid them by purchasing a lot of the back numbers to the amount of a thousand dollars. . . . It was thought best that assistance should be rendered to them in the way proposed . . . so that it might not be said that the concern is at present supported by the corporations or under their influence" (p. 222, from the *Hamilton Company Papers*).

7. John B. Andrews and W. D. P. Bliss, *History of Women in Trade Unions*, Bureau of Labor Report on Conditions of Women and Child Wage-Earners in the United States, vol. 10 (Washington, D.C.: Government Printing Office, 1911), p. 24. Quoting *Mechanics Free Press*, Jan. 17, 1829.

8. Ibid., p. 23, quoting *National Gazette*, Jan. 7, 1829.

9. Ibid., p. 27, quoting *Lowell Journal* and *Essex Tribute*, Feb. 22, 1834.

10. Ibid., p. 28, quoting *The Man*, Feb. 22, 1834.

11. Harriet H. Robinson, *Loom and Spindle, or Life Among the Early Mill Girls* (New York: Thomas Y. Crowell & Co., 1898), pp. 84–5.

12. Ibid., p. 84.

13. Andrews and Bliss, *Women in Trade Unions*, p. 30, from *National Laborer*, Oct. 29, 1836.

14. Robinson, *Looms and Spindle*, p. 85.

15. Philip Sheldon Foner, *History of the Labor Movement in the U.S.* (New York, 1947), vol. 1, p. 110. Taken from "An Address on the Origin and Progress of Avarice, and its Deleterious Effects on Human Happiness" (Boston, 1834).

16. Published anonymously in *Voice of Industry*, Feb. 20, 1846; quoted in Sumner, *History of Women in Industry*, p. 69.

17. Andrews and Bliss, *Women in Trade Unions*, p. 71, from *Voice of Industry*, June 5, 1845.

18. Hannah Josephson, *The Golden*

Threads (New York: Duell, Sloan & Pearce, 1949), p. 259.

19. Norman Ware, *The Industrial Worker, 1840–1860* (1924; reprint ed., Quadrangle Books, 1964), p. 137; quoting Massachusetts House Document no. 50 (1845).

20. Andrews and Bliss, *Women in Trade Unions*, p. 74, quoting *Voice of Industry*, Jan. 9, 1846.

21. Ibid., p. 74, quoting *Voice of Industry*, Nov. 28, 1846.

22. C. F. Ware, *New England Cotton Manufacture*, p. 280.

23. Andrews and Bliss, *Women in Trade Unions*, p. 72, from *Voice of Industry*, Feb. 27, 1846.

24. Foster Rhea Dulles, *Labor in America* (New York, 1960), p. 78. Also Ware, *Industrial Worker*, p. 10.

25. *Alistair Cook's America* (New York: Alfred A. Knopf, 1974), p. 275.

KATHRYN KISH SKLAR
Catharine Beecher:
Transforming the Teaching Profession

In the following essay Kathryn Kish Sklar describes the merger of economic and ideological concerns in the career of Catharine Beecher. By publicizing the appropriateness of teaching as a career for women, Beecher facilitated the entry of many women into the profession. In the process she also developed her own career, traveling widely, speaking in public frequently, and publishing popular books. Beecher made use of the familiar ideology that stressed women's "natural" docile and nurturing qualities and has been called the "Cult of True Womanhood." It was said, for example, that women had a duty to be teachers because their natural role as mothers suited them to the care of young children.

Within a single generation women replaced men in the ranks of teachers and were entrusted with classes that included boys as well as girls. It has been estimated that approximately one out of five white women in antebellum Massachusetts was a schoolteacher at some time in her life. Once the profession of teaching was "feminized" it would remain so; in 1970 more than 85 percent of the nation's elementary school teachers were women.

For the next decade and a half Catharine Beecher maintained the pace of life that she began in the summer of 1843. She sought out people . . . who were either themselves wealthy or could open doors to the wealth of other evangelical individuals and groups. She toured constantly in both East and West, raising funds, seek-

Excerpted from "Education at the West, 1843–1847," chap. 12 of *Catharine Beecher: A Study in American Domesticity* by Kathryn Kish Sklar (New Haven: Yale University Press, 1973). Copyright © 1973 by Yale University Press. Reprinted by permission of the author and the publisher. Notes have been renumbered.

ing sites for schools and seminaries, and recruiting teachers to occupy them. Her *Treatise [on Domestic Economy]* made her nationally known, and her frequent speaking tours kept her immediately in the public view. By the end of the 1840s she was one of the most widely known women in America.

Over the course of the decade, as she met with greater and greater success in promoting the primacy of women in American education, Catharine's public and private lives converged. Finally she had found a role commensurate with her personal needs and desires, and much of her achievement during this decade may have arisen from that congruence. As she traveled about the country advocating a special role for her sex, she became the living embodiment of that role. This new consistency in Catharine's life lent conviction to her activities and greatly enhanced her powers of persuasion. . . .

Catharine returned to Cincinnati in the fall of 1843. . . . She spent the winter striving to create a national organization to promote "the cause of popular education, and as intimately connected with it, the elevation of my sex by the opening of a profession for them as educators of the young." All that winter and spring she corresponded with prominent individuals in the East and West, soliciting their endorsement of such an organization.[1] . . .

. . . in the winter of 1845 she visited almost every major city in the East, delivering a standard speech and organizing local groups of church women to collect and forward funds and proselytize her views.[2]

Catharine's addresses were subsequently published in three volumes by Harpers. The first was entitled *The Evils Suffered by American Women and American Children: The Causes and the Remedy;* it was followed by *The Duty of American Women to Their Country;* and lastly, by *An Address to the Protestant Clergy of the United States.* These addresses clarified the ideas Catharine had evolved over the course of the last two decades. Now however like a practiced evangelist she played expertly upon the feelings and fears of her audience and ultimately brought them to commit themselves to her vision of a nation redeemed by women. The full meaning of Catharine's exhortation was not revealed until halfway through her addresses. First she gained her audiences' sympathy for the sufferings of masses of American children under cruel teachers and in degenerate environments. She quoted from several reports to state legislatures that described "the comfortless and dilapidated buildings, the unhung doors, broken sashes, absent panes, stilted benches, gaping walls, yawning roofs, and muddy moldering floors," of contemporary schools and "the self-styled teachers, who lash and dogmatize in these miserable tenements of humanity." Many teachers were "low, vulgar, obscene, intemperate," according to one report to the New York State legislature, "and utterly incompetent to teach anything good."[3]

To remedy this situation Catharine then proposed a national benevolent movement, similar to the temperance movement or the missionary boards, to raise money for teachers and schoolrooms. Yet Catharine's plan went even beyond the contemporary benevolent models. Her chief goal was to "elevate and dignify" her sex, and this goal was inextricably bound to her vision of a more consolidated society. The united effort of women in the East, combined with the moral influence of women in the West, would create homogeneous national institutions, Catharine asserted. The family, the school, and the social morality upon which these institutions were based would everywhere be similar. Sectional and ethnic diversities would give way to national unity as the influence of women increased.

To make her image of a unified society

more understandable to her audience, she explained that it was a Protestant parallel to the Catholic pattern of close interaction between social and religious forms. Protestant women should have the same social support for their religious and moral activities as Catholic nuns received from their society. She related the stories of many women she had known who were willing to sacrifice themselves to socially ameliorative efforts, but who had been rebuffed by public opinion and restricted to quiet domestic lives. "Had these ladies turned Catholic and offered their services to extend that church, they would instantly have found bishops, priests, Jesuits and all their subordinates at hand, to counsel and sustain; a strong *public sentiment* would have been created in their favor; while abundant funds would have been laid at their feet," she said.[4] Her plan envisioned a similar kind of cultural support for Protestant women. A web of interlocking social institutions, including the family, the school, and the church, would form a new cultural matrix within which women would assume a central role.

The ideological basis of Catharine's social theory was self-denial. The Catholic church's employment of self-denying women initially attracted Catharine to it as a model for her own plan. Yet Catharine emphasized that her notion of self-denial was different from the Catholic one. The Catholics had "a selfish and ascetic self-denial, aiming mainly to save *self* by inflictions and losses," Catharine said, whereas she advocated self-denial not as the means of personal salvation, but as the means of social cohesion.[5] . . . Self-denial was an inclusive virtue that could be practiced by wealthy and poor, converted and unconverted, by persons of all ages and both sexes. As the ideological basis of a national morality it was especially congenial to Catharine since women could be both the embodiment and the chief instructors of self-denial. It made possible an expanded cultural role for women as the exemplars and the teachers of a national morality.

To support this cultural role for women Catharine advocated three corollary ideas, each of which pointed toward a more consolidated American society. First, she said, women should abolish class distinctions among themselves and form one united social group. Catharine Beecher had earlier defended class distinctions as a part of the natural order of God's universe, but such divisions were no longer endorsed in her public writings. This change in her views was prompted in part by a visit she made to Lowell, Massachusetts, where she went to look for teachers. Catharine did not believe the Lowell owners' claims that factory work was a means of self-improvement for the women operatives. She concluded that at Lowell and in New York City women were deliberately exploited. "Work of all kinds is got from poor women, at prices that will not keep soul and body together," Catharine wrote, "and then the articles thus made are sold for prices that give monstrous profits to the capitalist, who thus grows rich on the hard labors of our sex."[6] Rather than participate in this kind of class exploitation, Catharine suggested women should donate their services to the cause of education. Although they might still be poor, their economic sacrifice would transcend class lines and benefit the whole nation instead of a self-interested class of businessmen.

While economic factors oppressed working-class women, social custom suppressed upper-class women. "The customs and prejudices of society forbid" educated young women from engaging in socially useful employments. Their sufferings were just as keen as those of working-class women, Catharine said, the only difference being that their spirits were starved instead of their bodies. "A little working of muslin and worsted, a little light reading, a little calling and shopping, and a great deal of the high stimulus of fashionable amusement, are all the ailment their starving spirits find," Catharine wrote. "The influence and the principle of *caste*," she maintained, must cease to operate on both these groups. Her solution was to secure "a proper education for all classes, and make productive labor honorable, by having all classes engage in it."[7]

The specific labor Catharine endorsed for both groups was teaching. Working-class women should leave the factories and seize the opportunity to go to the West as missionary teachers. Their places in the factories should be taken by men. Upper-class women, Catharine said, should do whatever they could to contribute to the "proper education" of American children. Whether by teaching themselves, or by raising funds, or by supervising schools in their community, all well-to-do women could do some productive labor for education. By their efforts, moreover, the public attitude toward the teaching profession could be changed. Teaching is regarded "as the most wearying drudgery, and few resort to it except from necessity," Catharine said, but by elevating the teaching profession into a "true and noble" one, and by making it the special "profession of a woman," women would be freed from the caste principles that suppressed them and enter into a new casteless, but elevated condition.[8] In effect Catharine would eliminate the extremes of class identity and fortify a middle-class social order.

The second corollary to the new social role Catharine described for women was that of fostering the nation's social conscience. Young women teachers in the West would be in the vanguard of settlement, and from them the character of the place would take its shape. "Soon, in all parts of our country, in each neglected village, or new settlement, the Christian female teacher will quietly take her station, collecting the ignorant children around her, teaching them habits of neatness, order and thrift; opening the book of knowledge, inspiring the principles of morality, and awakening the hope of immortality," she said.[9] . . . Catharine cited several examples of western settlement where the female teacher preceded the minister. Thus she asserted that a woman could be chiefly responsible for setting the moral tone of the community. A community could coalesce around women rather than the church.

The promotion of national unity was a third aspect of the new social role Catharine was defining for women. The special esteem in which American women were held meant that their united actions would have a nationwide effect. "It is the pride and honour of our country," she said, "that woman holds a commanding influence in the domestic and social circle, which is accorded to the sex in no other nation, and such as will make her wishes and efforts, if united for a benevolent and patriotic object, almost omnipotent." Women thus had the power to shape the character of the whole nation, and that character, Catharine said, would be one of a united nation rather than a collection of sections.[10] . . .

At the end of each address Catharine presented to her audience her plan for practical action. A committee of clergymen led by [Calvin] Stowe would, as soon as sufficient funds were raised for a salary, "appoint one man who shall act as an agent," giving his full time to the organization. The committee would also appoint "a Board of Managers, consisting of men from each of the principal Protestant denominations from each of the different sections of the country." In addition, local committees of women would raise funds "to aid in educating and locating missionary teachers." In the West such committees could aid in providing schools for those sent out. In both places the committees could publicize the cause. Lastly Catharine revealed how "every woman who feels an interest in the effort can contribute at least a small sum to promote it" by immediately purchasing Catharine's *Treatise on Domestic Economy* and her *Domestic Receipt Book,* since half the profits from the sale of these books was to be given to the cause.[11]

Catharine Beecher apparently misled her audience when she claimed that "the copyright interest in these two works is held by a board of gentlemen appointed for the purpose." Her original contract with Harper & Brothers, still preserved by Harper & Row, gave Catharine full control of the profits and did not mention a "board of gentlemen." Catharine's contract gave her 50 perecnt of the net profits, so she was correct in representing to her audience the fact that only half the price went to the publisher. But when she said that "Half the profits (after paying a moderate compensation to the author for the time and labour of preparing them, the amount to be decided by the above gentlemen) will be devoted to this object," she misrepresented the flow of power and profit between herself and the "gentlemen." For neither Stowe nor any of the other named Cincinnati clergymen would have been capable of questioning Catharine's use of the money that came to her from Harpers. Catharine had a reputation in her family of being "clever" to deal with financially, and it was extremely unlikely that Calvin Stowe would have crossed swords with his sister-in-law on financial issues. Later, when a salaried agent was found for the organization, he received his funds from the money he himself raised, not from the profits of Catharine's books.

Catharine's tactics in presenting herself and her cause to the public made her an enormously successful publicist. She sent circulars signed by Calvin Stowe to county newspapers and small-town clergymen throughout the East and West, asking for the names of women who might be willing to serve as missionary teachers and for the names of towns and villages where such teachers would be welcomed. The Catholic analogy and the ideology of self-denial made her efforts newsworthy, and to make the work of county editors easier she dispatched articles, such as the one entitled "Education at the West—Sisters of Charity," for newspapers to print alongside Stowe's circular.[12] The primary targets for Catharine's fund-raising efforts were the local groups of church women she organized in every city and town she visited.[13] She asked each group to make at least a hundred-dollar donation, this being the amount necessary to train and locate one teacher.

Catharine's efforts gained the endorsement of the most prominent American educators. Horace Mann, Henry Barnard, Thomas Burrowes, Samuel Lewis, and Gorham Abbot lent their support, and with each new endorsement by a national figure, Catharine's local fund-raising became more successful.[14] Catharine's tactic in each city was to plead her cause with the town's most eminent personage and, having gained his or her endorsement, to use it to build a substantial and active local committee. In this way she even drew into her cause those who traditionally opposed evangelical projects and especially opposed the Beecher family. . . .

By the spring of 1846 Catharine had delivered her addresses in most of the major cities of the East. Everywhere she called upon women to "save" their country from ignorance and immorality, and everywhere women responded. In Boston the Ladies Society for Promoting Education at the West donated several thousand dollars over the course of the decade to Catharine Beecher and her cause, and in other cities similar groups of women were organized by her into active proponents of her ideas on women and education. She corresponded with these groups constantly, relating her recent advances in other cities and exhorting her followers on to greater efforts. In a typical five-week period early in 1846 Catharine spoke in Pittsburgh, Baltimore, Washington, D.C., Philadelphia, New York City, Troy, Albany, and Hartford. She retraced her steps often, sometimes staying only one night in a place—long enough to deliver a public speech, encourage her old supporters, and welcome new ones. She traveled like a candidate for political office, moving quickly from one city to another, thereby promoting a large amount of newspaper coverage of her arrivals and departures.[15] . . .

In Albany in the spring of 1847 and in Hartford in the fall Catharine collected two groups of thirty-five young women for one month's training before they were sent to locations . . . in the West. The local women's committees provided room and board for Catharine and her young women. Catharine lectured the prospective teachers on how to meet all the difficulties that were to face them in the West: how to overcome the lack of books and proper schoolrooms; how to train children to good moral habits "when all domestic and social influences tend to weaken such habits"; how to impart spiritual training "without giving occasion for sectarian jealousy and alarm"; and how to preserve their health "from the risks of climate and the dangers of overexertion and excessive care." Catharine also lectured on the ways in which they could influence the community outside the schoolroom. They learned how to teach "the laws of health by the aid of simple drawings on the blackboard so that the children could copy them on slates to take home and explain to their parents," and how to teach certain branches of "domestic economy" so that parents would "be willing to adopt these improvements." Most of all they learned how to be moral examples that the rest of the community could imitate.[16]

Most of the seventy young women were New Englanders; only three came from New York and one from Pennsylvania. More than half of them went to Illinois and Indiana, seven crossed the Mississippi into Iowa, and a few went to Wisconsin, Michigan, Kentucky, and Tennessee. Each of them was expected to act as "a new source of moral power" in her community, and the reports they made at the end of the year revealed how seriously they took this charge.[17] . . .

The letters Catharine received from these teachers testified to the effectiveness of her training and to the tenacity of purpose she instilled. One woman went West to join a constituency that had migrated from North Carolina, Tennessee, and Germany and was met with a log cabin classroom holding forty-five pupils ranging in age from six to eighteen, and a community of hostile parents. "They seem desirous to have their children educated, but they differed so much about almost every thing, that they could not build a schoolhouse," she wrote Catharine.

> I was told, when I came, that they would not pay a teacher for more than three months in a year. At first, they were very suspicious, and watched me narrowly; but, through the blessing of my heavenly Father, I have gained their good will and confidence, so that they have provided me a good frame schoolhouse, with writing-desks and a blackboard, and they promise to support me all the year around.

Having proved herself in their eyes, she succeeded next in drawing both parents and children to a Sunday school. Then, because the nearest church was seven miles away and the people did not go to it, she persuaded them "to invite the nearest clergyman to preach" in her schoolhouse the next Sunday. This New England woman, though unused to frontier conditions, decided to stay on in the place even though she had to board "where there are eight children and the parents and only two rooms in the house," and she went without simple amenities such as candles and a place to bathe.[18] . . .

Developments shaping the teaching profession at this precise moment made the field especially receptive to Catharine Beecher's view that it properly belonged to women. Although female teachers began to replace men in some eastern states in the 1830s, the utility of that shift was not apparent to most state and local boards of education until 1840. What had begun as an improvised economy measure had by then proved to be a pedagogic as well as a fiscal improvement, and as these obvious benefits were discovered by state and local boards of education from 1840 to 1880, women gradually replaced their male predecessors in the teaching profession. By 1888 63 percent of American teachers were women, and in cities women constituted 90 percent of the teaching force.[19]

Although it is impossible to measure completely Catharine Beecher's impact on the profession, her publicizing in behalf of women did at least facilitate an otherwise confused transition period in the nation's schools. For the traditionally higher value attached to male labor blinded many communities to the advantages of female teachers, and as late as 1850 the state of Indiana viewed the female teacher as the exception rather than the rule.[20] The West was, on the whole, slower to employ women as teachers, perhaps because it attracted ample numbers of ambitious men who, typically, would teach for a brief period or even a few years before locating more lucrative commercial employment.[21] These male teachers were usually paid twice as much as female teachers, and a male teacher frequently brought fewer pedagogic talents to the job than a woman. In New York, one of the earliest states to shift to women teachers, the state board of regents in 1838 still assumed that teachers should be male, and they failed to approve the governor's request that normal schools be attached to female academies because they concluded that men, rather than women,

needed the normal training.[22] Therefore it was far from obvious to the American public that teaching was a woman's profession.

On the other hand the shift to women teachers was well enough along by 1843 to provide a solid factual basis for Catharine Beecher's claims on their behalf. In Massachusetts, the first state to promote the employment of women as teachers, women outnumbered men three to two in 1837 and two to one in 1842.[23] Many school districts had since the 1820s routinely employed women to teach the summer session, although they believed men were needed to "manage" the older boys present at the winter school session. Some New York districts learned in the 1820s that they could, with the state subsidy of half a teacher's salary, employ a woman to teach full-time and thus not have to bear any of the cost themselves.[24] As a leading educator pointed out later in the century, "the effective reason" women were employed in schools was that they were "cheaper than men." If they had not been cheaper, "they would not have replaced nine-tenths of the men in American public schools."[25]

The need for such educational economies became more critical in the 1830s and 1840s, when immigration and internal migration increased the population of many areas, but did not immediately increase the tax base. By reducing the school costs by hiring women, a district could accommodate its larger numbers of children without taxing itself at a higher rate.[26]

Three basic assumptions were used to justify these lower salaries for women: women, unlike men, did not have to support a family; women were only working temporarily until they married; and the free workings of the economic marketplace determined cheaper salaries for women. Women do not "expect to accumulate much property by this occupation; if it affords them a respectable support and a situation where they can be useful, it is as much as they demand," wrote the state superintendent of Ohio in 1839. He therefore urged "those counties who are in the habit of paying men for instructing little children" to hire women since "females would do it for less than half the sum and generally much better than men can."[27]

Catharine chose to exploit the short-term gains that these discriminatory practices brought to women, and her publicity on behalf of female teachers emphasized their willingness to work for less money. "To make education universal, it must be moderate in expense," Catherine wrote in a petition to Congress in 1853 for free normal schools for female teachers, "and women can afford to teach for one-half, or even less, the salary which men would ask, because the female teacher has only to sustain herself; she does not look forward to the duty of supporting a family, should she marry; nor has she the ambition to amass a fortune." Catharine also insisted that women's employment as teachers would not create a "celibate class" of women, but that their employment was only temporary, and would in fact prepare them to be better wives and mothers. By defining teaching as an extension of the duties of the home, Catharine presented her idea in a form most likely to gain widespread public support. "It is ordained by infinite wisdom, that, as in the family, so in the social state, the interests of young children and of women are one and the same," Catharine insisted.[28]

Since the profession had lower pay and status than most men qualified to teach could get elsewhere, since the economics of education called for even lower pay in the 1830s and 1840s, and since the schoolroom could be seen as functionally akin to the home, both public sentiment and economic facts supported Catharine Beecher's efforts to redefine the gender of the American teacher.

Notes

1. Catharine Beecher, *Educational Reminiscences and Suggestions* (New York, 1874), p. 101. Hereafter cited as CB, *Reminiscences*. . . .

2. CB, "Memoranda," 3 October 1844 to 7 June 1845, Beecher-Stowe Collection, Radcliffe College, Cambridge, Massachusetts.

3. CB, *The Evils Suffered by American Women and American Children: The Causes and the Remedy* (New York, 1846), p. 29.

4. CB, *An Address to the Protestant Clergy of the United States* (New York, 1846), p. 29.

5. Ibid., pp. 22–23; CB, *The Evils Suffered*, p. 16.

6. CB, "Memoranda," 29 November to 4 December 1844; CB, *The Evils Suffered*, pp. 6–9.

7. CB, *The Evils Suffered*, pp. 11–14.

8. Ibid., p. 11.

9. Ibid., pp. 9–10.

10. Ibid., p. 11.

11. CB, *The Duty of American Women to Their Country* (New York, 1845), pp. 112–31.

12. CB to Judge Lane, 26 July 1845, Ebenezer Lane Papers, Rutherford B. Hayes Library, Fremont, Ohio. CB undoubtedly knew that Elizabeth Seton had founded the first American religious community for women called "The Sisters of Charity" in 1810 and had soon thereafter opened the first parochial school free to children of all classes. Edward James et al., *Notable American Women, 1607–1950: A Biographical Dictionary*, 3 vols. (Cambridge, Mass., 1971), 3: 265.

13. CB, *Reminiscences*, p. 115.

14. Samuel Lewis was the state superintendent of schools for Ohio; Gorham Abbot, the brother of Jacob Abbot, was the director of a fashionable school for girls in New York City. CB also appealed to Rufus Choate, then the director of the Smithsonian Institution, and Mrs. James K. Polk, the nation's first lady, for their endorsements. See CB to The

Hon. Rufus Choate, 29 August 1846, Harriet Beecher Stowe Collection, Clifton Waller Barrett Library, University of Virginia; CB to Mrs. James K. Polk [1847], Hillhouse Family Papers, box 27, Sterling Memorial Library.

15. CB, "Memoranda," 21 March to 27 April 1846. Charles H. Foster, *An Errand of Mercy, The Evangelical United Front, 1790–1837* (Chapel Hill, 1960), p. 136, describes the traditional support New England women gave to education. The first female organizations in the country were formed for such a purpose—specifically to support men studying for the ministry. Early in the nineteenth century these female "cent societies" maintained 20 per cent of the ministerial students in New England. CB therefore drew on an organizational structure and a charitable predisposition that had existed among New England women for at least a generation.

16. William Slade, "Circular to the Friends of Popular Education in the United States," 15 May 1847, Increase Lapham Papers, State Historical Society of Wisconsin, Madison.

17. *First Annual Report of the General Agent of the Board of National Popular Education* (Hartford, 1848), pp. 15, 22–26.

18. CB, *The True Remedy for the Wrongs of Women* (Boston, 1851), pp. 163, 167.

19. Thomas Woody, *A History of Women's Education in the United States* (New York, 1929), 1:499.

20. Richard G. Boone, *A History of Education in Indiana* (New York, 1892), p. 142.

21. Michael Katz, *The Irony of Early School Reform: Innovation in Mid-Nineteenth Century Massachusetts* (Cambridge, Mass., 1968), pp. 57–58. Katz's evidence disproves the stereotype of the antebellum male teacher as a vacationing college student. His data suggests that teachers shifted to the ministry, commerce, and medicine. He concludes that "others may well have looked on teaching as a way both to stay alive and to establish a local reputation while waiting for the right business opportunity to appear." Paul Monroe, *Founding of the American Public School*

System (New York, 1940), 1:487: "In the newer settled regions of the Middle West men still predominated in the teaching profession throughout this period."

22. Elsie Garland Hobson, "Educational Legislation and Administration in the State of New York from 1772 to 1850," *Supplementary Educational Monographs* 3, no. 1 (Chicago, 1918): 75.

23. Woody, *History of Women's Education*, 1:497.

24. Hobson, "Educational Legislation," p. 66.

25. A comparison of salary rates for a three- to four-month period near the end of the 1840s compiled from the above sources reveals these differentials:

State	Year	Men	Women
Michigan	1847	$12.87	$5.74
Indiana	1850	12.00	6.00
Massachusetts	1848	24.51	8.07
Maine	c. 1848	15.40	4.80
New York	c. 1848	15.95	6.99
Ohio	c. 1848	15.42	8.73

Henry Barnard was practically alone in protesting this discriminatory practice. See "Report to the Secretary of the Board," *Connecticut Common School Journal* 1, no. 13 (1839): 163–64. Charles William Eliot, "Wise and Unwise Economy in Schools," *Atlantic Monthly*, no. 35 (June 1875):715, quoted in Katz, *Irony of Early School Reform*, p. 58.

26. Katz, *Irony of Early School Reform*, pp. 56–58.

27. Woody, *History of Women's Education*, 1:491.

28. Petition appeared in *Godey's Lady's Book* (Jaunary 1853), pp. 176–77. CB wrote Horace Mann: "The great purpose of a woman's life—the happy superintendence of a family—is accomplished all the better and easier by preliminary teaching in school. All the power she may develop here will come in use there" (CB to Horace Mann, in *Common School Journal* 5 [Boston, 1843]: 353).

CARROLL SMITH-ROSENBERG

The Female World of Love and Ritual: Relations between Women in Nineteenth-Century America

Women's associations with each other have traditionally been ignored by historians. One reason for this has been a fascination with public life; only women who were powerful in the same fashion as men or whose lives were intertwined with the lives of powerful men attracted the historical spotlight. The world of women was treated as wholly private or domestic, encompassing only family responsibilities. Women's diaries and letters were used primarily as a source of illustrative anecdote.

Carroll Smith-Rosenberg has read the letters and diaries of women in a strikingly original way. She evaluates nineteenth-century American society in much the same way an anthropologist might observe a distant culture. She describes relations between women as intellectually active, personally rewarding, mutually supportive, and socially creative. Smith-Rosenberg offers a radically new account of the relationship between the sexes in Victorian America. What revision does she suggest ought to be made in our traditional understanding of Victorian sexuality?

The female friendship of the nineteenth century, the long-lived, intimate, loving friendship between two women, is an excellent example of the type of historical phenomena which most historians know something about, which few have thought much about, and which virtually no one has written about.[1] It is one aspect of the female experience which consciously or unconsciously we have chosen to ignore. Yet an abundance of manuscript evidence suggests that eighteenth- and nineteenth-century women routinely formed emotional ties with other women. Such deeply felt, same-sex friendships were casually accepted in American society. Indeed, from at least the late eighteenth through the mid-nineteenth century, a female world of varied and yet highly structured relationships appears to have been an essential aspect of American society. These relationships ranged from the supportive love of sisters, through the enthusiasms of adolescent girls, to sensual avowals of love by mature women. It was a world in which men made but a shadowy appearance.[2]

Defining and analyzing same-sex relationships involves the historian in deeply problematical questions of method and interpretation. This is especially true since historians, influenced by Freud's libidinal theory, have discussed these relationships almost exclusively within the context of individual psychosexual developments or, to be more explicit, psychopathology.[3] Seeing same-sex relationships in terms of a dichotomy between normal and abnormal, they have sought the origins of such apparent deviance in childhood or adolescent trauma and detected the symptoms of "latent" homosexuality in the lives of both those who later became "overtly" homosexual and those who did not. Yet theories concerning the nature and origins of same-sex relationships are frequently contradictory or based on questionable or arbitrary data. In recent years such hypotheses have been subjected to criticism both from within and without the psychological professions. Historians who seek to work within a psychological framework, therefore, are faced with two hard questions: Do sound psychodynamic theories concerning the nature and origins of same-sex relationships exist? If so, does the historical datum exist which would permit the use of such dynamic models?

I would like to suggest an alternative approach to female friendships—one which would view them within a cultural and social setting rather than from an exclusively individual psychosexual perspective. Only by thus altering our approach will we be in the position to evaluate the appropriateness of particular dynamic interpretations. Intimate friendships between men and men and women and women existed in a larger world of social relations and social values. To interpret such friendships more fully they must be related to the structure of the American family and to the nature of sex-role divisions and of male-female relations both within the family and in society generally. The female friendship must not be seen in isolation; it must be analyzed as one aspect of women's overall relations with one another. The ties between moth-ers and daughters, sisters, female cousins and friends, at all stages of the female life cycle constitute the most suggestive framework for the historian to begin an analysis of intimacy and affection between women. Such an analysis would not only emphasize general cultural patterns rather than the internal dynamics of a particular family or childhood; it would shift the focus of the study from a concern with deviance to that of defining configurations of legitimate behavioral norms and options.[4]

This analysis will be based upon the correspondence and diaries of women and men in thirty-five families between the 1760s and the 1880s. These families, though limited in number, represented a broad range of the American middle class, from hard-pressed pioneer families and orphaned girls to daughters of the intellectual and social elite. It includes families from most geographic regions, rural and urban, and a spectrum of Protestant denominations ranging from Mormon to orthodox Quaker. Although scarcely a comprehensive sample of America's increasingly heterogeneous population, it does, I believe, reflect accurately the literate middle class to which the historian working with letters and diaries is necessarily bound. It has involved an analysis of many thousands of letters written to women friends, kin, husbands, brothers, and children at every period of life from adolescence to old age. Some collections encompass virtually entire life spans; one contains over 100,000 letters as well as diaries and account books. It is my contention that an analysis of women's private letters and diaries which were never intended to be published permits the historian to explore a very private world of emotional realities central both to women's lives and to the middle-class family in nineteenth-century America.[5]

The question of female friendships is peculiarly elusive; we know so little or perhaps have forgotten so much. An intriguing and almost alien form of human relationship, they flourished in a different social structure and amidst different sexual norms. Before attempting to reconstruct their social setting, therefore, it might be best first to describe two not atypical friendships. These two friendships, intense, loving, and openly avowed, began during the women's adolescence and, despite subsequent marriages and geographic separation, continued throughout their lives. For nearly half a century these women played a central emotional role in each other's lives, writing time and again of their love and of the pain of separation. Paradoxically to twentieth-century minds, their love appears to have been both sensual and platonic.

Sarah Butler Wister first met Jeannie Field Musgrove while vacationing with her family at Stockbridge, Massachusetts, in the summer of 1849.[6] Jeannie was then sixteen, Sarah fourteen. During two subsequent years spent together in boarding school, they formed a deep and intimate friendship. Sarah began to keep a bouquet of flowers before Jeannie's portrait and wrote complaining of the intensity and anguish of her affection.[7] Both young women assumed nom de plumes, Jeannie a female name, Sarah a male one; they would use these secret names into old age.[8] They frequently commented on the nature of their affection: "If the day should come," Sarah wrote Jeannie in the spring of 1861, "when you failed me either through your fault or my own, I would forswear all human friendship, thenceforth." A few months later Jeannie commented: "Gratitude is a word I should never use toward you. It is perhaps a misfortune of such intimacy and love that it makes one regard all kindness as a matter of course, as one has always found it, as natural as the embrace in meeting."[9]

Sarah's marriage altered neither the frequency of their correspondence nor their desire to be together. In 1864, when twenty-nine, married, and a mother, Sarah wrote to Jeannie: "I shall be entirely alone [this coming week]. I can give you no idea how desperately I shall want you. . . ." After one such visit Jeannie, then a spinster in New York, echoed Sarah's longing: "Dear darling Sarah! How I love you & how happy I have been! You are the joy of my life. . . . I cannot tell you how much happiness you gave me, nor how constantly it is all in my thoughts. . . . My darling how I long for the time when I shall see you. . . ." After another visit Jeannie wrote: "I want you to tell me in your next letter, to assure me, that I am your dearest. . . . I do not doubt you, & I am not jealous but I long to hear you say it once more & it seems already a long time since your voice fell on my ear. So just fill a quarter page with caresses & expressions of endearment. Your silly Angelina." Jeannie ended one letter: "Goodbye my dearest, dearest lover—ever your own Angelina." And another, "I will go to bed . . . [though] I could write all night—A thousand kisses—I love you with my whole soul—your Angelina."

When Jeannie finally married in 1870 at the age of thirty-seven, Sarah underwent a period of extreme anxiety. Two days before Jeannie's marriage Sarah, then in London, wrote desperately: "Dearest darling—How incessantly have I thought of you these eight days—all today—the entire uncertainty, the distance, the long silence—are all new features in my separation from you, grevious to be borne. . . . Oh Jeannie. I have thought & thought & yearned over you these two days. Are you married I wonder? My dearest love to you wherever and *who*ever you are."[10] Like many other women in this collection of thirty-five families, marriage brought Sarah and Jeannie physical separation; it did not cause emotional distance. Although at first they may have wondered how marriage would affect their relationship, their affection remained unabated throughout their lives, underscored by their loneliness and their desire to be together.[11]

During the same years that Jeannie and Sarah wrote of their love and need for each other, two slightly younger women began a similar odyssey of love, dependence and—ultimately—physical, though not emotional, separation. Molly and Helena met in 1868 while both attended the Cooper Institute School of Design for Women in New York City. For several years these young women studied and explored the city together, visited each other's families, and formed part of a social network of other artistic young women. Gradually, over the years, their initial friendship deepened into a close intimate bond which continued throughout their lives. The tone in the letters which Molly wrote to Helena changed over these years from "My dear Helena," and signed "your attached friend," to "My dearest Helena," "My Dearest," "My Beloved," and signed "Thine always" or "thine Molly."[12]

The letters they wrote to each other during these first five years permit us to reconstruct something of their relationship together. As Molly wrote in one early letter:

> I have not said to you in so many or so few words that I was happy with you during those few so incredibly short weeks but surely you do not need words to tell you what you must know. Those two or three days so dark without, so bright with firelight and contentment within I shall always remember as proof that, for a time, at least—I fancy for quite a long time—we might be sufficient for each other. We know that we can amuse each other for many idle hours together and now we know that we can also work together. And that means much, don't you think so?

She ended: "I shall return in a few days. Imagine yourself kissed many times by one who loved you so dearly."

The intensity and even physical nature of Molly's love was echoed in many of the letters she wrote during the next few years, as, for instance in this short thank-you note for a small present: "Imagine yourself kissed a dozen times my darling. Perhaps it is well for you that we are far apart. You might find my thanks so expressed rather overpowering. I have that delightful feeling that it doesn't matter much what I say or how I say it, since we shall meet so soon and forget in that moment that we were ever separated. . . . I shall see you soon and be content."[13]

At the end of the fifth year, however, several crises occurred. The relationship, at least in its intense form, ended, though Molly and Helena continued an intimate and complex relationship for the next half-century. The exact nature of these crises is not completely clear, but it seems to have involved Molly's decision not to live with Helena, as they had originally planned, but to remain at home because of parental insistence. Molly was now in her late twenties. Helena responded with anger and Molly became frantic at the thought that Helena would break off their relationship. Though she wrote distraught letters and made despairing attempts to see Helena, the relationship never regained its former ardor—possibly because Molly had a male suitor.[14] Within six months Helena had decided to marry a man who was, coincidentally, Molly's friend and publisher. Two years later Molly herself finally married. The letters toward the end of this period discuss the transition both women made to having male lovers—Molly spending much time reassuring Helena, who seemed depressed about the end of their relationship and with her forthcoming marriage.[15]

It is clearly difficult from a distance of 100 years and from a post-Freudian cultural perspective to decipher the complexities of Molly and Helena's relationship.

Certainly Molly and Helena were lovers—emotionally if not physically. The emotional intensity and pathos of their love becomes apparent in several letters Molly wrote Helena during their crisis: "I wanted so to put my arms round my girl of all the girls in the world and tell her . . . I love her as wives do love their husbands, as *friends* who have taken each other for life—and believe in her as I believe in my God. . . . If I didn't love you do you suppose I'd care about anything or have ridiculous notions and panics and behave like an old fool who ought to know better. I'm going to hang on to your skirts. . . . You can't get away from [my] love." Or as she wrote after Helena's decision to marry: "You know dear Helena, I really was in love with you. It was a passion such as I had never known until I saw you. I don't think it was the noblest way to love you." The theme of intense female love was one Molly again expressed in a letter she wrote to the man Helena was to marry: "Do you know sir, that until you came along I believe that she loved me almost as girls love their lovers. *I know I loved her so.* Don't you wonder that I can stand the sight of you." This was in a letter congratulating them on their forthcoming marriage.[16]

The essential question is not whether these women had genital contact and can therefore be defined as heterosexual or homosexual. The twentieth-century tendency to view human love and sexuality within a dichotomized universe of deviance and normality, genitality and platonic love, is alien to the emotions and attitudes of the nineteenth century and fundamentally distorts the nature of these women's emotional interaction. These letters are significant because they force us to place such female love in a particular historical context. There is every indication that these four women, their husbands and families—all eminently respectable and socially conservative—considered such love both socially acceptable and fully compatible with heterosexual marriage. Emotionally and cognitively, their heterosocial and their homosocial worlds were complementary.

One could argue, on the other hand, that these letters were but an example of the romantic rhetoric with which the nineteenth century surrounded the concept of friendship. Yet they possess an emotional intensity and a sensual and physical explicitness that is difficult to dismiss. Jeannie longed to hold Sarah in her arms; Molly mourned her physical isolation from Helena. Molly's love and devotion to Helena, the emotions that bound Jeannie and Sarah together, while perhaps a phenomenon of nineteenth-century society were not the less real for their Victorian origins. A survey of the correspondence and diaries of eighteenth- and nineteenth-century women indicates that Molly, Jeannie, and Sarah represented one very real behavioral and emotional option socially available to nineteenth-century women.

This is not to argue that individual needs, personalities, and family dynamics did not have a significant role in determining the nature of particular relationships. But the scholar must ask if it is historically possible and, if possible, important, to study the intensely individual aspects of psychosexual dynamics. Is it not the historian's first task to explore the social structure and the world view which made intense and sometimes sensual female love both a possible and an acceptable emotional option? From such a social perspective a new and quite different series of questions suggests itself. What emotional function did such female love serve? What was its place within the hetero- and homosocial worlds which women jointly inhabited? Did a spectrum of love-object choices exist in the nineteenth century across which some individuals, at least, were capable of moving? Without attempting to answer these questions it will be difficult to understand either nineteenth-century sexuality or the nineteenth-century family.

Several factors in American society between the mid-eighteenth and the mid-nineteenth centuries may well have permitted women to form a variety of close emotional relationships with other women. American society was characterized in large part by rigid gender-role differentiation within the family and within society as a whole, leading to the emotional segregation of women and men. The roles of daughter and mother shaded imperceptibly and ineluctably into each other, while the biological realities of frequent pregnancies, childbirth, nursing, and menopause bound women together in physical and emotional intimacy. It was within just such a social framework, I would argue, that a specifically female world did indeed develop, a world built around a generic and unself-conscious pattern of single-sex or homosocial networks. These supportive networks were institutionalized in social conventions or rituals which accompanied virtually every important event in a woman's life, from birth to death. Such female relationships were frequently supported and paralleled by severe social restrictions on intimacy between young men and women. Within such a world of emotional richness and complexity devotion to and love of other women became a plausible and socially accepted form of human interaction.

An abundance of printed and manuscript sources exists to support such a hypothesis. Etiquette books, advice books on child rearing, religious sermons, guides to young men and young women, medical texts, and school curricula all suggest that late eighteenth- and most nineteenth-century Americans assumed the existence of a world composed of distinctly male and female spheres, spheres determined by the immutable laws of God and nature.[17] The unpublished letters and diaries of Americans during this same period concur, detailing the existence of sexually segregated worlds inhabited by human beings with different values, expectations, and personalities. Contacts between men and women frequently partook of a formality and stiffness quite alien to twentieth-century America and which today we tend to define as "Victorian." Women, however, did not form an isolated and oppressed subcategory in male society. Their letters and diaries indicate that women's sphere had an essential integrity and dignity that grew out of women's shared experiences and mutual affection and that, despite the profound changes which affected American social structure and institutions between the 1760s and the 1870s, retained a constancy and predictability. The ways in which women thought of and interacted with each other remained unchanged. Continuity, not discontinuity, characterized this female world. Molly Hallock's and Jeannie Fields's words, emotions, and experiences have direct parallels in the 1760s and the 1790s.[18] There are indications in contemporary sociological and psychological literature that female closeness and support networks have continued into the twentieth century—not only among ethnic and working-class groups but even among the middle class.[19]

Most eighteenth- and nineteenth-century women lived within a world bounded by home, church, and the institution of visiting—that endless trooping of women to each others' homes for social purposes. It was a world inhabited by children and by other women.[20] Women helped each other with domestic chores and in times of sickness, sorrow, or trouble. Entire days, even weeks, might be spent almost exclusively with other women.[21] Urban and town women could devote virtually every day to visits, teas, or shopping trips with other women. Rural women developed a pattern of more extended visits that lasted weeks and sometimes months, at times even dislodging husbands from their beds and bedrooms so that dear friends might spend every hour of every day together.[22] When husbands traveled, wives routinely moved in with other women, invited women friends to teas and suppers, sat together sharing and comparing the letters they had received from other close women friends. Secrets were exchanged and cherished, and the husband's return at times viewed with some ambivalence.[23]

Summer vacations were frequently organized to permit old friends to meet at water spas or share a country home. In 1848, for example, a young matron wrote cheerfully to her husband about the delightful time she was having with five close women friends whom she had invited to spend the summer with her; he remained at home alone to face the heat of Philadelphia and a cholera epidemic.[24] Some ninety years earlier, two young Quaker girls commented upon the vacation their aunt had taken alone with another woman; their remarks were openly envious and tell us something of the emotional quality of these friendships: "I hear Aunt is gone with the Friend and wont be back for two weeks, fine times indeed I think the old friends had, taking their pleasure about the country . . . and have the advantage of that fine woman's conversation and instruction, while we poor young girls must spend all spring at home. . . . What a disappointment that we are not together. . . ."[25]

Friends did not form isolated dyads but were normally part of highly integrated networks. Knowing each other, perhaps related to each other, they played a central role in holding communities and kin systems together. Especially when families became geographically mobile women's long visits to each other and their frequent letters filled with discussions of marriages and births, illness and deaths, descriptions of growing children,

and reminiscences of times and people past provided an important sense of continuity in a rapidly changing society.[26] Central to this female world was an inner core of kin. The ties between sisters, first cousins, aunts, and nieces provided the underlying structure upon which groups of friends and their network of female relatives clustered. Although most of the women within this sample would appear to be living within isolated nuclear families, the emotional ties between nonresidential kin were deep and binding and provided one of the fundamental existential realities of women's lives.[27] Twenty years after Parke Lewis Butler moved with her husband to Louisiana, she sent her two daughters back to Virginia to attend school, live with their grandmother and aunt, and be integrated back into Virginia society.[28] The constant letters between Maria Inskeep and Fanny Hampton, sisters separated in their early twenties when Maria moved with her husband from New Jersey to Louisiana, held their families together, making it possible for their daughters to feel a part of their cousins' network of friends and interests.[29] The Ripley daughters, growing up in western Massachusetts in the early 1800s, spent months each year with their mother's sister and her family in distant Boston; these female cousins and their network of friends exchanged gossip-filled letters and gradually formed deeply loving and dependent ties.[30]

Women frequently spent their days within the social confines of such extended families. Sisters-in-law visited each other and, in some families, seemed to spend more time with each other than with their husbands. First cousins cared for each other's babies—for weeks or even months in times of sickness or childbirth. Sisters helped each other with housework, shopped and sewed for each other. Geographic separation was borne with difficulty. A sister's absence for even a week or two could cause loneliness and depression and would be bridged by frequent letters. Sibling rivalry was hardly unknown, but with separation or illness the theme of deep affection and dependency reemerged.[31]

Sisterly bonds continued across a lifetime. In her old age a rural Quaker matron, Martha Jefferis, wrote to her daughter Anne concerning her own half-sister, Phoebe: "In sister Phoebe I have a real friend—she studies my comfort and waits on me like a child. . . . She is exceedingly kind and this to all other homes (set aside yours) I would prefer—it is next to being with a daughter." Phoebe's own letters confirmed Martha's evaluation of her feelings. "Thou knowest my dear sister," Phoebe wrote, "there is no one . . . that exactly feels [for] thee as I do, for I think without boasting I can truly say that my desire is for thee."[32]

Such women, whether friends or relatives, assumed an emotional centrality in each others' lives. In their diaries and letters they wrote of the joy and contentment they felt in each others' company, their sense of isolation and despair when apart. The regularity of their correspondence underlines the sincerity of their words. Women named their daughters after one another and sought to integrate dear friends into their lives after marriage.[33] As one young bride wrote to an old friend shortly after her marriage: "I want to see you and talk with you and feel that we are united by the same bonds of sympathy and congeniality as ever."[34] After years of friendship one aging woman wrote of another: "Time cannot destroy the fascination of her manner . . . her voice is music to the ear. . . ."[35] Women made elaborate presents for each other, ranging from the Quakers' frugal pies and breads to painted velvet bags and phantom bouquets.[36] When a friend died, their grief was deeply felt. Martha Jefferis was unable to write to her daughter for three weeks because of the sorrow she felt at the death of a dear friend. Such distress

was not unusual. A generation earlier a young Massachusetts farm woman filled pages of her diary with her grief at the death of her "dearest friend" and transcribed the letters of condolence other women sent her. She marked the anniversary of Rachel's death each year in her diary, contrasting her faithfulness with that of Rachel's husband who had soon remarried.[37]

These female friendships served a number of emotional functions. Within this secure and empathetic world women could share sorrows, anxieties, and joys, confident that other women had experienced similar emotions. One mid-nineteenth-century rural matron in a letter to her daughter discussed this particular aspect of women's friendships: "To have such a friend as thyself to look to and sympathize with her—and enter into all her little needs and in whose bosom she could with freedom pour forth her joys and sorrows—such a friend would very much relieve the tedium of many a wearisome hour. . . ." A generation later Molly more informally underscored the importance of this same function in a letter to Helena: "Suppose I come down . . . [and] spend Sunday with you quietly," she wrote Helena ". . . that means talking all the time until you are relieved of all your latest troubles, and I of mine. . . ."[38] These were frequently troubles that apparently no man could understand. When Anne Jefferis Sheppard was first married, she and her older sister Edith (who then lived with Anne) wrote in detail to their mother of the severe depression and anxiety which they experienced. Moses Sheppard, Anne's husband, added cheerful postscripts to the sisters' letters—which he had clearly not read—remarking on Anne's and Edith's contentment. Theirs was an emotional world to which he had little access.[39]

This was, as well, a female world in which hostility and criticism of other women were discouraged, and thus a milieu in which women could develop a sense of inner security and self-esteem. As one young woman wrote to her mother's longtime friend: "I cannot sufficiently thank you for the kind unvaried affection & indulgence you have ever shown and expressed both by words and actions for me. . . . Happy would it be did all the world view me as you do, through the medium of kindness and forbearance."[40] They valued each other. Women, who had little status or power in the larger world of male concerns, possessed status and power in the lives and worlds of other women.[41]

An intimate mother-daughter relationship lay at the heart of this female world. The diaries and letters of both mothers and daughters attest to their closeness and mutual emotional dependency. Daughters routinely discussed their mother's health and activities with their own friends, expressed anxiety in cases of their mother's ill health and concern for her cares.[42] Expressions of hostility which we would today consider routine on the part of both mothers and daughters seem to have been uncommon indeed. On the contrary, this sample of families indicates that the normal relationship between mother and daughter was one of sympathy and understanding.[43] Only sickness or great geographic distance was allowed to cause extended separation. When marriage did result in such separation, both viewed the distance between them with distress.[44] Something of this sympathy and love between mothers and daughters is evident in a letter Sarah Alden Ripley, at age sixty-nine, wrote her youngest and recently married daughter: "You do not know how much I miss you, not only when I struggle in and out of my mortal envelop and pump my nightly potation and no longer pour into your sympathizing ear my senile gossip, but all the day I muse away, since the sound of your voice no longer rouses me to sympathy with your joys or sorrows. . . . You cannot

know how much I miss your affectionate demonstrations."[45] A dozen aging mothers in this sample of over thirty families echoed her sentiments.

Central to these mother-daughter relations is what might be described as an apprenticeship system. In those families where the daughter followed the mother into a life of traditional domesticity, mothers and other older women carefully trained daughters in the arts of housewifery and motherhood. Such training undoubtedly occurred throughout a girl's childhood but became more systematized, almost ritualistic, in the years following the end of her formal education and before her marriage. At this time a girl either returned home from boarding school or no longer divided her time between home and school. Rather, she devoted her energies on two tasks: mastering new domestic skills and participating in the visiting and social activities necessary to finding a husband. Under the careful supervision of their mothers and of older female relatives, such late-adolescent girls temporarily took over the household management from their mothers, tended their young nieces and nephews, and helped in childbirth, nursing, and weaning. Such experiences tied the generations together in shared skills and emotional interaction.[46]

Daughters were born into a female world. Their mother's life expectations and sympathetic network of friends and relations were among the first realities in the life of the developing child. As long as the mother's domestic role remained relatively stable and few viable alternatives competed with it, daughters tended to accept their mother's world and to turn automatically to other women for support and intimacy. It was within this closed and intimate female world that the young girl grew toward womanhood.

One could speculate at length concerning the absence of that mother-daughter hostility today considered almost inevitable to an adolescent's struggle for autonomy and self-identity. It is possible that taboos against female aggression and hostility were sufficiently strong to repress even that between mothers and their adolescent daughters. Yet these letters seem so alive and the interest of daughters in their mothers' affairs so vital and genuine that it is difficult to interpret their closeness exclusively in terms of repression and denial. The functional bonds that held mothers and daughters together in a world that permitted few alternatives to domesticity might well have created a source of mutuality and trust absent in societies where greater options were available for daughters than for mothers. Furthermore, the extended female network— a daughter's close ties with her own older sisters, cousins, and aunts—may well have permitted a diffusion and a relaxation of mother-daughter identification and so have aided a daughter in her struggle for identity and autonomy. None of these explanations are mutually exclusive; all may well have interacted to produce the degree of empathy evident in those letters and diaries.

At some point in adolescence, the young girl began to move outside the matrix of her mother's support group to develop a network of her own. Among the middle class, at least, this transition toward what was at the same time both a limited autonomy and a repetition of her mother's life seemed to have most frequently coincided with a girl's going to school. Indeed education appears to have played a crucial role in the lives of most of the families in this study. Attending school for a few months, for a year, or longer, was common even among daughters of relatively poor families, while middle-class girls routinely spent at least a year in boarding school.[47] These school years ordinarily marked a girl's first separation from home. They served to wean the daughter from her home, to train her in the essential social graces, and, ulti-

mately, to help introduce her into the marriage market. It was not infrequently a trying emotional experience for both mother and daughter.[48]

In this process of leaving one home and adjusting to another, the mother's friends and relatives played a key transitional role. Such older women routinely accepted the role of foster mother; they supervised the young girl's deportment, monitored her health and introduced her to their own network of female friends and kin.[49] Not infrequently women, friends from their own school years, arranged to send their daughters to the same school so that the girls might form bonds paralleling those their mothers had made. For years Molly and Helena wrote of their daughters' meeting and worried over each others' children. When Molly finally brought her daughter east to school, their first act on reaching New York was to meet Helena and her daughters. Elizabeth Bordley Gibson virtually adopted the daughters of her school chum, Eleanor Custis Lewis. The Lewis daughters soon began to write Elizabeth Gibson letters with the salutation "Dearest Mama." Eleuthera DuPont, attending boarding school in Philadelphia at roughly the same time as the Lewis girls, developed a parallel relationship with her mother's friend, Elizabeth McKie Smith. Eleuthera went to the same school and became a close friend of the Smith girls and eventually married their first cousin. During this period she routinely called Mrs. Smith "Mother." Indeed Eleuthera so internalized the sense of having two mothers that she casually wrote her sisters of her "Mamma's" visits at her "mother's" house—that is at Mrs. Smith's.[50]

Even more important to this process of maturation than their mother's friends were the female friends young women made at school. Young girls helped each other overcome homesickness and endure the crises of adolescence. They gossiped about beaux, incorporated each other into their own kinship systems, and attended and gave teas and balls together. Older girls in boarding school "adopted" younger ones, who called them "Mother."[51] Dear friends might indeed continue this pattern of adoption and mothering throughout their lives; one woman might routinely assume the nurturing role of pseudo-mother, the other the dependency role of daughter. The pseudomother performed for the other woman all the services which we normally associate with mothers; she went to absurd lengths to purchase items her "daughter" could have obtained from other sources, gave advice and functioned as an idealized figure in her "daughter's" imagination. Helena played such a role for Molly, as did Sarah for Jeannie. Elizabeth Bordley Gibson bought almost all Eleanor Parke Custis Lewis's necessities—from shoes and corset covers to bedding and harp strings—and sent them from Philadelphia to Virginia, a procedure that sometimes took months. Eleanor frequently asked Elizabeth to take back her purchases, have them redone, and argue with shopkeepers about prices. These were favors automatically asked and complied with. Anne Jefferis Sheppard made the analogy very explicitly in a letter to her own mother written shortly after Anne's marriage, when she was feeling depressed about their separation "Mary Paulen is truly kind, almost acts the part of a mother and trys to aid and *comfort me,* and also to *lighten my new cares.*"[52]

A comparison of the references to men and women in these young women's letters is striking. Boys were obviously indispensable to the elaborate courtship ritual girls engaged in. In these teenage letters and diaries, however, boys appear distant and warded off—an effect produced both by the girl's sense of bonding and by a highly developed and deprecatory whimsy. Girls joked among themselves about the conceit, poor looks or affectations of suitors. Rarely, especially in the eighteenth and early nineteenth centuries, were favorable remarks exchanged. Indeed, while hostility and criticism of other women were so rare as to seem almost tabooed, young women permitted themselves to express a great deal of hostility toward peer-group men.[53] When unacceptable suitors appeared, girls might even band together to harass them. When one such unfortunate came to court Sophie DuPont she hid in her room, first sending her sister Eleuthera to entertain him and then dispatching a number of urgent notes to her neighboring sister-in-law, cousins, and a visiting friend who all came to Sophie's support. A wild female romp ensued, ending only when Sophie banged into a door, lacerated her nose, and retired, with her female cohorts, to bed. Her brother and the presumably disconcerted suitor were left alone. These were not the antics of teenagers but of women in their early and mid-twenties.[54]

Even if young men were acceptable suitors, girls referred to them formally and obliquely: "The last week I received the unexpected intelligence of the arrival of a friend in Boston," Sarah Ripley wrote in her diary of the young man to whom she had been engaged for years and whom she would shortly marry. Harriet Manigault assiduously kept a lively and gossipy diary during the three years preceding her marriage, yet did not once comment upon her own engagement nor indeed make any personal references to her fiance—who was never identified as such but always referred to as Mr. Wilcox.[55] The point is not that these young women were hostile to young men. Far from it; they sought marriage and domesticity. Yet in these letters and diaries men appear as an other or out group, segregated into different schools, supported by their own male network of friends and kin, socialized to different behavior, and coached to a proper formality in courtship behavior. As a consequence, relations between young women and men frequently lacked the spontaneity and emotional intimacy that characterized the young girls' ties to each other.

Indeed, in sharp contrast to their distant relations with boys, young women's relations with each other were close, often frolicsome, and surprisingly long lasting and devoted. They wrote secret missives to each other, spent long solitary days with each other, curled up together in bed at night to whisper fantasies and secrets.[56] In 1862 one young woman in her early twenties described one such scene to an absent friend: "I have sat up to midnight listening to the confidences of Constance Kinney, whose heart was opened by that most charming of all situations, a seat on a bedside late at night, when all the household are asleep & only oneself & one's confidante survive in wakefulness. So she has told me all her loves and tried to get some confidences in return but being five or six years older than she, I know better. . . ."[57] Elizabeth Bordley and Nelly Parke Custis, teenagers in Philadelphia in the 1790s, routinely secreted themselves until late each night in Nelly's attic, where they each wrote a novel about the other.[58] Quite a few young women kept diaries, and it was a sign of special friendship to show their diaries to each other. The emotional quality of such exchanges emerges from the comments of one young girl who grew up along the Ohio frontier:

> Sisters CW and RT keep diaries & allow me the inestimable pleasure of reading them and in turn they see mine—but O shame covers my face when I think of it; theirs is so much better than mine, that every time. Then I think well now I *will* burn mine but upon second thought it would deprive me the pleasure of reading theirs, for I esteem it a very great privilege indeed, as well as very improving, as we lay our hearts open to each other, it heightens our love & helps to cherish & keep alive that sweet soothing friendship and endears us to each other by that soft attraction.[59]

Girls routinely slept together, kissed and hugged each other. Indeed, while waltzing with young men scandalized the otherwise flighty and highly fashionable Harriet Manigault, she considered waltzing with other young women not only acceptable but pleasant.[60]

Marriage followed adolescence. With increasing frequency in the nineteenth century, marriage involved a girl's traumatic removal from her mother and her mother's network. It involved, as well, adjustment to a husband, who, because he was male came to marriage with both a different world view and vastly different experiences. Not surprisingly, marriage was an event surrounded with supportive, almost ritualistic, practices. (Weddings are one of the last female rituals remaining in twentieth-century America.) Young women routinely spent the months preceding their marriage almost exclusively with other women—at neighborhood sewing bees and quilting parties or in a round of visits to geographically distant friends and relatives. Ostensibly they went to receive assistance in the practical preparations for their new home—sewing and quilting a trousseau and linen—but of equal importance, they appear to have gained emotional support and reassurance. Sarah Ripley spent over a month with friends and relatives in Boston and Hingham before her wedding; Parke Custis Lewis exchanged visits with her aunts and first cousins throughout Virginia.[61] Anne Jefferis, who married with some hesitation, spent virtually half a year in endless visiting with cousins, aunts, and friends. Despite their reassurance and support, however, she would not marry Moses Sheppard until her sister Edith and her cousin Rebecca moved into the groom's home, met his friends, and explored his personality.[62] The wedding did not take place until Edith wrote to Anne: "I can say in truth I am entirely willing thou shouldst follow him even away in the Jersey sands believing if thou are not happy in they future home it will not be any fault on his part. . . ."[63]

Sisters, cousins, and friends frequently accompanied newlyweds on their wedding night and wedding trip, which often involved additional family visiting. Such extensive visits presumably served to wean the daughter from her family of origin. As such they often contained a note of ambivalence. Nelly Custis, for example, reported homesickness and loneliness on her wedding trip. "I left my Beloved and revered Grandmamma with sincere regret," she wrote Elizabeth Bordley. "It was sometime before I could feel reconciled to traveling without her." Perhaps they also functioned to reassure the young woman herself, and her friends and kin, that though marriage might alter it would not destroy old bonds of intimacy and familiarity.[64]

Married life, too, was structured about a host of female rituals. Childbirth, especially the birth of the first child, became virtually a *rite de passage*, with a lengthy seclusion of the woman before and after delivery, severe restrictions on her activities, and finally a dramatic reemergence.[65] This seclusion was supervised by mothers, sisters, and loving friends. Nursing and weaning involved the advice and assistance of female friends and relatives. So did miscarriage.[66] Death, like birth, was structured around elaborate unisexed rituals. When Nelly Parke Custis Lewis rushed to nurse her daughter who was critically ill while away at school, Nelly received support, not from her husband, who remained on their plantation, but from her old school friend, Elizabeth Bordley. Elizabeth aided Nelly in caring for her dying daughter, cared for Nelly's other children, played a major role in the elaborate funeral arrangements (which the father did not attend), and frequently visited the girl's grave at the mother's request. For years Elizabeth continued to be the confidante of Nelly's anguished recollections of her lost daughter. These

memories, Nelly's letters make clear, were for Elizabeth alone. "Mr. L. knows nothing of this," was a frequent comment.[67] Virtually every collection of letters and diaries in my sample contained evidence of women turning to each other for comfort when facing the frequent and unavoidable deaths of the eighteenth and nineteenth centuries.[68] While mourning for her father's death, Sophie DuPont received elaborate letters and visits of condolence—all from women. No man wrote or visited Sophie to offer sympathy at her father's death.[69] Among rural Pennsylvania Quakers, death and mourning rituals assumed an even more extreme same-sex form, with men or women largely barred from the deathbeds of the other sex. Women relatives and friends slept with the dying woman, nursed her, and prepared her body for burial.[70]

Eighteenth- and nineteenth-century women thus lived in emotional proximity to each other. Friendships and intimacies followed the biological ebb and flow of women's lives. Marriage and pregnancy, childbirth and weaning, sickness and death involved physical and psychic trauma which comfort and sympathy made easier to bear. Intense bonds of love and intimacy bound together those women who, offering each other aid and sympathy, shared such stressful moments.

These bonds were often physical as well as emotional. An undeniably romantic and even sensual note frequently marked female relationships. This theme, significant throughout the stages of a woman's life, surfaced first during adolescence. As one teenager from a struggling pioneer family in the Ohio Valley wrote in her diary in 1808: "I laid with my dear R[ebecca] and a glorious good talk we had until about 4[A.M]—O how hard I do *love* her. . . ."[71] Only a few years later Bostonian Eunice Callender carved her initials and Sarah Ripley's into a favorite tree, along with a pledge of eternal love, and then waited breathlessly for

Sarah to discover and respond to her declaration of affection. The response appears to have been affirmative.[72] A half-century later urbane and sophisticated Katherine Wharton commented upon meeting an old school chum: "She was a great pet of mine at school & I thought as I watched her light figure how often I had held her in my arms—how dear she had once been to me." Katie maintained a long intimate friendship with another girl. When a young man began to court this friend seriously, Katie commented in her diary that she had never realized "how deeply I loved Eng and how fully." She wrote over and over again in that entry: "Indeed I love her!" and only with great reluctance left the city that summer since it meant also leaving Eng with Eng's new suitor.[73]

Peggy Emlen, a Quaker adolescent in Philadelphia in the 1760s, expressed similar feelings about her first cousin, Sally Logan. The girls sent love poems to each other (not unlike the ones Elizabeth Bordley wrote to Nellie Custis a generation later), took long solitary walks together, and even haunted the empty house of the other when one was out of town. Indeed Sally's absences from Philadelphia caused Peggy acute unhappines. So strong were Peggy's feelings that her brothers began to tease about her affection for Sally and threatened to steal Sally's letters, much to both girls' alarm. In one letter that Peggy wrote the absent Sally she elaborately described the depth and nature of her feelings: "I have not words to express my impatience to see My Dear Cousin, what would I not give just now for an hours sweet conversation with her, it seems as if I had a thousand things to say to thee, yet when I see thee, everything will be forgot thro' joy. . . . I have a very great friendship for several Girls yet it dont give me so much uneasiness at being absent from them as from thee. . . . [Let us] go and spend a day down at our place together and there unmolested enjoy each others company."[74]

Sarah Alden Ripley, a young, highly educated woman, formed a similar intense relationship, in this instance with a woman somewhat older than herself. The immediate bond of friendship rested on their atypically intense scholarly interests, but it soon involved strong emotions, at least on Sarah's part. "Friendship," she wrote Mary Emerson, "is fast twining about her willing captive the silken hands of dependence, a dependence so sweet who would renounce it for the apathy of self-sufficiency?" Subsequent letters became far more emotional, almost conspiratorial. Mary visited Sarah secretly in her room, or the two women crept away from family and friends to meet in a nearby woods. Sarah became jealous of Mary's other young friends. Mary's trips away from Boston also thrust Sarah into periods of anguished depression. Interestingly, the letters detailing their love were not destroyed but were preserved and even reprinted in a eulogistic biography of Sarah Alden Ripley.[75]

Tender letters between alodescent women, confessions of loneliness and emotional dependency, were not peculiar to Sarah Alden, Peggy Emlen, or Katie Wharton. They are found throughout the letters of the thirty-five families studied. They have, of course, their parallel today in the musings of many female adolescents. Yet these eighteenth- and nineteenth-century friendships lasted with undiminished, indeed often increased, intensity throughout the women's lives. Sarah Alden Ripley's first child was named after Mary Emerson. Nelly Custis Lewis's love for and dependence on Elizabeth Bordley Gibson only increased after her marriage. Eunice Callender remained enamored of her cousin Sarah Ripley for years and rejected as impossible the suggestion by another woman that their love might some day fade away.[76] Sophie

DuPont and her childhood friend, Clementina Smith, exchanged letters filled with love and dependency for forty years while another dear friend, Mary Black Couper, wrote of dreaming that she, Sophie, and her husband were all united in one marriage. Mary's letters to Sophie are filled with avowals of love and indications of ambivalence toward her own husband. Eliza Schlatter, another of Sophie's intimate friends, wrote to her at a time of crisis: "I wish I could be with you present in the body as well as the mind & heart— I would turn your *good husband out of bed*—and snuggle into you and we would have a long talk like old times in Pine St.—I want to tell you so many things that are not *writable*. . . ."[77]

Such mutual dependency and deep affection is a central existential reality coloring the world of supportive networks and rituals. In the case of Katie, Sophie, or Eunice—as with Molly, Jeannie, and Sarah—their need for closeness and support merged with more intense demands for a love which was at the same time both emotional and sensual. Perhaps the most explicit statement concerning women's lifelong friendships appeared in the letter abolitionist and reformer Mary Grew wrote about the same time, referring to her own love for her dear friend and lifelong companion, Margaret Burleigh. Grew wrote, in response to a letter of condolence from another woman on Burleigh's death: "Your words respecting my beloved friend touch me deeply. Evidently . . . you comprehend and appreciate, as few persons do . . . the nature of the relation which existed, which exists, between her and myself. Her only surviving niece . . . also does. To me it seems to have been a closer union than that of most marriages. We know there have been other such between two men and also between two women. And why should there not be. Love is spiritual, only passion is sexual."[78]

How then can we ultimately interpret these long-lived intimate female relationships and integrate them into our understanding of Victorian sexuality? Their ambivalent and romantic rhetoric presents us with an ultimate puzzle: the relationship along the spectrum of human emotions between love, sensuality, and sexuality.

One is tempted, as I have remarked, to compare Molly, Peggy, or Sophie's relationships with the friendships adolescent girls in the twentieth century routinely form—close friendships of great emotional intensity. Helene Deutsch and Clara Thompson have both described these friendships as emotionally necessary to a girl's psychosexual development. But, they warn, such friendships might shade into adolescent and postadolescent homosexuality.[79]

It is possible to speculate that in the twentieth century a number of cultural taboos evolved to cut short the homosocial ties of girlhood and to impel the emerging women of thirteen or fourteen toward heterosexual relationships. In contrast, nineteenth-century American society did not taboo close female relationships but rather recognized them as a socially viable form of human contact—and, as such, acceptable throughout a woman's life. Indeed it was not these homosocial ties that were inhibited but rather heterosexual leanings. While closeness, freedom of emotional expression, and uninhibited physical contact characterized women's relationships with each other, the opposite was frequently true of male-female relationships. One could thus argue that within such a world of female support, intimacy, and ritual it was only to be expected that adult women would turn trustingly and lovingly to each other. It was a behavior they had observed and learned since childhood. A different type of emotional landscape existed in the nineteenth century, one in which Molly and Helena's love became a natural development.

Of perhaps equal significance are the implications we can garner from this framework for the understanding of heterosexual marriages in the nineteenth century. If men and women grew up as they did in relatively homogeneous and segregated sexual groups, then marriage represented a major problem in adjustment. From this perspective we could interpret much of the emotional stiffness and distance that we associate with Victorian marriage as a structural consequence of contemporary sex-role differentiation and gender-role socialization. With marriage both women and men had to adjust to life with a person who was, in essence, a member of an alien group.

I have thus far substituted a cultural or psychosocial for a psychosexual interpretation of women's emotional bonding. But there are psychosexual implications in this model which I think it only fair to make more explicit. Despite Sigmund Freud's insistence on the bisexuality of us all or the recent American Psychiatric Association decision on homosexuality, many psychiatrists today tend explicitly or implicitly to view homosexuality as a totally alien or pathological behavior—as totally unlike heterosexuality. I suspect that in essence they may have adopted an explanatory model similar to the one used in discussing schizophrenia. As a psychiatrist can speak of schizophrenia and of a borderline schizophrenic personality as both ultimately and fundamentally different from a normal or neurotic personality, so they also think of both homosexuality and latent homosexuality as states totally different from heterosexuality. With this

rapidly dichotomous model of asumption, "latent homosexuality" becomes the indication of a disease in progress—seeds of a pathology which belie the reality of an individual's heterosexuality.

Yet at the same time we are well aware that cultural values can effect choices in the gender of a person's sexual partner. We, for instance, do not necessarily consider homosexual-object choice among men in prison, on shipboard or in boarding schools a necessary indication of pathology. I would urge that we expand this relativistic model and hypothesize that a number of cultures might well tolerate or even encourage diversity in sexual and nonsexual relations. Based on my research into this nineteenth-century world of female intimacy, I would further suggest that rather than seeing a gulf between the normal and the abnormal we view sexual and emotional impulses as part of a continuum or spectrum of affect gradations strongly affected by cultural norms and arrangements, a continuum influenced in part by observed and thus learned behavior. At one end of the continuum lies committed heterosexuality, at the other uncompromising homosexuality; between, a wide latitude of emotions and sexual feelings. Certain cultures and environments permit individuals a great deal of freedom in moving across this spectrum. I would like to suggest that the nineteenth century was such a cultural environment. That is, the supposedly repressive and destructive Victorian sexual ethos may have been more flexible and responsive to the needs of particular individuals than those of mid-twentieth century.

Notes

1. The most notable exception to this rule is now eleven years old: William R. Taylor and Christopher Lasch, "Two 'Kindred Spirits': Sorority and Family in New England, 1839–1846," *New England Quarterly* 36 (1963):25–41. Taylor has made a valuable contribution to the history of women and the history of the family with his concept of

"sororial" relations. I do not, however, accept the Taylor-Lasch thesis that female friendships developed in the mid-nineteenth century because of geographic mobility and the breakup of the colonial family. I have found these friendships as frequently in the eighteenth century as in the nineteenth and would hypothesize that the geographic mobility of the mid-nineteenth century eroded them as it did so many other traditional social institutions. Helen Vendler (*Review of Notable American Women, 1607–1950*, ed. Edward James and Janet James, *New York Times*, [November 5, 1972]: sec. 7) points out the significance of these friendships.

2. I do not wish to deny the importance of women's relations with particular men. Obviously, women were close to brothers, husbands, fathers, and sons. However, there is evidence that despite such closeness relationships between men and women differed in both emotional texture and frequency from those between women. Women's relations with each other, although they played a central role in the American family and American society, have been so seldom examined either by general social historians or by historians of the family that I wish in this article simply to examine their nature and analyze their implications for our understanding of social relations and social structure. I have discussed some aspects of male-female relationships in two articles: "Puberty to Menopause: The Cycle of Femininity in Nineteenth-Century America," *Feminist Studies* 1 (1973): 58–72, and, with Charles Rosenberg, "The Female Animal: Medical and Biological Views of Women in 19th Century America," *Journal of American History* 59 (1973):331–56.

3. See Freud's classic paper on homosexuality, "Three Essays on the Theory of Sexuality," in *The Standard Edition of the Complete Psychological Works of Sigmund Freud*, trans. James Strachey (London: Hogarth Press, 1953), 7:135–72. The essays originally appeared in 1905. Prof. Roy Shafer, Department of Psychiatry, Yale University, has pointed out that Freud's view of sexual behavior was strongly influenced by nineteenth-century evolutionary thought. Within Freud's schema, genital heterosexuality marked the height of human development (Schafer, "Problems in Freud's Psychology of Women," *Journal of the American Psychoanalytic Association* 22 [1974]:459–85).

4. For a novel and most important exposition of one theory of behavioral norms and options and its application to the study of human sexuality, see Charles Rosenberg,

"Sexuality, Class and Role," *American Quarterly* 25 (1973):131–53.

5. See, e.g., the letters of Peggy Emlen to Sally Logan, 1768–72, Wells Morris Collection, Box 1, Historical Society of Pennsylvania; and the Eleanor Parke Custis Lewis Letters, Historical Society of Pennsylvania, Philadelphia.

6. Sarah Butler Wister was the daughter of Fanny Kemble and Pierce Butler. In 1859 she married a Philadelphia physician, Owen Wister. The novelist Owen Wister is her son. Jeannie Field Musgrove was the half-orphaned daughter of constitutional lawyer and New York Republican politician David Dudley Field. Their correspondence (1855–98) is in the Sarah Butler Wister Papers, Wister Family Papers, Historical Society of Pennsylvania.

7. Sarah Butler, Butler Place, S.C., to Jeannie Field, New York, September 14, 1855.

8. See, e.g., Sarah Butler Wister, Germantown, Pa., to Jeannie Field, New York, September 25, 1862, October 21, 1863; or Jeannie Field, New York, to Sarah Butler Wister, Germantown, July 3, 1861, January 23 and July 12, 1863.

9. Sarah Butler Wister, Germantown, to Jeannie Field, New York, June 5, 1861, February 29, 1864; Jeannie Field to Sarah Butler Wister, November 22, 1861, January 4 and June 14, 1963.

10. Sarah Butler Wister, London, to Jeannie Field Musgrove, New York, June 18 and August 3, 1870.

11. See, e.g., two of Sarah's letters to Jeannie: December 21, 1873, July 16, 1878.

12. This is the 1868–1920 correspondence between Mary Hallock Foote and Helena, a New York friend (the Mary Hallock Foote Papers are in the Manuscript Division, Stanford University). Wallace E. Stegner has written a fictionalized biography of Mary Hallock Foote (*Angle of Repose* [Garden City, N.Y.: Doubleday & Co., 1971]). See, as well, her autobiography: Mary Hallock Foote, *A Victorian Gentlewoman in the Far West: The Reminiscences of Mary Hallock Foote*, ed. Rodman W. Paul (San Marino, Calif.: Huntington Library, 1972). In many ways these letters are typical of those women wrote to other women. Women frequently began letters to each other with salutations such as "Dearest," "My Most Beloved," "You Darling Girl," and signed them "tenderly" or "to my dear dear sweet friend, good-bye." Without the least self-consciousness, one woman in her frequent letters to a female friend referred to her husband as "my other

love." She was by no means unique. See, e.g., Annie to Charlene Van Vleck Anderson, Appleton, Wis., June 10, 1871, Anderson Family Papers, Manuscript Division, Stanford University; Maggie to Emily Howland, Philadelphia, July 12, 1851, Howland Family Papers, Phoebe King Collection, Friends Historical Library, Swarthmore College; Mary Jane Burleigh to Emily Howland, Sherwood, N.Y., March 27, 1872, Howland Family Papers, Sophia Smith Collection, Smith College; Mary Black Couper to Sophia Madeleine DuPont, Wilmington, Del.: n.d. [1834] (two letters), Samuel Francis DuPont Papers, Eleutherian Mills Foundation, Wilmington, Del.; Phoebe Middleton, Concordville, Pa., to Martha Jefferis, Chester County, Pa., February 22, 1848; and see in general the correspondence (1838–49) between Rebecca Biddle of Philadelphia and Martha Jefferis, Chester County, Pa., Jefferis Family Correspondence, Chester County Historical Society, West Chester, Pa.; Phoebe Bradford Diary, June 7 and July 13, 1832, Historical Society of Pennsylvania; Sarah Alden Ripley, to Abba Allyn, Boston, n.d. [1818–20], and Sarah Alden Ripley to Sophia Bradford, November 30, 1854, in the Sarah Alden Ripley Correspondence, Schlesinger Library, Radcliffe College; Fanny Canby Ferris to Anne Biddle, Philadelphia, October 11 and November 19, 1811, December 26, 1813, Fanny Canby to Mary Canby, May 27, 1801, Mary R. Garrigues to Mary Canby, five letters n.d. [1802–8], Anne Biddle to Mary Canby, two letters n.d., May 16, July 13, and November 24, 1806, June 14, 1807, June 5, 1808, Anne Sterling Biddle Family Papers, Friends Historical Society, Swarthmore College; Harriet Manigault Wilcox Diary, August 7, 1814, Historical Society of Pennsylvania. See as well the correspondence between Harriet Manigault Wilcox's mother, Mrs. Gabriel Manigault, Philadelphia, and Mrs. Henry Middleton, Charleston, S.C., between 1810 and 1830, Cadwalader Collection, J. Francis Fisher Section, Historical Society of Pennsylvania. The basis and nature of such friendships can be seen in the comments of Sarah Alden Ripley to her sister-in-law and longtime friend, Sophia Bradford: "Hearing that you are not well reminds me of what it would be to lose your loving society. We have kept step together through a long piece of road in the weary journey of life. We have loved the same beings and wept together over their graves" (Mrs. O. J. Wister and Miss Agnes Irwin, eds., *Worthy Women of Our First Century* [Philadelphia: J. B. Lippincott & Co., 1877] p. 195).

13. Mary Hallock [Foote] to Helena, n.d. [1869–70], n.d. [1871–72], Folder 1, Mary Hallock Foote Letters, Manuscript Division, Stanford University.

14. Mary Hallock [Foote] to Helena, September 15 and 23, 1873, n.d. [October 1873], October 12, 1873.

15. Mary Hallock [Foote] to Helena, n.d. [January 1874], n.d. [Spring 1874].

16. Mary Hallock [Foote] to Helena, September 23, 1873; Mary Hallock [Foote] to Richard, December 13, 1873. Molly's and Helena's relationship continued for the rest of their lives. Molly's letters are filled with tender and intimate references, as when she wrote, twenty years later and from 2,000 miles away: "It isn't because you are good that I love you—but for the essence of you which is like perfume" (n.d. [1890s?]).

17. I am in the midst of a larger study of adult gender-roles and gender-role socialization in America, 1785–1895. For a discussion of social attitudes toward appropriate male and female roles, see Barbara Welter, "The Cult of True Womanhood: 1820–1860," *American Quarterly* 18 (Summer 1966):151–74; Anne Firor Scott, *The Southern Lady: From Pedestal to Politics, 1830–1930* (Chicago: University of Chicago Press, 1970), chaps. 1–2; Smith-Rosenberg and Rosenberg.

18. See, e.g., the letters of Peggy Emlen to Sally Logan, 1768–72, Wells Morris Collection, Box 1, Historical Society of Pennsylvania; and the Eleanor Parke Custis Lewis Letters, Historical Society of Pennsylvania.

19. See esp. Elizabeth Botts, *Family and Social Network* (London: Tavistock Publications, 1957); Michael Young and Peter Willmott, *Family and Kinship in East London*, rev. ed. (Baltimore: Penguin Books, 1964).

20. This pattern seemed to cross class barriers. A letter that an Irish domestic wrote in the 1830s contains seventeen separate references to women and but only seven to men, most of whom were relatives and two of whom were infant brothers living with her mother and mentioned in relation to her mother (Ann McGrann, Philadelphia, to Sophie M. DuPont, Philadelphia, July 3, 1834, Sophie Madeleine DuPont Letters, Eleutherian Mills Foundation).

21. Harriet Manigault Diary, June 28, 1814, and passim; Jeannie Field, New York, to Sarah Butler Wister, Germantown, April 19, 1963; Phoebe Bradford Diary, January 30, February 19, March 4, August 11, and October 14, 1832, Historical Society of Pennsylvania; Sophie M. DuPont, Brandywine, to

Henry DuPont, Germantown, July 9, 1827, Eleutherian Mills Foundation.

22. Martha Jefferis to Anne Jefferis Sheppard, July 9, 1843; Anne Jefferis Sheppard to Martha Jefferis, June 28, 1846; Ann Sterling Biddle Papers, passim, Biddle Family Papers, Friends Historical Society, Swarthmore College; Eleanor Parke Custis Lewis, Virginia, to Elizabeth Bordley Gibson, Philadelphia, November 24 and December 4, 1820, November 6, 1821.

23. Phoebe Bradford Diary, January 13, November 16–19, 1832, April 26 and May 7, 1833; Abigail Brackett Lyman to Mrs. Catling, Litchfied, Conn., May 3, 1801, collection in private hands; Martha Jefferis to Anne Jefferis Sheppard, August 28, 1845.

24. Lisa Mitchell Diary, 1860s, passim, Manuscript Division, Tulane University; Eleanor Parke Custis Lewis to Elizabeth Bordley [Gibson] February 5, 1822; Jeannie McCall, Cedar Park, to Peter McCall, Philadelphia, June 30, 1849, McCall Section, Cadwalader Collection, Historical Society of Pennsylvania.

25. Peggy Emlen to Sally Logan, May 3, 1769.

26. For a prime example of this type of letter, see Eleanor Parke Custis Lewis to Elizabeth Bordley Gibson, passim; or Fanny Canby to Mary Canby, Philadelphia, May 27, 1801; or Sophie M. DuPont, Brandywine, to Henry DuPont, Germantown, February 4, 1832.

27. Place of residence is not the only variable significance in characterizing family structure. Strong emotional ties and frequent visiting and correspondence can unite families that do not live under one roof. Demographic studies based on household structure alone fail to reflect such emotional and even economic ties between families.

28. Eleanor Parke Custis Lewis to Elizabeth Bordley Gibson, April 20 and September 25, 1848.

29. Maria Inskeep to Fanny Hampton Correspondence, 1823–60, Inskeep Collection, Tulane University Library.

30. Eunice Callender, Boston, to Sarah Ripley [Stearns], September 24 and October 29, 1803, February 16, 1805, April 29 and October 9, 1806, May 26, 1810.

31. Sophie DuPont filled her letters to her younger brother Henry (with whom she had been assigned to correspond while he was at boarding school) with accounts of family visiting (see, e.g., December 13, 1827, January 10 and March 9, 1828, February 4 and March 10, 1832; also Sophie M. DuPont to Victorine Du-

Pont Bauday, September 26 and December 4, 1827, February 22, 1828; Sophie M. DuPont, Brandywine, to Clementina B. Smith, Philadelphia, January 15, 1830; Eleuthera DuPont, Brandywine, to Victorine DuPont Bauday, Philadelphia, April 17, 1821, October 20, 1826; Evelina DuPont [Biderman] to Victorine DuPont Bauday, October 18, 1816). Other examples, from the Historical Society of Pennsylvania, are Harriet Manigault [Wilcox] Diary, August 17, September 8, October 19 and 22, December 22, 1814; Jane Zook, West Town School, Chester County, Pa., to Mary Zook, November 13, December 7 and 11, 1870, February 26, 1871; Eleanor Parke Custis [Lewis] to Elizabeth Bordley [Gibson], March 30, 1796, February 7 and March 20, 1798; Jeannie McCall to Peter McCall, Philadelphia, November 12, 1847; Mary B. Ashew Diary, July 11 and 13, August 17, Summer and October 1858, and, from a private collection, Edith Jefferis to Anne Jefferis Sheppard, November 1841, April 5, 1842; Abigail Brackett Lyman, Northampton, Mass., to Mrs. Catling, Litchfield, Conn., May 13, 1801; Abigail Brackett Lyman, Northampton, to Mary Lord, August 11, 1800. Mary Hallock Foote vacationed with her sister, her sister's children, her aunt, and a female cousin in the summer of 1874; cousins frequently visited the Hallock farm in Milton, N.Y. In later years Molly and her sister Bessie set up a joint household in Boise, Idaho (Mary Hallock Foote to Helena, July [1874?] and passim). Jeannie Field, after initially disliking her sister-in-law, Laura, became very close to her, calling her "my little sister" and at times spending virtually every day with her (Jeannie Field [Musgrove] New York, to Sarah Butler Wister, Germantown, March 1, 8, and 15, and May 9, 1863).

32. Martha Jefferis to Anne Jefferis Sheppard, January 12, 1845; Phoebe Middleton to Martha Jefferis, February 22, 1848. A number of other women remained close to sisters and sisters-in-law across a long lifetime (Phoebe Bradford Diary, June 7, 1832, and Sarah Alden Ripley to Sophia Bradford, cited in Wister and Irwin, p. 195).

33. Rebecca Biddle to Martha Jefferis, 1838–49, passim; Martha Jefferis to Anne Jefferis Sheppard, July 6, 1846; Anne Jefferis Sheppard to Rachael Jefferis, January 16, 1865; Sarah Foulke Farquhar [Emlen] Diary, September 22, 1813, Friends Historical Library, Swarthmore College; Mary Garrigues to Mary Canby [Biddle], 1802–8, passim; Anne Biddle to Mary Canby [Biddle], May 16, July 13, and November 24, 1806, June 14, 1807, June 5, 1808.

34. Sarah Alden Ripley to Abba Allyn, n.d., Schlesinger Library.

35. Phoebe Bradford Diary, July 13, 1832.

36. Mary Hallock [Foote] to Helena, December 23 [1868 or 1869]; Phoebe Bradford Diary, December 8, 1832; Martha Jefferis and Anne Jefferis Sheppard letters, passim.

37. Martha Jefferis to Anne Jefferis Sheppard, August 3, 1849; Sarah Ripley [Stearns] Diary, November 12, 1808, January 8, 1811. An interesting note of hostility or rivalry is present in Sarah Ripley's diary entry. Sarah evidently deeply resented the husband's rapid remarriage.

38. Martha Jefferis to Edith Jefferis, March 15, 1841; Mary Hallock Foote to Helena, n.d. [1874–75?]; see also Jeannie Field, New York, to Sarah Butler Wister, Germantown, May 5, 1863, Emily Howland Diary, December 1879, Howland Family Papers.

39. Anne Jefferis Sheppard to Martha Jefferis, September 29, 1841.

40. Frances Parke Lewis to Elizabeth Bordley Gibson, April 29, 1821.

41. Mary Jane Burleigh, Mount Pleasant, S.C., to Emily Howland, Sherwood N.Y., March 27, 1872, Howland Family Papers; Emily Howland Diary, September 16, 1879, January 21 and 23, 1880; Mary Black Couper, New Castle, Del., to Sophie M. DuPont, Brandywine, April 7, 1834.

42. Harriet Manigault Diary, August 15, 21, and 23, 1814, Historical Society of Pennsylvania; Polly [Simmons] to Sophie Madeleine DuPont, February 1822; Sophie Madeleine DuPont to Victorine Bauday, December 4, 1827; Sophie Madeleine DuPont to Clementina Beach Smith, July 24, 1828, August 19, 1829; Clementina Beach Smith to Sophie Madeleine DuPont, April 29, 1831; Mary Black Couper to Sophie Madeleine DuPont, December 24, 1828, July 21, 1834. This pattern appears to have crossed class lines. When a former Sunday school student of Sophie DuPont's (and the daughter of a worker in her father's factory) wrote to Sophie she discussed her mother's health and activities quite naturally (Ann McGrann to Sophie Madeleine DuPont, August 25, 1832; see also Elizbeath Bordley to Martha, n.d. [1797]; Eleanor Parke Custis [Lewis] to Elizabeth Bordley [Gibson], May 13, 1796, July 1, 1798; Peggy Emlen to Sally Logan, January 8, 1786. All but the Emlen/Logan letters are in the Eleanor Parke Custis Lewis Correspondence, Historical Society of Pennsylvania).

43. Mrs. S. S. Dalton, "Autobiography," (Circle Valley, Utah, 1876), pp. 21–22, Bancroft Library, University of California, Berke-ley; Sarah Foulke Emlen Diary, April 1809; Louisa G. Van Vleck, Appleton, Wis., to Charlena Van Vleck Anderson, Göttingen, n.d. [1875], Harriet Manigault Diary, August 16, 1814, July 14, 1815; Sarah Alden Ripley to Sophy Fisher [early 1860s], quoted in Wister and Irwin (n. 12 above), p. 212. The Jefferis family papers are filled with empathetic letters between Martha and her daughters, Anne and Edith. See, e.g., Martha Jefferis to Edith Jefferis, December 26, 1836, March 11, 1837, March 15, 1841; Anne Jefferis Sheppard to Martha Jefferis, March 17, 1841, January 17, 1847; Martha Jefferis to Anne Jefferis Sheppard, April 17, 1848, April 30, 1849. A representative letter is this of March 9, 1837 from Edith to Martha: "My heart can fully respond to the language of my own precious Mother, the absence has not diminished our affection for each other, but has, if possible, strengthened the bonds that have united us together & I have had to remark how we had been permitted to mingle in sweet fellowship and have been strengthened to bear one another's burdens. . . ."

44. Abigail Brackett Lyman, Boston, to Mrs. Abigail Brackett (daughter to mother), n.d. [1797], June 3, 1800; Sarah Alden Ripley wrote weekly to her daughter, Sophy Ripley Fisher, after the latter's marriage (Sarah Alden Ripley Correspondence, passim); Phoebe Bradford Diary, February 25, 1833, passim, 1832–33; Louisa G. Van Vleck to Charlena Van Vleck Anderson, December 15, 1873, July 4, August 15 and 29, September 19, and November 9, 1875. Eleanor Parke Custis Lewis's long correspondence with Elizabeth Bordley Gibson contains evidence of her anxiety at leaving her foster mother's home at various times during her adolescence and at her marriage, and her own longing for her daughters, both of whom had married and moved to Louisiana (Eleanor Parke Custis [Lewis] to Elizabeth Bordley [Gibson], October 13, 1795, November 4, 1799, passim, 1820s and 1830s). Anne Jefferis Sheppard experienced a great deal of anxiety on moving two days' journey from her mother at the time of her marriage. This loneliness and sense of isolation persisted through her marriage until, finally a widow, she returned to live with her mother (Anne Jefferis Sheppard to Martha Jefferis, April 1841, October 16, 1842, April 2, May 22, and October 12, 1844, September 3, 1845, January 17, 1847, May 16, June 3, and October 31, 1849; Anne Jefferis Sheppard to Susanna Lightfoot, March 23, 1845, and to Joshua Jefferis, May 14 1854). Daughters evidently frequently slept with

their mothers—into adulthood (Harriet Mani-gault [Wilcox] Diary, February 19, 1815; Eleanor Parke Custis Lewis to Elizabeth Bordley Gibson, October 10, 1832). Daughters also frequently asked mothers to live with them and professed delight when they did so. See, e.g., Sarah Alden Ripley's comments to George Simmons, October 6, 1844, in Wister and Irwin, p. 185: "It is no longer 'Mother and Charles came out one day and returned the next,' for mother is one of us: she has entered the penetratice, been initiated into the mystery of the household gods, . . . Her divertissement is to mend the stockings . . . whiten sheets and napkins, . . . and take a stroll at evening with me to talk of our children, to compare our experiences, what we have learned and what we have suffered, and, last of all, to complete with pears and melons the cheerful circle about the solar lamp. . . ." We did find a few exceptions to this mother-daughter felicity (M.B. Ashew Diary, November 19, 1857, April 10 and May 17, 1858). Sarah Foulke Emlen was at first very hostile to her stepmother (Sarah Foulke Emlen Diary, August 9, 1807), but they later developed a warm supportive relationship.

45. Sarah Alden Ripley to Sophy Thayer, n.d. [1861].

46. Mary Hallock Foote to Helena [winter 1873] (no. 52); Jossie, Stevens Point, Wis., to Charlena Van Vleck [Anderson], Appleton, Wis., October 24, 1870; Pollie Chandler, Green Bay, Wis., to Charlena Van Vleck [Anderson], Appleton, n.d. [1870]; Eleuthera DuPont to Sophie DuPont, September 5, 1829; Sophie DuPont to Eleuthera DuPont, December 1827; Sophie DuPont to Victorine Bauday, December 4, 1827; Mary Gilpin to Sophie DuPont, September 26, 1827; Sarah Ripley Stearns Diary, April 2, 1809; Jeannie McCall to Peter McCall, October 27 [late 1840s]. Eleanor Parke Custis Lewis's correspondence with Elizabeth Bordley Gibson describes such an apprenticeship system over two generations—that of her childhood and that of her daughters. Indeed Eleanor Lewis's own apprenticeship was quite formal. She was deliberately separated from her foster mother in order to spend a winter of domesticity with her married sisters and her remarried mother. It was clearly felt that her foster mother's (Martha Washington) home at the nation's capital was not an appropriate place to develop domestic talents (October 13, 1795, March 30, May 13, and [summer] 1796, March 18 and April 27, 1797, October 1827).

47. Education was not limited to the daughters of the well-to-do. Sarah Foulke Emlen, the daughter of an Ohio Valley frontier farmer, for instance, attended day school for several years during the early 1800s. Sarah Ripley Stearns, the daughter of a shopkeeper in Greenfield, Mass., attended a boarding school for but three months, yet the experience seemed very important to her. Mrs. S. S. Dalton, a Mormon woman from Utah, attended a series of poor country schools and greatly valued her opportunity, though she also expressed a great deal of guilt for the sacrifices her mother made to make her education possible (Sarah Foulke Emlen Journal, Sarah Ripley Stearns Diary, Mrs. S. S. Dalton, "Autobiography").

48. Maria Revere to her mother [Mrs. Paul Revere], June 13, 1801, Paul Revere Papers, Massachusetts Historical Society. In a letter to Elizabeth Bordley Gibson, March 28, 1847, Eleanor Parke Custis Lewis from Virginia discussed the anxiety her daughter felt when her granddaughters left home to go to boarding school. Eleuthera DuPont was very homesick when away at school in Philadelphia in the early 1820s (Eleuthera DuPont, Philadelphia, to Victorine Bauday, Wilmington, Del., April 7, 1821; Eleuthera DuPont to Sophie Madeleine DuPont, Wilmington, Del., February and April 3, 1821).

49. Elizabeth Bordley Gibson, a Philadelphia matron, played such a role for the daughters and nieces of her lifelong friend, Eleanor Parke Custis Lewis, a Virginia planter's wife (Eleanor Parke Custis Lewis to Elizabeth Bordley Gibson, January 29, 1833, March 19, 1826, and passim through the collection). The wife of Thomas Gurney Smith played a similar role for Sophie and Eleuthera DuPont (see, e.g., Eleuthera DuPont to Sophie Madeleine DuPont, May 22, 1825; Rest Cope to Philema P. Swayne [niece] West Town School, Chester County, Pa., April 8, 1829, Friends Historical Library, Swarthmore College). For a view of such a social pattern over three generations, see the letters and diaries of three generations of Manigault women in Philadelphia: Mrs. Gabrielle Manigault, her daughter, Harriet Manigault Wilcox, and granddaughter, Charlotte Wilcox McCall. Unfortunately the papers of the three women are not in one family collection (Mrs. Henry Middleton, Charleston, S.C., to Mrs. Gabrielle Manigault, n.d. [mid 1800s]; Harriet Manigault Diary, vol. 1; December 1, 1813, June 28, 1814; Charlotte Wilcox McCall Diary, vol. 1, 1842, passim. All in Historical Society of Philadelphia).

50. Frances Parke Lewis, Woodlawn, Va., to Elizabeth Bordley Gibson, Philadelphia,

April 11, 1821, Lewis Correspondence; Eleuthera DuPont, Philadelphia, to Victorine DuPont Bauday, Brandywine, December 8, 1821, January 31, 1822; Eleuthera DuPont, Brandywine, to Margaretta Lammont [DuPont], Philadelphia, May 1823.

51. Sarah Ripley Stearns Diary, March 9 and 25, 1810; Peggy Emlen to Sally Logan, March and July 4, 1769; Harriet Manigault [Wilcox] Diary, vol. 1, December 1, 1813, June 28 and September 18, 1814, August 10, 1815; Charlotte Wilcox McCall Diary, 1842, passim; Fanny Canby to Mary Canby, May 27, 1801, March 17, 1804; Deborah Cope, West Town School, to Rest Cope, Philadelphia, July 9, 1828, Chester County Historical Society, West Chester, Pa.; Anne Zook, West Town School, to Mary Zook, Philadelphia, January 30, 1866, Chester County Historical Society, West Chester, Pa.; Mary Gilpin to Sophie Madeleine DuPont, February 25, 1829; Eleanor Parke Custis [Lewis] to Elizabeth Bordley [Gibson], April 27, July 2, and September 8, 1797, June 30, 1799, December 29, 1820; Frances Parke Lewis to Elizabeth Bordley Gibson, December 20, 1820.

52. Anne Jefferis Sheppard to Martha Jefferis, March 17, 1841.

53. Peggy Emlen to Sally Logan, March 1769, Mount Vernon, Va.; Eleanor Parke Custis [Lewis] to Elizabeth Bordley [Gibson], Philadelphia, April 27, 1797, June 30, 1799; Jeannie Field, New York to Sarah Butler Wister, Germantown, July 3, 1861, January 16, 1863, Harriet Manigault Diary, August 3 and 11–13, 1814; Eunice Callender, Boston, to Sarah Ripley [Stearns], Greenfield, May 4, 1809. I found one exception to this inhibition of female hostility. This was the diary of Charlotte Wilcox McCall, Philadelphia (see, e.g., her March 23, 1842 entry).

54. Sophie M. DuPont and Eleuthera DuPont, Brandywine, to Victorine DuPont Bauday, Philadelphia, January 25, 1832.

55. Sarah Ripley [Stearns] Diary and Harriet Manigault Diary, passim.

56. Sophie Madeleine DuPont to Eleuthera DuPont, December 1827; Clementina Beach Smith to Sophie Madeleine DuPont, December 26, 1828; Sarah Faulke Emlen Diary, July 21, 1808, March 30, 1809; Annie Hethroe, Ellington, Wis., to Charlena Van Vleck [Anderson], Appleton, Wis., April 23, 1865; Frances Parke Lewis, Woodlawn, Va., to Elizabeth Bordley [Gibson], Philadelphia, December 20, 1820; Fanny Ferris to Debby Ferris, West Town School, Chester County, Pa., May 29, 1826. An excellent example of the warmth of women's comments about each other and

the reserved nature of their references to men are seen in two entries in Sarah Ripley Stearn's diary. On January 8, 1811 she commented about a young woman friend: "The amiable Mrs. White of Princeton . . . one of the loveliest most interesting creatures I ever knew, young fair and blooming . . . beloved by everyone . . . formed to please & to charm. . . ." She referred to the man she ultimately married always as "my friend" or "a friend" (February 2 or April 23, 1810).

57. Jeannie Field, New York, to Sarah Butler Wister, Germantown, April 6, 1862.

58. Elizabeth Bordley Gibson, introductory statement to the Eleanor Parke Custis Lewis Letters [1850s], Historical Society of Pennsylvania.

59. Sarah Foulke [Emlen] Diary, March 30, 1809.

60. Harriet Manigault Diary, May 26, 1815.

61. Sarah Ripley [Stearns] Diary, May 17 and October 2, 1812; Eleanor Parke Custis Lewis to Elizabeth Bordley Gibson, April 23, 1826; Rebecca Ralston, Philadelphia, to Victorine DuPont [Bauday], Brandywine, September 27, 1813.

62. Anne Jefferis to Martha Jefferis, November 22 and 27, 1840, January 13 and March 17, 1841; Edith Jefferis, Greenwich, N.J., to Anne Jefferis, Philadelphia, January 31, February 6 and February 1841.

63. Edith Jefferis to Anne Jefferis, January 31, 1841.

64. Eleanor Parke Custis Lewis to Elizabeth Bordley, November 4, 1799. Eleanor and her daughter Parke experienced similar sorrow and anxiety when Parke married and moved to Cincinnati (Eleanor Parke Custis Lewis to Elizabeth Bordley Gibson, April 23, 1826). Helena DeKay visited Mary Hallock the month before her marriage; Mary Hallock was an attendant at the wedding; Helena again visited Molly about three weeks after her marriage; and then Molly went with Helena and spent a week with Helena and Richard in their new apartment (Mary Hallock [Foote] to Helena DeKay Gilder [Spring 1874] (no. 61), May 10, 1874 [May 1874], June 14, 1874 [Summer 1874]. See also Anne Biddle, Philadelphia, to Clement Biddle (brother), Wilmington, March 12 and May 27, 1827; Eunice Callender, Boston, to Sarah Ripley [Stearns], Greenfield, Mass., August 3, 1807, January 26, 1808; Victorine DuPont Bauday, Philadelphia, to Evelina DuPont [Biderman], Brandywine, November 25 and 26, December 1, 1813; Peggy Emlen to Sally Logan, n.d. [1769–70?]; Jeannie Field, New

York, to Sarah Butler Wister, Germantown, July 3, 1861).

65. Mary Hallock to Helena DeKay Gilder [1876] (no. 81); n.d. (no. 83), March 3, 1884; Mary Ashew Diary, vol. 2, September-January, 1860; Louisa Van Vleck to Charlena Van Vleck Anderson, n.d. [1875]; Sophie DuPont to Henry DuPont, July 24, 1827; Benjamin Ferris to William Canby, February 13, 1805; Benjamin Ferris to Mary Canby Biddle, December 20, 1825; Anne Jefferis Sheppard to Martha Jefferis, September 15, 1884; Martha Jefferis to Anne Jefferis Sheppard, July 4, 1843, May 5, 1844, May 3, 1847, July 17, 1849; Jeannie McCall to Peter McCall, November 26, 1847, n.d. [late 1840s]. A graphic description of the ritual surrounding a first birth is found in Abigail Lyman's letter to her husband Erastus Lyman, October 18, 1810.

66. Fanny Ferris to Anne Biddle, November 19, 1811; Eleanor Parke Custis Lewis to Elizabeth Bordley Gibson, November 4, 1799, April 27, 1827; Martha Jefferis to Anne Jefferis Sheppard, January 31, 1843, April 4, 1844; Martha Jefferis to Phoebe Sharpless Middleton, June 4, 1846; Anne Jefferis Sheppard to Martha Jefferis, August 20, 1843, February 12, 1844; Maria Inskeep, New Orleans, to Mrs. Fanny G. Hampton, Bridgeton, N.J., September 22, 1848; Benjamin Ferris to Mary Canby, February 14, 1805; Fanny Ferris to Mary Canby [Biddle], December 2, 1816.

67. Eleanor Parke Custis Lewis to Elizabeth Bordley Gibson, October-November 1820, passim.

68. Emily Howland to Hannah, September 30, 1866; Emily Howland Diary, February 8, 11, and 27, 1880; Phoebe Bradford Diary, April 12 and 13, and August 4, 1833; Eunice Callender, Boston, to Sarah Ripley [Stearns], Greenwich, Mass., September 11, 1802, August 26, 1810; Mrs. H. Middleton, Charleston, to Mrs. Gabrielle Manigault, Philadelphia, n.d. [mid 1800s]; Mrs. H. C. Paul to Mrs. Jeannie McCall, Philadelphia, n.d. [1840s]; Sarah Butler Wister, Germantown, to Jeannie Field [Musgrove], New York, April 22, 1864; Jeannie Field [Musgrove] to Sarah Butler Wister, August 25, 1861, July 6, 1862; S. B. Raudolph to Elizabeth Bordley [Gibson], n.d. [1790s]. For an example of similar letters between men, see Henry Wright to Peter McCall, December 10, 1852; Charles McCall to Peter McCall, January 4, 1860, March 22, 1864; R. Mercer to Peter McCall, November 29, 1872.

69. Mary Black [Couper] to Sophie Madeleine DuPont, February 1827, [November 1, 1834], November 12, 1834, two letters [late

November 1834]; Eliza Schlatter to Sophie Madeleine DuPont, November 2, 1834.

70. For a few of the references to death rituals in the Jefferis papers see: Martha Jefferis to Anne Jefferis Sheppard, September 28, 1843, August 21 and September 25, 1844, January 11, 1846, summer 1848, passim; Anne Jefferis Sheppard to Martha Jefferis, August 20, 1843; Anne Jefferis Sheppard to Rachel Jefferis, March 17, 1863, February 9, 1868. For other Quaker families, see Rachel Biddle to Anne Biddle, July 23, 1854; Sarah Foulke Farquhar [Emlen] Diary, April 30, 1811, February 14, 1812; Fanny Ferris to Mary Canby, August 31, 1810. This is not to argue that men and women did not mourn together. Yet in many families women aided and comforted women and men, men. The same-sex death ritual was one emotional option available to nineteenth-century Americans.

71. Sarah Foulke [Emlen] Diary, December 29, 1808.

72. Eunice Callender, Boston, to Sarah Ripley [Stearns], Greenfield, Mass., May 24, 1803.

73. Katherine Johnstone Brinley [Wharton] Journal, April 26, May 30, and May 29, 1856, Historical Society of Pennsylvania.

74. A series of roughly fourteen letters written by Peggy Emlen to Sally Logan (1768–71) has been preserved in the Wells Morris Collection, Box 1, Historical Society of Pennsylvania (see esp. May 3 and July 4, 1769, January 8, 1768).

75. The Sarah Alden Ripley Collection, the Arthur M. Schlesinger, Sr., Library, Radcliffe College, contains a number of Sarah Alden Ripley's letters to Mary Emerson. Most of these are undated, but they extend over a number of years and contain letters written both before and after Sarah's marriage. The eulogistic biographical sketch appeared in Wister and Irwin (n. 12 above). It should be noted that Sarah Butler Wister was one of the editors who sensitively selected Sarah's letters.

76. See Sarah Alden Ripley to Mary Emerson, November 19, 1823. Sarah Alden Ripley routinely, and one must assume ritualistically, read Mary Emerson's letters to her infant daughter, Mary. Eleanor Parke Custis Lewis reported doing the same with Elizabeth Bordley Gibson's letters, passim. Eunice Callender, Boston, to Sarah Ripley [Stearns], October 19, 1808.

77. Mary Black Couper to Sophie M. DuPont, March 5, 1832. The Clementina Smith–Sophie DuPont coresspondence of 1,678 letters is in the Sophie DuPont Correspondence.

The quotation is from Eliza Schlatter, Mount Holly, N.J., to Sophie DuPont, Brandywine, August 24, 1834. I am indebted to Anthony Wallace for informing me about this collection.

78. Mary Grew, Providence, R.I., to Isabel Howland, Sherwood, N.Y., April 27, 1892,

Howland Correspondence, Sophia Smith Collection, Smith College.

79. Helena Deutsch, *Psychology of Women* (New York: Grune & Stratton, 1944), vol. 1, chaps. 1–3; Clara Thompson, *On Women,* ed. Maurice Green (New York: New American Library, 1971).

JAMES C. MOHR
Abortion in America

If we observe nineteenth-century society through women's eyes, surely no statistic was as significant as the one that marked the decline in the average number of children borne by each woman. Childbirth was a time of terror; as James C. Mohr shows, many women sought actively to control the number of times they faced it. When unsuccessful in avoiding pregnancies, they attempted to abort them. The methods of the times were dangerous, but until the 1840s the women were rarely censured by the community if fetal movement had not been felt. The vigorous attack on abortion after 1840 may well have been a response to the growing willingness of married women to attempt it. After 1840 an act that had been dealt with in a biological context was given ideological overtones. What does the debate on abortion policy reveal about public attitudes toward women and their place in the family and in society?

ABORTION IN AMERICA, 1800–1825

In the absence of any legislation whatsoever on the subject of abortion in the United States in 1800, the legal status of the practice was governed by the traditional British common law as interpreted by the local courts of the new American states. For centuries prior to 1800 the key to the common law's attitude toward abortion had been a phenomenon associated with normal gestation known as quickening. Quickening was the first perception of fetal movement by the pregnant woman herself. Quickening generally occurred near the midpoint of gestation, late in the fourth or early in the fifth month, though it could and still does vary a good deal from one woman to another.

Excerpted from "Abortion in America, 1800–1825" and "The Social Character of Abortion in America, 1840–1880" chaps. 1 and 4 of *Abortion in America: The Origins and Evolution of National Policy, 1800–1900* by James C. Mohr (New York: Oxford University Press, 1978). Copyright © 1978 by Oxford University Press. Reprinted by permission. Notes have been renumbered.

The common law did not formally recognize the existence of a fetus in criminal cases until it had quickened. After quickening, the expulsion and destruction of a fetus without due cause was considered a crime, because the fetus itself had manifested some semblance of a separate existence: the ability to move. The crime was qualitatively different from the destruction of a human being, however, and punished less harshly. Before quickening, actions that had the effect of terminating what turned out to have been an early pregnancy were not considered criminal under the common law in effect in England and the United States in 1800.[1]

Both practical and moral arguments lay behind the quickening distinction. Practically, because no reliable tests for pregnancy existed in the early nineteenth century, quickening alone could confirm with absolute certainty that a woman really was pregnant. Prior to quickening, each of the telltale signs of pregnancy could, at least in theory, be explained in alternative ways by physicians of the day. Hence, either a doctor or a woman herself could take actions designed to restore menstrual flow after one or more missed periods on the assumption that something might be unnaturally "blocking" or "obstructing" her normal cycles, and if left untreated the obstruction would wreak real harm upon the woman. Medically, the procedures for removing a blockage were the same as those for inducing an early abortion. Not until the obstruction moved could either a physician or a woman, regardless of their suspicions, be completely certain that it was a "natural" blockage—a pregnancy—rather than a potentially dangerous situation. Morally, the question of whether or not a fetus was "alive" had been the subject of philosophical and religious debate among honest people for at least 5000 years. The quickening doctrine itself appears to have entered the British common law tradition by way of the tangled disputes of medieval theologians over whether or not an impregnated ovum possessed a soul.[2] The upshot was that American women in 1800 were legally free to attempt to terminate a condition that might turn out to have been a pregnancy until the existence of that pregnancy was incontrovertibly confirmed by the perception of fetal movement.

An ability to suspend one's modern preconceptions and to accept the early nineteenth century on its own terms regarding the distinction between quick and unquick is absolutely crucial to an understanding of the evolution of abortion policy in the United States. However doubtful the notion appears to modern readers, the distinction was virtually universal in America during the early decades of the nineteenth century and accepted in good faith. Perhaps the strongest evidence of the tenacity and universality of the doctrine in the United States was the fact that American courts pointedly sustained the most lenient implications of the quickening doctrine even after the British themselves had abandoned them. . . .

Because women believed themselves to be carrying inert non-beings prior to quickening, a potential for life rather than life itself, and because the common law permitted them to attempt to rid themselves of suspected and unwanted pregnancies up to the point when the potential for life gave a sure sign that it was developing into something actually alive, some American women did practice abortion in the early decades of the nineteenth century. One piece of evidence for this conclusion was the ready access American women had to abortifacient information from 1800 onward. A chief source of such information was the home medical literature of the era.

Home medical manuals characteristically contained abortifacient information in two different sections. One listed in explicit detail a number of procedures that might release "obstructed menses" and the other identified a number of specific things to be avoided in a suspected pregnancy because they were thought to bring on abortion. Americans probably consulted William Buchan's *Domestic Medicine* more frequently than any other home medical guide during the first decades of the nineteenth century.[3] Buchan suggested several courses of action designed to restore menstrual flow if a period was missed. These included bloodletting, bathing, iron and quinine concoctions, and if those failed, "a tea-spoonful of the tincture of black hellebore [a violent purgative] . . . twice aday in a cup of warm water." Four pages later he listed among "the common causes" of abortion "great evacuations [and] vomiting," exactly as would be produced by the treatment he urged for suppressed menses. Later in pregnancy a venturesome, or desperate, woman could try some of the other abortion inducers he ticked off: "violent exercise; raising great weights; reaching too high; jumping, or stepping from an eminence; strokes [strong blows] on the belly; [and] falls."[4] . . .

Like most early abortion material, Buchan's . . . advice harked back to almost primordial or instinctual methods of ending a pregnancy. Bloodletting, for example, was evidently thought to serve as a surrogate period; it was hoped that bleeding from any part of the body might have the same flushing effect upon the womb that menstrual bleeding was known to have. This primitive folk belief lingered long into the nineteenth century, well after bleeding was abandoned as medical therapy in other kinds of cases, and it was common for abortionists as late as the 1870s to pull a tooth as part of their routine.[5] . . .

In addition to home medical guides and health manuals addressed to women, abortions and abortifacient information were also available in the United States from midwives and midwifery texts.[6] . . .

Herbal healers, the so-called Indian

doctors, and various other irregular practitioners also helped spread abortifacient information in the United States during the early decades of the nineteenth century. Their surviving pamphlets, of which Peter Smith's 1813 brochure entitled "The Indian Doctor's Dispensary" is an example, contained abortifacient recipes that typically combined the better-known cathartics with native North American ingredients thought to have emmenagogic properties. For "obstructed menses" Smith recommended a concoction he called "Dr. Reeder's chalybeate." The key ingredients were myrrh and aloes, combined with liquor, sugar, vinegar, iron dust, ivy, and Virginia or seneca snakeroot.[7] A sweet-and-sour cocktail like that may or may not have induced abortion, but must certainly have jolted the system of any woman who tried one. . . .

Finally, and most importantly, America's regular physicians, those who had formal medical training either in the United States or in Great Britain or had been apprenticed under a regular doctor, clearly possessed the physiological knowledge and the surgical techniques necessary to terminate a pregnancy by mechanical means. They knew that dilation of the cervix at virtually any stage of gestation would generally bring on uterine contractions that would in turn lead to the expulsion of the contents of the uterus. They knew that any irritation introduced into the uterus would have the same effect. They knew that rupturing the amniotic sac, especially in the middle and later months of pregnancy, would usually also induce contractions and expulsion, regardless of whether the fetus was viable. Indeed, they were taught in their lecture courses and in their textbooks various procedures much more complex than a simple abortion, such as in utero decapitation and fetal pulverization, processes they were instructed to employ in lieu of the even more horribly dangerous Caesarean section. Like the general public, they knew the drugs and herbs most commonly used as abortifacients and emmenagogues, and also like the general public, they believed such preparations to have been frequently effective.[8] . . .

This placed great pressure on physicians to provide what amounted to abortion services early in pregnancy. An unmarried girl who feared herself pregnant, for example, could approach her family doctor and ask to be treated for menstrual blockage. If he hoped to retain the girl and her family as future patients, the physician would have little choice but to accept the girl's assessment of the situation, even if he suspected otherwise. He realized that every member of his profession would testify to the fact that he had no totally reliable means of distinguishing between an early pregnancy, on the one hand, and the amenorrhea that the girl claimed, on the other. Consequently, he treated for obstruction, which involved exactly the same procedures he would have used to induce an early abortion, and wittingly or unwittingly terminated the pregnancy. Regular physicians were also asked to bring to a safe conclusion abortions that irregulars or women themselves had initiated. . . . And through all of this the physician might bear in mind that he could never be held legally guilty of wrongdoing. No statutes existed anywhere in the United States on the subject of abortion, and the common law . . . considered abortion actionable only after a pregnancy had quickened. No wonder then that Heber C. Kimball, recalling his courtship with a woman he married in 1822, claimed that she had been "taught . . . in our young days, when she got into the family way, to send for a doctor and get rid of the child"; a course that she followed.[9]

In summary, then, the practice of aborting unwanted pregnancies was, if not common, almost certainly not rare in the United States during the first decades of the nineteenth century. A knowledge of various drugs, potions, and techniques was available from home medical guides, from health books for women, from midwives and irregular practitioners, and from trained physicians. Substantial evidence suggests that many American women sought abortions, tried the standard techniques of the day, and no doubt succeeded some proportion of the time in terminating unwanted pregnancies. Moreover, this practice was neither morally nor legally wrong in the eyes of the vast majority of Americans, provided it was accomplished before quickening.

The actual number of abortions in the United States prior to the advent of any statutes regulating its practice simply cannot be known. But an equally significant piece of information about those abortions can be gleaned from the historical record. It concerns the women who were having them. Virtually every observer through the middle of the 1830s believed that an overwhelming percentage of the American women who sought and succeeded in having abortions did so because they feared the social consequences of an illegitimate pregnancy, not because they wanted to limit their fertility per se. The doctor who uncovered the use of snakeroot as an abortifacient, for example, related that in all of the many instances he heard about "it was taken by women who had indulged in illegitimate love."[10]

In short, abortion was not thought to be a means of family limitation in the United States, at least on any significant scale, through the first third of the nineteenth century. This was hardly surprising in a largely rural and essentially preindustrial society, whose birthrates were exceeding any ever recorded in a European nation.[11] One could, along with medical student [Thomas] Massie, be less than enthusiastic about such an "unnatural" practice as abortion, yet tolerate it as the "recourse . . . of the victim of passion . . . the child of nature" who was driven by "an unrelenting world" unable to forgive any "deviation from what they have termed virtue."[12] Consequently, Americans in the early nineteenth century could and did look the other way when they encountered abortion. Nothing in their medical knowledge or in the rulings of their courts compelled them to do otherwise, and, as Massie indicated, there was considerable compassion for the women involved. It would be nearly midcentury before the perception of who was having abortions for what reasons would begin to shift in the United States, and that shift would prove to be one of the critical developments in the evolution of American abortion policy.

A final point remains to be made about abortion in the United States during the first decades of the nineteenth century. Most observers appeared to consider it relatively safe, at least by the medical standards of the day, rather than extremely dangerous. . . . This too must have reassured women who decided to risk an abortion before quickening. According to the lecture notes of one of his best students, Walter Channing told his Harvard classes that abortion could be troublesome when produced by external blows, because severe internal hemorrhage would be likely, but that generally considered, "abortion [was] not so dangerous as commonly supposed."[13]

The significance of these opinions lay less in whether or not they were accurate than in the fact that writers on abortion, including physicians, saw no reason to stress the dangers attendant to the process. Far from it. They were skeptical about poisons and purgatives, but appear to have assessed physically induced abortions as medically acceptable risks by the standards of the day, especially if brought on during the period of pregnancy when both popular belief and the public courts condoned them anyhow. Here again was a significant early perception that would later change. That change, like the shift

in the perception of who was having abortions for what purposes, would also have an impact on the evolution of American abortion policy. . . .

THE SOCIAL CHARACTER OF ABORTION IN AMERICA, 1840–1880

Before 1840 abortion was perceived in the United States primarily as a recourse of the desperate, especially of the young woman in trouble who feared the wrath of an overexacting society. After 1840, however, evidence began to accumulate that the social character of the practice had changed. A high proportion of the women whose abortions contributed to the soaring incidence of that practice in the United States between 1840 and 1880 appeared to be married, native-born, Protestant women, frequently of middle- or upper-class status. The data came from disparate sources, some biased and some not, but in the end proved compelling.

Even before the availability of reliable evidence confirmed that the nation's birthrates were starting to plummet, observers noticed that abortion more and more frequently involved married women rather than single women in trouble. Professor Hugh L. Hodge of the University of Pennsylvania, one of the first physicians in the United States to speak out about abortion in anything approaching a public forum, lectured his introductory obstetrics students in 1839 that abortion was fast becoming a prominent feature of American life. Hodge still considered women trying "to destroy the fruit of illicit pleasure" to be the ones most often seeking abortions, but he alerted his students to the fact that "married women, also, from the fear of labor, from indisposition to have the care, the expense, or the trouble of children, or some other motive" were more and more frequently requesting "that the embryo be destroyed by their medical attendant." Hodge attributed a good deal of this activity to the quickening doctrine, which allowed "women whose moral character is, in other respects, without reproach; mothers who are devoted, with an ardent and self-denying affection, to the children who already constitute[d] their family [to be] perfectly indifferent respecting the foetus in the utero."[14] . . .

Opinion was divided regarding the social status of the women who accounted for the great upsurge of abortion during the middle period of the nineteenth century. While most observers agreed "all classes of society, rich and poor" were involved to some extent, many thought that the middle and upper classes practiced abortion more extensively than the lower classes.[15] The Michigan State Medical Society in 1859 declared that abortion "pervade[d] all ranks" in that state.[16] The Medical Society of Buffalo pointed out that same year "now we have ladies, yes, *educated and refined ladies*" involved as well.[17] On the other hand, court cases revealed at least a sprinkling of lower-class women, servant girls, and the like. . . .

Although the going price for an abortion varied tremendously according to place, time, practitioner, and patient, abortions appear to have been generally quite expensive. Regular physicians testified repeatedly throughout the period that the abortion business was enormously lucrative. Those doctors pledged not to perform abortions bitterly resented men like the Boston botanic indicted for manslaughter in an abortion case in 1851, who posted $8000 bond and returned to his offices, at a time when the average university professor in the United States earned under $2000 per year.[18] . . .

When women turned from regulars to the commercial abortionists, the prices were still not cheap. Itinerants and irregulars generally tried to charge whatever they judged the traffic would bear, which could vary anywhere from $5 to $500. During the 1840s, for example, Madame Restell charged $5 for an initial visit and

diagnosis, then negotiated the price of the operation "according to the wealth and liberality of the parties." In a case for which she was indicted in 1846 she asked a young woman about "her beau's circumstances" before quoting a figure, and then tried to get $100 when she found out the man was a reasonably successful manufacturer's representative. The man thought that was too costly, and only after extensive haggling among go-betweens was a $75 fee agreed upon.[19] . . .

Despite the apparent gradual leveling of prices, however, the abortion business remained a profitable commercial venture well into the 1870s. Anthony Comstock, the single-minded leader of a massive anti-obscenity campaign launched in the United States during the 1870s, kept meticulous and extensive records of all of the people he helped arrest while operating as a special agent of the Post Office Department. Between 1872 and 1880 Comstock and his associates aided in the indictment of 55 persons whom Comstock identified as abortionists. The vast majority were very wealthy and posted large bonds with ease. . . .

. . . abortion entered the mainstream of American life during the middle decades of the nineteenth century. While the unmarried and the socially desperate continued to have recourse to it as they had earlier in the century, abortion also became highly visible, much more frequently practiced, and quite common as a means of family limitation among white, Protestant, native-born wives of middle- and upper-class standing. These dramatic changes, in turn, evoked sharp comment from two ideologically opposed groups in American society, each of which either directly or indirectly blamed the other for the shift in abortion patterns. On one side of the debate were the antifeminists, led by regular physicians, and on the other side were the nation's feminists. Both groups agreed that abortion had become a large-scale and socially significant phenomenon in American life, but they disagreed over the reasons why.

Before examining the two chief explanations put forward by contemporaries for the striking shifts in the incidence and the character of abortion in the United States after 1840, two observations may be worth making. First, it is never easy to understand why people do what they do even in the most straightforward of situations; it is nearly impossible to know with certainty the different reasons, rational and irrational, why people in the past might have taken such a psychologically loaded action as the termination of a suspected pregnancy. Second, most participants on both sides of the contemporary debate over why so many American women began to practice abortion after 1840 actually devoted most of their attention to the question of why American women wanted to limit their fertility. This confirmed that abortion was important between 1840 and 1880 primarily as a means of family limitation, but such discussions offer only marginal help in understanding why so many American women turned to abortion itself as a means toward that end.

Cultural anthropologists argue that abortion has been practiced widely and frequently in pre-industrial societies at least in part because "it is a woman's method [of limiting fertility] and can be practiced without the man's knowledge."[20] This implies a sort of women's conspiracy to limit population, which would be difficult to demonstrate in the context of nineteenth-century America. Nonetheless, there is some evidence, though it must be considered carefully, to suggest that an American variant of this proposition may have been at least one of the reasons why abortion became such a common form of family limitation in the United States during the period. A number of physicians, as will become evident, certainly believed that one of the keys to the upsurge of abortion was the fact that it was a

uniquely female practice, which men could neither control nor prevent. . . .

Earlier in the century observers had alleged that the tract literature and lectures of the women's rights movement advocated family planning and disseminated abortifacient information.[21] In 1859 Harvard professor Walter Channing reported the opinion that "women for whom this office of foeticide, unborn-child-killing, is committed, are *strong-minded*," and no later writer ever accused them of being weak-minded.[22] . . .

The most common variant of the view that abortion was a manifestation of the women's rights movement hinged upon the word "fashion." Over and over men claimed that women who aborted did so because they cared more about scratching for a better perch in society than they did about raising children. They dared not waste time on the latter lest they fall behind in the former. Women, in short, were accused of being aggressively self-indulgent. Some women, for example, had "the effrontery to say boldly, that they have neither the time nor inclination to nurse babies"; others exhibited "self-indulgence in most disgusting forms"; and many of the women practicing abortion were described as more interested in "selfish and personal ends" or "fast living" than in the maternity for which God had supposedly created them.[23] . . . For this reason, some doctors urged that feticide be made a legal ground for divorce.[24] A substantial number of writers between 1840 and 1880, in other words, were willing to portray women who had abortions as domestic subversives. . . .

Notwithstanding the possibility that recourse to abortion sometimes reflected the rising consciousness of the women who had them, and notwithstanding the fact that some males, especially regular physicians, were distinctly uneasy about the practice because of what its ultimate effects upon the social position of women might be, the relationship between abortion and feminism in the nineteenth century nevertheless remained indirect and ironical. This becomes evident when the arguments of the feminists themselves are analyzed. One of the most forceful early statements of what subsequently became the feminist position on abortion was made in the 1850s in a volume entitled *The Unwelcome Child*.[25] The author, Henry C. Wright, asserted that women alone had the right to say when they would become pregnant and blamed the tremendous outburst of abortion in America on selfishly sensual husbands. Wright's volume was more interesting than other similar tracts, however, because he published a large number of letters from women detailing the circumstances under which they had sought abortions.

One of Wright's letters was from a woman who had her first abortion in 1841, because her one-year-old first born was sick and her husband was earning almost nothing. She "consulted a lady friend, and by her persuasion and assistance, killed" the fetus she was carrying. When she found herself pregnant again shortly thereafter she "consulted a physician. . . . He was ready with his logic, his medicines and instruments, and told me how to destroy it. After experimenting on myself three months, I was successful. I killed my child about five months after conception." She steeled herself to go full term with her next pregnancy and to "endure" an addition to her impoverished and unhappy household. When pregnant again she "employed a doctor, to kill my child, and in the destruction of it . . . ended my power to be a mother." The woman's point throughout, however, was that abortion "was most repulsive" to her and her recourse to it "rendered [her] an object of loathing to [her]self." Abortion was not a purposeful female conspiracy, but an undesirable necessity forced by thoughtless men. As this woman put it: "I was the veriest slave alive."[26] . . .

The attitudes expressed by Wright's correspondents in the 1840s and 1850s became the basis of the official position of American feminists toward abortion after the Civil War. As Elizabeth Cady Stanton phrased it, the practice was one more result of "the degradation of woman" in the nineteenth century, not of woman's rising consciousness or expanding opportunities outside the home.[27] . . . The remedy to the problem of abortion in the United States, in their view, was not legalized abortion open to all but *"the education and enfranchisement of women"* which would make abortion unnecessary in a future world of egalitarian respect and sexual discretion.[28] In short, most feminists, though they agreed completely with other observers that abortion was endemic in America by midcentury, did not blame the increase on the rising ambitions of women but asserted with Matilda E. J. Gage "that this crime of 'child murder,' 'abortion,' 'infanticide,' lies at the door of the male sex."[29] The *Woman's Advocate* of Dayton, Ohio, put it even more forcefully in 1869: "Till men learn to check their sensualism, and leave their wives free to choose their periods of maternity, let us hear no more invectives against women for the destruction of prospective unwelcome children, whose dispositions, made miserable by unhappy ante-natal conditions, would only make their lives a curse to themselves and others."[30] . . .

Despite the blame and recrimination evoked by the great upsurge of abortion in the United States in the nineteenth century, some of which was directed at women and some at men, it appears likely that most decisions to use abortion probably involved couples conferring together, not just men imposing their wills or women acting unilaterally, and that abortion was the result of diffuse pressures, not merely the rising consciousness of women or the tyrannical aggressions of men. American men and women wanted to express their sexuality and mutual affections, on the one hand, and to limit their fertility, on the other. Abortion was neither desirable nor undesirable in itself, but rather one of the few available means of reconciling and realizing those two higher priorities. And it seems likely that the man and woman agreed to both of those higher priorities in most instances, thus somewhat mooting in advance the question of which one was more responsible for the decisions that made abortion a common phenomenon in mid-nineteenth-century America.[31]

Court records provide one source of evidence for the mutuality of most abortion decisions. Almost every nineteenth-century abortion case that was written up, whether in the popular press, in medical journals, or in the official proceedings of state supreme courts, involved the agreement of both the man and the woman. There is no record of any man ever having sued any woman for aborting his child. . . .

Perhaps the best evidence for the likely mutuality of most abortion decisions is contained in the diary that Lester Frank Ward, who later became one of America's most famous sociologists, kept as a newly-wed in the 1860s. Though Ward was unique in writing down the intimate decisions that he and his wife had to make, the couple seemed otherwise typical young Americans, almost as Tocqueville might have described them, anxious for further education and ambitious to get ahead quickly. Both Ward and his wife understood that a child would overburden their limited resources and reduce the probability of ever realizing either their individual goals of self-improvement or their mutual goals as a couple. They avoided pregnancy in pre-marital intercourse, then continued to avoid it after their marriage

in August 1862. Not until early in 1864 did Lizzie Ward become pregnant. In March, without consulting her husband, she obtained "an effective remedy" from a local woman, which made her very sick for two days but helped her to terminate her pregnancy. She probably took this action after missing three or four periods; it was still early enough in gestation that her husband did not realize she was pregnant but late enough that lactation had begun. Ward noted in his diary that "the proof" she had been pregnant was "the milk" that appeared after the abortion.[32]

Anti-feminists might have portrayed Lizzie Ward's action as diabolical, a betrayal of duty. Feminists might have viewed it as the only recourse open to a female who wanted both to further her own education and to remain on good terms with an ambitious spouse who would certainly have sacrificed his wife's goals to child-rearing, while he pursued his own. But the decision was really the result of a pre-existing consensus between the two of them. Though Ward had not been party to the process in a legal or direct sense, which may go some distance toward confirming the role of abortion as a more uniquely female method of family limitation than contraception, he was clearly delighted that his wife was "out of danger" and would not be having a child. After this brush with family responsibility, the Wards tried a number of new methods of contraception, which they presumably hoped would be more effective than whatever they had been using to avoid pregnancy before Lizzie had to resort to abortion. These included both "pills" and "instruments." Not until the summer of 1865, after Ward had obtained a decent job in Washington, did the couple have a baby.[33]

Abortion had been for the Wards what it apparently also was for many other American couples: an acceptable means toward a mutually desirable end, one of the only ways they had to allow themselves both to express their sexuality and affection toward each other with some degree of frequency and to postpone family responsibilities until they thought they were better prepared to raise children. The line of acceptability for most Americans trying to reconcile these twin priorities ran just about where Lizzie Ward had drawn it. Infanticide, the destruction of a baby after its birth, was clearly unacceptable, and so was abortion after quickening, though that was a much grayer area than infanticide. But abortion before quickening, like contraception itself, was an appropriate and legally permissible method of avoiding unwanted children. And it had one great advantage, as the Wards learned, over contraception: it worked. As more and more women began to practice abortion, however, and as the practice changed from being invisible to being visible, from being quantitatively insignificant to being a systematic practice that terminated a substantial number of pregnancies after 1840, and from being almost entirely a recourse of the desperate and the socially marginal to being a commonly employed procedure among the middle and upper classes of American society, state legislators decided to reassess their policies toward the practice. Between 1840 and 1860 law-makers in several states began to respond to the increase of abortion in American life.

NOTES

1. The quickening doctrine went back to the thirteenth century in England and was well established by the time Coke wrote his famous commentaries in the first half of the seventeenth century. On quickening in the common law see Cyril C. Means, Jr., "The Law of New York concerning Abortion and the Status of the Foetus, 1664–1968: A Case of Cessation of Constitutionality," *New York Law Forum*, XIV, No. 3 (Fall 1968), 419–426.

2. Ibid. 411–419, and John T. Noonan, Jr., "An Almost Absolute Value in History," in John T. Noonan, Jr., ed., *The Morality of Abortion* (Cambridge, Mass., 1970), 1–59, represent two learned summaries, from different perspectives, on the long philosophical debate over the legal status of abortion in the Western world since the time of the Greeks.

3. The full title was *Domestic Medicine, or a Treatise on the Prevention and Cure of Diseases by Regimen and Simple Medicines.* Buchan's volume was published in Philadelphia as early as 1782, where it went through many editions. The 1816 edition, published in New Haven, Connecticut, carried the subtitle: *With an Appendix, Containing a Dispensatory for the Use of Private Practitioners.* This remarkably successful book continued to be reprinted in America through 1850.

4. Buchan, *Domestic Medicine*, 400, 403–404.

5. See, for example, Frederick Hollick, *Diseases of Women, Their Causes and Cure Familiarly Explained: With Practical Hints for Their Prevention, and for the Preservation of Female Health: For Every Female's Private Use* (New York, 1849), 150; Edward H. Dixon, *Woman and Her Diseases, from the Cradle to the Grave: Adapted Exclusively to Her Instruction in the Physiology of Her System, and All the Diseases of Her Critical Periods* (New York, 1847), 254–255. . . .

6. For the continued reputation of midwives as abortionists in nineteenth-century America see George Ellington, *The Women of New York, or the Under-World of the Great City* (New York, 1869), 399–400.

7. Peter Smith, "The Indian Doctor's Dispensary, Being Father Peter Smith's Advice Respecting Diseases and Their Cure; Consisting of Prescriptions for Many Complaints: And a Description of Medicines, Simple and Compound, Showing Their Virtues and How to Apply Them," [1813] reproduced in J. U. Lloyd, ed., *Bulletin of the Lloyd Library of Botany, Pharmacy and Materia Medica* (1901), Bull. #2, Reproduction Series #2, 46–47.

8. John Burns, *Observations on Abortion: Containing an Account of the Manner in Which It Takes Place, the Causes Which Produce It, and the Method of Preventing or Treating It* (Troy, New York, 1808), 73–81. . . .

9. Heber C. Kimball in the *Journal of Discourses*, 26 vols. (Liverpool, 1857), V, 91–92. Kimball, it should be pointed out, was not an unbiased observer, which was probably why he would testify so straightforwardly

about abortion. He was a leader of the Mormon church in Utah in 1857 when he made the statement quoted, and the Mormons, who were under attack on the polygamy issue, frequently counterattacked by pointing out how common abortion was in the East. I am greatly indebted to Dr. Lester Bush for this and other references to abortion in the *Journal of Discourses*.

10. Thomas Massie, "An Experimental Inquiry into the Properties of the Polygala Senega," in Charles Caldwell, ed., *Medical Theses, Selected from among the Inaugural Dissertations, Published and Defended by the Graduates in Medicine, of the University of Pennsylvania, and of Other Medical Schools in the United States* (Philadelphia, 1806), 203.

11. Between 1800 and 1830 the population profile of the United States corresponded closely to an ideal type identified and recognized by many different historical demographers, though the different scholars call the type by different names. William Petersen's widely used *Population* (New York, 3rd ed., 1975), 15, labels it the "underdeveloped" type and identifies its characteristics as a mixed economy, high fertility rates, falling mortality rates, and very high rates of population growth.

12. Massie, "Polygala Senega," 204.

13. John G. Metcalf, student notebooks written while attending Dr. Walter Channing's lectures of midwifery at Harvard Medical School, 1825–1826 (Countway Library, Harvard Medical School), entry for December 27, 1825. There had been cases of abortion induced by blows to the belly tried in British courts in the eighteenth century.

14. Hugh L. Hodge in Francis Wharton and Moreton Stillé, *Treatise on Medical Jurisprudence* (Philadelphia, 1855), 270. Hodge did not publish the lecture he gave in 1839 until 1854.

15. "Report on Criminal Abortion," *Transactions of the American Medical Association*, XII (1859), 75.

16. E. P. Christian, "Report to the State Medical Society on Criminal Abortions," *Peninsular & Independent Medical Journal*, II, 135.

17. "Criminal Abortions," *Buffalo Medical Journal and Monthly Review*, XIV (1859), 249.

18. *Boston Medical and Surgical Journal*, XLIV, No. 14 (May 7, 1851), 288. For an excellent example of this bitterness and jealousy see Worthington Hooker, *Physician and Patient . . .* (New York, 1849), passim, and especially 405–408. The estimate on income

is from Colin B. Burke, "The Quiet Influence" (Ph.D. dissertation, Washington University of St. Louis, 1973), 69, Table 2.19.

19. A Physician of New-York, *Trial of Madame Restell, For Producing Abortion on the Person of Maria Bodine, to which is added, a Full Account of her Life & Horrible Practices: Together with Prostitution in New-York; Its Extent—Causes—and Effects upon Society* (New York, 1847), 3–4, 10.

20. Kingsley Davis and Judith Blake, "Social Structure and Fertility: An Analytical Framework," *Economic Development and Cultural Change*, IV, No. 3 (April 1956), 230.

21. Hooker, *Physician and Patient*, 93; James Reed, *From Private Vice to Public Virtue: The Birth Control Movement and American Society since 1830* (New York, 1978), chaps. 1–5.

22. Walter Channing, "Effects of Criminal Abortion," *Boston Medical and Surgical Journal*, LX (March 17, 1859), 135.

23. E. M. Buckingham, "Criminal Abortion," *Cincinnati Lancet & Observer*, X (March 1867), 141; Channing, "Effects of Criminal Abortion," 135; J. C. Stone, "Report on the Subject of Criminal Abortion," *Transactions of the Iowa State Medical Society*, I (1867), 29; J. Miller, "Criminal Abortion," *The Kansas City Medical Record*, I (Aug. 1884), 296.

24. H. Gibbons, Sr., "On Feticide," *Pacific Medical and Surgical Journal* (San Francisco), XXI, No. 3 (Aug. 1879), 97–111; H. C. Markham, "Foeticide and Its Prevention," *Journal of the American Medical Association*, XI, No. 23 (Dec. 8, 1888), 805–806.

25. Henry C. Wright, *The Unwelcome Child; or, the Crime of an Undesigned and Undesired Maternity* (Boston, 1860). The volume was copyrighted in 1858.

26. Ibid., 65–69.

27. E[lizabeth] C[ady] S[tanton], "Infanticide and Prostitution," *Revolution*, I, No. 5 (Feb. 5, 1868), 65.

28. Ibid. For the same point reiterated see "Child Murder," in ibid. I, No. 10 (March 12, 1868), 146–147 and ibid. I, No. 18 (May 1868), 279.

29. Ibid., I, No. 14 (April 9, 1868), 215–216.

30. E. V. B., "Restellism, and the N.Y. Medical Gazette," *Woman's Advocate* (Dayton, Ohio), I, No. 20 (April 8, 1869), 16. Note the reference to the belief in antenatal character formation that was used, as here implied, as another rationale for abortion during the nineteenth century.

31. Carl N. Degler is one of those who

has argued persuasively that nineteenth-century American women were very much aware of their own sexuality and desirous, morality books notwithstanding, of expressing it: "What Ought To Be and What Was: Women's Sexuality in the Nineteenth Cen-

tury," *American Historical Review*, LXXIX, No. 5 (Dec. 1974), 1467–1490.

32. Lester Ward, *Young Ward's Diary*, Bernhard J. Stern, ed. (New York, 1935), 140.

33. Ibid. 150, 152–153, 174.

LOIS W. BANNER
Elizabeth Cady Stanton:
Early Marriage and Feminist Rebellion

No issue is so useful a warning against applying to women generalizations about men than is the matter of citizenship. Women were citizens (if they were born or naturalized in the United States, and if they were not slaves), but they could not vote. "I am tired of explaining this charming system of equality and independence," sneers a fictional woman created by the first American novelist, Charles Brockden Brown. Real abolitionists asked plaintively, "Are we aliens because we are women?"*

Most histories leap to the conclusion that since women did not vote they were not part of the political community. Yet throughout the nineteenth century non-voting citizens tried to influence public policy. Individual women sent private petitions to legislatures; philanthropic groups established charities when public pensions failed. Women turned the temperance movement into their own; they joined the abolitionist movement and shaped its campaigns. In 1839–40, in fact, the national abolitionist movement splintered over the issue of whether women could be full members of the association, hold office, and speak in public. When in 1848 Elizabeth Cady Stanton formulated the Declaration of Sentiments (document 2 in Essential Documents) as an echo of the Declaration of Independence, she was attempting to bring the status of women into belated congruence with the changes made for men by the founders' generation.

Stanton was particularly sensitive to the interrelationship of public and pri-

* Charles Brockden Brown, *Alcuin: A Dialogue* (1798), ed. Lee R. Edwards (New York: Grossman Publishers, 1971), p. 23.

vate life. The defense of women's rights that she developed and her attention to married women's property rights demonstrate her recognition of the interrelationship of economics and politics. As Lois W. Banner shows, Stanton's political career emerged out of issues with which she began to wrestle in her private life. Throughout her long career she would have important things to say about the major issues that confronted American society.

The Stantons traveled to London in 1840 for the antislavery cause. But Cady Stanton returned six months later affected not so much by the plight of the slaves as by the situation of women.

The London Anti-Slavery Convention welcomed Henry Stanton as a leading American abolitionist and named him its secretary. Antislavery societies throughout the British Isles invited him to speak. Influential reformers entertained them, and Cady Stanton could hardly believe that she actually met people she "had so long worshipped from afar." The Stantons toured London, journeyed through Ireland and Scotland, and spent time in Paris.

Meetings and discussions with the American women delegates at the convention, however, impressed Cady Stanton more profoundly than the sights or the antislavery issue. The American Anti-Slavery Society, founded in 1833, had divided in 1839 over allowing women to participate in its affairs. New York members, fearing that any association with feminism would undermine abolitionism, wanted women's societies kept separate from the organizations of men. In 1840 they would take leading roles in moving abolitionism boldly into the male world of politics by founding the Liberty party. The Boston and Philadelphia supporters of William Lloyd Garrison, who retained control of the American society, held that both sexes should participate equally in the same societies. In support of their positions, both groups sent delegates to the London convention. But only among the Garrisonians were women to be found.

Before she arrived in London, Cady Stanton's sympathies lay with the New Yorkers. Her husband, active in forming the Liberty party, sided with his New York colleagues, as did Gerrit Smith and the Welds. . . .

Her attitude changed when they reached London. The Stantons were lodged in the same boarding house as the women delegates, and they had meals together. Cady Stanton sat next to Lucretia Mott, a renowned Philadelphia Quaker preacher, twenty years her senior, who was the acknowledged leader of the American women representatives. The first night at dinner, despite Birney's frowns and her husband's nudgings under the table, Cady Stanton supported Mott's arguments for woman's equal participation in the antislavery societies. Cady Stanton had always been fascinated by Quaker women, who were allowed to speak in public and to become ministers and who, like Mott and the Grimké sisters, often took on public roles as reformers. Indeed, Mott was different from the women Cady Stanton knew. She was gentle, serene, and good humored, although she questioned all creeds; she was at peace with herself in defying society's dogmas about women's behavior; and she had the self-confidence to challenge men directly. During the weeks in London, Cady Stanton continually sought Mott out and solicited her views on social and theological issues. Spellbound, she witnessed Mott preach in a London Unitarian church. It was the first time she had heard a woman speak in public before an audience which included men.

At the convention, too, Cady Stanton became Mott's confederate. The question of whether the women should even be accepted as delegates preempted the first days of the meeting. The conservatives were in control. The women were not permitted to speak on their own behalf nor to sit on the convention floor. Instead, they were relegated to a curtained gallery at one end of the hall. Henry Stanton was sufficiently sensitive to his wife's feelings that he, alone among the New Yorkers, spoke in favor of seating the women. Yet, in contrast to William Lloyd Garrison, who was also present, he did not leave his seat on the convention floor to join the women in the gallery. Nor did his advocacy of the women approach the fervor of Wendell Phillips, a patrician Boston Garrisonian whose new wife had been largely responsible for his conversion to antislavery. Wendell and Ann Phillips were also on their wedding trip; the comparison was not lost on Cady Stanton.

The acrimonious debates canvassed all possible arguments for women's subordination. Cady Stanton found the exchanges "such refined torture as I had never before experienced." The only relief was "the placid comments and smiles of derision that passed around the distinguished circle of women." Barred from speaking at the convention, the women engaged in long debates with the men at their boarding house. . . . Cady Stanton resolved her anger by a decision to act. She proposed to Lucretia Mott that they hold a woman's rights convention as soon as they returned to the United States, and Mott agreed.

That gathering was not to take place until 1848. Time and other concerns intervened. . . .

During the first eight years of her marriage, domesticity dominated Cady Stanton's life. . . .

. . . Decorating, cleaning, and gardening fascinated her, especially after the Stantons moved into their own home in Boston. Cooking became a passion: "I spent half my time preserving, pickling, and experimenting with new dishes." While still in Johnstown, her first son, Daniel, was born, followed by two more sons, Henry and Gerrit, born during the Boston years. Motherhood added another absorbing interest.

Caring for her children engaged her intellect as well as her emotions. From the birth of her first child, she questioned accepted procedures. The local Johnstown woman she hired as a nurse for Daniel swaddled the infant, tightly wrapping him in strips of cloth which prevented the movement of arms and legs, in the belief that new limbs needed support during the first year of life. She closed the windows to keep out supposed evil substances from the air outside. She counseled Cady Stanton to feed the baby continuously, in the belief that an unfilled stomach caused colic and rickets. She kept on hand an arsenal of herbal concoctions and soothing syrups, many of which contained laudanum, an opium derivative. Despite these attentions, the child cried constantly. Distraught, Cady Stanton "wept, prayed, and philosophized by turns."

She then turned to the available literature on child rearing. Rejecting most treatises as useless, she found validation of both homeopathic medical advice and her common sense in an 1840 work on infant care by Andrew Combe, a Scottish physician and the younger brother of the phrenologist George Combe. Defying her husband, her parents, and her male doctor, she threw off the swaddling clothes, opened the windows to let in fresh air, threw away the medicines, and nursed the baby on a regular schedule during the day and not at night. The results were striking. Although the new schedule monopolized her time as much as the nurse's procedures, the baby stopped crying. And there were other, more personal benefits.

She claimed through this experience to have learned "another lesson in self-reliance." Moreover, her involvement in infant care had important ramifications for her later feminist thought, in which she would identify maternity as a key factor in human development.

In neither Johnstown nor Boston did Cady Stanton entirely forego activities outside the home or forget her earlier interest in woman's rights. In both places she found time to study theology, law, and history—particularly as they pertained to women. Before she left Johnstown she took an interest in the Married Women's Property Act, introduced in the New York State legislature in 1836 and designed to give married women control over their property. The bill had garnered considerable public support, particularly from the wealthy, whose daughters' dowries and inheritances were prey to the debts of bankrupt and improvident sons-in-law. The bill, however, dealt only with property rights; it did not address any of the other legal inequalities of women. . . .

In 1842 she made her first public speech in Johnstown, not on woman's rights or the property bill for married women, but on the respectable subject of temperance. Her insecurity was evidenced by the fact that she did no more than mention the inflammatory issue of woman's rights in the speech. Nor was she any bolder in private conversation. Defensively, she wrote to Lucretia Mott that she did her best to interject the issue into social discourse. But Cady Stanton did not yet have the courage and self-confidence that speaking out for woman's rights required.

The Stantons' move to Boston in 1843 placed her in the intellectual and reform center of the nation. Margaret Fuller, the transcendentalist intellectual and feminist ideologue whose conversational gatherings with Boston women were renowned, had already left the city. But Cady Stanton seized every opportunity to go to concerts, lectures, plays, and church services. She faithfully attended temperance, peace, prison, and antislavery reform conventions. She met Emerson and Hawthorne and visited Brook Farm, the transcendentalist commune near Boston—an experience which almost converted her to communitarianism. She remained for the most part a private person, however. Although she collected signatures on antislavery petitions, she did not become a leader in any of the reform organizations. On separate occasions she discussed holding a woman's rights convention with both Lucretia Mott and black abolitionist Frederick Douglass, a recent escapee from slavery whom she converted to woman's rights advocacy, but again she did nothing further actually to implement the project.

Yet too public an association with the Garrisonian leaders of Boston reform might have undermined Henry Stanton's political career. Besides, Cady Stanton still found housekeeping fulfilling, and religious exploration doubly absorbing in the national center of religious liberalism. . . .

So wary did Boston make her of reform activities that she continued her woman's rights activity instead in New York, not in Massachusetts, where, in fact, woman's rights petitions were not circulated until 1848 and a married woman's property bill not drafted until 1854. During long visits to her family, both in Johnstown and in Albany, she continued to circulate petitions on behalf of the Married Women's Property Act, still pending before the legislature. In Albany, she lobbied on behalf of the bill among the legislators, many of whom she encountered in local society. Again her efforts were modest. But the experience gave Cady Stanton useful training in politics and in defending her position before male opponents.

In 1847, after four years in Boston, the Stantons moved to Seneca Falls, New York. Stanton suffered from chronic lung congestion in Boston's damp climate; he had failed to win elective office despite several attempts; and he was dissatisfied with the shady ethics of his law partner. . . . Seneca Falls was a growing town, holding out professional possibilities, and it was near the reform centers of Rochester and Buffalo. Down the road in Auburn lived Lucretia Mott's sister, Martha Wright, as well as William Henry Seward, reform governor and antislavery politician. In the nearby town of Waterloo was a large community of reform Quakers.

Yet the situation did not work out as expected. Before the move Cady Stanton worried that Henry would be unhappy in a small town. But the reverse proved to be the case. The years in Johnstown and Boston had been fulfilling for her; the initial months in Seneca Falls were not. Life in her new community revealed years of accumulated grievances, often only dimly perceived at the time. To cope with her discontent and to legitimate her own desire for a broader sphere of action, she began seriously to consider the timeliness of a woman's rights convention. Once again she successfully overcame depression through action; this time her movement toward what, in Emersonian terms, she often called "self-reliance" was almost complete.

More than anything else, Cady Stanton traced her discontent in Seneca Falls to the burden of increased housework. In Johnstown the Stantons had lived with her parents, and in Boston she had always found capable servants. But in provincial Seneca Falls such help seemed unavailable. Her house was only a block away from the town's most imposing avenue, along which the wealthy factory owners and merchants lived. But her street was not paved; it was dusty; and the business district of town, containing shops and churches and meeting places, was a good mile or two away.

Domestic tasks that had charmed her in Johnstown and Boston now bored her. Her three children, boys of eight, six, and three, were difficult to manage, and their activities left the house in an uproar. From a nearby community of Irish laborers came regular complaints that her boys threw rocks. The lakes of the area were fertile breeding grounds for mosquitoes, and respiratory ailments were common. Her children, it seemed, were constantly sick. For the first time in many years, Cady Stanton felt directly and personally oppressed as a woman.

Yet other, deeper reasons lay behind her discontent. In later years dusty streets and minor illnesses did not bother her, and she regained her pleasure in domestic tasks. She would then find substitutes for Boston's cultural life by organizing a town discussion group, advising neighbors, and bringing friends to Seneca Falls. But at the moment, all the grievances of her life in a small town converged with one other mounting problem: her marriage to Henry Stanton.

Strong-willed and opinionated, Stanton was not easy to live with. Ten years Cady Stanton's senior, married for the first time at thirty-five, he was set in his ways. His kindly but nonetheless patronizing control is evident in an 1843 letter in which he addressed her as "My Dearest Daughter." Two women abolitionist friends who had traveled with the Stantons for a brief time in 1840 privately commented on Stanton's overbearing treatment of his wife.

Moreover, as a lawyer and politician Stanton simply did not meet the promise of his early career. Although he devoted enormous time and energy to volunteer party activism, his attempts at elective office, except for two terms in the New York Senate, failed. . . .

Increasingly he left home for long periods on business trips and political assignments. He was absent at the birth of at least two of his children. Whenever possible, he journeyed to Washington to witness the debates in Congress and mingle informally with the politicians. Eventually he became the Washington reporter for the *New York Tribune*. His enthusiasm for politics went beyond the desire to effect social change. He was equally drawn to its masculine nature and the easy camaraderie of men whose careers were based on pleasing others and who usually left their families at home. On the way to Washington, he invariably detoured to Albany to exchange gossip with the state's master politician, Thurlow Weed, on whose newspaper, the *Rochester Telegraph*, he had worked as a reporter in his prereform days. In 1857 Susan B. Anthony noted that Stanton had spent his usual seven months in Washington, pursuing, as she sarcastically put it, "Political Air Castles." Increasingly Cady Stanton resented his absences and, even more, his freedom to do what he wanted. In 1848 she wrote to a friend of her great love for Henry; in 1858 she poured out her discontent to Anthony. "How rebellious it makes me feel when I see Henry going about where and how he pleases," she wrote. "He can walk at will through the whole wide world or shut himself up alone. As I contrast his freedom with my bondage I feel that, because of the false position of women I have been compelled to hold all my noblest aspirations in abeyance in order to be a wife, a mother, a nurse, a cook, a household drudge."

Stanton's behavior at home also bothered her. The derisive descriptions of American husbands in her writings were clearly modeled after him. The once doting lover had become staid and indifferent, absorbed in his career and his interests outside the home. His pipe and his evening newspapers were irritants that symbolized all the rest. Buried behind his ritual reading, he answered his wife's questions with a vacant stare, while the children were carefully schooled not to disturb "his devotions to his God, his evening paper."

Henry Stanton was not entirely to blame for Cady Stanton's discontent.

Both husband and wife liked to live well, but Stanton's income was never large. Daniel Cady gave them their houses in both Boston and Seneca Falls in addition to other financial aid. Nor was Cady Stanton, increasingly strong-willed and opinionated, easy to live with. As early as 1840, on her postwedding visit, the Welds were concerned about Cady Stanton's fashionable ways, and they worried that Henry Stanton was not, in fact, strong enough to guide her in the direction of self-denial and reform. Her son Gerrit contended that his father often went on trips because his mother regularly filled the house with so many visitors that there was hardly room to move. Moreover, after 1848, Cady Stanton's well-known feminism was an obstacle to Stanton's political career, for her reform involvement challenged entrenched cultural conventions about the proper role of women. During Stanton's 1850 campaign for the state senate, a furor was raised because Cady Stanton was wearing the bloomer reform dress, which substituted short skirts and trousers for women's regular long, restrictive dress. Cady Stanton and several other feminists, notably Seneca Falls' editor and Assistant Postmaster Amelia Bloomer, had designed it, and Bloomer's name had quickly been attached to it. Cady Stanton's feminism almost cost Stanton his one elective office.

The Stantons' sexual relationship also was probably a source of frustration. In contrast to many of her contemporaries, Cady Stanton was aware of woman's sexuality, and she agreed with an 1853 phrenological analysis of herself as "able to enjoy the connubial relationship in a high degree." But in her public writings she consistently rated mental and spiritual relationships as more fulfilling than sexual ones and criticized the unregulated sexual drives of men. Her ambivalence about sex probably derived partly from her ambivalence about her own fertility. The Stantons did not practice birth control. Historians now think that knowledge of birth control was widespread in nineteenth-century America. But in her later life Cady Stanton implied that during her childbearing years she was ignorant of such techniques. The many children she bore indicates that she rejected abstinence, although she later stated that at some point after the birth of her third son, Gerrit, in 1845, she began to practice her own eugenic theories about conceiving children only when husband and wife were in optimal condition. The lack of power over her reproductive life increased Cady Stanton's sense of subordination and eventually contributed to the centrality of the birth control message in her feminist theory and activism. In the Seneca Falls years it added to the frustration of an already strained marital relationship.

Despite their difficulties, Cady Stanton never considered divorcing Henry Stanton. She vigorously denied contemporary attacks that her liberal ideas about divorce grew out of her negative experiences with men and insisted that they derived from observations of the experiences of other women, particularly of a childhood friend who discovered shortly after her wedding that her husband had married her only for her dowry. . . .

Cady Stanton expected an enormous amount from marriage: an intense emotional and intellectual relationship, a sense of total union with a soul mate whom she could "reverence and worship as a God." Her writings extolled this kind of union and contrasted it to the usual marriage held together by emotional need, legal entanglement, or the tyranny of husband over wife. Occasionally, however, she described other kinds of imperfect, but workable unions. One such relationship involved two opposite personalities both powerfully attracted to one another and in constant conflict, reflecting her own situation.

Merry and carefree Elizabeth Cady had married strong and sensible Henry Stanton; the romantic idealist and feminist was linked to the pragmatic politician. Yet by and large Henry Stanton did not interfere in her reform activities, no small gesture from a man of his era. He acquiesced to her changes in their marriage ceremony, and did not refuse to be seen with her in bloomer dress, although Susan Anthony claimed that he finally opposed it. As a New York state senator he introduced several woman's rights petitions into the legislature, and he helped her draft the resolutions for the Seneca Falls convention. Although she complained in 1855 that he opposed her advocacy of woman's rights, he rarely interfered with her later career, even when for many months of the year she abandoned her domestic role for nationwide lecture tours and left him at home with responsibility for the family. In 1862 he was the catalyst behind the Woman's Loyal National League, designed to mount a petition campaign to end slavery. At the 1869 organizing meeting of the National Woman Suffrage Association he supported his wife's proposal that membership be limited to women, stating that "he had been drilled for twenty years privately, and he was convinced that women could do it better alone."

Yet there were tensions during all these years. Infuriated, Stanton refused to attend the 1848 woman's rights convention when his wife introduced a resolution for woman suffrage. He was a spokesman for political antislavery; she became a Garrisonian. He supported the Republican stand on Reconstruction, while Cady Stanton mounted a campaign against the antifeminist Fourteenth and Fifteenth Amendments. Returning to his Democratic identification, he supported Horace Greeley for president in 1872, despite his wife's support of Ulysses S. Grant and her bitter controversy over woman's rights with Greeley, a former friend and early supporter of the woman's movement.

Cady Stanton often mused about the unhappy marriages of great men. But it was a self-indulgent half-truth when she implied to her son in 1898 that the function of work in her life had been to "heal her sorrows." Her drive for work, for regular and stimulating occupation, was intense. On some level she discerned that competition with her husband had caused a basic friction in their marriage. Writing after Stanton's death, she recalled how her young son Theodore had praised a speech he heard his father deliver while criticizing one of hers. Rather than accepting the judgment, she traced her son's preference to society's belief in men's superiority. She was perturbed at losing even so minor a competition to Stanton.

Yet the Stantons ultimately worked out some mutually satisfactory arrangement. When the news of Stanton's death reached her while she was visiting her daughter in England in 1887, she felt a deep loss and regretted "every unkind, ungracious word, every act of coldness and neglect." In his autobiography, largely a catalogue of his career, Stanton mentioned his wife only once, referring to her formally, along with Susan B. Anthony, as the leader of the American woman's movement. "We lived together, without more than the usual matrimonial friction, for nearly half a century" was the judgment of her marriage in Cady Stanton's autobiography.

That Cady Stanton became a reformer had little to do with any sense of status discontent, of having lost her social position as the daughter of a wealthy judge and the granddaughter of the patrician Livingstons—whether because of her reform activities or because the rise of new commercial elites in economically expanding America had challenged the holders of old wealth for social predominance. Rather than feeling displaced as a daughter of the old elite, she was in sympathy with the new economic order. A committed individualist, she liked laissez faire economics. The egalitarian rhetoric of the Democratic party appealed to her. She chose to make her friends among reformers and individuals outside of the social elite. She liked elegance, but her style of life was informal, not patrician. If anything, her privileged background gave her the motivation and the assurance to reject her past, as many reformers and radicals have often done, such as Gerrit Smith, Wendell Phillips, and the Grimké sisters in her own day, all of whom traced their origins to the elite.

Cady Stanton's decision to become a reformer was an outgrowth of her upbringing, her experiences, her intelligence, her reading, her maternal instincts, and her sensitivity to others. Had she been completely satisfied with her marriage, she might have been content to remain in the background. But once she had made her personal discontent public, the course of events and her considerable ability propelled her into a position of leadership.

In July 1848, after the Stantons had lived in Seneca Falls for nearly a year, Martha Wright, Lucretia Mott's sister, informed Cady Stanton that Mott was due to visit and invited her to spend July 13 with Quaker friends in Waterloo. Present on that occasion were Jane Hunt and Mary McClintock, in addition to Wright, Mott, and Cady Stanton. In the course of conversation, Cady Stanton so eloquently expressed her discontent that she and the others, deeply moved, agreed to convene a woman's rights convention and issue a statement of grievances.

The decision was not as precipitous as it seems at first glance. In April 1848, the New York State legislature had finally passed the Married Women's Property Act. Other states, too, had begun to modify their statutes. Cady Stanton knew that Lucretia Mott regularly visited her sister each year at the time of the regional Quaker meeting. After years of antislavery work, Mott had considerable expertise in the planning of such conventions. The intention of the women at Waterloo was to mobilize reform sentiment only in the immediate Seneca Falls area; they announced the meeting only in the local newspaper and, since it was harvest season, expected a small attendance.

They called the convention for July 19 and 20 and spent a day drawing up an agenda and a declaration of grievances. Developing the latter document occupied most of their time. Again Cady Stanton was the guiding force. She chose the 1776 Declaration of Independence as the model and did most of the actual writing, keeping close to the original phraseology of the eighteenth-century document but substituting the word "male" for the name of "King George." Finding that the Declaration of Independence included eighteen grievances, the women in Waterloo spent most of one day combing law books and other documents to find eighteen injustices of their own. The unexpected difficulty of the task was both frustrating and exhilarating, and, drawing on Cady Stanton's particular love of fun, they teased each other about the actuality of their individual oppression. But they felt the gravity of their position as pioneers in a new and radical reform, and laughter relieved their tension.

A half century of feminist thought and writing lay behind their endeavors. They were all familiar with Mary Wollstonecraft's *Vindication of the Rights of Woman* (1792), the first modern feminist treatise; with Sarah Grimké's *Letters on the Equality of the Sexes* (1838); and with Margaret Fuller's *Woman in the Nineteenth Century* (1845). In contrast to these longer works, they intended to present a short and compelling list of grievances on the order of the lawyer's briefs which had been an important part of Cady Stanton's education.

In the end they did not have far to search to discover woman's wrongs. Although married women in some states had secured the right to their own property, they still had no legal right to their earnings or to their children. They could not testify against their husbands in court. Single women could own property, but they paid taxes on it without enjoying the right to vote—the very issue of "taxation without representation" that had triggered the American Revolution. In all occupations women were paid much less than men. The double standard of morality required women to remain virgins until married and then faithful to their husbands, while male indiscretions were condoned. No liberal arts college, with the exception of Oberlin, admitted women. With the exception of writing and school-teaching the professions were closed to them. Not until 1869 would an Iowa woman be licensed to practice law, and the graduation of Elizabeth Blackwell from Geneva Medical College in nearby Geneva, New York, only a month before the convention was the first episode in a long struggle to secure the regular training and licensing of women in medicine. To Cady Stanton and the others the list of grievances justified the charge of tyranny. In this document they held man to blame for woman's state. "He has endeavored, in every way that he could, to destroy her confidence in her own powers, to lessen her self-respect, and to make her willing to lead a dependent and abject life." In a lengthy series of resolutions, Cady Stanton and the others called for an end to all discrimination based on sex.

Cady Stanton's appropriation of the Declaration of Independence was a brilliant propagandistic stroke. She thereby connected her cause to a powerful American symbol of liberty. She adopted the celebrated felicity of expression of Thomas Jefferson, the author of the original document, who was, in his own time, a proponent of human rights—at least for white men. As did many radicals after her, using the 1776 declaration as the basis of their creeds and manifestoes, she astutely placed her movement within the mainstream of the American tradition and reiterated her own loyalty to the revolutionary generation, whom she often identified as "fathers" of the feminists, at least in revolutionary temper. Moreover, her manifesto was in tune with the popular, democratic revolutions against monarchical rule which were sweeping European states in 1848.

Despite the boldness of their action in calling the convention, Cady Stanton and her confederates were seized by insecurity when the convention opened in a local Methodist chapel. On the spot, none of them had sufficient self-possession to chair the meeting. They pressed James Mott, Lucretia Mott's husband, into service, even though the women had previously agreed that men should not take part in the event. But their audience of 300 was much larger than they had expected, and it included forty men. The Waterloo Quakers were there in full force, as were representatives from the Rochester reform community, including black abolitionist Frederick Douglass. In Seneca Falls the meeting was a major event, and it attracted many townspeople, including aggrieved women factory workers, committed reformers, and the curious.

The first day of the convention was devoted to speeches by Mott, McClintock, and Cady Stanton, among others. When Cady Stanton took the podium, the prospect was so threatening, she later recalled, that she felt like "suddenly abandoning all her principles and running away." Amelia Bloomer, who along with her husband managed the Seneca Falls post office, contended that Cady Stanton spoke so softly it was impossible to hear her. Yet by the second day, which was devoted to reading the Declaration of Sentiments and voting on its resolutions, Cady Stanton was sufficiently bold to electrify the meeting with a new and controversial resolution. She proposed that the Declaration of Sentiments demand suffrage for women. All other resolutions passed unanimously. But only a bare majority voted in favor of

suffrage and only after an eloquent speech by Frederick Douglass.

The Quakers at the convention opposed the demand for suffrage because, as pacifists, they abjured any participation in a polity that condoned war as national policy. But there was much more to the opposition than that. Henry Stanton, the reformer, helped his wife draft the resolutions for the convention. But Stanton, the politician, refused to attend when his wife decided to introduce the suffrage resolution. Even Lucretia Mott contended that the demand would make them appear ridiculous.

The exclusive right to vote, Stanton and Mott knew, was central to male political hegemony. Early in the century state legislatures had disenfranchised women in the states where colonial voting rights were still theirs, just as they had disenfranchised free blacks in the 1820s and 1830s when they eliminated property qualifications for voting and instituted universal male suffrage. The democratization of American politics coincided with an increasing conservatism with regard to the position of women and an increasing tendency to define their proper role as domestic. Democracy and the free enterprise economy created a volatile social order in which neither status nor income was entirely secure. In compensation, the society reinforced traditional definitions of separate masculine and feminine spheres of behavior, particularly after the woman's rights movement challenged it. Republican ideology, which was a legacy of the Revolution, and the religious revivals of the 1820s and 1830s, in which most converts were women, both centered on purifying the nation; and both regarded woman's natural virtue and influence in the home as primary agents of national regeneration. The rough worlds of business and politics were for men; women provided a secure haven in the home and through it attempted to institute moral reformation.

The average politician, patterning himself after Andrew Jackson, strove to be forceful and aggressive. Martin Van Buren was ridiculed for his elegant manners: the age's worst epithet, "man-milliner," with its pejorative reference to effete male hatmakers, dogged him throughout his career. William Henry Harrison underscored his identify by adopting as his symbols the coonskin cap and the whiskey barrel—potent symbols of masculinity. The political world was masculine, its competitiveness symbolized by party battles and ritualized by tempestuous elections, in which heavy drinking and fist fights were the order of the day at the saloons and barber shops where many polls were set up. When Lucretia Mott described the demand for suffrage as "ridiculous," she meant that the culture would view the entry of women into the political world as so outlandish as to seem comical.

To Cady Stanton, the daughter of a statesman and the wife of a politician, the political world was neither strange nor impregnable. For years her husband had argued that politics was the key to abolitionist success; it was a primary source of power in the democratic polity. It was no less the key to feminist success, Cady Stanton came to understand, and the vote was the first step. Nor was suffrage potentially as culturally explosive as other radical ideas, like divorce reform or birth control, which were becoming crucial to Cady Stanton's emerging ideology, and which she avoided at Seneca Falls. In her personal experience and her own ideology, the demand for suffrage was pragmatic, not radical.

Furthermore, for years Cady Stanton had resented her husband's preoccupation with politics. It is not surprising that she chose the issue of woman's access to politics as her first significant act of feminist rebellion. As early as the spring before the convention she had approached New York legislator Ansel Bascom, a former classmate at Johnstown Academy and a Seneca Falls neighbor, to suggest that he introduce a woman suffrage bill before the legislature. In addition, in August 1848, just a few weeks after the Seneca Falls convention, political abolitionists, among whom Henry Stanton was prominent, were to meet to form a new Free-Soil party that would appeal as much to the economic ambitions of Northerners as to their antislavery sentiment. Henry Stanton stormed out of Seneca Falls; any connection with the controversial issue of woman suffrage might seriously damage the future of the new party, as well as his own career within it.

In advocating a position that varied from that of other feminists, Cady Stanton established her mature reform style. Within the context of reform politics and prevailing social attitudes, the emphasis on enfranchisement was radical. It was calculated to shock woman's rights advocates into a stand that would directly confront social prejudices and prove that they lacked neither courage nor commitment. . . . Cady Stanton gave a number of explanations for introducing the suffrage resolutions in the 1848 convention. . . .

[Her primary model in this behavior was] William Lloyd Garrison. She had criticized his militant style during the London Anti-Slavery Convention and in 1841 declared her support for her husband's advocacy of political action. But even then she was wavering, writing of her partial conversion to Garrison's ideas. His early support of woman's rights always impressed her. Nor did she forget his willingness to choose principle over politics; his role in the abolitionist movement as prophet and moralist deeply appealed to her. Garrisonian strategy recognized that the number of dedicated abolitionists was too small ever to be more than a pressure group and that the very nature of politics inevitably compromised their goals. The key to antislavery success lay therefore in changing public opinion and not in party action. . . .

Throughout her career Cady Stanton was pulled toward the opposite poles of politics and morality and of partisan maneuver and direct confrontation. That she usually chose confrontation and a high moral stance over indirect political methods had much to do with her emotional makeup. Politics was not really congenial to her. Independent by nature, with a childlike love of surprises, impatient of partial solutions and unable to tolerate delay, the political mode of moderation, compromise, and slow progress did not fit her. Rather she preferred to shock her colleagues, to stir them out of complacency, to arouse their passions through introducing issues they had not considered. Furthermore, emotionally volatile, powerful in personality, and liking extravagant praise, the platform and the lecture hall, not the assembly chamber, appealed to her. She loved the theater and often suggested that acting was an exciting career for women. She became a brilliant interpreter of feminist ethics as a writer and orator and not as a political strategist. She attributed her successful effort for suffrage at Seneca Falls to arguments delivered from the public podium and not in private conversation.

Had the Seneca Falls convention not occurred, the woman's rights movement would nonetheless have shortly come into being. Groups in Ohio and Massachusetts were contemplating action, and the Seneca Falls declaration called for similar meetings throughout the nation. Indeed, Boston reform women, former associates of Cady Stanton, in 1850 organized the first woman's rights convention purposefully designed to be national in scope in the reform center of Worcester, Massachusetts. Nonetheless the legend of the primacy of Seneca Falls was quickly established. No other meeting produced such a powerful document as its Declaration of Sentiments, and the immediate and na-

tionwide reaction of the press quickly gained it public notoriety. The telegraph and the newly formed Associated Press quickly disseminated the news of the meeting. Until then, newspapers had paid little attention to woman's rights activities; all those present at Seneca Falls were amazed at the ferocity of the medium's response.

Somewhere they had touched a raw nerve. Whether out of fear or disdain, whether because all editors were men and most newspapers were quasi-official organs for political parties, the press was vituperative in denouncing the meeting. They advanced charges that would become characteristic of the opposition to feminism throughout the century: the leaders were frustrated old maids; the demands were unnecessary because most American women, pampered by husbands and fathers, were satisfied with their lots; and abandonment of the domestic sphere threatened marriage, the family, and the entire social order.

Cady Stanton later asserted that, had she realized the furor the convention would rouse, she would never have called it. Indeed, she opposed having a woman chair a convention held two weeks later in Rochester to continue the discussions. Of the 100 men and women who signed the declaration, many retracted their signatures under pressure from relatives. When Daniel Cady heard about the meeting, he hurried to Seneca Falls, along with his son-in-law, Daniel Eaton, whose wife Harriet had been visiting Cady Stanton and had signed the declaration. Under pressure from her father and her husband, Harriet retracted her signature and returned home. But despite the entreaties of her father, Cady Stanton refused to withdraw her name. She would not recant. In calling the Seneca Falls convention, in writing the declaration, in holding firm for suffrage, she had taken her stand. In the process, she had found herself.

DOCUMENTS: Political Oratory

SOJOURNER TRUTH
"And a'n't I a woman?"

Our only account of impassioned oratory by this black abolitionist comes from the pen of Frances D. Gage, who chaired a large women's rights meeting in Akron, Ohio, in May 1851. Sojourner Truth had already achieved renown as an effective abolitionist speaker, although it is clear from Gage's account that the people at the Akron meeting regarded her as a pariah. In the 1850s and 1860s she toured the upper Midwest, speaking on behalf of antislavery and women's rights. Her presence at a meeting of white women, however, was exceptional. Black abolitionists split from the white movement in the 1850s, and few black women seem to have been welcomed at white women's rights meetings.

May 29, 1851

There were very few women in those days who dared to "speak in meeting"; and the august teachers of the people were seemingly getting the better of us, while the boys in the galleries, and the sneerers among the pews, were hugely enjoying the discomfiture, as they supposed, of the "strong-minded." Some of the tender-skinned friends were on the point of losing dignity, and the atmosphere betokened a storm. When, slowly from her seat in the corner rose Sojourner Truth, who, till now, had scarcely lifted her head. "Don't let her speak!" gasped half a dozen in my ear. She moved slowly and solemnly to the front, laid her old bonnet at her feet, and turned her great speaking eyes to me. There was a hissing sound of disapprobation above and below. I rose and announced "Sojourner Truth," and begged the audience to keep silence for a few moments.

The tumult subsided at once, and every eye was fixed on this almost Amazon form, which stood nearly six feet high, head erect, and eyes piercing the upper air like one in a dream. At her first word there was a profound hush. She spoke in deep tones, which, though not loud, reached every ear in the house, and away through the throng at the doors and windows.

"Wall, chilern, whar dar is so much racket dar must be somethin' out o' kilter. I tink dat 'twixt de niggers of de Souf and de womin at de Norf, all talkin' 'bout rights, de white men will be in a fix pretty soon. But what's all dis here talkin' 'bout?

"Dat man ober dar say dat womin needs to be helped into carriages, and lifted ober ditches, and to hab de best

Excerpted from Frances D. Gage, Reminiscences of Sojourner Truth in *History of Woman Suffrage*, edited by Elizabeth Cady Stanton, Susan B. Anthony, and Matilda Joslyn Gage, vol. 1 (New York: Fowler & Wells, 1881), pp. 115–17.

place everywhar. Nobody eber helps me into carriages, or ober mud-puddles, or gibs me any best place!" And raising herself to her full height, and her voice to a pitch like rolling thunder, she asked. "And a'n't I a woman? Look at me! Look at my arm! (and she bared her right arm to the shoulder, showing her tremendous muscular power). I have ploughed, and planted, and gathered into barns, and no man could head me! And a'n't I a woman? I could work as much and eat as much as a man—when I could get it—and bear de lash as well! And a'n't I a woman? I have borne thirteen chilern, and seen 'em mos' all sold off to slavery, and when I cried out with my mother's grief, none but Jesus heard me! And a'n't I a woman?

"Den dey talks 'bout dis ting in de head; what dis dey call it?" ("Intellect," whispered some one near.) "Dat's it, honey. What's dat got to do wid womin's rights or nigger's rights? If my cup won't hold but a pint, and yourn holds a quart, wouldn't ye be mean not to let me have my little half-measure full?" And she pointed her significant finger, and sent a keen glance at the minister who had made the argument. The cheering was long and loud.

"Den dat little man in black dar, he say women can't have as much rights as men, 'cause Christ wan't a woman! Whar did your Christ come from?" Rolling thunder couldn't have stilled that crowd, as did those deep, wonderful tones, as she stood there with outstretched arms and eyes of fire. Raising her voice still louder, she repeated, "Whar did your Christ come from? From God and a woman! Man had nothin' to do with Him." Oh, what a rebuke that was to that little man.

Turning again to another objector, she took up the defense of Mother Eve. I can not follow her through it all. It was pointed, and witty, and solemn; eliciting at almost every sentence deafening applause; and she ended by asserting: "If de fust woman God ever made was strong enough to turn de world upside down all alone, dese women togedder (and she glanced her eye over the platform) ought to be able to turn it back, and get it right side up again! And now dey is asking to do it, de men better let 'em." Long-continued cheering greeted this. "'Bleeged to ye for hearin' on me, and now ole Sojourner hasn't got nothin' more to say."

Amid roars of applause, she returned to her corner, leaving more than one of us with streaming eyes, and hearts beating with gratitude. She had taken us up in her strong arms and carried us safely over the slough of difficulty turning the whole tide in our favor.

MARY C. VAUGHAN
"We would act as well as endure"

Temperance was a more popular reform movement among women than abolition and probably accounted for more recruits to the women's rights cause. Mary C. Vaughan's speech at an Albany, New York, temperance meeting suggests some of the issues to which women responded that led them from a concern over alcoholism to one for women's rights. Which sex does Vaughan think is most likely to abuse alcohol? Who does she think most requires protection? Note that, at the end, Vaughan mentions "the true woman"; what does Vaughan imply are the characteristics of a "true woman"?

January 28, 1852

We have met to consider what we, as women, can do and may do, to forward the temperance reform. We have met, because, as members of the human family, we share in all the sufferings which error and crime bring upon the race, and because we are learning that our part in the drama of life is something beside inactive suffering and passive endurance. We would act as well as endure; and we meet here to-day because many of us have been trying to act, and we would combine our individual experiences, and together devise plans for the future, out of which shall arise well-based hopes of good results to humanity. We are aware that this proceeding of ours, this calling together of a body of women to deliberate publicly upon plans to carry out a specified reform, will rub rather harshly upon the mould of prejudice, which has gathered thick upon the common mind.

. . . There are plenty of women, as well as men, who can labor for reforms without neglecting business or duty. It is an error that clings most tenaciously to the public mind, that because a part of the sex are wives and mothers and have absorbing duties, that all the sex should be denied any other sphere of effort. To deprive every unmarried woman, spinster, or widow, or every childless wife, of the power of exercising her warm sympathies for the good of others, is to deprive her of the greatest happiness of which she is capable; to rob her highest faculties of their legitimate operation and reward; to belittle and narrow her mind; to dwarf her affections; to turn the harmonies of her nature to discord; and, as the human mind must be active, to compel her to employ hers with low and grovelling thoughts, which lead to contemptible actions.

There is no reform in which woman can act better or more appropriately than temperance. I know not how she can re-

Excerpted from Mary C. Vaughan, Address, Daughters of Temperance Assembly, in *History of Woman Suffrage*, edited by Elizabeth Cady Stanton, Susan B. Anthony, and Matilda Joslyn Gage, vol. 1 (New York: Fowler & Wells, 1881), pp. 476–78.

sist or turn aside from the duty of acting in this; its effects fall so crushingly upon her and those whose interests are identical with her own; she has so often seen its slow, insidious, but not the less surely fatal advances, gaining upon its victim; she has seen the intellect which was her dearest pride, debased; the affections which were her life-giving springs of action, estranged; the children once loved, abused, disgraced and impoverished; the home once an earthly paradise, rendered a fit abode for lost spirits; has felt in her own person all the misery, degradation, and woe of the drunkard's wife; has shrunk from revilings and cowered beneath blows; has labored and toiled to have her poor earnings transferred to the rum-seller's ill-gotten hoard; while her children, ragged, fireless, poor, starving, gathered shivering about her, and with hollow eyes, from which all smiles had fled, begged vainly for the bread she had not to bestow. Oh! the misery, the utter, hopeless misery of the drunkard's wife!

. . . We account it no reason why we should desist, when conscience, an awakened sense of duty, and aroused heart-sympathies, would lead us to show ourselves something different than an impersonation of the vague ideal which has been named, Woman, and with which woman has long striven to identify herself. A creature all softness and sensibility, who must necessarily enjoy and suffer in the extreme, while sharing with man the pleasures and the ills of life; bearing happiness meekly, and sorrow with fortitude; gentle, mild, submissive, forbearing under all circumstances; a softened reflex of the opinions and ideas of the masculines who, by relationship, hold mastery over her; without individualism, a mere adjunct of man, the chief object of whose creation was to adorn and beautify his existence, or to minister to some form of his selfishness. This is nearly the masculine idea of womanhood, and poor womanhood strives to personify it. But not all women. This is an age of iconoclasms; and daring hands are raised to sweep from its pedestal, and dash to fragments, this false image of woman. We care not how soon, if the true woman but takes its place.

SUSAN B. ANTHONY
"Guaranteed to us and our daughters forever"

The capstone of the celebration of the Centennial was a public reading of the Declaration of Independence in Independence Square, Philadelphia, by a descendant of a signer, Richard Henry Lee. Elizabeth Cady Stanton, who was then president of the National Woman Suffrage Association, asked permission to present silently a women's protest and a written Declaration of Rights. The re-

Excerpted from Susan B. Anthony, Declaration of Rights for Women by the National Woman Suffrage Association, in *History of Woman Suffrage*, edited by Elizabeth Cady Stanton, Susan B. Anthony, and Matilda Joslyn Gage, vol. 3 (Rochester, N.Y.: Susan B. Anthony, 1886), pp. 31–34.

quest was denied. "Tomorrow we propose to celebrate what we have done the last hundred years," replied the president of the official ceremonies, "not what we have failed to do."

Led by suffragist Susan B. Anthony, five women appeared at the official reading, distributing copies of their declaration. After this mildly disruptive gesture they withdrew to the other side of Independence Hall, where they staged a counter-Centennial and Anthony read the following address. Compare it to the Declaration of Sentiments (document 2 in Essential Documents) of twenty-eight years before. Note the splendid oratorical flourish of the final paragraph.

July 4, 1876

While the nation is buoyant with patriotism, and all hearts are attuned to praise, it is with sorrow we come to strike the one discordant note, on this one-hundredth anniversary of our country's birth. When subjects of kings, emperors, and czars, from the old world join in our national jubilee, shall the women of the republic refuse to lay their hands with benedictions on the nation's head? Surveying America's exposition, surpassing in magnificence those of London, Paris, and Vienna, shall we not rejoice at the success of the youngest rival among the nations of the earth? May not our hearts, in unison with all, swell with pride at our great achievements as a people; our free speech, free press, free schools, free church, and the rapid progress we have made in material wealth, trade, commerce and the inventive arts? And we do rejoice in the success, thus far, of our experiment of self-government. Our faith is firm and unwavering in the broad principles of human rights proclaimed in 1776, not only as abstract truths, but as the corner stones of a republic. Yet we cannot forget, even in this glad hour, that while all men of every race, and clime, and condition, have been invested with the full rights of citizenship under our hospitable flag, all women still suffer the degradation of disfranchisement.

The history of our country the past hundred years has been a series of assumptions and usurpations of power over woman, in direct opposition to the principles of just government, acknowledged by the United States as its foundation. . . .

And for the violation of these fundamental principles of our government, we arraign our rulers on this Fourth day of July, 1876,—and these are our articles of impeachment:

Bills of attainder have been passed by the introduction of the word "male" into all the State constitutions, denying to women the right of suffrage, and thereby making sex a crime—an exercise of power clearly forbidden in article 1, sections 9, 10, of the United States constitution. . . .

The right of trial by a jury of one's peers was so jealousy guarded that States refused to ratify the original constitution until it was guaranteed by the sixth amendment. And yet the women of this nation have never been allowed a jury of their peers—being tried in all cases by men, native, and foreign, educated and ignorant, virtuous and vicious. Young girls have been arraigned in our courts for the crime of infanticide; tried, convicted, hanged—victims, perchance, of judge, jurors, advocates—while no woman's voice could be heard in their defense. . . .

Taxation without representation, the immediate cause of the rebellion of the colonies against Great Britain, is one of the grievous wrongs the women of this country have suffered during the century. Deploring war, with all the demoralization that follows in its train, we have been taxed to support standing armies, with their waste of life and wealth. Believing in temperance, we have been taxed to support the vice, crime and pauperism of the liquor traffic. While we suffer its wrongs and abuses infinitely more than man, we have no power to protect our sons against this giant evil. . . .

Unequal codes for men and women. Held by law a perpetual minor, deemed incapable of self-protection, even in the industries of the world, woman is denied equality of rights. The fact of sex, not the quantity or quality of work, in most cases, decides the pay and position; and because of this injustice thousands of fatherless girls are compelled to choose between a life of shame and starvation. Laws catering to man's vices have created two codes of morals in which penalties are graded according to the political status of the offender. Under such laws, women are fined and imprisoned if found alone in the streets, or in public places of resort, at certain hours. Under the pretense of regulating public morals, police officers seizing the occupants of disreputable houses, march the women in platoons to prison, while the men, partners in their guilt, go free. . . .

Representation of woman has had no place in the nation's thought. Since the incorporation of the thirteen original States, twenty-four have been admitted to the Union, not one of which has recognized woman's right of self-government. On this birthday of our national liberties, July Fourth, 1876, Colorado, like all her elder sisters, comes into the Union with the invidious word "male" in her constitution. . . .

The judiciary above the nation has proved itself but the echo of the party in power, by upholding and enforcing laws that are opposed to the spirit and letter of the constitution. When the slave power was dominant, the Supreme Court decided that a black man was not a citizen, because he had not the right to vote; and when the constitution was so amended as to make all persons citizens, the same high tribunal decided that a woman, though a citizen, had not the right to vote. Such vacillating interpretations of constitutional law unsettle our faith in judicial authority, and undermine the liberties of the whole people.

These articles of impeachment against our rulers we now submit to the impartial judgment of the people. To all these wrongs and oppressions woman has not submitted in silence and resignation. From the beginning of the century, when Abigail Adams, the wife of one president and mother of another, said, "We will not hold ourselves bound to obey laws in which we have no voice or representation," until now, woman's discontent has been steadily increasing, culminating nearly thirty years ago in a simultaneous movement among the women of the nation, demanding the right of suffrage. In making our just demands, a higher motive than the pride of sex inspires us; we feel that national safety and stability depend on the complete recognition of the broad principles of our government. Woman's degraded, helpless position is the weak point in our institutions today; a disturbing force everywhere, severing family ties, filling our asylums with the deaf, the dumb, the blind; our prisons with criminals, our cities with drunkenness and prostitution; our homes with disease and death. It was the boast of the founders of the republic, that the rights for which they contended were the rights of human nature. If these rights are ignored in the case of one-half the people, the nation is surely preparing for its downfall. Governments try themselves. The recognition of a governing and a governed class is incompatible with the first principles of freedom. Woman has not been a heedless spectator of the events of this century, nor a dull listener to the grand arguments for the equal rights of humanity. From the earliest history of our country woman has shown equal devotion with man to the cause of freedom, and has stood firmly by his side in its defense. Together, they have made this country what it is. Woman's wealth, thought and labor have cemeted the stones of every monument man has reared to liberty.

And now, at the close of a hundred years, as the hour-hand of the great clock that marks the centuries points to 1876, we declare our faith in the principles of self-government; our full equality with man in natural rights; that woman was made first for her own happiness, with the absolute right to herself—to all the opportunities and advantages life affords for her complete development; and we deny that dogma of the centuries, incorporated in the codes of all nations—that woman was made for man—her best interests, in all cases, to be sacrificed to his will. We ask of our rulers, at this hour, no special privileges, no special legislation. We ask justice, we ask equality, we ask that all the civil and political rights that belong to citizens of the United States, be guaranteed to us and our daughters forever.

Medical Examination at Ellis Island
"*The day of the emigrants' arrival in New York was the nearest earthly likeness to th*
final day of Judgment, when we have to prove our fitness to enter Heaven." The word
were those of a sympathetic journalist who shared the anxiety-ridden experience awai
ing immigrants at the port of entry, usually Ellis Island. Failing the medical test coul
mean deportation. Brown Brothers

II~B~

Industrializing America
1880–1920

Americans triumphantly celebrated the end of the nineteenth century. They had secured sectional unity between North and South and the benefits of continental expansion. The industrial revolution, dominated by the vision and organizational genius of a few hard-driving, ruthless entrepreneurs, had transformed a wilderness into a new landscape, crisscrossed by railroads and telegraph and telephone lines and dotted with foundries, factories, and mills. Sprawling cities and industrial centers lured native and immigrant alike with the promise of a new job and a fresh start. As the urban population increased from 15 million in 1880 to 45 million in 1910, America's farmers expanded their output not only to feed this nation's teeming cities but those of Europe as well. American technology provided its own "miracles." The Brooklyn Bridge, upon completion in 1883, was the longest suspension bridge in the world. Serving thousands of daily commuters between Brooklyn and Manhattan, it stood as a symbol not only of the technological achievements of the American people but of the emergence of a new nation—industrial, urban, and ethnically diverse.

Maturing as an economic power in an age of imperialism, America was fast becoming an international power as well. Competing with Europe in a worldwide quest for new trade outlets, the United States picked up new territories along with new markets. Acquisition of Alaska (1867) was followed by involvement in—and ultimately annexation of—Samoa (1872) and Hawaii (1898). After a "splendid little war" with Spain, this nation was left with Puerto Rico, Guam, and the Philippines. Eager to protect strategic interests in the Pacific, the United States acquired the right to construct an interoceanic canal to be owned by the new country of Panama but under American control. The Panama Canal, another triumph of American engineering, was one of many developments portending this nation's willingness to intervene in the affairs of other nations to the south in order to establish hemispheric dominance and protect American investments.

The economic expansion that had enabled, and indeed encouraged, this former British colony to create its own imperial system did not occur painlessly. The populist movement of the 1890s, for example, expressed the anger of agrarians who attacked the injustices of an economic system that victimized farmers while benefiting industrial, railroad, and banking interests. The growing socialist movement was but one expression of workers' discontent with an industrial order in which 5 percent of the population owned nearly half the nation's property while more than a third of its 76 million people in 1910 lived below the poverty line. Living conditions were no better than working conditions for the millions trapped in the poverty and misery of teeming urban ghettos. Cities, ill prepared to cope with rapid population growth, were governed inadequately and often dishonestly by politicians whose base of support lay in wards populated by immigrants inexperienced with American politics and grateful for services provided by the "machine."

Attempting to steer a middle course between radicalism and reaction, many Americans at the turn of the century turned to progressivism, participating in a multifaceted coalition of reformers that included insurgent intellectuals and university professors, Christian "social gospelers," women activists, investigative reporters, business and professional men, farmers, and laborers. A diverse lot dedicated to a variety of goals, progressives generally agreed on certain basic propositions. Government, particularly at the local and state level, must be made more democratic, honest, and efficient; monopolies must be controlled and big business made more responsive to the public interest; natural resources must be used more rationally; social conditions must be made more just and humane and the environment in which people lived and worked made safer. Extending to international affairs this same concern for order and reform, they agreed that in the wake of World War I the postwar world created must be progressive as well. Although their efforts to meet the needs of this new urban, industrial society were sometimes contradictory and not always successful, progressives laid the foundations of the modern welfare state.

Technology, industrialization, immigration, urbanization, domestic reform, and international involvement: these were the developments shaping American life between 1880 and 1920, and they involved women as well as men. Women, many from southern and eastern Europe, moved to cities, seeking there some measure of economic survival and family stability. Women worked on farms and in factories, some emerging as populist agitators, socialist activists, and labor organizers. Women also became progressives and pacificists, serving in the vanguard of those struggling for economic and social justice and international peace.

Historians have customarily acknowledged these women with little more than a cursory nod toward such figures as Mary Elizabeth Lease, the populist orator who urged farmers "to raise less corn and more hell"; Mary Harris ("Mother") Jones, the fiery labor agitator who became a symbol of defiance wherever strikers gathered; and, of course, Jane Addams, the humanitarian reformer whose settlement house work made her a relentless foe of political corruption and economic exploitation. Although historians usually include women's winning the vote among progressive achievements, they have been reluctant to examine the ways in which men and women differed in their experiences of industrial work and technological change. Even in studying reform most historians of progressivism have focused on males, whether as business, professional, or political elites or as working-class voters. Suppose, however, we reverse this emphasis, exploring progressivism as one example of the way in which the inclusion of women's experience prompts a refocusing of what we know about this much studied era in American reform.

We should begin by reversing the relation of women reformers to progressivism. Instead of focusing on them as part of a reform coalition, let us, for the moment, view progressivism as part of women's history, looking especially at the way in which women steadily moved from the domestic into the public sphere, in the process changing both. The first stage of that process we can locate in the early years of the republic when women as "Republican Mothers" assumed a role that made their domestic domain of education and nurture into a schoolroom for the next generation of virtuous citizens. This acknowledgment of the mother's private domain as a public trust helped to establish women—in the ideal, at least—as public persons with public responsibilities, even if exercised within the privacy of the family. At an ever-accelerating pace between 1820 and 1880—the dates are approximations—women expanded that role into what might be called "Reformist Motherhood." Instead of influencing the public domain indirectly through the lives of their sons, women began to extend their role as nurturer and teacher of morals from the domestic sphere into the public sphere through church, missionary, and moral reform groups. Women sought to make the world conform more strictly to values taught in the home—sexual responsibility and restraint for men as well as women, self-discipline for those who used strong drink, charity and rehabilitation for those who were entrapped by poverty and crime, sympathy and justice for Afro-Americans.

Between 1880 and 1920 a new role developed that might be called "Political Motherhood." Increasing numbers of women joined the Woman's Christian Temperance Union (WCTU), the Young Women's Christian Association

(YWCA), the settlement house movement, the General Federation of Women's Clubs, the National Association of Colored Women, the Children's Aid Society, the National Child Labor Committee, the National Consumers' League, the Pure Food Association, and a host of others. (By 1920, for example, the WCTU had 800,000 members, the General Federation of Women's Clubs nearly one million.) Through these organizations and related activities, women enlarged still further their sphere in public life where once only men had acted. They worked to protect industrial workers, especially women and children, to clean up local politics as well as unsanitary slaughterhouses and polluted water supplies, to promote health, education, social welfare, and mental hygiene. Even big business was no longer "off limits" to women as Ida Tarbell proved when she exposed the corrupt practices used by John D. Rockefeller to create his oil empire. In their rejection of an individualism that, in the hands of such men, had become exploitative, and in their willingness to use government at all levels to create a more humane, caring community, women were thinking and acting in ways that were quintessentially progressive.

In transforming women's sphere from the private, family-oriented world of domesticity into the formerly male world of politics and public policy, a major change was occurring. The "womanhood" identified with "mothering" was becoming less a biological fact—giving birth to children—and more a political role with new ideological dimensions. The traditional word *motherhood* was being reshaped so as to justify women's assuming new, ever-more-public responsibilities. Women now clearly meant to transform the domestic housekeeping responsibilities of their grandmothers into an attack on the worst abuses of an urban, industrial society. The household now included marketplace and city hall.

Viewed in this context, prohibition, a progressive reform often regarded as a political aberration, can be seen as the logical extension of women's traditional concern for those women and children who were so often the victims of alcohol-related abuse. Indeed, such protection seemed as necessary and as logical as legislation abolishing child labor or limiting the hours of working women whose health as potential mothers would affect the health of the next generation. In this context, too, suffrage marks the final step in the movement out of the domestic sphere into the political sphere. That women should justify the need to vote in terms of their domestic responsibilities, a justification criticized by some historians, becomes quite consistent. That, too, must be viewed as part of a long process in which the drive to enlarge women's sphere came through gradual transformation of ideals identified with an older domesticity into a new and broader sense of responsibility appropriate for a public sphere itself changing under the impact of industrialization, immigration, and urbanization.

What, then, have we accomplished through this exercise of taking women out of the progressive coalition and putting progressivism into women's history?

We discover first of all that female reformers were not merely one group among many in the progressive coalition. Women's perspective quite as much as their participation gave progressivism much of its ideological direction as well as its momentum. Indeed, we can even say that the progressive perspective was, in large part, the appropriation by male reformers of those ideas most intimately associated with the social perspective of women, almost literally the application to society of moral issues nurtured in women's domain. The significance of this achievement is understood, however, only when we include women's experience as basic, *not incidental*, to how we view the past. Refocusing history is, to be sure, a complicated task, but this one example—women and progressivism—suggests how we may begin to view afresh the first two decades of the twentieth century.

DOCUMENTS: Working for Wages

DAVID M. KATZMAN
Seven Days a Week: Domestic Work

For women who needed to work outside the home, domestic service has always been one of the limited job options available. Housekeeping was, after all presumed to be "women's work." By 1900 over one-third of the wage-earning women in this country were employed as domestics or waitresses. Many were either immigrants or the daughters of immigrants from Europe; others were Afro-Americans. The lot of such women was not easy, especially in the years before the invention of the labor-saving appliances that became common fixtures in middle-class households by 1920. Note the number of tasks expected of a domestic in a single-servant household, the long hours, the low pay, the necessity of always being at the "beck-and-call" of the mistress, and the lack of time of one's own. Because of these factors, many women of European background left domestic service for jobs in factories or shops, leaving black women—victims of even greater discrimination—to form a larger proportion of domestic workers.

The best way of illustrating the daily and weekly cycles is to follow a general household worker through a part of her week's work. Inez Godman recorded her activities on a typical workday in 1901. She worked in a Northern home, doing all the work except the wash. She had negotiated a 75¢-a-week reduction in wages to $2.75 in return for her mistress hiring the wash out. Godman began work on a Wednesday afternoon and immediately prepared the dinner. Apparently no time was allotted for her to adjust to her new work and living environment. Wearing the apron and cap provided her, she served the meal. After cleaning up the kitchen and dining room, she prepared bread dough; her mistress had become "weary of baker's stuff." At 9:00 P.M. she was through for the day.[1]

On Thursday she rose at 6:00 A.M. and served breakfast an hour later. By 9:30 A.M. the kitchen and dining room had been cleaned, and her weekly chores began. She spent two hours cleaning the sitting room. "Everything had to be carried into the adjoining room, and there was much china and bric-a-brac," she wrote. The carpet had to be moved, and each slat of the Venetian blinds wiped clean. Twice she had to go to the kitchen

Excerpted from "Household Work," chap. 3 of *Seven Days a Week: Women and Domestic Service in Industrializing America* by David M. Katzman (New York: Oxford University Press, 1978). Copyright © 1978 by Oxford University Press. Reprinted by permission. Notes have been renumbered.

to check the bread she was baking (it had risen overnight), and five times she had to answer the doorbell. Lunch required an hour of preparation, and she served her mistress at one. Already she had worked seven hours: "I was thankful for a chance to sit, and dawdled over my lunch for half an hour." By 2:30 P.M. the kitchen and dining room were clean again, and her mistress suggested Godman clean the kitchen floor. Afterwards, she rested in her room from 3:20 to 4:00 P.M. At 4:00 she had to go downstairs to heat the oven and begin the evening meal. "Dinner was a complex meal," she explained, "and coming at night when I was tired was always something of a worry. To have the different courses ready at just the right moment, to be sure that nothing burned or curdled while I was waiting on the table, to think quickly and act calmly; all this meant weariness."[2]

The alternation of the daily and weekly chores continued during each day. On Friday after breakfast she cleaned the halls, stairs, vestibule, and bathroom: "It was heavy work, for the halls were carpeted with moquette, but I sat on the stairs as I swept them with a whisk broom, thus saving my feet." Before lunch she had gone to the market, then returned and made the midday meal. After cleaning the kitchen and dining room and doing the weekly cleaning of the refrigerator, she wearily climbed to her room. She passed her mistress, who "sat with a flushed face still sewing." She offered to help, and her mistress responded: "I don't know how to rush sewing but I wish to wear this skirt to-morrow, and if you *would* do it I would like to rest." Godman finished it in half an hour. She still had another hour of rest, since she was cooking fish for dinner and would not have to light the oven. She could rest until 4:30. She was rewarded for doing the skirt; her employer gave her Saturday evening off, since she was going out to dinner.[3]

Sunday was filled with daily chores,

but Godman was pressed for time because she had to help her mistress dress for church. She rushed and managed to finish by 2:00 P.M. so she could attend a Sunday school class. That night she served a light supper and managed to retire at 8:00 P.M. On Monday morning she cleaned the dining room, polished silver, did the marketing, and baked bread. Since guests were invited to dinner that evening she worked straight through her afternoon break, and did not finish cleaning up until 10:00 P.M. Monday had turned into a sixteen-hour workday, including time for meals. The laundress came on Tuesday, and Godman spent all afternoon plus all day Wednesday and part of Thursday between her daily chores and ironing. But Thursday began a new weekly cycle. Wisely her mistress went out for lunch that first week so Godman could complete the ironing and clean the sitting room without having to make lunch and clean up. She finished the ironing at 11:00 A.M. Thursday and then went to the sitting room. She simply rested there for an hour, then cleaned the room in just twenty minutes. Though she thought it looked clean, she knew it was not thoroughly done. Each week she failed to complete the ironing on Wednesday; it was physically impossible for her. The result was that Thursday was "a hard day, for my lady did not go out to luncheon after that first week, and with her in the house I could not slight the work nor stop to rest. Every Thursday night I was ready to collapse.[4]

Inez Godman's full workdays are typical. Daily chores for the maid-of-all-work included lighting fires (in stoves, for hot water, in winter fireplaces or furnaces), preparing and serving meals and cleaning up, making beds, doing light dusting, sweeping or scrubbing front steps and porch, answering the doorbell, and running errands. The weekly cycle, dominated by washing, ironing, and heavy cleaning, was more physically demanding. A typical week would begin with washing on Monday, ironing on Tuesday, and mending on Wednesday. On Thursday the dining room would be thoroughly cleaned, including the polishing of silver and glass. On Friday the house would be swept and the windows cleaned. Saturday would entail major housecleaning—the kitchen, cellar, and rooms not cleaned thoroughly on other days—and then perhaps breadbaking. Repetition of tasks made the work monotonous, but the complaint heard most seemed to be that of physical fatigue and tiredness. Over and over again women mentioned how they often collapsed in bed at the end of the day, too tired to read or even take a bath. "If one of the twelve labors of Hercules had been to solve the servant girl problem," one servant wrote, "he never would have had the reputation he has."[5]

NOTES

1. Inez A. Godman, "Ten Weeks in a Kitchen," *Independent* LIII (October 17, 1901), 2459.

2. Ibid., p. 2460.

3. Ibid.

4. Ibid., p. 2461.

5. Catherine Owen, *Progressive Housekeeping: Keeping House Without Knowing How*, and *Knowing How to Keep House Well* (Boston and New York, 1896), p. 14; "A Servant Girl's Letter," *Independent* LIV (January 2, 1902), 37.

ELIZABETH BEARDSLEY BUTLER
Women and the Trades

In 1907 a team of writers and social workers descended on the city of Pittsburgh. The new Russell Sage Foundation had decided to make its first major project an effort to put social work and philanthropy on a new footing. The young men and women who worked on the project intended to report social conditions dispassionately and help Pittsburgh's own charity workers to develop a rational set of priorities for improving life in a heavily industrialized city. It was clear that baskets of food at Christmas were not enough.

Their survey of conditions resulted in six significant volumes of description and analysis. Entitled *The Pittsburgh Survey*, these volumes became a classic document in the history of American social work.

The project was directed by Paul U. Kellogg, only twenty-eight years old but already an experienced social worker and journalist. He hired Lewis Hine, then

Excerpted from "Workers and Workrooms" and "The Metal Trades," chaps. 1 and 13 of *Women and the Trades: Pittsburgh, 1907–1908* by Elizabeth Beardsley Butler (New York: Charities Publication Committee, 1909). Copyright © 1909 by the Russell Sage Foundation. Tables have been omitted.

an unknown amateur photographer, to accompany the investigators. Hine's photographs are important documents in the history of photojournalism. Among the authors of the individual volumes were Margaret Byington, whose sensitive book *Homestead* documented "the sense of powerlessness that pervaded everything the [immigrant] families thought and did"; Crystal Eastman, who would proceed from her book on *Work Accidents and the Law* to a significant career on the New York State Industrial Commission; and Elizabeth Beardsley Butler, who wrote the first book in the series, *Women and the Trades*. Occupational segregation in Pittsburgh was particularly severe, since women did not work in the steel mills.

Women and the Trades was startling. It attacked many assumptions middle-class Americans made about women's work. Most women did not work for pin money. Working conditions were not reasonable or safe. Evidence like that collected by Butler would provide important support for those who wished to establish protective legislation for working women (see, e.g., *Muller* v. *Oregon*, document 8 in Essential Documents).

WORKERS AND WORKROOMS

Pittsburgh as a workshop for women seems a contradiction in terms. Workshop this city is, but a workshop which calls for the labor of men. To dig crude ores, to fuse and forge them, are not among the lighter handicrafts at which women can readily be employed. Look down from Mount Washington at the merging of the two dull brown rivers, at the irregular succession of bridges, at scows and small river craft slowly finding way from wharf to wharf; and on either shore, at the black enclosures, gleaming now with leaping flames, now with the steady white-hot glow of Bessemer converters, but everywhere swarthy from the rising columns of black smoke. The cry of the dwarfs under the earth, the first metal smiths, rings again in the blows of the miners' tools and in the shouts of gangs of furnacemen and engine crews in the recesses of the mills.

Nevertheless, in this city whose prosperity is founded in steel, iron and coal, there has come into being beside the men a group of co-laborers. If we listen closely enough, we hear the cry of the dwarfs

not only from gangs of furnacemen, but from the girl thread makers at the screw and bolt works, and from the strong-armed women who fashion sand cores in foundries planned like Alberich's smithy in the underworld. And if we listen still more closely, we shall hear answering voices in many other workrooms, in the hum of machines in a garment factory, in the steady turn of metal rolls in a laundry, and even in the clip of the stogy roller's knife in a tenement loft. For Pittsburgh is not only a great workshop, it is many workshops; and in these workshops women stand beside the men. Forced by individual and group necessities, they have found a place in industry in the steel district of the Alleghenies.

Various selective forces have played a part in recruiting these women, in the teeth of the tonnage industries that shut them out. The influence of climate, the commercial wants of a rich producing district and the demands of a great laboring force as consumers, can readily be seen in tracing the development of the trades which employ them. As the shopping center of a nest of mill towns, Pittsburgh gives employment to over 6,000 saleswomen. The city is also an office center for plants and mines; and the printing trades, alive in every city, have taken on character, and with almost no edition work, turn out the ledgers and office paper of the big companies. In walking through the business streets, you are impressed by the number and size of the commercial stationers. They fairly flourish on every corner, and the function of Pittsburgh's pressrooms and binderies is to supply them. Pittsburgh's location and its knot of railroad lines have made it a distributing point within a radius of 200 miles for articles of use and wear. Scattered industrial plants make brooms and brushes, caskets, trunks and suit-cases, and cork. The manufactories of foodstuffs (canned goods, crackers and candy) were first called into being by the demands of neighboring counties in Ohio, West Virginia and Pennsylvania, but now they supply national markets. The success of the stogy industry is traceable in large measure to the demand for cheap tobacco of workingmen who for forty miles along the rivers are busy at metals or coal or steel. Similarly, garment trades came into being to supply cheap jeans and railroad jumpers by the hundred thousands. Moreover, no making of fine garments, no textile manufacture, could persist in this region of smoke-clouds. The city sets its seal upon fabrics. They survive by their wearing qualities and by their ability to withstand smoke and grime and fog. Although the growth of the city and of neighboring towns developed a market for a greater variety of goods, workmen's overalls are still the staple article of trade.

All of these Pittsburgh industries have recruited women as wage-earners. . . .

Altogether, 22,185 women wage-earners, excluding agricultural and professional workers and domestic servants, are employed in Pittsburgh. These figures are based on a careful census of the women-employing trades, made during the winter of 1907–8. This working force is distributed in 449 factories and shops and stores. . . .

Surveying the city, then, we see English-speaking girls holding the positions for which a few months' training and some intelligence are needed, a knowledge of English, or of reading and writing. The Italian girl, hindered by tradition, scarcely figures, but within a limited circle of industries, immigrant Jewesses hold positions beside girls of native birth. We see much inferior and unpleasant work yielded to Slavic immigrants, and we see these newcomers, sometimes by sheer physical strength, sometimes by personal indifference and a low standard, competing on the basis of lower wages for men's work which otherwise would never have been given to girls to do. Workrooms that would not long be tolerated for American women have been regarded with indifference for the Slavs, perhaps because of our inability to share the sensations of a foreigner. The place of the Slav, scrubbing floors and sorting onions for canners, packing crackers, stripping tobacco for stogy makers, and trimming bolts for the metal workers, is lowest industrially among the women workers of Pittsburgh. It is the place of the woman who is fighting her way, but has not yet thought where she is going. Marriage is not suffered to act as a hindrance. A determination to work and to earn is uppermost.

Our survey of the city shows us more than this. We see that since the days of settlement and mill town, Pittsburgh has become an industrial center whose workrooms give hire to more than 22,000 wage-earning women. These women have left household work and home industry for the field of collective service. From doing the whole of a thing and from knowing the user, the younger generation has gradually found its work more and more minutely subdivided; the individual worker makes not even a whole hinge, but a tenth part of it, and knows neither the use nor the destination of the finished product. She does not know the relation of her fraction of the work to the other fractions nor to the product as a whole,— and she works with a speed unknown to the houseworker. These younger women have pushed past the traditional activities of cleaning and cooking and sewing. Relatively few are occupied even by the congregate form of these industries, such as the laundries and garment factories. They have not only gone into pressrooms and binderies, into cork factories, and workrooms where candies are made and fruit is preserved, but they help to finish the glass tumblers that the men in the next room blow, they make the cores for the foundrymen, they are among the shapers of metals for lamps and for hinges and bolts and screws. In a district that is pre-eminent for the making of steel and iron and the products of steel and iron, women have gained a foothold in industries that seemed wholly in the hands of men. If mere numbers were the criterion, in the discussion of occupations which follows the Pittsburgh saleswomen should demand our first attention; but it has been the task of this investigation to consider primarily these factory trades where women are extending the boundaries of their industrial activity.

Pittsburgh as a city of wage-earning women is seen in all this to be not a contradiction in terms, but an actuality. From river to river, women have rapidly come to share in the modern industrial life of the city. It is a movement 22,000 strong. An industrial movement which makes for cheapness, or for efficiency, or for the utilization of a hitherto only partially utilized labor force, cannot be turned back by any theory as to its inappropriateness. But our survey shows us still other and more fundamental issues to be reckoned with in this situation. Many of these women are put to work at wages below the cost of subsistence, for hours longer than the measure of their strength, in buildings and at ill-constructed machines which cannot but injure their health, and at processes which must handicap heavily the development of both body and mind. Industrial movements and practices which lead to such consequences may not easily be stayed, yet they may be directed and controlled by law and by public opinion grounded on considerations of the social welfare. To this end the investigation has sought more thorough knowledge of conditions under which women work in the industries than has hitherto been available to the public, to the progressive individual employer, or to the women themselves. The study has thrown light on how the occupations of women and of men are related, how far women have reached the point of self-support, and what the social effect of their work seems to be.

The numbers of women workers in competitive industry are greater, not less, than they were fifty years ago, or twenty-five years ago, or ten years ago. There is every indication that these numbers will continue actually and proportionately to increase. We have no reason to think that the problems presented by the industrial employment of women will be solved by a cessation of that employment. But there is reasonable prospect that through change in the conditions of their labor much that seems evil in it may be done away, and the participation of women in industry may become a force of permanent value.

THE METAL TRADES

Men in the Pittsburgh metal trades, in the steel mills, the foundries, the machine shops, are doing work that is both heavy and difficult. They are carrying loads of crude ore, they are running engines, mixing metals in crucibles or operating the levers which move huge, sensitive electric cranes. The product at which they work is measured in tons of metal or reduced to threads and mechanical parts accurate to the thousandth part of an inch. It is shaped into rails and carwheels and tubes, into electric motors and delicate and intricate machinery. Women also have found work to do in these plants, but their product is of a different order. Instead of the brass parts of an engine, they make the sand cores for the molds in which the brass takes form. Instead of electric motors, they make the simplest and smallest of the coils of which the motor is built. Instead of steel rails, they trim the bolts with which the rails are fastened down. They split mica for the insulators which are built by men; they assemble the parts of small metal novelties; they feed light hinges into a machine, or solder tin, or dip pieces of tinware into enamel. They have nothing to do with the great ingots or with the fashioning or assembling of involved machinery; rather they handle the small pieces of brass or aluminum or steel which are needed in such quantities that the process of making them can be turned into a mere series of repetitions, or they tend machines which they do not control or understand. Their product is used either in preparation for the final metal shaping, as in the case of sand cores, or it is finishing work, as japanning, after the metal has been shaped.

Light as the product is, subsidiary as the process often is, the work done by women is a significant part of the metal trades of Pittsburgh. The number of women [1,954], too, is significant. Only two other factory trades, stogy making and laundry work, exceed metal work in the number of women employed. . . .

FOUNDRIES

Fifty core makers work in the largest foundry core room which employs women in Pittsburgh. All are women. Through the narrow entrance you can see them moving about among wreaths of coal smoke and black dust, working on molds at their benches, or carrying trays to the ovens. Some are Polish girls, round featured, with high foreheads and fair hair;

others are peasant women of the Hungarian type, strong and mature, their dark hair roughly combed back, their waist half open and their sleeves rolled high. Muscular and dark of skin, they strike you as an incarnation of the activities of smoking ovens, boiling crucibles and iron soft with fierce heat. The dim light through windows encrusted with black dust hardly reaches to the rows of ovens in the centre of the room, and even the glare of an electric bulb cannot dispel the impression of unreality and remoteness.

The benches of the core makers are on either side of the ovens, ranged through seventy feet of drifting dust. Each girl has her little heaps of different kinds of sand, her mold and shaping tools. She makes the sand cores and carries them, a trayful at a time, weighing sometimes ten pounds, sometimes twenty, sometimes fifty, to the ovens to be baked hard. Her work may be on cores with vents and spikes, or on simple finger-shaped cores which pay the makers $.10 a 1000. Quick girls can make three a minute or 10,000 a day. The large intricate cores which fit into big machines are not made by girls, but by men in another room.

Altogether the seven core rooms which make use of women core makers employed 159 women in 1907. Some are with brass foundries, some are operated in connection with malleable iron companies, while others are adjuncts to machine shops. In some foundries two or three women supplement the work of men and in others women make all the cores. They are employed irrespective of the kind of foundry so long as the work is not too heavy or too intricate for them to handle. The cores which they make of sand are set in the molds into which the hot metal is poured. In this way a hollow metal shape is produced, lighter and easier to handle than would be the solid metal.

The core room is, of course, but an adjunct to the foundry; core making a subsidiary process; and the convenience of other departments is consulted first in the laying out of the plant. Sometimes part of the foundry itself is used as a core room. Sometimes a space is set apart between machines, or a narrow bit of a room is partitioned off on the floor above. For example, in one case twelve girls work in a loft above a brass foundry. The fumes from the brass find their way up the narrow stairway leading to the loft and out through the one window at the end of the room. The girls stand at their benches in the midst of the dust and fumes. In every core room but one the ovens are either in the room or close beside it. This one plant provides a workplace apart from machinery and dust, in a clean, freshly painted room lighted by side windows and a skylight. High stools are placed at the tables and girls can sit at their work.

The influence of the machinists' union has closed some of the core rooms at 5:30 P.M. Others close at five, but all the foundries save one obtain a ten-hour day by cutting short the rest time at noon. . . .

Unlike men core makers, women are paid by the piece. As trades go, the returns are not high, if we take into consideration the length of time spent in learning. It is two years before a girl is considered expert. In some places, the girls do not earn more than $1.00 a day after they have learned, but $1.25 is more usual, and in two foundries the core makers regularly draw a day's pay of $1.40. An American girl who had worked for five years, said that she usually made from $7.00 to $8.00 a week, although in poor weeks she had fallen as low as $6.00. Once she had made $10.50, and sometimes at long intervals she had made $9.00, but such wages as these were by no means to be regarded as regular earnings. Much of the time her work was on finger-shaped cores with vents, that paid $.07 a 100, and very often on "round liners" for Kelso couplers. These round liners are finger-shaped with vent and

spike. They pay $.12 a 100, and an experienced girl can turn out from 1,200 to 1,500 a day. These cores are the lightest in weight and are set 13 on a tray, a total weight of not over 10 pounds; but other kinds of cores are set 58 on a tray and weigh from 20 to 25 pounds, if not more. There is a tradition in the core room of this foundry that a girl once made $2.00 a day at a new kind of work and that when the firm found it out, the rate was cut so that no girl thereafter should be able to make more than $1.50, or a maximum, rarely reached, of $1.85. Another foundry has a fixed maximum of $1.75, but 20 out of the 30 women whom it employs do not exceed $1.00 or at most $1.20 a day.

One dollar and twenty-five cents may be regarded as the mean wage of the women core makers in Pittsburgh. For unorganized men, employed on the small work at which girls are otherwise used, the minimum day's pay is $2.50. I am told by men in the trade that there are 500 core makers in Pittsburgh and the North Side, and that 75 per cent of them are organized. The union rate of wages is $3.50 a day up. That nearly a fourth of all the core makers should be women, would seem at first sight to indicate that this, too, is a trade for which men and women are competing, and that the greater cheapness of women workers is winning them ground. They get $1.25 less a day than the unorganized men; $2.25 less than the union scale. The union, to combat this tendency, admits no women to its membership and prohibits the employment of women in core rooms with union men; its aim is to force women out of the occupation as it increases the number of union shops.

Yet it is only in part true that women in this trade are actively competing with men. A line of cleavage separates the kinds of work at which they are severally employed. The heavy work, the cores of intricate design that require for their making long training and the skill of a craftsman—these cores are made by men. It is the men in the trade who know what kinds of sand to use and how to combine several cores in one. Women are used for the simpler, more obvious things, for the stock shapes of cores which can be learned in a few weeks. The core maker's trade, as men know it, is not by any means in women's hands. No women are apprenticed to learn the work in all its ramifications.

In the more difficult branches of the trade, therefore, there is no active competition between men and women. Yet potentially there is real competition. The small work, as well as the large, was at one time in the hands of men. Except where the union has been strong enough to force a shop to employ only men in the core room, the small work has been given over to women. The proportion of women in the trade is great enough to be menacing, in that they are doing the work at half the price of unorganized, and at a third the price of organized, men. Within a few years they have crept into shops that the public and even people in the trade still suppose to be employing men. They are doing the men's work. They are themselves carrying the trays and handling the tools. Except for the natural limitations to their work on heavy cores and the artificial limitations to their trade apprenticeship, these women core makers are in a fair way to become not only numerically important in the core rooms of machine shops, but economically effective in depressing the wages of the men.

PAULINE NEWMAN
The Triangle Shirtwaist Factory

One of the earliest industries in which women found employment was the garment industry. Based in New York City—the port of entry for millions of immigrants—the industry provided countless married women with piecework to take back to dimly lit tenements where they often enlisted the help of grandmothers and children. By the end of the nineteenth century much of the work had been transferred to sweatshops notorious for their low wages and squalid working conditions. Later the work was done in small factories such as the Triangle Shirtwaist Factory. This building became the scene of one of the great industrial tragedies in New York City's history. Although the factory contained several elevators and two staircases, the eight-story wooden building had no sprinkler system; the doors to the fire escapes were locked to prevent outdoor relaxation. When fire broke out in 1911, five hundred employees—many of them young Jewish and Italian women—were trapped behind locked doors. Some jumped to

Adapted from "Pauline Newman," in *American Mosaic: The Immigrant Experience in the Words of Those Who Lived It*, edited by Joan Morrison and Charlotte Fox Zabusky (New York: E. P. Dutton, 1980), pp. 9–14. Copyright © 1980 by Joan Morrison and Charlotte Fox Zabusky. Reprinted by permission of the publisher.

their death; others burned or asphyxiated inside. Altogether the fire claimed the lives of 146 women. Viewing their charred bodies on the street, one reporter recalled that some of these same women had gone on strike only the year before to demand decent wages, more sanitary working conditions, and safety precautions.

One of the strikers was Pauline Newman, who had worked at the Triangle Factory until she became an organizer for the International Ladies Garment Workers Union (ILGWU). Its educational director until her death in 1986, Newman conveys in this brief account a sense of what it was like to be a garment worker in the early twentieth century. She also expresses the indomitable spirit of these early women organizers who carried on a tradition established by their predecessors in the Lowell mills.

A cousin of mine worked for the Triangle Shirtwaist Company and she got me on there in October of 1901. It was probably the largest shirtwaist factory in the city of New York then. They had more than two hundred operators, cutters, examiners, finishers. Altogether more than four hundred people on two floors. The fire took place on one floor, the floor where we worked. You've probably heard about that. But that was years later.

We started work at seven-thirty in the morning, and during the busy season we worked until nine in the evening. They didn't pay you any overtime and they didn't give you anything for supper money. Sometimes they'd give you a little apple pie if you had to work very late. That was all. Very generous.

What I had to do was not really very difficult. It was just monotonous. When the shirtwaists were finished at the machine there were some threads that were left, and all the youngsters—we had a corner on the floor that resembled a kindergarten—we were given little scissors to cut the threads off. It wasn't heavy work, but it was monotonous, because you did the same thing from seven-thirty in the morning till nine at night.

Well, of course, there were [child labor] laws on the books, but no one bothered to enforce them. The employers were always tipped off if there was going to be an inspection. "Quick," they'd say, "into the boxes!" And we children would climb into the big boxes the finished shirts were stored in. Then some shirts were piled on top of us, and when the inspector came—no children. The factory always got an okay from the inspector, and I suppose someone at City Hall got a little something, too.

The employers didn't recognize anyone working for them as a human being. You were not allowed to sing. Operators would have liked to have sung, because they, too, had the same thing to do and weren't allowed to sing. We weren't allowed to talk to each other. Oh, no, they would sneak up behind if you were found talking to your next colleague. You were admonished: "If you keep on you'll be fired." If you went to the toilet and you were there longer than the floor lady thought you should be, you would be laid off for half a day and sent home. And, of course, that meant no pay. You were not allowed to have your lunch on the fire escape in the summertime. The door was locked to keep us in. That's why so many people were trapped when the fire broke out.

My pay was $1.50 a week no matter how many hours I worked. My sisters made $6.00 a week; and the cutters, they were the skilled workers, they might get as much as $12.00. The employers had a sign in the elevator that said: "If you don't come in on Sunday, don't come in on Monday." You were expected to work every day if they needed you and the pay was the same whether you worked extra or not. You had to be there at seven-thirty, so you got up at five-thirty, took the horse car, then the electric trolley to Greene Street, to be there on time. . . .

I stopped working at the Triangle Factory during the strike in 1909 and I didn't go back. The union sent me out to raise money for the strikers. I apparently was able to articulate my feelings and opinions about the criminal conditions, and they didn't have anyone else who could do better, so they assigned me. And I was successful getting money. After my first speech before the Central Trade and Labor Council I got front-page publicity, including my picture. I was only about fifteen then. Everybody saw it. Wealthy women were curious and they asked me if I would speak to them in their homes. I said I would if they would contribute to the strike, and they agreed. So I spent my time from November to the end of March upstate in New York, speaking to the ladies of the Four Hundred [the elite of New York's society] and sending money back. . . .

We didn't gain very much at the end of the strike. I think the hours were reduced to fifty-six a week or something like that. We got a 10 percent increase in wages. I think that the best thing that the strike did was to lay a foundation on which to build a union. There was so much feeling against unions then. The judge, when one of our girls came before him, said to her: "You're not striking against your employer, you know, young lady. You're striking against God," and sentenced her to two weeks on Blackwell's Island, which is now Welfare Island. And a lot of them got a taste of the club. . . .

After the 1909 strike I worked with the union, organizing in Philadelphia and Cleveland and other places, so I wasn't at the Triangle Shirtwaist Factory when the fire broke out, but a lot of my friends were. I was in Philadelphia for the union and, of course, someone from here called me immediately and I came back. It's very difficult to describe the feeling because I knew the place and I knew so many of the girls. The thing that bothered me was the employers got a lawyer. How anyone could have *defended* them!—because I'm quite sure that the fire was planned for insurance purposes. And no one is going to convince me otherwise. And when they testified that the door to the fire escape was open, it was a lie! It was never open. Locked all the time. One hundred and forty-six people were sacrificed, and the judge fined Blank and Harris seventy-five dollars!

Conditions were dreadful in those days. But there was something that is lacking today and I think it was the devotion and the belief. We *believed* in what we were doing. We fought and we bled and we died. Today they don't have to.

You sit down at the table, you negotiate with the employers, you ask for 20 percent, they say 15, but the girls are working. People are working. They're not disturbed, and when the negotiations are over they get the increases. They don't really have to fight. Of course, they'll belong to the union and they'll go on strike if you tell them to, but it's the inner faith that people had in those days that I don't see today. It was a terrible time, but it was interesting. I'm glad I lived then.

Even when things were terrible, I always had that faith . . . Only now, I'm a little discouraged sometimes when I see the workers spending their free hours watching television—trash. We fought so hard for those hours and they waste them. We used to read Tolstoy, Dickens, Shelley, by candlelight, and they watch the "Hollywood Squares." Well, they're free to do what they want. That's what we fought for.

ALICE KESSLER-HARRIS
Where Are the Organized Women Workers?

Because so many wage-earning women in the early twentieth century were young, single women who regarded their work as a temporary necessity until rescued by marriage, male labor leaders—and historians—usually assumed that women workers had little interest in joining unions. Alice Kessler-Harris explores this assumption and other barriers to the organization of women workers. She demonstrates with particular effectiveness how unionization was inhibited by fears of job competition on the part of male workers and the conviction of male trade unionists and employers alike that woman's proper place of work was in the home. She also calls attention to the ambivalent position of women like Rose Schneiderman, who had the difficult task of mediating between working women and middle-class reformers. The result, Kessler-Harris points out, was not only the division of the working class on the basis of gender but the perpetuation of an underclass of workers whose experience with wage work is still characterized by "sex typing" that limits job options, by low pay whatever the job involved, and by the absence of significant union membership.

"The Organization of Women," wrote Fannia Cohn, an officer of the International Ladies Garment Workers Union to William Green, newly elected president of the American Federation of Labor, "is not merely a moral question, but also an economic one. Men will never be certain with their conditions unless the conditions of the millions of women are improved."[1] Her letter touched a home truth and yet in 1925, the year in which Cohn's letter was written, the A. F. of L., after nearly forty years of organizing, remained profoundly ambivalent about the fate of more than eight million wage-earning women.

During these four decades of industrial growth, the women who worked in the industrial labor force had not passively waited to be organized. Yet their best efforts had been tinged with failure. Figures for union members are notoriously unreliable, and estimates fluctuate widely. But something like 3.3 percent of the women who were engaged in industrial occupations in 1900 were organized into trade unions. As low as that figure was, it was to decline even further. Around 1902 and 1903 trade union membership among women began to decrease, reaching a low of 1.5 percent in 1910. Then, a surge of organization among garment workers lifted it upwards. A reasonable estimate might put

"Where Are the Organized Women Workers?" by Alice Kessler-Harris, in *Feminist Studies* 3, no. 1/2 (Fall 1975):92–110. Copyright © 1975 by Feminist Studies, Inc. Reprinted by permission of the publisher, Feminist Studies, Inc., c/o Women's Studies Program, University of Maryland, College Park, Maryland 20742.

6.6 percent of wage-earning women into trade unions by 1920. In a decade that saw little change in the relative proportion of female and male workers, the proportion of women who were trade union members quadrupled, increasing at more than twice the rate for trade union members in general. Even so, the relative numbers of wage-earning women who were trade union members remained tiny. One in every five men in the industrial workforce belonged to a union, compared to one in every fifteen women. Although more than 20 percent of the labor force was female, less than 8 percent of organized workers were women. And five years later, when Fannia Cohn was urging William Green, to pay attention to female workers, these startling gains had already been eroded.[2]

Figures like these have led historians of the working class to join turn-of-the-century labor organizers in lamenting the difficulty of unionizing female workers. Typically, historians argue that the traditional place of women in families, as well as their position in the workforce, inhibited trade unionism. Statistical overviews suggest that these arguments have much to be said for them. At the turn of the century, most wage-earning women were young temporary workers who looked to marriage as a way to escape the shop or factory. Eighty-five percent of these women were unmarried and nearly half were under twenty-five years old. Most women worked at traditionally hard-to-organize unskilled jobs: a third were domestic servants and almost one quarter worked in the garment and textile industries. The remainder were scattered in a variety of industrial and service jobs, including the tobacco and boot and shoe industries, department stores, and laundries. Wage-earning women often came from groups without a union tradition: about one-half of all working women were immigrants or their daughters who shared rural backgrounds. In

the cities, that figure sometimes climbed to 90 percent.[3]

For all these reasons, women in the labor force unionized with difficulty. Yet the dramatic fluctuations in the proportions of organized working women testify to their potential for organization. And the large numbers of unions in which the proportion of women enrolled exceeded their numbers in the industry urge us to seek further explanations for the small proportions of women who actually became union members.[4]

No apparent change either in the type of women who worked or in the structure of jobs explains the post-1902 decline in the proportion of unionized women. On the contrary, several trends would suggest the potential for a rise in their numbers. The decline began just at the point when union membership was increasing dramatically after the devastating depression of 1893–1897. The proportion of first-generation immigrant women who were working dropped after the turn of the century only to be matched by an increase in the proportion of their Americanized daughters who worked. Married women entered the labor force in larger numbers suggesting at once a more permanent commitment to jobs and greater need for the security unions could provide. Large declines in the proportion of domestic workers reduced the numbers of women in these isolated, low-paying, and traditionally hard-to-organize jobs. At the same time, increases in office and clerical workers, department store clerks, and factory operatives, offered fertile areas for promoting unionization among women. Strenuous organizing campaigns by and among women in all these areas achieved few results.

Although cultural background, traditional roles, and social expectations hindered some unionizing efforts, they were clearly not insurmountable barriers. Given a chance, women were devoted and successful union members, convinced that unionism would serve them as it seemed to be serving their brothers. In the words of a seventeen-year-old textile worker, "We all work hard for a mean living. Our boys belong to the miners' union so their wages are better than ours. So I figured that girls must have a union. Women must act like men, ain't?"[5] In the garment workers union where women were the majority of members, they often served as shop "chairladies" and reached positions of minor importance in the union structure. Faige Shapiro recalled how her union activity began at the insistence of a business agent but quickly became an absorbing interest. In these unions, women arrested on picket lines thought highly enough of the union to try to save it bail money by offering to spend the night in jail before they returned to the line in the morning.[6]

In mixed unions, women often led men in militant actions. Iowa cigar makers reported in 1899 that some striking men had resumed work, while the women were standing pat.[7] Boot and shoe workers in Massachusetts were reported in 1905 to be tough bargainers. "It is harder to induce women to compromise," said their president, "they are more likely to hold out to the bitter end . . . to obtain exactly what they want."[8] The great uprising of 1909 in which 20,000 women walked out of New York's garment shops occurred over the objections of the male leadership, striking terror into the hearts of Jewish men afraid "of the security of their jobs."[9] Polish "spool girls" protesting a rate cut in the textile mills of Chicopee, Massachusetts, refused their union's suggestion that they arbitrate and won a resounding victory. Swedish women enrolled in a Chicago Custom Clothing Makers local, lost a battle against their bosses' attempts to subdivide and speed up the sewing process when the United Garment Workers union, largely male, agreed to the bosses' conditions. The bosses promptly locked out the women forcing many to come to

terms and others to seek new jobs.[10] At the turn of the century, female garment workers in San Francisco and tobacco strippers, overall and sheepskin workers, and telephone operators in Boston ran highly successful sex-segregated unions.[11]

If traditional explanations for women's failure to organize extensively in this period are not satisfying, they nevertheless offer clues to understanding the unionization process among women. They reveal the superficiality of the question frequently asked by male organizers and historians alike: "Why don't women organize?" And they encourage us to adopt economist Theresa Wolfson's more sensitive formulation: "Where are the organized women workers?"[12] For when we stop asking why women have not organized themselves, we are led to ask how women were, and are, kept out of unions.

The key to this question lies, I think, in looking at the function that wage-earning women have historically played in the capitalist mode of production. Most women entered the labor force out of economic necessity. They were encouraged by expanding technology and the continuing division of labor which in the last half of the nineteenth century reduced the need for skilled workers and increased the demand for cheap labor. Like immigrant men, and blacks today, women formed a large reservoir of unskilled workers. But they offered employers additional advantages. They were often at the mercy of whatever jobs happened to be available in the towns where their husbands or fathers worked, and they willingly took jobs that offered no access to upward mobility. Their extraordinarily low pay and exploitative working conditions enabled employers to speed up the process of capital accumulation. Their labor was critical to industrial expansion, yet they were expected to have few job-related aspirations and to look forward instead to eventual marriage. Under these circumstances, employers had a special incentive to resist unionization among women. As John Andrews, writing in the 1911 Report on the Condition of Women and Child Wage Earners, put it: ". . . the moment she organizes a union and seeks by organization to secure better wages she diminishes or destroys what is to the employer her chief value."[13]

If the rising numbers of working women are any gauge, women for the most part nicely filled the expectations of employers. Traditional social roles and the submissive behavior expected of women with primary attachments to home and family precisely complemented the needs of their bosses. To those women whose old world or American family norms encouraged more aggressive and worldly behavior— Russian Jews, for example—unionization came easier. Yet, for the most part, women fought on two fronts: against the weight of tradition and expectation, and against employers. If that were not enough, there was yet a third battlefront.

Unionists, if they thought about it at all, were well aware of women's special economic role. Samuel Gompers, head of the American Federation of Labor, editorialized in 1911 that some companies had "taken on women not so much to give them work as to make dividends fatter."[14] In a competitive labor market unionists tended to be suspicious of women who worked for wages and to regard them as potentially threatening to men's jobs. "Every woman employed," wrote an editor in the A. F. of L. journal, *American Federationist*, "displaces a man and adds one more to the idle contingent that are fixing wages at the lowest limit."[15]

Since employers clearly had important economic incentives for hiring women, male trade unionists felt they had either to eliminate that incentive, or to offer noneconomic reasons for restricting women's labor-force participation. In the early 1900s they tried to do both. In order to reduce the economic threat, organized labor repeatedly affirmed a commitment to

unionize women wage earners and to extract equal pay for them. Yet trade unionists simultaneously argued that women's contributions to the home and their duties as mothers were so valuable that women ought not to be in the labor force at all. Their use of the home-and-motherhood argument had two negative effects: it sustained the self-image on which the particular exploitation of women rested, and it provided employers with a weapon to turn against the working class as a whole.

Buttressed by the grim realities of exploitative working conditions and the difficulties of caring for children while working ten or more hours a day, and supported by well-intentioned social reformers, the argument to eliminate women from the work force, in the end, held sway. It was, of course, impossible to achieve, so the A. F. of L. continued to organize women and to demand equal pay for equal work. But genuine ambivalence tempered its efforts. The end result was to divide the working-class firmly along gender lines and to confirm women's position as a permanently threatening underclass of workers who finally resorted to the protection of middle-class reformers and legislators to ameliorate intolerable working conditions. The pattern offers us some lessons about what happens to the work force when one part of it attacks another.

The published sources of the A. F. of L. reveal some of the attitudes underlying A. F. of L. actions, and I have focused attention on these because I want to illustrate not only how open and prevalent the argument was, but because the A. F. of L.'s affiliated unions together constituted the largest body of collective working-class opinion. We have amassed enough evidence by now to know that the A. F. of L. was a conservative force whose relatively privileged members sacrificed the larger issues of working-class solidarity for a piece of the capitalist pie. In the creation of what labor economist Selig Perlman called "a joint partnership of organized labor and organized capital," the Federation cooperated extensively with corporation-dominated government agencies, sought to exclude immigrants, and supported an imperialist foreign policy.[16] Its mechanisms for dealing with the huge numbers of women entering the labor force are still unclear. Yet they are an integral part of the puzzle surrounding the interaction of ideological and economic forces in regulating labor market participation.

In the period from 1897 to 1920, the A. F. of L. underwent dramatic expansion. It consolidated and confirmed its leadership over a number of independent unions, including the dying Knights of Labor. Membership increased from about 265,000 members in 1897 to more than four million by 1920, and included four-fifths of all organized workers. In the same period, the proportion of women working in the industrial labor force climbed rapidly. Rapid and heady expansion offered a golden opportunity for organizers. That they didn't take advantage of it is one of the most important facts in the history of labor organizing in America.

Union leaders were sure that women did not belong in the workforce. Anxious about losing jobs to these low-paid workers, they tried instead to drive women out of the labor force. "It is the so-called competition of the unorganized defenseless woman worker, the girl and the wife, that often tends to reduce the wages of the father and husband," proclaimed Samuel Gompers.[17] And the *American Federationist* was filled with tales of men displaced by women and children. "One house in St. Louis now pays $4 per week to women where men got $16," snapped the journal in 1896. "A local typewriter company has placed 200 women to take the place of unorganized men," announced an organizer in 1903.[18]

The Federation's fears had some basis. In the late nineteenth and early twentieth century, new technology and techniques of efficiency pioneered by Frederick Taylor eroded the control and the jobs of skilled workmen, replacing them with managerial experts and the unskilled and semiskilled. Skilled members of the A. F. of L. who might appropriately have directed their anger at the way technology was being manipulated, lashed out instead at women who dared to work. Gompers offers a good example. In an article published in 1904, he declared, "The ingenuity of man to produce the world's wealth easier than ever before, is utilized as a means to pauperize the worker, to supplant the man by the woman and the woman by the child. . . ."[19] Some of the least appropriate bitterness was expressed by Thomas O'Donnell, secretary of the National Spinners Union whose constituency, once largely female, had been replaced by men after the Civil War. The advent of simple electric-powered machinery caused him to complain that "the manufacturers have been trying for years to discourage us by dispensing with the spinning mule and substituting female and child labor for that of the old time skilled spinners. . . ."[20]

Real anxieties about competition from women stimulated and supported rationalizations about woman's role as wife and mother. Working men had argued even before the Civil War that women belonged at home, and both the harsh conditions of labor and the demands of rearing a family supported their contention. But the women who worked for wages in the early 1900s were overwhelmingly single, and often supported widowed mothers and younger siblings with their meagre pay. An argument that could have been used to improve conditions for all workers was directed at eliminating women from the work force entirely. By the early 1900s it had become an irrepressible chorus. "The great principle for which we fight," said the A. F. of L.'s treasurer in 1905, "is opposed to taking . . . the women from their homes to put them in the factory and the sweatshop."[21] "We stand for the principle," said another A. F. of L. member, "that it is wrong to permit any of the female sex of our country to be forced to work, as we believe that the man should be provided with a fair wage in order to keep his female relatives from going to work. The man is the provider and should receive enough for his labor to give his family a respectable living."[22] And yet a third proclaimed, "Respect for women is apt to decrease when they are compelled to work in the factory or the store. . . . More respect for women brings less degeneration and more marriages . . . if women labor in factories and similar institutions they bring forth weak children who are not educated to become strong and good citizens."[23] No language was too forceful or too dramatic. "The demand for female labor," wrote an official of the Boston Central Labor Union in 1897, is "an insidious assault upon the home . . . it is the knife of the assassin, aimed at the family circle."[24] The *American Federationist* romanticized the role of women's jobs at home, extolling the virtues of refined and moral mothers, of good cooking and even of beautiful needlework and embroidery.[25]

These sentiments did not entirely prevent the A. F. of L. from attempting to unionize women. Gompers editorialized on the subject in 1904: "We . . . shall bend every energy for our fellow workmen to organize and unite in trade unions; to federate their effort without regard to . . . sex."[26] Yet the limited commitment implied by the wish that women would get out of the work force altogether was tinged with the conviction and perhaps the hope that women would in the end, fail. The Federation's first female organizer, Mary Kenny, had been appointed as early as 1892. But the Federation had supported her only half-heartedly and allowed her position to expire when she gave up the job to marry. It was 1908 before the organization appointed another woman,

Annie Fitzgerald, as full-time organizer. While Gompers and others conceded the "full and free opportunity for women to work whenever and wherever necessity requires," Gompers did not address himself to the problem of how to determine which women were admissible by these standards, and his actions revealed that he thought their numbers relatively few.[27] The A. F. of L. repeatedly called for an end to discriminatory pay for women and men: "Equal compensation for equal service performed."[28] The demand was a double-edged sword. While it presumably protected all workers from cheap labor, in the context of the early 1900s labor market it often functioned to deprive women of jobs. The Boston Typographical Union, noted one observer, saw "its only safety in maintaining the principle of equal pay for men and women. . . ."[29] Officials must have been aware that equal compensation for women often meant that employers would as soon replace them with men. It was no anomaly, then, to find an A. F. of L. organizer say of his daughters in 1919 that though he had "two girls at work [he] . . . wouldn't think of having them belong to a labor organization."[30]

When the A. F. of L. did organize women, its major incentive was often the need to protect the earning power of men. Women were admitted to unions after men recognized them as competitors better controlled from within than allowed to compete from without. "It has been the policy of my associates and myself," wrote Gompers in 1906, "to throw open wide the doors of our organization and invite the working girls and working women to membership for their and our common protection."[31] *American Federationist* articles that began with pleas that women stay out of the work force concluded with equally impassioned pleas to organize those who were already in it. Alice Woodbridge, writing in 1894, concluded an argument that women who worked for wages were neglecting their duties to their "fellow creatures" with the following statement: "It is to the interest of both sexes that women should organize . . . until we are well organized there is little hope of success among organizations of men."[32] The A. F. of L. officially acknowledged competition as a primary motivation for organizing women in 1923. "Unorganized they constitute a menace to standards established through collective action. Not only for their protection, but for the protection of men . . . there should be organization of all women. . . ."[33]

These were not of course the only circumstances of which men suspended their hostility toward women's unions. Occasionally in small towns female and male unions in different industries supported each other against the hostile attacks of employers. Minersville, Pennsylvania miners, for example, physically ousted railroad detectives who tried to break up a meeting of female textile workers.[34] The women in this case were the daughters, sisters and sweethearts of miners. Far from competing with men for jobs, women were helping to support the same families as the miners. Similarly, women and men in newly established industries could cooperate more effectively in unionizing together. The garment industry saw parallel but equally effective organization among its various branches. Though female organizers complained bitterly of the way they were treated, male leadership depended on the numerical majority of female workers to bargain successfully with employers and did not deny women admission. Yet, even here, union leadership successfully eliminated "home work" without offering to the grossly underpaid and often needy female workers who did it a way of recouping their financial losses.

Occasional exceptions notwithstanding, the general consequence of union attitudes toward women was to isolate them from the male work force. Repeatedly women who organized themselves into unions applied for entry to the appropriate parent body only to be turned down or simply ignored. Pauline Newman, who had organized and collected dues from a group of candy makers in Philadelphia, in 1910 offered to continue to work with them if the International Bakery and Confectionery Workers union would issue a charter. The International stalled and put them off until the employers began to discharge the leaders and the group disintegrated.[35] Waitresses in Norfolk, Virginia, suffered a similar fate. Mildred Rankin, who requested a charter for a group of fifteen, was assured by the local A. F. of L. organizer that she was wasting her time. "The girls were all getting too much money to be interested," was his comment on denying the request.[36] New York's International Typographical Union refused to issue female copyholders a charter on the grounds that they were insufficiently skilled. When the group applied to the parent A. F. of L. for recognition, they were refused on the grounds that they were within the ITU's jurisdiction. The Women's Trade Union League got little satisfaction when it raised this issue with the A. F. of L.'s executive council the following year. Though the Federation had agreed to issue charters to black workers excluded from all-white unions, it refused to accord the same privilege to women. The parent body agreed only to "take up the subject with the trade unions and to endeavor to reach an understanding" as far as women were concerned.[37]

A strong union could simply cut women out of the kinds of jobs held by unionized men. This form of segmenting the labor market ran parallel to, and sometimes contradicted the interests of employers who would have preferred cheap labor. A Binghamton, New York printing establishment, for example, could not hire women linotype operators because "the men's union would not allow it."[38] The technique was as useful for excluding racial minorities as it was for restricting women.[39] Like appeals to racist beliefs, arguments based on the natural weakness of women worked well as a rationale, as the following examples will indicate. Mary Dreier, then President of the New York Chapter of the Women's Trade Union League, recalled a union of tobacco workers whose leaders refused to admit women because "they could only do poor sort of work . . . , because women had no colour discrimination."[40] A Boston metal polishers union refused to admit women. "We don't want them," an official told a Women's Bureau interviewer. "Women can only do one kind of work while men can polish anything from iron to gold and frame the smallest part to the largest," and besides, he added, "metal polishing is bad for the health."[41]

Women were often excluded from unions in less direct but equally effective ways. The International Retail Clerks Union charged an initiation fee of $3, and dues of 50¢ a month. Hilda Svenson, a local organizer in 1914, complained that she had been unable to negotiate a compromise with the International. "We want to be affiliated with them," she commented, "but on account of the dues and initiation fee we feel it is too high at the present time for the salaries that the girls in New York are getting."[42] Sometimes union pay scales were set so high that the employer would not pay the appropriate wage to women. Joining the union could mean that a female printer would lose her job, so women simply refused to join.

Though the A. F. of L. supported its few female organizers only half-heartedly, male organizers complained of the difficulty of organizing women. Social propriety hindered them from talking to women in private or about moral or sanitary issues. Women felt keenly the absence of aid. When the Pennsylvania State Federation of Labor offered to finance the Philadelphia Women's Trade Union League's program for organizing women, its secretary pleaded with Rose Schneiderman to

take the job. "We have never had a wise head to advise, or an experienced worker," she wrote.[43]

But even membership in a union led by men guaranteed little to women. Such well-known tactics as locating meetings in saloons, scheduling them at late hours, and ridiculing women who dared to speak deprived women of full participation. And unions often deliberately sabotaged their female members. Fifteen hundred female street railway conductors and ticket agents, dues-paying members of New York City's Amalgamated Street Workers Union, complained in 1919 that their brother union members had supported a reformers' bill to deprive them of their jobs. When the women discovered they had been betrayed they resigned from the union and formed their own organization sending women throughout the state to Albany "to show them that they . . . were able to take care of their own health and morals." To no avail. Eight hundred of the 1500 women lost their jobs and the remaining 700 continued to work only at reduced hours.[44] Supporting union men was not likely to benefit women either. Mary Anderson, newly appointed head of the Women's Bureau, got a frantic telegram from a WTUL organizer in Joliet, Illinois, early in 1919. The women in a Joliet steel plant who, in return for the promise of protection, had supported unionized men in a recent strike, were fighting desperately for jobs that the union now insisted they give up. The company wanted to retain the women, but union men argued the work was too heavy for them.[45]

As the idea of home-and-motherhood was used to exclude women from unions, so it enabled unionized workers to join legislatures and middle-class reformers in restricting women's hours and regulating their working condition through protective labor legislation. The issue for the Federation's skilled and elite corps of male workers was clearly competition. Their wives did not work for wages, and most could afford to keep their daughters outside the marketplace. In an effort to preserve limited opportunity, they attacked fellow workers who were women, attempting to deny them access to certain kinds of jobs. Abused by employers who valued women primarily for their "cheap labor," women were isolated by male workers who were afraid their wages and their jobs would fall victim to the competition. Arguments used by male workers may have undercut their own positions, confirming the existence of a permanent underclass of workers and locking men psychologically and economically into positions of sole economic responsibility for their families. Appeals to morality and to the duties of motherhood obscured the economic issues involved, encouraging women and men alike to see women as impermanent workers whose major commitment would be to families and not to wage earning. Women would, therefore, require the special protection of the state for their presumably limited wage-earning lives.

The argument reached back at least as far as the 1880s and it was firmly rooted in the idea that the well-being of the state depended on the health of future mothers. But the line between the interests of the state and those of working men was finely drawn, and occasionally a protagonist demonstrated confusion about the issue. A few examples will illustrate the point. The cigar maker, Adolph Strasser, testifying before a Congressional Committee in 1882, concluded a diatribe against the number of women entering the trade with a plea to restrict them. "Why?" asked his questioner. "Because," replied Strasser, "I claim that it is the duty of the government to protect the weak and the females are considered among the weak in society."[46] Nearly forty years later, a Women's Bureau investigator reported that the Secretary of the Amalgamated Clothing Workers Union, fearful that women were taking jobs from men, had argued that women were "going into industry so fast that home life is very much in danger, not to mention the propagation of the race."[47] As the idea spread, it took on new forms, leading a Boston streetcar union secretary to acknowledge that "he would not care to see [women] employed as conductors. . . . It coarsened [them] to handle rough crowds on cars."[48] But in more sophisticated form, the argument for protective legislation appeared as a patriotic appeal to enlightened national self-interest. "Women may be adults," argued one A. F. of L. columnist in 1900, "and why should we class them as children? Because it is to the interest of all of us that female labor should be limited so as not to injure the motherhood and family life of a nation."[49] Sometimes pleas were more dramatic. In a piece entitled, "The Kingdom of God and Modern Industry," Ira Howerth, a sociologist writing for the *American Federationist*, asserted:

> The highest courts in some of our states declare that a law limiting the hours of labor for these women is unconstitutional. It may be so, but if it is so, so much the worse for the state. The state or nation that permits its women to stunt their bodies and dwarf their minds by over-exertion in insanitary [sic] stores and mills and factories is thereby signing its own death warrant. For the degeneracy of women is the degeneracy of the race. A people can never be any better than its mothers.[50]

Gompers, as well as other Federation officials, at first opposed the idea of legislation. But in the period following World War I, their attitudes changed, perhaps as a result of what seemed like an enormous increase in the number of women in the industrial labor force. The A. F. of L. encouraged the Department of Labor to set up a Women's Bureau to defend the interests of wage earning women.[51] The Bureau, on investigation, found that many union officials viewed unionization and protective legislation as alternate means to the same goal: better working conditions. Sara Conboy, United Textile Workers' official and a WTUL activist, told a Women's Bureau interviewer that she believed in "legislation to limit long hours of work for women where and when the union [was] not strong enough to limit hours."[52] Some unionized workers thought legislation surer and faster or remarked that it was more dependable than possibly untrustworthy union leaders. A. J. Muste, then secretary of the Amalgamated Textile Workers Union of America, preferred unionization, but was said to have believed that legislation did not hinder organization and might be essential in industries with many women and minors.[53] But some women union leaders were not so sanguine. Fannia Cohn of the International Garment Workers Union only reluctantly acquiesced to the need for protective legislation. "I did not think the problem of working women could be solved in any other way than the problem of working men and that is through trade union organization," she wrote in 1927, "but considering that very few women are as yet organized into trade unions, it would be folly to agitate against protective legislation."[54] Cohn laid the problems of female workers on the absence of organization.

In any event, exclusion from unions merely confirmed the discomfort many women felt about participating in meetings. Italian and Southern families disliked their daughters going out in the evenings. Married and self-supporting women and widows had household duties at which they spent after-work hours. Women who attended meetings often participated reluctantly. They found the long discussions dull and were often intimidated by the preponderance of men. Men, for their part, resented the indifference of the women and further excluded them from leadership roles, thereby discouraging more women from attending. Even fines failed to spark attendance. Some women preferred to pay them rather than to go to the meeting.[55]

Self-images that derived from a pa-ternalistic society joined ethnic ties in hindering unionization. Wage-earning women, anxious to marry, were sometimes reluctant to join unions for what they felt would be a temporary period. Occasionally, another role conflict was expressed: "No nice girl would belong to one," said one young woman.[56] An ILG organizer commented that most women who did not want to join a union claimed that "the boss is good to us and we have nothing to complain about and we don't want to join the union."[57] A woman who resisted unionization told an organizer that she knew "that $6 a week is not enough pay but the Lord helps me out. He always provides . . . I won't ever join a union. The Lord doesn't want me to."[58] A recent convert to unionism apologized for her former reticence. She had always scabbed because church people disapproved of unions. Moreover she and her sister had only with difficulty, she told an organizer, overcome their fear of the Italian men who were organizing their factory.[59]

Exceptions to this pattern occurred most often among women whose ethnic backgrounds encouraged both wage labor and a high level of social consciousness, as in the American Jewish community for example. Young Jewish women constituted the bulk of the membership of the International Ladies Garment Workers Union in the period from 1910 to 1920. Their rapid organization and faithful tenure is responsible for at least one quarter of the increased number of unionized women in the second decade of the twentieth century. And yet, they were unskilled and semiskilled workers, employed in small, scattered shops, and theoretically among the least organizable workers. These women, unionized at their own initiative, formed the backbone of the ILGWU, which had originally been directed toward organizing the skilled, male, cutters in the trade.

As it became clear to many laboring women that unionists would offer them little help, many women turned to such middle-class allies as the Women's Trade Union League. Established in 1905, the WTUL, an organization founded by female unionists and upper-middle-class reformers, offered needed financial and moral support for militant activity. Its paternalistic and benevolent style was not unfamiliar to women and those who came from immigrant families seemed particularly impressed with its Americanizing aspects. Young immigrant girls spoke with awe of the "fine ladies" of the WTUL and did not object to the folk-dancing classes that were part of the Chicago League's program.[60] But help from these nonwage-earning women came at a price. Working women who became involved in the WTUL moved quickly from working-class militance to the search for individual social mobility through vocational training, legislation, and the social refinements that provided access to better paying and rapidly increasing clerical and secretarial jobs. Rose Schneiderman illustrates this syndrome well. Beginning as a fiery organizer of the hat and cap makers, she moved through the WTUL to become Secretary of the New York State Department of Labor. Like the WTUL, which had begun by organizing women into trade unions, she began in the 1920s to devote herself to attaining protective legislation, even borrowing some of the arguments used by men who did not wish women to compete with them.

By this time many working women were themselves moving in the direction of legislative solutions to exploitative working conditions. It seemed to be the most accessible solution to the problems of exploitation. Female workers interviewed by the Women's Bureau at first felt that both women and men should be included in any legislation. Later, they asked that office workers be exempted.[61] Other women acquiesced reluctantly. "I have always been afraid," wrote a supervisor in a Virginia silk mill, "that if laws were made discriminating for women, it would work a hardship upon them." By

1923 she had changed her mind: ". . . it would in time raise the entire standard rather than make it hard for women."[62] As women came to accept the necessity for legislation, they, like men, saw it as an alternative to unionization and rationalized its function in terms of their female "roles." A Women's Bureau agent noted of the reactions to a 48-hour law passed in Massachusetts that "the girls felt that legislation establishing a 48-hour week was more 'dignified' and permanent than one obtained through the union as it was not so likely to be taken away."[63] By the mid-1920s only business and professional women remained staunchly opposed to protective legislation.

Within this framework of trade-union ambivalence and the real need of wage-earning women for some form of protection employers who were particularly anxious that women not unionize pressed their advantage. Using crude techniques, rationalized by the home-and-motherhood argument, they contributed more than their share toward keeping women out of unions. In the small businesses in which women most often worked, employers used a variety of techniques to discourage organization, some of them familiar to men. Department store employees whose union membership became known were commonly fired. Many stores had spy systems so that employees could not trust their coworkers. Blacklists were common. A representative of the year-old retail clerks union testifying before a Congressional Committee in 1914 was afraid even to reveal the number of members in her union. Owners of New York's garment shops, fighting a losing battle by 1910, nevertheless frequently discharged employees who were thought to be active organizers or union members.[64]

Other tactics were no more subtle. Employers often played on ethnic and racial tensions in order to prevent women from unionizing. Rose Schneiderman, who formed the Hat and Cap Makers Union in 1903, fought against bosses who urged immigrant workers to stick to the "American shop"—a euphemism for an antiunion shop. Jewish owners sometimes hired only Italian workers who were thought to be less prone to unionization than Jews.[65] Others hired "landsmen" from the same old country community, hoping that fraternal instincts might keep them from striking. Blacks were played off against whites. Waitresses picketing Knab's restaurant in Chicago were met with counterpickets paid by the employers. A representative of the waitresses union reported indignantly that the employer "placed colored pickets on the street, colored women who wore signs like this 'Gee, I ain't mad at nobody and nobody ain't mad at Knab.' " When the nonunion pickets attracted a crowd, police moved in and arrested the union members. The women were further discouraged by trials engineered by employers who had previously given "every policeman a turkey free."[66]

Police routinely broke up picket lines and outdoor union meetings. Women who were accused of obstructing traffic or were incited into slapping provocateurs were arrested. More importantly, women who might have been interested in unionization were intimidated by police who surrounded open air meetings or by department store detectives who mingled obtrusively with potential recruits. Department store owners diverted workers from street meetings by locking all but one set of doors or sending trucks, horns honking full blast, to parade up and down the street in which a meeting was scheduled.[67]

Small employers formed mutual assistance associations to help them resist their employees' attempts to unionize. The Chicago Restaurant Keepers Association, for example, denied membership to any "person, firm or corporation . . . having signed agreements with any labor organization."[68] Garment manufacturers in both New York and Chicago created protective associations to combat what they called "the spreading evil of unionism."[69] In small towns, the power of town officials was called into play. Ann Washington Craton, organizing textile workers in Minersville, Pennsylvania, was warned by the town burgess: "You are to let our girls alone . . . Mr. Demsky will shut the factory down rather than have a union. . . . The town council brought this factory here to provide work for worthy widows and poor girls. We don't intend to have any trouble about it."[70]

Employers justified continued refusal to promote women or to offer them access to good jobs on the grounds that women's major contribution was to home and family. When they were challenged with the argument that bad working conditions were detrimental to that end, they responded slowly with paternalistic amelioration of the worst conditions and finally by acquiescing to protective labor legislation. Often concessions to workers were an effort to undercut mounting union strength, as for example when department store owners voluntarily closed their shops one evening a week. Some employers introduced welfare work in their factories, providing social workers, or other women, to help smooth relationships between them and their female employees. Mutual benefit associations, sometimes resembling company unions, were a more familiar tactic. Though they were presumably cooperative and designed to incorporate input from workers, membership in them was compulsory and dues of ten to twenty-five cents per month were deducted from wages. In return employees got sickness and health benefits of varying amounts but only after several months of continuous employment. A 1925 investigation of one widely publicized cooperative association operated by Filene's department store in Boston revealed that in all its twelve years, only store executives had ever served on its board of directors.[71]

Manufacturers seemed to prefer legislation regulating the hours and conditions of women's work to seeing their workers join unions. One, for example, told the Women's Bureau of the Department of Labor that a uniform 48-hour week for women would equalize competition and would, in any event, only confirm existing conditions in some shops. Some went even further hoping for federal legislation that would provide uniform standards nationwide.[72]

When occasionally employers found it in their interests to encourage unionism they did so in return for certain very specific advantages. One of these was the union label. In the garment industry the label on overalls in certain parts of the country assured higher sales. To acquire the right to use it, some employers rushed into contracts with the United Garment Workers and quite deliberately urged their workers into the union.[73] New York garment manufacturers negotiated a preferential union shop, higher wages, and shorter hours with the ILGWU in return for which the union agreed to discipline its members and to protect employers against strikes. The garment manufacturers' protective association urged employers to "make every effort to increase the membership in the union so that its officers may have complete control of the workers and be enabled to discipline them when necessary."[74] Southern textile mill owners, otherwise violently opposed to unions, were similarly interested in the disciplinary functions of unionism. They would, an observer reported, modify their opposition "if the purposes of the union were to improve the educational, moral and social conditions of the workers."[75]

In general, however, employers made valiant attempts to keep women out of unions. The paternalism, benevolence, and welfare they offered in compensation were supported by other sectors of their society, including the trade unions. Middle-class reformers and government investigators had long viewed the harsh conditions under which women worked as detrimental to the preservation of home and family, and government regulation or voluntary employer programs seemed to many an adequate alternative. Unions played into this competitive structure adopting the home-and-motherhood argument to restrict women's labor-force participation. In the process they encouraged women to see their interests apart from those of male workers.

Limited labor-force opportunities, protective labor legislation and virtual exclusion from labor unions institutionalized women's isolation from the mainstream of labor. Not accidentally, these tendencies confirmed traditional women's roles, already nurtured by many ethnic groups and sustained by prevailing American norms. Together they translated into special behavior on the part of female workers that isolated them still further from male workers and added up to special treatment as members of the labor force.

In acquiescing, women perhaps bowed to the inevitable, seeking for themselves the goals of employers who preferred not to see them in unions, of male workers who hoped thereby both to limit competition and to share in the advantages gained, and of middle-class reformers who felt they were helping to preserve home and motherhood. Echoing labor union arguments of twenty years earlier, Women's Bureau head Mary Anderson defended protective legislation in 1925 on the grounds that such laws were necessary to conserve the health of the nation's women.[76]

A final consequence for women was to lead them to search for jobs in non-sex-stereotyped sectors of the labor market. Employers' needs in the rapidly expanding white-collar sector led women increasingly toward secretarial and clerical work. Vocational education to train women for office jobs, teaching, and social work expanded rapidly in the early twentieth century. Working women rationalized these jobs as steps up the occupational ladder; state and local governments and employers provided financial aid; and middle-class women launched a campaign to encourage women to accept vocational training.[77] It took an astute union woman like Fannia Cohn to see what was happening. She drew a sharp line between her own function as educational director of the International Ladies Garment Workers Union and the functions of the new schools. Her hope was to train women to be better union members, not to get them out of the working class.

The parallel development of protective legislation and vocational education confirmed for many working women their marginal positions in the labor force, positions they continued to rationalize with obeisance to marriage and the fam-ily. As Alice Henry said of an earlier group of female wage-earners, "They did not realize that women were within the scope of the labor movement."[78] Fannia Cohn understood what that meant. That hard-headed and clear-sighted official of the ILGWU prefaced a call for a revolution in society's view of women with a plea for an end to competition between working women and men. Because it was destructive for all workers, she argued, "this competition must be abolished once and for all, not because it is immoral, yes inhuman, but because it is impractical, it does not pay."[79] But in the first two decades of the twentieth century, moral arguments prevailed—releasing some women from some of the misery of toil, but simultaneously confirming their place in those jobs most conducive to exploitation.

NOTES

Abbreviations: WB/NA: Women's Bureau collection, Record Group no. 86, National Archives; CIR: Final Report and Testimony of the Commission on Industrial Relations, Senate Documents, vol. 21, 64th Congress, 1st session, vol. 3, 1914; AF: American Federationist.

1. Fannia Cohn to William Green, March 6, 1925. Fannia Cohn collection, New York Public Library, Box 4.

2. Figures are derived from John Andrews and W. D. P. Bliss, History of Women in Trade Unions, Report on the Condition of Women and Child Wage Earners in the U.S. (Washington, D.C.: G.P.O., 1911), vol. 10, pp. 136–39; Leo Wolman, Ebb and Flow in Trade Unionism (New York: National Bureau of Economic Research, 1936), pp. 74, 116; Leo Wolman, The Growth of American Trade Unions, 1880–1923 (New York: National Bureau of Economic Research, 1923), chapter 5. Wolman estimates that about 40 percent of organized women were in the three garment industry unions: ILGWU, Amalgamated Clothing Workers, and United Garment Workers, unions that had been either literally or virtually nonexistent before 1910. See Wolman, and Alice Henry, Women and the Labor Movement (New York: George Doran, 1923), chapter 4, for discussions of the difficulty of collecting trade union figures. Henry illustrates the numbers of women in specific unions.

3. The proportion of foreign-born and native-born and native-born daughters of foreign-born women declined slightly in this period and women continued to shift from manual sectors to low-level clerical sectors of the work force. See U.S. Census, 14th Census of Populations (Washington, D.C.: G.P.O.: 1920), vol. 3, p. 15. Such occupations as taking in boarders, homework, and working on husbands' farms or in family businesses are not counted by census takers. Including these legitimate forms of labor would create drastic upward revisions in the proportion of working women, but we have no way of knowing by how much. The figures include black women, more than 40 percent of whom worked for wages, compared to about 20 percent of white women. However, about 32 percent of married black women worked, compared to less than 6 percent of married white women. Black wage-earning women are far more heavily concentrated in agricultural and domestic service jobs than their white counterparts. Figures are from Joseph Hill, Women in Gainful Oc-

cupations: 1870–1920, Census Monographs, no. 9 (Washington, D.C.: G.P.O., 1929), chapters 5 and 9; Janet Hooks, Women's Occupations Through Seven Decades, Women's Bureau Bulletin, no. 218 (Washington, D.C.: G.P.O., 1947), pp. 37, 39.

4. Andrews and Bliss, History of Women in Trade Unions, pp. 138–39. Even before the great uprising of 1909–1910, women, who made up 63 percent of the workers in the garment trades, represented 70 percent of the trade union members. This is all the more remarkable because their skill levels did not, by and large, match those of men. 32.5 percent of hat and cap makers were women, and 54 percent of union members were women. Women made up 50 percent of bookbinders, and 40 percent of the trade union members in that industry.

5. Ann Blankenhorn, miscellaneous notes, chapter 2, p. 12, file no. 23, box no. 1, Ann Craton Blankenhorn collection, Archives of Labor History, Wayne State University. For another example, see interview with Netti Chandler, Virginia Home visits, Bulletin no. 10, accession no. 51A101, WB/NA.

6. Interview with Faigele Shapiro, August 6, 1964. Amerikaner Yiddishe Geschichte Bel-pe, YIVO, pp. 2, 7.

7. AF 6 (November 1899):228.

8. Quoted in Andrews and Bliss, History of Women in Trade Unions, p. 173.

9. New York Women's Trade Union League, Report of the Proceedings, 4th Annual Conference of Trade Union Women, October 9, 10, 1926, p. 18.

10. Vera Shlakman, Economic History of a Factory Town: A Study of Chicopee, Massachusetts, Smith College Studies in History, vol. 20, no. 1–4 (October 1934–July 1935), p. 216; Andrews and Bliss, History of Women in Trade Unions, p. 166.

11. Andrews and Bliss, History of Women in Trade Unions, p. 168; Massachusetts Women's Trade Union League, The History of Trade Unionism among Women in Boston (Boston: WTUL, n.d., but c. 1907) pp. 22, 23.

12. Theresa Wolfson, "Where Are the Organized Women Workers?" AF 32 (June 1925):455–57.

13. Andrews and Bliss, History of Women in Trade Unions, p. 151.

14. AF 17 (November 1911), p. 896. James Kenneally, "Women and Trade Unions," Labor History 14 (Winter 1973), describes, but does not explain, the A. F. of L's mixed feelings.

15. Eva McDonald Valesh, "Women and Labor," AF 3 (February 1896):222.

16. Selig Perlman, A History of Trade Unionism in the U.S. (New York: Macmillan, 1923), p. 166. For illustrations of A. F. of L. policies see James Weinstein, The Corporate Ideal in the Liberal State: 1900–1918 (Boston: Beacon Press, 1968), especially chapters 1 and 2; Ronald Radosh, American Labor and United States Foreign Policy (New York: Vintage, 1970); Stanley Aronowitz, False Promises (New York: McGraw-Hill, 1973).

17. Samuel Gompers, "Should the Wife Help Support the Family?" AF 13 (January 1906):36. See also Stuart Reid, "The Joy of Labor? Plutocracy's Hypocritical Sermonizing Exposed—A Satire," AF 11 (November 1904): 977–78.

18. "Mainly Progressive," AF 3 (March 1896):16; "What Our Organizers Are Doing," AF 10 (April 1903):370.

19. Editorial, AF 11 (July 1904):584.

20. "Trade Union History," AF 9 (November 1902):871.

21. John Safford, "The Good That Trade Unions Do," part I, AF 9 (July 1902):353, 358; "Talks on Labor," AF 12 (November 1905):846.

22. William Gilthorpe, "Advancement," AF 17 (October 1910):847.

23. Safford, "The Good That Trade Unions Do," part 2, AF 9 (August 1902):423.

24. Edward O'Donnell, "Women as Breadwinners: The Error of the Age," AF 4 (October 1897):186. The article continued: "The wholesale employment of women in the various handicrafts must gradually unsex them as it most assuredly is demoralizing them, or stripping them of that modest demeanor that lends a charm to their kind, while it numerically strengthens the multitudinous army of loafers, paupers, tramps and policemen."

25. Safford, "The Good That Trade Unions Do," part 1, pp. 357–58.

26. Gompers, "Should the Wife Help Support the Family?" p. 36.

27. Ibid. See also Louis Vigoreux, "Social Results of the Labor Movement in America," AF 6 (April 1899):25.

28. Women's Labor Resolution, AF 5 (January 1899):220; "Talks on Labor," AF 10 (June 1903):477.

29. Massachusetts, WTUL, History of Trade Unionism Among Women in Boston, p. 13; Elizabeth Baker, Technology and Women's Work (New York: Columbia University Press, 1964), p. 33.

30. Mildred Rankin to Mrs. Raymond Robins, March 30, 1919, Margaret Dreier Robins Collection, University of Florida, Gainesville, Florida. In 1918, two women members of the federation offered a resolu-

tion to the national convention urging the addition of two women to the all-male executive board. It was quietly suppressed.

31. Gompers, "Should the Wife Help Support the Family?" p. 36.

32. Alice Woodbridge, "Women's Labor," *AF* 1 (April 1894):66–67; Valesh, "Women and Labor," p. 222; and Massachusetts WTUL, *History*, p. 32. 2.

33. WTUL Action of Policies, pp. 3, 8, box 4, accession no. 55A556, WB/NA: Proceedings of the A. F. of L. convention, 1923. See also Massachusetts WTUL, *History of Trade Unionism Among Women in Boston*, p. 32.

34. Blankenhorn manuscript notes, chapter 4, p. 17, box 1, file no. 24. Such examples of family unity are not unusual in the mine/mill towns of Western Pennsylvania and the Appalachian mountains. Women helped to picket during strikes, provided essential support services, and sometimes spearheaded attacks against mine management.

35. Pauline Newman, interview, undated, Amerikaner Yiddisher Geschichte Bel-pe, p. 21, YIVO. Gladys Boone, *The Women's Trade Union League in Great Britain and the U.S.A.* (New York: Columbia University Press, 1942), p. 166, recounts a similar incident as having taken place in 1918. I suspect that it might be the same one and that her date is incorrect. Andrews and Bliss, *History of Women in Trade Unions*, p. 149, notes that women practically disappeared from this union between 1905 and 1910—a period in which master bakers were rapidly being eliminated by machinery.

36. Mildred Rankin to Mrs. Raymond Robins, March 30, 1919, Robins papers.

37. Boone, *The Women's Trade Union League*, p. 167; Alice Henry, *Women in the Labor Movement* (New York: Doran, 1923): 102.

38. Interview with Vail Ballou Press, Effects of Legislation: Night Work Schedule, New York, NA/WB.

39. See for example Rankin to Robins, March 30, 1919; and M. E. Jackson, "The Colored Woman in Industry," *Crisis* 17 (November 1918):14.

40. New York Women's Trade Union League, *Report of the Proceedings*, 4th Conference, p. 14.

41. Undated interviews, unions, for Bulletin no. 65, NA/WB.

42. Testimony of Hilda Svenson, C.I.R., p. 2307; the testimony was taken in June 1914.

43. Florence Sanville to Rose Schneiderman, November 28, 1917, Rose Schneiderman

collection. Tamiment Institute library, box A 94. For examples of union discrimination see Massachusetts WTUL, *History of Trade Unionism Among Women in Boston*, p. 13; Andrews and Bliss, *History of Women in Trade Unions*, pp. 156, 157; Alice Henry, *The Trade Union Woman* (New York: Burt Franklin, 1973), p. 150.

44. Testimonies, box 15, accession no. 51A101, WB/NA. The women had been hired when the war broke out.

45. Emma Steghagen to Mary Anderson, January 15, 1919, WTUL Action on Policies, accession no. 55A556, WB/NA.

46. United States Education and Labor Committee, *Report Upon the Relations Between Capital and Labor* (Washington, D.C., G.P.O., 1882), vol. 1, p. 453. See Andrews and Bliss, *History of Women in Trade Unions*, p. 94, for Strasser's often-quoted "We cannot drive the females out of the trade but we can restrict their daily quota of labor through factory laws," and p. 155 of the same volume for Samuel Gompers' fears of female competition as expressed in 1887.

47. Interview with Mr. Salerno, Amalgamated Clothing Workers, interviews, unions, accession no. 51A101, WB/NA.

48. Interview with Mr. Hurley, July 1919, Women Street Car Conductors, accession no. 51A101, WB/NA.

49. Sir Lyon Playfair, "Children and Female Labor," *AF* 7 (April 1900):103. See also Martha Moore Avery, "Boston Kitchen Help Organize," *AF* 10 (April 1903):259, 260.

50. Ira Howerth, "The Kingdom of God in Modern Industry," *AF* 14 (August 1907): 544.

51. Mary Anderson, "The Federal Government Recognizes Problems of Women in Industry," *AF* 32 (June 1925):453.

52. Individual interviews, Massachusetts, April 12, 1920, accession no. 51A101, WB/NA. Her perference rested on the union's ability to ask for wage raises to compensate for the reduction in hours.

53. Individual interviews, Massachusetts and New Jersey, accession no. 51A101, WB/NA. See especially interviews with A. J. Muste, Mr. Sims, Secretary of the Weavers union, and Amalgamated meeting of workers at Princeton Worsted Mills. These are undated but must have occurred in early 1921.

54. Fannia Cohn to Dr. Marion Phillips, September 13, 1827, Fannia Cohn Collection, box 4.

55. Interviews with Tony Salerno, Amalgamated Clothing Workers Union and Hat and Cap Makers Local 7, Boston, individual interviews, unions, accession no. 51A101,

BW/NA. Massachusetts WTUL, *History of Trade Unionism Among Women in Boston*, p. 11.

56. Lizzie Swank Holmes, "Women Workers of Chicago," *AF* 12 (August 1905): 507–10; Eva McDonald Valesh, "Women in Welfare Work," *AF* 15 (April 1908):282–84; "Mainly Progressive," *AF* 3 (March 1896): 16.

57. Shapiro, p. 25.

58. *Justice* (April 19, 1919):2.

59. Blankenhorn manuscript notes, chapter 13, p. 4, box 1, file 25.

60. For example, see Mary Dreier, address to New York WTUL in *Report of the Proceedings*, 4th conference, 1926, p. 14. Dreier refers in this speech to the difficulty the WTUL had getting female workers to serve on the executive board at first. See Nancy Schrom Dye, "Creating a Feminist Alliance: Sisterhood and Class Conflict in the New York WTUL, 1903–1914," *Feminist Studies* 2 (1975):24–38. Kenneally, "Women and Trade Unions," treats the WTUL's relations with the A. F. of L. at length.

61. Individual interviews, California, effects of legislation, accession no. 51A101, WB/NA.

62. Quoted in a letter from Mary Van Kleeck to Mary Anderson, February 2, 1923, Mary Van Kleeck collection, Smith College, unsorted.

63. Breman and O'Brien, individual interviews, Massachusetts, accession no. 51A101, WB/NA. Such sentiments must, however, be treated cautiously. We know, for example, that the National Consumers' League in Philadelphia orchestrated an anti-E.R.A. letter-writing campaign by wage-earning women in 1922. The league urged women to write letters arguing that the E.R.A. would limit or eliminate protective labor legislation. See Barbara Klazcynska, "Working Women in Philadelphia: 1900–1930," (Ph.D. dissertation, Temple University, 1975). Janice Hedges and Stephen Bemis point out that most "protective" legislation has now been invalidated by EEOC decisions. "Sex Stereotyping: Its Decline in Skilled Trades," *Monthly Labor Review* 97 (May 1974):18.

64. Sylvia Shulman, testimony, CIR, pp. 2285, 2292; Hilda Svenson, testimony, CIR, pp. 2311, 2317; Elizabeth Dutcher, testimony, CIR, p. 2392. Exceptions sometimes occurred in small western towns where workers would not patronize nonunion stores. Dutcher testified that 75 employees of Macy's were discharged in 1907 after they attended a union ball. Svenson, CIR, p. 2307; Lillian Mallach

to David Dubinsky, December 18, 1964, YIVO. See also minutes of the Waistmakers Conference, January 10, 1911, ILGWU, Ladies Waist and Dress Makers Union file, Rose Schneiderman collection, Tamiment, box A 95.

65. Rose Schneiderman with Lucy Goldthwaite, *All for One* (New York: Paul Erickson, 1967):59, Shapiro, p. 9.

66. Elizabeth Maloney testimony, CIR, pp. 3246–47. See also M. E. Jackson, "The Colored Woman in Industry," pp. 12–17.

67. Agnes Nestor, testimony, CIR, p. 3389; Elizabeth Dutcher testimony, CIR, p. 2405.

68. Elizabeth Maloney testimony, CIR, p. 3245.

69. Leon Stein, *The Triangle Fire* (Philadelphia: J. P. Lippincott, 1952), Nestor, CIR, p. 3382.

70. Blankenhorn, manuscript notes, chapter 4, p. 17, file 24, box 1.

71. Nestor, CIR, p. 3382; Svenson, CIR, p. 3382 and Svenson, CIR, p. 2308, reveal the degree to which this was an attempt to undercut union strength; see also an unsigned typescript entitled "Personnel and Management in a Retail Store: A Study of the Personnel Policies and Practices of William Filene's Sons Co., Boston, Mass.," p. 14, in the Mary Van Kleeck collection, unsorted, Smith College; and Marie Obenauer and Charles Verrill, *Wage Earning Women in Stores and Factories*, Report on the Condition of Women and Child Wage Earners (Washington, D.C.: G.P.O., 1911), vol. 5, p. 48; Svenson, CIR, p. 2309.

72. See Cambridge Paper Box Company, Long Hour Day Schedule, accession no. 51A101, WB/NA.

73. Andrews and Bliss, *History of Women in Trade Unions*, p. 169.

74. U.S. Department of Labor, Bureau of Labor Statistics, Bulletin no. 145, 1914, p. 37.

75. *The Cotton Textile Industry*, Report on the Condition of Women and Child Wage Earners (Washington, D.C.: G.P.O., 1910), vol. 1, p. 608.

76. Mary Anderson, "Industrial Standards for Women," *AF* 32 (July 1925):21.

77. See Massachusetts WTUL, *History of Trade Unionism Among Women in Boston*, pp. 7, 32; New York WTUL, *Report of the Proceedings*, 4th Conference, p. 21.

78. Henry, *Women and the Labor Movement*, p. 108.

79. Typescript of "Complete Equality Between Men and Women," from the December 1917 issue of the *Ladies Garment Worker*, Fannia Cohn collection, box 7.

DOCUMENTS: *Struggling for Educational Opportunities*

ZITKALA-ŠA
The School Days of an Indian Girl

Education has long been regarded as a key to the upward economic and social mobility inherent in the American dream. School was (and is) also a means of instructing "outsiders" in the values and behavior of the dominant culture. Although the early settlers of the original thirteen colonies were, in fact, the "outsiders," they and their descendants regarded Amerindians as such. Because Euroamericans measured all other cultures by their own, federal officials and missionaries alike thought *all* women should conform in their behavior and dress to the standard set by white middle-class women. Amerindian women were regarded with great consternation because the work they did was judged unsuitable and the leisure behavior they engaged in viewed as immoral. Although they were perceived as "backward," many Indian women in fact enjoyed greater responsibilities and economic independence than did their Euroamerican counterparts.

While Indian women may have had reason to welcome some aspects of modernization, the process of acculturation was often traumatic, as this account of a Sioux Indian girl, Zitkala-Ša, makes clear. Zitkala-Ša, as Gertrude Simmons Bonnin, went on to have an active career as an author and reformer.* To what extent did her mother anticipate that the experience at the mission school would be difficult? What evidence is there to suggest that she herself was involved in the process of acculturation?

The first turning away from the easy, natural flow of my life occurred in an early spring. It was in my eighth year; in the month of March, I afterward learned. At this age I knew but one language, and that was my mother's native tongue.

From some of my playmates I heard

---

* Bonnin's interesting life is described at length by Mary E. Young in *Notable American Women, 1607–1950: A Biographical Dictionary*, ed. Edward T. James, Janet Wilson James, and Paul Boyer (Cambridge, Mass., 1971), 1:198–200.

Excerpted from "Impressions of an Indian Childhood," "The School Days of an Indian Girl," and "An Indian Teacher among Indians" by Zitkala-Ša, *Atlantic Monthly* 85 (January, February, and March 1900):45–47, 186–87, and 386.

that two paleface missionaries were in our village. They were from that class of white men who wore big hats and carried large hearts, they said. Running direct to my mother, I began to question her why these two strangers were among us. She told me, after I had teased much, that they had come to take away Indian boys and girls to the East. My mother did not seem to want me to talk about them. But in a day or two, I gleaned many wonderful stories from my playfellows concerning the strangers.

"Mother, my friend Judéwin is going home with the missionaries. She is going to a more beautiful country than ours; the palefaces told her so!" I said wistfully, wishing in my heart that I too might go.

Mother sat in a chair, and I was hanging on her knee. Within the last two seasons my big brother Dawée had returned from a three years' education in the East, and his coming back influenced my mother to take a farther step from her native way of living. First it was a change from the buffalo skin to the white man's canvas that covered our wigwam. Now she had given up her wigwam of slender poles, to live, a foreigner, in a home of clumsy logs.

Judéwin had told me of the great tree where grew red, red apples; and how we could reach out our hands and pick all the red apples we could eat. I had never seen apple trees. I had never tasted more than a dozen red apples in my life; and when I heard of the orchards of the East, I was eager to roam among them. The missionaries smiled into my eyes, and patted my head. I wondered how mother could say such hard words against them.

"Mother, ask them if little girls may have all the red apples they want, when they go East," I whispered aloud, in my excitement.

The interpreter heard me, and answered: "Yes, little girl, the nice red apples are for those who pick them; and

you will have a ride on the iron horse if you go with these good people."

I had never seen a train, and he knew it.

"Mother, I'm going East! I like big red apples, and I want to ride on the iron horse! Mother, say yes!" I pleaded.

My mother said nothing. The missionaries waited in silence; and my eyes began to blur with tears, though I struggled to choke them back. The corners of my mouth twitched, and my mother saw me.

"I am not ready to give you any word," she said to them. "Tomorrow I shall send you my answer by my son."

With this they left us. Alone with my mother, I yielded to my tears, and cried aloud, shaking my head so as not to hear what she was saying to me. This was the first time I had ever been so unwilling to give up my own desire that I refused to harken to my mother's voice.

There was a solemn silence in our home that night. Before I went to bed I begged the Great Spirit to make my mother willing I should go with the missionaries.

The next morning came, and my mother called me to her side. "My daughter, do you still persist in wishing to leave your mother?" she asked.

"Oh, mother, it is not that I wish to leave you, but I want to see the wonderful Eastern land," I answered. . . .

. . . My brother Dawée came for mother's decision. I dropped my play, and crept close to my aunt.

"Yes, Dawée, my daughter, though she does not understand what it all means, is anxious to go. She will need an education when she is grown, for then there will be fewer real Dakotas, and many more palefaces. This tearing her away, so young, from her mother is necessary, if I would have her an educated woman. The palefaces, who owe us a large debt for stolen lands, have begun to pay a tardy justice in offering some education to our children. But I know my daughter must suffer keenly in this experiment. For her sake, I dread to tell you my reply to the missionaries. Go, tell them that they may take my little daughter, and that the Great Spirit shall not fail to reward them according to their hearts."

Wrapped in my heavy blanket, I walked with my mother to the carriage that was soon to take us to the iron horse. I was happy. I met my playmates, who were also wearing their best thick blankets. We showed one another our new beaded moccasins, and the width of the belts that girdled our new dresses. Soon we were being drawn rapidly away by the white man's horses. When I saw the lonely figure of my mother vanish in the distance, a sense of regret settled heavily upon me. I felt suddenly weak, as if I might fall limp to the ground. I was in the hands of strangers whom my mother did not fully trust. I no longer felt free to be myself, or to voice my own feelings. The tears trickled down my cheeks, and I buried my face in the folds of my blanket. Now the first step, parting me from my mother, was taken, and all my belated tears availed nothing.

Having driven thirty miles to the ferryboat, we crossed the Missouri in the evening. Then riding again a few miles eastward, we stopped before a massive brick building. I looked at it in amazement, and with a vague misgiving, for in our village I had never seen so large a house. Trembling with fear and distrust of the palefaces, my teeth chattering from the chilly ride, I crept noiselessly in my soft moccasins along the narrow hall, keeping very close to the bare wall. I was as frightened and bewildered as the captured young of a wild creature.

The first day in the land of apples was a bitter-cold one; for the snow still covered the ground, and the trees were bare. A large bell rang for breakfast, its loud metallic voice crashing through the belfry overhead and into our sensitive ears. The annoying clatter of shoes on bare floors gave us no peace. The constant clash of harsh noises, with an undercurrent of many voices murmuring an unknown tongue, made a bedlam within which I was securely tied. And though my spirit tore itself in struggling for its lost freedom, all was useless.

A paleface woman, with white hair, came up after us. We were placed in a line of girls who were marching into the dining room. These were Indian girls, in stiff shoes and closely clinging dresses. The small girls wore sleeved aprons and shingled hair. As I walked noiselessly in my soft moccasins, I felt like sinking to the floor, for my blanket had been stripped from my shoulders. I looked hard at the Indian girls, who seemed not to care that they were even more immodestly dressed than I, in their tightly fitting clothes. While we marched in, the boys entered at an opposite door. I watched for the three young braves who came in our party. I spied them in the rear ranks, looking as uncomfortable as I felt. . . .

. . . Late in the morning, my friend Judéwin gave me a terrible warning. Judéwin knew a few words of English; and she had overheard the paleface woman talk about cutting our long, heavy hair. Our mothers had taught us that only unskilled warriors who were captured had their hair shingled by the enemy. Among our people, short hair was worn by mourners, and shingled hair by cowards!

We discussed our fate some moments, and when Judéwin said, "We have to submit, because they are strong," I rebelled.

"No, I will not submit! I will struggle first!" I answered.

I watched my chance, and when no one noticed I disappeared. I crept up the stairs as quietly as I could in my squeaking shoes,—my moccasins had been exchanged for shoes. Along the hall I passed, without knowing whither I was going. Turning aside to an open door, I found a large room with three white beds in it.

The windows were covered with dark green curtains, which made the room very dim. Thankful that no one was there, I directed my steps toward the corner farthest from the door. On my hands and knees I crawled under the bed, and cuddled myself in the dark corner.

From my hiding place I peered out, shuddering with fear whenever I heard footsteps near by. Though in the hall loud voices were calling my name, and I knew that even Judéwin was searching for me, I did not open my mouth to answer. Then the steps were quickened and the voices became excited. The sounds came nearer and nearer. Women and girls entered the room. I held my breath, and watched them open closet doors and peep behind large trunks. Some one threw up the curtains, and the room was filled with sudden light. What caused them to stoop and look under the bed I do not know. I remember being dragged out, though I resisted by kicking and scratching wildly. In spite of myself, I was carried downstairs and tied fast in a chair.

I cried aloud, shaking my head all the while until I felt the cold blades of the scissors against my neck, and heard them gnaw off one of my thick braids. Then I lost my spirit. Since the day I was taken from my mother I had suffered extreme indignities. People had stared at me. I had been tossed about in the air like a wooden puppet. And now my long hair was shingled like a coward's! In my anguish I moaned for my mother, but no one came to comfort me. Not a soul reasoned quietly with me, as my own mother used to do; for now I was only one of many little animals driven by a herder. . . .

. . . Now, as I look back upon the recent past, I see it from a distance, as a whole. I remember how, from morning till evening, many specimens of civilized peoples visited the Indian school. The city folks with canes and eyeglasses, the countrymen with sunburnt cheeks and clumsy feet, forgot their relative social ranks in an ignorant curiosity. Both sorts of these Christian palefaces were alike astounded at seeing the children of savage warriors so docile and industrious.

As answers to their shallow inquiries they received the students' sample work to look upon. Examining the neatly figured pages, and gazing upon the Indian girls and boys bending over their books, the white visitors walked out of the schoolhouse well satisfied: they were educating the children of the red man! They were paying a liberal fee to the government employees in whose able hands lay the small forest of Indian timber.

In this fashion many have passed idly through the Indian schools during the last decade, afterward to boast of their charity to the North American Indian. But few there are who have paused to question whether real life or long-lasting death lies beneath this semblance of civilization.

MARY ANTIN
The School Days of an Immigrant Girl

Education was also a means of acculturation for the millions of immigrant children who came to this country between 1880 and 1920. Predominantly southern or eastern Europeans, they were set apart by differences of religion as well as language—many were Catholic or Jewish. Mary Antin (the name has been Anglicized), a young Jewish girl from the Russian town of Polotzk, communicates in the following account her enormous yearning for education and her boundless enthusiasm for her new home.

That the public school of Chelsea, Massachusetts, provided happier memories for Mary Antin than did the missionary school for Zitkala-Ša can be explained in part by the greater sensitivity of Antin's teachers. Equally important was the fact that Antin was able to remain with her family and within her ethnic community. The process of acculturation was also made easier by the fact that her father, who had preceded his family to Boston, was eager to embrace things American. More important, he attached a high value to education, as did most Jews, although, as among other ethnic groups, greater sacrifices were likely to be made on behalf of sons than daughters. That this should be the case is not surprising given the greater earning potential of males. What neither essay reveals fully is the extent to which, in a period of intense racial and ethnic prejudice, many "old-stock" Americans believed that education for such girls should serve only to prepare them for domestic service in their own homes or the homes of others, irrespective of individual aspirations and abilities. How important was it to Mary Antin's educational development that her father did *not* share that assumption? In what ways was he supportive of her?

Father himself conducted us to school. He would not have delegated that mission to the President of the United States. He had awaited the day with impatience equal to mine, and the visions he saw as he hurried us over the sun-flecked pavements transcended all my dreams. Almost his first act on landing on American soil, three years before, had been his application for naturalization. He had taken the remaining steps in the process with eager promptness, and at the earliest moment allowed by the law, he became a citizen of the United States. It is true that he had left home in search of bread for his hungry family, but he went blessing the necessity

Excerpted from "The Promised Land" and "Initiation," chaps. 9 and 10 of *The Promised Land* by Mary Antin (Boston: Houghton Mifflin, 1912).

that drove him to America. The boasted freedom of the New World meant to him far more than the right to reside, travel, and work wherever he pleased; it meant the freedom to speak his thoughts, to throw off the shackles of superstition, to test his own fate, unhindered by political or religious tyranny. . . .

. . . His struggle for a bare living left him no time to take advantage of the public evening school; but he lost nothing of what was to be learned through reading, through attendance at public meetings, through exercising the rights of citizenship. Even here he was hindered by a natural inability to acquire the English language. In time, indeed, he learned to read, to follow a conversation or lecture; but he never learned to write correctly, and his pronunciation remains extremely foreign to this day.

If education, culture, the higher life were shining things to be worshipped from afar, he had still a means left whereby he could draw one step nearer to them. He could send his children to school, to learn all those things that he knew by fame to be desirable. The common school, at least, perhaps high school; for one or two, perhaps even college! His children should be students, should fill his house with books and intellectual company; and thus he would walk by proxy in the Elysian Fields of liberal learning. As for the children themselves, he knew no surer way to their advancement and happiness.

So it was with a heart full of longing and hope that my father led us to school on that first day. He took long strides in his eagerness, the rest of us running and hopping to keep up. . . .

I was not a bit too large for my little chair and desk in the baby class, but my mind, of course, was too mature by six or seven years for the work. So as soon as I could understand what the teacher said in class, I was advanced to the second grade. This was within a week after Miss Nixon took me in hand. But I do not mean to give my dear teacher all the credit for my rapid progress, nor even half the credit. I shall divide it with her on behalf of my race and my family. I was Jew enough to have an aptitude for language in general, and to bend my mind earnestly to my task; I was Antin enough to read each lesson with my heart, which gave me an inkling of what was coming next, and so carried me along by leaps and bounds. As for the teacher, she could best explain what theory she followed in teaching us foreigners to read. . . .

There were about half a dozen of us beginners in English, in age from six to fifteen. Miss Nixon made a special class of us, and aided us so skilfully and earnestly in our endeavors to "see-a-cat," and "hear-a-dog-bark," and "look-at-the-hen," that we turned over page after page of the ravishing history, eager to find out how the common world looked, smelled, and tasted in the strange speech. The teacher knew just when to let us help each other out with a word in our own tongue,—it happened that we were all Jews,—and so, working all together, we actually covered more ground in a lesson than the native classes, composed entirely of the little tots. . . .

Whenever the teachers did anything special to help me over my private difficulties, my gratitude went out to them, silently. . . . Dear Miss Carrol, of the second grade, would be amazed to hear what small things I remember, all because I was so impressed at the time with her readiness and sweetness in taking notice of my difficulties.

Says Miss Carrol, looking straight at me:—

"If Johnnie has three marbles, and Charlie has twice as many, how many marbles has Charlie?"

I raise my hand for permission to speak.

"Teacher, I don't know vhat is tvice."

Teacher beckons me to her, and whispers to me the meaning of the strange word, and I am able to write the sum correctly. It's all in the day's work with her; with me, it is a special act of kindness and efficiency. . . .

If I was eager and diligent, my teachers did not sleep. As fast as my knowledge of English allowed, they advanced me from grade to grade, without reference to the usual schedule of promotions. My father was right, when he often said, in discussing my prospects, that ability would be promptly recognized in the public schools. Rapid as was my progress, on account of the advantages with which I started, some of the other "green" pupils were not far behind me; within a grade or two, by the end of the year. . . .

This is the document, copied from an educational journal, a tattered copy of which lies in my lap as I write—treasured for fifteen years, you see, by my vanity.

EDITOR "PRIMARY EDUCATION":—

This is the uncorrected paper of a Russian child twelve years old, who had studied English only four months. She had never, until September, been to school even in her own country and has heard English spoken *only* at school. I shall be glad if the paper of my pupil and the above explanation may appear in your paper.

CHELSEA, MASS.   M. S. DILLINGHAM

SNOW

Snow is frozen moisture which comes from the clouds.

Now the snow is coming down in feather-flakes, which makes nice snow-balls. But there is still one kind of snow more. This kind of snow is called snow-crystals, for it comes down in little curly balls. These snow-crystals aren't quiet as good for snow-balls as feather-flakes, for they (the snow-crystals) are dry: so they can't keep together as feather-flakes do.

The snow is dear to some children for they like sleighing.

As I said at the top—the snow comes from the clouds.

Now the trees are bare, and no flowers are to see in the fields and gardens, (we all know why) and the whole world seems like asleep without the happy birds songs which left us till spring. But the snow which drove away all these pretty and happy things, try, (as I think) not to make us at all unhappy; they covered up the branches of the trees, the fields, the gardens and houses, and the whole world looks like dressed in a beautiful white—instead of green—dress, with the sky looking down on it with a pale face.

And so the people can find some joy in it, too, without the happy summer.

MARY ANTIN

. . . So here was my teacher, the moment she saw that I could give a good paraphrase of her talk on "Snow," bent on finding out what more I could do. One day she asked me if I had ever written poetry. I had not, but I went home and tried. I believe it was more snow, and I know it was wretched. . . . But Miss Dillingham was not discouraged. She saw that I had no idea of metre, so she proceeded to teach me. We repeated miles of poetry together, smooth lines that sang themselves, mostly out of Longfellow. Then I would go home and write—oh, about the snow in our back yard!—but when Miss Dillingham came to read my verses, they limped and they lagged and they dragged, and there was no tune that would fit them.

At last came the moment of illumination: I saw where my trouble lay. I had supposed that my lines matched when they had an equal number of syllables, taking no account of accent. Now I knew better; now I could write poetry! The everlasting snow melted at last, and the mud puddles dried in the spring sun, and the grass on the common was green, and still I wrote poetry! . . .

Making fair allowance for my youth, retarded education, and strangeness to the language, it must still be admitted that I never wrote good verse. But I loved to read it. My half-hours with Miss Dillingham were full of delight for me, quite apart from my new-born ambition to become a writer. What, then, was my joy, when Miss Dillingham, just before locking up her desk one evening, presented me with a volume of Longfellow's poems! It was a thin volume of selections, but to me it was a bottomless treasure. I had never owned a book before. The sense of possession alone was a source of bliss, and this book I already knew and loved. And so Miss Dillingham, who was my first American friend, and who first put my name in print, was also the one to start my library. . . .

About the middle of the year I was promoted to the grammar school. Then it was that I walked on air. For I said to myself that I was a *student* now, in earnest, not merely a school-girl learning to spell and cipher. I was going to learn out-of-the-way things, things that had nothing to do with ordinary life—things to *know*. When I walked home afternoons, with the great big geography book under my arm, it seemed to me that the earth was conscious of my step. Sometimes I carried home half the books in my desk, not because I should need them, but because I loved to hold them; and also because I loved to be seen carrying books. It was a badge of scholarship, and I was proud of it. I remembered the days in Vitebsk when I used to watch my cousin Hirshel start for school in the morning, every thread of his student's uniform, every worn copybook in his satchel, glorified in my envious eyes. And now I was myself as he: aye, greater than he; for I knew English, and I could write poetry. . . .

How long would you say, wise reader, it takes to make an American? By the middle of my second year in school I had reached the sixth grade. When, after the Christmas holidays, we began to study the life of Washington, running through a summary of the Revolution, and the early days of the Republic, it seemed to me that all my reading and study had been idle until then. The reader, the arithmetic, the song book, that had so fascinated me until now, became suddenly sober exercise books, tools wherewith to hew a way to the source of inspiration. When the teacher read to us out of a big

book with many bookmarks in it, I sat rigid with attention in my little chair, my hands tightly clasped on the edge of my desk; and I painfully held my breath, to prevent sighs of disappointment escaping, as I saw the teacher skip the parts between bookmarks. When the class read, and it came my turn, my voice shook and the book trembled in my hands. I could not pronounce the name of George Washington without a pause. Never had I prayed, never had I chanted the songs of David, never had I called upon the Most Holy, in such utter reverence and worship as I repeated the simple sentences of my child's story of the patriot. I gazed with adoration at the portraits of George and Martha Washington, till I could see them with my eyes shut. . . .

On the day of the Washington celebration I recited a poem that I had composed in my enthusiasm. But "composed" is not the word. The process of putting on paper the sentiments that seethed in my soul was really very discomposing. I dug the words out of my heart, squeezed the rhymes out of my brain, forced the missing syllables out of their hiding-places in the dictionary. . . .

When I had done, I was myself impressed with the length, gravity, and nobility of my poem. My father was overcome with emotion as he read it. His hands trembled as he held the paper to the light, and the mist gathered in his eyes. My teacher, Miss Dwight, was plainly astonished at my performance, and said many kind things, and asked many questions; all of which I took very solemnly, like one who had been in the clouds and returned to earth with a sign upon him. When Miss Dwight asked me to read my poem to the class on the day of celebration, I readily consented. It was not in me to refuse a chance to tell my schoolmates what I thought of George Washington. . . .

I can laugh now at the impossible metres, the grandiose phrases, the verbose repetitions of my poem. . . .

He whose courage, will, amazing bravery,
  Did free his land from a despot's rule,
From man's greatest evil, almost slavery,
  And all that's taught in tyranny's school,

Who gave his land its liberty,
  Who was he?

'T was he who e'er will be our pride,
  Immortal Washington,
Who always did in truth confide,
  We hail our Washington!

The best of the verses were no better than these, but the children listened. They had to. Presently I gave them news, declaring that Washington

> Wrote the famous Constitution;
>   sacred's the hand
> That this blessed guide to man had
>   given, which says, "One
> And all of mankind are alike,
>   excepting none."

This was received in respectful silence, possibly because the other Fellow Citizens were as hazy about historical facts as I at this point. "Hurrah for Washington!" they understood, and "Three cheers for the Red, White, and Blue!" was only to be expected on that occasion. But there ran a special note through my poem—a thought that only Israel Rubinstein or Beckie Aronovitch could have fully understood, besides myself. For I made myself the spokesman of the "luckless sons of Abraham," saying—

> Then we weary Hebrew children at last
>   found rest
> In the land where reigned Freedom,
>   and like a nest
> To homeless birds your land proved to
>   us, and therefore

Will we gratefully sing your praise
  evermore. . . .

If I had been satisfied with my poem in the first place, the applause with which it was received by my teachers and schoolmates convinced me that I had produced a very fine thing indeed. So the person, whoever it was,—perhaps my father—who suggested that my tribute to Washington ought to be printed, did not find me difficult to persuade. When I had achieved an absolutely perfect copy of my verses, at the expense of a dozen sheets of blue-ruled note paper, I crossed the Mystic River to Boston and boldly invaded Newspaper Row. . . .

When the paper with my poem in it arrived, the whole house pounced upon it at once. . . . It occupied a gratifying amount of space, and was introduced by a flattering biographical sketch of the author—the *author!*—the material for which the friendly editor had artfully drawn from me during that happy interview. And my name, as I had prophesied, was at the bottom!

When the excitement in the house had subsided, my father took all the change out of the cash drawer and went to buy up the "Herald." He did not count the pennies. He just bought "Heralds," all he could lay his hands on, and distributed them gratis to all our friends, relatives, and acquaintances; to all who could read, and to some who could not. For weeks he carried a clipping from the "Herald" in his breast pocket, and few were the occasions when he did not manage to introduce it into the conversation. He treasured that clipping as for years he had treasured the letters I wrote him from Polotzk.

M. CAREY THOMAS
"The passionate desire of women . . . for higher education"

The way Americans have viewed intellectual activity among women tells us a great deal about what they believed to be woman's proper role. By the late nineteenth and early twentieth centuries a slightly higher proportion of girls than boys were attending school, and girls were increasing their lead over boys in the upper age group. College, however, was another matter. Families that sent sons to college as a matter of course might understandably be reluctant to extend that same opportunity to their daughters when medical experts warned that too much exposure to the "impedimenta of libraries" could leave young female graduates incapable of performing their normal reproductive functions.

M. Carey Thomas conveys with particular effectiveness the yearnings of the young college-bound women of her generation. When she later became president of Bryn Mawr College, one of several elite women's colleges founded in the latter half of the nineteenth century, she strongly disagreed with those who argued that the primary purpose of a woman's education was to prepare her for marriage and motherhood. Insisting that the Bryn Mawr student enter college with the same qualifications in Greek, Latin, and mathematics required of her male counterpart at Harvard or Yale, Thomas expected Bryn Mawr graduates to lead lives as productive, economically independent women, finding, as did men, "their greatest happiness in congenial work."* Note her insistence on the importance of having women scholars who could serve as role models for their students.

The passionate desire of women of my generation for higher education was accompanied thruout its course by the awful doubt, felt by women themselves as well as by men, as to whether women as a sex were physically and mentally fit for it. I think I can best make this clear to you if I refer briefly to my own experience. I cannot remember the time when I was not sure that studying and going to college were the things above all others which I wished to do. I was always wondering whether it could be really true, as every one thought, that boys were cleverer than girls. Indeed, I cared so much that I never dared to ask any grown-up person the direct question, not even my father or mother, because I feared to hear the reply.

* M. Carey Thomas, "The Future of Women's Higher Education," in *Mount Holyoke College: The Seventy-Fifth Anniversary* (South Hadley, Mass., 1913), p. 104.

Excerpted from "Present Tendencies in Women's College and University Education" by M. Carey Thomas, in *Educational Review* 30 (1908):64–85.

I remember often praying about it, and begging God that if it were true that because I was a girl I could not successfully master Greek and go to college and understand things to kill me at once, as I could not bear to live in such an unjust world. When I was a little older I read the Bible entirely thru with passionate eagerness because I had heard it said that it proved that women were inferior to men. Those were not the days of the higher criticism. I can remember weeping over the account of Adam and Eve because it seemed to me that the curse pronounced on Eve might imperil girls' going to college; and to this day I can never read many parts of the Pauline epistles without feeling again the sinking of the heart with which I used to hurry over the verses referring to women's keeping silence in the churches and asking their husbands at home. . . .

It was not to be wondered at that we were uncertain in those old days as to the ultimate result of women's education. Before I myself went to college I had never seen but one college woman. I had heard that such a woman was staying at the house of an acquaintance. I went to see her with fear. Even if she had appeared in hoofs and horns I was determined to go to college all the same. But it was a relief to find this Vassar graduate tall and handsome and dressed like other women. When, five years later, I went to Leipzig to study after I had been graduated from Cornell, my mother used to write me that my name was never mentioned to her by the women of her acquaintance. I was thought by them to be as much of a disgrace to my family as if I had eloped with the coachman. Now, women who have been to college are as plentiful as blackberries on summer hedges. Even my native city of Baltimore is full of them, and women who have in addition studied in Germany are regarded with becoming deference by the very Baltimore women who disapproved of me.

During the quarter of the century of the existence of the Association of Collegiate Alumnae [now American Association of University Women] two generations of college women have reached mature life, and the older generation is now just passing off the stage. We are therefore better prepared than ever before to give an account of what has been definitely accomplished, and to predict what will be the tendencies of women's college and university education in the future.

The curriculum of our women's colleges has steadily stiffened. Women, both in separate, and in coeducational colleges, seem to prefer the old-fashioned, so-called disciplinary studies. They disregard the so-called accomplishments. I believe that to-day more women than men are receiving a thoro college education, even altho in most cases they are receiving it sitting side by side with men in the same college lecture rooms.

The old type of untrained woman teacher has practically disappeared from women's colleges. Her place is being taken by ardent young women scholars who have qualified themselves by long years of graduate study for advanced teaching. Even the old-fashioned untrained matron, or house-mother, is swiftly being replaced in girls' schools, as well as in women's colleges, by the college-bred warden or director.

We did not know when we began whether women's health could stand the strain of college education. We were haunted in those early days by the clanging chains of that gloomy little specter, Dr. Edward H. Clarke's *Sex in Education*. With trepidation of spirit I made my mother read it, and was much cheered by her remark that, as neither she, nor any of the women she knew, had ever seen girls or women of the kind described in Dr. Clarke's book, we might as well act as if they did not exist. Still, we did not *know* whether colleges might not produce a crop of just such invalids. Doctors insisted that they would. We women could not be sure until we had tried the experiment. Now we have tried it, and tried it for more than a generation, and we know that college women are not only not invalids, but that they are better physically than other women in their own class of life. We know that girls are growing stronger and more athletic. Girls enter college each year in better physical condition. For the past four years I have myself questioned closely all our entering classes, and often their mothers as well. I find that an average of sixty per cent. enter college absolutely and in every respect well, and that less than thirty per cent. make, or need to make, any periodic difference whatever in exercise, or study, from year's end to year's end. This result is very different from that obtained by physicians and others writing in recent magazines and medical journals. These alarmists give grewsome statistics from high schools and women's colleges, which they are very careful not to name. Probably they are investigating girls whose general hygienic conditions are bad. . . .

We are now living in the midst of great and, I believe on the whole beneficent, social changes which are preparing the way for the coming economic independence of women. Like the closely allied diminishing birth rate, but unlike the higher education of women, this great change in opinion and practise seems to have come about almost without our knowledge, certainly without our conscious coöperation. The passionate desire of the women of my generation for a college education seems, as we study it now in the light of coming events, to have been a part of this greater movement.

In order to prepare for this economic independence, we should expect to see what is now taking place. Colleges for women and college departments of co-educational universities are attended by ever-increasing numbers of women students. In seven of the largest western universities women already outnumber men in the college departments.

A liberal college course prepares women for their great profession of teaching. College women have proved to be such admirably efficient teachers that they are driving other women out of the field. Until other means of self-support are as easy for women as teaching, more and more women who intend to teach will go to college. Such women will elect first of all the subjects taught by women in the high schools, such as Latin, history, and the languages. They will avoid chemistry, physics, and other sciences which are usually taught by men. Until all women become self-supporting, more women than men will go to college for culture, especially in the west, and such women will tend to elect the great disciplinary studies which men neglect because they are intrinsically more difficult and seem at first sight less practical. For these obvious reasons certain college courses are therefore already crowded by women and almost deserted by men in many of the coeducational universities.

And just because women have shown such an aptitude for a true college education and such delight in it, we must be careful to maintain it for them in its integrity. We must see to it that its disciplinary quality is not lowered by the insertion of so-called practical courses which are falsely supposed to prepare for life. Women are rapidly coming to control women's college education. It rests with us to decide whether we shall barter for a mess of pottage the inheritance of the girls of this generation which the girls of my generation agonized to obtain for themselves and for other girls. . . .

I believe also that every women's college ought to maintain . . . a graduate school of philosophy of the highest grade. . . .

. . . The highest service which colleges can render to their time is to discover and foster imaginative and constructive genius.

Such genius unquestionably needs opportunity for its highest development. This is peculiarly the case with women students. As I watch their gallant struggles I sometimes think that the very stars in their courses are conspiring against them. Women scholars can assist women students, as men can not, to tide over the first discouragements of a life of intellectual reunification. Ability of the kind I am speaking of is, of course, very rare, but for this reason it is precious beyond all other human products. . . .

The time has now come for those of us who are in control of women's education to bend ourselves to the task of creating academic conditions favorable for the development of this kind of creative ability. We should at once begin to found research chairs for women at all our women's colleges, with three or four hours a week research teaching and the rest of the time free for independent investigation. We should reserve all the traveling fellowships in our gift for women who have given evidence, however slight, of power to do research work. We should bring pressure on our state universities to give such women opportunities to compete for professors' chairs. In the four women suffrage states this can be accomplished in the twinkling of an eye: it will only be necessary for women's organizations to vote for university regents with proper opinions. The Johns Hopkins University situated in conservative Baltimore has two women on its academic staff who are lecturing to men. Why can not all chairs in the arts departments of universities, that is, in the college and school of philosophy, be thrown open to the competition of women? This is the next advance to be made in women's education—the last and greatest battle to be won.

MARY McLEOD BETHUNE
"How the Bethune-Cookman college campus started"

Mary McLeod Bethune was one of the most distinguished educators of her generation. The daughter of slaves, she received her early education from missionary teachers. Like others of her race who saw education as a key to racial advancement at a time when the white South was indifferent if not hostile to the aspirations of Afro-Americans, Bethune faced extraordinary obstacles. When she began a little school at Daytona Beach, Florida, in 1904, America was entering an era of reform. Yet even most northern progressives—with the notable exception of women such as Mary White Ovington, one of the founders of the National Association for the Advancement of Colored People—shared the racist

Excerpted from "Faith That Moved a Dump Heap" by Mary McLeod Bethune, in *Who, The Magazine about People* 1, no. 3 (June 1941):31–35, 54.

assumptions of that era, believing that the future of black women, like immigrant women, lay in domestic service. Bethune had larger dreams. Because of her courage, energy, and vision she was able to keep her little school afloat with her intrepid fund raising, guiding its growth from grammar school to high school and to what finally became an accredited four-year college. President of the institution from its founding until her resignation in 1942, she remained a trustee of Bethune-Cookman College until her death in 1955. She was an activist and held many important posts within the black community, founding such organizations as the National Association of Colored Women's Clubs and the National Council of Negro Women. A national figure as well, she served in the Roosevelt administration during the 1930s, advising the president on minority affairs. She was also involved in early efforts on behalf of the United Nations. Her many offices and honors, however, never diverted her from her primary purpose—the pursuit of full citizenship rights for all black Americans.

On October 3, 1904, I opened the doors of my school, with an enrollment of five little girls, aged from eight to twelve, whose parents paid me fifty cents' weekly tuition. My own child was the only boy in the school. Though I hadn't a penny left, I considered cash money as the smallest part of my resources. I had faith in a living God, faith in myself, and a desire to serve. . . .

We burned logs and used the charred splinters as pencils, and mashed elderberries for ink. I begged strangers for a broom, a lamp, a bit of cretonne to put around the packing case which served as my desk. I haunted the city dump and the trash piles behind hotels, retrieving discarded linen and kitchenware, cracked dishes, broken chairs, pieces of old lumber. Everything was scoured and mended. This was part of the training to salvage, to reconstruct, to make bricks without straw. As parents began gradually to leave their children overnight, I had to provide sleeping accommodations. I took corn sacks for mattresses. Then I picked Spanish moss from trees, dried and cured it, and used it as a substitute for mattress hair.

The school expanded fast. In less than two years I had 250 pupils. In desperation I hired a large hall next to my original little cottage, and used it as a combined dormitory and classroom. I concentrated more and more on girls, as I felt they especially were hampered by lack of educational opportunities. . . .

I had many volunteer workers and a few regular teachers, who were paid from fifteen to twenty-five dollars a month and board. I was supposed to keep the balance of the funds for my own pocket, but there was never any balance—only a yawning hole. I wore old clothes sent me by mission boards, recut and redesigned for me in our dress-making classes. At last I saw that our only solution was to stop renting space, and to buy and build our own college.

Near by was a field, popularly called Hell's Hole, which was used as a dumping ground. I approached the owner, determined to buy it. The price was $250. In a daze, he finally agreed to take five dollars down, and the balance in two years. I promised to be back in a few days with the initial payment. He never knew it, but I didn't have five dollars. I raised this sum selling ice cream and sweet-potato pies to the workmen on construction jobs, and I took the owner his money in small change wrapped in my handkerchief.

That's how the Bethune-Cookman college campus started. . . .

As the school expanded, whenever I saw a need for some training or service we did not supply, I schemed to add it to our curriculum. Sometimes that took years. When I came to Florida, there were no hospitals where a Negro could go. A student became critically ill with appendicitis, so I went to a local hospital and begged a white physician to take her in and operate. My pleas were so desperate he finally agreed. A few days after the operation, I visited my pupil.

When I appeared at the front door of the hospital, the nurse ordered me around to the back way. I thrust her aside—and found my little girl segregated in a corner of the porch behind the kitchen. Even my toes clenched with rage.

That decided me. I called on three of my faithful friends, asking them to buy a little cottage behind our school as a hospital. They agreed, and we started with two beds.

From this humble start grew a fully equipped twenty-bed hospital—our college infirmary and a refuge for the needy throughout the state. It was staffed by white and black physicians and by our own student nurses. We ran this hospital for twenty years as part of our contribution to community life; but a short time ago, to ease our financial burden, the city took it over.

Gradually, as educational facilities expanded and there were other places where small children could go, we put the emphasis on high-school and junior-college training. In 1922, Cookman College, a men's school, the first in the state for the higher education of Negroes, amalgamated with us. The combined coeducational college, now run under the auspices of the Methodist Episcopal Church, is called Bethune-Cookman College. We have fourteen modern buildings, a beautiful campus of thirty-two acres, an enrollment in regular and summer sessions of 600 students, a faculty and staff of thirty-two, and 1,800 graduates. The college property, now valued at more than $800,000, is entirely unencumbered.

When I walk through the campus, with its stately palms and well-kept lawns, and think back to the dump-heap foundation, I rub my eyes and pinch myself. And I remember my childish visions in the cotton fields.

But values cannot be calculated in ledger figures and property. More than all else the college has fulfilled my ideals of distinctive training and service. Extending far beyond the immediate sphere of its graduates and students, it has already enriched the lives of 100,000 Negroes.

In 1934, President Franklin D. Roosevelt appointed me director of the division of Negro affairs of the National Youth Administration. My main task now is to supervise the training provided for 600,-000 Negro children, and I have to run the college by remote control. Every few weeks, however, I snatch a day or so and return to my beloved home.

This is a strenuous program. The doctor shakes his head and says, "Mrs. Bethune, slow down a little. Relax! Take it just a little easier." I promise to reform, but in an hour the promise is forgotten.

For I am my mother's daughter, and the drums of Africa still beat in my heart. They will not let me rest while there is a single Negro boy or girl without a chance to prove his worth.

DOCUMENT: *Reforming America*

FLORENCE KELLEY
The Women at Hull House

Hull House was a pioneering social settlement, established in Chicago in 1889 by twenty-nine-year-old Jane Addams. In the years to come it would be the model for settlement houses in cities all across America, staffed by women and men who shared Addams's vision and were caught up in the excitement of developing the new field of professional social service. They represented, as we have suggested in our introduction to this section, a distinctive female component in American progressivism.

In the following account, Florence Kelley describes her first encounter with the women of Hull House. It was no accident that Kelley was drawn to this novel institution or that she was soon put in charge of the Chicago inquiry into sweated labor. Preparation for a career as a reformer had begun as a young girl when her father, a Republican congressman from Pennsylvania, shared with her his voluminous library, his commitment to female suffrage, and his own concern over the economic exploitation that accompanied the industrial development he believed so essential to America. Further preparation occurred at Cornell, one of the few co-ed institutions in the country, where Kelley wrote her thesis on legislation affecting women and children. Denied permission to enroll in law school at the University of Pennsylvania because of her sex, she went to Switzerland for further study at the University of Zurich. There her passion for economic and social justice was reinforced by contact with Marxism and young radicals in the student body. Returning home in 1886, Kelley began five years later at Hull House a distinguished career as an advocate for legislation protecting women and children from exploitation in the workplace.

On a snowy morning between Christmas 1891 and New Year's 1892, I arrived at Hull House, Chicago, a little before breakfast time, and found there Henry Standing Bear, a Kickapoo Indian, waiting for the front door to be opened. It was Miss Addams who opened it, holding on her left arm a singularly unattractive, fat, pudgy baby belonging to the cook, who was behindhand with breakfast. Miss Addams was a little hindered in her movements by a super-energetic kindergarten child,

Excerpted from "I Go to Work" by Florence Kelley, in the *Survey* 58, no. 5 (June 1, 1927): 271–74.

left by its mother while she went to a sweatshop for a bundle of cloaks to be finished.

We were welcomed as though we had been invited. We stayed, Henry Standing Bear as helper to the engineer several months, when he returned to his tribe; and I as a resident seven happy, active years until May 1, 1899, when I returned to New York City to enter upon the work in which I have since been engaged as secretary of the National Consumers' League.

I cannot remember ever again seeing Miss Addams hold a baby, but that first picture of her gently keeping the little Italian girl back from charging out into the snow, closing the door against the blast of wintry wind off Lake Michigan, and tranquilly welcoming these newcomers, is as clear today as it was at that moment.

Henry Standing Bear had been camping under a wooden sidewalk which surrounded a vacant lot in the neighborhood, with two or three members of his tribe. They had been precariously employed by a vendor of a hair improver, who had now gone into bankruptcy leaving his employes a melancholy Christmas holiday. Though a graduate of a government Indian school, he had been trained to no way of earning his living and was a dreadful human commentary upon Uncle Sam's treatment of his wards in the Nineties.

At breakfast on that eventful morning, there were present Ellen Gates Starr, friend of many years and fellow-founder of Hull-House with Jane Addams; Jennie Dow, a delightful young volunteer kindergartner, whose good sense and joyous good humor found for her unfailing daily reward for great physical exertion. She spent vast energy visiting the homes of her Italian pupils, persuading their mothers to remove at least two or three times during the winter their layers of dresses, and give them a thorough sponge-bath in the sympathetic and reassuring pres-

ence of their kindergartner, Mary Keyser, who had followed Miss Addams from the family home in Cedarville and throughout the remainder of her life relieved Miss Addams of all household care. This was a full-time professional job where such unforeseen arrivals as Henry Standing Bear's and mine were daily episodes in the place which Miss Addams' steadfast will has made and kept, through war and peace, a center of hospitality for people and for ideas.

Julia Lathrop, then recently appointed county visitor for Cook County for those dependent families who received outdoor relief in money or in kind, was mentioned as away for the holidays with her family at Rockford, Illinois. Miss Lathrop, later a member of the Illinois State Board of Charities and from 1912 to 1921 through its first nine creative years, chief of the Children's Bureau at Washington, was then and is now a pillar of Hull-House. Two others of the permanent group were Edward L. Burchard, for many years curator of the Field Museum; and Anna Farnsworth, an agreeable woman of leisure and means, happy to be hostess-on-call to some and all who appeared at the front door from breakfast until midnight seven days a week. That was before the squalid, recent social convention had been set up, according to which everyone, however abundant and well assured her income, must earn her own living or be censured as a parasite. Miss Farnsworth's gracious gifts of free time and abundant good-will for counseling perplexed immigrants, finding comfortable quarters for old people who could do little work but not fend for themselves in the labor market, providing happy Saturdays in the parks for little groups of school children whose mothers worked away from home, were among the Settlement's early enrichments of the neighborhood life.

Reaching Hull-House that winter day was no small undertaking. The streets between car-track and curb were piled mountain high with coal-black frozen snow. The street cars, drawn by horses, were frequently blocked by a fallen horse harnessed to a heavily laden wagon. Whenever that happened, the long procession of vehicles stopped short until the horse was restored to its feet or, as sometimes occurred, was shot and lifted to the top of the snow, there to remain until the next thaw facilitated its removal.

Nor were these difficulties in the way of travel minimized by free use of the telephone. In all weathers and through all depths of snow and slush and sleet, we used to navigate across Halsted Street, the thirty-miles-long thoroughfare which Hull-House faced, to a drug store where we paid ten cents a call, stood throughout the process, and incidentally confided our business to the druggist and to any English-speaking neighbors who might happen in.

A superb embodiment of youth in the Mississippi Valley was Mary Kenney. Born in Keokuk, Iowa, of Irish immigrant parents, she had moved with her mother to a nearby brick tenement house, a distinguished three-story edifice in that region of drab one- and two-story frame cottages, in order to be a close neighbor to Hull-House and participate in its efforts to improve industrial conditions. Her volunteer work was with self-supporting, wage-earning young women whom she hoped to form into powerful, permanent trade unions. Tall, erect, broad-shouldered, with ruddy face and shining eyes, she carried hope and confidence whithersoever she went. Her rich Irish voice and friendly smile inspired men, women and children alike to do what she wished. Her undertakings prospered and throve.

A highly skilled printer, she was employed by a company which gave preference to union employes. As a numberer she earned fourteen dollars a week, supporting herself and her lovely old mother on that wage. Hers was the initiative in making of the brick tenement a cooperative house for working girls known as the Jane Club, a large part of the success of which was for many years due to the gentle sweetness of Mrs. Kenney, who mothered the cooperators as though they had been her own.

Although this was an entirely self-governing undertaking, Miss Addams was elected year after year an honorary director, having underwritten the experiment from the beginning. Later a friend of the Settlement, as a first step towards an endowment, paid for a building planned for the convenience of the cooperators, the rent going to Hull-House. This became a model for the Eleanor Clubs and countless other cooperative home clubs for self-supporting women scattered over the great city and growing with its growth during the past quarter century. . . .

In my first year at Hull-House, Carroll D. Wright, U. S. commissioner of commerce and labor, in charge of a federal study of the slums of great cities, entrusted me with the Chicago part of the enquiry. With a group of schedule men under my guidance, we canvassed a square mile extending from Hull-House on the west to State Street on the east, and several long blocks south. In this area we encountered people of eighteen nationalities.

Hull-House was, we soon discovered, surrounded in every direction by homework carried on under the sweating system. From the age of eighteen months few children able to sit in high chairs at tables were safe from being required to pull basting threads. In the Hull-House kindergarten children used with pleasure blunt, coarse needles for sewing bright silk into perforated outlines of horses, dogs, cats, parrots, and less known creatures on cards. They did this in the intervals between singing, modeling and playing active games. At home they used equally coarse sharp needles for sewing buttons on garments. The contrast was a hideously painful one to witness, especially when the children fell asleep at their work in their homes.

Out of this inquiry, amplified by Hull-House residents and other volunteers, grew the volume published under the title Hull-House Maps and Papers. One Map showed the distribution of the polyglot peoples. Another exhibited their incomes (taken by permission from the federal schedules) indicated in colors, ranging from gold which meant twenty dollars or more total a week for a family, to black which was five dollars or less total family income. There was precious little gold and a superabundance of black on that income map!

The discoveries as to home work under the sweating system thus recorded and charted in 1892 (that first year of my residence) led to the appointment at the opening of the legislature of 1893, of a legislative commission of enquiry into employment of women and chilldren in manufacture, for which Mary Kenney and I volunteered as guides. Because we knew our neighborhood, we could and did show the commissioners sights that few legislators had then beheld; among them unparalleled congestion in frame cottages which looked decent enough, though drab and uninviting, under their thick coats of soft coal soot. One member of the Commission would never enter any sweatshop, but stood in the street while the others went in, explaining that he had young children and feared to carry them some infection.

This Commission had been intended as a sop to labor and a sinecure, a protracted junket to Chicago, for a number of rural legislators. Our overwhelming hospitality and devotion to the thoroughness and success of their investigation, by personally conducted visits to sweat-shops, though irksome in the extreme to the lawgivers, ended in a report so compendious, so readable, so surprising that they presented it with pride to the legislature. We had offered it to them under the modest title, Memorandum for Legislative Commission of 1893. They renamed it. The subject was a new one in Chicago. For the press the sweating system was that winter a sensation. No one was yet blasé.

With backing from labor, from Hull-House, from the Henry Demarest Lloyds and their numberless friends, the Commission and the report carried almost without opposition a bill applying to manufacture, and prescribing a maximum working day not to exceed eight hours for women, girls and children, together with child labor safeguards based on laws then existing in New York and Ohio, and quite advanced. There was a drastic requirement in the interest of the public health that tenement houses be searched for garments in process of manufacture, and goods found exposed in homes to contagious diseases be destroyed on the spot. Owners of goods produced under the sweating system were required to furnish to the inspectors on demand complete lists of names and addresses of both contractors and home workers.

The bill created a state factory inspection department on which was conferred power, with regard to tenement-made goods found on infected premises, unique in this country in 1893. Illinois changed, at a single stride, from no legislation restricting working hours in manufacture for men, women or children, by day, by night, or by the week, to a maximum eight-hour-day for girls and for women of all ages, in all branches of manufacture. . . .

. . . When the new law took effect, and its usefulness depended upon the personnel prescribed in the text to enforce it,

Governor Altgeld offered the position of chief inspector to Mr. Lloyd, who declined it and recommended me. I was accordingly made chief state inspector of factories, the first and so far as I know, the only woman to serve in that office in any state. . . .

My first effort to apply the penalty for employing children below the age of sixteen years without the prescribed working paper, led me to the office of the district attorney for Cook County. This was a brisk young politician with no interest whatever in the new law and less in the fate of the persons for whose benefit it existed. The evidence in the case I laid before him was complete. An eleven-year-old boy, illegally engaged to gild cheap picture frames by means of a poisonous fluid, had lost the use of his right arm, which was paralyzed. There was no compensation law and no prohibition of work in hazardous occupations. There was only a penalty of twenty dollars for employing a child without the required certificate. The young official looked at me with impudent surprise and said in a tone of astonishment:

"Are you calculating on *my* taking this case?"

I said: "I thought you were the district attorney."

"Well," he said, "suppose I am. You bring me this evidence this week against some little two-by-six cheap picture-frame maker, and how do I know you won't bring me a suit against Marshall Field next week? Don't count on me. I'm overloaded. I wouldn't reach this case inside of two years, taking it in its order."

That day I registered as a student in the Law School of Northwestern University for the approaching fall term, and received in June, 1894, a degree from that University whose graduates were automatically empowered to practice before the Supreme Court of Illinois. Credit was given for my reading law with Father in Washington in 1882, my study in Zurich, and one year in the senior class in Chicago. The lectures were given in the evening and did not interfere with my administrative work.

BLANCHE WIESEN COOK
Female Support Networks and Political Activism: Lillian Wald, Crystal Eastman, Emma Goldman

---

In her passion to create a more just and humane society, Florence Kelley was typical of a remarkable generation of female reformers and radicals. As a divorcée (she had married in Zurich) and the mother of three children, she

Excerpted from "Female Support Networks and Political Activism: Lillian Wald, Crystal Eastman, Emma Goldman" by Blanche Wiesen Cook, in *Chrysalis* 3 (1977):43–61. Copyright © 1977 by Blanche Wiesen Cook. Reprinted by permission of the author. Notes have been renumbered.

did not typify her many colleagues who, like Jane Addams, were single and childless. Writing about those women in the 1950s, historian Ray Ginger strongly suggested that exciting, useful, and important as their work might be, it was ultimately best understood as a compromise "that helped to reconcile so many brilliant women to an unmarried, childless, career-cloistered life."* This last phrase may tell us more about the assumptions of its author and popular attitudes of the 1950s than it does of the way Jane Addams viewed her own life. Did *she* think her career was a compromise, valuable primarily as consolation for a marriage and children she could not have?

The sensitive essay that follows reflects a very different interpretation of the choices Addams and her friends made. It is a particularly good example of the way in which historians' interpretations may be shaped by the cultural climate in which they write; virtually all of the material Blanche Wiesen Cook uses was available to Ray Ginger.

What does Cook mean by the phrase "female support networks"? To what extent does her interpretation extend the suggestion made in the last paragraph of Carroll Smith-Rosenberg's essay "The Female World of Love and Ritual" (part IIA)? How does Cook evoke private lives in order to point toward a more precise understanding of the ways in which these women built public careers?

In Vera Brittain's *Testament of Friendship,* the biography of her beloved friend Winifred Holtby, the British activist and author wrote that

> From the days of Homer the friendships of men have enjoyed glory and acclamation, but the friendships of women, in spite of Ruth and Naomi, have usually been not merely unsung, but mocked, belittled and falsely interpreted. . . .[1]

Part of the problem is general in scope and involves a distorted vision of the historian's craft that is no longer operable. Historians of my generation were trained to believe that the proper study of our past should be limited to the activities of great men—the wars of kings, the hero's quest for power. We were taught that the personal was separate from the political and that emotions were irrelevant to history.

Recent history and the movements of the sixties, the decade of our professional

maturing, have revealed the absurdity of that tradition. It has become clear that in history, no less than in life, our personal choices and the nature of our human relationships were and remain inseparable from our political, our public efforts. Once the personal impact of such confined historical perspective emerged, the need for revision became clear.

In my own work, ten years of work on the historical peace movement—studies that included such significant women as Lillian Wald, Jane Addams, Crystal Eastman, and Emma Goldman—I had focused entirely on women's political contributions. I wrote about their programs for social justice and their opposition to international war. Nothing else. Whenever I came across a love letter by Lillian Wald, for example, I would note "love letter," and move on.

This paper is the result of a long overdue recognition that the personal is the political: that networks of love and sup-

* Ray Ginger, *Altgeld's America* (New York, 1958), p. 139.

port are crucial to our ability as women to work in a hostile world where we are not in fact expected to survive. And it comes out of a recognition that frequently the networks of love and support that enable politically and professionally active women to function independently and intensively consist largely of other women.

LILLIAN WALD,
CRYSTAL EASTMAN,
EMMA GOLDMAN

Beyond their commitment to economic and social change and their opposition to America's entrance into World War I, Lillian Wald, Crystal Eastman, Emma Goldman, and Jane Addams had very little in common. They are of different generations, represent contrary political solutions, and in private lives reflect a broad range of choice. Yet all four women expanded the narrow contours of women's role and all four left a legacy of struggle against poverty and discrimination.

Jane Addams and Lillian Wald were progressive social reformers. The most famous of the settlement-house crusaders, Wald created the Henry Street Settlement and Visiting Nurse Service in New York while Addams founded Hull-House in Chicago.

Crystal Eastman, a generation younger than Addams and Wald, was an attorney and journalist who investigated labor conditions and work accidents. In 1907 she authored New York State's first workman's compensation law, which became the model for most such laws in the United States. One of the three founders of Alice Paul's Congressional Union for suffrage, Eastman was a socialist and radical feminist who believed in "free love."

More outspoken and less respectful of authority than Addams and Wald, Eastman nevertheless worked closely with

them in the peace movement. Wald was president of the American Union Against Militarism, the parent organization of the American Civil Liberties Union, and Eastman was its executive secretary. Addams was president of the Woman's Peace Party (renamed the Women's International League for Peace and Freedom), and Eastman, also one of its founders, was president of the New York branch. Their differences of temperament and tactics tell us much about the nature of the women's movement during the rapidly changing era of World War I.[2]

Emma Goldman was outside their company, but always in the vanguard of their activity. Addams, Wald, and Eastman worked to improve immigrant and labor conditions. Goldman, an anarchist immigrant worker, sought to recreate society. They worked within the law to modify it. Goldman worked without the law to replace it with anarchist principles of voluntary communism.

Goldman frequently visited the Nurses' Settlement on Henry Street and liked Lillian Wald and her co-workers, particularly Lavinia Dock, well enough. She thought them "women of ideals, capable of fine, generous deeds." But she disapproved of their work and feared that their activities created "snobbery among the very people they were trying to help." Although Jane Addams was influenced by anarchist writings, Goldman regarded her even more critically. She thought Addams an elitist snob.[3]

Emma Goldman's work with Crystal Eastman on behalf of birth control, the legalization of prostitution, and free speech in wartime was also dissatisfying. They agreed on more issues: but when Eastman and her circle were on the same picket line or in the same park distributing birth-control literature with Goldman and her allies, only Goldman's group would be arrested. That was the nature of class in America.

Wald, Eastman, and Addams worked

to keep America out of war through the American Union Against Militarism (AUAM). They dined at the White House with Wilson and his advisors. They hired professional lobbyists to influence Congress, Goldman worked through the Antimilitarist League and spoke throughout the United States on the capitalist nature of war and the cruelties of the class system. When she was arrested, the Civil Liberties Bureau of the AUAM defended her; but the members of the AUAM were not themselves arrested. Goldman's wartime activities resulted in her deportation. Wald and Addams received commendations from the government because, in addition to their anti-war work, they allowed their settlement houses to be used as conscription centers.[4]

As different as their political visions and choice of strategies were, Addams and Wald, Eastman and Goldman were dedicated to a future society that guaranteed economic security and the full development of individual potential for women and men on the basis of absolute equality. Reformists, socialist, anarchist, all four women made contributions toward progressive change that are today being dismantled. The playgrounds, parks, and school lunch facilities they built are falling apart all over America because of lack of funding and a callous disregard for the needs of our country's children. The free-speech and human-rights issues they heralded are today facing a reawakened backlash that features the needs of "national security" and a fundamentalist Christianity that seems more appropriate to the seventeenth century.

The Historical Denial of Lesbianism

The vigor and strength of these four women, born daughters in a society that reared daughters to be dependent and servile, cannot be explained without an understanding of their support networks and the nature of their private lives. Their lifestyles varied as dramatically as did their public activities from the prescribed norm of "wife-mother in obedient service to husband-father" that their culture and their era valued above all.

Of the four women, only Emma Goldman relied predominantly on men for emotional sustenance and political support. Although she was close to many anarchist and radical women, there were few with whom she had intimate and lasting relations. The kind of communal and noncompetitive intimacy of the settlement houses or the younger feminist movement Crystal Eastman was associated with was never a feature of Goldman's life.

Yet throughout her life, Goldman wrote, she "longed for a friend of my own sex, a kindred spirit with whom I could share the innermost thoughts and feelings I could not express to men. . . . Instead of friendship from women I had met with much antagonism, petty envy and jealousy because men liked me." There were exceptions, and Goldman listed them in her autobiography. But basically, she concluded, "there was no personal, intimate point of contact."[5]

Like Goldman, Crystal Eastman was also surrounded by men who shared her work, her vision, and her commitment to social change. Unlike Goldman, she had a feminist support group as well. Her allies consisted of her husband (particularly her second husband, Walter Fuller), her brother Max, and the women who were her friends, many of them from childhood and Vassar until her early death in 1928. Eastman's comrades were the "new women" of Greenwich Village. Radical feminists and socialists, they considered men splendid lovers and friends, but they believed that women needed the more egalitarian support of other women. For Crystal Eastman and her associates this was not only an emotional choice, it was a political necessity.

Jane Addams and Lillian Wald were involved almost exclusively with women who remained throughout their lives a nurturing source of love and support.

Henry Street and Hull House were staffed by their closest friends, who, night and day, made possible their unrelenting schedules.

In the past, historians tended to ignore the crucial role played by the networks of love and support that have been the very sources of strength that enabled political women to function. Women's friendships were obscured and trivialized. Whether heterosexual or homosexual, the private lives of political women were declared beyond the acceptable boundaries of historical inquiry. As a result, much of our history and the facts that define our heritage have been removed from our consciousness. Homophobia, a bigotry that declares woman-loving women an evil before God or a mental disease or both, has served to erase the very aspects of our history that would have enabled us to deal healthfully with what has been for most lesbians an isolating and cruel experience. Homophobia has also erased a variety of role-models whose existence would tend to obliterate crude and dehumanizing stereotypes. . . .

This denial has persisted over time. The figures that serve as the frontispiece for Dolores Klaich's book *Woman + Woman* symbolize the problem. We see a sculpture, dated c. 200 B.C., of two women in a tender and erotic embrace. It has been called by the curators of the British Museum, "Women Gossiping."

Similarly, companionate women who have lived together all their adult lives have been branded "lonely spinsters." When their letters might reveal their love, their papers have often been rendered unavailable.* Interpreting Freud through a Victorian prism and thinking it enlight-

* See Dolores Klaich, *Woman + Woman: Attitudes Toward Lesbianism* (Morrow, 1974). The recently successful pressure to open the Mary E. Woolley Papers at Mt. Holyoke is a case in point. The famous college president lived with the chairwoman of the English Department, Jeannette Marks, for many years. They were lovers. When that fact was discovered their papers were closed.

ened, male historians have concluded that the settlement-house reformers were asexual women who sublimated their passionate energies into their work. Since they were not recognizably "dykes" on the order of Radclyffe Hall or Gertrude Stein, and they always functioned too successfully to be called "sick," the historical evidence was juggled to deny the meaning of their lifestyles altogether.

So, for example, William O'Neill can refer to the 40-year relationship between Mary Rozet Smith and Jane Addams as that of "spouse-surrogates" and then conclude: "Finally, one suspects, the very qualities that led [Addams] to reject the family claim prevented her from experiencing the human reality that she celebrated in her writings and defied convention to encounter. She gave her time, money, and talents entirely to the interests of the poor. . . . In a sense she rejected the personal claims upon her, . . . and remained largely untouched by the passionate currents that swirled around her. The crowning irony of Jane Addams's life, therefore, was that she compromised her intellect for the sake of human experiences which her nature prevented her from having. Life, as she meant the term, forever eluded her."[6]

Allen Davis observes a different phenomenon. "It would be easy to misunderstand," Davis writes, the friendship and affection between Jane Addams and her early companion Ellen Gates Starr. Quoting Gordon Haight, Davis concludes: " 'The Victorian conception of love between those of the same sex cannot be fairly understood by an age steeped in Freud—where they say only beautiful friendship, the modern reader suspects perversion.' "[7]

It is important to understand the language here. We are being told that, since Jane Addams was a conventional lady with pearls, her intense "romantic attachments" to other women could not possibly be suspected of "perversion." As a result, the perfectly ordinary nature of women's differing sexual preferences has been denied expression. Without information and history, we have become ignorant of the range of our choices. Repression and conformity have been fostered and an entire generation of activist and passionate women branded by historians, on no evidence whatsoever, as "asexual."

Our prejudices are such that it has been considered less critical—kinder, even—to label a woman "asexual" rather than "lesbian." . . .

More sensitive than most male historians, Allen Davis notes that although the romantic words and the love letters "can be easily misinterpreted," what is important is "that many unmarried women drew warmth and strength from their supportive relationships with other women." But he concludes that "whether or not these women were actually lesbians is essentially irrelevant."[8]

If we lived in a society where individual choice and the diversity of our human rhythms were honored, the actuality of lesbianism would in fact be irrelevant. But we live in a society where children are taken away from lesbian mothers, where teachers are fired for bedroom activities, where in June 1976 the Supreme Court endorsed the imprisonment of consenting adults for homosexual relations, and where as I sit typing this paper—in June 1977—the radio announces that Dade County, Florida, by a vote of 2:1, has supported Anita Bryant's hate campaign against homosexuals.

Such legal and social manifestations of bigotry and repression have been reinforced and are validated by the historical rejection and denial of diversity in general and of independent and alternative lifestyles among women in particular. It is the very conventionality of women like Jane Addams and Lillian Wald that is significant. Not until our society fully accepts as moral and ordinary the wide range of personal choice will differences be "essentially irrelevant."

As I think about Anita Bryant's campaign to "Save Our Children" from homosexuality, my thoughts turn to Lillian Wald, who insisted that every New York City public school should have a trained nurse in residence and who established free lunch programs for the city's school children. My thoughts then turn to Jane Addams, who, in an essay called, "Women, War and Babies," wrote:

> As women we are the custodians of the life of the ages and we will not longer consent to its reckless destruction. We are particularly charged with the future of childhood, the care of the helpless and the unfortunate, and we will not longer endure without protest that added burden of maimed and invalid men and poverty-stricken women and orphans which war places on us.
>
> We have built by the patient drudgery of the past the basic foundations of the home and of peaceful industry; we will not longer endure that hoary evil which in an hour destroys or tolerate that denial of the sovereignty of reason and justice by which war and all that makes for war today render impotent the idealism of the race.[9]

And in the wake of the first mid-twentieth-century American vote to discriminate against an entire group of people,[10] my thoughts turn again to Lillian Wald and Jane Addams, who campaigned for the creation of the United States Children's Bureau. That bureau set up programs throughout the United States to care for battered wives and battered children; it crusaded against child labor and for humane child care.[11] Yet Anita Bryant would demand that we save our children from Jane Addams if Anita Bryant knew that Jane Addams slept in the same house, in the same room, in the same bed with Mary Rozet Smith for 40 years. (And when they travelled, Addams even wired ahead to order a large double bed for their hotel room.)

Because difference arouses fear and condemnation, there are serious methodological problems involved in writing about women who, for political and economic reasons, kept their private lives as secret as possible. The advent of the homosexual "closet" at the end of the nineteenth century was not accidental. Oscar Wilde had, after all, been released from prison on 19 May 1897. In addition to the criminal stigma now attached to homosexuality, a sudden explosion of "scientific" publications on "sexual disorders" and "perversions" appeared at the turn of the century. Nancy Sahli, historian and archivist, reports that in the first series of 16 volumes of the *Index Catalogue of the Library of the Surgeon General's Office, U.S. Army,* covering the years 1740 to 1895, only one article ("A Case of Man-Impersonation") dealt specifically with lesbians. In the second series, published between 1896 and 1916, there were over 90 books and 566 articles listed that related to women's "perversions," "inversions," and "disorders."[12]

Secrecy is not a surprising response to this psychoanalytic assault. How then, male historians continually ask, do you know these women were lesbians? Even if we were to assume that Addams and Smith never in 40 years in the same bed touched each other, we can still argue that they were lesbians because they chose each other. Women who love women, who choose women to nurture and support and to create a living environment in which to work creatively and independently, are lesbians.

It may seem elementary to state here that lesbians cannot be defined simply as women who practice certain physical rites together. Unfortunately, the heterosexist image—and sometimes even the feminist image—of the lesbian is defined by sexual behavior alone, and sexual in the most limited sense. It therefore seems important to reiterate that physical love between women is one expression of a whole range of emotions and responses to each other that involves all the mysteries of our human nature. Women-related women feel attraction, yearning, and excitement with women. Nobody and no theory has yet explained why for some women, despite all cultural conditioning and societal penalties, both intellectual and emotional excitement are aroused in response to women.

LILLIAN WALD

Besides, there *is* evidence of these women's lesbianism. Although Lillian Wald's two volumes of memoirs are about as personal as her entry in *Who's Who among American Women,* her letters underscore the absurdity of a taxi conversation that Mabel Hyde Kittredge reported to Wald after a meeting at Henry Street:

1st man:	*Those women are really lonely.*
Second man:	*Why under the sun are they lonely?*
1st man:	*Any woman is lonely without a man.*

Unlike Jane Addams, Lillian Wald seems not to have had one particular "great friend," and the chronology of the women in her life, with their comings and goings, is impossible to follow. There are gaps and surprises throughout over 150 boxes of correspondence. But all of Lillian Wald's companions appear to have been friends for life.

Wald's basic support group consisted of the long-term residents of Henry Street, Ysabella Waters, Anne Goodrich, Florence Kelley, Helene MacDowell, and Lavinia L. Dock. They worked together on all projects, lived and vacationed together for over 50 years, and, often in company with the women of Hull House, travelled together to Europe, Japan, Mexico, and the West Indies.

But the letters are insufficient to tell us the specifics of her life. There are turmoils that we will probably never know anything about—upheavals that result, for example, in a 10-year hiatus in Wald's correspondence with Lavinia Dock. This hiatus, combined with the fact that in November 1915, after 20 years, "Docky" moved out of the Henry Street Settlement and, in an icy and formal note of March 1916, even resigned from the Henry Street Corporation, remains unexplained. There is also the puzzling fact that Dock, the ardent suffragist, feminist and socialist, a pioneer of American nursing education and organization, appears to be R. L. Duffus' major source of information—beyond Wald herself—for his 1938 biography, *Lillian Wald: Neighbor and Crusader*. The first letter to appear in the collection after Dock's 1916 resignation is dated 1925 and implies that the two women have not had a long-term falling out at all:

> why-dear-I was imagining you radiating around the town telling about Mexico and here you are in the hospital just like any commonplace person—oh dear oh dear! . . . Dearest I would scrape up some money if you need—you have often done the same for me . . . and I am not telling anyone that you are ill and in the hospital for I know how you would dislike being thought just a mere mortal. . . .[13]

It is clear from another letter that Dock went to New York to be with Wald during her first operation. She wrote Wald's nurse that she was so relieved the tumor turned out to be benign that "for the first time my knees wobbled as I went down the steps to go to the train. . . ." The next week Dock wrote to Wald: "Dearest—I'm not sure whether to give you letters yet so I haven't written before and just send this line to tell you that you do your illnesses and recoveries in the same dazzling form and with the same vivacity and originality as all your other deeds; With Love/Ever yours/ Docky."

Why then did Dock leave? Was there a personal reason? A new lover? An old anger? Or was it connected with the polit-

ical differences that emerged between them in 1915 when Wald became more absorbed by antimilitarist activities and Dock, also a pacifist, joined the radical suffragist movement of Alice Paul's Congressional Union? All the evidence indicates that the only significant differences between these women at this time were political. Their lives were dedicated to work each regarded as just and right. When they disagreed so intensively that they could no longer support and nurture each other's activities, they temporarily parted. . . .

During the war, while Wald was meeting with President Wilson and being as conciliatory as possible on behalf of the peace movement, Dock and the militant suffragists were infuriating official Washington, getting themselves arrested, and generally aggravating the very people Wald was attempting to persuade—and for a different purpose.

Dock considered Paul's Congressional Union "fresh-young-glorious." She wrote to Paul in June 1915: "Pay no attention to criticism. Go right ahead with your splendid daring and resourcefulness of youth." Dock reacted furiously to criticism that the Congressional Union's confrontational tactics not only harmed the suffrage movement but threatened the peace movement. And Lillian Wald was one of the leading critics of such tactics. On this issue they disagreed utterly. Dock was adamant: "And what is this terrible burden of responsibility and anxiety now resting on the American Men's President? Is it arising from anything women have done or are going to do? Not at all. . . . I can't see it—surely there could be no more appropriate moment for women to press forward with their demand for a voice—women—who are at this moment going on errands of peace—and who are being called a national menace for doing so—followed wherever he goes, by the demand which, so long as it remains unanswered shows a painful insincerity in those rounded and sonorous paragraphs on American ideals and American freedom that he utters so eloquently. . . ."[14]

Five months after this exchange, Lavinia Dock moved permanently out of her Henry Street home of 20 years. I have not yet found one correspondence between her and Wald that deals with the event. And all Wald says about Dock in *Windows on Henry Street* is that "Everyone admired her, none feared her, though she was sometimes very fierce in her denunciations. Reputed a man-hater, we knew her as a lover of mankind."

WALD'S OTHER SUPPORT NETWORK

There were two other categories of women close to Wald and the settlement. The first consisted of affluent women such as Irene and Alice Lewisohn and Rita Morgenthau. Younger than Wald, they admired her and regarded her as a maternal figure. She in turn nurtured their spirits, supported their ambitions, and provided them with sustaining and secure friendship. They, together with Wald's "friend of friends" Jacob Schiff, contributed tirelessly and abundantly to Henry Street. The Lewisohns founded the Neighborhood Play House and supported the famous music and dance education projects that continue to this day. They were also coworkers in the Woman's Peace Party and the American Union Against Militarism. On occasion they travelled with Wald. And they wrote numerous letters of affection and devotion to their dear "Lady Light." Alice Lewisohn frequently signed her letters "Your Baby Alice." One letter from Irene, conveying love and gratitude after a trip the Lewisohn sisters took with Ysabella Waters and Wald, is replicated in the collection by scores of others:

Why attempt to tell a clairvoyant all that is in one's mind? You know even better than I what those months of companion-

ship with you and Sister Waters have meant. For way and beyond even the joys of our wanderings I have some memories that are holier by far than temples or graves or blossoms. A fireside romance and a moonlight night are among the treasures carefully guarded. . . . As an offering for such inspirations, I am making a special vow to be and to do. . . . Much of my heart to you!

Wald's closest friend among the younger nonresidents appears to have been Rita Wallach Morgenthau, who generally signed her letters with love from "Your Daughter," "Your Foolish Daughter," or "Your Spoiled Child." However much Wald may have spoiled her "adoptive daughters," the very fact of her nurturing presence helped establish the nature of their life's work; and their work focused on social change and the education, dance, and theatre programs they created.[15] . . .

All of Wald's friends and correspondents wrote of how she inspired them, fired their imaginations, and directed their lives to greater heights of consciousness and activity. Lavinia Dock referred to this quality in a letter to Duffus for his biography of Wald: "She believed absolutely in human nature and as a result the best of it was shown to her. People just naturally turned their best natures to her scrutiny and developed what she perceived in them, when it had been dormant and unseen in them before. I remember often being greatly impressed by this inner vision that she had. . . ."[16]

The last group of women involved with Wald and the settlement differed basically from the other two. Although they also served as residents or volunteered their time to Henry Street, they were "society women" perhaps more interested in Wald than in social change. Such long-term residents as Dock, Waters, and MacDowell, and Wald's younger friends, Morgenthau and the Lewisohns, supported Wald emotionally and politically and shared collectively in all her interests. The society women, however, attempted to possess or monopolize Wald, lamented that her activities kept her from them, and were finally rebuffed in what must have been thoroughly specific terms. Generally they fell into that trap that Margaret Anderson defined so well: "In real love you want the other person's good. In romantic love you want the other person."[17]

Lillian Wald had structured her life to avoid becoming anybody's possession. While she did get involved in emotional enthusiasms, as soon as the woman involved sought to redirect her priorities Wald's enthusiasm evaporated.

The clearest representatives of the society group were Mabel Hyde Kittredge and Helen Arthur. Both women were rich "uptowners" who spent many years "downtown." Both were highly educated, hardworking, and demanding. Both devoted their time to good works, in large part because their friendship with Wald encouraged them to think politically, and not because social change was their life's commitment. But they were loyal. Kittredge, for example, evidently left Henry Street because Wald encouraged her to do so. Yet she continued to be involved in settlement activities, helped organize the free lunch program in public schools in 1908, and founded the Association of Practical Housekeeping Centers that operated as a subsidiary organization for many years.

To understand Lillian Wald fully, it is necessary to deal with her relationship with Mabel Hyde Kittredge. Kittredge's demands seem on occasion outrageous, and her biases are transparent. Yet it is clear that for a time Wald was not only smitten by this lady, but relied upon her for comfort and trusted her deeply.

A Park Avenue socialite who frequently played bridge whist all night after she had played in a golf tournament all day, Kittredge was the daughter of

Reverend Abbott E. Kittredge of the prominent Madison Avenue Church. After she had lived at Henry Street for several years, she wrote to Wald on 28 April 1904 that she understood Wald's objections to what appears to have been a moment of flagrant ethnic bigotry: "I believe that I will never again say 'my people and *your* people.' It may be that even though I have no prejudice I have used words and expressions that have done something to keep the lines drawn between the two peoples. . . ."

Whatever her views, it appears that when Wald was troubled she turned for a time to Kittredge. In a long letter of tender assurance and sensible advice to Wald concerning a bereaved friend, Kittredge wrote:

> . . . I seemed to hold you in my arms and whisper all this. . . . If you want me to stay all night tomorrow night just say so when you see me. . . . Please dont feel that I keep before me the signs of sorrow that you trusted me enough to let me see —of the things of Thursday evening that are consciously with me are first the fact that in a slight degree I can share with you the pain that you suffer. Then I can hear you say "I love you"—and again and again I can see in your eyes the strength, and the power and the truth that I love but the confidence in yourself not there. All this I have before me— never a thought of weakness because you dared to be human. Why dear I knew that you were human before Thursday night— I think though that our love never seemed quite so real a thing before then. Good night.

But after 1904 most of Kittredge's letters became competitive—Kittredge *vs.* humanity in their claims on Wald's attentions. Wald evidently reserved one night in the week for Kittredge and then occasionally cancelled their date, infuriating her friend:

> Just because you have reformed on Tuesday night—I havent got to give you en-

tirely to humanity. I am human too and tonight I'd keep you up until—well later than Miss MacDowell would approve of—if I had you. . . .

On a similar evening Kittredge wrote that she had just done two very sensible things, not telephoned to say good night and torn up a whiny letter:

But what business has a great grown woman like myself to sit up in her night-clothes and write nothings. . . . I am getting altogether too close to you Lady Wald—or is it . . . all those doors that you have pushed open for me? Half open-dear-just half open. And then I come up here and grow hungry for more knowledge. . . . And I feel that my strength ends and love you so. . . . I can feel your arms around me as you say I really must go.

When Wald cancelled a visit to Kittredge at Monmouth Beach, she wrote: "And so the verdict has gone forth—I can't have you. . . . But even you must want the ocean at times instead of Henry Street. . . ."

Wald did want the ocean at times. More than that, she sought the relaxation and comfort of Kittredge's friendship. During a business trip that was evidently particularly hectic, Wald wrote to Kittredge from Chattanooga that she looked forward to long, quiet, cosy evenings on the back porch. Kittredge replied that Wald's letter "was a real life-giving thing." But she no longer believed that Wald would actually make such free time possible and wrote: "When Lady Lillian is that cosy time to be? Miss MacDowell says not after midnight and your humanity world would not let me have you before. 'Long evenings on the back porch'—it sounds fine—and improbable. . . ."

Eventually Kittredge's jealousy extended from humanity in general to the residents of Henry Street in particular:

If you think that I wasnt damned mad today it is simply that I have inherited

so much self-control and sweetness from my minister parent that the fact was hidden. . . .

There are times when to know that Miss Clark is standing behind one curtain, Miss MacDowell behind another and to feel an endless lot of people forever pressing the door or presenting unsigned papers makes me lack that perfect sympathy with "work for others" as exemplified by a settlement. No wonder I am called "one of your crushes." . . . It is kiss and run or run without kissing—there really isnt time for anything else. . . .

After what appears to have been for Kittredge a particularly difficult Christmas season, she gave up entirely the competition for Wald's affections:

These may be "Merry" days but they starve one to death as far as any satisfaction in calm, every day loving and talking goes. . . . I would very much like to meet you on a desert island or a farm where the people cease from coming and the weary are at rest—will the day ever come? Or is that white ring, those long, lazy drives, the quiet and the yellow trees only a lost dream? And yet you love me—the plant on my table tells me so. The new coffee tray tells me so . . . and a look that I see in your eyes makes me sure. . . .

Refusing to participate, evidently for the first time, in Henry Street's Christmas festivities, Kittredge wrote that she was

. . . not loveless nor lonely. I am free and strong and alive and awfully happy—But someway as I think back over this year, I believe that I needed you—it may be as much as the others— . . . I know that it would be a loss out of my life if my thoughts of you, my love for you and my confidence in you were taken away—I don't believe they ever could be less than they are tonight. . . .[18]

Judging from the letters, whatever gap the loss of Mabel Hyde Kittredge's friendship may have opened Wald seems to have filled by that summer. Wald vacationed through August and September

1906 with another society woman, Helen Arthur, an attorney and director of the research department of the Woman's Municipal League. Helen Arthur seems to have been more spontaneous and less complaining than Kittredge; and she had a sense of humor. . . .

Arthur was also more dependent on Wald, and in this relationship Wald's maternal aspects were more evident. She coaxed Arthur out of repeated depressions, encouraged her law practice, managed her finances, and kept her bankbook so that she would not overspend. This last made Arthur pout, especially during one Christmas season when she wrote to Wald that she tried to buy "exactly 28 presents for $10 worth of currency without visiting the 5 and 10 cent store which is, I regret to say, not on the Consumer's League list! If you were at 265 Henry Street—I should hold you up for my bankbook—What's vacation money compared to Christmas toys—Surely it is more blessed to give than to receive interest on deposits! Couldn't you be an old dear and let me rob it for a month? Please, mommy."

When Wald travelled, Arthur wrote long newsy letters about her law cases and activities; but they all concluded or began with a note of despair that her good mother had left her sad or naughty "son" all alone: "Such a strange feeling— no one to telephone me no 'Hello-de-e-ar' to listen for—Rainy horrid day outside and a lonesome atmosphere within. . . ." At another time she wrote "I am as near blue tonight as green can ever get and if I just had my nicest mommy to snuggle up to and talk it out straight for her son, I'd feel less like a disbarred judge. . . . Couldnt you write me a note and tell me—something?"

Eventually, Wald's busy schedule resulted in disappointments, cancelled dates, loneliness for Arthur, and what must have been for Wald familiar letters of discontent:

Dearest, nothing could have relieved the gloom of this day except the presence of the one person her secretary notified me not to expect. . . . Now that I am being severely left alone—I have much time to spend in my own room—the walls of which formerly saw . . . me only from 2 until 7 a.m. . . . I've put you—the dear old you in your silver frame on my desk and close to me when I write and I shoved my decanter and cigarette case to the other side—if I had you, the real you instead of one-ten-thousandth part of you I might shove the unworthy things way off—Summertime has spoiled the judge who longs to get back to your comfortable lap and the delights of kicking her pajammaed legs in peace and comfort instead of being solicitously hustled from your room at 10 o'clock. . . .

In another letter, Arthur, like so many others, expressed her desire to live up to Wald's expectations of her: "If only I could pull out of my easy ways—the pleasant vices which hinder me so. . . ." But her physical longing for Wald was equally powerful. The two combined to explain Wald's magnetism: "If only August and September, 1906 were all the year round for me, but their memories stay by and perhaps some day you'll be proud of your small judge. . . . I think so often of the hundreds who remember you with affection and of the tens who openly adore you and I appreciate a little what it all means and I'm grateful to think that your arms have been close around me and that you did once upon a time, kiss me goodnight and even good morning, and I am your lonesome little/Judge."

Arthur, more than many others, was genuinely mindful of Wald's time and her emotional needs. On 30 January 1907, she wrote that "Little by little there is being brought in upon me, the presumption of my love for you—the selfishness of its demands, the triviality of its complaints— and more slowly still, is coming the realization of what it ought to bring to you and what I mean it shall. . . ."[19]

Whatever special friend came or went in Lillian Wald's life, the women of Henry Street, the residents who called themselves her "steadies," were the mainstay of her support. The women in Wald's communal family served each other as well as society. There was nothing self-sacrificing about that community: It was a positive choice. For Wald it was the essential key to her life—and the only aspect of her personal life about which she wrote clearly. On the 40th anniversary of the settlement, Wald wrote: "I came with very little program of what could or should be done. I was perhaps conscious only of a passionate desire to have people, who had been separated and who for various causes were not likely to come together, know each other that they might sympathize and understand the problems and difficulties of each other. I made no sacrifices. My friend Mary Brewster [the first coworker at Henry Street] and I were engrossed in the edifice which was taking form and in which my friends and I might dwell together."[20]

Wald and her friends lived together for over 50 years. At the end, during long years of pain and poor health, she was surrounded by love and support. After her first operation, Mabel Hyde Kittredge wrote to Wald that "at least you must feel that this is a world full of friends and love and sympathy. I hope all the bread you ever cast upon any waters has come back fresh and lovely and so much as to be a surprise. . . ." On the morning of her death, Lillian Wald turned to her nurse and said, "I'm a very happy woman . . . because I've had so many people to love, and so many to love me."[21]

The letters in the Wald collections document only a fragment of her life, and they raise as many questions as they answer. Because we can never know the intimate details of people's lives if they are censored, withheld, or destroyed, we are confined to the details we have. But the details we have make it abundantly clear that Lillian Wald lived in a homosocial world that was also erotic. Her primary emotional needs and desires were fulfilled by women. She was woman-supported, woman-allied. Once that has been established, it becomes entirely unnecessary to pursue evidence of a specific variety of genital contact. Beyond a certain point, we get into fairly small-minded questions of technique. Since society's presumption of heterosexuality stops short of any inquiry as to what the husband and wife do atop their conjugal bed, it is only to indulge our prejudices that we demand "evidence" of lesbianism from conventional or famous women. Insistence on genital evidence of proof for a lesbian identity derives from a male model that has very little to do with the love, support, and sensuality that exist among women.

EMMA GOLDMAN

Emma Goldman wrote vividly about the difficulties faced by people who attempt to express themselves in harmony with their own nature. In a 1906 essay, "The Child and Its Enemies," she wrote that society employs all its forces to mould out of all our human differences a thing of dehumanized, patterned regularity: "Every institution . . . , the family, the state, our moral codes, sees in every strong, beautiful uncompromising personality a deadly enemy." Every effort is made, from earliest infancy, "to cramp human emotion and originality of thought" in order to create "a patient work slave, professional automaton, taxpaying citizen, or righteous moralist." To that end, all the child's questions "are met with narrow, conventional, ridiculous replies mostly based on falsehoods." Thus uniformity and order, rather than "eternal change, thousandfold variation, continual innovation," have become the hallmarks of our culture.

The full implications of our brutally

deforming institutions were clear to Goldman: "Since every effort in our educational life seems to be directed toward making of the child a being foreign to itself, it must of necessity produce individuals foreign to one another. . . ."[22]

Urged to deny the secrets within our natures and to reject the differences of others, we are taught to be fearful of ourselves and contemptuous of others. Separated from ourselves and isolated from each other, we are encouraged to huddle together for comfort under the socially acceptable banners of racism, sexism, classism, and homophobia. While people are called "human resources" in advanced industrial societies, we are discouraged from seeing the ways in which we are all connected. We are thus rendered powerless and immobilized by our prejudices. This is not an accident.

Ardent feminists and fiercely independent, Emma Goldman and Crystal Eastman depended on men for the comradeship and pleasure Lillian Wald and Jane Addams sought from women. Far more specific about their sexual orientation, Eastman and Goldman wrote about their private lives and their commitment to free love. They made it clear that they refused to be trapped by conventional or legal arrangements such as marriage.

Both were, in the larger sense, maternal women. Crystal Eastman considered the status of the unmarried mother and decided to get married largely for the sake of the two children she would have. Emma Goldman nurtured all her friends and associates. According to Kate Richards O'Hare, Emma Goldman while in prison was, above all, "the tender cosmic mother."

Contrary to the popular notions of "free love" as promiscuous and amoral, Goldman's long-term relations with the men she loved—Sasha Berkman, Ed Brady, Ben Reitman, Max Baginsky, and Hippolyte Havel—were nurturing and tender on her part and devoted and supportive on theirs. They worked for her and cared for her. Ed Brady enabled her to go to Europe to study. Ben Reitman, her manager, served as her "advance man"; he raised money for *Mother Earth* and arranged her speaking tours. These men did not possess her, control her, dominate her, or expect from her more than she would give freely because she loved them as a free woman.

Free love, for Emma Goldman and Crystal Eastman meant simply love given freely to the lover of one's choice. Both rejected the notion that love was a limited commodity. They believed that it was an undefinable sentiment that expanded in proportion to the number of people who evoked it. Possession and jealousy were anathema to them. They rejected the notion that women were love objects to be married into the service and control of men.

Despite the clarity of their writings, their views were frequently misunderstood. The refusal of Eastman and Goldman to separate the personal from the political, their contempt for sham and hypocrisy, and their unfaltering openness about the most intimate subjects horrified their contemporaries. Among the social reformers with whom Crystal Eastman worked, she acquired a reputation as a reckless revolutionary. Her attitudes on free love and her frank affirmation of women's right to physical sexuality appeared hedonistic and horrible. A frequent contributor to feminist journals, her attitudes and behavior—notably her "affairs," divorce, and remarriage were perceived as scandalous. After years of leadership in the peace movement, as founder and president of the Woman's Peace Party of New York and as executive director of the American Union Against Militarism, she was blocked from attending the second meeting at the Hague in 1919 by a committee chaired by Jane Addams, specifically because of Eastman's radical socialism and her espousal of free love.[23]

The reaction of the older social-reform women such as Jane Addams to Crystal

Eastman's lifestyle is not explained by the simple fact that the sword of bigotry is many-edged. The failure of Jane Addams and most social-reform women to analyze traditional assumptions about marriage and sexuality is another byproduct of the societal pressure that kept alternative lifestyles of any kind in the closet for so many years. The settlement-house women were supplicants to the rich on behalf of the poor. Steadfast about their priorities, they frequently made political decisions which were not in harmony with their lives and which locked them into a conservative public position regarding such issues as sexuality.

CRYSTAL EASTMAN'S VISION

Emma Goldman was adamant in her opposition to marriage, which she considered an economic arrangement. Since a wife's body is "capital to be exploited and manipulated, she came to look on success as the size of her husband's income." For Goldman marriage was the very antithesis of love. Why, she asked, should two people who love each other get married? Marriage is an arbitrary, mercenary, legal tie; while it does not bind, it fetters. Only love is free. Love for Emma was "the strongest and deepest element in all life; . . . love, the freest, the most powerful moulder of human destiny; how can such an all-compelling force be synonymous with that poor State-and-Church begotten weed, marriage?"[24]

Although Crystal Eastman shared Goldman's views on marriage, she married twice. But she was not limited or stifled in these marriages and arranged them to suit both her work and her emotional needs. According to one of her closest friends, Jeannette Lowe, Crystal Eastman was free—"You would not believe how free she was."[25] Vigorous and bold, Crystal Eastman discarded her first marriage with alacrity and then sought to revolutionize the institution. In her own life she extended the contours of marriage beyond recognition. During the first years of her second marriage, she and her husband, her brother Max, and several of their friends lived communally.

After the war she, her two children, and her husband, Walter Fuller, lived in England "under two roofs" as ordinary lovers. "He keeps a change of clothes and all the essentials for night and morning comfort at my house, as might a favorite and frequent guest." They phoned each other daily and often met for the theatre or dinner or at a friend's house. After the evening's entertainment they decided, "like married lovers," whether to part on the street or go home together. "Marriage under two roofs makes room for moods." As for the children, "without a scowling father around for breakfast, the entire day began cheerfully. . . ."

Crystal Eastman was, above all, a feminist. She considered the true feminist the most radical member of society. The true feminist, Eastman wrote, begins with the knowledge "that the vast majority of women as well as men are without property, and are of necessity bread and butter slaves under a system which allows the very sources of life to be privately owned by a few, and she counts herself a loyal soldier in the working-class army that is marching to overthrow that system." But she had no illusions about where men in that army placed women. "If we should graduate into communism tomorrow . . . man's attitude to his wife would not be changed." For Eastman, the creation of a communistic society based on sex equality was the task of the organized feminist movement.[26]

Unlike Emma Goldman, who lived almost exclusively among men, Crystal Eastman always had a feminist support group of considerable importance to her life. She was supported by women with whom she had deep and lasting relations: many of the ardent suffragists of the Congressional Union, her friends from Vassar who worked with her in the Woman's Peace Party of New York and who were part of her communal family in Greenwich Village. On several occasions she lived with one or more of these friends, and her experiences enabled her to write in "Now We Can Begin":

> Two business women can "make a home" together without either one being over-burdened or over-bored. It is because they both know how and both feel responsible.
>
> But it is a rare man who can marry one of them and continue the home-making partnership. Yet if there are no children, there is nothing essentially different in the combination. Two self-supporting adults decide to make a home together: if both are women it is a pleasant partnership, more fun than work; if one is a man, it is almost never a partnership— the woman simply adds running the home to her regular outside job. Unless she is very strong, it is too much for her, she gets tired and bitter over it, and finally perhaps gives up her outside work and condemns herself to the tiresome half-job of housekeeping for two.

Crystal Eastman evidently solved that problem for herself by spending her summers in the south of France with Jeannette Lowe and their children, leaving her husband under his separate roof and in his separate country.

Throughout the postwar years Eastman had planned to write a book about women. But in 1928, one year after returning to New York to look for new work, she died of a kidney ailment. She was 47 years old, and her death came as a shock to her friends. Claude McKay wrote: "Crystal Eastman was a great-hearted woman whose life was big with primitive and exceptional gestures. She never wrote that Book of Woman which was imprinted on her mind. She was poor, and fettered with a family. She had a grand idea for a group of us to go off to write in some quiet corner of the world, where living was cheap and easy. But it couldn't be realized. And

so life was cheated of one contribution about women that no other woman could write."[27]

EMMA GOLDMAN AND WOMEN

Emma Goldman's lack of a feminist support group did not affect her adversely until the postwar years. Before and during the war she was surrounded by her anarchist comrades and Ben Reitman. But even then her friends found Reitman distasteful and tended to admonish Goldman for her choice of lovers. Sasha Beckman in particular hated Reitman because he was not dedicated to the revolution, anarchism, or even social change. Margaret Anderson thought that the "fantastic" Dr. Reitman was not "so bad if you could hastily drop all your ideas as to how human beings should look and act. . . ." But Emma loved him and wrote that he "gave without measure or restraint. His best years, his tremendous zest for work, he had devoted to me. It is not unusual for a woman to do as much for the man she loves. Thousands of my sex had sacrificed their own talents and ambitions for the sake of the man. But few men had done so for women. Ben was one of the few; he had dedicated himself completely to my interests."[28] . . .

. . . Before the war Goldman idealized heterosexual relations. In many of her writings she scorned the bourgeois American feminists whose "narrow puritanical vision banished man as a disturber and doubtful character out of their emotional life. . . ." In a March 1906 essay, "The Tragedy of Woman's Emancipation," she argued that the "greatest shortcoming" of the feminist movement was "its narrow respectabilities which produce an emptiness in woman's soul that will not let her drink from the fountain of life." In September 1915 she published a similar editorial in *Mother Earth* by one "R.A.P.," who argued that "American feminists are the exponents of a new slavery," which denied sexual activity, encouraged inhibition, and crusaded against the "sexual victimization of virtuous females by some low, vulgar male." R.A.P. judged the bourgeois feminist movement classist and hypocritical and of "no interest except as an amusing and typical instance of feminine intellectual homosexuality."[29]

This is not to imply that Emma Goldman was homophobic in any intellectual or traditional sense. On the contrary, she was the only woman in America who defended homosexuality in general and the [rights] of Oscar Wilde in particular. Although she was absolute about a person's right to sexual choice, she felt a profound ambivalence about lesbianism, as a lifestyle. She believed that "the body, in all its splendid sensuality, had to be reclaimed from the repressive hands of the prudes and the philistines." When she was criticized by her comrades for dealing with such "unnatural themes as homosexuality," thereby increasing the difficulties of the already misunderstood anarchist movement, she persisted. "I minded the censors of my own ranks as little as I did those in the enemy's camp." Censorship from her comrades had, she wrote, "the same effect on me as police persecution; it made me . . . more determined to plead for every victim, be it of social wrong or of moral prejudice."[30]

There is even some evidence that Goldman may have experimented with a woman herself. The 1912 letters of an anarchist worker, Almeda Sperry, to Goldman are very one-sided. They consist in part of affirmations of passionate love by Sperry and apparent rebuffs by Goldman. These do not deter Sperry, who evidently luxuriated for a time in a state of unrequited yearning: "God how I dream of you! You say that you would like to have me near you always if you were a man, or if you felt as I do. I would not if I could. . . ." In response to Goldman's queries about Sperry's feelings toward men, she replies: "If you mean have I ever loved a man I will frankly say that I never *saw* a man. No, I have never deeply loved any man." Sperry was, however, married, and several letters refer to her affection for her husband.

Then, in the summer of 1912, the letters take a different turn. Sperry thanks Goldman for addressing her with terms of endearment, and . . . she tells Goldman to know, just before she sleeps, that "I kiss your body with biting kisses—I inhale the sweet pungent odor of you and you plead with me for relief." A month later Sperry refers to the week they spent together after all in the country:

Dearest, I have been flitting about from one thing to another . . . to quell my terrible longing for you . . . I am . . . seized with a fire that races over my body in recurrent waves. My last thoughts at night are of you . . . and that hellish alarm clock is losing some of its terrors for me for my first waking thoughts are of you.

Dear, that day you were so kind to me and afterwards took me in your arms, your beautiful throat, that I kissed with a reverent tenderness. . . .

Do you know, sweet cherry-blossom, that my week with you has filled me with such an energy, such an eagerness to become worthy of your friendship, that I feel that I must either use my intensity towards living up to my best self or ending it all quickly in one last, grand debauch. . . .

How I wish I [were] with you on the farm! You are so sweet in the mornings —your eyes are like violets and you seem to forget, for a time, the sorrows of the world. And your bosom—ah, your sweet bosom, unconfined.[31]

There is nothing simple about Goldman's attitude toward lesbianism. She never refers to Almeda Sperry, and it is impossible to know the significance of this correspondence in her life. Her absolute commitment to personal liberty and her total respect for individual choice prompted Magnus Hirschfeld, a leading homosexual rights advocate in Germany and the founder of the Humanitarian Committee, organized in 1897, to write that Goldman was the "only human being of importance in America to carry the issue of homosexual love to the broadest layers of the public."[32]

But in a long article in the 1923 Yearbook of Hirschfeld's committee, Goldman critizes an earlier article on Louise Michel in puzzling terms. Goldman reaffirms her political commitment to free sexual choice and affirms her disinterest in "protecting" Louise Michel from the charge of lesbianism. "Louise Michel's service to humanity and her great work of social liberation are such that they can be neither enlarged nor reduced, whatever her sexual habits were." Then follows a long tirade against minorities who claim for themselves all the earth's significant people, and a longer analysis of why it would be "nonsensical" to assume that Louise Michel was a lesbian. In an ultimately vague and paradoxical paragraph, Goldman concludes: "In short, Louise Michel was a complete woman, free of all the prejudices and traditions which for centuries held women in chains and degraded them to household slaves and objects of sexual lust. The new woman celebrated her resurrection in the figure of Louise, the woman capable of heroic deeds but one who remains a woman in her passion and in her love."[33]

It appears that, in Goldman's mind, to be a lesbian was an absolute right, and nothing nasty about it. But it was also to be rendered somehow less a woman.

EMMA GOLDMAN IN EXILE

In the long years of Emma Goldman's exile, years made lonelier by her political isolation, she wrote a series of letters that explored the difficulties and the pain of being a free and independent woman without a support group that provided emotional nurturance as well as a shared vision of the work to be done. After two years of disappointment in Soviet Russia, Goldman travelled back and forth between England, France, and Germany, seeking to rebuild her shattered life and attempting to convince her friends on the left that her critical analysis of the Soviet experiment was correct. In these letters she revealed the toll on her spirit taken by her personal loneliness and her political isolation. Also revealed is the brutal double standard to which even advanced women in progressive anarchist circles are subjected if their friendships are limited to men. On 28 May 1925 she wrote to Berkman:

> I agree with you that both men and women need some person who really cares. The woman needs it more and finds it impossible to meet anyone when she has reached a certain age. That is her tragedy. . . . I think in the case of one who gave out so much in her life, it is doubly tragic not to have anyone, to really be quite alone. . . . I am consumed by longing for love and affection for some human being of my own.[34] . . .

As Goldman looked back over her life while in exile, even the good times seemed bitter. In a heartbreaking letter to Sasha she deals with the sexist double standard of her closest comrades:

> Where did you ever get the idea that I suspected you of being jealous of Ben in any sexual sense. . . . What I did suspect—more than that what I knew—was that you are a prig who constantly worries about what the comrades will say and how it will affect the movement when you yourself lived your life to suit yourself, I mean as far as women are concerned. It was painful to me, at the time, as it has been on many other occasions, to see you fly the movement in the face a hundred times and then condemn me for doing the same. . . . Do I mean to deny Ben's faults? Of course not, my dear. . . . I knew Ben inside and out two weeks after we went on tour; I not only knew but loathed his sensational ways, his bombast, his braggadocio, and his

promiscuity, which lacked the least sense of selection. But above all that there was something large, primitive, unpremeditated, and simple about Ben which had terrific charm. Had you and the other friends concerned in my salvation recognized this . . . instead of writing to the university to find out about his medical degree (which the boy never could forget). . . . Ben would not have become a renegade. . . . The trouble with you was . . . as with all our comrades, you are a puritan at heart. . . .

I have been too long in the movement not to know how narrow and moral it is, how unforgiving and lacking in understanding toward everyone different from them. . . . You will repeat your objections to Ben were because . . . "he did not belong in our ranks." All right, but what were your objections to Arthur Swenson? He never was in our ranks. Why did you treat him like a dog after he came to Berlin? Why did you fail to understand the terrific turmoil the boy created in my being? . . . Of course it is nonsense to say that the attitude of men and women in their love to younger people is the same. . . . It is nothing of the kind. . . . Hundreds of men marry women much younger than themselves; they have circles of friends; they are accepted by the world. Everybody objects, resents, in fact dislikes a woman who lives with a younger man; they think her a god-damned fool; no doubt she is that, but it is not the business or concern of friends to make her look and feel like a fool. . . .

In another letter Emma tried to console Sasha after the sudden departure of his former lover Fitzie. Secretary of the Provincetown Players, Eleanor Fitzgerald had been Sasha's companion until his arrest during World War I. In 1928 she arrived in St. Tropez to be with Djuna Barnes and to visit Berkman. Although the events are unclear, Goldman's letters of explanation for Fitzie's behavior over several years formulate her own reflections on the struggle of women to be liberated: "Here we have been worrying about who

should meet Fitzie, then that crazy Djuna kidnaps her. Damned fool. . . . Really, the Lesbians are a crazy lot. Their antagonism to the male is almost a disease with them. I simply cant bear such narrowness. . . ."

By implication, Goldman denied that Fitzie's affair with Barnes might have been a positive choice. To understand Fitzie, Goldman wrote, it was necessary to understand that all her relations with men had been disastrous. Her tragedy "is the tragedy of all emancipated women, myself included. We are still rooted in the old soil, though our visions are of the future and our desire is to be free and independent. . . . It is a longing for fulfillment which very few modern women find because most men too are rooted in the old tradition. They too want the woman as wife and mother in the old sense, and the new medium has not yet been devised, I mean the way of being wife, mother, friend and yet retain one's complete freedom. Will it ever? . . ."[35]

Emma Goldman doubted it. Ultimately she even doubted that women could enjoy real satisfaction even physically with men. After a lifetime of celebrating woman's absolute right to full sexual pleasure, there is something intensively poignant about a letter to Dr. Samuel D. Schmalhausen in which she implied that all through the years the pleasure she received from the men she loved had been inadequate. Schmalhausen had written *Woman's Coming of Age*, and on 26 January 1935 Goldman wrote that ever since her "intellectual awakening" she had had the same thought. Namely,

that the sex of the man lasts from the moment of its dominant motivation to its climax. After that the brute has done of his share. The brute can go to sleep. Not so the woman. The climax of the embrace, far from leaving her relaxed or stupefied as it does the man, raises all her sensibilities to the highest pitch. All her yearning for love, affection, tenderness becomes more vibrant and carries her to ecstatic heights. At that moment she needs the understanding of and communion with her mate perhaps more than the physical. But the brute is asleep and she remains in her own world far removed from him. I know this from my personal experience and experiences of scores of women who have talked freely with me. I am certain that the cause for the conflict between the sexes which continues to exist regardless of woman's emancipation is due to the differences in quality of the sex embrace. Perhaps it will always be that way. Certainly I find very few men who have the same need, or who know how to minister that of the woman's. Naturally, I felt elated to read your analysis . . . which actually expresses what I have felt and voiced for well nigh 45 years. . . .[36]

Despite anger, isolation, and disappointment, Emma Goldman remained active and enthusiastic to the end of her life. After her despondent years in London, several friends presented her with a cottage on St. Tropez: "Georgette LeBlanc, Margaret Anderson, Peggy Guggenheim, Lawrence Vail and many others came for an hour or a day to discuss serious matters or in jolly company." Life in St. Tropez, Goldman wrote, restored her health and her "fighting spirit." It was there that she decided to write her memoirs, tour Canada, and cable friends in the United States for loans to continue her important work, now focused mainly in Spain.[37] But she never found the one great friend who could understand her empty places, and she never acknowledged the value of feminist alliances for active women whose very activity, depths of passion, and committed independence alienated them from the men with whom they worked and struggled.

Lillian Wald, Jane Addams, Crystal Eastman, and Emma Goldman all had visions of social change and economic justice that, 60 years later, we have yet to see fulfilled. They lived as they did at a time when, as Vera Brittain noted, women were programmed to monopolize their husbands, dominate their sons, possess their daughters, and make fetishes of their kitchens and shrines of their homes. These four women present a range of choices and affinities that were charged with courage, experiment, fulfillment, and intensity. In viewing women of the past it has been a common practice to assume that feminists, spinsters, woman-related women, and most women engaged in social reform were asexual, self-denying, and puritanical, sublimating their sexual passions in their work. Even today the myth persists that women unattached to men are lonely, bitter, and without community; that women who are political activists working with men can function effectively without a support network of women. In the lives of Wald, Addams, and Eastman, we see clearly the energy and strength they received from feminist networks. Crystal Eastman's feminism drew upon and allowed her to appreciate the woman-identification of her lesbian friends. On the other hand, despite Emma Goldman's intellectual and political identification with the oppressed, including women and homosexuals, she never did understand or identify with the feminist movement, and she never did find a friend of her own sex, "a kindred spirit with whom she could share her innermost thoughts and feelings."

For Jane Addams and Lillian Wald, service to humanity and leadership in public life were constantly refueled by their female support communities and by personal relationships with women who gave them passionate loyalty and love. The power of communities of independent women, and of the love between individual women, expressed not only sensually but in a range of ways, is part of the history that has been taken from us by heterosexist culture. To recognize this history is to recognize our own personal forces of energy and courage and the power to change.

NOTES

1. See Vera Brittain, *Testament of Friendship: The Story of Winifred Holtby* (London: Macmillan, 1947), p. 2: "Within the framework of this biography I have tried to tell . . . the story of a friendship which continued unbroken and unspoilt for sixteen incomparable years. . . ."

2. See Blanche Wiesen Cook, "Democracy in Wartime: Antimilitarism in England and the United States, 1914–1918," *American Studies* (Spring 1972), reprinted in Charles Chatfield, ed., *Peace Movements in America* (Schocken Books, 1973), pp. 39–57; Cook, "Woodrow Wilson and the Antimilitarists, 1914–1918" (unpublished Ph.D. dissertation, The Johns Hopkins University, 1970); and Cook, ed., *Toward the Great Change: Crystal and Max Eastman on Feminism, Antimilitarism and Revolution* (Garland Publishing, 1976).

3. Emma Goldman, *Living My Life*, Vol. I (Dover Reprint, 1970), pp. 160, 375, passim.

4. Blanche Wiesen Cook, "The Woman's Peace Party: Collaboration and Non-Cooperation," *Peace and Change* (Fall 1972), pp. 36 ff.

5. Goldman, op. cit., pp. 157–160.

6. William O'Neill, *Everyone Was Brave: Feminism in America* (Quadrangle, 1969), p. 120.

7. Allen Davis, *American Heroine: The Life and Legend of Jane Addams* (Oxford University Press, 1973), p. 46.

8. Davis, op. cit., p. 91.

9. Jane Addams, "Women, War and Babies" (31 July 1915), reprinted in Allen Davis, ed., *Jane Addams on Peace, War and International Understanding, 1895–1932* (Garland Publishing, 1976).

10. George Will, "How Far Out of the Closet?" *Newsweek*, 3 May 1977, p. 92.

11. For information about the U.S. Children's Bureau, see Nancy P. Weiss, "The Children's Bureau: A Case Study of Women's Voluntary Networks," an unpublished paper presented at the Berkshire Conference on the History of Women, 10 June 1976, Bryn Mawr.

12. See Nancy Sahli's unpublished paper, "Changing Patterns of Sexuality and Female Interaction in Nineteenth-Century America," presented at the Berkshire Conference, 11 June 1976, pp. 12–13.

13. Lillian Wald's correspondence is divided between the New York Public Library and Columbia University. See Dock to Wald, 27 April 1925; 10 May 1925; 10 March 1916, Columbia University.

14. Lavinia Dock's correspondence with the Congressional Union is in the Woman's Party Papers, Library of Congress. See especially Dock to Paul, 8 September 1914, tray 1, box 6; 28 June 1915, New York, tray 1, box 6; Dock to C.U., 22 May 1915, tray 1, box 5.

15. Irene Lewisohn to Dear Lady Light, n.d., Wald Papers, Columbia. This probably refers to a round-the-world trip that lasted six months (1910). See R. L. Duffus, *Lillian Wald* (Macmillan, 1938), pp. 123 ff.; Rita Morgenthau to Wald, 1 January 1905, box 14, . . . Wald Papers, Columbia.

16. Dock to Duffus, 28 May 1936, in Duffus, op. cit., pp. 346–347.

17. Margaret Anderson, *The Fiery Fountains* (Horizon Press, 1969 [1951]), p. 84.

18. Mabel Hyde Kittredge to Wald, 28 April 1904; all Kittredge letters, Wald Papers, Columbia.

19. Helen Arthur's correspondence with Wald is generally undated between 1906 and 1908. Ibid.

20. Wald quoted in Duffus, op. cit., p. 55.

21. Kittredge to Wald, 11 May 1925, Wald Papers, Columbia; George V. Alger, Oral History, Columbia, pp. 251–252; Allen Reznick, "Lillian Wald: The Years at Henry Street" (unpublished Ph.D. dissertation, University of Wisconsin, 1973), p. ii.

22. Emma Goldman, "The Child and Its Enemies," *Mother Earth* (April 1906), pp. 107–109.

23. A long correspondence to block Eastman's participation at the Hague may be found in the Balch and Addams Papers at the Swarthmore College Peace Collection; see especially Lucia Ames Mead to Emily Green Balch, Balch Papers. See also Nan Bauer Maglin, "Early Feminist Fiction: The Dilemma of Personal Life," *Prospects* (1976), pp. 167 ff., for an overview of the reformists' unwillingness to deal with changing social and sexual mores.

24. See Richard Drinnon, *Rebel in Paradise: A Biography of Emma Goldman* (University of Chicago Press, 1961), pp. 149–151; and Goldman, "Marriage and Love," in Alix Shulman, ed., *Red Emma Speaks* (Vintage, 1972), pp. 158 ff. See also Shulman, *To the Barricades: The Anarchist Life of Emma Goldman* (Crowell, 1971).

25. Jeannette Lowe to author, 27 March 1973.

26. Crystal Eastman, "Marriage under Two Roofs" (1923); "Feminists Must Fight" (1924); and "Now We Can Begin" (1920)—all reprinted in Blanche Wiesen Cook, Toward the Great Change.

27. Claude McKay, A Long Way from Home (Harcourt, 1970 [1935]), pp. 154–155.

28. Margaret Anderson, My Thirty Years' War (Corici, Friede, 1930), pp. 54–55; Goldman, Living My Life, Vol. II, p. 694.

29. Goldman, "The Tragedy of Woman's Emancipation," Mother Earth (No. 3, 1906), pp. 9–18 (reprinted in Red Emma Speaks); R.A.P., "Feminism in America," Mother Earth (February 1915), pp. 392–394.

30. Goldman, Living My Life, Vol. I, p. 555.

31. See Sperry to Goldman in Jonathan

Katz, Gay American History (Crowell, 1976), pp. 523–530.

32. John Lauritsen and David Thorstad, The Early Homosexual Rights Movement, 1864–1935 (Times Change Press, 1974), pp. 36–37.

33. Katz, op. cit., pp. 376–380.

34. Richard and Anna Maria Drinnon, eds., Nowhere At Home: Letters From Exile of Emma Goldman and Alexander Berkman (Schocken Books, 1975), p. 128.

35. Ibid., pp. 132–133, p. 86.

36. Goldman to Dr. Samuel Schmulhausen, 26 January 1935, Golrman Papers, Labadie Collection, University of Michigan.

37. Goldman, Living My Life, Vol. II, pp. 985–986; see also Goldman to Margaret Anderson, ed., The Little Review Anthology (Horizon Press, 1953), p. 363.

DOLORES HAYDEN
The Grand Domestic Revolution:
The Feminist Paradise Palace

The commitment to social change propelling women such as Jane Addams and Florence Kelley to seek political reforms that would end women's oppression in the workplace prompted other women to focus on women's oppression in the home. Charlotte Perkins Gilman, an author, charismatic lecturer, and noted feminist, argued that not until women were able to achieve economic independence through work outside the home and release from domestic drudgery within the home would they be able to realize their full human potential. Liberation, she believed, could come through collective domesticity achieved through the building of private kitchenless houses and apartments connected to central kitchens and day care centers.

One of Gilman's disciples, Henrietta Rodman, sought to implement these ideas in a feminist apartment house in New York City. While such a venture would not be "political" in the traditional sense, contemporary feminists argue

Excerpted from "Domestic Evolution or Domestic Revolution?" chap. 9 of The Grand Domestic Revolution: A History of Feminist Designs for American Homes, Neighborhoods, and Cities by Dolores Hayden (Cambridge, Mass.: MIT Press, 1981). Copyright © 1981 by The Massachusetts Institute of Technology. Reprinted by permission. Notes have been renumbered.

that private domestic arrangements have a political dimension. Assignment of household tasks reflects power relationships.

In what sense was Rodman trying to achieve a collective solution to problems faced by a new generation of professional women confronted individually with combining career and family, wage work and domestic work? Why was the issue of "professional" domestic workers versus redistribution of household labor between the sexes such a troublesome one for Rodman and her associates? Has their dilemma been solved? Whose dilemma is it?

In April 1914, Henrietta Rodman, active in New York feminist and socialist circles, founded the Feminist Alliance. Rodman had been involved in many trade union struggles in New York, and had won recognition for her drive to organize the public schoolteachers. Now, wishing to attack broader issues, she recruited some wealthy women active in Crystal Eastman's Congressional Union for Woman Suffrage as well as some middle-class professional women and their husbands. In addition to attempting to have women admitted to law and medical schools, the Feminist Alliance won a campaign for maternity leaves for teachers (previously New York's Board of Education had fired teachers who became mothers). They demanded American women's rights to retain their citizenship if they married foreigners. In their more sociable moments they held a fancy dress ball where guests were invited to come in women's costumes ranging from primitive to futuristic.[1]

Most ambitious of their projects was the Feminist Apartment House. Charlotte Perkins Gilman had described it in detail; Rodman was determined to see it built. . . . In 1906, Gilman had written:

> We have so arranged life, that a man may have a home and family, love, companionship, domesticity, and fatherhood, yet remain an active citizen of age and country. We have so arranged life, on the other hand, that a woman must "choose"; must either live alone, unloved, uncompanied, uncared for, homeless, childless, with her work in the world for sole consolation; or

give up all world-service for the joys of love, motherhood, and domestic service.[2]

The settlement houses inhabited by career women were the great exception to Gilman's generalization. Rodman and the other members of the Feminist Alliance were determined to rearrange home life so that women could combine a career and marriage successfully, by creating women's housing less tied to specific types of work than the settlement houses. They planned to offer an organization similar to the Jane Club run by women workers, but to construct an edifice equal to the apartment hotels built for male residents with varied occupations.

The group hired Max G. Heidelberg, a radical New York architect, to design their building. He had both socialist and feminist interests as an activist on housing issues in the Cooperative League of America and as a member of the Executive Committee of the National Birth Control League.[3] For the Alliance, Heidelberg designed a twelve-story building for a site near Greenwich Village, including kitchenless apartments, collective housekeeping facilities, and a roof-top nursery school. The building of about four hundred rooms, divided into one hundred and seventy one-to-four-room suites, required a capital of half a million dollars.[4] In the ambitious calculations about its size and quality, the project resembled A. T. Stewart's ill-fated Woman's Hotel of 1878, but the Alliance's project was to be controlled by its residents and to provide day care for the children of employed women, thus recognizing that family and paid work for women were not incompatible activities.

Rodman believed that Alva Belmont, Fanny Villard, and other wealthy investors would guarantee most of the capital. Villard had worked for decades with the New York Diet Kitchen Association which provided food for the poor, and with various nurseries and kindergartens, the National Household Economic Association, three suffrage groups, and the Women's Peace Party. Her husband was a cofounder of the Edison General Electric Company. Alva Belmont had come to feminism late in her life but was a heavy contributor to suffrage causes, the Women's Trade Union League, and Max Eastman's magazine, *The Masses*. Most important, she had been a flamboyant patron of architecture in her earlier days as a reigning society matron. Richard Morris Hunt had built her a three-million-dollar pseudo-French chateau at Fifth Avenue and Fifty-Second Street in 1881, a two-million dollar "cottage" at Newport in 1892, and another estate at Sands Points, Long Island. To Rodman she appeared a likely supporter for this feminist architectural enterprise.

In addition to $480,000 from wealthy patrons, the organizers hoped to raise one year's rent in advance from the residents, the rather small sum of $20,000. Single women could live in the building, as well as married women with their children and husbands; all resident parents, male and female, were expected to help with child care. Rodman said: "I maintain that every child has a right to a real father, one who has sufficient leisure to take a real interest in his children."[5] She planned that the building would be staffed by "trained help from the domestic science departments of the high schools," working eight-hour days, in order that the resident career women would be freed from chores. . . . The professional women assured themselves that they would make things much easier for the domestic workers, with good wages and limited hours. Yet Rodman conceded that her real interest was not in helping domestic workers but in providing a home for employed, educated women. Having won teachers the right to marry, she was now attempting to provide housing which would support them and other professionals while they struggled with both careers and children.

Heidelberg, who chaired the Feminist Alliance's Committee on the Socialization of the Primitive Industries of Women, made some attempt to eliminate domestic drudgery through design. There would be no wallpaper and no picture moldings. All corners would be rounded, all bathtubs would be built in, all windows would pivot, all beds would fold into the walls, and all hardware would be dull-finished.[6] Of course, the women with high school training in domestic science would still be cleaning inside the built in bathtubs, if not under them, and washing the pivoting windows.

Rodman wanted to believe that new domestic technology and the professionalization of housework would solve all domestic problems, but her husband, Herman de Frem, was more alert to the economic and social issues involved. As Executive Secretary of the Feminist Alliance, he claimed there was a need for greater democracy in the house and argued that "it should be made cooperative in every sense."[7] Rodman, steeped in Gilman's polemics against cooperation in housekeeping, claimed that cooperators would not actually get as much work done as paid "professionals." While the discussion raged, the project was criticized from outside as a "feminist paradise palace" by Laura Fay-Smith, writing in the *New York Times*.

Fay-Smith sneered at feminism and railed at women who refused the "responsibilities" of motherhood. A militant antifeminist, . . . she argued that if nature had intended women to be feminists, then women of the future would be square-shouldered, flat-chested, and equipped with "large feet on which to stand their ground." They would be born with "money as their only standard of value." Fay-Smith asserted that true women know their place is at home, as mothers, because this was what nature had ordered. She fired a parting complaint: "The feminist wants to hire other women to do what she ought to do herself; she wants to climb high above the harsh labors of the house, on the shoulders of the women whose hard necessity compels them to be paid servants."[8] In her portrayal of conflict between women as employers and employees, Fay-Smith did identify a problem that the feminist organizers could not resolve: how to escape from stereotypes about "women's" work without exploiting women of a lower economic class.

By refusing to shift one half of the domestic burden back on to men, the women of the Feminist Alliance separated themselves from the "professional" domestic workers whom they planned to employ. No one asked how the "professional" domestic workers could also be mothers. Debate centered on whether or not a feminist apartment hotel promoted or destroyed "natural" motherhood for middle-class women. No critic picked up on Rodman's scrutiny of "natural" fatherhood, and asked what "real men" ought to do around the house. No one asked how the professionals who were supporting themselves and their children could survive without their jobs. In the last rounds of the debate, the editors of the *New York Times* actually agreed with the Feminist Alliance's assertion that removing housework from the house was desirable, but the editors reproved the activists for mixing up this technological and social advance with feminism, "whatever that may be," and thereby "making a difficult problem harder."[9]

The *New York Post* analyzed all of the Feminist Alliance's economic calculations, questioning whether child care could cost only sixty-five cents per day, with a ratio of one nurse to every five babies, and one kindergarten teacher to every ten pupils.

They questioned as well whether or not the cost of apartments, with meals, could average ten dollars per week, and concluded: "The only wonder is why, if women teachers, literary workers, and musicians can be fed on 53 cents a day, there should be such a clamor for a minimum wage for shop girls."[10]

Ultimately the alliance between elderly, wealthy women interested in suffrage and philanthropy, and younger women and men who were cultural radicals, socialists, and feminists broke down. "Motherhood" had been the point of public attack, but the unresolved problems of domestic service versus domestic cooperation caused the group's internal disagreements. The struggle to unite socialism and feminism was at a very early stage. Feminists with capital who could afford the new physical environment for collective domestic work never thought of voluntarily sharing that domestic work themselves. Men and women with socialist sympathies who defended the Feminist Alliance's project in *The Masses* had no analysis of the conflicts of either gender or economic class involved in reorganizing domestic work.[11] The problems of housewives and servants were still very little understood, although almost half a century had passed since Steven Pearl Andrews and Victoria Woodhull had attempted to promote apartment hotels for everyone as part of a "grand domestic revolution" in New York City. The closer such domestic projects got to practical realization, the greater the ideological difficulties seemed to be. Not one feminist woman nor one socialist man in Rodman's group (with the possible exception of her husband), wanted to do any domestic work themselves. Talk as they might about the dignity of labor, or about creating good jobs for well-trained workers, no one wanted to be a well-trained domestic worker. Everyone wanted to pay someone else to do this job, but they were never prepared to pay more than they earned themselves as writers, or teachers, or white-collar workers.

NOTES

1. June Sochen, *The New Woman: Feminism in Greenwich Village, 1910–1920* (New York: Quadrangle, 1972), 3–25. Born in New York in 1878, Rodman attended Teachers College at Columbia University, and became an English teacher in New York public schools. She was a socialist and a believer in free love who enjoyed a lively circle of feminist and radical friends in Greenwich Village, including Crystal Eastman, Ida Rauh, Floyd Dell, and Max Eastman. She led five hundred schoolteachers in the Teachers Association in support of the striking seamstresses and shirtwaist makers in New York. In Paterson, New Jersey, Rodman also led a demonstration in support of free speech for Elizabeth Gurley Flynn, the militant Industrial Workers of the World organizer who called Rodman, "a truly remarkable woman" who was never afraid of Red-baiting. Elizabeth Gurley Flynn, *The Rebel Girl: An Autobiography, My First Life (1906–26)* (1955; New York: International Publishers, 1973), 117, 172.

2. Charlotte Perkins Gilman, "The Passing of Matrimony," *Harper's Bazaar*, 40 (June 1906), 496.

3. Heidelberg and his partner Harry A. Jacobs designed an orphanage about this time, but I can find no other information on his practice. See Clara de L. Berg, "A New Home Ideal for the Orphan," *Craftsman*, 27 (January 1915), 441–444. The National Birth Control League directors are listed in *The Masses*, 10 (April 1917), 35.

4. "Feminists Design a New Type Home," *New York Times*, April 5, 1914. Mary M. Huth of the University of Rochester Library kindly provided this reference in the *New York Times*, and the following ones.

5. George MacAdam, "Feminist Apartment House to Solve Baby Problem," *New York Times*, Section 5, January 24, 1915, 9.

6. "Feminists Debate Plans for a House," *New York Times*, April 22, 1914.

7. Ibid.

8. Laura Fay-Smith, "That Feminist Paradise Palace," *New York Times*, April 25, 1915, Section 5, 21.

9. "A Difficult Problem Made Harder," editorial, *New York Times*, April 23, 1914, 12. Also see "Feminists' Model Home," *New York Times*, May 13, 1914, 22; "Feminists Plan a Home," *New York Times*, April 16, 1914, 3.

10. "Futurist Baby Raising," editorial, *New York Evening Post*, June 17, 1914. Of course this was why Engels objected to all philanthropic housing reform programs in *The Housing Question*.

11. May Wood Simons, "Co-operation and Housewives," *The Masses*, woman's number 1 (December 1911); K. W. Baker, "'Raising' Babies," *The Masses*, 6 (February 1916).

ANNE F. SCOTT and ANDREW M. SCOTT
One Half the People:
The Fight for Woman Suffrage

Enfranchisement of women is part of many histories: the history of suffrage, of democracy, of social reform, of popular movements, and of women. It is a story

Excerpted from "Turning the Corner: 1896–1916" and "Victory: 1917–1920," chaps. 3 and 4 of *One Half the People: The Fight for Woman Suffrage* by Anne F. Scott and Andrew M. Scott (Philadelphia: J. B. Lippincott, 1975). Copyright © 1975 by J. B. Lippincott Company. Reprinted by permission of University of Illinois Press. Notes have been renumbered and cross-references adjusted.

bound up with defense of privilege and fear of reform. Yet despite conservative attacks on woman suffrage as a major innovation that would undermine the sexual-social division of labor by permitting women to invade the male world of politics, some historians have accused suffragists of diverting attention from feminism and women's "real" problems to the ritual of casting the ballot. This view, however, ignores the historic role of suffrage as symbolic of the rights of citizens to participate in shaping the future of the republic for their own benefit as well as that of others. It also ignores the sharp challenge to tradition that occurred when women broke out of the domestic sphere into the traditionally male public sphere. If women could do little about their subordinate status within the family in the nineteenth century, they could, as the historian Ellen Du Bois has pointed out, *bypass* the family or private sphere and focus on the public sphere, demanding as citizens and as voters the right to participate directly as individuals, not indirectly as an extension of their positions as wives and mothers.

The following selection shows how in the first two decades of the twentieth century politically adept and energetic suffragists were able to establish the public role of women as a legitimate, constitutional right. Although later generations would have to develop the full meaning of this achievement, winning the vote was essential to establishing the principle that women's rights were "public" and that citizenship was not limited by sex.

TURNING THE CORNER, 1896–1916

NEW ORGANIZATIONAL FERVOR

"Progressivism" brought a change in the atmosphere of politics, and of the suffrage movement. Young people were attracted to social and political action, and enthusiasm was joined with willingness to cross class lines, study economic questions, and engage in public demonstrations. This energy was evident in the growth of local suffrage groups, and in the formation of new kinds of groups alongside the traditional ones. While NAWSA's [National American Woman Suffrage Association] National Board did not immediately reflect the change, an increase in membership and the emergence of new leaders took place in many communities. After years of slow growth the suffrage movement was in the process of developing a mass base.

In Massachusetts a group of young women in 1901 had created two important new organizations: the Boston Equal Suffrage Association for Good Government and the College Equal Suffrage League, both aimed at reaching members of the community who had hitherto been indifferent to suffrage. Maud Wood Park, just out of Radcliffe, formed the College Equal Suffrage League. The idea proved so timely that she was soon being asked to help with similar groups in other states.

Meantime the Boston Equal Suffrage Association was experimenting with bold new kinds of campaigning: going door-to-door in Boston in every kind of neighborhood, or sending groups of women on a trolley tour of the state, to make suffrage speeches at every stop along the interurban line. Outdoor meetings, set up spontaneously wherever a crowd could be found, brought the message to people who would never have gone to a suffrage meeting on their own. Timid at first, the women took courage from experience and were soon enjoying themselves as well as recruiting new supporters.[1]

Young American women were increasingly aware of the rise of a militant wing in the English suffrage movement. In 1903 Emmeline and Christabel Pankhurst, members of the Labour Party, had launched the Women's Social and Political Union, and by 1905 they were experimenting with dramatic tactics. After they had heckled candidates for Parliament by demanding that they state a position on woman suffrage, members of the union, when they spit upon policemen attempting to quiet them and organized a protest meeting outside the hall, were arrested and sent to jail. For the first time the English press began to pay considerable attention to the suffrage movement. The lesson was not lost on impatient young Americans, who were themselves engaged in developing new and more colorful tactics.

Harriot Stanton Blatch, daughter of Elizabeth Cady Stanton, had come back to New York after years in England during which she had moved in radical circles. Shocked by the inertia of the traditional suffrage groups, she set about organizing the Equality League of Self-Supporting Women, drawing from a new source (women employed in factories, laundries and garment shops) and using such tactics as open air meetings, silent pickets, women poll watchers, and suffrage parades. She brought Mrs. Pankhurst and other English militants to speak in New York, and was adroit in gaining publicity. In a comparatively short time the Equality League recruited nineteen thousand members.

Inez Milholland exemplified one new style of leader. She had organized two-thirds of the Vassar student body in a college suffrage league before her graduation in 1909. Turned down at a number of law schools, she finally got a law degree from New York University, joined Mrs.

Blatch's Equality League of Self-Supporting Women, and divided her time between legislative hearings and suffrage parades on the one hand, and picket lines in the interest of the shirtwaist and laundry workers' strikes on the other. She became a Socialist, and edited a "Department for Women" in *McClure's Magazine*. She was only the most flamboyant of a number of college women who came on the scene in the first decade of the century and added a new dimension to suffrage leadership.

In July 1911 the Philadelphia *Public Ledger* carried a notice that a wagon load of women speakers had appeared on a street corner, adding: "The spectacle of a woman with a wagon for a platform pleading for the use of the ballot was so novel that the audience was quick to respond, . . ." Nor was the new wave confined to the eastern seaboard or to big cities. In Boone, Iowa, the state's annual suffrage convention in 1908 was addressed by two English militants. A spontaneous parade followed, and even Anna Howard Shaw, there to represent NAWSA, was carried along by the spirit of the affair and gave an open air speech at the end.[2]

Between 1910 and 1913 campaigns in three states showed what new energy and careful organization could do. The first was in the state of Washington, where Mrs. Emma DeVoe (who had learned her political methods under Mrs. Catt's tutelage) ran a quiet campaign based on carefully planned district-by-district organization. Suffrage won almost two to one, and a wave of enthusiasm spread through the movement.

Even more encouraging was the California campaign which began in the spring of 1911. There women combined every new technique they knew of, making use of automobiles (still something of a novelty), contests, billboards and detailed organization aimed at getting out the vote and insuring a fair election. Money and help came from suffragists all over the country. The key to success, Eleanor Flexner concluded, was close attention to small town and village meetings, parlor talks, and "small groups organized where previously there had been no visible signs of interest in woman suffrage."[3] The California victory, though narrow, was enough. Women could now vote in six western states.

The third major breakthrough came in Illinois where the Equal Suffrage Association, with the help of Progressives in the legislature, put through a bill granting women the right to vote in presidential elections, a measure which did not require a constitutional amendment. There, too, the organization for the legislative campaign was impressively thorough. For the first time in a state east of the Mississippi (and a large populous state at that), women would be able to vote in presidential elections. Morale rose again.

INTERNAL CHANGES IN THE MOVEMENT

Members of NAWSA, including some on the National Board, were beginning to demand that a clear-cut political strategy be found to take advantage of what was clearly a new opportunity. Between 1910 and 1916 the board was in turmoil, and experienced considerable turnover. For a time it seemed that the organization might destroy itself through internal conflict.

Two young women who had lived in England and taken part in the militant movement there became a focal point of conflict and eventually precipitated a significant reorganization. Alice Paul and Lucy Burns came back to the United States in 1910, helped initiate the use of new methods in Pennsylvania, and in 1912 offered their services to NAWSA for the purpose of organizing a new drive for a national amendment. The board welcomed them, and dispatched them to Washington as its Congressional Committee. It was not long before they made their presence felt.

Woodrow Wilson, arriving for his inauguration on March 3, 1913 and finding no crowd at the station, was told the people were all watching a suffrage parade. Alice Paul could not have planned it better: crowds in town for the inauguration, rowdies undeterred by the police, troops from Fort Belvoir to the rescue, and indignant congressmen demanding an investigation of the police department for its failure to protect a lawful demonstration, dramatized the suffrage cause.

It was not long, however, before members of the NAWSA board began to recognize some important differences between their own philosophy and that of Paul and Burns. Not only had the two young women organized and raised money for a separate lobbying group which they called the Congressional Union, but they were also ready to operate on a different set of political assumptions. Their English experience led them to believe that effective political action required holding the party in power responsible for policy decisions. Since the Democratic party controlled both houses of Congress and the presidency, they reasoned that all Democrats, those who had supported suffrage as well as those who had opposed it, should be held responsible if no action was taken on the suffrage amendment. They proposed to organize women to oppose Democrats in all the suffrage states.

NAWSA had always held to the view that in the American Congress men of both parties would be needed to make up two-thirds in each house, and had therefore insisted on a nonpartisan policy. Suffragists who had worked actively for the Progressive party had been criticized on just this ground.

Paul and Burns failed to understand the essential difference between the English parliamentary system and the United States system. In England the executive had a working majority in Parliament, party discipline was strong, and Parliament could grant the vote to women by a simple legislative act. In the United States the achievement of woman suffrage required that both houses of Congress pass a proposed amendment by a two-thirds vote and that the legislatures or special conventions in three-quarters of the states approve it. Furthermore, party discipline is notoriously weak in this system, and when most measures pass legislatures they are approved by coalitions comprised of members from both of the major parties. Suffrage needed every legislative friend it could find, and it made little sense to oppose supporters in the name of a principle—party responsibility—which was not understood in American politics.

At the 1913 convention, after much discussion, the NAWSA board withdrew its support from Paul and Burns who went their own way thereafter, first in the Congressional Union, then in the National Woman's Party. For the second time the suffrage movement was divided. Few long-lived reform movements escape factionalism, and when splits occur they are apt to separate the radical from the relatively conservative, the venturesome from the cautious, and are likely to revolve around questions of strategy and tactics. This new division was reminiscent of the earlier cleavage between the National and the American associations. Then Lucy Stone and the Bostonians had emphasized moderation, and had tried to avoid extreme actions that might antagonize friends and neutrals. Stanton and Anthony had been prepared to press ahead, letting the chips fall where they might. Now the NAWSA had fallen into comfortable and conservative ways, and was flanked on the left by the more militant Congressional Union.

Events had outrun the leaders of the NAWSA. While new life was stirring in many states, and the Congressional Union was generating excitement in Washington, the board appeared to be plodding along with no clear political strategy. Discontent within the organization was exacerbated by controversy over the board's decision to support a new constitutional amendment, the so-called Shafroth-Palmer amendment, which would have thrown the suffrage issue once again back to the states. On March 19, 1914, for the first time in the twentieth century, the federal amendment was brought to a vote in the Senate, and overwhelmingly defeated. Of the sixty-nine members voting, thirty-four opposed. A roll call in the House on January 12, 1915 was similarly discouraging: yeas 174, nays 204. Discontent came to a head in 1915 after the defeat, despite excellent and imaginative campaigns, of constitutional amendments in four crucial eastern states. Many members of NAWSA called for Carrie Chapman Catt to take the presidency.

In 1887, as a talented young widow with some legal training and experience in education and journalism already behind her, Carrie Chapman had joined the Iowa Woman Suffrage Association. Within two years she was organizing all over the state, and in 1890 Iowa had sent her to the national convention. Her marriage the following year to George Catt had taken her first to Seattle and then to New York, but not out of suffrage activity. She campaigned in South Dakota, Colorado and Idaho, winning in the latter two states. In Idaho she first experimented with an organization based on election districts. She next headed the Organization Committee of NAWSA, and then was president for four years. During the period immediately after her husband's death she had spent a good deal of time organizing the International Suffrage Alliance, and then had returned to New York where she organized the Woman Suffrage party, and began preparing for the referendum which finally came in 1915. In the meantime, methods she had helped to develop contributed to the victories in Washington, California, and Illinois. When the 1915 campaign in New York got forty-two percent of the vote, she had at once launched the next campaign aimed at 1917.

It was this record which led the discontented members of NAWSA to fix their hopes on Mrs. Catt. At the 1915 convention she was persuaded to take the presidency, on the condition that she could choose her own board. She went to work at once to turn NAWSA into a tightly organized, effective force. Now both suffrage organizations were ready to campaign seriously for a national amendment.

Moving Towards a National Amendment: The Election of 1916

The two groups approached the task with different philosophies, and as time went by the divergence would grow. Under Mrs. Catt's leadership, NAWSA would depend upon a high degree of organizational coherence; a close relationship between local, state and national workers, a mass base, careful, low-key lobbying, and ladylike behavior. The Congressional Union also believed in organization, and it tried to develop a base in the country, especially in the suffrage states. But, in addition, Alice Paul believed in dramatic action, the symbolic gesture, headlines, and in a small, disciplined group of activists. As the union moved further in this direction, NAWSA would take pains to separate itself from its flamboyant activities, and especially to keep the distinction clear in the minds of congressmen.

It is hard now to avoid concluding that the existence of the militant group was important. The temper of the times called for a vigorous pursuit of the goal. Once again, as in the 1868 division, the two groups stimulated each other. Indeed, the challenge from the Congressional Union was part of the stimulus which led to Mrs. Catt's election, and for that reason NAWSA owed the union an unacknowledged debt.

With the Congressional Union and NAWSA both at work the militants could press ahead with shock tactics, while the more conservative group could develop its careful organization based on congres-

sional districts. It was a good one-two punch, as events in 1916 would demonstrate.

That was an important year for woman suffrage. In June NAWSA organized a giant parade to the Republican National Convention being held in Chicago. On a cold, windy, rainy day ten thousand women marched to the convention hall and the *New York Times* reported that some politicians felt this was "the pluckiest thing they ever knew women to do." The Republicans came out for suffrage but in a disappointing states' rights plank. They "recognized the right of each state to settle this question for itself." When the Democrats met in St. Louis, delegates walked to the convention hall through streets lined with women wearing yellow sashes and carrying yellow parasols to remind them of the suffrage issue. After an acrimonious floor debate the Democrats, too, came out for suffrage "state, by state, on the same terms as men."

Carrie Chapman Catt responded by calling an emergency convention to meet in September to which she invited both presidential candidates. Wilson came and, using notes supplied to him by Alice Stone Blackwell, declared his support for suffrage but added ambiguously "we will not quarrel in the long run as to the method of it." Charles Evans Hughes, the Republican candidate, did not accept the invitation but had already endorsed suffrage by federal amendment. Both parties were beginning to contend for the suffrage votes that had gone to the Progressive party in 1912.

During this convention state presidents and officers of the national association met in secret to hear what would come to be called Mrs. Catt's "Winning Plan." The essence of the plan was that suffragists should move forward on *all* fronts, and each state was given responsibilities depending on its particular status. The eleven full suffrage states and Illinois were to get resolutions from their legislatures memorializing the Congress to submit the federal amendment. In others, referendum campaigns were the task at hand; in some states, campaigns for presidential suffrage, and in the South campaigns for primary suffrage—all aimed at increasing the number of electoral votes which women could influence. Representatives of thirty-six state associations signed a compact to carry out these plans and to keep them secret until they revealed themselves in action. Insofar as possible, the opposition was to be caught napping.

As for the federal amendment, work in Washington was to be organized at a new level of intensity. Just before the Atlantic City convention Mrs. Catt had written to Maud Wood Park:

> I do feel keenly that the turn of the road has come. . . . I really believe that we might pull off a campaign which would mean the vote within the next six years if we could secure a Board of officers who would have sufficient momentum, confidence and working power in them. . . .
>
> Come! My dear Mrs. Park, gird on your armor once more. . . .[4]

That Atlantic City convention gave the National Board—Carrie Chapman Catt's board—authority to direct all the activities of the organization. A million dollar budget was authorized and Mrs. Park and quite a few others did "gird on their armor" and move to Washington for the duration of the struggle.

When Woodrow Wilson surveyed his prospects for reelection in 1916 it was clear that his best hope lay in attracting the votes of many citizens who in 1912 had cast their ballots for Theodore Roosevelt. Accordingly, under his aggressive leadership, the Congress that summer had adopted a number of measures which progressives considered a test of his commitment to their position, especially the Keating-Owen Child Labor Bill. Accordingly, too, he had gone to the NAWSA convention and made his tantalizing statement, opening the door to his eventual support of the federal amendment.

As in 1914, the Congressional Union took the position that since the Democrats had controlled the government for four years *all* Democrats must be opposed. NAWSA held to its careful bipartisanship, supporting its friends in either party. With war going on in Europe, peace was a major issue, and on a platform of peace and progressivism Wilson went to the country, polling nearly three million votes beyond what he had received in 1912.

The *New York Times* postelection analysis indicated that women voters had helped to swell this number and had contributed significantly to his victory in California, Idaho, Utah and Arizona. The Woman's Party effort to persuade women to vote against all Democrats had not, apparently, hurt the president very much except in Illinois.[5]

The immediate tactics of the two suffrage organizations had pulled in opposite directions. The failure of the Woman's Party tactic was not surprising since it was based on an erroneous conception of the American political process. Even though its objective was quixotic, however, the campaign contributed to the growing momentum of the suffrage movement. While the Congressional Union in *The Suffragist* of November 11, 1916 asserted that "the Democratic campaign in the West consisted almost entirely of an attempt to combat the Woman's Party attack," other suffragists were content to give women credit for helping Wilson win, and to let all politicians draw the obvious lesson. Women now voted in states totalling nearly a hundred electoral votes. Candidates had to take notice.

If the *New York Times* is any test, the press, too, was taking increasing notice. From December 1915 to March 1916, only six suffrage stories appeared on the first five pages of the *Times*, and many that did appear were printed along with engagement, marriage, birth and death notices. By July coverage began to pick up, and two and three column articles replaced the earlier brief paragraphs. By late summer editorials and letters to the editor appeared in considerable numbers, including a protracted argument over the right of the federal government to impose woman suffrage on states which had previously defeated state constitutional amendments.[6]

The Sixty-fourth Congress met on December 4, 1916 to hear President Wilson read his message to Congress. Now safely reelected, he did not mention woman suffrage. While he spoke representatives of the Congressional Union seated in the gallery quietly unfurled a large banner: "Mr. President, What Will You Do For Woman Suffrage?" The press reported that after a moment's pause he continued reading, but it was a question that neither Wilson nor the American nation could sidestep much longer.[7]

Four more years of hard work lay ahead for suffragists, but by the end of 1916 the corner had been turned. The ideological and political spectrum had shifted to the left, and in the process woman suffrage had been legitimized in the minds of many Americans. It was rapidly picking up support among women and men in all parts of the country.

After a period of stagnation, new energies and new tactical ideas emerged within the movement and precipitated a division. The new organization, modelled to some extent on that of the English militants, had found its way to new and dramatic tactics.[8] Its emergence, its vigor, and its tactics all served to challenge the National American Woman Suffrage Association and led to its reinvigoration. Though neither organization had much use for the other, they supplemented one another very well. In the atmosphere of progressivism the question was no longer whether women would have the vote in the United States, but only when.

VICTORY: 1917–1920

WINNING PLANS

For suffragists, scattering from the NAWSA emergency convention to pick up their assigned tasks or gathering in intense conference around Alice Paul at the "Little White House" on LaFayette Square, the fall of 1916 was an exciting time to be alive. Suffrage was suddenly a major issue; newspapers and magazines were full of it, the environment was more accepting than it had ever been, four million women in eleven states could now vote, and members of both organizations were in fine fettle. Women were increasingly exhilarated by the experience of concentrated, demanding work for a high cause, one which was at last making visible progress. An English militant could have been speaking for them all when she wrote: "All the time, watching, attacking, defending, moving and counter-moving! . . . how glorious those . . . days were! To lose the personal in the great impersonal is to live!"[9] For many women the suffrage movement gave a meaning and force to life that would be remembered with keen nostalgia in later years.

The essence of Mrs. Catt's "Winning Plan" was careful coordination of work in the states with lobbying in Washington. In order for women in the congressional districts to do their job, they were supplied with a steady flow of precise information, along with constant reminders to send letters of appreciation to every member of Congress who did anything to help the cause. They were responsible for building every kind of pressure from home: resolutions of all sorts, letters from politically active men, news of mass meetings— whatever they could drum up. The flow of information from Washington required a major effort at that end. Mrs. Park described what she saw when she arrived to join the Congressional Committee:

> . . . file cases holding . . . 531 portfolios, 96 for the Senate and 435 for the House . . . provided . . . all the known data about a senator or representative. There were printed sketches of his life; there were facts supplied by our members in the state about his personal, political, business and religious affiliations; there were

reports of interviews . . . there was everything that could be discovered about his stand on woman suffrage and more or less about his views on other public questions. . . .[10]

From time to time groups of women from individual states would journey to Washington at their own expense to add their efforts to those of the regular members of the NAWSA Congressional Committee. In January 1917, for example, twenty-nine women arrived from sixteen states. Mrs. Catt's later judgment was that no group ever came to know the inside of Congress as suffragists did.

The Congressional Union deployed smaller numbers in its lobbying effort, but these members were equally diligent— walking the corridors of the House and Senate office buildings by day, and gathering in the evening to exchange information and plot the next step. The Congressional Union also kept full and careful files and sought to use its information in much the same way as did NAWSA.

Although the two groups made similar organizational preparations for lobbying they had different self-images. This was reflected to some extent in the manner in which they conducted their congressional activities. Mrs. Park was concerned with finding just the right woman to make a favorable impression on the member being interviewed. She always sent a woman from a man's own region if possible, recognizing the difficulty a New England woman might have, for example, with a congressman from Georgia. She thought on balance her most successful lobbyists were women from the Middle-West, middle-aged, and "rather too dressy," but "possessed of much common sense and understanding of politics in general, as well as of the men from their districts." They impressed the members, she thought, as substantial citizens of the type who had great weight with office holders.[11]

Congressional Union women did not pride themselves on diplomacy; rather the contrary:

Here was an army of young Amazons who looked them [congressmen] straight in the eye, who were absolutely informed, who knew their rights, who were not to be frightened by bluster, put off by rudeness, or thwarted either by delay or political trickery. They never lost their tempers and they never gave up. . . . They were young and they believed they could do the impossible. . . .[12]

There was a measure of fantasy in this description, and doubtless the constant emphasis upon the youth and vigor of Congressional Union women contributed to the friction between the two groups. Neither Mrs. Park in her late thirties nor Mrs. Catt in her fifties felt themselves ready to be put out to pasture.

NAWSA was by now the largest voluntary organization in the country. Two million women, slowly being organized along lines of political jurisdictions, learning the ways of politics, were beginning to make their weight felt. A conference set up to train local people for more effective work in their congressional districts gave evidence of a sense of growing confidence when it adopted a resolution to the effect that if the Sixty-fifth Congress should fail to submit the federal suffrage amendment before the 1918 election, the association would "select a sufficient number of Senators and Representatives for replacement" to assure passage by the Sixty-sixth.[13]

The Texas congressional chairman was an example of the new breed NAWSA was developing: she arrived in Washington well acquainted with the situation in most Texas districts, and went off at once for interviews on Capital Hill. Coming back to Suffrage House at night she remarked of one Texas member, "There is nothing we can do but retire him. That is what we will have to do."[14]

Every new achievement in the states added to the stock of "good news" the congressional committee found so helpful in Washington. In one eight-month period in 1917 the number of electoral votes dependent in part on women jumped from 91 to 172. Good news indeed.[15]

With the help of Wilson's close friend Helen Hamilton Gardener ("a woman of genius," Maud Wood Park wrote, "who was to teach me almost everything of value I came to know during those years in Washington") NAWSA kept up a steady pressure on the president. Mrs. Gardener was infinitely polite and diplomatic.

Not so the Congressional Union. Convinced that Wilson could and should do more to push the Congress, on January 10, 1917, pickets appeared at the White House bearing banners with such slogans as MR. PRESIDENT! HOW LONG MUST WOMEN WAIT FOR LIBERTY? As Wilson went out for his afternoon drive, fine words from his own writings on democracy were waved before him. On inauguration day a thousand women walked slowly round and round the executive mansion.

The president whom they were trying to recruit to their cause was, by this time, almost wholly preoccupied with the implications of the European War for the United States. In January he had laid before the Congress his "Peace without Victory" message describing the kind of settlement he hoped would be reached among the warring powers. His grand hope was that the United States, from a position of strict neutrality, would be able to bring both sides to the peace table, and lead them to a new era in international relations. In the end, he got not peace but war. By the end of February the Germans had made it clear that they were determined to sink every ship in the war zones they could, neutral and belligerent alike. This, Wilson felt, the United States could not tolerate. This new Congress was summoned into special session to receive the president's war message, and on April 6 it declared war on the Central Powers. There were many pacifists among suffrage workers, and these watched with pride as Jeannette Rankin of Montana, the first woman to be elected to the Congress, cast one of the fifty votes against the war resolution. There was also some dismay as other suffrage leaders counted the possible cost of being identified with Miss Rankin's presumed lack of patriotism.

The war changed the situation in which the suffrage campaign was conducted. Mrs. Catt had foreseen the possibility that war would come, and in February the Executive Council of NAWSA, after long debate, had decided to pledge service to the government if war should come, but decided also that it would continue the suffrage effort without relaxation. The National Woman's Party, which now encompassed the Congressional Union, decided in convention that while individual members could do as their consciences dictated, the organization as such would take no part in war work. It would continue to work for woman suffrage and for that alone, believing that in so doing it would "serve the highest interest of the country."[16]

MILITANT AND EFFECTIVE TACTICS

Picketing of the White House by the Woman's Party had proceeded peacefully at first, but in the summer of 1917 the placards became more provocative. The president was called "Kaiser Wilson" and Russian envoys from the Kerensky government arriving at the White House were greeted with signs warning them that there was no real democracy in the United States. Onlookers were provoked, skirmishes broke out, and in time arrests began. More than two hundred women were arrested, and ninety-seven sentenced to jail for "obstructing the sidewalk." The newspapers reported every incident, usually on the front pages. In jail the women protested their miserable conditions and rough handling, demanded to be treated as the political prisoners they felt themselves to be, and finally went on a hunger strike. Embarrassed and outmaneuvered, the administration dropped the charges and released the prisoners.

The women of NAWSA and many of

their friends in Congress were sure these militant tactics hurt the movement and slowed the progress of the amendment. The Woman's Party insisted that the reverse was true, and took credit for the favorable report which came from the Senate Committee on Woman Suffrage on September 15, and for the long-delayed appointment of a House Committee on Woman Suffrage on September 24, accomplishments which NAWSA thought "we came very near losing because of their activities."[17]

Probably the militant tactics did more good than harm. Nervousness about what the radical women might do next encouraged both Congress and the president to make concessions and to embrace the more conservative suffragists as the lesser evil. The sequence here, as elsewhere, illustrates the usefulness of a radical faction in a reform movement. But for the rivalry and complementarity of the two, the federal amendment might have been delayed for years, though neither faction was prepared, then or later, to recognize the contribution of the other.

While the country slowly geared itself to fight a war, suffragists in New York were busier and better organized than ever before. In November the suffrage referendum there carried by an impressive margin of one hundred thousand votes. This was dramatic progress, especially at a time when much energy of activist women was going to war work. When the Sixty-fifth Congress met for its regular session in December, women in Washington could tell the difference the New York referendum result had made in their reception on the Hill.

Almost immediately the House adopted the prohibition amendment, which removed another obstacle. The liquor interests had long feared that women voters would enact prohibition; if prohibition was coming anyway there was no reason to waste time and effort fighting woman suffrage. Maud Wood Park noted that

"Many wet opponents . . . felt their chief reason for objection was gone."[18]

President Wilson was coming to believe that both party necessity and his own position as an international leader required him to support a federal suffrage amendment. On January 4, 1918 the *New York Times* reported that Theodore Roosevelt had written the Republican National Committee urging that everything possible be done to persuade Republican congressmen to vote for the amendment, and suggesting that a woman from each suffrage state be added to the National Committee itself. Five days later Wilson advised a delegation of Democrats to vote for the amendment "as an act of right and justice to the women of the country and of the world." On the same day in a private letter he said that though he hesitated to volunteer advice to congressmen, when anyone asked he advised them to vote for the amendment.[19]

In the first issue of *The Revolution* in 1868 Elizabeth Cady Stanton had foreseen a time when party necessity would force men to vote for woman suffrage. That time had finally arrived. As each additional state adopted suffrage, national party leaders became more respectful. The women's vote had become a factor in many election calculations.

On January 10, 1918 the House of Representatives witnessed one of those dramas of which myths are made: galleries packed with tense, waiting women; sick men brought from their beds to vote; a New York congressman leaving the deathbed of his suffragist wife to cast his ballot. Only six members failed to vote (or to be paired)—itself an indication of how important the amendment had become since 1915 when forty-one had failed to be recorded. When the roll call ended there were 274 yeas and 136 nay votes—the necessary two-thirds had finally been achieved.

Thirty-three New Yorkers had voted yes, twenty-two more than in 1915. Eighteen percent of the southern representatives now voted for the bill; two percent had voted yes in 1915. And while ninety percent of the men from suffrage states had voted yes, so had half those from nonsuffrage states, a gain from the thirty-six percent in 1915. While the increase in the number of suffrage states was the most vital factor in victory, the increase in suffrage sentiment in nonsuffrage states was also very helpful.

As women poured out of the galleries a Woman's Party member from Massachusetts struck up the doxology. The marble halls reverberated to the sound of "Praise God from which all blessings flow . . ." and for a few minutes NAWSA and Woman's Party members sang in harmony.

BATTLE FOR THE SENATE

God's blessing did not flow all at once, however, for there was still the Senate to be conquered, and that body proved itself capable of resistance to both popular and presidential pressure. Six-year terms protected senators from the immediate impact of public opinion, and though direct election had been in effect since 1913, one-third of the members still held their seats courtesy of a state legislature. Ten prosuffrage senators had died during the Sixty-fifth congress. And then there was the South. Southern senators from one-party states had less to fear from competition at election time, and more dread of the possible consequences of a federal amendment. Southern women were flocking to the cause: Senator Simmons from North Carolina, for one, heard often from his daughters on the subject, but his vote was not changed. Many southern women came, bearing petitions and other evidence of the change of opinion back home. A petition signed by one thousand of the country's "best known" men added to the pressure on the Senate.

Still NAWSA's careful check list indicated that two additional votes were needed for the required two-thirds. The women praised the courage of Louisiana Senator Ransdell who supported suffrage as a matter of justice, while admitting that many of his constituents did not agree, and gave grudging admiration to McCumber of North Dakota who said he would vote for the amendment despite his own convictions, because his state had granted women the vote.

During the winter and spring of 1918 both suffrage organizations tried to recruit two more senators. On May 22 Wilson said ruefully that he had done everything he could think of, to no avail. Mass meetings were organized throughout the country, and on July 13 a massive demonstration was mounted on Boston Common. Conventions of the American Federation of Labor and the National Education Association among others called for action.

By July 17, in response to Mrs. Park's urgent plea, 554 resolutions had come in from a variety of organizations. Indiana alone supplied 120, and only Delaware and Georgia failed to send any.[20] The Democratic National Committee voted unanimously to support the amendment; the Republicans had already done so.

In August the Woman's Party once again took to the streets, and a new round of arrests began. In September the pickets added a new twist—burning Wilson's speeches before the White House gate, once again accusing him of hypocrisy, despite his by now vigorous efforts on behalf of the amendment. (Between June and August he made personal pleas to eight antisuffrage senators.) Twice the Senate had seemed ready to vote; twice the chairman of the Woman Suffrage Committee, Senator A. A. Jones, had withdrawn the amendment rather than risk defeat. Then, on September 26, he moved to take it up.

After five days of debate in which all the old arguments were once again rehearsed, the president took the extraordinary step of appearing in person to plead for a favorable vote. He argued that the suffrage amendment was vital to "the winning of the war and to the energies alike of preparation and of battle." It was also, he said, ". . . vital to the right solution of the great problems we must settle . . . when the war is over."[21] Other members of his party were saying, not so publicly, that the fall elections might well turn upon the passage of the amendment. Neither the president nor the prosuffrage Democrats prevailed; the roll call was taken and still two votes were needed for a two-thirds majority.

The *New York Tribune* reported that Republicans expected to gain Progressive votes in November as a result of the intransigence on the part of southern Democrats, and suggested that both houses of Congress might change hands as a result. It thought the voters would rebuke senators who had voted "no," since the United States "will not long support a Senate that insists upon being more reactionary and less progressive than the British House of Lords." The *New York World* could "find no evidence of consistency or principle," saying that the adverse vote "represented personal prejudice rather than adherence to any known theory of government." David Lawrence writing in the *Evening Post* reported that northern and western Democrats were indeed worried about the election. "It is truly an extraordinary situation," he said with some wonder, "and woman is at the bottom of it all."[22]

On October 25 Wilson again took an unusual step when he asked the voters to return a Democratic Congress to help him end the war and win the peace. When the dust settled after the election the Republicans had gained twenty-five seats in the House, and six in the Senate. This election has sometimes been interpreted as a sharp rebuke to the president, but one of the country's leading political scientists assessed the change, at the time, as about normal for off year elections.

Republicans gained six seats in Ohio, four each in Indiana and Kansas, three each in New York, Pennsylvania, Missouri and Nebraska, two in Colorado, and one each in California, and West Virginia. All but five of these were suffrage states. However, Democrats also defeated Republicans for particular seats in New York, New Jersey, Pennsylvania, California, Nevada, and Oklahoma, so generalization is impossible. The chances are that local situations were as important in many races as national issues.[23]

NAWSA had lived up to its threat to select recalcitrant senators for defeat, and had chosen four, two from each party, as objects of special campaign efforts. Somewhat to their own amazement, by excellent organization of women in both states, Republican Senator Weeks in Massachusetts and Democratic Senator Saulsbury in Delaware were defeated. The other two, Moses of New Hampshire and Baird of New Jersey were returned, but with diminished majorities. Unless death once again took off prosuffrage senators, the precious two votes were now assured.

But the women were taking no chances. After yet another failure to get a favorable vote in the lameduck session of the Sixty-fifth Congress, they turned all their energy toward making sure of the Sixtysixth. Resolutions again poured in: twenty-four state legislatures asked the Congress to submit the amendment.

Wilson, in Paris for the peace talks, continued to urge support upon hesitant Democrats. The fall elections had added three more full suffrage states and six more presidential suffrage states, as well as bringing primary suffrage in Arkansas and Texas. Women could now vote for presidential electors in thirty states for a total of 339 electoral votes. The "Winning Plan" was working. The House, with 117 new members, passed the amendment for a second time, this time by a vote of 304 to 89. Of all the new men voting, only six voted no! Two hundred and twenty-four of those voting yes came from suffrage states, and eighty from nonsuffrage ones. Thirty percent of the southerners were now voting yes, a significant change in sentiment since the first roll call in 1915. All six Arkansas congressmen, three of four from Florida, and ten of seventeen from Texas swelled the southern contribution. Only Mississippi and South Carolina remained solidly "no."

Then, at long last, came June 4 when the Senate was to vote once again. This time it bowed to the inevitable, but just barely. Even now, when the amendment was certain to pass, there was no rush to get on the bandwagon: thirty senators still voted no. Of the thirteen new men, however, eleven voted for the amendment. The women took no time for rejoicing: they were already busy with the drive for ratification.

RATIFICATION: THE FINAL STEP

A constitutional amendment must be approved by legislatures (or special conventions) in three-fourths of the states. The federal system had presented American suffragists with difficult political and legal problems from the beginning and the difficulties were to continue to the very end. The magic number was thirty-six, and eleven ratifications came in the first month. The next five months brought eleven more ratifications. While the proponents of suffrage needed the support of thirty-six states, opponents had to hold only *thirteen* states to block ratification, and the opposition was never more active.

With an eye on the electoral votes already affected by women suffrage, the national committees of both parties urged speedy ratification. As is usual with state legislators, however, local conditions were more important than the preferences of national leaders. Weary, but by now experienced, local suffrage organizations went to work. Armed with well-researched

lists of governors and legislators they began again the process of persuasion. Mrs. Catt travelled where ever she was needed and the Woman's Party deployed its organizers.

By August 1920 thirty-five states had ratified and only one state remained in which ratification was deemed feasible before the presidential election. A special session of the Tennessee legislature was scheduled to begin on August 9 and suffragists and opponents poured into Nashville. It was a wild ten days. The liquor interests, railroad lobby and manufacturers lobby were all active. Opponents of suffrage set up shop on the 8th floor of the Hermitage Hotel and "dispensed Old Bourbon and moonshine whisky with lavish insistence."[24] There was considerable intoxication and on one dismal night, reports circulated that the entire legislature was drunk. In any case by August 13 state senators were sober enough to ratify the amendment by a vote of twenty-five to four.

The contest now swirled around the lower House. There were rumors of deals and bribes and offers of loans on attractive terms. Supporters the suffragists had counted on mysteriously defected, and it was alleged that an attempt was made to kidnap a suffrage member. The vote was so close that it turned on the decision of twenty-four-year-old Harry Burn, the youngest member of the legislature. In the end he supported suffrage because, so legend has it, his mother urged him to "help Mrs. Catt." The amendment carried by forty-nine to forty-seven.

In the early morning hours of August 26, 1920 the United States secretary of state issued a formal proclamation, and the struggle was over. Seventy-two years had passed since the women at Seneca Falls resolved to "seek their sacred right to the elective franchise." Everywhere in the United States women had the legal right to vote.

Notes

1. See Sharon Hartman Storm, "Leadership and Tactics in the American Woman Suffrage Movement: A New Perspective from Massachusetts," *Journal of American History* 62 (Sept. 1975), pp. 262–82.

2. See Harriot Stanton Blatch, *Challenging Years* (New York: G.P. Putnam's Sons, 1940), pp. 91–242. Caroline Katzenstein, *Lifting the Curtain* (Philadelphia: Dorrance and Company, 1955), pp. 46–47. Louise Noun, *Strong Minded Women* (Ames: The Iowa State University Press, 1969), pp. 246–247, and the *Woman's Journal*, 1905–1910 for evidence of the growing influence of English militant methods in the American suffrage movement. Enthusiastic crowds turned out to hear Mrs. Pankhurst, the leader of the English militants, in New York in 1909 and in Boston in 1910.

3. Eleanor Flexner, *Century of Struggle* (Cambridge: Harvard University Press, 1958), p. 256.

4. Carrie Chapman Catt to Maud Wood Park, August 30, 1916, Maud Wood Park Papers, Schlesinger Library, Radcliffe College, Cambridge, Massachusetts.

5. See *New York Times*, Nov. 12, 1916. The analysis is based on observations of local politicians and correspondents; no survey data of the kind which we might have now was available. The only place where women's vote could be accurately measured was Illinois (since women there could vote only for president). In that state women voted more heavily for Charles Evans Hughes, the Republican candidate, than did the men.

6. We are indebted to an unpublished paper by Myla Taylor, Duke University student, for this information.

7. Inez Haynes Irwin, *The Story of the Woman's Party* (New York: Harcourt-Brace, 1921), pp. 185–86.

8. It is important to note that woman suffrage as an international movement had spread widely since New Zealand enfranchised its women in 1893. Australia, Austria, Canada, Czechoslovakia, Denmark, England, Finland, Germany, Hungary, Ireland, Mexico, Norway, Poland, Russia, and Scotland all had woman suffrage before 1919. See Ross Evans Paulson, *Women's Suffrage and Temperance* (Glenview, Illinois: Scott-Foresman, 1973) for . . . discussion of the international suffrage movement.

9. Christabel Pankhurst, *Unshackled: The Story of How We Won the Vote* (London: Hutchinson, 1959), p. 83. Such a spirit supplies great energy to a social movement; it pervades the personal documents of the women who did the work in NAWSA and in the Woman's Party. By the time of the first House victory in January 1918 many members of Congress had come to share the sense of a great cause, and some went to extraordinary lengths to insure the success of the amendment on that occasion. The feeling of solidarity in a good cause is powerful.

10. Maud Wood Park, *Front Door Lobby* (Boston: Beacon Press, 1960. Copyright © 1960 by Edna Lamprey Stantial. Reprinted by permission of Beacon Press), p. 19.

11. Park, *Front Door Lobby*, p. 44.

12. Irwin, *Story of the Woman's Party*, p. 334.

13. Carrie Chapman Catt and Nettie R. Shuler, *Woman Suffrage and Politics* (New York: Charles Scribner's Sons, 1923), p. 318. The figure of two million is based on Aileen Kraditor's careful estimates. See *Ideas of the Woman Suffrage Movement* (New York: Columbia University Press, 1965), p. 45.

14. Ethel Smith to Maud Wood Park, October 10, 1917, Maud Wood Park Papers, Schlesinger Library, Cambridge, Massachusetts.

15. Park, *Front Door Lobby*, p. 71.

16. Doris Stevens, *Jailed for Freedom* (New York: Boni and Liveright, 1920), p. 82.

17. Loretta Zimmerman, "Alice Paul and the National Woman's Party" (doctoral dissertation, Tulane University, 1964), p. 241.

18. Report of the National Congressional Committee, December 1, 1917–January 11, 1918, Maud Wood Park Papers, Schlesinger Library, Cambridge, Massachusetts.

19. Ray Stannard Baker, *Woodrow Wilson: Life and Letters* (New York: Doubleday Page and Co., 1927), vol. VII, p. 460.

20. Memo in Maud Wood Park Papers, Schlesinger Library, Cambridge, Massachusetts. These papers are filled with information concerning the effort to turn the Senate around.

21. U.S., Congress, Senate, Document 284, 65th Cong., 1st sess.

22. These comments were reported in *The Literary Digest* 59 (October 12, 1918), pp. 12–13.

23. P. Orman Ray, "American Government and Politics," *American Political Science Review* 12, no. 1 (Feb. 1910), pp. 80–84.

24. Catt and Shuler, *Woman Suffrage*, p. 442. See also A. Elizabeth Taylor, *The Woman Suffrage Movement in Tennessee* (New York: Bookman Associates, 1957), chapter 7.

DOCUMENT: Controlling Reproduction

MARGARET SANGER
My Fight for Birth Control

Nowhere does gender matter more than in the area of reproduction. The contrast between the high fertility of newly arriving immigrants and the low birth rate among old-stock Americans around the turn of the century prompted such leaders as Theodore Roosevelt to lament "race suicide" and to exhort women of the "proper sort" to perform their maternal functions in the selfless fashion dictated by time and tradition. Viewed through women's eyes, however, these population trends looked different, as this selection on the beginnings of the birth control movement dramatically illustrates. While a few radicals such as Emma Goldman saw contraception as a means of liberating women by restoring to them control over their own bodies and thereby lessening their economic dependence on men, it was Margaret Higgins Sanger whose name would become most closely linked with the crusade for birth control.

The factors that propelled Sanger—always a complex personality—to leadership were many. One of eleven children, she helped bury her mother, who died of tuberculosis. Young Margaret, however, was convinced that it was the passion of her father who lived to be eighty which was the real cause of her mother's death. A nursing career also shaped Sanger's thinking, as the following account suggests. Arrested under the Comstock Law (document 6 in Essential Documents) for publication of a newspaper advocating contraception, she fled in 1914 to England with her husband and three children. There she met the famous British psychologist and sex expert, Havelock Ellis, who further convinced her that sexual experience should be separated from reproduction, enabling couples to enhance the quality of their sexual relationship. Returning to New York, the Sangers continued their activities on behalf of birth control. The opening of the Brownsville clinic in 1916, recounted here, resulted in still further confrontation with authorities. The hunger strike of Sanger's sister, Ethel Byrne, a nurse at the clinic, was followed by Sanger's own trial. Convicted of "maintaining a public nuisance," she was sentenced to thirty days in the workhouse. Ever the icono-

Excerpted from "Awakening and Revolt," "A 'Public Nuisance,' " and "Hunger Strike," chaps. 3, 12, and 13 of *My Fight for Birth Control* by Margaret Sanger (New York: Farrar & Reinhart, 1931). Copyright © 1931 by Margaret Sanger. Reprinted by permission of Grant Sanger. Cross-references have been adjusted.

clast and rebel, she gave talks to other inmates on sex hygiene when the matrons were out of sight. Divorcing William Sanger, she subsequently married a wealthy oil man who contributed liberally to the American Birth Control League, which she founded in 1921.

Important financial aid would also come in later years from the wealthy feminist, Katherine McCormick, who shared Sanger's commitment to research in contraception. In the early 1950s McCormick provided funds for experiments in endocrinology that led to the development of the birth control pill. At a time when few scientists thought an oral contraceptive was possible, the insistence of Sanger and McCormick that every woman had the right to control her own body helped bring about a major breakthrough in medical technology. In 1960 "the pill" became available to the public. The timing was propitious, for it coincided with a period of sexual liberation that, while proving in some respects to be a mixed blessing for women, also coincided with new recognition of the intensity of their sexual drive and capacity for sexual pleasure.

Although Sanger saw the development of an oral contraceptive as another victory in a long and difficult struggle for reproductive freedom, others viewed the birth control movement differently. Arguments that limiting family size could not only free women's energies for social reform but prevent the world's poor from producing children they were unable to care for met with opposition from women themselves in the early years of Sanger's crusade. Some feared that birth control would contribute to promiscuity; others feared it would deny women the dignity that was theirs by virtue of motherhood. The Roman Catholic Church was unrelenting in its opposition, maintaining that the use of contraceptives is a sin. Among groups in the self-styled profamily movement of the 1980s Sanger is still being angrily attacked. Her contribution to the lives of modern American women remains a matter of political debate. Birth control is not only a technical way of spacing and limiting children so as to benefit both mother and child but is part of a larger debate about the extent to which women should be able to control their own reproductive lives.

AWAKENING AND REVOLT

Early in the year 1912 I came to a sudden realization that my work as a nurse and my activities in social service were entirely palliative and consequently futile and useless to relieve the misery I saw all about me. . . .

It is among the mothers here that the most difficult problems arise—the outcasts of society with theft, filth, perjury, cruelty, brutality oozing from beneath.

Ignorance and neglect go on day by day; children born to breathe but a few hours and pass out of life; pregnant women toiling early and late to give food to four or five children, always hungry; boarders taken into homes where there is not sufficient room for the family; little girls eight and ten years of age sleeping in the same room with dirty, foul smelling, loathsome men; women whose weary, pregnant, shapeless bodies refuse to accommodate themselves to the husbands' desires find husbands looking with lustful eyes upon other women, sometimes upon their own little daughters, six and seven years of age.

In this atmosphere abortions and birth become the main theme of conversation. On Saturday nights I have seen groups of fifty to one hundred women going into questionable offices well known in the community for cheap abortions. I asked several women what took place there, and they all gave the same reply: a quick examination, a probe inserted into the uterus and turned a few times to disturb the fertilized ovum, and then the woman was sent home. Usually the flow began the next day and often continued four or five weeks. Sometimes an ambulance carried the victim to the hospital for a curetage, and if she returned home at all she was looked upon as a lucky woman.

This state of things became a nightmare with me. There seemed no sense to it all, no reason for such waste of mother life, no right to exhaust women's vitality and to throw them on the scrap-heap before the age of thirty-five.

Everywhere I looked, misery and fear stalked—men fearful of losing their jobs, women fearful that even worse conditions might come upon them. The menace of another pregnancy hung like a sword over the head of every poor woman I came in contact with that year. The question which met me was always the same: What can I do to keep from it? or, What can I do to get out of this? Sometimes they talked among themselves bitterly.

"It's the rich that know the tricks," they'd say, "while we have all the kids." Then, if the women were Roman Catholics, they talked about "Yankee tricks," and asked me if I knew what the Protestants did to keep their families down. When I said that I didn't believe that the rich knew much more than they did I was laughed at and suspected of holding back information for money. They would nudge each other and say something about pay-

ing me before I left the case if I would reveal the "secret." . . .

I heard over and over again of their desperate efforts at bringing themselves "around"—drinking various herb-teas, taking drops of turpentine on sugar, steaming over a chamber of boiling coffee or of turpentine water, rolling down stairs, and finally inserting slippery-elm sticks, or knitting needles, or shoe hooks into the uterus. I used to shudder with horror as I heard the details and, worse yet, learned of the conditions *behind the reason* for such desperate actions.

. . . Each time I returned it was to hear that Mrs. Cohen had been carried to a hospital but had never come back, that Mrs. Kelly had sent the children to a neighbor's and had put her head into the gas oven to end her misery. Many of the women had consulted midwives, social workers and doctors at the dispensary and asked a way to limit their families, but they were denied this help, sometimes indignantly or gruffly, sometimes jokingly; but always knowledge was denied them. Life for them had but one choice: either to abandon themselves to incessant childbearing, or to terminate their pregnancies through abortions. Is it any wonder they resigned themselves hopelessly, as the Jewish and Italian mothers, or fell into drunkenness, as the Irish and Scotch? The latter were often beaten by husbands, as well as by their sons and daughters. They were driven and cowed, and only as beasts of burden were allowed to exist. . . .

They claimed my thoughts night and day. One by one these women, with their worried, sad, pensive and ageing faces would marshal themselves before me in my dreams, sometimes appealingly, sometimes accusingly. I could not escape from the facts of their misery, neither was I able to see the way out of their problems and their troubles. . . .

Finally the thing began to shape itself, to become accumulative during the three weeks I spent in the home of a desperately sick woman living on Grand Street, a lower section of New York's East Side.

Mrs. Sacks was only twenty-eight years old; her husband, an unskilled worker, thirty-two. Three children, aged five, three and one, were none too strong nor sturdy, and it took all the earnings of the father and the ingenuity of the mother to keep them clean, provide them with air and proper food, and give them a chance to grow into decent manhood and womanhood.

Both parents were devoted to these children and to each other. The woman had become pregnant and had taken various drugs and purgatives, as advised by her neighbors. Then, in desperation, she had used some instrument lent to her by a friend. She was found prostrate on the floor amidst the crying children when her husband returned from work. Neighbors advised against the ambulance, and a friendly doctor was called. The husband would not hear of her going to a hospital, and as a little money had been saved in the bank a nurse was called and the battle for that precious life began.

. . . The three-room apartment was turned into a hospital for the dying patient. Never had I worked so fast, so concentratedly as I did to keep alive that little mother. . . .

. . . July's sultry days and nights were melted into a torpid inferno. Day after day, night after night, I slept only in brief snatches, ever too anxious about the condition of that feeble heart bravely carrying on, to stay long from the bedside of the patient. With but one toilet for the building and that on the floor below, everything had to be carried down for disposal, while ice, food and other necessities had to be carried three flights up. It was one of those old airshaft buildings of which there were several thousands then standing in New York City.

At the end of two weeks recovery was in sight, and at the end of three weeks I was preparing to leave the fragile patient to take up the ordinary duties of her life including those of wifehood and motherhood. . . .

But as the hour for my departure came nearer, her anxiety increased, and finally with trembling voice she said: "Another baby will finish me, I suppose."

"It's too early to talk about that," I said, and resolved that I would turn the question over to the doctor for his advice. When he came I said: "Mrs. Sacks is worried about having another baby."

"She well might be," replied the doctor, and then he stood before her and said: "Any more such capers, young woman, and there will be no need to call me."

"Yes, yes—I know, Doctor," said the patient with trembling voice, "but," and she hesitated as if it took all of her courage to say it, "*what* can I do to prevent getting that way again?"

"Oh ho!" laughed the doctor good naturedly, "You want your cake while you eat it too, do you? Well, it can't be done." Then, familiarly slapping her on the back and picking up his hat and bag to depart, he said: "I'll tell you the only sure thing to do. Tell Jake to sleep on the roof!"

With those words he closed the door and went down the stairs, leaving us both petrified and stunned.

Tears sprang to my eyes, and a lump came in my throat as I looked at that face before me. It was stamped with sheer horror. I thought for a moment she might have gone insane, but she conquered her feelings, whatever they may have been, and turning to me in desperation said: "He can't understand, can he?—he's a man after all—but you do, don't you? You're a woman and you'll tell me the secret and I'll never tell it to a soul."

She clasped her hands as if in prayer, she leaned over and looked straight into my eyes and beseechingly implored me to tell her something—something I *really did not know.* . . .

I had to turn away from that imploring face. I could not answer her then. I quieted her as best I could. She saw that I was moved by the tears in my eyes. I promised that I would come back in a few days and tell her what she wanted to know. The few simple means of limiting the family like *coitus interruptus* or the condom were laughed at by the neighboring women when told these were the means used by men in the well-to-do families. That was not believed, and I knew such an answer would be swept aside as useless were I to tell her this at such a time. . . .

The intelligent reasoning of the young mother—how to *prevent* getting that way again—how sensible, how just she had been—yes, I promised myself I'd go back and have a long talk with her and tell her more, and perhaps she would not laugh but would believe that those methods were all that were really known.

But time flew past, and weeks rolled into months. . . . I was about to retire one night three months later when the telephone rang and an agitated man's voice begged me to come at once to help his wife who was sick again. It was the husband of Mrs. Sacks, and I intuitively knew before I left the telephone that it was almost useless to go.

. . . I arrived a few minutes after the doctor, the same one who had given her such noble advice. The woman was dying. She was unconscious. She died within ten minutes after my arrival. It was the same result, the same story told a thousand times before—death from abortion. She had become pregnant, had used drugs, had then consulted a five-dollar professional abortionist, and death followed.

The doctor shook his head as he rose from listening for the heart beat. . . . The gentle woman, the devoted mother, the loving wife had passed on leaving behind her a frantic husband, helpless in his loneliness, bewildered in his helplessness as he paced up and down the room, hands clenching his head, moaning "My God! My God! My God!"

The Revolution came—but not as it has been pictured nor as history relates that revolutions have come. . . .

After I left that desolate house I walked and walked and walked; for hours and hours I kept on, bag in hand, thinking, regretting, dreading to stop; fearful of my conscience, dreading to face my own accusing soul. At three in the morning I arrived home still clutching a heavy load the weight of which I was quite unconscious.

. . . As I stood at the window and looked out, the miseries and problems of that sleeping city arose before me in a clear vision like a panorama: crowded homes, too many children; babies dying in infancy; mothers overworked; baby nurseries; children neglected and hungry —mothers so nervously wrought they could not give the little things the comfort nor care they needed; mothers half sick most of their lives—"always ailing, never failing"; women made into drudges; children working in cellars; children aged six and seven pushed into the labor market to help earn a living; another baby on the way; still another; yet another; a baby born dead—great relief; an older child dies—sorrow, but nevertheless relief—insurance helps; a mother's death—children scattered into institutions; the father, desperate, drunken; he slinks away to become an outcast in a society which has trapped him.

. . . There was only one thing to be done: call out, start the alarm, set the heather on fire! Awaken the womanhood of America to free the motherhood of the world! I released from my almost paralyzed hand the nursing bag which unconsciously I had clutched, threw it across the room, tore the uniform from my body, flung it into a corner, and renounced all palliative work forever.

I would never go back again to nurse

women's ailing bodies while their miseries were as vast as the stars. I was now finished with superficial cures, with doctors and nurses and social workers who were brought face to face with this overwhelming truth of women's needs and yet turned to pass on the other side. They must be made to see these facts. I resolved that women should have knowledge of contraception. They have every right to know about their own bodies. I would strike out—I would scream from the housetops. I would tell the world what was going on in the lives of these poor women. I *would* be heard. No matter what it should cost. *I would be heard.* . . .

I announced to my family the following day that I had finished nursing, that I would never go on another case—and I never have.

I asked doctors what one could do and was told I'd better keep off that subject or Anthony Comstock would get me. I was told that there were laws against that sort of thing. This was the reply from every medical man and woman I approached. . . .

A "PUBLIC NUISANCE"

The selection of a place for the first birth control clinic was of the greatest importance. No one could actually tell how it would be received in any neighborhood. I thought of all the possible difficulties: The indifference of women's organizations, the ignorance of the workers themselves, the resentment of social agencies, the opposition of the medical profession. Then there was the law—the law of New York State.

Section 1142 was definite. It stated that *no one* could give information to prevent conception to *anyone* for any reason. There was, however, Section 1145, which distinctly stated that physicians (*only*) could give advice to prevent conception for the cure or prevention of disease. I inquired about the section, and was told by two attorneys and several physicians that this clause was an exception to 1142 referring only to venereal disease. But anyway, as I was not a physician, it could not protect me. Dared I risk it?

I began to think of the doctors I knew. Several who had previously promised now refused. I wrote, telephoned, asked friends to ask other friends to help me find a woman doctor to help me demonstrate the need of a birth control clinic in New York. None could be found. No one wanted to go to jail. No one cared to test out the law. Perhaps it would have to be done without a doctor. But it had to be done; that I knew.

Fania Mindell, an enthusiastic young worker in the cause, had come on from Chicago to help me. Together we tramped the streets on that dreary day in early October, through a driving rainstorm, to find the best location at the cheapest terms possible . . .

Finally at 46 Amboy Street, in the Brownsville section of Brooklyn, we found a friendly landlord with a good place vacant at fifty dollars a month rental; and Brownsville was settled on. It was one of the most thickly populated sections. It had a large population of working class Jews, always interested in health measures, always tolerant of new ideas, willing to listen and to accept advice whenever the health of mother or children was involved. I knew that here there would at least be no breaking of windows, no hurling of insults into our teeth; but I was scarcely prepared for the popular support, the sympathy and friendly help given us in that neighborhood from that day to this. . . .

With a small bundle of handbills and a large amount of zeal, we fared forth each morning in a house-to-house canvass of the district in which the clinic was located. Every family in that great district received a "dodger" printed in English, Yiddish and Italian. . . .

Women of every race and creed flocked to the clinic with the determination not to have any more children than their health could stand or their husbands could support. Jews and Christians, Protestants and Roman Catholics alike made their confessions to us, whatever they may have professed at home or in the church. Some did not dare talk this over with their husbands; and some came urged on by their husbands. Men themselves came after work; and some brought timid, embarassed wives, apologetically dragging a string of little children. . . .

When I asked a bright little Roman Catholic woman what she would say to the priest when he learned that she had been to the Clinic, she answered indignantly: "It's none of his business. My husband has a weak heart and works only four days a week. He gets twelve dollars, and we can barely live on it now. We have enough children."

Her friend, sitting by, nodded a vigorous approval. "When I was married," she broke in, "the priest told us to have lots of children, and we listened to him. I had fifteen. Six are living. Nine baby funerals in our house. I am thirty-six years old now. Look at me! I look sixty."

As I walked home that night, I made a mental calculation of fifteen baptismal fees, nine funeral expenses, masses and candles for the repose of nine little souls, the physical suffering of the mother, and the emotional suffering of both parents; and I asked myself, "Was it fair? Is this the price of Christianity?" . . .

Ethel Byrne, who is my sister and a trained nurse, assisted me in advising, explaining, and demonstrating to the women how to prevent conception. As all of our 488 records were confiscated by the detectives who later arrested us for violation of the New York State law, it is difficult to tell exactly how many more women came in those days to seek advice; but we estimate that it was far more than five hundred. As in any new enterprise, false reports were maliciously spread about the clinic; weird stories without the slightest foundation of truth. We talked plain talk and give plain facts to the women who came there. We kept a record of every applicant. All were mothers; most of them had large families.

It was whispered about that the police were to raid the place for abortions. We had no fear of that accusation. We were trying to spare mothers the necessity of that ordeal by giving them proper contraceptive information. . . .

The arrest and raid on the Brooklyn clinic was spectacular. There was no need of a large force of plain clothes men to drag off a trio of decent, serious women who were testing out a law on a fundamental principle. My federal arrest, on the contrary, had been assigned to intelligent men. One had to respect the dignity of their mission; but the New York city officials seem to use tactics suitable only for crooks, bandits and burglars. We were not surprised at being arrested, but the shock and horror of it was that a *woman*, with a squad of five plain clothes men, conducted the raid and made the arrest. A woman—the irony of it!

I refused to close down the clinic, hoping that a court decision would allow us to continue such necessary work. I was to be disappointed. Pressure was brought upon the landlord, and we were dispossessed by the law as a "public nuisance." In Holland the clinics were called "public utilities."

When the policewoman entered the clinic with her squad of plain clothes men and announced the arrest of Miss Mindell and myself (Mrs. Byrne was not present at the time and her arrest followed later), the room was crowded to suffocation with women waiting in the outer room. The police began bullying these mothers, asking them questions, writing down their names in order to subpoena them to testify against us at the trial. These women, always afraid of trouble which the very presence of a policeman signifies, screamed and cried aloud. The children on their laps screamed, too. It was like a panic for a few minutes until I walked into the room where they were stampeding and begged them to be quiet and not to get excited. I assured them that nothing could happen to them, that I was under arrest but they would be allowed to return home in a few minutes. That quieted them. The men were blocking the door to prevent anyone from leaving, but I finally persuaded them to allow these women to return to their homes, unmolested though terribly frightened by it all.

. . . The patrol wagon came rattling through the streets to our door, and at length Miss Mindell and I took our seats within and were taken to the police station. . . .

HUNGER STRIKE

Out of that spectacular raid, which resulted in an avalanche of nation-wide publicity in the daily press, four separate and distinct cases resulted:

Mrs. Ethel Byrne, my sister, was charged with violating Section 1142 of the Penal Code, designed to prevent dissemination of birth control information.

Miss Fania Mindell was charged with having sold an allegedly indecent book entitled "What Every Girl Should Know" written by Margaret Sanger.

I was charged with having conducted a clinic at 46 Amboy Street, Brooklyn, in violation of the same section of the Penal Code.

Having re-opened the clinic, I was arrested on a charge of "maintaining a public nuisance," in violation of Section 1530 of the Penal Code.

The three of us were held for trial in the Court of Special Sessions, with bail fixed at $500 each. This meant that our cases would be decided by three judges appointed by the Mayor and not by a jury. . . .

My sister was found guilty, and on January 22 she was sentenced to thirty days in the Workhouse. A writ of habeas corpus as a means of suspending sentence during appeal was refused by Supreme Court Justice Callahan. She spent the night in jail.

Ethel Byrne promptly declared a hunger strike. I knew that she would not flinch. Quiet, taciturn, with a will of steel hidden by a diffident air, schooled by her long training as a professional nurse, she announced briefly that she would neither eat, drink, nor work until her release. Commissioner of Correction Burdette G. Lewis promptly announced that she would be permitted to see no one but her attorney.

While the newspapers were reporting—always on the front page—the condition of the hunger striker, plans were hastened for a monster mass meeting of protest, to be held in Carnegie Hall. Helen Todd acted as chairman, and Dr. Mary Halton was an additional speaker. The hall was crowded by a huge audience of all classes. The women patients of the Brownsville clinic were given places of honor on the platform. The salvos of applause which greeted me showed that intelligent opinion was strongly behind us, and did much to give me the courage to fight with renewed strength for the immediate release of Ethel Byrne.

This meeting was acclaimed by the press as a "triumph of women, for women, by women." The meeting was said to have struck the right note—that of being instructive and persuasive, instead of agitational.

In the meantime, Ethel Byrne's refusal to eat and drink was crowding all other news off the front pages of the New York papers. Her defiance was sharpening the issue between self-respecting citizens and the existing law, which was denounced on every street corner as hypocritical. In the subway crowds, on street-corners, everywhere people gathered, the case was discussed. "They are imprisoning a woman for teaching physiological facts!" I heard one man exclaim. . . .

"It makes little difference whether I starve or not," she replied, through her attorney, "so long as this outrageous arrest calls attention to the archaic laws which would prevent our telling the truth about the facts of life. With eight thousand deaths a year in New York State from illegal operations on women, one more death won't make much difference."

All this served to convince the now panic-stricken Mr. Lewis [Commissioner of Correction in charge of Blackwell's Island] that Mrs. Byrne was different, after all, from the alcoholics and drug addicts who had given him his previous experience, and with whom he had gallantly compared her. When she had gone 103 hours without food, he established a precedent in American prison annals. He ordered her forcibly fed. She was the first woman so treated in this country. . . .

The truth was that Mrs. Byrne was in a critical condition after being rolled in a blanket and having milk, eggs and a stimulant forced into her stomach through a rubber tube. I realized this as soon as I heard that she was "passive under the feeding." Nothing but loss of strength could have lessened the power of her resistance to such authority. Nothing but brutality could have reduced her fiery spirit to acquiescence. I was desperate; torn between admiration for what she was doing and misery over what I feared might be the result.

On January 31st, a committee headed by Mrs. Amos Pinchot, Jessie Ashley and myself went to Albany for the purpose of asking Governor Whitman to appoint a commission to investigate birth control and make a report to the state legislature. Governor Whitman, a wise, fair, intelligent executive and statesman, received us, and listened to our exposition of the economic and moral necessity for birth control; the medical theory behind its justification. He promised to consider appointing the commission. During the interview Miss Jessie Ashley introduced the subject of Mrs. Byrne's treatment on Blackwell's Island and the anxiety we felt about her condition. We tried to make him see the outrage committed by the state in making anyone suffer for so just a cause. The Governor offered Mrs. Byrne a pardon on condition that she would not continue to disseminate birth control information. . . .

When we left Albany that day, I had the promise of a provisional pardon for Mrs. Byrne, but best of all I had in my purse a letter from the Governor to the authorities at Blackwell's Island authorizing me to see her. I was shocked and horrified when, in the late afternoon of February 1st, I saw my sister. She was lying semi-conscious on a cot in a dark corner of the prison cell. . . .

There was not time to inform her of the conditions of her pardon, and moreover she was too ill to face the question. I still believe that I was right in accepting the conditions which the Governor imposed. There was no other course. I saw that she was dangerously ill, that nothing further was to be gained by her keeping on, and that her death would have been a terrible calamity. Her life was what mattered to me, regardless of her future activities. . . .

At any rate, by the time she was released the subject was a burning issue. Newspapers which previously had ignored the case, had to mention a matter important enough to bring the Governor of the State from Albany to New York.

The Torch Relay, Opening the National Women's Conference, Houston, Texas, 1977
The torch, brought by runners from Seneca Falls to Houston, symbolized the link be-
tween those early feminists who drafted the Declaration of Sentiments and their con-
temporary counterparts who assembled to present new proposals designed to achieve
the still-elusive goal of equality. From left to right: Billie Jean King, Susan B. Anthony
II, Bella Abzug, Sylvia Ortiz, Peggy Kokernot, Michele Cearcy, Betty Friedan. Photo-
graph by Diana Mara Henry

III

Modern America
1920-85

The years between 1920 and 1980 have, in the main, been years of crisis. Domestically, innovations in technology, management, and marketing transformed an industrial nation into a consumer society. But consumption did not automatically bring the good life that advertisers promised. In the early years after World War I Americans were plagued by tensions that erupted into strikes, attacks upon radicals, and indiscriminate accusations of communism. The climate of suspicion and anxiety brought out the uglier aspects of American society—the Ku Klux Klan enjoyed a brief rebirth. Conflict between generations underscored anxiety over the continuing erosion of Victorian moral standards. Although elements of progressivism persisted, successive Republican administrations pursued policies designed primarily to benefit American corporations on the assumption that the prosperity of the few would bring prosperity to the many. Whether the assumption was true or not, the collapse of corporate America brought collapse to all after the stock market crash of 1929.

The resulting depression crippled industry and left 20 percent of the labor force unemployed. In 1932, after the Hoover administration had failed to produce recovery, voters turned to Franklin Delano Roosevelt and the Democrats. Promising a "new deal" at a time when people were homeless and starving, Roosevelt launched a program of economic recovery and reform, much of it improvised, not all of it successful, and some of it far less radical and extensive than many critics had wished. The result, however, was that in its efforts to cope with economic disaster, the Roosevelt administration redefined the responsibility of the federal government to its citizens. Relief and work programs were provided, unemployment compensation and minimum wages and hours legislation passed, old-age pensions introduced, individual savings accounts insured, farm prices supported, farm ownership encouraged, farm and home mortgages guaranteed, rural houses electrified, and regional development and soil conservation promoted. The welfare state had arrived. Presidents of both parties would subsequently expand it, designing their own programs to benefit the American people. In the process other changes accelerated by international crises occurred: growth in the power of the presidency, in the size of the federal bueraucracy, and in the level of government spending.

If domestic events had occupied the attention of most Americans in previous years, Nazi aggression and Japan's attack upon Pearl Harbor in 1941 thrust their country into a new international role. Mobilized for total war along conventional lines, Americans were psychologically unprepared for their entry into the new atomic age as citizens of the strongest industrial and military power in world history. The implications of these new developments were scarcely understood when tensions between the United States and its former ally, the USSR, escalated into a "cold" war. The expansion of Russian hegemony in eastern Europe and the victory of Chinese communists in a bloody civil war convinced key policy makers that this nation would have to pursue a vigorous policy to "contain" communism throughout the world. If historians cannot agree on the process that led to cold war, they can agree that the persistent confrontations between East and West during the 1950s profoundly affected American life. Viewing North Korea's invasion of South Korea as proof of Russia's drive for world domination and convinced that the credibility of "containment" was at stake, the Truman administration sent troops to check communist aggression. In the United States there was another kind of warfare. Fearing domestic subversion, anticommunists during the McCarthy era purged government, organized labor, the entertainment industry, and schools and universities of communists—real and alleged. Dissent had become tantamount to disloyalty. By the mid-1950s it was axiomatic to some Americans that any critique of American foreign policy or American society—even if justified—was communist inspired. It was not surprising, therefore, that in the 1960s and 1970s blacks and women who wished to improve their social position should be accused of leftist and un-American sympathies. Many Americans, however, weary of conflict and crisis, had long since sought refuge in suburban privatism and the affluent consumerism of the postwar years.

The election of John Fitzgerald Kennedy in 1960 promised energy and optimism. The succeeding years exemplified both, but not in the manner anticipated. Blacks refused to be intimidated any longer by appeals to "gradualism" or threats of violence. They forced white America to address domestic problems too long deferred; they also provided insight, tactics, rhetoric, and impetus to a resurgent feminist movement. Through the vivid images conveyed to them by television, Americans faced a new and disorderly world. Blacks, Chicanos, Indians, students, women, and protesters against the Vietnam War—all confronted the nation in its living rooms. America seemed to be disintegrating. Convinced that protest had become anarchy, middle America elected Richard M. Nixon in 1968 and again in 1972. But the candidate of "law and order" became the president who put himself above the law. His successors tried to repair the damage done the nation's highest office. In some measure, they succeeded. However, they also faced overwhelming economic problems. These became so grave that the American people would elect a conservative to the presidency in 1980 and re-elect him in 1984—one whose "old-fashioned values" kept him from supporting an amendment to give women equal rights under the Constitution. The time of social reform was over. The expansive mood of the 1960s disintegrated in the face of anxiety over the unemployment, inflation, rising energy costs, and declining productivity. Foreign relations were no consolation. There was the embarrassment of Vietnam and the danger of Soviet aggression, the weakening ties with our allies, and a greater interdependence of the industrial nations and the Third World. Looking ahead to the remaining years of the century, a distinguished historian observed that this nation's vaunted capacity for self-renewal would be "sorely tested." Few would disagree.[1]

Recounting these successive decades in traditional fashion suggests the difficulty of specifying the impact of women's experience. During an era when international developments assumed increasing importance, women were simply not part of the inner councils that debated issues of national security. Women were, of course, included in other aspects of historical experience. As shoppers in the 1920s, they purchased new consumer goods. As unemployed laborers and as wives and daughters of unemployed laborers and dispossessed farmers, they shared the economic problems of the Depression; as members of the Roosevelt administration, they shared in the search for solutions. As industrial workers and as members of the armed forces during World War II, women filled critical jobs in a time of labor shortages and contributed to an allied victory. We can even incorporate women into the Washington drama of the McCarthy era, recognizing that women were among the victims of repressive practices and also among the critics of the practitioners. Margaret Chase Smith was one of the first senators to denounce the " 'know-nothing suspect everything' attitudes" that had transformed the Senate into a "forum of hate and character assassination."[2] The women participating in Women Strike for Peace also played a role in discrediting the inquisition, as Amy Swerdlow demonstrates in her account of their confrontation with the House Un-American Activities Committee.

Including women, even in this cursory fashion, requires recognition of differing experiences that are gender related. Two examples come immediately to mind. The first concerns the differing experience of male and female industrial workers employed during World War II. For working-class men wartime jobs provided a foundation on which to build a secure future in a postwar era of full employment. For working-class women the jobs were only a temporary bonus that they forfeited to returning veterans. Although no long-term study exists to support firm conclusions, there is reason to believe that many of the women who lost their jobs were heads of households. Some may have found low-paying jobs as clerical workers, beauticians, waitresses, or domestics, but in 1947 the increases in the number of women listed as unemployed—as actively seeking work—may have "foreshadow[ed] the great shift among poor women onto unemployment and later welfare rolls." One need not push that hypothesis further to conclude that wartime industrial employment could constitute economically a new beginning—or an end—depending on gender.

A second example concerns participation in the protest movements that shattered the complacency of the affluent society, transforming the 1960s into a decade of self-criticism and turmoil. Two groups in the vanguard of the struggle were the Student Nonviolent Coordinating Committee (SNCC), part of the militant wing of the civil rights movement, and the Students for a Democratic Society (SDS), an organization of the New Left. Both attracted young white women who shared with their male counterparts a commitment to equality. But while men in these organizations often assumed leadership roles, women found themselves functioning in traditional fashion as housekeepers and sexual partners. That this should be so in movements dedicated to radical change, and above all to equality, seemed an inconsistency of such magnitude that women began to organize on their own behalf.

Including women's experience, even as it differed significantly from that of men, does not in itself refocus history, although it does remind us that attention only to public events and international relations can divert us from understanding how most people lived. The process of refocusing history can occur successfully only when we have a fuller understanding of the way gender has affected *all* aspects of human life. We know, for example, that technological developments have been basic to the development of a modern economy. Yet we have only begun to probe the way in which gender has affected technological development. In the garment industry, women have long been employed as seamstresses, sewing being work women have traditionally done and therefore not a skill to command high wages. Men have been employed at higher pay as cutters and pressers. In part because of gender-related wage differentials, little technological change has occurred in sewing since the invention of the sewing machine, according to Ruth Schwartz Cowan.[3] Yet substantial change has occurred in the ancillary process of cutting and pressing. If the relationship between gender, the price of labor, and technological innovation has eluded us in the past, it need not do so in the future. The situation of women sewing-machine operators is but one area in which scholarship informed by the insights of contemporary feminism has begun to capture a larger portion of historical reality. As feminist scholars—male as well as female—restore women to history, comparing both the differences and similarities in the experiences of both sexes and valuing the experience of both, we can begin to refocus history. We must search then for a new paradigm that will enable us to find a past in which, as Gerda Lerner suggests, both *"men and women* are the measure of significance."[4]

Notes

1. William E. Leuchtenburg, *A Troubled Feast: American Society since 1945* (New York, 1973), p. 270.

2. *Congressional Record*, 96 (June 1, 1950):7894–95.

3. Ruth Schwartz Cowan, "From Virginia Dare to Virginia Slims: Women and Technology in American Life," *Technology and Culture* 20 (1979):51–63.

4. Gerda Lerner, *The Majority Finds Its Past: Placing Women in History* (New York, 1979), p. 180.

RUTH SCHWARTZ COWAN
The "Industrial Revolution" in the Home: Household Technology and Social Change in the Twentieth Century

The industrial technology that changed factory work also changed housework; the washing machine replaced the washtub just as the power loom replaced the handloom. Yet the impact of changing household technology on household workers has been little explored. In the following essay Ruth Schwartz Cowan examines how housework changed with the introduction of a variety of labor-saving appliances and the aggressive use of advertising designed to promote their sale. What emerges is a job that has changed in structure. Less burdensome physically, housework became no less time consuming as new duties were added and the work itself invested with new expectations and greater emotional content. What Cowan describes, in part, is the transition from the nineteenth-century mistress of the household who directed a servant's work to the twentieth-century middle-class housewife who, as jane-of-all-trades—laundress, scrub woman, gardener, nursemaid, chauffeur, and cook—was expected to find self-fulfillment in housework. What does this assumption suggest about the role of ideology as well as technology in defining work? What has happened to Henrietta Rodman's vision of "the grand domestic revolution" that technology and the "professionalization" of housework would bring about? In what sense is the individual housewife more isolated than ever?

When we think about the interaction between technology and society, we tend to think in fairly grandiose terms: massive computers invading the workplace, railroad tracks cutting through vast wildernesses, armies of women and children toiling in the mills. These grand visions have blinded us to an important and rather peculiar technological revolution which has been going on right under our noses: the technological revolution in the home. This revolution has transformed the conduct of our daily lives, but in somewhat unexpected ways. The industrialization of the home was a process very different from the industrialization of other means of production, and the impact of that process was neither what we have been led to believe it was nor what students of the other industrial revolutions would have been led to predict.

Some years ago sociologists of the functionalist school formulated an explanation of the impact of industrial technology on the modern family. Although that explanation was not empirically verified, it has become almost universally accepted.[1] Despite some differences in emphasis, the basic tenets of the traditional interpretation can be roughly summarized as follows:

Before industrialization the family was the basic social unit. Most families were rural, large, and self-sustaining; they produced and processed almost everything that was needed for their own support and for trading in the marketplace, while at the same time performing a host of other functions ranging from mutual protection to entertainment. In these preindustrial families women (adult women, that is) had a lot to do, and their time was almost entirely absorbed by household tasks. Under industrialization the family is much less important. The household is no longer the focus of production; production for the marketplace and production for sustenance have been removed to other locations. Families are smaller and they are urban rather than rural. The number of social functions they perform is much reduced, until almost all that remains is consumption, socialization of small children, and tension management. As their functions diminished, families became atomized; the social bonds that had held them together were loosened. In these postindustrial families women have very little to do, and the tasks with which they fill their time have lost the social utility that they once possessed. Modern women are in trouble, the analysis goes, because modern families are in trouble; and modern families are in trouble because industrial technology has either eliminated or eased almost all their former functions, but modern ideologies have not kept pace with the change. The results of this time lag are several: some women suffer from role anxiety, others land in the divorce courts, some enter the labor market, and others take to burning their brassieres and demanding liberation.

This sociological analysis is a cultural artifact of vast importance. Many Americans believe that it is true and act upon that belief in various ways: some hope to reestablish family solidarity by relearning lost productive crafts—baking bread, tending a vegetable garden—others dismiss the women's liberation movement as "simply a bunch of affluent housewives who have nothing better to do with their time." As disparate as they may seem, these reactions have a common ideological source—the standard sociological analysis of the impact of technological change on family life.

As a theory this functionalist approach has much to recommend it, but at present we have very little evidence to back it up. Family history is an infant discipline, and what evidence it has produced in recent years does not lend credence to the standard view.[2] Phillippe Ariès has shown, for example, that in France the ideal of the small nuclear family predates industrialization by more than a century.[3] Historical demographers working on data from English and French families have been surprised to find that most families were quite small and that several generations did not ordinarily reside together; the extended family, which is supposed to have been the rule in preindustrial societies, did not occur in colonial New England either.[4] Rural English families routinely employed domestic servants, and even very small English villages had their butchers and bakers and candlestick makers; all these persons must have eased some of the chores that would otherwise have been the housewife's burden.[5] Preindustrial housewives no doubt had much with which to occupy their time, but we may have reason to wonder whether there was quite as much pressure on them as sociological orthodoxy has led us to suppose. The large rural family that was sufficient unto itself back there on the prairies may have been limited to the prairies—or it may never have existed at all (except, that is, in the reveries of sociologists).

Even if all the empirical evidence were to mesh with the functionalist theory, the theory would still have problems, because its logical structure is rather weak. Comparing the average farm family in 1750 (assuming that you knew what that family was like) with the average urban family in 1950 in order to discover the significant social changes that had occurred is an exercise rather like comparing apples with oranges; the differences between the fruits may have nothing to do with the differences in their evolution. Transferring the analogy to the case at hand, what we really need to know is the difference, say, between an urban laboring family of 1750 and an urban laboring family 100 and then 200 years later, or the difference between the rural nonfarm middle classes in all three centuries, or the difference between the urban rich yesterday and today. Surely in each of these cases the analyses will look very different from what we have been led to expect. As a guess we might find that for the urban laboring families the changes have been precisely the opposite of what the model predicted; that is, that their family structure is much firmer today than it was in centuries past. Similarly, for the rural nonfarm middle class the results might be equally surprising; we might find that married women of that class rarely did any housework at all in 1890 because they had farm girls as servants, whereas in 1950 they bore the full brunt of the work themselves. I could go on, but the point is, I hope, clear: in order to verify or falsify the functionalist theory, it will be necessary to know more than we presently do about the impact of industrialization on families of similar classes and geographical locations.

With this problem in mind I have, for the purposes of this initial study, deliberately limited myself to one kind of technological change affecting one aspect of family life in only one of the many social classes of families that might have been considered. What happened, I asked, to middle-class American women when the implements with which they did their everyday household work changed? Did the technological change in household appliances have any effect upon the structure of American households, or upon the ideologies that governed the behavior of American women, or upon the functions that families needed to perform? Middle-class American women were defined as actual or potential readers of the better-quality women's magazines, such as the *Ladies' Home Journal, American Home, Parents' Magazine, Good Housekeeping,* and *McCall's.*[6] Nonfictional material (articles and advertisements) in those magazines was used as a partial indicator of some of the technological and social changes that were occurring.

The *Ladies' Home Journal* has been in continuous publication since 1886. A casual survey of the nonfiction in the *Journal* yields the immediate impression that that decade between the end of World War I and the beginning of the depression witnessed the most drastic changes in patterns of household work. Statistical data bear out this impression. Before 1918, for example, illustrations of homes lit by gaslight could still be found in the *Journal;* by 1928 gaslight had disappeared. In 1917 only one-quarter (24.3 percent) of the dwellings in the United States had been electrified, but by 1920 this figure had doubled (47.4 percent—for rural nonfarm and urban dwellings), and by 1930 four-fifths of all households had been electrified.[7] If electrification had meant simply the change from gas or oil lamps to electric lights, the changes in the housewife's routines might not have been very great (except for eliminating the chore of cleaning and filling oil lamps); but changes in lighting were the least of the changes that electrification implied. Small electric appliances followed quickly on the heels of the electric light, and some of those augured much more profound changes in the housewife's routine.

Ironing, for example, had traditionally been one of the most dreadful household chores, especially in warm weather when the kitchen stove had to be kept hot for the better part of the day; irons were heavy and they had to be returned to the stove frequently to be reheated. Electric irons eased a good part of this burden.[8] They were relatively inexpensive and very quickly replaced their predecessors; advertisements for electric irons first began to appear in the ladies' magazines after the war, and by the end of the decade the old flatiron had disappeared; by 1929 a survey of 100 Ford employees revealed that ninety-eight of them had the new electric irons in their homes.[9]

Data on the diffusion of electric washing machines are somewhat harder to come by; but it is clear from the advertisements in the magazines, particularly advertisements for laundry soap, that by the middle of the 1920s those machines could be found in a significant number of homes. The washing machine is depicted just about as frequently as the laundry tub by the middle of the 1920s; in 1929, forty-nine out of those 100 Ford workers had the machines in their homes. The washing machines did not drastically reduce the time that had to be spent on household laundry, as they did not go through their cycles automatically and did not spin dry; the housewife had to stand guard, stopping and starting the machine at appropriate times, adding soap, sometimes attaching the drain pipes, and putting the clothes through the wringer manually. The machines did, however, reduce a good part of the drudgery that once had been associated with washday, and this was a matter of no small consequence.[10] Soap powers appeared on the market in the early 1920s, thus eliminating the need to scrape and boil bars of laundry soap.[11] By the end of the 1920s Blue Monday must have been considerably less blue for some housewives—and probably considerably less "Monday," for with an electric iron, a washing machine, and a hot water heater, there was no reason to limit the washing to just one day of the week.

Like the routines of washing the laundry, the routines of personal hygiene must have been transformed for many households during the 1920s—the years of the bathroom mania.[12] More and more bathrooms were built in older homes, and new homes began to include them as a matter of course. Before the war most bathroom fixtures (tubs, sinks, and toilets) were made out of porcelain by hand; each bathroom was custom-made for the house in which it was installed. After the war industrialization descended upon the bathroom industry; cast iron enamelware went into mass production and fittings were standardized. In 1921 the dollar value of the production of enameled sanitary fixtures was $2.4 million, the same as it had been in 1915. By 1923, just two years later, that figure had doubled to $4.8 million; it rose again, to $5.1 million, in 1925.[13] The first recessed, double-shell cast iron enameled bathtub was put on the market in the early 1920s. A decade later the standard American bathroom had achieved its standard American form: the recessed tub, plus tiled floors and walls, brass plumbing, a single-unit toilet, an enameled sink, and a medicine chest, all set into a small room which was very often 5 feet square.[14] The bathroom evolved more quickly than any other room of the house; its standardized form was accomplished in just over a decade.

Along with bathrooms came modernized systems for heating hot water: 61 percent of the homes in Zanesville, Ohio, had indoor plumbing with centrally heated water by 1926, and 83 percent of the homes valued over $2,000 in Muncie, Indiana, had hot and cold running water by 1935.[15] These figures may not be typical of small American cities (or even large American cities) at those times, but they do jibe with the impression that one gets from the magazines: after 1918 references to hot water heated on the kitchen range, either for laundering or for bathing, become increasingly difficult to find.

Similarly, during the 1920s many homes were outfitted with central heating; in Muncie most of the homes of the business class had basement heating in 1924; by 1935 Federal Emergency Relief Administration data for the city indicated that only 22.4 percent of the dwellings valued over $2,000 were still heated by a kitchen stove.[16] What all these changes meant in terms of new habits for the average housewife is somewhat hard to calculate; changes there must have been, but it is difficult to know whether those changes produced an overall saving of labor and/or time. Some chores were eliminated—hauling water, heating water on the stove, maintaining the kitchen fire—but other chores were added—most notably the chore of keeping yet another room scrupulously clean.

It is not, however, difficult to be certain about the changing habits that were associated with the new American kitchen—a kitchen from which the coal stove had disappeared. In Muncie in 1924, cooking with gas was done in two out of three homes; in 1935 only 5 percent of the homes valued over $2,000 still had coal or wood stoves for cooking.[17] After 1918 advertisements for coal and wood stoves disappeared from the Ladies' Home Journal; stove manufacturers purveyed only their gas, oil, or electric models. Articles giving advice to homemakers on how to deal with the trials and tribulations of starting, stoking, and maintaining a coal or a wood fire also disappeared. Thus it seems a safe assumption that most middle-class homes had switched to the new method of cooking by the time the depression began. The change in routine that was predicated on the change from coal or wood to gas or oil was profound; aside from the elimination of such chores as loading the fuel and removing the ashes, the new stoves

were much easier to light, maintain, and regulate (even when they did not have thermostats, as the earliest models did not).[18] Kitchens were, in addition, much easier to clean when they did not have coal dust regularly tracked through them; one writer in the Ladies' Home Journal estimated that kitchen cleaning was reduced by one-half when coal stoves were eliminated.[19]

Along with new stoves came new foodstuffs and new dietary habits. Canned foods had been on the market since the middle of the nineteenth century, but they did not become an appreciable part of the standard middle-class diet until the 1920s—if the recipes given in cookbooks and in women's magazines are a reliable guide. By 1918 the variety of foods available in cans had been considerably expanded from the peas, corn, and succotash of the nineteenth century; an American housewife with sufficient means could have purchased almost any fruit or vegetable and quite a surprising array of ready-made meals in a can—from Heinz's spaghetti in meat sauce to Purity Cross's lobster à la Newburg. By the middle of the 1920s home canning was becoming a lost art. Canning recipes were relegated to the back pages of the women's magazines; the business-class wives of Muncie reported that, while their mothers had once spent the better part of the summer and fall canning, they themselves rarely put up anything, except an occasional jelly or batch of tomatoes.[20] In part this was also due to changes in the technology of marketing food; increased use of refrigerated railroad cars during this period meant that fresh fruits and vegetables were in the markets all year round at reasonable prices.[21] By the early 1920s convenience foods were also appearing on American tables: cold breakfast cereals, pancake mixes, bouillon cubes, and packaged desserts could be found. Wartime shortages accustomed Americans to eating much lighter meals than they had previously been wont to do; and as fewer family members were taking all their meals at home (businessmen started to eat lunch in restaurants downtown, and factories and schools began installing cafeterias), there was simply less cooking to be done, and what there was of it was easier to do.[22]

Many of the changes just described—from hand power to electric power, from coal and wood to gas and oil as fuels for cooking, from one-room heating to central heating, from pumping water to running water—are enormous technological changes. Changes of a similar dimension, either in the fundamental technology of an industry, in the diffusion of that technology, or in the routines of workers, would have long since been labeled an "industrial revolution." The change from the laundry tub to the washing machine is no less profound than the change from the hand loom to the power loom; the change from pumping water to turning on a water faucet is no less destructive of traditional habits than the change from manual to electric calculating. It seems odd to speak of an "industrial revolution" connected with housework, odd because we are talking about the technology of such homely things, and odd because we are not accustomed to thinking of housewives as a labor force or of housework as an economic commodity—but despite this oddity, I think the term is altogether appropriate.

In this case other questions come immediately to mind, questions that we do not hesitate to ask, say, about textile workers in Britain in the early nineteenth century, but we have never thought to ask about housewives in America in the twentieth century. What happened to this particular work force when the technology of its work was revolutionized? Did structural changes occur? Were new jobs created for which new skills were required? Can we discern new ideologies that influenced the behavior of the workers?

The answer to all of these questions, surprisingly enough, seems to be yes.

There were marked structural changes in the work force, changes that increased the work load and the job description of the workers that remained. New jobs were created for which new skills were required; these jobs were not physically burdensome, but they may have taken up as much time as the jobs they had replaced. New ideologies were also created, ideologies which reinforced new behavioral patterns, patterns that we might not have been led to expect if we had followed the sociologists' model to the letter. Middle-class housewives, the women who must have first felt the impact of the new household technology, were not flocking into the divorce courts or the labor market or the forums of political protest in the years immediately after the revolution in their work. What they were doing was sterilizing baby bottles, shepherding their children to dancing classes and music lessons, planning nutritious meals, shopping for new clothes, studying child psychology, and hand stitching color-coordinated curtains—all of which chores (and others like them) the standard sociological model has apparently not provided for.

The significant change in the structure of the household labor force was the disappearance of paid and unpaid servants (unmarried daughters, maiden aunts, and grandparents fall in the latter category) as household workers—and the imposition of the entire job on the housewife herself. Leaving aside for a moment the question of which was cause and which effect (did the disappearance of the servant create a demand for the new technology, or did the new technology make the servant obsolete?), the phenomenon itself is relatively easy to document. Before World War I, when illustrators in the women's magazines depicted women doing housework, the women were very often servants. When the lady of the house was drawn, she was often the person being served, or she was supervising the serving, or she was adding an elegant finishing touch to the work. Nursemaids diapered babies, seamstresses pinned up hems, waitresses served meals, laundresses did the wash, and cooks did the cooking. By the end of the 1920s the servants had disappeared from those illustrations; all those jobs were being done by housewives—elegantly manicured and coiffed, to be sure, but housewives nonetheless.

If we are tempted to suppose that illustrations in advertisements are not a reliable indicator of structural changes of this sort, we can corroborate the changes in other ways. Apparently, the illustrators really did know whereof they drew. Statistically the number of persons throughout the country employed in household service dropped from 1,851,000 in 1910 to 1,411,000 in 1920, while the number of households enumerated in the census rose from 20.3 million to 24.4 million.[23] In Indiana the ratio of households to servants increased from 13.5/1 in 1890 to 30.5/1 in 1920, and in the country as a whole the number of paid domestic servants per 1,000 population dropped from 98.9 in 1900 to 58.0 in 1920.[24] The business-class housewives of Muncie reported that they employed approximately one-half as many woman-hours of domestic service as their mothers had done.[25]

In case we are tempted to doubt these statistics (and indeed statistics about household labor are particularly unreliable, as the labor is often transient, part-time, or simply unreported), we can turn to articles on the servant problem, the disappearance of unpaid family workers, the design of kitchens, or to architectural drawings for houses. All of this evidence reiterates the same point: qualified servants were difficult to find; their wages had risen and their numbers fallen; houses were being designed without maid's rooms; daughters and unmarried aunts were finding jobs downtown; kitchens were being designed for housewives, not for servants.[26] The first home with a kitchen that was not an entirely separate room was designed by Frank Lloyd Wright in

1934.[27] In 1937 Emily Post invented a new character for her etiquette books: Mrs. Three-in-One, the woman who is her own cook, waitress, and hostess.[28] There must have been many new Mrs. Three-in-Ones abroad in the land during the 1930s.

As the number of household assistants declined, the number of household tasks increased. The middle-class housewife was expected to demonstrate competence at several tasks that previously had not existed at all. Child care is the most obvious example. The average housewife had fewer children than her mother had had, but she was expected to do things for her children that her mother would never have dreamed of doing: to prepare their special infant formulas; sterilize their bottles, weigh them every day, see to it that they ate nutritionally balanced meals, keep them isolated and confined when they had even the slightest illness, consult with their teachers frequently, and chauffeur them to dancing lessons, and evening parties.[29] There was very little Freudianism in this new attitude toward child care: mothers were not spending more time and effort on their children because they feared the psychological trauma of separation, but because competent nursemaids could not be found, and the new theories of child care required constant attention from well-informed persons—persons who were willing and able to read about the latest discoveries in nutrition, in the control of contagious diseases, or in the techniques of behavioral psychology. These persons simply had to be their mothers.

Consumption of economic goods provides another example of the housewife's expanded job description; like child care, the new tasks associated with consumption were not necessarily physically burdensome, but they were time consuming, and they required the acquisition of new skills.[30] Home economists and the editors of women's magazines tried to teach housewives to spend their money wisely. The present generation of housewives, it was argued, had been reared by mothers who did not ordinarily shop for things like clothing, bed linens, or towels; consequently modern housewives did not know how to shop and would have to be taught. Furthermore, their mothers had not been accustomed to the wide variety of goods that were now available in the modern marketplace; the new housewives had to be taught not just to be consumers, but to be informed consumers.[31] Several contemporary observers believed that shopping and shopping wisely were occupying increasing amounts of housewives' time.[32]

Several of these contemporary observers also believed that standards of household care changed during the decade of the 1920s.[33] The discovery of the "household germ" led to almost fetishistic concern about the cleanliness of the home. The amount and frequency of laundering probably increased, as bed linen and underwear were changed more often, children's clothes were made increasingly out of washable fabrics, and men's shirts no longer had replaceable collars and cuffs.[34] Unfortunately all these changes in standards are difficult to document, being changes in the things that people regard as so insignificant as to be unworthy of comment; the improvement in standards seems a likely possibility, but not something that can be proved.

In any event we do have various time studies which demonstrate somewhat surprisingly that housewives with conveniences were spending just as much time on household duties as were housewives without them—or, to put it another way, housework, like so many other types of work, expands to fill the time available. A study comparing the time spent per week in housework by 288 farm families and 154 town families in Oregon in 1928 revealed 61 hours spent by farm wives and 63.4 hours by town wives; in 1929 a U.S. Department of Agriculture study of families in various states produced almost identical results.[35] Surely if the standard sociological model were valid, housewives in towns, where presumably the benefits of specialization and electrification were most likely to be available, should have been spending far less time at their work than their rural sisters. However, just after World War II economists at Bryn Mawr College reported the same phenomenon: 60.55 hours spent by farm housewives, 78.35 hours by women in small cities, 80.57 hours by women in large ones—precisely the reverse of the results that were expected.[36] A recent survey of time studies conducted between 1920 and 1970 concludes that the time spent on housework by nonemployed housewives has remained remarkably constant throughout the period.[37] All these results point in the same direction: mechanization of the household meant that time expended on some jobs decreased, but also that new jobs were substituted, and in some cases—notably laundering—time expenditures for old jobs increased because of higher standards. The advantages of mechanization may be somewhat more dubious than they seem at first glance.

As the job of the housewife changed, the connected ideologies also changed; there was a clearly perceptible difference in the attitudes that women brought to housework before and after World War I.[38] Before the war the trials of doing housework in a servantless home were discussed and they were regarded as just that—trials, necessary chores that had to be got through until a qualified servant could be found. After the war, housework changed: it was no longer a trial and a chore, but something quite different—an emotional "trip." Laundering was not just laundering, but an expression of love; the housewife who truly loved her family would protect them from the embarrassment of tattletale gray. Feeding the family was not just feeding the family, but a way to express the housewife's artistic inclinations and a way to encourage feelings of family loyalty and affection. Diapering the baby was not just diapering, but a time to build the baby's sense of security and love for the mother. Cleaning the bathroom sink was not just cleaning, but an exercise of protective maternal instincts, providing a way for the housewife to keep her family safe from disease. Tasks of this emotional magnitude could not possibly be delegated to servants, even assuming that qualified servants could be found.

Women who failed at these new household tasks were bound to feel guilt about their failure. If I had to choose one word to characterize the temper of the women's magazines during the 1920s, it would be "guilt." Readers of the better-quality women's magazines are portrayed as feeling guilty a good lot of the time, and when they are not guilty they are embarrassed: guilty if their infants have not gained enough weight, embarrassed if their drains are clogged, guilty if their children go to school in soiled clothes, guilty if all the germs behind the bathroom sink are not eradicated, guilty if they fail to notice the first signs of an oncoming cold, embarrassed if accused of having body odor, guilty if their sons go to school without good breakfasts, guilty if their daughters are unpopular because of old-fashioned, or unironed, or—heaven forbid—dirty dresses. In earlier times women were made to feel guilty if they abandoned their children or were too free with their affections. In the years after World War I, American women were made to feel guilty about sending their children to school in scuffed shoes. Between the two kinds of guilt there is a world of difference.

Let us return for a moment to the sociological model with which this essay began. The model predicts that changing patterns of household work will be correlated with at least two striking indicators of social change: the divorce rate and the rate of married women's labor force participation. That correlation may indeed exist, but it certainly is not reflected in the women's magazines of the 1920s and 1930s; divorce and full-time paid employment were not part of the life-style or the life pattern of the middle-class housewife as she was idealized in her magazines.

There were social changes attendant upon the introduction of modern technology into the home, but they were not the changes that the traditional functionalist model predicts; on this point a close analysis of the statistical data corroborates the impression conveyed in the magazines. The divorce rate was indeed rising during the years between the wars, but it was not rising nearly so fast for the middle and upper classes (who had, presumably, easier access to the new technology) as it was for the lower classes. By almost every gauge of socioeconomic status—income, prestige of husband's work, education—the divorce rate is higher for persons lower on the socioeconomic scale—and this is a phenomenon that has been constant over time.[39]

The supposed connection between improved household technology and married women's labor force participation seems just as dubious, and on the same grounds. The single socioeconomic factor which correlates most strongly (in cross-sectional studies) with married women's employment is husband's income, and the correlation is strongly negative; the higher his income, the less likely it will be that she is working.[40] Women's labor force participation increased during the 1920s but this increase was due to the influx of single women into the force. Married women's participation increased slightly during those years, but that increase was largely in factory labor—precisely the kind of work that middle-class women (who were, again, much more likely to have labor-saving devices at home) were least likely to do.[41] If there were a necessary connection between the improvement of household technology and either of these two social indicators, we would expect the data to be precisely the reverse of what in fact has occurred: women in the higher social classes should have fewer functions at home and should therefore be more (rather than less) likely to seek paid employment or divorce.

Thus for middle-class American housewives between the wars, the social changes that we can document are not the social changes that the functionalist model predicts; rather than changes in divorce or patterns of paid employment, we find changes in the structure of the work force, in its skills, and in its ideology. These social changes were concomitant with a series of technological changes in the equipment that was used to do the work. What is the relationship between these two series of phenomena? Is it possible to demonstrate causality or the direction of that causality? Was the decline in the number of households employing servants a cause or an effect of the mechanization of those households? Both are, after all, equally possible. The declining supply of household servants, as well as their rising wages, may have stimulated a demand for new appliances at the same time that the acquisition of new appliances may have made householders less inclined to employ the laborers who were on the market. Are there any techniques available to the historian to help us answer these questions?

In order to establish causality, we need to find a connecting link between the two sets of phenomena, a mechanism that, in real life, could have made the causality work. In this case a connecting link, and intervening agent between the social and the technological changes, comes immediately to mind: the advertiser—by which term I mean a combination of the manufacturer of the new goods, the advertising agent who promoted the goods, and the periodical that published the promotion. All the new devices and new foodstuffs that were being offered to American households were being manufactured and marketed by large companies which had considerable amounts of capital invested in their production: General Electric, Procter & Gamble, General Foods, Lever Brothers, Frigidaire, Campbell's, Del Monte, American Can, Atlantic & Pacific Tea—these were all well-established firms by the time the houshold revolution began, and they were all in a position to pay for national advertising campaigns to promote their new products and services. And pay they did; one reason for the expanding size and number of women's magazines in the 1920s was no doubt, the expansion in revenues from available advertisers.[42]

Those national advertising campaigns were likely to have been powerful stimulators of the social changes that occurred in the household labor force; the advertisers probably did not initiate the changes, but they certainly encouraged them. Most of the advertising campaigns manifestly worked, so they must have touched upon areas of real concern for American housewives. Appliance ads specifically suggested that the acquisition of one gadget or another would make it possible to fire the maid, spend more time with the children, or have the afternoon free for shopping.[43] Similarly, many advertisements played upon the embarrassment and guilt which were now associated with household work. Ralston, Cream of Wheat, and Ovaltine were not themselves responsible for the compulsive practice of weighing infants and children repeatedly (after every meal for newborns, every day in infancy, every week later on), but the manufacturers certainly did not stint on capitalizing upon the guilt that women apparently felt if their offspring did not gain the required amounts of weight.[44]

And yet again, many of the earliest attempts to spread "wise" consumer practices were undertaken by large corporations and the magazines that desired their advertising; mail-order shopping guides, "product-testing" services, pseudoinformative pamphlets, and other such promotional devices were all techniques for urging the housewife to buy new things under the guise of training her in her role as skilled consumer.[45]

Thus the advertisers could well be called the "ideologues" of the 1920s, encouraging certain very specific social changes—as ideologues are wont to do. Not surprisingly, the changes that occurred were precisely the ones that would gladden the hearts and fatten the purses of the advertisers; fewer household servants meant a greater demand for labor- and time-saving devices; more household tasks for women meant more and more specialized products that they would need to buy; more guilt and embarrassment about their failure to succeed at their work meant a greater likelihood that they would buy the products that were intended to minimize that failure. Happy, full-time housewives in intact families spend a lot of money to maintain their households; divorced women and working women do not. The advertisers may not have created the image of the ideal American housewife that dominated the 1920s— the woman who cheerfully and skillfully set about making everyone in her family perfectly happy and perfectly healthy— but they certainly helped to perpetuate it.

The role of the advertiser as connecting link between social change and technological change is at this juncture simply a hypothesis, with nothing much more to recommend it than an argument from plausibility. Further research may serve to test the hypothesis, but testing it may not settle the question of which was cause and which effect—if that question can ever be settled definitively in historical work. What seems most likely in this case, as in so many others, is that cause and effect are not separable, that there is a dynamic interaction between the social changes that married women were experiencing and the technological changes that were occurring in their homes. Viewed this way, the disappearance of competent servants becomes one of the factors that stimulated the mechanization of homes, and this mechanization of homes becomes a factor (though by no means the only one) in the disappearance of servants. Similarly, the emotionalization of housework becomes both cause and effect of the mechanization of that work; and the expansion of time spent on new tasks becomes both cause and effect of the introduction of time-saving devices. For example the social pressure to spend more time in child care may have led to a decision to purchase the devices; once purchased, the devices could indeed have been used to save time—although often they were not.

If one holds the question of causality in abeyance, the example of household work still has some useful lessons to teach about the general problem of technology and social change. The standard sociological model for the impact of modern technology on family life clearly needs some revision: at least for middle-class nonrural American families in the twentieth century, the social changes were not the ones that the standard model predicts. In these families the functions of at least one member, the housewife, have increased rather than decreased and the dissolution of family life has not in fact occurred.

Our standard notions about what happens to a work force under the pressure of technological change may also need revision. When industries become mechanized and rationalized, we expect certain general changes in the work force to occur: its structure becomes more highly differentiated, individual workers become more specialized, managerial functions increase, and the emotional context of the work disappears. On all four counts our expectations are reversed with regard to household work. The work force became less rather than more differentiated as domestic servants, unmarried daughters, maiden aunts, and grandparents left the household and as chores which had once been performed by commercial agencies (laundries, delivery services, milkmen) were delegated to the housewife. The individual workers also became less specialized; the new housewife was now responsible for every aspect of life in her household, from scrubbing the bathroom floor to keeping abreast of the latest literature in child psychology.

The housewife is just about the only unspecialized worker left in America—a veritable jane-of-all-trades at a time when the jacks-of-all-trades have disappeared. As her work became generalized the housewife was also proletarianized: formerly she was ideally the manager of several other subordinate workers; now she was idealized as the manager and the worker combined. Her managerial functions have not entirely disappeared, but they have certainly diminished and have been replaced by simple manual labor; the middle-class, fairly well educated housewife ceased to be a personnel manager and became, instead, a chauffeur, charwoman, and short-order cook. The implications

of this phenomenon, the proletarianization of a work force that had previously seen itself as predominantly managerial, deserve to be explored at greater length than is possible here, because I suspect that they will explain certain aspects of the women's liberation movement of the 1960s and 1970s which have previously eluded explanation: why, for example, the movement's greatest strength lies in social and economic groups who seem, on the surface at least, to need it least—women who are white, well-educated, and middle-class.

Finally, instead of desensitizing the emotions that were connected with household work, the industrial revolution in the home seems to have heightened the emotional context of the work, until a woman's sense of self-worth became a function of her success at arranging bits of fruit to form a clown's face in a gelatin salad. That pervasive social illness, which Betty Friedan characterized as "the problem that has no name," arose not among workers who found that their labor brought no emotional satisfaction, but among workers who found that their work was invested with emotional weight far out of proportion to its own inherent value: "How long," a friend of mine is fond of asking, "can we continue to believe that we will have orgasms while waxing the kitchen floor?"

NOTES

1. For some classic statements of the standard view, see W. F. Ogburn and M. F. Nimkoff, *Technology and the Changing Family* (Cambridge, Mass., 1955); Robert F. Winch, *The Modern Family* (New York, 1952); and William J. Goode, *The Family* (Englewood Cliffs, N.J., 1964).

2. This point is made by Peter Laslett in "The Comparative History of Household and Family," in *The American Family in Social Historical Perspective*, ed. Michael Gordon (New York, 1973), pp. 28–29.

3. Phillippe Ariès, *Centuries of Child-

hood: A Social History of Family Life* (New York, 1960).

4. See Laslett, pp. 20–24; and Philip J. Greven, "Family Structure in Seventeenth Century Andover, Massachusetts," *William and Mary Quarterly* 23 (1966):234–56.

5. Peter Laslett, *The World We Have Lost* (New York, 1965), passim.

6. For purposes of historical inquiry, this definition of middle-class status corresponds to a sociological reality, although it is not, admittedly, very rigorous. Our contemporary experience confirms that there are class dif-

ferences reflected in magazines, and this situation seems to have existed in the past as well. On this issue see Robert S. Lynd and Helen M. Lynd, *Middletown: A Study in Contemporary American Culture* (New York, 1929), pp. 240–44, where the marked difference in magazines subscribed to by the business-class wives as opposed to the working-class wives is discussed; Salme Steinberg, "Reformer in the Marketplace: E. W. Bok and *The Ladies' Home Journal*" (Ph.D. diss., Johns Hopkins University, 1973), where the conscious attempt of the publisher to attract a middle-class audience is discussed; and Lee Rainwater et al., *Workingman's Wife* (New York, 1959), which was commissioned by the publisher of working-class women's magazines in an attempt to understand the attitudinal differences between working-class and middle-class women.

7. *Historical Statistics of the United States, Colonial Times to 1957* (Washington, D.C., 1960), p. 510.

8. The gas iron, which was available to women whose homes were supplied with natural gas, was an earlier improvement on the old-fashioned flatiron, but this kind of iron is so rarely mentioned in the sources that I used for this survey that I am unable to determine the extent of its diffusion.

9. Hazel Kyrk, *Economic Problems of the Family* (New York, 1933), p. 368, reporting a study in *Monthly Labor Review* 30 (1930): 1209–52.

10. Although this point seems intuitively obvious, there is some evidence that it may not be true. Studies of energy expenditure during housework have indicated that by far the greatest effort is expended in hauling and lifting the wet wash, tasks which were not eliminated by the introduction of washing machines. In addition, if the introduction of the machines served to increase the total amount of wash that was done by the housewife, this would tend to cancel the energy-saving effects of the machines themselves.

11. Rinso was the first granulated soap; it came on the market in 1918. Lux Flakes had been available since 1906; however it was not intended to be a general laundry product but rather one for laundering delicate fabrics. "Lever Brothers," *Fortune* 26 (November 1940): 95.

12. I take this account, and the term, from Lynd and Lynd, p. 97. Obviously, there were many American homes that had bathrooms before the 1920s, particularly urban row houses, and I have found no way of determining whether the increases of the 1920s

were more marked than in previous decades. The rural situation was quite different from the urban; the President's Conference on Home Building and Home Ownership reported that in the late 1920s, 71 percent of the urban families surveyed had bathrooms, but only 33 percent of the rural families did (John M. Gries and James Ford, eds., *Homemaking, Home Furnishing and Information Services*, President's Conference on Home Building and Home Ownership, vol. 10 [Washington, D.C., 1932], p. 13).

13. The data above came from Siegfried Giedion, *Mechanization Takes Command* (New York, 1948), pp. 685–703.

14. For a description of the standard bathroom see Helen Sprackling, "The Modern Bathroom," *Parents' Magazine* 8 (February 1933): 25.

15. *Zanesville, Ohio and Thirty-six Other American Cities* (New York, 1927), p. 65. Also see Robert S. Lynd and Helen M. Lynd, *Middletown in Transition* (New York, 1936), p. 537. Middletown is Muncie, Indiana.

16. Lynd and Lynd, *Middletown*, p. 96, and *Middletown in Transition*, p. 539.

17. Lynd and Lynd, *Middletown*, p. 98, and *Middletown in Transition*, p. 562.

18. On the advantages of the new stoves, see *Boston Cooking School Cookbook* (Boston, 1916), pp. 15–20; and Russell Lynes, *The Domesticated Americans* (New York, 1957), pp. 119–20.

19. "How To Save Coal While Cooking," *Ladies' Home Journal* 25 (January 1908): 44.

20. Lynd and Lynd, *Middletown*, p. 156.

21. Ibid.; see also "Safeway Stores," *Fortune* 26 (October 1940): 60.

22. Lynd and Lynd, *Middletown*, pp. 134–35 and 153–54.

23. *Historical Statistics*, pp. 16 and 77.

24. For Indiana data, see Lynd and Lynd, *Middletown*, p. 169. For national data, see D. L. Kaplan and M. Claire Casey, *Occupational Trends in the United States, 1900–1950*, U.S. Bureau of the Census Working Paper no. 5 (Washington, D.C., 1958), table 6. The extreme drop in numbers of servants between 1910 and 1920 also lends credence to the notion that this demographic factor stimulated the industrial revolution in housework.

25. Lynd and Lynd, *Middletown*, p. 169.

26. On the disappearance of maiden aunts, unmarried daughters, and grandparents, see Lynd and Lynd, *Middletown*, pp. 25, 99, and 110; Edward Bok, "Editorial," *American Home* 1 (October 1928): 15; "How to Buy Life Insurance," *Ladies' Home Journal* 45 (March 1928): 35. The house plans ap-

peared every month in *American Home,* which began publication in 1928. On kitchen design, see Giedion, pp. 603–21; "Editorial," *Ladies' Home Journal* 45 (April 1928):36; advertisement for Hoosier kitchen cabinets, *Ladies' Home Journal* 45 (April 1928):117. Articles on servant problems include "The Vanishing Servant Girl," *Ladies' Home Journal* 35 (May 1918):48; "Housework, Then and Now," *American Home* 8 (June 1932): 128; "The Servant Problem," *Fortune* 24 (March 1938):80–84; and *Report of the YWCA Commission on Domestic Service* (Los Angeles, 1915).

27. Giedion, p. 619. Wright's new kitchen was installed in the Malcolm Willey House, Minneapolis.

28. Emily Post, *Etiquette: The Blue Book of Social Usage,* 5th ed. rev. (New York, 1937), p. 823.

29. This analysis is based upon various child-care articles that appeared during the period in the *Ladies' Home Journal, American Home,* and *Parents' Magazine.* See also Lynd and Lynd, *Middletown,* chap. 11.

30. John Kenneth Galbraith has remarked upon the advent of woman as consumer in *Economics and the Public Purpose* (Boston, 1973), pp. 29–37.

31. There was a sharp reduction in the number of patterns for home sewing offered by the women's magazines during the 1920s; the patterns were replaced by articles on "what is available in the shops this season." On consumer education see, for example, "How to Buy Towels," *Ladies' Home Journal* 45 (February 1928):134; "Buying Table Linen," *Ladies' Home Journal* 45 (March 1928:43; and "When the Bride Goes Shopping," *American Home* 1 (January 1928):370.

32. See, for example, Lynd and Lynd, *Middletown,* pp. 176 and 196; and Margaret G. Reid, *Economics of Household Production* (New York, 1934), chap. 13.

33. See Reid, pp. 64–68; and Kyrk, p. 98.

34. See advertisement for Cleanliness Institute—"Self-respect thrives on soap and water," *Ladies' Home Journal* 45 (February 1928): 107. On changing bed linen, see "When the Bride Goes Shopping," *American Home* 1 (January 1928): 370. On laundering children's clothes, see, "Making a Layette," *Ladies' Home Journal* 45 (January 1928):20; and Josephine Baker, "The Youngest Generation," *Ladies' Home Journal* 45 (March 1928): 185.

35. As reported in Kyrk, p. 51.

36. Bryn Mawr College Department of Social Economy, *Women During the War and After* (Philadelphia, 1945); and Ethel Goldwater, "Woman's Place," *Commentary* 4 (December 1947):578–85.

37. JoAnn Vanek, "Keeping Busy: Time Spent in Housework, United States, 1920–1970" (Ph.D. diss., University of Michigan, 1973). Vanek reports an average of 53 hours per week over the whole period. This figure is significantly lower than the figures reported above, because each time study of housework has been done on a different basis, including different activities under the aegis of housework, and using different methods of reporting time expenditures; the Bryn Mawr and Oregon studies are useful for the comparative figures that they report internally, but they cannot easily be compared with each other.

38. This analysis is based upon my reading of the middle-class women's magazines between 1918 and 1930. For detailed documentation see my paper "Two Washes in the Morning and a Bridge Party at Night: The American Housewife between the Wars," *Women's Studies* 3 (1976):147–72. It is quite possible that the appearance of guilt as a strong element in advertising is more the result of new techniques developed by the advertising industry than the result of attitudinal changes in the audience—a possibility that I had not considered when doing the initial research for this paper. See A. Michael McMahon, "An American Courtship: Psychologists and Advertising Theory in the Progressive Era," *American Studies* 13 (1972): 5–18.

39. For a summary of the literature on differential divorce rates, see Winch, p. 706; and William J. Goode, *After Divorce* (New York, 1956), p. 44. The earliest papers demonstrating this differential rate appeared in 1927, 1935, and 1939.

40. For a summary of the literature on married women's labor force participation, see Juanita Kreps, *Sex in the Marketplace: American Women at Work* (Baltimore, 1971), pp. 19–24.

41. Valerie Kincaid Oppenheimer, *The Female Labor Force in the United States,* Population Monograph Series, no. 5 (Berkeley, 1970), pp. 1–15; and Lynd and Lynd, *Middletown,* pp. 124–27.

42. On the expanding size, number, and influence of women's magazines during the 1920s, see Lynd and Lynd, *Middletown,* pp. 150 and 240–44.

43. See, for example, the advertising campaigns of General Electric and Hotpoint from 1918 through the rest of the decade of the

1920s; both campaigns stressed the likelihood that electric appliances would become a thrifty replacement for domestic servants.

44. The practice of carefully observing children's weight was initiated by medical authorities, national and local governments, and social welfare agencies, as part of the campaign to improve child health which began about the time of World War I.

45. These practices were ubiquitous. *American Home*, for example, which was published by Doubleday, assisted its advertisers by publishing a list of informative pamphlets that readers could obtain; devoting half a page to an index of its advertisers specifically naming manufacturer's and list prices in articles about products and services allotting almost one-quarter of the magazine to a mail-order shopping guide which was not (at least ostensibly) paid advertisement and as part of its editorial policy, urging its readers to buy new goods.

JACQUELYN DOWD HALL
Disorderly Women: Gender and Labor Militancy in the Appalachian South

For many women the workplace included factory or mill as well as home. Factories in the 1920s were rent by strikes as workers whose wages were already low tried to cope with innovations designed to increase productivity. Southern textile mills, always the employer of large numbers of women, were especially vulnerable.

Jacquelyn Dowd Hall focuses on one of the many strikes exploding across the South in that tumultuous decade, exploring female activism in an essay that calls into question old stereotypes about southern workers as individualistic, docile, and "hard to organize." In this important study, Hall illuminates the distinctive style of collective action that the women of Elizabethton, Tennessee, employed and the self-concepts and family networks on which that style relied.

The rising sun "made a sort of halo around the crown of Cross Mountain" as Flossie Cole climbed into a neighbor's Model T and headed west down the gravel road to Elizabethton, bound for work in a rayon plant. Emerging from Stony Creek hollow, the car joined a caravan of buses and self-styled "taxis" brimming with young people from dozens of tiny communities strung along the creek branches and nestled in the coves of the Blue Ridge Mountains of East Tennessee. The caravan picked up speed as it hit paved roads and crossed the Watauga River bridge, passing beneath a sign advertising the county seat's new-found identity as

Excerpted from "Disorderly Women: Gender and Labor Militancy in the Appalachian South" by Jacquelyn Dowd Hall, in *Journal of American History* 73 (1986):354–82. Copyright © 1986 by Jacquelyn Dowd Hall. Condensed and reprinted by permission of the author. Notes have been renumbered.

a "City of Power." By the time Cole reached the factory gate, it was 7:00 A.M., time to begin another ten-hour day as a reeler at the American Glanzstoff plant.[1]

The machines whirred, and work began as usual. But the reeling room stirred with anticipation. The day before, March 12, 1929, all but seventeen of the 360 women in the inspection room next door had walked off their jobs. Now they were gathered at the factory gate, refusing to work but ready to negotiate. When 9:00 A.M. approached and the plant manager failed to appear, they broke past the guards and rushed through the plant, urging their co-workers out on strike. By 1:40 P.M. the machines were idle and the plant was closed.

The Elizabethton conflict rocked Carter County and made national headlines. Before March ended, the spirit of protest had jumped the Blue Ridge and spread through the Piedmont. Gastonia, Marion, and Danville saw the most bitter conflicts, but dozens of towns were shocked by an unexpected workers' revolt.[2]

The textile industry has always been a stronghold of women's labor, and women were central to these events. They were noted by contemporaries, sometimes as leaders, more often as pathetic mill girls or as "Amazons" providing comic relief.[3] In historical renditions they have dropped out of sight. The result has been thin description: a one-dimensional view of labor conflict that fails to take culture and community into account.

Elizabethton, of course, is not unusual in this regard. United recently, historians of trade unionism, like trade unionists themselves, neglected women, while historians of women concentrated on the Northeast and the middle class. There were few scholarly challenges to the assumption that women workers in general and southern women in particular were "hard to organize" and that women as family members exercised a conservative

pull against class cohesion. Instances of female militancy were seen and not seen.[4] Because they contradicted conventional wisdom, they were easily dismissed.

Recent scholarship has revised that formulation by unearthing an impressive record of female activism. But our task is not only to describe and celebrate but also to contextualize, and thus to understand. In Elizabethton the preindustrial background, the structure of the work force and the industry, the global forces that impinged on local events—these particularities of time and place conditioned women's choices and shaped their identities. Equally important was a private world traditionally pushed to the margins of labor history. Female friendships and sexuality, cross-generational and cross-class alliances, the incorporation of new consumer desires into a dynamic regional culture—these too energized women's participation. Women in turn were historical subjects, helping to create the circumstances from which the strike arose and guiding by their actions the course the conflict took.

With gender at the center of analysis, unexpected dimensions come into view. Chief among them is the strike's erotic undercurrent, its sexual theme. The activists of Elizabethton belonged to a venerable tradition of "disorderly women," women who, in times of political upheaval, embody tensions that are half-conscious or only dimly understood.[5] Beneath the surface of a conflict that pitted workers and farmers against a new middle class in the town lay an inner world of fantasy, gender ideology, and sexual style.

The melding of narrative and analysis that follows has two major goals. The first is a fresh reading of an important episode in southern labor history, employing a female angle of vision to reveal aspects of the conflict that have been overlooked or misunderstood. The second is a close look at women's distinctive forms of collective action, using language and gesture as points of entry to a culture.

The Elizabethton story may also help to make a more general point. Based as it is on what Michel Foucault has termed "local" or "subjugated" knowledge, that is, perceptions that seem idiosyncratic, naive, and irrelevant to historical explanation, this study highlights the limitations of conventional categories.[6] The women of Elizabethton were neither traditionalists acting on family values nor market-oriented individualists, neither peculiar mountaineers nor familiar modern women. Their irreverence and inventiveness shatter stereotypes and illuminate the intricacies of working-class women's lives.

In 1925 the J. P. Bemberg Company of Barmen, Germany, manufacturer of high-quality rayon yarn by an exclusive stretch spinning process, began pouring the thick concrete floors of its first United States subsidiary. Three years later Germany's leading producer of viscose yarn, the Vereinigte Glanzstoff Fabriken, A.G., of Elberfeld opened a jointly managed branch nearby. A post–World War I fashion revolution, combined with protective tariffs, had spurred the American rayon industry's spectacular growth. As one industry publicist put it, "With long skirts, cotton stockings were quite in order; but with short skirts, nothing would do except sheer, smooth stockings. . . . It was on the trim legs of post-war flappers, it has been said, that rayon first stepped out into big business." Dominated by a handful of European giants, the rayon industry clustered along the Appalachian mountain chain. By World War II, over 70 percent of American rayon production took place in the southern states, with 50 percent of the national total in Virginia and Tennessee alone.[7]

When the Bemberg and Glanzstoff companies chose East Tennessee as a site for overseas expansion, they came to a region that has occupied a peculiar place in the American economy and imagination. Since its "discovery" by local-color writers in the 1870s, southern Appalachia has been seen as a land "where time stood still." Mountain people have been romanticized as "our contemporary ancestors" or maligned as "latter-day white barbarians." Central to both images is the notion of a people untouched by modernity. In fact, as a generation of regional scholars has now made clear, the key to modern Appalachian history lies not in the region's isolation but in its role as a source of raw materials and an outlet for investment in a capitalist world economy.[8]

Frontier families had settled the fertile Watauga River Valley around Elizabethton before the Revolution. Later arrivals pushed farther up the mountains into the hollows carved by fast-falling creeks. Stony Creek is the oldest and largest of those creek-bed communities. Here descendants of the original settlers cultivated their own small plots, grazed livestock in woods that custom held open to all, hunted and fished in an ancient hardwood forest, mined iron ore, made whiskey, spun cloth, and bartered with local merchants for what they could not produce at home.

In the 1880s East Tennessee's timber and mineral resources attracted the attention of capitalists in the United States and abroad, and an era of land speculation and railroad building began. The railroads opened the way to timber barons, who stripped away the forests, leaving hillsides stark and vulnerable to erosion. Farmers abandoned their fields to follow the march of the logging camps. Left behind, women and children did their best to pick up the slack.[9] But by the time Carter County was "timbered out" in the 1920s, farm families had crept upward to the barren ridge lands or grown dependent on "steady work and cash wages."

Meanwhile, in Elizabethton, the county seat, an aggressive new class of bankers, lawyers, and businessmen served as brokers for outside developers, speculated in land, invested in homegrown factories, and looked beyond the hills for their standards of "push, progress and prosperity."[10]

Carter County, however, lacked Appalachia's grand prize: The rush for coal that devastated other parts of the mountains had bypassed that part of East Tennessee. Nor had county farmers been absorbed into the cotton kingdom, with its exploitative credit system and spreading tenancy. To be sure, they were increasingly hard pressed. As arable land disappeared, farms were divided and redivided. In 1880 the average rural family had supported itself on 140 acres of land; by 1920 it was making do on slightly more than 52 acres. Yet however diminished their circumstances, 84.5 percent still owned their own land.[11] The economic base that sustained traditional expectations of independence, production for use, and neighborly reciprocity tottered but did not give way.

The coming of the rayon plants represented a coup for Elizabethton's aspiring businessmen, who wooed investors with promises of free land, tax exemptions, and cheap labor. But at first the whole county seemed to share the boom-town spirit. Men from Stony Creek, Gap Creek, and other mountain hamlets built the cavernous mills, then stayed on to learn the chemical processes that transformed the cellulose from wood pulp and cotton linters (the short fibers that remain on cotton seeds after longer, spinnable fibers are removed) into "artificial silk." Women vied for jobs in the textile division where they wound, reeled, twisted, and inspected the rayon yarn. Yet for all the excitement it engendered, industrialization in Carter County retained a distinctly rural cast. Although Elizabethton's population tripled (from 2,749 in

1920 to 8,093 in 1930), the rayon workers confounded predictions of spectacular urban growth, for most remained in the countryside, riding to work on chartered buses and trains or in taxis driven by neighbors and friends.

Women made up approximately 37 percent of the 3,213 workers in the mills. Most were under twenty-one, but many were as young as twelve or, more commonly, fourteen. By contrast, the work force contained a large proportion of older, married men. Those men, together with a smaller number of teenage boys, dominated the chemical division, while young women processed the finished yarn.[12]

Whether married or single, town- or country-bred, the men who labored in the rayon plants followed in the footsteps of fathers, and sometimes grandfathers, who had combined farming with a variety of wage-earning occupations. To a greater extent than we might expect, young women who had grown up in Elizabethton could also look to earlier models of gainful labor. A search of the 1910 manuscript census found 20 percent (97/507) of women aged fourteen and over in paid occupations. The largest proportion (29.6 percent) were cooks and servants. But close behind were women in what mountain people called "public work": wage-earning labor performed outside a household setting. For rayon workers from the countryside it was a different story. Only 5.2 percent of adult women on Stony Creek were gainfully employed (33/638). Nineteen of these were farmers. The rest—except for one music teacher—were servants or washerwomen.[13]

These contrasts are telling, and from them we can surmise two things. The first is that industrialization did not burst upon a static, conflict free "traditional" world. The women who beat a path to the rayon plants came from families that had already been drawn into an economy where money was a key to survival. The second is that the timber industry, which attracted Carter County's men, undermined its agricultural base, and destroyed its natural resources, created few opportunities for rural women. No wonder that farm daughters in the mills counted their blessings and looked on themselves as pioneers.

Whether they sought work out of family need or for more individualistic reasons, these "factory girls" saw their jobs as a hopeful gamble rather than a desperate last resort, and they remembered the moment with astounding precision. "I'll never forget the day they hired me at Bemberg," said Flossie Cole. "We went down right in front of it. They'd come out and they'd say, 'You and you and you,' and they'd hire so many. And that day I was standing there and he picked out two or three more and he looked at me and he said, 'You.' It thrilled me to death." She worked 56 hours that week and took home $8.16.[14]

Such pay scales were low even for the southern textile industry, and workers quickly found their income eaten away by the cost of commuting or of boarding in town. When the strike came it focused on the issue of Glanzstoff women's wages, which lagged behind those at the older Bemberg plant. But workers had other grievances as well. Caustic chemicals were used to turn cellulose into a viscous fluid that was then forced through spinnerets, thimble-shaped nozzles pierced with tiny holes. The fine, individual streams coagulated into rayon filaments in an acid bath. In the chemical division men waded through water and acid, exposed all day to a lethal spray. Women labored under less dangerous conditions, but for longer hours and less pay. Paid by the piece, they complained of rising production quotas and what everyone referred to as "hard rules."[15]

Women in particular were singled out for petty regulations, aimed not just at extracting labor but at shaping deportment as well. They were forbidden to wear makeup; in some departments they were required to purchase uniforms. Most galling of all was company surveillance of the washroom. According to Bessie Edens, who was promoted to "forelady" in the twisting room, "men could do what they wanted to in their own department," but women had to get a pass to leave the shop floor. "If we went to the bathroom, they'd follow us," Flossie Cole confirmed, "'fraid we'd stay a minute too long." If they did, their pay was docked; one too many trips and they lost their jobs.[16]

Complaints about the washroom may have had other meanings as well. When asked how she heard that a strike was brewing, Nettie Reece cited "bathroom gossip."[17] As the company well knew, the women's washroom, where only a forelady, not a male supervisor could go, might serve as a communications center, a hub of gossip where complaints were aired and plans were formulated.

The German origins of the plant managers contributed to the tension. Once the strike began, union organizers were quick to play on images of an "imported Prussian autocracy." The frontier republicanism of the mountains shaded easily into post-World War I Americanism as strikers demanded their rights as "natural-born American citizens" oppressed by a "latter day industrialism." In that they had much in common with other twentieth-century workers, for whom the democratic values articulated during the war became a rallying cry for social justice at home. The nationality of the managers helped throw those values into sharp relief.[18]

The strike came on March 12, 1929, led by women in Glanzstoff inspection department, by what one observer called "girls in their teens [who] decided not to put up with the present conditions any longer." The county court immediately issued injunctions forbidding all demonstrations against the company. When strikers ignored the injunctions, the governor sent in the National Guard. The strikers secured a charter from the American Federation of Labor's United Textile Workers union (UTW). Meeting in a place called the Tabernacle, built for religious revivals, they listened to a Baptist preacher from Stony Creek warn: "The hand of oppression is growing on our people. . . . You women work for practically nothing. You must come together and say that such things must cease to be." Each night more workers "came forward" to take the union oath.[19]

Meanwhile, UTW and Federal Conciliation Service officials arrived on the scene. On March 22 they reached a "gentlemen's agreement" by which the company promised a new wage scale for "good girl help" and agreed not to discriminate against union members. The strikers returned to work, but the conflict was far from over. Higher paychecks never materialized; union members began losing their jobs. On April 4 local businessmen kidnapped two union organizers and ran them out of town. Eleven days later the workers responded with what most observers agreed was a "spontaneous and complete walkout."[20]

This time the conflict quickly escalated. More troops arrived, and the plants became fortresses, with machine guns on the rooftops and armed guardsmen on the ground. The company sent buses manned by soldiers farther up the hollows to recruit new workers and escort them back to town. Pickets blocked narrow mountain roads. Houses were blown up; the town water main was dynamited. An estimated 1,250 individuals were arrested in confrontations with the National Guard.[21]

As far as can be determined, no women were involved in barn burnings and dynamitings—what Bessie Edens referred to as "the rough . . . stuff" that accompanied the second strike. Men "went

places that we didn't go," explained Christine Galliher. "They had big dark secrets . . . the men did." But when it came to public demonstrations women held center stage. At the outset "hundreds of girls" had ridden down main street "in buses and taxis, shouting and laughing at people who watched them from windows and doorsteps." Now they blocked the road at Gap Creek and refused soldiers' orders that they walk twelve miles to jail in town. "And there was one girl that was awful tough in the bunch. . . . She said, 'No, by God. We didn't walk out here, and we're not walking back!' And she sat her hind end down in the middle of the road, and we all sat down with her. And the law used tear gas on us! . . . And it nearly put our eyes out, but we still wouldn't walk back to town." In Elizabethton after picket duty, women marched down the "Bemberg Highway . . . draped in the American flag and carrying the colors"—thereby forcing the guardsmen to present arms each time they passed. Inventive, playful, and shrewd, the women's tactics encouraged a holiday spirit. They may also have deflected violence and garnered community support.[22]

Laughter was among the women's most effective weapons. But beneath high spirits the terms of battle had begun to change. Local organizers were hobbled by a national union that lacked the resources and commitment to sustain the strike. Instead of translating workers' grievances into a compelling challenge, the UTW pared their demands down to the bone. On May 26, six weeks after the strike began, the union agreed to a settlement that made no mention of wages, hours, working conditions, or union recognition. The company's only concession was a promise not to discriminate against union members. The workers were less than enthusiastic. According to one reporter, "It took nine speeches and a lot of question answering lasting two and a half hours to get the strikers to accept the terms."[23]

The press, for the most part, greeted the settlement as a workers' victory, or at least a satisfactory resolution of the conflict. Anna Weinstock, the first woman to serve as a federal conciliator, was credited with bringing the company to the bargaining table and was pictured as the heroine of the event. "SETTLED BY A WOMAN!" headlined one journal. "This is the fact that astounds American newspaper editors." "Five feet five inches and 120 pounds of femininity; clean cut, even features"—and so on, in great detail. Little was made of Weinstock's own working-class origins. She was simply a "new woman," come to the rescue of a backward mountain folk. The strikers themselves dropped quickly from view.[24]

From the outside, the conflict at Elizabethton looked like a straightforward case of labor-management strife. But it appeared quite different from within. Everyone interviewed put the blame for low wages on an alliance between the German managers and the "leading citizens" of the town. Preserved in the oral tradition is the story of how the "town fathers" promised the company a supply of cheap and unorganized labor. Bessie Edens put it this way: They told the company that "women wasn't used to working, and they'd work for almost nothing, and the men would work for low wages. That's the way they got the plant here." In this version of events the strike was part of a long-term struggle, with development-minded townspeople on one side and workers, farmers, and country merchants on the other.[25]

Workers' roots in the countryside encouraged resistance and helped them to mobilize support once the strike began. "These workers have come so recently from the farms and mountains . . . and are of such independent spirit," Alfred Hoffman observed, "that they 'Don't care if they do lose their jobs' and cannot be scared." Asked by reporters what would happen if strike activity cost them their

jobs, one woman remarked, "I haven't forgotten to use a hoe," while another said, "We'll go back to the farm."[26] Such threats were not just bravado. High levels of farm ownership sustained cultural independence. Within the internal economy of families, individual fortunes were cushioned by reciprocity; an orientation toward subsistence survived side by side with the desire for cash and store-bought goods.

Stony Creek farmers were solidly behind the sons and daughters they sent to the factories, as were the small shopkeepers who relied on farmers for their trade. In county politics Stony Creekers had historically marshaled a block vote against the town. In 1929 Stony Creek's own J. M. Moreland was county sheriff, and he openly took the strikers' side. A strike leader in the twisting room ran a country store and drove his working neighbors into town. "That's why he was pretty well accepted as their leader," said a fellow worker. "Some of them were cousins and other relations. Some of them traded at his store. Some of them rode in his taxi. All intertwined."[27]

The National Guard had divided loyalties. Parading past the plants, the strikers "waved to and called the first names of the guardsmen, for most of the young men in uniforms [were friends of] the men and girls on strike." Even when the local unit was fortified by outside recruits, fraternizing continued. Nettie Reece, like a number of her girlfriends, met her future husband that way; she saw him on the street and "knew that was mine right there." Some guardsmen went further and simply refused to serve. "The use of the National Guard here was the dirtiest deal ever pulled," one protested. "I turned in my equipment when I was ordered to go out and patrol the road. I was dropped from the payroll two weeks later."[28]

In this context of family- and community-based resistance, women had important roles to play. Farm mothers nurtured the strikers' independence simply by cleaving to the land, passing on to their children a heritage at odds with the values of the new order and maintaining family production as a hedge against the uncertainties of a market economy. But the situation of farm mothers had other effects as well, and it would be a mistake to push the argument for continuity too far. As their husbands ranged widely in search of wage labor, women's work intensified while their status—now tied to earning power—declined. The female strikers of Elizabethton saw their mothers as resourceful and strong but also as increasingly isolated and hard pressed. Most important, they no longer looked to their mothers' lives as patterns for their own.[29]

The summer after the strike, Bessie Edens attended the Southern Summer School for Women Workers, a workers' education project in North Carolina, where she set the group on its ear with an impassioned defense of women's rights:

> It is nothing new for married women to work. They have always worked. . . . Women have always worked harder than men and always had to look up to the man and feel that they were weaker and inferior. . . . If we women would not be so submissive and take every thing for granted, if we would awake and stand up for our rights, this world would be a better place to live in, at least it would be better for the women.

> Some girls think that as long as mother takes in washings, keeps ten or twelve boarders or perhaps takes in sewing, she isn't working. But I say that either one of the three is as hard work as women could do. So if they do that at home and don't get any wages for it, why would it not be all right for them to go to a factory and receive pay for what they do?

Edens had been the oldest of ten children. She had dreamed of going to nursing school, but her poverty-stricken parents had opposed her plan. At fifteen, she had gone to work as a servant. "Then I'd come back when Momma had a baby and wait on her, and help if she needed me in any way." Asked fifty years later about a daughter's place on a hardscrabble farm, Edens replied: "The girls were supposed to do housework and work in the fields. They were supposed to be slaves."[30]

Bessie Edens was unusual in her articulation of a working-class feminism. But scattered through the life histories written by other students are echoes of her general themes. Read in the context of farm daughters' lives—their first-hand exposure to rural poverty, their yearnings for a more expansive world—these stories reflect the "structure of feeling" women brought to the rayon plants and then to the picket line and union hall.[31] Women such as Edens, it seems, sensed the devaluation of women's handicraft labor in the face of cheap consumer goods. They feared the long arm of their mothers' fate, resented their fathers' distant authority, and envied their brothers' exploits away from home. By opting for work in the rayon plants, they struck out for their own place in a changing world. When low wages, high costs, and autocratic managers affronted their dignity and dashed their hopes, they were the first to revolt.

The Elizabethton story thus presents another pattern in the female protest tradition. In coal-mining communities a rigid division of labor and women's hardships in company towns have resulted, paradoxically, in the notable militancy of miners' wives. By contrast, tobacco factories have tended to employ married women, whose job commitments and associational lives enable them to assume leadership roles in sustained organizing drives. In yet other circumstances, such as the early New England textile mills or the union insurgency of the 1920s and 1930s, single women initiated independent strikes or provided strong support for male-led, mixed-sex campaigns. Where, as in Elizabethton, people were mobilized as family and community members rather than as individual workers, non-wage-earning women could provide essential support. Once in motion, their daughters might outdo men in militancy, perhaps because they had fewer dependents than their male co-workers and could fall back more easily on parental resources, perhaps because the peer culture and increased independence encouraged by factory labor stirred boldness and inspired experimentation.[32]

The fact of women's initiative and participation in collective action is instructive. Even more intriguing is the gender-based symbolism of their protest style. Through dress, language, and gesture, female strikers expressed a complex cultural identity and turned it to their own rebellious purposes.

Consider, for instance, Trixie Perry and a woman who called herself "Texas Bill." Twenty-eight-year-old Trixie Perry was a reeler in the Glanzstoff plant. She had apparently become pregnant ten years before, had married briefly and then divorced, giving her son her maiden name. Her father was a butcher and a farmer, and she lived near her family on the edge of town. Trixie later moved into Elizabethton. She never remarried but went on to have several more children by other men. Texas Bill's background is more elusive. All we know is that she came from out of state, lived in a boardinghouse, and claimed to have been married twice before she arrived in town. These two friends were ringleaders on the picket line. Both were charged with violating the injunction, and both were brought to trial.[33]

Trixie Perry took the stand in a dress sewn from red, white, and blue bunting and a cap made of a small American flag. The prosecuting attorney began his cross-examination:

"You have a United States flag as a cap on your head?"

"Yes."

"Wear it all the time?"

"Whenever I take a notion."

"You are dressed in a United States flag, and the colors?"

"I guess so, I was born under it, guess I have a right to."

The main charge was that Perry and her friend had drawn a line across the road at Gap Creek and dared the soldiers to cross it. Above all they were accused of taunting the National Guard. The defense attorney, a fiery local lawyer playing to a sympathetic crowd, did not deny the charges. Instead, he used the women to mock the government's case. Had Trixie Perry threatened a lieutenant? "He rammed a gun in my face and I told him to take it out or I would knock it out." Had she blocked the road? "A little thing like me block a big road?" What had she said to the threat of a tear gas bomb? "That little old fire cracker of a thing, it won't go off."[34]

Texas Bill was an even bigger hit with the crowd. The defense attorney called her the "Wild Man From Borneo." A guard said she was "the wildest human being I've ever seen." Texas Bill both affirmed and subverted her reputation. Her nickname came from her habit of wearing "cowboy" clothes. But when it was her turn to testify, she "strutted on the stand" in a fashionable black picture hat and a black coat. Besides her other transgressions, she was accused of grabbing a soldier's gun and aiming it at him. What was she doing on the road so early in the morning? "I take a walk every morning before breakfast for my health," Texas replied with what a reporter described as "an assumed ladylike dignity."[35]

Witnesses for the prosecution took pains to contradict Texas Bill's "assumed ladylike dignity." A guardsman complained that she called him a " 'God damned yellow son-of-a-bitch,' and then branched out from that." Texas offered no defense: "When that soldier stuck his gun in my face, that did make me mad and I did cuss a little bit and don't deny it." Far from discrediting the strikers, the soldiers' testimony added to their own embarrassment and the audience's delight. In tune with the crowd, the defense attorney "enjoyed making the guards admit they had been 'assaulted' . . . by 16 and 18-year-old girls."[36]

Mock gentility, transgressive laughter, male egos on the line—the mix made for wonderful theater, and proved effective in court as well. The judge reserved maximum sentences for three especially aggressive men; all the women and most of the men were found not guilty or were lightly fined. In the end even those convictions were overturned by the state court of appeals.[37]

Trixie Perry and Texas Bill certainly donned the role of "disorderly woman." Since, presumably, only extraordinary circumstances call forth feminine aggression, women's assaults against persons and property constitute a powerful witness against injustice. At the same time, since women are considered less rational and taken less seriously than men, they may meet less resistance and be punished less severely for their crimes.[38]

But Trixie Perry and Texas Bill were not just out of line in their public acts; they also led unconventional private lives. It was this erotic subtext that most horrified officialdom and amused the courtroom crowd. The only extended discussion of the strike that appears in the city council minutes resulted in a resolution that read in part:

WHEREAS, it has come to [our] attention . . . that the moral tone of this community has been lowered by reason of men and women congregating in various houses and meeting-places in Elizabethton and there practicing lewdness all hours of the night, in defiance of morality, law and order. . . .

NOW, THEREFORE, BE IT RESOLVED, that the police force of the City arrest and place in the City Jail those who are violating the laws by practicing lewdness within the City of Elizabethton. . . .[39]

Union representatives apparently shared, indeed anticipated, the councilmen's concern. Worried by rumors that unemployed women were resorting to prostitution, they had already announced to the press that 25 percent of the strikers had been sent back to their hillside homes, "chiefly young single girls whom we want to keep off the streets." The townsmen and the trade unionists were thus united in drawing a line between good women and bad, with respectability being measured not only by chastity but by nuances of style and language as well.[40] In the heat of the trial, the question of whether or not women—as workers—had violated the injunction took second place to questions about their status *as women*, as members of their sex. Had they cursed? Had they been on the road at odd hours of the day or night? Was Texas Bill a lady or a "wild man from Borneo"? Fearing that "lewd women" might discredit the organizing drive, the organizers tried to send them home. To protect the community's "moral tone," the city council threatened to lock them up.

There is nothing extraordinary about this association between sexual misbehavior and women's labor militancy. Since strikers are often young single women who violate gender conventions by invading public space customarily reserved for men (and sometimes frequented by prostitutes)—and since female aggressiveness stirs up fears of women's sexual power—opponents have often undercut union organizing drives by insinuations of prostitution or promiscuity. Fearing guilt by association, "respectable" women stay away.[41]

What is impressive here is how Trixie Perry and Texas Bill handled the dichotomy between ladyhood and lewdness, good girls and bad. Using words that, for women in particular, were ordinarily taboo, they refused deference and signaled disrespect. Making no secret of their sexual experience, they combined flirtation with fierceness on the picket line and adopted a provocative courtroom style. And yet, with the language of dress—a cap made of an American flag, an elegant wide-brimmed hat—they claimed their rights as citizens and their place in the female community.

Moreover, that community upheld their claims. The defense attorney chose unruly women as his star witnesses, and the courtroom spectators enthusiastically cheered them on. The prosecuting attorney recommended dismissal of the charges against all the women on trial except Trixie Perry, Texas Bill, and a "hoodlum" named Lucille Ratliffe, on the grounds that the rest came from "good families." Yet in the court transcripts, few differences can be discerned in the behavior of good girls and bad. The other female defendants may have been less flamboyant, but they were no less sharp-tongued. Was Vivian King a member of the UTW? "Yes, and proud of it." Had she been picketing? "Yes, proud of that." What was a young married woman named Dorothy Oxindine doing on Gap Creek at five o'clock in the morning? "Out airing." Did Lena May Jones "holler out 'scab'"? "No, I think the statement made was 'I wouldn't be a scab' and 'Why don't you come and join our organization.'" Did she laugh at a soldier and tell him his gun wouldn't shoot? "I didn't tell him it wouldn't shoot, but I laughed at him . . . and told him he was too much of a man to shoot a lady."[42]

Interviewed over fifty years later, strike participants still refused to make invidious distinctions between themselves and women like Trixie Perry and Texas Bill. Bessie Edens was a settled, self-educated, married woman. But she was also a self-described "daredevil on the picket line," secure in the knowledge that she had a knife hidden in her drawstring underwear. To Edens, who came from a mountain hamlet called Hampton, the chief distinction did not lie between herself and

rougher women. It lay between herself and merchants' wives who blamed the trouble on "those hussies from Hampton." When asked what she thought of Trixie Perry and Texas Bill, she answered simply, "There were some girls like that involved. But I didn't care. They did their part."[43]

Nettie Reece, who lived at home with parents who were "pretty particular with [their] daughters," shared Bessie Edens's attitude. After passing along the town gossip about Trixie Perry, she was anxious to make sure her meaning was not misconstrued. "Trixie was not a woman who sold her body," she emphasized. "She just had a big desire for sex. . . . And when she had a cause to fight for, she'd fight." Reece then went on to establish Perry's claim to a certain kind of respectability. After the strike Perry became a hard-working restaurant cook. She was a good neighbor: "If anybody got sick, she was there to wait on them." The children she bore out of wedlock did well in life, and they "never throwed [their mother] aside."[44]

Industrialization, as we know, changed the nature of work, the meaning of time. In Carter County it entailed a shift of economic and political power from the countryside to the town. At issue too were more intimate matters of fantasy, culture, and style.

Implicit in the conflict were two different sexual systems. One, subscribed to by union officials and the local middle class, mandated chastity before marriage, men as breadwinners, and women as housewives in the home. The other, rooted in a rural past and adapted to working-class life, recognized liaisons established without the benefit of clergy or license fees and allowed legitimacy to be broadly construed. It was unfamiliar with—or pragmatic about—prostitution. It circumscribed women's roles without investing in abstract standards of femininity. It was, in short, a society that might produce a Trixie Perry or defend "hussies from Hampton" against the snubs of merchants' wives.

This is not to say that the women of Elizabethton were simply acting on tradition. On the contrary, the strikers dressed the persona of the disorderly woman in unmistakably modern garb. Women's behavior on the witness stand presupposed a certain sophistication: A passing familiarity allowed them to parody ladyhood and to thumb a nose at the genteel standards of the town. Combining garments from the local past with fragments of an expansive consumer culture, the women of Elizabethton assembled their own version of a brash, irreverent Jazz Age style.

By the early 1920s radios and Model T's had joined railroads and mail-order catalogs as conduits to the larger world. Record companies had discovered hill-country music and East Tennessee's first country-music stars were recording hits that transformed ballad singing, fiddle playing, and banjo picking into one of America's great popular-music sounds. The banjo itself was an Afro-American instrument that had come to the mountains with the railroad gangs. Such cultural interchanges multiplied during the 1920s as rural traditions met the unheavals of industrial life. The result was an explosion of musical creativity—in the hills of Tennessee no less than in New York City and other cosmopolitan centers.[45] Arriving for work in the rayon plants, young people brought with them the useable past of the countryside, but they quickly assimilated the speeded-up rhythms of a changing world.

Work-related peer groups formed a bridge between traditional loyalties and a novel youth culture. Whether married or single, living with parents or on their own, women participated in the strike in same-sex groups. Sisters boarded, worked, and demonstrated together. Girlfriends teamed up in groups or pairs. Trixie Perry and Texas Bill were a case in point.

But there were others as well. Nettie Reece joined the union with her parents' approval but also with her whole school girl gang in tow. Ethel and M. C. Ashworth, ages eighteen and seventeen, respectively, came from Virginia to work in the plants. "Hollering and singing [in a] Ford touring car," they were arrested in a demonstration at Watauga Point. Ida and Evelyn Heaton boarded together on Donna Avenue. Evelyn Heaton was hit by a car on the picket line, swore out a warrant, and had the commander of the National Guard placed under arrest. After the strike she was blacklisted, and Ida attended the Southern Summer School.[46]

The sudden gathering of young people in the town nourished new patterns of heterosociability, and the strike's erotic undercurrent surfaced not only in Trixie Perry's "big desire for sex" but also in the behavior of her more conventional peers. The loyalties of the national guardsmen were divided, but their sympathy was obvious, as was their interest in the female strikers. Most of the Elizabethton women were in their teens or early twenties, the usual age of marriage in the region, and the strike provided unaccustomed opportunities for courtship. Rather than choosing a neighbor they had known all their lives, under watchful parental eyes, women flirted on the picket lines or the shop floor. Romance and politics commingled in the excitement of the moment, flowering in a spectrum of behavior—from the outrageousness of Trixie Perry to a spate of marriages among other girls.

What needs emphasis here is the dynamic quality of working-class women's culture—a quality that is sometimes lost in static oppositions between modernism and traditionalism, individualism and family values, consumer and producer mentalities. This is especially important where regional history has been so thoroughly mythologized. Appalachian culture, like all living cultures, embraced continuity and discontinuity, indigenous and borrowed elements.[47] As surely as Anna Weinstock—or Alabama's Zelda Fitzgerald—or any city flapper, the Elizabethton strikers were "new women," making their way in a world their mothers could not have known but carrying with them values handed down through the female line.

Two vignettes may serve to illustrate that process of grounded change.

Flossie Cole's mother, known by everyone on Stony Creek as "Aunt Tine," was Sheriff Moreland's sister, but that didn't keep her from harboring cardplayers, buckdancers, and whiskey drinkers in her home. Aunt Tine was also a seamstress who "could look at a picture in a catalog and cut a pattern and make a dress just like it." But like most of her friends, Cole jumped at the chance for store-bought clothes: "That first paycheck, that was it . . . I think I bought me some new clothes with the first check I got. I bought me a new pair of shoes and a dress and a hat. Can you imagine someone going to a plant with a hat on? I had a blue dress and black shoes—patent leather, honey, with real high heels—and a blue hat." Nevertheless, before Cole left home in the morning for her job in the rayon plant, Aunt Tine made sure that around her neck—beneath the new blue dress—she wore a bag of asafetida, a strong-smelling resin, a folk remedy to protect her from diseases that might be circulating in the town.[48]

Second, there is visual evidence: a set of sixteen-millimeter films made by the company in order to identify—and to blacklist—workers who participated in the union. In those films groups of smiling women traipse along the picket line dressed in up-to-date clothes.[49] Yet federal conciliator Anna Weinstock, speaking to an interviewer forty years later, pictured them in sunbonnets, and barefooted. "They were," she explained, "what we would normally call hillbillies": women who "never get away from their shacks."[50] This could be seen as the treachery of

memory, a problem of retrospection. But it is also an illustration of the power of stereotypes, of how cultural difference is registered as backwardness, of how images of poverty and backwardness hide the realities of working-class women's lives.

The strike, as we know, was defeated. Participants were blacklisted. The Great Depression settled over the mountains, rekindling reliance on older ways of making do. Flossie Cole, for instance, had been new to factory labor, but she was no stranger to women's work. While her brothers had followed their father's lead to the coal mines, she had pursued the two most common occupations of the poorest mountain girls: agricultural labor and domestic service. "We would hire out and stay with people until they got through with us and then go back home. And when we got back home, it was workin' in the corn or wash for people." When Cole lost her job after the strike she went back to domestic service, "back to the drudge house," as she put it.[51]

Young women had poured eagerly into the rayon mills, drawn at least in part by the promise of independence, romance and adventure. As hard times deepened, such motives paled beside stark necessity. Two statistics make the point: The percentage of Carter County women who were gainfully employed held steady through the thirties. But by the end of the period a larger proportion than before worked as servants in other people's homes. When Flossie Cole went "back to the drudge house," she had plenty of company.[52]

Still, despite subsequent hardships, the spirit of the 1920s flickered on. Setting out to explore the strike through oral-history interviews, we expected to find disclaimers or silences. Instead, we heard unfaded memories and no regrets. "I knew I wasn't going to get to go back, and I didn't care," said Bessie Edens. "I wrote them a letter and told them I didn't care whether they took me back or not. I didn't! If I'd starved I wouldn't of cared, because I knew what I was a'doing when I helped to pull it. And I've never regretted it in any way. . . . And it did help the people, and it's helped the town and the country."[53] For those, like Edens, who went on to the Southern Summer School or remained active in the union, the strike was a pivot around which the political convictions and personal aspirations of a lifetime turned. For them, there were intangible rewards: a subtle deepening of individual power, a belief that they had made history and that later generations benefited from what they had done.

The strike, of course, made a fainter impression on other lives. Women's rebelliousness neither redefined gender roles nor overcame economic dependency. Their desire for the trappings of modernity could blur into a self-limiting consumerism. An ideology of romance could end in sexual danger or a married woman's burdensome double day. Still, the women of Elizabethton left a legacy. A norm of female public work, a new style of sexual expressiveness, the entry of women into public space and political struggles previously monopolized by men—all these pushed against traditional constraints even as they created new vulnerabilities. The farm daughters who left home for the rayon plants pioneered a new pattern of female experience, and they created for their post-World War II daughters an environment far different from the one they, in their youth, had known. It would be up to later generations to wrestle with the costs of commercialization and to elaborate a vision that embraced economic justice and community solidarity as well as women's liberation.[54]

Notes

This study began as a collaborative endeavor with Sara Evans of the University of Minnesota, who helped to gather many of the interviews on which I have relied. Rosemarie Hester and Jennifer Dowd also joined me on trips to the mountains, and I benefited from their companionship, ideas, and research. I owe a special debt to Christopher Daly, Lu Ann Jones, Robert Korstad, James Leloudis, and Mary Murphy, with whom I am co-writing a more general study of southern textile workers. Others who commented thoughtfully on various drafts of this essay were Judith Bennett, Carol Berkin, Mari Jo Buhle, Jane De Hart-Mathews, Amy Glass, Alice Kessler-Harris, Suzanne Lebsock, Barbara Melosh, Anne Firor Scott, Joan W. Scott, and David Whisnant. Christine Stansell in particular helped me sort out thorny issues along the way. Thanks to Aliza Blachman, Emily Jernberg, and Ben Pranger for research assistance.

1. Dan Crowe, Old Town and the Covered Bridge (Johnson City, Tenn., 1977), 32, 71; Florence (Cole) Grindstaff interview by Jacquelyn Hall, July 10, 1981 (in Hall's possession).

2. For this strike wave, see, Tom Tippett, When Southern Labor Stirs (New York, 1931); James A. Hodges, "Challenge to the New South: The Great Textile Strike in Elizabethton, Tennessee, 1929," Tennessee Historical Quarterly, 23 (Dec. 1964), 343–57; Irving Bernstein, The Lean Years: A History of the American Worker, 1920–1933 (Boston, 1960), 1–43; and George B. Tindall, The Emergence of the New South, 1913–1945 (Baton Rouge, 1967), 341–53.

3. Contemporary observations include, Knoxville News Sentinel, May 17, 1929; Florence Kelley, "Our Newest South," Survey, June 15, 1929, pp. 342–44; Matilda Lindsay, "Women Hold Key to Unionization of Dixie," Machinists' Monthly Journal 41 (Sept. 1929), 638–39, 684; Sherwood Anderson, "Elizabethton, Tennessee," Nation, May 1, 1929, pp. 526–27.

4. Anne Firor Scott, "On Seeing and Not Seeing: A Case of Historical Invisibility," Journal of American History, 71 (June 1984), 7–8.

5. Natalie Zemon Davis, Society and Culture in Early Modern France (Stanford, 1975), 124–51. For this phenomenon in the New

World, see Laurel Thatcher Ulrich, *Good Wives: Image and Reality in the Lives of Women in Northern New England, 1650–1750* (New York, 1982), 191–97.

6. Michel Foucault, *Power/Knowledge: Selected Interviews and Other Writings, 1972–1977*, trans. and ed. Colin Gordon (New York, 1980), 81.

7. Joseph Leeming, *Rayon: The First Man-Made Fiber* (Brooklyn, 1950), 1–82; Jesse W. Markham, *Competition in the Rayon Industry* (Cambridge, Mass., 1952), 1–38, 97, 186, 193, 209.

8. Bruce Roberts and Nancy Roberts, *Where Time Stood Still: A Portrait of Appalachia* (New York, 1970); William Goodell Frost, "Our Contemporary Ancestors in the Southern Mountains," *Atlantic Monthly*, 83 (March 1899), 311; Arnold J. Toynbee, *A Study of History* (2 vols., New York, 1947), II, 312; Henry D. Shapiro, *Appalachia on Our Mind: The Southern Mountains and Mountaineers in the American Consciousness, 1870–1920* (Chapel Hill, 1978); Ronald D Eller, *Miners, Millhands, and Mountaineers: Industrialization of the Appalachian South, 1880–1930* (Knoxville, 1982).

9. For this preindustrial economy, and its transformation, see Eller, *Miners, Millhands, and Mountaineers*, 3–38, 86–127. Information on Carter County is drawn from John F. Holly, "Elizabethton, Tennessee: A Case Study of Southern Industrialization" (Ph.D. diss., Clark University, 1949), 1–121; and Alfred Hoffmann, "The Mountineer in Industry," *Mountain Life and Work*, 5 (Jan. 1930), 2–7.

10. *Mountaineer*, Dec. 28, Dec. 31, 1887.

11. U.S. Department of the Interior, Census Office, *Report on the Productions of Agriculture as Returned at the Tenth Census (June 1, 1880)* (Washington, 1883), 84–85, 132, 169; U.S. Department of Commerce, Bureau of the Census, *Fourteenth Census of the United States Taken in the Year 1920: Agriculture*, vol. VI, pt. 2 (Washington, 1922), 446–47.

12. Holly, "Elizabethton, Tennessee," 123, 133–38, 156, 198; U.S. Congress, Senate, Committee on Manufactures, *Working Conditions of the Textile Industry in North Carolina, South Carolina, and Tennessee*, 71 Cong., 1 sess., May 8, 9, and 20, 1929, p. 95; Henry Schuettler interview by Hall, n.d. [1981] (in Hall's possession).

13. Thirteenth Census of the United States, 1910, Manuscript Population Schedule, Carter County, Tenn., district 7; ibid., district 15; ibid., district 10; ibid., district 12.

14. Grindstaff interview.

15. *Scraps of Work and Play*, Southern Summer School for Women Workers in Industry, Burnsville, N.C., July 11–Aug. 23, 1929, typescript, pp. 21–22, 24, box 111, American Labor Education Service Records (Martin P. Catherwood Library, New York State School of Industrial and Labor Relations, Cornell University, Ithaca, N.Y.); Bessie Edens interview by Mary Frederickson, Aug. 14, 1975, pp. 1–2, 31–32, Southern Oral History Program Collection, Southern Historical Collection (Wilson Library, University of North Carolina at Chapel Hill) [hereafter SOHP].

16. Edens interview, Aug. 14, 1975, p. 32; Grindstaff interview.

17. Nettie Reece [pseud.] interview by Hall, May 18 and 19, 1983 (in Hall's possession).

18. *Knoxville News Sentinel*, May 13, 1929; *American Bemberg Corporation v. George Miller, et al.*, East Tennessee District Supreme Court, Jan. 29, 1930, record of evidence, typescript, box 660 (Tennessee State Library and Archives, Nashville) [hereafter Record of Evidence]. For such uses of Americanism, see David Alan Corbin, *Life, Work, and Rebellion in the Coal Fields: The Southern West Virginia Miners, 1880–1922* (Urbana, 1981), 236–52.

19. *Knoxville News Sentinel*, March 14, 1929; Christine (Hinkle) Galliher and Dave Galliher interview by Hall, Aug. 8, 1979, pp. 8–9, SOHP; Tom Tippett, "Southern Situation," speech typescript, meeting held at the National Board, May 15, 1929, p. 3, box 25, Young Women's Christian Association Papers, Sophia Smith Collection (Smith College, Northampton, Mass.); Tom Tippett, "Impressions of Situation at Elizabethton, Tenn. May 10, 11, 1929," typescript, p. 1, ibid.

20. *Knoxville News Sentinel*, March 20, March 29, 1929; "Instructions for Adjustment of Wage Scale for Girl Help," March 15, 1929, Records of the Conciliation Service, RG 280 (National Archives); Committee of Striking Workers[,] Members of United Textile Workers of America to the Honorable Herbert Hoover, April 16, 1929, ibid.; "Preliminary Report of Commissioner of Conciliation," April 16, 1929, ibid.

21. Dr. J. A. Hardin to Hon. H. H. Horton, May 16, 1929, box 12, Governor Henry H. Horton Papers (Tennessee State Library and Archives); *Knoxville News Sentinel*, May 6, May 10, May 12, May 14, May 19, May 24, 1929.

22. Edens interview, Aug. 14, 1975, pp. 40, 49; Galliher interview, 33; *Knoxville News Sentinel*, March 15, May 16, 1929.

23. *Knoxville News Sentinel*, May 27, 1929; Ina Nell (Hinkle) Harrison interview by Hall, Aug. 8, 1979, p. 2, SOHP; Mary Heaton Vorse, "Rayon Strikers Reluctantly Accept Settlement," press release, May 27, 1929, box 156, Mary Heaton Vorse Papers, Archives of Labor and Urban Affairs (Walter P. Reuther Library, Wayne State University, Detroit, Mich.).

24. "Rays of Sunshine in the Rayon War," *Literary Digest*, June 8, 1929, p. 12; *Charlotte Observer*, June 2, 1929; *Raleigh News and Observer*, May 24, 1929.

25. Edens interview, Aug. 14, 1975, pp. 43–44; Myrtle Simmerly interview by Hall, May 18, 1983 (in Hall's possession); Ollie Hardin interview by Hall and Sara Evans, Aug. 9, 1979 (in Hall's possession); Effie (Hardin) Carson interview by Hall and Evans, Aug. 6, 1979, p. 41, SOHP; Holly, "Elizabethton, Tennessee," 306–307.

26. James Myers, "Field Notes: Textile Strikes in the South," box 374, Archive Union Files (Martin P. Catherwood Library); *Raleigh News and Observer*, March 15, 1929.

27. Hoffmann, "Mountaineer in Industry," 2–5; Robert (Bob) Moreland and Barbara Moreland interview by Hall, July 11, 1981 (in Hall's possession); *Knoxville News Sentinel*, March 15, 1929; Honard Ward interview by Hall, n.d. [1981] (in Hall's possession).

28. *Knoxville News Sentinel*, May 15, 1929; Reece interview; Duane McCracken, *Strike Injunctions in the New South* (Chapel Hill, 1931), 246.

29. For the argument that precisely because they are "left behind" by the economic developments that pull men into wage labor, woman-centered families may harbor alternative or oppositional values, see Mina Davis Caulfield, "Imperialism, the Family, and Cultures of Resistance," *Socialist Revolution*, 4 (Oct. 1974), 67–85; and Helen Matthews Lewis, Sue Easterling Kobak, and Linda Johnson, "Family, Religion and Colonialism in Central Appalachia or Bury My Rifle at Big Stone Gap," in *Colonialism in Modern America: The Appalachian Case*, ed. Helen Matthews Lewis, Linda Johnson, and Don Askins (Boone, N.C., 1978), 113–39.

30. Bessie Edens, "Why a Married Woman Should Work," in *Scraps of Work and Play*, 30–31; Edens interview, Aug. 14, 1975, pp. 14, 21, 34–35; Bessie Edens interview by Hall, Aug. 5, 1979 (in Hall's possession); Millie

Sample, "Impressions," Aug. 1931, box 9, American Labor Education Service Records.

31. Mirion Bonner, "Behind the Southern Textile Strikes," *Nation*, Oct. 2, 1929, pp. 351–52; "Scraps From Our Lives," in *Scraps of Work and Play*, 5–11; Raymond Williams, *The Long Revolution* (London, 1961), 48–71.

32. Corbin, *Life, Work, and Rebellion*, 92–93; Louise A. Tilly, "Paths of Proletarianization: Organization of Production, Sexual Division of Labor, and Women's Collective Action," *Signs* 7 (Winter 1981), 400–17; Thomas Dublin, *Women at Work: The Transformation of Work and Community in Lowell, Massachusetts, 1826–1860* (New York, 1979), esp. 86–131; Sharon Hartman Strom, "Challenging 'Woman's Place': Feminism, the Left, and Industrial Unionism in the 1930s," *Feminist Studies*, 9 (Summer 1983), 359–86; Alice Kessler-Harris, *Out to Work: A History of Wage-Earning Women in the United States* (New York, 1982), 160.

33. *Elizabethton Star*, Nov. 14, 1953, Jan. 31, 1986; Reece interview; Carson interview, 25; Nellie Bowers interview by Hall, May 15, 1983 (in Hall's possession); *Knoxville News Sentinel*, May 17, May 18, 1929.

34. Record of Evidence.

35. *Knoxville News Sentinel*, May 17, 1929.

36. Ibid.; Record of Evidence.

37. *American Bemberg Corporation v. George Miller, et al.*, minute books "Q" and "R," Chancery Court minutes, Carter County, Tenn., July 22, 1929 (Carter County Courthouse, Elizabethton, Tenn.); *American Bemberg Corporation v. George Miller, et al.*, Court of Appeals, #1, Sept. 5, 1930 (Supreme Court and Courts of Appeal, State of Tennessee, Knoxville).

38. Davis, *Society and Culture in Early Modern France*, 124–51; Ulrich, *Good Wives*, 191–97.

39. Elizabethton City Council, Minutes, May 23, 1929, Minute Book, vol. 5, pp. 356–57 (City Hall, Elizabethton, Tenn.).

40. *Knoxville News Sentinel*, May 5, 1929; Myers, "Field Notes." For working-class standards of respectability and sexual morality, see Kathy Peiss, *Cheap Amusements: Working Women and Leisure in Turn-of-the-Century New York* (Philadelphia, 1986), esp. 88–114.

41. See for instance, Alice Kessler-Harris, "The Autobiography of Ann Washington Craton," *Signs*, 1 (Summer 1976), 1019–37.

42. *Knoxville News Sentinel*, May 18, 1929; Record of Evidence.

43. Edens interview, Aug. 5, 1979.

44. Reece interview, May 19, 1983.

45. Charles K. Wolfe, *Tennessee Strings: The Story of Country Music in Tennessee* (Knoxville, 1977), 22–90; Barry O'Connell, "Dick Boggs, Musician and Coal Miner," *Appalachian Journal*, 11 (Autumn-Winter 1983–84), 48.

46. *Miller's Elizabethton, Tenn., City Directory*, 1930; Reece interview; Record of Evidence; *Knoxville News Sentinel*, May 16, May 17, 1929; Kelley, "Our Newest South," 343; "Analysis of Union List," Oct. 21, 1929, Records of the Conciliation Service.

47. David E. Whisnant, *All That is Native and Fine: The Politics of Culture in an American Region* (Chapel Hill, 1983), 48.

48. Grindstaff interview; Moreland interview.

49. *Knoxville Journal*, April 22, 1929; sixteen-millimeter film (1 reel), ca. 1929, Helen Raulston Collection, Archives of Appalachia (East Tennessee State University, Johnson City); sixteen-millimeter film (20 reels), ca. 1927–1928, Bemberg Industry Records (Tennessee State Library and Archives). Mimi Conway drew my attention to these films, and, more important, helped prevent their loss or destruction when the Bemberg plant closed.

50. Anna Weinstock Schneider interview by Julia Blodgett Curtis, 1969, pp. 161, 166, 172–3, 177, Anna Weinstock Schneider Papers, box 1 (Martin P. Catherwood Library).

51. Grindstaff interview.

52. Bureau of the Census, *Fifteenth Census of the United States: 1930. Population*, vol. III, pt. 2 (Washington, 1932), p. 909; U.S. Department of Commerce, Bureau of the Census, *Sixteenth Census of the United States: 1940. Population*, vol. II, pt. 6 (Washington, 1943), 616.

53. Edens interview, Aug. 14, 1975, p. 50.

54. For similar conclusions about first-generation immigrant workers, see Peiss, *Cheap Amusements*, 185–88; and Elizabeth Ewen, *Immigrant Women in the Land of Dollars: Life and Culture on the Lower East Side, 1890–1925* (New York, 1985), 264–69.

MARGARET JARMAN HAGOOD
Of the Tenant Child as Mother to the Woman

In the midst of the Great Depression, President Franklin D. Roosevelt identified the South as the nation's number one "problem." Farm tenancy, sharecropping, eroding land, grinding poverty, and persistent illiteracy plagued the region; it also had the lowest rate of urbanization and the highest birth rate in the nation. These problems were human as well as economic, and they attracted the attention of a remarkable nucleus of scholars at the University of North Carolina at Chapel Hill who were interested not only in documentation but also in solutions. One of this small group was Margaret Jarman Hagood, who visited 254 carefully selected tenant houses in Piedmont North Carolina, Georgia, and Alabama to study "mothers of the South," as her book would be entitled when published in 1939. She brought to her task a fine blending of attributes that lent credibility

Excerpted from "Of the Tenant Child as Mother to the Woman," chap. 13 of *Mothers of the South: Portraiture of the White Tenant Farm Woman* by Margaret Jarman Hagood (Chapel Hill: University of North Carolina Press, 1939). Copyright © 1939 by the University of North Carolina Press. Reprinted by permission of the publisher.

to her work. As a professional sociologist, she used scientific methods of inquiry. As a wife and mother, she used the experience she shared with other women to overcome barriers of class and education so that she might enter the "distinctly feminine culture . . . centered around mating, child care and home-making" that she believed existed among these tenant farm women. (Note the woman's world that Carroll Smith-Rosenberg found among women of a different class and generation, part IIA.) The portraits resulting from Hagood's study provide a glimpse into the lives of women who bore their poverty and powerlessness with stoic courage and strength. Hagood's study shows how cotton, tobacco, and children—the economic production of society and the physical *reproduction* of society—were intertwined in the lives of rural southern women.

The story of the tenant child begins more than a quarter of a century ago. On Monday ten-year-old Mollie woke up when her mother lifted the stove lid and began making the fire. She slipped from underneath the cover easily, so as not to disturb her little brother, and took down her last year's red dress, which had been fleecy and warm, but now was slick and thin. Their bed was in the log kitchen of the Goodwin's two-room cabin, which would be warm enough in a half hour for the sickly knee-baby, who slept with Mollie, to face the December morning. . . .

Mollie's plump arms stretched tight the seams of her outgrown dress, and as she leaned over to pick up fresh wood for the fire, she felt her dress split at the shoulder. She wondered what she would do the washing in if she couldn't get into the old dress next Monday or the one after that. Her father's rule was that her two new dresses of the same cotton fleece lined material, one red and one blue, must never be worn except for school or Sunday School. She had no sisters to hand down clothes to her, for the other four children were boys. Some girls she knew wore overalls for working, but her father would not allow that either. A wicked thought came to her mind—maybe if she had nothing to wear to wash in next Monday, she wouldn't have to wash and instead could go to school with her broth-

ers. She could iron on Tuesday inside the house in her underwear—then a vision of her mother bending over the wash tubs, moaning with the pain in her back, made her put aside the daydream of a washless Monday.

After breakfast Mollie's older brother cut wood and started a fire under the wash pot while she and the brother next younger drew and carried water from the well. Then the boys left for the mile walk to the one-teacher school and Mollie started back for the house to get up the clothes. She lingered on the way, debating whether her father's overalls, stiff with a week's accumulation of winter mud and stable stains, were harder to wash than the baby's soiled diapers. They *were* harder, but the odor from the diapers made you feel you couldn't go on. It was a sensory symbol of babies, of her sick mother, of crying, little brothers, and now was vaguely mixed with her distaste for what two girl friends had told her at recess last week about how babies come. Mollie tried not to think about this and hoped she never had any babies.

The school bell's ringing interrupted her musing and reminded Mollie of how much she wanted to be there. Her dress was as new as any in school and its color still bright. The teacher had smiled approvingly at Mollie last week when the visiting preacher pinched her dimpled cheek and said, "Miss Grace, you have a fine looking bunch of little girls." Mollie thought now of having, when she was grown, a dress like Miss Grace's Sunday one. The bell stopped ringing and Mollie resolved to stop thinking and to work very hard and fast. Once before she had finished all the washing in time to go back with the boys after dinner. And so she scrubbed with all her force against the washboard and paid no attention to the pain from her knuckles scraped raw.

By dinner time all the clothes were on the line and the first ones out already frozen stiff. Mollie, numbed by cold and fatigue, ate peas, fat pork, and cornbread without joining in the family talk. When she got up from the table, her back ached—she wondered how many years of washing it would take to make it as bent over as her mother's. She changed to her new dress in time to set off for the afternoon session of school. She pulled herself together to respond to the teacher's beaming look of approval for having come to school that afternoon, and then relaxed into a lethargy from weariness and missed words she knew in the Third Reader and was spelled down quickly. . . .

One stormy winter night three months before Mollie was twelve, she was put to bed early. Her father moved the trundle bed from the main room and all the children went to sleep in the kitchen—all but Mollie. She had a terrible feeling of impending disaster to her mother and herself. When she had asked her mother about babies not long before, her mother had told her she was going to have another and that something would happen to Mollie soon, too. From the front room Mollie heard groans and knew her mother was suffering. Her own body began to ache. Her mother's sounds grew louder and each time an anguished scream reached Mollie's ears, a shooting pain went through her. Hardly daring, Mollie reached down under the cover and felt that her legs were wet. All the boys were

asleep and so she drew back the cover and in the moonlight saw black stains which had come from her body. Suddenly she thought she was having a baby. She tried to scream like her mother, but the terror of the realization paralyzed her. Fright overwhelmed her until she was no longer conscious of pain. She remained motionless for a long time, knowing and feeling nothing but a horrible fear of disgrace and dread. Then she became aware that the moaning in the next room had stopped and that someone had unlatched the kitchen door. Trembling, she eased out of bed and crept into her mother's room. There was a new baby lying on one side, but she slipped into the other side of the bed and nestled against her mother. The relaxing warmth and comfort of another's body released the inner tensions and Mollie melted into tears and weak, low sobs. Her mother stroked her but said nothing. She lay there for some minutes until the Negro "granny" said she must leave her mother and led her back to bed. Early in the morning she hid the soiled bedclothes in a corner until she could wash them secretly in the creek and found some cloths in her mother's drawer which she asked for without giving any reason. Not for two years, when a girl friend told her, did she have any instruction about how to fix and wear sanitary pads.

The summer Mollie was fourteen her mother persuaded Ben to buy her a silk dress. Mollie had worked so well that year that her father, in an appreciative mood, took her to town and let her select the material, which was a glamorous, changeable, rose and green taffeta. Mrs. Bynum helped her make it, and when her father consented to take the whole family to a Fourth of July celebration ten miles away, Mollie's cup overflowed with joy. She rolled up her hair in rags the night before. She helped bathe and dress the younger children two hours before leaving time so that she might extract the full delight from dressing leisurely in her new clothes for the first time. By eight o'clock in the morning, the family, now nine, piled into the wagon and set off. To keep from going through the county seat, they cut through a shorter, back road, which was rocky and went over steep hills. The boys got out and pushed on the worst places, but Mollie sat on the bench with her mother and father—accorded special privileges because of her new dress. The jolting and hot sun bearing down were unnoticed for the joy anticipated in being the most beautifully dressed girl at the celebration. Mollie was scarcely aware of her family in the wagon as she rode along with her head in the clouds.

They reached the tabernacle, where there were to be political speeches interspersed with hymn singing contests between churches. Mollie hopped down lightly and was about to run over to join a group of girls she knew when her mother, climbing over the edge of the wagon more slowly, called her back and took her a few steps away from the wagon.

"Your dress is ruined behind," she whispered to Mollie, "you'll have to set still over here by this tree all day." Excitement and the jolting had brought on her menstrual period early and the realization of this brought about a flush of hot shame which obliterated the festive scene of picnic tables and merry people. Mollie's heart seemed to close up and with it her capacity to perceive or respond. Passively she allowed herself to be led to a sheltered spot under an oak with protruding roots which afforded a seat. The loss of her life's triumph and the indescribable embarrassment kept her from comprehending meanings. She felt that she was dead and after awhile she leaned against the tree and slept. No one approached, for there seemed to be a tacit understanding of her plight. Late in the afternoon she rode home without speaking to her family. The next day she and her mother were unable to remove the stain from her dress and the beautiful taffeta was never worn. Her father never bought her another silk dress.

Two years later, Mollie finished the seventh grade at sixteen. The other girls were now having boys drop by their houses, but Ben Goodwin was known for his sternness and none came to see Mollie.

That summer one of Mrs. Bynum's many nieces went to a town in another county to work in a tobacco factory and her sister reveled in telling Mollie about the money she made and spent. They planned what sort of things Mollie could buy if she were to go to work in town. After weeks of whispered plans, the sister in town arranged for Mollie to have a job weighing and wrapping cigarettes. Without even telling her mother, Mollie bundled up her clothes and left early one morning, just as the cotton picking season was beginning. A neighbor boy drove her to town and she went to a relative of Ben's to board.

For four months Mollie worked in the tobacco factory and exulted in making $20 a week. This was during the postwar boom period and labor was scarce. As fast as the money came in, she spent $15 for a coat, $11 for hightop shoes, $8 for a hat, and smaller amounts for slippers, dresses, beads, and brooches. There were five other women boarding in the same house and Mollie's greatest delight was in the just-before-bedtime lunches they shared. Each one chipped in a nickel every night for cheese, crackers, and fancy canned things. Mollie had never before eaten "store bought" food and had never had even one cent to spend on self-indulgence. After she had bought an entire outfit of new clothes, she went to a county fair with the women. A boy who worked in the cigarette factory asked her to go with him, but she thought she would have a better time with the other women. This boy always hung around Mollie in the factory and said things she thought were fresh, but the landlady wouldn't allow her to go out with him. Once in December he asked Mollie to marry him but she laughed and said, "Why should I marry and keep house and have babies when I've got such a good job and can buy myself such fine clothes?"

Just before Christmas Ben Goodwin got someone to write a letter to Mollie for him. He told her she had to come back home, but that he would make arrangements for her to live during the week with an aunt in the county seat so that she could go to high school in town. Mollie cried and at first said she wouldn't go, but in the end she knew she had to mind her father. She spent her last week's wages buying presents for all the family and went home on Christmas Eve. The next day her mother took flu and one by one the children came down with it. The weakly brother's flu went into pneumonia and finally into tuberculosis, which required so much waiting on that Mollie didn't get to start to school after all.

The following summer Mollie's mother gave birth to her ninth child. It was in the daytime and the baby came in a hurry. No one was in the house except Mollie and the sick brother in the back room. Ben had gone for a doctor but not soon enough and the doctor did not get there in time. The suffering woman begged for help but Mollie did not know what to do. She even pled with Mollie to kill her and put an end to her tortures. Finally the baby was born, but with the covers pulled up so that Mollie could not see. The mother wrapped the baby up and let it lie there until the doctor came and cut the cord.

With a sick brother, a sickly mother, and a new baby in the house, Mollie had a busy summer. About the only times she had off from household duties were when she spent the night with her cousins or with Mrs. Bynum's nieces. On one such night the young people all went to watch a Negro revival meeting. While they were standing on the outside listening to the shouting through the windows, a man who knew some of the boys came up and joined them. His name was Jim and he was ten years older than Mollie, but he "took a shine" to her from their first meeting. For the rest of the summer he rode his mule for nine miles to come to see her whenever she could spend a night away from home, as Ben was still adamant about no sports coming into his house.

In the fall the brother was better and the original plan for Mollie to go to school in town was feasible. Because Ben had no buggy of his own, and because he wished so much to have his favorite daughter at home on week-ends, he finally consented for Jim to drive her out on Fridays and back to town on Sundays. His mule was the fastest one for miles around, but walked very slowly when Jim was taking Mollie home. This was when they did their courting, for Jim was never permitted to linger after delivering Mollie to her parents. He pressed his suit with urgency, for he was nearly thirty and felt it was time for him to be getting married. Mollie wasn't enjoying going back to school after being out for a year, since she was older than the town girls in her grade and felt awkward with them. She liked Jim although she never felt gay or excited with him the way she did with younger boys. She still did not want to think of marrying and settling down to repeat her mother's life—ruining her health and looks with overwork and childbearing. She made one last appeal to her father to let her go back to work in the cigarette factory, for her one-time job has remained to this day a symbol of money for clothes and luxuries. Ben would not consent, however; he said that factories were no place for his women-folks and that she could never go back. And so Mollie gave Jim a lukewarm "yes" and they planned to marry on Christmas Day. . . .

Five years later Mollie was pregnant for the third time. She felt very hopeful because this was "the kickingest baby you ever felt." Her first child had been a girl, but a terrible disappointment to Mollie in looks. At four she was big, cumbersome, awkward, and slow moving, resembling her two-hundred-pound father so much that he was frequently told, "You couldn't deny that child if you wanted to!" The second baby was a boy, weakly and always crying just like the little brother Mollie used to sleep with and take care of. The alertness of the child she was now carrying promised better success.

Mollie showed more interest in everything that spring and summer. Jim's family had left them to go live and work in a cotton mill town and for the first time they were "tending" a farm and living in a house alone. Their family of four was the smallest she had ever cooked, cleaned, and washed for, and their tobacco crop looked good in July. She was glad Jim was raising tobacco instead of cotton because it meant more money in the fall. He was still kind about buying her one Sunday dress every year with the first tobacco money he got. Mollie was still pretty at twenty-three and during her nine months of pregnancy she often daydreamed of the child, who was to be a pert, attractive daughter whom she could dress daintily.

In midsummer when her time was nearing, the baby suddenly stopped moving one night, "right short like." Mollie knew that minute the baby was dead and alarmed she woke up Jim and told him about it. He reassured her, but on her insistence the next morning went to

town and told the doctor about it. The doctor said there was nothing to do but wait, although it was eleven days before labor set in. The delivery was difficult for the dead fetus had begun disintegrating. The body was too much in pieces to be dressed for burial but they showed Mollie the face of her little girl and she thought it was the prettiest she had ever seen. Blood poison, complications, and a long illness afterwards made Mollie temporarily infertile and she had no more children for ten years.

At thirty-seven Mollie is again pregnant. She is not bitter about it, although she wishes doctors would tell you what to do when they say, "Now you shouldn't have any more children." She was quite surprised when she found she was "that way" four years ago, but she made up her mind she wouldn't hope or imagine anything because, "it's like counting your chickens before they're hatched." Then, too, Mollie has had many lessons in disappointment since her baby died. Several years there was not enough money even to "pay out," much less to buy the annual Sunday dress. Jim can't understand why he hasn't been able to buy a team. Of course, his labor force is small, but Mollie and the oldest daughter do almost full-time work in the summer. He has moved from one place to another in several counties trying to change his luck, but it has done no good. Mollie's greatest disappointment, next to the death of her pretty baby, was the year when they were living in a county where the land is supposed to be the best in the State for tobacco. Jim decided his luck had changed at last, for a week before time to begin priming, his tobacco was looking the finest of any crop he'd ever raised. He was so confident over the proceeds it would bring that he promised to give Mollie not only a finer dress than usual, but a permanent wave as soon as they sold the first load of tobacco. Mollie's straight hair had always been a source of dissatisfaction to her and she felt an almost girlish glow of anticipation over the thought of curls. Then hail came and tore the leaves, battered down the stalks, and ruined their tobacco crop. They had to sell their cow that year to pay up what they owed their landlord for furnishing.

And so Mollie, hoping no longer, was none the less delighted when her fourth child was again a pretty girl—not so pretty as the dead one, and a little plump, but much more nearly a replica of herself. Mollie began selling eggs to bring in a little money all during the year so she could buy cloth to make her daughter pretty clothes. At three now the little girl, always clean and dainty with a hair ribbon, seems incongruous with the meagerly furnished, not too well kept, three-room log cabin in which the family live.

Mollie has already laid down the law that this child shall never have to do field work or heavy household tasks. She must go to school regularly and get an education so she can get a job early—"maybe a beauty parlor job"—and get away from farming with its hardships. . . .

Mollie doesn't worry too much about the child yet to be born. She is sorry about the trouble it will be, but she accepts the "Lord's will" here as she does when they have a bad crop year. She no longer expects to realize the goals of life herself, but has transferred her efforts to achieving them for her daughter. Last year she even chose to forego the Sunday dress in order to buy a fur-trimmed coat for her baby. And yet Mollie is cheerful, except when impatient with her two older children, and works routinely at her farm and housework without complaint.

WILLIAM H. CHAFE
Eleanor Roosevelt

Eleanor Roosevelt's limitless energy, humanitarian zeal, and compassion made her the most active First Lady in the nation's history. A complex woman with a difficult childhood and great inner doubts, she created a public life for herself that both preceded and extended well beyond the White House years. This process is skillfully and sensitively traced in this brief biography. Note the importance that women played in Eleanor Roosevelt's intellectual and political development: the impact of school mistress Marie Souvestre, the influence and support provided by a female reform network that included women who had come to prominence in the progressive era—Rose Schneiderman, Maud Swartz, and Mary Dreier of the Women's Trade Union League and Mary Dewson of

Expanded version of "Eleanor Roosevelt" by William H. Chafe, in *Notable American Women: The Modern Period*, edited by Barbara Sicherman and Carol Hurd Green (Cambridge, Mass.: Belknap Press of Harvard University Press, 1980), pp. 595–601. Copyright © 1980 by Radcliffe College. Reprinted by permission of the publisher.

the Consumers' League. Included, too, were female activists in the Democratic party such as Marion Dickerman and Nancy Cook as well as women in the Roosevelt administration such as Lorena Hickok. (That women can be at odds with each other over the appropriate roles they should play is exemplified in Eleanor Roosevelt's conflict with her husband's mother.) In what sense can Eleanor Roosevelt be said to have encompassed within her own life the long pilgrimage of millions of women over more than one life span during the nineteenth and twentieth centuries? Note how she moved from dependency to influence to power, from anonymity to repute to leadership, from reliance on a male-dominated structure to female "networks" to public activity to political influence, from the private world of her father's house to the United Nations. Is it easy to make a distinction between Eleanor Roosevelt the person and Eleanor Roosevelt the symbol?

Anna Eleanor Roosevelt was born in New York City [on October 11, 1884], the first child of Elliott and Anna (Hall) Roosevelt. Descended on both sides from distinguished colonial families active in commerce, banking, and politics, Eleanor seemed destined to enjoy all the benefits of class and privilege. By the time she was ten, both her parents had died, as had a younger brother, leaving Eleanor and her second brother, Hall, as the only survivors.

From that point forward, Eleanor Roosevelt's life was characterized by paradox. A woman of remarkable self-control, she yet reached out to touch the world in profoundly emotional ways. Although committed to the traditional idea of women as primarily responsible to husband and family, she personified the strength of the independent woman. Both by fate and by will, she became the most important public woman of the twentieth century.

Eleanor Roosevelt remembered herself as "a solemn child, without beauty. I seemed like a little old woman entirely lacking in the spontaneous joy and mirth of youth." She experienced emotional rejection early: her mother called her "granny" and, at least in Eleanor's memory, warmly embraced her son while being only "kindly and indifferent" to her little

girl. From most of her family young Eleanor received the message that she was "very plain," almost ugly, and certainly "old-fashioned." When her parents died, she went to live with her maternal grandmother, who was equally without warmth. As a cousin later remarked: "It was the grimmest childhood I had ever known. Who did she have? Nobody."

In fact, she had one person—her father. "He was the one great love of my life as a child," she later wrote," and . . . like many childlren, I have lived a dream life with him." Described by his friends as "charming, impetuous . . . generous, [and] friendly," Elliott Roosevelt developed with Eleanor an intimacy that seemed almost magical. "As soon as I could talk," she recalled, "I went into his dressing room every morning and chattered to him . . . I even danced with him." She dreamed of the time when she and her father "would have a life of our own together."

But Elliott Roosevelt's capacity for ebullient play and love also contained the seeds of self-destruction. He was never able to provide stability for himself and his family, and his emotional imbalance caused his banishment from the household. He nourished the relationship with Eleanor through letters to "father's own little Nell," writing of "the wonderful long rides" that he wanted them to enjoy together. But when his long-awaited visits occurred, they often ended in disaster, as when he left Eleanor with the doorman at his club, promising to return but going off on a drunken spree. The pain of betrayal was exceeded only by a depth of love for the man who she believed to be "the only person who really cared."

The emotional void caused by her father's death persisted until, at the age of fifteen, she enrolled at Allenswood, a girls' school outside of London presided over by Marie Souvestre. The daughter of the French philosopher and radical Emil Souvestre, she passionately embraced unpopular causes, staunchly defending Dreyfus in France and the cause of the Boers in South Africa. Souvestre provided for Eleanor a deeply needed emotional bond, confiding in her as they toured the continent together, and expressing the affection that made it possible for the younger woman to flower. Roosevelt remembered the years at Allenswood as "the happiest years" of her life: "Whatever I have become since had its seeds in those three years of contact with a liberal mind and strong personality."

Souvestre's imprint was not lost when Eleanor Roosevelt returned to New York City at seventeen to come out in society. Even in the rush of parties and dances, she kept her eye on the more serious world of ideas and social service. Mlle. Souvestre had written her in 1901: "even when success comes, as I'm sure it will, bear in mind that there are more quiet and enviable joys than to be among the most sought after women at a ball." Heeding the injunction, Eleanor Roosevelt plunged into settlement house work and social activities.

Much of Eleanor Roosevelt's subsequent political life can be traced to this early involvement with social reform. At the age of eighteen she joined the National Consumers' League. Headed by Flor-

ence Kelley, the League was committed to securing health and safety for workers—especially women—in clothing factories and sweat shops. Visiting these workplaces, Eleanor learned firsthand the misery of the working poor and developed a lifelong commitment to their needs. At the same time, she joined the Junior League and commenced work at the Rivington Street Settlement House where she taught calisthenics and dancing and witnessed both the deprivation of the poor and the courage of slum dwellers who sought to improve their lot. Eleanor Roosevelt discovered that she preferred social work to debutant parties. More and more, she came to be recognized as a key member of the social reform network in New York City.

At the same time, Eleanor Roosevelt was secretly planning to marry her cousin Franklin Roosevelt. Like Elliott Roosevelt, his godfather, Franklin was spontaneous, warm, and gregarious. But Franklin Roosevelt also possessed good sense and singleness of purpose. Eleanor Roosevelt saw in him the spark of life that she remembered from her father; he, in turn, saw in her the discipline that would curb his own instincts toward excess.

After their marriage on March 17, 1905, the young Roosevelts settled in New York City while Franklin finished his law studies at Columbia University. For the next fifteen years Eleanor Roosevelt's public activities gave way to other concerns. Sara Roosevelt, Franklin's mother, objected to her work at the settlement house because she might bring home diseases. The Roosevelts' first child, Anna, was born within a year (1906), James the next year, and two years later Franklin. Eleanor Roosevelt cherished her children, but it was not a happy time. Her mother-in-law dominated the household, and she came to feel that "Franklin's children were more my mother-in-law's children than they were mine." Fearing that she would hurt her husband and lose his affection, Eleanor Roosevelt did not rebel; but she did experience a profound sense of inadequacy about her abilities as a wife and mother which continued throughout her life. The death of her third child, seven months after his birth, only reinforced her pain and unhappiness. Three additional children were born in the next six years, Elliott in 1910, Franklin in 1914, and John in 1916. Eleanor Roosevelt was devoted to each of her children, yet motherhood could not be fulfilling in a household ruled by a grandmother who referred to the children as "my children . . . your mother only bore you."

Between 1910 and the beginning of World War I, Eleanor Roosevelt's activities revolved increasingly around her husband's growing political career. Elected as the Democratic assemblyman from Dutchess County, N.Y., in 1910, Franklin Roosevelt rapidly became a leader of insurgent anti-Tammany forces in Albany and Eleanor Roosevelt found herself organizing frequent social-political gatherings. In 1913 he was appointed assistant secretary of the navy and she became expert at hosting multiple social events while managing a large household and moving everyone to Campobello in New Brunswick during the summer, then to Hyde Park, and back to Washington.

The entry of the United States into World War I in 1917 provided Eleanor Roosevelt, as her biographer Joseph Lash has noted, with "a reason acceptable to her conscience to free herself of the social duties that she hated, to concentrate less on her household, and plunge into work that fitted her aptitude." She rose at 5:00 A.M. to coordinate activities at Washington's Union Station canteen for soldiers on their way to training camps, took charge of Red Cross activities, supervised the knitting rooms at the navy department, and spoke at patriotic rallies. Her interest in social welfare led to her drive to improve conditions at St. Elizabeth's Hospital for the mentally ill, while her

sensitivity to suffering came forth in the visits she paid to wounded soldiers. "[My son] always loved to see you come in," one mother wrote. "You always brought a ray of sunshine."

The war served as a transition for Eleanor Roosevelt's reemergence as a public personality during the 1920s. After Franklin Roosevelt's unsuccessful campaign for the vice-presidency on James Cox's ticket in 1920, the family returned to New York where Eleanor became active in the League of Women Voters. At the time of her marriage, she had opposed suffrage, thinking it inconsistent with women's proper role; now she coordinated the League's legislative program, keeping track of bills that came before the Albany legislature, drafting laws providing for equal representation for men and women, and working with Esther Lape and Elizabeth Reid on the League's lobbying activities. In 1922 she also joined the Women's Trade Union League—then viewed as "left-leaning"—and found friends as well as political allies within the organization. In addition to working for programs such as maximum hours and minimum wages for women, she helped raise funds for WTUL headquarters in New York City. Her warm ties to first- and second-generation immigrants like Rose Schneiderman and Maud Swartz highlighted how far she had moved from the upper-class provincialism of her early years.

When her husband was paralyzed by polio in 1921, Eleanor Roosevelt's public life expanded still further as she became his personal representative in the political arena. With the aid of Louis Howe, Franklin Roosevelt's political mentor who had become her own close friend, she first mobilized Dutchess County women, then moved on to the state Democratic party, organizing all but five counties by 1924. "Organization," she noted, "is something to which [the men] are always ready to take off their hats." No one did the job better. Leading a delegation to the Democratic National Convention in 1924, she fought for equal pay legislation, the child labor amendment, and other planks endorsed by women reformers.

By 1928, Eleanor Roosevelt had become a political leader in her own right. Once just a political wife, she gradually extended that role into a vehicle for asserting her own personality and goals. She headed up the national women's campaign for the Democratic party in 1928, making sure that the party appealed to independent voters, to minorities, and to women. After Franklin Roosevelt's election as governor of New York, she was instrumental in securing Frances Perkins's appointment as the state's industrial commissioner. She dictated as many as a hundred letters a day, spoke to countless groups, and acted as an advocate of social reform and women's issues.

Eleanor Roosevelt's talent for combining partisan political activity with devotion to social welfare causes made her the center of an ever-growing female reform network. Her associates included Marion Dickerman and Nancy Cook, former suffragists and Democratic party loyalists; Mary Dewson, who was president of the New York Consumers' League from 1925 to 1931; and Mary Dreier of the WTUL. She walked on picket lines with Rose Schneiderman, edited the *Women's Democratic News*, and advised the League of Women Voters on political tactics. Not only did her political sophistication grow, but she also learned to uphold her beliefs even if she caused "disagreement or unpleasant feelings." By standing up for women in politics, she provided a model for others to follow.

During the 1932 campaign which led to her husband's election to the presidency, Eleanor Roosevelt coordinated the activities of the Women's Division of the Democratic National Committee, working with Mary Dewson to mobilize thousands

of women precinct workers. After the election, Dewson took over direction of the Women's Division. She corresponded daily with Eleanor Roosevelt both about appointing women to office and about securing action on issues that would appeal to minorities, women, and such professional groups as educators and social workers. Together they brought to Washington an unprecedented number of dynamic women activists. Ellen Woodward, Hilda Worthington Smith and Florence Kerr all held executive offices in the Works Progress Administration, while Lorena Hickok acted as eyes and ears for WPA director Harry Hopkins as she traveled across the country to observe the impact of the New Deal's relief program. Mary Anderson, Director of the Women's Bureau, recalled that women government officials had formerly dined together in a small university club. "Now," she said, "there are so many of them that we need a hall."

Eleanor Roosevelt also provided a national forum for transmitting the views and concerns of these women. At regular press conferences for women reporters, she introduced Mary McLeod Bethune and other women leaders to talk about their work with the administration. These sessions provided new status and prestige for the female press corps; they also underlined the importance to Eleanor Roosevelt of women's issues and created a community of women reporters and government workers.

As a result of Eleanor Roosevelt's activities, women achieved a strong voice in the New Deal. The percentage of women appointed as post masters, for example, shot up from 17.6 percent in 1930 to 26 percent between 1932 and 1938. Eleanor Roosevelt's own political role was best seen in the 1936 reelection drive when she used the educational approach developed by the Women's Division in 1932 as a primary campaign weapon. More than 60,000 women precinct workers canvassed the electorate and for the first time women received equal representation on the Democratic platform committee, an event described by the *New York Times* as "the biggest coup for women in years."

Eleanor Roosevelt's fear that there would be no active role available to her as first lady had been unfounded. She toured the country repeatedly, surveying conditions in the coal mines, visiting relief projects, and speaking out for the human rights of the disadvantaged. Through her syndicated newspaper column "My Day," which first appeared in January 1936, and through radio programs and lectures, she reached millions and communicated to the country her deep compassion for those who suffered. At the White House, in turn, she acted as advocate of the poor and disenfranchised. "No one who ever saw Eleanor Roosevelt sit down facing her husband, and holding his eyes firmly, say to him 'Franklin, I think you should . . . or, Franklin, surely you will not' . . . will ever forget the experience," Rexford Tugwell wrote. She had become, as columnist Raymond Clapper noted a "Cabinet Minister without portfolio—the most influential woman of our times."

But if Eleanor Roosevelt had achieved an unparalleled measure of political influence, it was in place of, rather than because of, an intimate personal relationship with her husband. Probably at no time after their first few years together did Franklin and Eleanor Roosevelt achieve the degree of intimacy that she once described as caring so much that a look and the sound of a voice would tell all. Not only did Sara Roosevelt remain a dominant presence, but Franklin had embarked on his own interests and enthusiasms, often different from those of his wife. The dissimilarities in their temperaments became a permanent barrier. While he loved to party, she held back, telling her daughter Anna in a letter from Warm Springs, Ga., in 1934, that she "always felt like a spoil-sport and policeman here . . . I'm an idiotic puritan and I wish I had the right kind of sense of humor and could enjoy certain things. At least, thank God, none of you chilldren have inherited that streak in me."

During his years as assistant secretary of the navy, Franklin Roosevelt had often indulged his fun-loving instinct, causing a lasting breach in the marriage. When his wife was away, his frequent companion had been Lucy Mercer, Eleanor's social secretary. Over time, their relationship became intimate. Eleanor Roosevelt learned of the affair in 1918 and offered to divorce him. Although Franklin refused her offer, and Sara Roosevelt engineered an agreement for them to stay together if her son stopped seeing Lucy Mercer, Eleanor Roosevelt's marriage would never again achieve the magical possibility of being "for life, for death."

Some observers have connected Eleanor Roosevelt's reemergence as a public figure with her profound anger at her husband's betrayal. Yet her activism predated her discovery of the Mercer affair, going back to World War I and the settlement house years, and was rooted ultimately in her relationship with Mlle. Souvestre. The Lucy Mercer affair, like Franklin's polio, reinforced her move toward public self-assertion, but did not in itself cause a transformation. What it did cause was a gradual reallocation of emotional energy away from her husband. Throughout the 1920s a warmth of tone and feeling continued in her letters to and about him. Yet gradually their lives became more separate. She might be jealous of his secretary, Missy LeHand, or even of her daughter Anna, for the ease with which they supplied Franklin Roosevelt with fun and enjoyment. But part of her also accepted the idea that others must provide what she could not give. In a poignant piece entitled "On Being Forty-five," written for *Vogue* in 1930, Eleanor Roosevelt wrote that by middle-age a woman must recognize that the romantic dreams of youth are over. "We should know that happiness does not come from the seeking, that it is never ours by right, but we earn it through giving of ourselves." Above all, she concluded, the forty-five-year-old woman "must keep an open and speculative mind . . . [to] be ready to go out and try new adventures, create new work for others as well as herself, and strike deep roots in some community where her presence will make a difference to the lives of others."

Taking her own advice, Eleanor Roosevelt transferred her emotional attachments to others. Women reformers provided intimate friendship as well as political camaraderie. In 1926 she had moved with Nancy Cook and Marion Dickerman into Val-Kill, a newly constructed cottage at Hyde Park. The event accurately symbolized her growing detachment from Franklin and his mother. Although she returned to "the big house" at Hyde Park when her husband was present, it was always with a sense of resentment and regret. She and Dickerman purchased Todhunter, a private school in New York City where Eleanor Roosevelt taught three days a week even after Franklin was elected governor of New York. The three women also jointly managed a furniture crafts factory at Val-Kill. After 1920, she and Louis Howe developed profound bonds of affection and support, each carrying the other loyally through crises with Franklin and the vicissitudes of party politics. Harry Hopkins, director of the WPA, also became an intimate. But her most carefree relationship was probably that with Earl Miller, a former state trooper and subsequently a bodyguard for the Roosevelt family who became a close companion. Miller encouraged her to drive her own car, take up horseback riding again, and develop confidence in her personality.

With these and others, Eleanor Roosevelt developed a rich emotional life. Although she frequently appeared cold and distant, she passionately cared for her children and friends. Writing to her daughter Anna on Christmas Eve in 1935, she noted: "It was hard to decorate the tree or get things distributed without you . . . and if anyone says much I shall weep." She expressed similar affection in daily letters to Lorena Hickok, the former journalist and assistant to Harry Hopkins, who moved to Hyde Park after a falling-out occurred between Eleanor Roosevelt and Marion Dickerman and Nancy Cook in the late 1930s. Most surprising of all, perhaps, she poured out her feelings to distant correspondents, answering the many pleas for help which came to her with either a sensitive letter, an admonition to a federal agency to take action, or even a personal check. The poor wrote to her because they knew she cared, and in caring, she found an outlet for her powerful emotional needs.

The same compassion was manifested in Eleanor Roosevelt's advocacy of the oppressed. Hearing about the struggle of Appalachian farmers to reclaim their land, she became a champion of the Arthurdale (W. Va.) Resettlement Administration project and devoted her lecture fees as well as her influence to help the community. She invited to the White House representatives of poor southern textile workers and northern garment workers, seating them next to the president at dinner so that he might hear of their plight. She and Franklin Roosevelt had worked out a tacit understanding which permitted her to bring the cause of the oppressed to his attention, and allowed him, in turn, to use her activism as a means of building alliances with groups to his left. Although the president frequently refused to act as she wished, the dispossessed at least had an advocate.

Largely because of Eleanor Roosevelt, the issue of civil rights for black Americans received a hearing at the White House. Although like most white Americans she had grown up in an environment suffused with racism and nativism, she was one of the few voices in the administration insisting that racial discrimination had no place in American life. As always, she led by example. At a 1939 Birmingham meeting inaugurating the Southern Conference on Human Welfare, she placed her chair so that it straddled the black and white sides of the aisle, thereby confounding local authorities who insisted on segregation. She resigned in the same year from the Daughters of the American Revolution after they denied the black artist Marian Anderson permission to perform at Constitution Hall. Instead, and in part through Eleanor Roosevelt's intervention, Anderson sang to 75,000 people from the Lincoln Memorial.

Eleanor Roosevelt also acted as behind-the-scenes lobbyist for civil rights legislation. With alacrity she accepted the suggestion of Walter White, executive secretary of the NAACP, that she act as an intermediary with the president in the association's attempt to secure legislation defining lynching as a federal crime. She also agreed to be a patron of an NAACP-sponsored exhibit in New York City of paintings and drawings dealing with lynching, and attended the showing. Although she lost out in her campaign for the president's strong endorsement of an antilynching bill, she had communicated to him her anger that "one could get nothing done." Continuing to speak forthrightly for the cause of civil rights, she addressed the NAACP's annual meeting in June 1939 and joined the biracial protest organization a few weeks later. As the threat of war increased, Eleanor Roosevelt joined her Negro friends in arguing vigorously for administration action to eliminate discrimination in the armed services and in defense employment. Although civil rights forces were not satisfied with the administration's response,

the positive changes that did occur were due in large part to their alliance with Eleanor Roosevelt.

She brought the same fervor to her identification with young people. Fearing that a whole generation might be lost to democracy because of the depression, she reached out to make contact with them. Despite warnings from White House aides, between 1936 and 1940 Eleanor Roosevelt became deeply involved in the activities of the American Student Union and the American Youth Congress, groups committed to a democratic socialist program of massively expanded social welfare programs. She advanced their point of view in White House circles, and invited them to meet the president. Although she was later betrayed by some of her young allies who followed the Communist party line and denounced the European war as imperialistic after the Nazi-Soviet Non-Aggression Pact of 1939, she continued to believe in the importance of remaining open to dissent. "I have never said anywhere that I would rather see young people sympathetic with communism," Eleanor Roosevelt wrote. "But I have said I would rather see the young people actively at work, even if I considered they were doing things that were a mistake."

With the onset of World War II, Roosevelt persisted in her efforts for the disadvantaged. She insisted that administration officials consult women activists and incorporate roles for women as a major part of their planning for wartime operations, and she intervened repeatedly with war production agencies as well as the military to advocate fairer treatment for black Americans. When it seemed that many New Deal social welfare programs would be threatened by war, Eleanor Roosevelt became their defender. Increasingly she devoted herself to the dream of international cooperation, aware more than most of the revolution rising in Africa and Asia, and of the dangers posed by the threats of postwar conflict.

But her energies in the war were directed primarily to human needs. When Jewish refugees seeking a haven from Nazi persecution received less than an enthusiastic response from the State Department, Eleanor Roosevelt served as their advocate. Families separated by war always found an ally when they sought her help, and wounded veterans in army hospitals far from home received from her visits the cherished message that someone cared.

As the war proceeded, the worlds of Franklin and Eleanor Roosevelt became still more separate. They were frequently adversaries and the president was less able to tolerate her advocacy of unpopular causes. In search of release from the unbearable pressures of the war, he had come to rely on the gaiety and laughter of his daughter Anna, and other women companions, including Lucy Mercer Rutherford, who, unknown to Eleanor, was with Franklin Roosevelt in Warm Springs when he died of a cerebral hemorrhage in April 1945.

With great discipline and dignity, Eleanor Roosevelt bore both the pain of Franklin's death and the circumstances surrounding it. Her first concern was with carrying forward the policies in which they had both believed despite their disagreements. Writing later about their relationship, she commented: "He might have been happier with a wife who had been completely uncritical. That I was never able to be and he had to find it in some other people. Nevertheless, I think that I sometimes acted as a spur . . . I was one of those who served his purposes." What she did not say was that Franklin Roosevelt had served her purposes as well. Though they never retrieved their early intimacy, they had created an unparalleled partnership to respond to the needs of a nation in crisis.

Not long after her husband's death, Eleanor Roosevelt told a reporter: "The story is over." But no one who cared so much for so many causes, and was so effective a leader, could long remain on the sidelines. Over the next decade and a half, she continued to be the most effective woman in American politics. In long letters to President Harry S Truman, she implored the administration to push forward with civil rights, maintain the Fair Employment Practices Commission, develop a foreign policy able to cope with the needs of other nations, and work toward a world system where atom bombs would cease to be a negotiating chip in international relations.

Appropriately, President Truman nominated Eleanor Roosevelt as a United States delegate to the United Nations. There she argued, debated, and lobbied for the creation of a document on human rights that would embody standards which civilized humankind would accept as sacred and inalienable. Finally on Dec. 10, 1948, the Universal Declaration of Human Rights, fundamentally shaped by her, passed the General Assembly. Delegates rose in a standing ovation to the woman who more than anyone else had come to symbolize the cause of human rights. Even those in the United States who had most opposed her applauded: "I want to say that I take back everything I ever said about her," Michigan Senator Arthur Vandenberg commented, "and believe me, it's been plenty." At times during the New Deal a figure of scorn among some conservatives, Eleanor Roosevelt was fast becoming a national heroine.

The cause of world peace and the desire to help the victims of war quickly became central to Roosevelt's efforts. In moving speeches that vividly portrayed the suffering wrought by war, she sought to educate the United States to its postwar responsibilities. She had traveled through England noting the names of all the young men who had died during the war, she told an audience. "There is a feeling that spreads over the land," she said, "the feel of civilization that of itself might have a hard time coming back." If the United States wished to avoid such a world, it must help those who had suffered, and avoid isolationism.

Although Eleanor Roosevelt disagreed profoundly with some of the military aspects of United States foreign policy, she supported the broad outlines of its response to the Soviet Union in the developing cold war. In debates at the UN she learned quickly that Soviet delegates could be hypocritical, and on more than one occasion she responded to their charges of injustice in America by proposing that each country submit to investigation of its social conditions—a suggestion the Soviets refused. She refused in 1947 to support the newly formed Progressive party with its platform of accommodation toward the Soviet Union, and instead spearheaded the drive to build Americans for Democratic Action, a group which espoused social reforms at home and support of Truman's foreign policy.

Throughout the 1950s Eleanor Roosevelt remained a singular public figure, able to galvanize the attention of millions by her statements. She became one of the staunchest advocates of Israel, argued vigorously for civil rights, and spoke forcefully against the witch hunts of McCarthyism. When Dwight D. Eisenhower became president in 1953 she resigned her UN post, but she continued to work tirelessly through the American Association for the United Nations to mobilize public support for international cooperation. She also gave unstintingly of her time to the election campaigns in 1952 and 1956 of her friend Adlai Stevenson, who brought to politics a wit and sophistication that she admired.

The private sphere, however, remained most precious. "The people I love," Eleanor Roosevelt wrote her friend and physician David Gurewitsch, "mean more to me than all the public things. I only do the public things because there are a few close people whom I love dearly and who

matter to me above everything else." The Roosevelt children remained as much a trial as a comfort. After Franklin Roosevelt's death, she lived at Val-Kill with her secretary, Malvina Thompson (1893–1953), and her son Elliott and his family. More often than not, family gatherings degenerated into bitter arguments. But her grandchildren brought joy as did friends, old and new.

As she entered her seventies, Eleanor Roosevelt had become the first lady of the world. Traveling to India, Japan, and the Soviet Union, she spoke for the best that was in America. Although she did not initially approve of John F. Kennedy and would have much preferred to see Adlai Stevenson nominated again in 1960, she lived to see the spirit of impatience and reform return to Washington. In 1962 she sponsored hearings in Washington, D.C., where young civil rights workers testified about the judicial and police harassment of black protesters in the south.

It was fitting that Eleanor Roosevelt's last major official position was to chair President Kennedy's Commission on the Status of Women, to which she was appointed in December 1961. More than anyone else of her generation she had exemplified the political independence and personal autonomy that were abiding themes of the women's movement. Eleanor Roosevelt had not been a militant feminist and, like most social reformers, she had opposed the Equal Rights Amendment (ERA) until the mid-1940s, believing that it would jeopardize protective labor legislation for women. During the depression she accepted the popular view that, at least temporarily, some married women should leave the labor force to improve the chances of the unemployed. On occasion, she also adopted male-oriented definitions of fulfillment. "You are successful," she wrote in a 1931 article, "when your husband feels that he has been a success and that life has been worthwhile."

But on the issue of women's equality as

in so many other areas, Roosevelt most often affirmed the inalienable right of the human spirit to grow and seek fulfillment. Brought up amidst anti-Semitic and anti-Negro attitudes, she had transcended her past to become one of the strongest champions of minority rights. Once opposed to suffrage, she had grown to exemplify women's aspirations for a full life in politics.

There was, in fact, a direct line from Mlle. Souvestre's advocacy of intellectual independence to Eleanor Roosevelt's involvement in the settlement house to her subsequent embrace of women's political activism in the 1920s and 1930s, and her final role as leader of the Commission on the Status of Women. She had personified not only the right of women to act as equals with men in the political sphere, but the passion of social activists to ease pain, alleviate suffering, and affirm solidarity with the unequal and disenfranchised of the world.

Eleanor Roosevelt participated in the activities of the Women's Commission until August 1962, testifying on behalf of equal pay laws at a congressional hearing in April of that year. She died at her home in New York City [on November 7, 1962] from a rare form of tuberculosis. Twenty years earlier she had written: "You can never really live anyone else's life, not even your child's. The influence you exert is through your own life and what you've become yourself."

Despite disappointment and tragedy, Eleanor Roosevelt had followed her own advice. "What other single human being," Adlai Stevenson asked at her memorial service, "has touched and transformed the existence of so many? . . . She walked in the slums . . . of the world, not on a tour of inspection . . . but as one who could not feel contentment when others were hungry." Because of her life, millions of others may have experienced a new sense of possibility. She would have wished for nothing more.

RUTH MILKMAN

Redefining "Women's Work": The Sexual Division of Labor in the Auto Industry during World War II

As a nation struggling with depression began fighting its second world war, unemployment lines quickly vanished. Manpower shortages meant that women would once again move into jobs in industry, experiencing new vocational opportunities, a lessening of discrimination based on marital status, age, and race, and public praise for their wartime contribution as workers. The potential provided by the war for refashioning gender roles was enormous, but the results

Excerpted from "Redefining 'Women's Work': The Sexual Division of Labor in the Auto Industry during World War II" by Ruth Milkman, in *Feminist Studies* 8 (1982):337–72. Copyright © 1982 Ruth Milkman. Reprinted by permission of the author. Notes have been renumbered and tables omitted.

were disappointing. The expectation was that once the men came home, women would happily exchange industrial tools for broom and mop or a new vacuum cleaner and baby bottle. Polls showed that up to 85 percent of these women needed to continue working and expected that job seniority would entitle them to return after veterans had been absorbed in the work force.

The sex/gender system was deeply ingrained in American society, even—indeed especially—in the labor market, as Ruth Milkman demonstrates in this study of the persistence with which job segregation was maintained at a time when the very survival of democracy was at stake. To what extent have attitudes to working women described earlier by Kessler-Harris (part IIB) changed?

Note Milkman's argument that occupational sex typing becomes even more important when women's labor force participation increases. How does job segregation help to explain the fact that for the past thirty years women in the labor force have earned roughly 55 cents for every $1.00 earned by men? Even a college education provides no immunity against the earnings gap; a working woman with four or more years of college has an average income only slightly above that of a man *without* a high school diploma. Do you agree with Milkman's assertion that both class consciousness and gender consciousness are essential to bringing about social and economic change?

INTRODUCTION

Feminists have deliberately idealized the experience of women workers during World War II. . . . The stunning imagery of female strength and versatility captured in photographs of women industrial workers in the 1940s has become a mainstay of contemporary "feminist realism." . . .

A closer look at the actual experience of women industrial workers during the war years, however, suggests that the retrospective feminist construction of their place in history is apocryphal. Women were hired to do "men's jobs" during the war on a scale unparalleled before or since, but this was in no way the result of a feminist campaign. In basic industries like auto, employers were initially quite resistant to the idea of hiring women for war work. They did so only when the supply of male labor had been completely exhausted because of military conscription on the one hand and the rapid expansion of demand for labor to produce military hardware on the other. It was not a change in management beliefs about women's capabilities in industry that led to their incorporation into jobs previously considered suitable only for men, but rather the male labor shortage during the war years which led to the change in management's beliefs.

Once women were drawn upon to meet the need for labor in war-bloated "heavy" industries, moreover, they were not randomly incorporated into "men's jobs" as vacancies occurred. Instead, *new* patterns of occupational segregation by sex were established "for the duration" within sectors of the economy previously monopolized by men. So Rosie the Riveter did a "man's job," but more often than not she worked in a predominantly female department or job classification.[1]

The wartime experience of women in industry is a fruitful object of feminist analysis, then, but for reasons opposite to those generally presumed. The economic mobilization led to a shift in the location of the boundaries between "men's" and "women's" work, not the elimination of those boundaries. The persistence of segregation during the war, in the face of a massive influx of women into the labor force and a dramatic upheaval in the previously established sexual division of labor, poses quite starkly the fundamental problem of explaining how and why job segregation by sex is maintained and reproduced over and over again throughout the history of capitalist development.[2]

The underlying forces that continually reproduce segregation within the supposedly "impersonal" wage labor market remain obscure if the problem is approached at the level of the individual employer or firm. Once women have been introduced into the paid labor force at a lower cost than men, one would expect that the relentless efforts of capital to maximize profits would lead employers to substitute women for men whenever possible, at least until the costs of female and male labor power are equalized. It appears quite irrational for management to differentiate rigidly between women and men workers, as if they were truly noninterchangeable sources of labor power. . . .

Collectively, capital benefits from the existence of gender divisions within the working class in that they—like racial and other intraclass cleavages—foster political disunity within what might otherwise be a stronger source of opposition to capital.[3] In addition, and crucially, segregation by sex within the wage labor market helps to secure the daily and generational reproduction of the working class through the unpaid household labor of women, by denying female workers a living wage and maintaining their economic dependence on men and on families. At the same time, the sexual division of labor in the household is exactly what constitutes women as a source of "cheap" and expendable labor to begin with.[4]

Of course, not only collective capital but also male workers benefit from job segregation by sex, at least in the short term. Not only do men receive higher wages than women within the wage labor market, but the concentration of women in poorly paid, insecure jobs ensures that women will perform personal services for men in the household even if they also work for pay. While capital, not the male work force, generally controls the process of job definition and allocation, insofar as men mobilize themselves to maintain the subordination of women within the wage labor market, the interest of collective capital in a gender-segregated labor market is reinforced.

But if male workers pursued their *class* interest, rather than seek to maintain their position as a privileged gender, they would mobilize *against* job segregation by sex. Male workers have a class interest in working-class unity. Job segregation by sex, even as it reinforces male power over women, threatens at the same time to undercut the bargaining power of male labor vis-à-vis capital, precisely because of the "cheapness" of female labor. In short, the class interest and what might be called the gender interest of male workers directly conflict with one another. Historically, the apparent domination of men's gender interest over their class interest in shaping their relationship to job segregation by sex must be explained, not presumed from the outset as inevitable or "given." It is crucial for feminists to understand the specific historical conditions under which male workers' class interests might predominate over their gender interests, if we are to have any hope of successfully eliminating job segregation. . . .

. . . the interest of collective capital is reinforced by the gender interest of male workers in job segregation by sex and its rationalizing ideology of occupational sex typing. Both these interests are served by the maintenance of the family as an institution of social reproduction based on unpaid female labor. Women's participation in wage labor on equal terms with men would ultimately undermine the unequal sexual division of labor in the household. Access to an individual wage, even on terms unequal to men, erodes the structure of women's economic dependence on men and on families. This is precisely why, rather than disappearing as women's labor force participation increases, occupational sex typing persists and indeed becomes ever more important: it constructs women's "primary" commitment as devotion to home and family, whether or not they also work for pay.

This interdependence between the circumscribed roles of women in the family and in the labor market, which has been observed in a wide range of circumstances by feminist scholars, helps explain the particular case of the reconstruction of job segregation by sex within the mobilized economy of the early 1940s. During the World War II years, married women and mothers poured into the labor force in massive numbers for the first time, posing an unprecedented threat to family stability.[5] Thus, far from being rendered unnecessary by the exigencies of the war emergency, job segregation was more crucial than ever before at this juncture. The sex typing of the jobs newly opened to women "for the duration" reconciled women's new economic situation with their traditional position as guardians of the hearth. This was manifested in the pervasive wartime propaganda image of "woman's place" on the nation's production lines, which portrayed women's war work in industry as a temporary extension of domesticity.

The World War II experience not only reveals the resilience of the structure of job segregation by sex and of the *general* ideology of sexual division which legitimates it, but it also renders completely transparent the specific *idiom* of sex typing, which is flexibly applied to whatever jobs women and men happen to be doing.

Jobs which had previously been cast in terms suggestive of the very quintessence of masculinity were suddenly endowed with femininity and glamour "for the duration." The propaganda newsreel *Glamour Girls of '43*, for example, suggested:

> Instead of cutting the lines of a dress, this woman cuts the pattern of aircraft parts. Instead of baking cake, this woman is cooking gears to reduce the tension in the gears after use. . . . They are taking to welding as if the rod were a needle and the metal a length of cloth to be sewn. After a short apprenticeship, this woman can operate a drill press just as easily as a juice extractor in her own kitchen. And a lathe will hold no more terrors for her than an electric washing machine.[6]

Virtually any job could be labeled as "woman's work" in this way. [This is not to say, however, that management had a free hand in the labeling process.] . . .

Employers must take account of a range of economic considerations in their hiring decisions: not only the available supplies of female and male labor and their relative costs, but also such factors as the proportion of a firm's capital outlays made up by wages, and the ease with which labor costs can be passed on to consumers. There are also political constraints which limit, or potentially limit, management's freedom in allocating jobs to women and men. For example, the greater the actual or anticipated male resistance to feminization, the less likely an employer may be to attempt it. Managerial initiatives affecting the sexual division of labor may become objects of political struggle for women and/or men workers, especially when the sex-specific supply-and-demand equilibrium in a labor market is disrupted—which occurs quite regularly in a dynamic capitalist economy. Usually these struggles are over marginal changes in the sexual division of labor, but there are times when more dramatic shifts in the structure of the labor market take place, presenting political opportunities for a broader challenge to the sexual division of wage labor as a whole. The large-scale economic dislocations associated with the mobilization for World War II and the subsequent postwar reconversion presented one such historical opportunity. . . .

. . . The upheaval in the sexual division of labor precipitated by the wartime mobilization was particularly dramatic in basic manufacturing industries such as auto. While women's labor force participation increased by 50 percent in the economy as a whole between 1940 and 1944, in heavy "war industries" the number of women rose 460 percent during that period, and in the auto industry the increase was an astounding 600 percent.[7] Clearly the auto industry was by no means typical of the economy as a whole in regard to the changes that occurred in the sexual division of labor. Yet, precisely because the shifts in the position of women were so extensive and so rapid, the auto industry experience is especially revealing. It offers a magnified view of the reproduction of job segregation by sex, a process that is always occuring.

Politically, the situation in the auto industry in the 1940s is also of special interest. The young auto workers' union, the United Automobile Workers—Congress of Industrial Organizations (UAW-CIO), was the largest union in the country during the war, boasting over 1 million members in 1945, 28 percent of whom were female.[8] It was also one of the most progressive unions on questions of discrimination—although this was saying very little, and there were certainly instances of UAW-management collusion at the expense of women workers. Still, in the absence of an organized feminist movement during this period, the UAW became a crucial avenue for political challenges to management on sexual division of labor issues. The union set up a

Women's Bureau in 1944, and prior to that it was instrumental in several precedent-setting cases involving the issue of "equal pay for equal work." The auto industry was quite unusual in this respect as well, but here again its very atypicality is illuminating: it suggests the limits and possibilities of political challenges to the managerial construction of the sexual division of labor in this period.

"WOMEN'S WORK" IN THE PREWAR AUTO INDUSTRY

Automotive manufacturing relied on an overwhelmingly male work force in the years before World War II, with women accounting for less than one-tenth of its labor force throughout that period. The revolutionary organization of production around the moving assembly line laid the basis for auto's development as a high-wage, capital-intensive industry, in which employers had relatively little incentive to substitute female labor for its more expensive male equivalent. While the representation of women in the industry was abnormally low, women auto workers were concentrated in a relatively small number of jobs and in particular branches of the industry, consistent with the broader pattern of job segregation by sex found throughout the nation's economy. Although small numbers of women could be found scattered through many departments of the plants, they were clustered primarily in the upholstery or "cut-and-sew" divisions of body plants, and in small parts assembly.[9]

Although women auto workers earned wages higher than those available in most other fields of female employment, throughout the industry women's wages were far below men's. In 1925, the average hourly earnings of female workers in the auto industry were forty-seven cents, compared with a seventy-three cent average for men.[10] Although there were occasional incidents of women being substituted for men, and at lower pay, what is much more striking is that management was never particularly interested in pursuing a policy of large-scale feminization. The supreme lever of control over labor in the industry was machinery, and especially the assembly line—centerpiece of the Fordist revolution. Mechanization was carried forward to such a degree that wages became a relatively small component of costs. The announcement of the legendary Five-Dollar Day by the Ford Motor Company in 1914 quickly established the industry's reputation as a *high*-wage industry. Under these conditions, female substitution had little to recommend it.[11]

Jobs were clearly defined as "male" or "female" during this period, with none of the subtlety with which segregation by sex would later come to be disguised in the face of challenges to the legitimacy of discrimination. . . . A 1925 government survey of motor vehicle manufacturing found women in only 22 of the 110 occupational groups enumerated for the industry, and over two-thirds of the women were working in just four of these classifications. When a similar survey was conducted fifteen years later, the situation was virtually unchanged.[12] . . .

The idiom in which the sexual division of labor in the prewar auto industry was cast stressed the suitability of women for "light" or "delicate" work in accounting for their concentration in particular job classifications. "In finishing, polishing, and upholstery, where much handwork is required," wrote one observer in 1929, "they [women] are considered fast workers." In another typical rendition, it was suggested that women were especially well represented in the parts branch of this industry "since they are adept at assembly of light units."[13] . . .

Yet the actual sexual division of labor in the prewar auto industry bore at best a limited relationship to such factors. The majority of jobs done by both women and

men in the industry were repetitive operations, and most required some degree of manual "dexterity." There were also some "women's jobs" which required substantial physical exertion. And firms varied to some degree in the way in which they constructed the sexual division of labor, despite an overall similarity in the organization of production. It seems that whatever jobs women were assigned to in a given plant came to be viewed as requiring a feminine touch, although exactly the same positions might be deemed suited only for men elsewhere in the industry. Thus in 1926 the *Wall Street Journal* reported that women crane operators at the Hudson Motor Company who lifted motors and carried them to the chassis were "more sensitive and accurate than men," while at other auto firms this was an exclusively male occupation.[14]

Once firmly established, the sexual division of labor in the auto industry remained remarkably stable during the years before the war. Even during the economic depression of the 1930s, when the auto industry underwent a severe profitability crisis, there was surprisingly little change in the sexual division of labor. Although there were occasional efforts to substitute women for men to save on labor costs, in general the ideology of sexual division reigned supreme even in the face of the extraordinary economic circumstances of the depression decade. While the incentive for substituting female labor for male was more compelling than it had been previously, so was the social ideology that decried the employment of women so long as men were unemployed. . . .

The 1930s brought a political transformation to the auto industry as well as changed economic circumstancees. In the second half of the decade, management's recognition of the UAW profoundly altered the character of labor relations in the auto industry, where unions had never been able to establish a foothold before.

For the UAW, as for other CIO unions in this period, it followed from the logic of industrial unionism that the minority of women production workers should be organized along with the much more numerous male work force. The CIO also had a serious commitment to opposing all forms of employment discrimination, although it lacked any special commitment to challenging sexual inequality as such. This reflected the weakness of feminism in the interwar period, as well as the hardy tradition of male domination within the labor movement itself.

Women auto workers still benefited enormously from unionization. Women's average hourly wages in the industry jumped from fifty-four cents in 1936 to sixty-five cents two years later, while men's rose from eighty-one to ninety-eight cents over the same period.[15] And the institutionalization of seniority systems gave women workers some protection from sexual favoritism and sexual harassment for the first time, although frequently there were separate seniority lists for women and men.[16] Yet the UAW's main concern in this period was with consolidating its organizational gains generally, and issues concerning women specifically were rather low on its list of priorities. In the 1930s, the union never mounted a serious challenge to the sexual division of labor in industry or to the pervasive social ideology of "woman's place" which supplied it with such a compelling rationale.

Indeed, to the degree that the UAW became involved in conflicts with management affecting the sexual division of labor at all, the primary result was the consolidation of the existing pattern of female employment, not the dissolution of the boundaries between "women's work" and "men's work." When management did attempt female substitution, male workers could now resist it more effectively than before the introduction of collective bargaining. Sex differentials

in wages and separate seniority systems, established by management in the pre-union era, were now institutionalized in many local contracts. Although the principle of nondiscrimination embedded in the new industrial unionism provided the basis for a challenge to sex discrimination, it would be many years before such a struggle materialized.

During the 1930s, then, the auto industry remained predominantly male with a clearly demarcated "woman's place" in its various divisions, essentially unchanged in this respect from the non-union era. It was not the political forces unleashed with unionization, but the economic impact of World War II that exploded the traditional sexual division of labor in the auto industry.

REDEFINING "WOMEN'S WORK" IN THE WARTIME AUTO INDUSTRY

The immediate impact of U.S. entry into World War II on the auto industry was a complete shutdown of production. Consumer production of cars and trucks was banned shortly after Pearl Harbor, and in February 1942 the last car rolled off the assembly line. There followed massive layoffs of auto workers, as the industry retooled for war production, and "conversion unemployment" was particularly pronounced among women auto workers. The number and proportion of women in the industry therefore dropped in the first part of 1942, but this was followed by a sudden rise in the representation of women as demand for labor outstripped the available supply of men. In April 1942, only one of every twenty auto production workers was a woman; eighteen months later, one out of four workers in the industry's plants was female.[17]

Initially, women war workers in the auto industry were employed only in jobs that had long before been established within the industry as "women's work."

Although a U.S. Employment Service survey of war work in early 1942 found that women could capably perform the tasks required in 80 percent of job classifications, UAW woman-employing plants showed women in only 28 percent of the classifications, on average, in July of that year. "The chief classifications on which they were employed," the UAW reported, "were assembly, inspection, drill press, punch press, sewing machines, filing, and packing."[18] Such positions had long before been associated with women.

Even as the supply of male labor was being depleted, auto employers were loath to forsake their prewar hiring preference for white male workers. . . . Ultimately the federal government intervened, setting male employment ceilings and giving the War Manpower Commission (WMC) the power to enforce them. "Over our strenuous objections," Detroit WMC director Edward Cushman recalls, "the Ford Motor Company began hiring 17, 18 and 19 year old men. And we kept drafting them."[19] Women, as well as blacks and other industrial minorities, were only incorporated into the automotive labor force when there was no longer any possibility of continuing to hire white men.

Management footdragging applied doubly to black women. "The [black] men are o.k. on unskilled jobs," reported one government representative, summarizing the attitude of auto industry employers toward black workers in mid-1943, "but the women are a drug [sic] on the market." Geraldine Bledsoe of the U.S. Employment Service in Detroit complained publicly in October of 1942 that over one thousand black women had completed vocational training courses, "and yet they go day after day to the plants and are turned down." By mid-1943, the WMC estimated that twenty-eight thousand black women were available for war work in Detroit, but that most war plants would employ them only as janitors, matrons, and government inspectors. By the

war's end, Detroit auto plants had hired black women in substantial numbers, but this was only after all other sources of labor had been fully exhausted.[20]

The auto firms had always actively recruited male labor from the South, and they continued to do so during the mobilization period. But Detroit, where the vast bulk of the industry's production took place, could not accommodate male in-migrants and their families on the scale that the rapid wartime expansion of the industry would have required. Housing and transportation facilities were limited, and with wartime restrictions on construction and rationing of scarce materials, the deficit could not be met. Moreover, the entire nation was facing a male labor shortage. It was these circumstances that generated government pressure on the auto firms to hire women. The WPB threatened to withhold additional war contracts from Detroit manufacturers, and even to remove existing contracts if in-migration to the Motor City was not stemmed. The alternative to continued in-migration, the WPB urged in mid-1942, was recruiting women for war work:

> The recruitment of local women who are not now in the labor market is free from the disadvantages or limitations of the other methods of meeting the labor deficit. Local women workers will not require new housing, transportation or other facilities. They do not create a possible future relief burden. Each woman who is recruited will reduce the necessary in-migration correspondingly and thus reduce or eliminate the need for transferring contracts elsewhere.[21]

The government pressured the auto firms to hire women, but made no effort whatsoever to influence their placement within the industry once management let them into the factory gates. The U.S. Employment Service routinely filled employer job openings which called for specific numbers of women and men, and while ceilings were imposed on the number of men who could be allocated to each plant, employers had a free hand in placing women and men in particular jobs within this constraint.[22] . . .

. . . In 45 percent of the plants with sexually mixed work forces responding to a survey conducted in mid-1944 by the UAW Women's Bureau, jobs were formally set up on a "male" and "female" basis.[23] And it is extremely unlikely that women were more fully integrated into the range of job classifications in the other 55 percent. A case in point is the Ford River Rouge plant. The available data do not offer a very detailed breakdown, yet a great deal of segregation is apparent. In December 1943, when women's employment in the industry was at its wartime peak, women made up 16 percent of the work force at the Rouge plant. Over one-half of the occupational groups listed in the company's internal factory count included women, but 62 percent of the women workers were clustered in just 20 of the 416 job categories. And nearly two-thirds of the job groups were at least 90 percent male.[24]

Management was quick to offer a rationale for the concentration of women in certain kinds of jobs and their exclusion from others, just as it had done in the prewar period. "Womanpower differs from manpower as oil fuel differs from coal," proclaimed the trade journal *Automotive War Production* in October 1943, "and an understanding of the characteristics of the energy involved was needed for obtaining best results." Although it was being applied to a larger and quite different set of jobs, the basic characterization of women's abilities and limitations was familiar. "On certain kinds of operations—the very ones requiring high manipulative skill—women were found to be a whole lot quicker and more efficient than men," reported the article.

Engineering womanpower means realizing fully that women are not only different from men in such things as lifting power and arm reach—but in many other ways that pertain to their physiological and their social functions. To understand these things does not mean to exclude women from *the jobs for which they are peculiarly adapted*, and where they can help to win this war. It merely means using them as women, and not as men.[25]

Repeatedly stressed was the lesser physical strength of the average woman worker. "Woman isn't just a 'smaller man,' " the industry's organ pointed out.

Compensations in production processes must be made to allow for the fact that the average woman is only 35 per cent muscle in comparison to the average man's 41 per cent. Moreover, industrial studies have shown that only 54 per cent of woman's weight is strength, as against man's 87 per cent, and that the hand squeeze of the average woman exerts only 48 pounds of pressure, against man's 81 pounds.[26]

This emphasis on the physical limitations of women workers had a dual character. Not only did it provide a justification for the sexual division of labor, but it also served as the basis for increased mechanization and work simplification. "To adjust women's jobs to such [physical] differences, automotive plants have added more mechanical aids such as conveyors, chain hoists and load lifters." Although production technology was already quite advanced in auto relative to other industries, the pace of change accelerated during the war period. This was due at least as much to the combined impact of the labor shortage and the opportunity to introduce new technology at government expense as to the desire to make jobs easier for female workers, but the latter was particularly stressed by the industry's spokespersons.[27]

There was a contradiction in the management literature on women's war work.

It simultaneously stressed the fact that "women are being trained in skills that were considered exclusively in man's domain" and their special suitability for "delicate war jobs."[28] The link between these two seemingly conflicting kinds of statements was made primarily through analogies between "women's work" in the home and in the war plants. "Why should men, who from childhood on never so much as sewed on buttons," inquired one manager, "be expected to handle delicate instruments better than women who have plied embroidery needles, knitting needles and darning needles all their lives?"[29]

Glamour was a related theme in the idiom through which women's war work was demarcated as female. As if calculated to assure women—and men—that war work need not involve a loss of femininity, depictions of women's new work roles were constantly overlaid with allusions to their stylish dress and attractive appearance. "A pretty young inspector in blue slacks pushes a gauge—a cylindrical plug with a diamond-pointed push-button on its side—through the shaft's hollow chamber," was a typical rendition.[30] Such statements, like the housework analogies, effectively reconciled woman's position in what had previously been "men's jobs" with traditional images of femininity.

Ultimately, what lay behind the mixed message that war jobs were at once "men's" and "women's" jobs was an unambiguous point: women *could* do "men's work," but they were only expected to do it temporarily. The ideological definition of women's war work explicitly included the provision that they would gracefully withdraw from their "men's jobs" when the war ended and the rightful owners returned. Women, as everyone knew, were in heavy industry "for the duration." This theme would become much more prominent in the immediate aftermath of the war, but it was a constant undercurrent from the beginning.

Women had always been stereotyped as temporary workers in any case, and the sex typing of jobs prior to the war had helped to ensure that even if they were gainfully employed, women would continue to view themselves as women first, workers second. Now this aspect of the relationship between women and paid work took on new importance, because the reserves of "womanpower" drawn on by the war industries included married women, and even mothers of young children, in unprecedented numbers. A study by the Automotive Council for War Production noted that of 12,000 women employed during the war by one large automotive firm in Detroit, 40 percent were married with children, and another 28 percent were married without children. Another study by the WPB in 1943 also found that 40 percent of the 150,000 women war workers employed in Detroit were mothers. "With the existing prejudice against employing women over forty, the overwhelming majority of these women workers are young mothers with children under 16."[31]

This was exactly the group of women least likely to have been employed in the prewar years. "In this time of pressure for added labor supply," the U.S. Women's Bureau reported, "the married women for the first time in this country's history exceeded single women in the employed group."[32] The representation of married women in the auto industry was especially large, probably due to the vigorous effort to recruit local female labor in Detroit. Some firms went so far as to make a deliberate effort to recruit the wives and daughters of men whom they had employed prior to the war. The Detroit Vickers aircraft plant, for example, had a policy of hiring "members of men's families who have gone to forces so that when these men come back there will be less of a problem in getting the women out of the jobs to give them back to the men."[33]

This dramatic rise in employment of married women in the war mobilization period raised the long-standing tension between women's commitment to marriage and family and their status as individual members of the paid work force to a qualitatively different level. Prior to the war, unmarried women, young wives with no children, and self-supporting widowed, divorced, and separated women had constituted the bulk of the female labor force. With the inclusion of married women and mothers in this group during wartime, the ideology of occupational sex typing which linked women's roles in the family and in paid work, far from disintegrating under the impact of the war emergency, was infused with new energy.

The wartime idiom of job segregation by sex combined such familiar prewar themes as women's dexterity and lack of physical strength with a new emphasis on the value of women's multivaried experience doing housework and an unrelenting glamourization of their new work roles. That the construction of a "woman's place" in the wartime auto industry was achieved so quickly and effectively owed much to the power of this elaborate ideology of occupational sex labeling. Although the initiative came from management, neither unions nor rank-and-file workers—of either gender—offered much resistance to the *general* principle of differentiation of jobs into "female" and "male" categories. Nor was the idiom of "woman's place" in the war effort ever frontally challenged. There was a great deal of conflict, however, over the location of the boundaries between the female and male labor markets within the wartime auto industry, and over wage differentials between these newly constituted markets.

AMBIGUITY AND LABOR-MANAGEMENT CONFLICT OVER "WOMEN'S WORK"

"Will you please advise me on our particular job as to what is considered as major assembly and what is considered as minor assembly?" inquired the President of UAW Local 249 of Mauro Garcia, an international representative of the union's Ford Department, in July 1943. "We cannot agree down here [Kansas City, Missouri] as to where we should draw the line. . . . Also, what is considered a light drill press and what is considered a heavy drill press?" Garcia in turn wrote to the Ford Motor Company's Rate Department with the same questions, saying, "I do not know what method you use in determining these classifications."[34]

This is one example of a dilemma which pervaded the auto industry, and other war industries as well, in the aftermath of conversion. How to go about classifying the new sets of jobs which had come into existence "for the duration" was ambiguous not only for management, but also for workers themselves—both female and male. There was of course some resemblance between many of the new war jobs and their predecessors in the peacetime auto industry, but the conversion process with its attendant technological changes and the dramatic shifts in the composition of the labor force combined to create tremendous disarray in what had before the war been a relatively stable system of job organization. Although in this example the issue of gender was not explicitly broached, distinctions like "heavy" and "light," or "major" and "minor" more often than not coincided with the sexual division of labor in this period. The problem of ambiguity in job classifications was not limited to the dilemma of where to assign sex labels, but this issue was central to the more general case illustrated here. It is also clear from this example that the UAW viewed these matters as management's province, at least initially.

Not only in classification systems but also in actual job content, "heavy" and "light" tended to differentiate women's and men's jobs. Yet where the line should be drawn between the two was always ambiguous, and its arbitrariness—along with that of the accompanying wage differentials—became completely transparent in this period. "Except that there is a division as to what's heavy and what's light, there's no difference in men [sic] and women's jobs," Irene Young remarked at a UAW Women's Conference in February 1942:

> This is a carry-over from procedure they have had years ago. They just decide what our [sic] women's jobs and what are men's jobs. Men get all the way from ten to 20¢ more on the same job. We have many women doing similar types of work —I have seen a lot of men working alongside women and getting more pay for the same work. It is that sort of thing that has caused a certain amount of the split between women and men.

Moreover, Young pointed out, there were many women in the plants whose jobs were physically taxing, protective legislation notwithstanding. "We have today any number of women who are doing heavy work, who lack safety devices," she said.[35] . . .

Eleanor Brenthal, another delegate at the conference, explained that women often accepted such working conditions because they feared that their very right to employment was at stake. "Women are to blame in some cases," she said. "We decided this work was very heavy. When the shop committee came to agree that this work was too hard for us, we denied it. We were afraid that if we couldn't do this particular heavy work we'd be put out on the street. We said

we agreed to do that work, but it was too heavy." Clearly women's placement in the industry's labor force was by no means consistently linked to their physique—and Brenthal for one would have been more satisfied if it had been. "Someone should point out to us just what work we are suited for," she concluded.[36]

Young and Brenthal were speaking on the basis of their prewar experience in the auto industry. But it was obvious to everyone at the conference that the war presented a situation where such problems would be compounded. Many delegates expressed uncertainty as to which jobs were suited for women. "How would you determine whether a job was too difficult . . . ?" Bernice Cut wanted to know. "If they asked me to work on a lathe machine—would you label that as a man's job?" another delegate inquired. Yet a third woman pointed out. "Some of our sisters are stronger than others— they could handle jobs that would about kill some of our other sisters in one or two days. How will we manage to distinguish this?"[37]

In response to such comments as these, UAW Secretary-Treasurer George Addes articulated the union's policy on this issue at the conference. He said that

> First of all under this program you train the women for a particular job and machine. If said employer should assign women to jobs that are strenuous, too difficult because of the heaviness of the work; or materials that are detrimental, then it becomes a problem for the local union negotiating committee and the management to determine the type of work they should be placed on for the time being. Of course, when the male help is gone and these jobs must be filled it must be decided which jobs women are capable of performing—the jobs must be classified.[38]

Again, it was the union's official policy to leave initial decisions on such matters to management, and then to negotiate any necessary adjustments. None of the women at the conference objected to the idea of using some system of job classification arrived at in this way—on the contrary, they hoped it might protect them from assignment to overly strenuous jobs. Evidence that such abuses had occurred in the prewar period only served to reinforce the women's support for a more systematic classification of jobs.

This view, however, was soon proven naive. The union historically had developed other principles of job assignment which conflicted with the notion that women should be placed on the lighter jobs. There were numerous changes that management was manipulating the sexual division of labor in the mobilization period in ways calculated to undermine the seniority-based job preference rights of the prewar (that is, predominantly male) labor force. George Romney, testifying before the U.S. Senate hearings on "Manpower Problems in Detroit" in 1945 in his capacity as head of the Automotive Council for War Production, cited such a case:

> On September 13, 1943, company Y tried to discontinue the placement of men on jobs that women would be able to handle. Since that date, the company has tried on numerous occasions to effect this policy but each attempt has been met by positive union resistance. On May 26, 1944, a survey of the company's plants revealed that over 400 jobs then being held by men could be performed by women. Again the management requested, and the union refused, the replacement of these men by women, even though the management offered to guarantee the rates of the men so transferred. . . . To date the union has not granted such approval.
> The types of jobs to be vacated by men and filled by women were varied, but all were considered to be light enough for women to fill. The union's reasons for not granting approvals seemed to be that the men, for the most part, had worked

long periods of time to acquire these lighter jobs, and did not feel that they should be removed from them just so the jobs could be filled by women.[39]

There were also numerous grievances of this sort filed by the UAW against General Motors (GM) in late 1943 and early 1944. . . .

What provoked these union challenges was not a belief that the idiom of sex typing (on which all parties seemed to agree) had been incorrectly applied. Rather, the central concern was that management was undercutting the seniority principle as a factor in job placement. Thus the evolution of the sexual division of labor in the war years became entangled with political and economic conflicts which involved a range of other issues. The ways in which management, the union, and rank-and-file workers defined and sought to advance their respective interests in relation to the sexual division of labor were determined in the larger context of labor relations and shop floor politics. . . .

For the majority of the new women auto workers, the chance to work in a unionized basic industry, in virtually any job category, meant an enormous improvement in their economic circumstances. For example, 68 percent of the women employed at the Ford Willow Run bomber plant earned at least three times as much in their war jobs than in their prewar jobs, while this was true for less than 15 percent of the men.[40] This dramatic improvement in their wages was not the result of any political effort on the part of women who got war jobs in the auto industry, but it reflected the historical development of the industry as one paying relatively high wages. Under such circumstances, it is not surprising that most women were relatively indifferent to their placement within what was in any case a completely new and unfamiliar system of job classification.

... the situation would be very different in the immediate postwar period, when the gains woman had made in the war years were directly threatened. Women would be the protagonists in the battles that ensued over the sexual division of labor in the course of postwar reconversion. But during the mobilization period, the struggles were generally waged between management and the predominantly male prewar labor force, and the interests of women workers lacked any politically effective vehicle for their expression. . . .

THE VARIABILITY OF MALE INTERESTS: FROM EXCLUSION TO "EQUAL PAY"

On the eve of U.S. entry into the war, in October 1941, there was a strike at a newly built defense plant owned by the Kelsey-Hayes Wheel Company in Plymouth, Michigan. Although it took place before anyone could fully comprehend the unprecedented scale on which female labor would have to be incorporated into the auto industry, this strike clearly posed the issues which would have to be confronted in establishing the wartime sexual division of labor. . . .

The two-day work stoppage was the culmination of a conflict between the company and the union which had been the subject of negotiations for some weeks prior to the October 28 walkout. On October 15, the UAW had filed a strike notice against Kelsey-Hayes demanding a wage increase and "the removal of all girl employes from machine work which, it [the UAW] contends, is a man's job." Negotiations over these issues were continuing when workers discovered that two women had been hired on the night shift, and walked out at midnight in protest, because the company had agreed to hire no more women pending the outcome of the negotiations. Significantly, "the strikers had no ob-

jection to women being hired, ordinarily on other jobs in the plant." But because women in the plant received a maximum of eighty-five cents per hour, while men earned one dollar per hour, "workers feared the company would replace men with women workers in order to reduce labor expenses."[41]

The strike was successful. The union and the company settled upon the following working arrangement:

> It was agreed by the Company that girls would not be used on any Screw Machine Operations, nor would they be used on Profiling operations. The Company would use them, however, on Filing wherever possible, on Inspection (Bench) where they can be utilized, and on small assemblies wherever they can be utilized.
>
> Female employees at no time will exceed 25% of the total.[42]

Thus the main object of the walkout was achieved: the exclusion of women from "men's jobs." The union did not object to women being employed at lower wage rates than men's, providing they were confined to "women's jobs," as stipulated in this agreement. Indeed, the maximum pay rates negotiated for the female job classifications established after the strike were 88¢ for women with two years' seniority or more, and 85¢ for those with less than two years. Men's maximum rates under the new agreement, in contrast, ranged from $1.01 to $1.13 in the various classifications they occupied.[43]

In this case, the effect of the union's action in clarifying and then enforcing the system of job segregation by sex is obvious, but the circumstances behind the strike make the matter more complex. In the face of a shortage of male labor, management sought to take advantage of the lower wages historically paid to women by breaking down the existing pattern of job segregation by sex. It was this assault on their own wage standards which provoked the strike in defense of the extant sexual division of labor. . . .

The demand to exclude women from what had previously been regarded by everyone as male job classifications was male labor's first line of defense in the mobilization period—as it had been in many earlier historical episodes of this type, particularly in the craft union era. After the no-strike pledge, there were wildcat strike actions opposing the hiring of women. . . . And there were other ways to pursue the objective of excluding women from particular jobs besides going on strike, notably refusing to break in new workers properly, or actively obstructing their work.

The various exclusionary tactics male auto workers employed, while at times successful in the short term (as at Kelsey-Hayes), became less and less viable as the rising demand for labor and the rapid exhaustion of the male labor supply forced a break with the old sexual division of labor. Once it became clear that resistance to the inclusion of women in the industry's male preserves was doomed to failure, a new set of tactics emerged. These were of two basic types. First, the union undertook various efforts to ensure that women's employment in "men's jobs" would be limited to the period of the war emergency—by such means as separate seniority lists, special agreements providing for the integration of women "for the duration" only, or by giving the newly hired workers "trainee" status, with limited seniority rights. Such arrangements affected the sexual division of labor in the industry not during the war but in the postwar period, however. It was the second set of tactics that had the greatest impact on the wartime sexual division of labor. . . .

. . . the demand for "equal pay for equal work" became the central focus of the struggles shaping the wartime sexual division of labor. This demand was not a new one in the 1940s—it had been the UAW's standard defense against the actual or potential replacement of men with women. But before the war, actual incidents of such replacement had been relatively rare. It was only with the disruption of the sexual division of labor in the mobilization period that the union's long-standing fears of large-scale female replacement really materialized. Worse, there was every reason to fear that any wage cuts made while women occupied any given position would affect men after the war, when the job reverted to them. And the wartime wage freeze meant that equal pay demands were one of the few avenues of any kind for the pursuit of substantial wage increases.

Some companies readily agreed to adopt a policy of equal rates for women, without a protracted struggle (though perhaps in anticipation of one if women were paid less on "men's jobs"). Ford's recruitment handbills for the giant Willow Run bomber plant advertised the firm's policy: "Women paid same rates as men," and Ford as well as Studebaker and Vultee signed national contracts with the UAW which had equal pay clauses.[44] Because a great deal of war production was done under "cost-plus" war contracts, under which the wage bill was passed directly on to the government, and because the expectation was that women's war jobs would revert to men after the war in any event, "equal pay for equal work" was a sensible policy for many managements.

But there were also numerous disputes over the question of equal pay in the wartime auto industry. The most important was a WLB case the UAW brought against GM in 1942. The board's decision in this case was widely regarded as a milestone in the development of government policy on the issue, and it firmly established the equal pay principle in board practice. "Wages should be paid to female employees on the principle of equal pay for equal work," the September 26, 1942, decision stated. "There should be no discrimination between employees whose production is substantially the same on comparable jobs." The WLB ordered GM and the UAW to include an equal pay clause in their contract as well, and they did so.[45]

Subsequently, however, major disputes developed over the implementation of the equal pay principle as embodied in the contract, and when negotiations failed to resolve the matter, the UAW requested arbitration in June 1943. At three GM plants, hearings were held before WLB arbitrator William Simkin, who issued a decision on July 31, which was later sustained by the National WLB. The issue in this case, typical of equal pay disputes, was whether or not jobs being done by women were "comparable in quantity and quality" to those jobs done by men. . . .

Simkin baldly acknowledged the ambiguity surrounding the assignment of sex labels to the jobs in question in a section of his decision aptly entitled, "WOMAN'S JOB OR MAN'S JOB?" He noted that "exact and certain allocation of a specific operation to a given type is by no means easy."[46] But ultimately he accepted, at least in part, the arguments put forward by GM which detailed why all the jobs in question were appropriate for women and distinct from the "men's jobs" to which the union insisted they were comparable. GM's case was cast entirely in terms of the idiom of job segregation by sex, stressing that women did physically "light" work and had fewer responsibilities than men, as well as insisting that most of women's war jobs resembled their prewar jobs. Typical was the statement that "it is not possible to assign to a woman all the duties that over a period of time can be assigned to a male janitor because of her physical capacity. Often the janitors are called on to do heavy work such as moving furniture. . . ."[47]

The arbitrator ruled that the existing wage differentials were too wide to be justified by the variation in content between "men's" and "women's" jobs, but also perpetuated what had been *sex* differentials in wages in a new, if thinly disguised form: as differentials between "light" and "heavy" work. . . .

> Under the principle of equal pay for equal work, sex differentials are no longer proper. The principle . . . however, is consistent with differences in rates which are based upon differences in job content. It is upon this basis that the arbitrator *substituted* for the classifications "Inspection—Receiving—Male" and "Inspection—Receiving—Female" the classifications of "Inspection—Receiving—Heavy" and "Inspection—Receiving—Light" and fixed the rate for the former at $1.14 per hour and for the latter at $1.04 per hour. Roughly, the new classification "Inspection—Receiving—Heavy" corresponds to the former classification "Inspection—Receiving—Male" and the "Inspection—Receiving—Light" to the former classification "Inspection—Receiving—Female." *Rates of each classification imply whether the employees are men or women.*[48]

Thus was the sexual division of labor recodified "for the duration."

The main reason the UAW opposed making any distinction between "heavy" and "light" work, or "men's" and "women's" work, was that it feared *men's* postwar wages would be lowered as a result or that women would permanently replace men after the war, and at lower pay. But the union's position in these equal pay struggles was radically different from its stance in the 1941 Kelsey-Hayes strike. Then, the UAW had defended the division of jobs into "male" and "female"; now it wanted to eliminate any such distinction. Management's position had also made a 180-degree turn. Yet in both the Kelsey-Hayes strike and the equal pay disputes, the stakes were the same: male wage levels and male employment security. The crucial difference was that, at

Kelsey-Hayes, the male workers feared women would permanently replace them, and so they tried to exclude women from employment altogether. A short time later, however, the war made women's presence in the auto industry necessary, and now the same fear of permanent replacement by women led men to fight against sex discrimination in pay. This shift in how male auto workers defined their interests in the 1940s suggests that men's interests in relation to the sexual division of labor are not fixed. Sometimes, men's interest in preserving their power and privileges "as men"—their *gender* interest—prevails; but under certain conditions their *class* interest in opposing sex discrimination and supporting their female co-workers prevails instead. Struggles between male workers and management, then, can work for or against women workers, depending on the particular situation.

But if the demand for equal pay challenged wage discrimination by sex, it did so in a very limited way. The very formulation of the issue as "equal pay for equal work" precluded from the outset the general equalization of work between women and men. The struggle was explicitly confined to determining whether women within a relatively small spectrum of occupational categories were indeed engaged in "men's work," or work similar enough to "men's work" to merit similar compensation. Although the ensuing debate revealed the arbitrary aspect of the sex labeling of jobs, at the same time it reinforced the legitimacy of the sexual division of labor as a whole. Indeed, the previously established pattern of job segregation was elevated into the reference point for determining the legitimacy of particular claims for equal pay, at the margin between "women's" and "men's" jobs. A more radical formulation of the issue, as in the struggles being waged today for "equal pay for comparable worth," would have to not merely challenge the pay rates

of those jobs at the margin, but also put forth a critique of the entire structure of job segregation and the systematic undervaluing of women's work.[49] . . .

CONCLUSION

The changes in the sexual division of labor in the auto industry during the mobilization for World War II illustrate the way in which job segregation by sex can be reproduced in the face of dramatic changes in the economic setting. Although neither the war period nor the auto experience is typical in women's labor history, that job segregation was reconstituted under such extreme circumstances—in a high-wage industry and in a situation in which women's incorporation into basic industry's work force was construed as temporary—suggests the resilience of the ideology of sex typing and the job segregation it enforces. . . .

In the absence of an organized feminist movement or consciousness, the only vehicle for political struggle over the sexual division of labor in this period was the labor movement. The UAW did challenge managerial initiatives in this area during the mobilization, most importantly in the form of demands for "equal pay for equal work." Here the conflict was essentially between male auto workers and management, as women were new to both the industry and the union and were not yet a politically effective force. In addition, just securing access to "men's jobs" in the auto plants brought such a dramatic improvement in women workers' status and pay that the sexual division of labor *within* the wartime industry understandably did not preoccupy them.

During the postwar reconversion, when these gains were threatened and when women had accumulated some political experience, they would mobilize in opposition to management's effort to return to the prewar sexual division of labor in the auto industry. In the mobilization period, however, women and men alike generally accepted as legitimate the overall idiom of the sexual division of labor in that industry. The struggles which took place focused on where the boundaries between women's and men's work should be drawn, without questioning the existence of such boundaries, as the equal pay example well illustrates. Ultimately, then, despite the

dramatic upheaval in women's position in the work force during the war, the ideology of sex typing retained its power for both workers and management in the auto industry. In the absence of either a more fully developed class consciousness or a feminist movement, there was really no political basis for a sustained challenge to job segregation and the ideology of gender division which underpins it.

NOTES

Special thanks to Ava Baron, Eileen Boris, David Brody, Michael Burawoy, Nancy Gabin, Marty Glaberman, Heidi Hartmann, David Matza, Ros Petchesky, Michael Rogin, and Judy Stacey for their comments on earlier versions of this paper.

1. Karen Skold has documented the wartime pattern of job segregation by sex in the shipbuilding industry in her article, "The Job He Left Behind: Women and Shipyard Workers in Portland, Oregon during World War II," in Women, War, and Revolution, ed. Carol R. Berkin and Clara M. Lovett (New York: Holmes, Meier, 1980). . . . My dissertation . . . also documents wartime job segregation in the electrical manufacturing industry. See Ruth Milkman, "The Reproduction of Job Segregation by Sex: A Study of the Changing Sexual Division of Labor in the Auto and Electrical Manufacturing Industries in the 1940s" (Ph.D dissertation, University of California at Berkeley, 1981).

2. To be sure, the existence of a clearly defined sexual division of labor is not peculiar to capitalist societies—quite the contrary. Yet the persistence and reproduction of job segregation within capitalist relations of production presents a distinct theoretical problem—and an especially paradoxical one. Indeed, the development of capitalism was expected by friend and foe alike eventually to eliminate such "ascriptive" characteristics as sex (and race) from the process of allocating people to places within the social division of labor, and above all in the wage labor market. Both Karl Marx and Max Weber predicted this in the nineteenth century, and the same expectation has been expressed by many twentieth-century Marxist writers and by mainstream social scientists. Today it is im-

possible to defend the view that capitalism is incompatible with a rigid sexual division of labor outside the home. . . . Yet an adequate theoretical account of the continuous reproduction of job segregation by sex in capitalist societies has yet to be developed. . . .

3. This consideration is stressed in the literature on "labor market segmentation" developed by Marxist economists. See, for example, Richard Edwards, Michael Reich, and David Gordon, eds., Labor Market Segmentation (Lexington, Mass.: D.C. Heath and Co., 1975). . . .

4. This dynamic has been discussed extensively in Marxist feminist literature. See especially . . . Heidi Hartmann, "Capitalism, Patriarchy, and Job Segregation by Sex," in Women and the Workplace: The Implications of Occupational Segregation, ed. Martha Blaxall and Barbara Reagan (Chicago: University of Chicago Press, 1976).

5. The war years produced a "family crisis" with many parallels to that of our own time and aroused many of the same concerns among contemporaries. This is discussed indirectly in Karen Anderson, Wartime Women: Sex Roles, Family Relations and the Status of Women in World War II (Westport, Conn.: Greenwood Press, 1981), chap. 3.

6. The transcript of this newsreel was made available to me by the Rosie the Riveter Film Project, Emeryville, California. Additional examples of the wartime idiom are cited below.

7. U.S. Department of Labor, Women's Bureau, Changes in Women's Employment during the War (1944), Special Bulletin No. 20, p. 15; and U.S. Department of Labor,

Bureau of Labor Statistics, *Women in Factories* (1947), p. 7.

8. U.S. Department of Labor, Women's Bureau, *Women Union Leaders Speak* (1945), p. 32. (Mimeographed.)

9. Statistics on the representation of women in the auto industry for this period are scattered and not entirely consistent. The 1930 Census reported that women were 7 percent of all workers employed by the industry, and the 1940 Census enumeration produced a figure of 9 percent. . . .

10. U.S. Department of Labor, Bureau of Labor Statistics, *Wages and Hours of Labor in the Motor Vehicle Industry: 1925*, Bulletin No. 438 (1927), pp. 2–3.

11. Even in the depression decade, when wage cuts were endemic throughout the economy, the weekly earnings of auto factory workers averaged 24 percent above the average for all manufacturing industry. . . .

12. Computed from data in Bureau of Labor Statistics, *Wages and Hours of Labor*, pp. 2–3; and U.S. Department of Labor, Bureau of Labor Statistics, *Wage Structure of the Motor-Vehicle Industry*, Bulletin No. 706 (1942), pp. 23–24. . . .

13. Robert W. Dunn, *Labor and Automobiles* (New York: International Publishers, 1929), p. 74; William McPherson, "Automobiles," in *How Collective Bargaining Works*, ed. Harry A. Millis (New York: Twentieth Century Fund, 1942), p. 576.

14. *Wall Street Journal*, 22 November 1926, cited in Dunn, *Labor and Automobiles*, p. 74. For evidence that this was generally an exclusively male occupation, see Bureau of Labor Statistics, *Wages and Hours of Labor*.

15. "Annual Averages of Hourly and Weekly Earnings and Average Hours per Week for Male and Female Wage Earners in the Automobile Industry," 28 June 1944, in UAW Research Department Collection, Wayne State University Archives of Labor History and Urban Affairs, Detroit, Michigan (hereafter cited as WSUA), Box 10, Folder 10–19: "Employment, Detroit, 1941–1947."

16. See U.S. Department of Labor, Bureau of Labor Statistics, "Seniority in the Automobile Industry," by Jonas Silver and Everett Kassalow, 1944, pp. 25–27. (Mimeographed.)

17. On conversion, see Barton J. Bernstein, "The Automobile Industry and the Coming of the Second World War," *Southwestern Social Science Quarterly* 47 (June 1966): 22–33; and Alan Clive, *State of War: Michigan in World War II* (Ann Arbor: University of Michigan Press, 1979), pp. 18–42.

The best statistics on the changing representation of women in the industry are those published by the Bureau of Labor Statistics, *Women in Factories*. . . .

18. "Women in War Industries," *UAW Research Report*, 2 (September 1942), p. 1.

19. "Meeting for Discussion on Labor Supply and Future Labor Requirements," 26 June 1942, Detroit, Michigan, pp. 30–31 of transcript, in Records of the War Production Board—Record Group 179, National Archives (henceforth RG 179—NA), Box 1016, Folder: "241.11R Labor—Women—Recruiting Drive" . . .

20. Memorandum from Anthony Luchek to Joseph D. Keenan, 14 July 1943, "Degree of Utilization of Negro Workers . . . ," in RG 179—NA, Box 1017, Folder: "241.3 Labor Negroes." . . . Black employment in the Detroit auto industry rose from about 4 percent in the prewar period to 15 percent of the labor force in 1945. See . . . August Meier and Elliott Rudwick, *Black Detroit and the Rise of the UAW* (New York: Oxford University Press, 1979), p. 213.

21. On prewar recruitment by auto firms, see Blanche Bernstein, "Hiring Policies in the Automobile Industry," Works Projects Association National Research Project (1937), marked "not for publication," copy in the W. Ellison Chalmers Collection, WSUA, Box 1. On wartime migration and the problems associated with it, see Clive, *State of War*, pp. 94–95, 172. The government report cited is an "Outline of Proposed Drive to Recruit Women for War Work in Wayne County Area," attached to memorandum from Ernest Kanzler to John L. Lovett, 3 July 1942, in RG 179—NA, Box 1016, Folder: "241.11R Labor—Women—Recruiting Drive."

22. U.S. Congress, Senate, *Manpower Problem in Detroit*, Hearings before a Special Committee Investigating the National Defense Program, 79th Cong., 1st Session, March 9–13, 1945, pp. 13534, 13638.

23. Computed from the questionnaires from this survey by the writer. The questionnaires (unprocessed) are in the UAW War Policy Division—Women's Bureau Collection, WSUA, Series 1, Box 5, Folders 5–10, 5–11, and 5–12.

24. Computed by the writer from "Ford Motor Company—Rouge Plant, Factory Count, December 14, 1943." This is one of several years' worth of weekly "Factory Counts" in Acc. 732, Ford Archives, Box 1.

25. "Engineers of Womanpower," *Automotive War Production* 2 (October 1943):4–5

(emphasis added). This magazine was published monthly, starting in March 1942, by the Automotive Council for War Production.

26. "Provisions in Plants for Physical Differences Enable Women to Handle Variety of War Jobs," *Automotive War Production* 2 (September 1943):7.

27. Ibid. Also see "Technological Advances in Automotive Plants Help to Combat Growing Manpower Crisis," *Automotive War Production* 2 (September 1943):3; and "Automotive Industry Reducing War Costs through Improved Production Techniques, *Automotive War Production* 2 (March 1943):3.

28. "Women Work for Victory," *Automotive War Production* 1 (November 1942): 4; "Engineers of Womanpower," p. 4.

29. "Engineers of Womanpower," p. 4.

30. Ibid., p. 4.

31. "New Workers," Manpower Reports No. 10 (Published by the Manpower Division, Automotive Council for War Production), p. 4; and "Problems of Women War Workers in Detroit," 20 August 1943, p. 2, by Anne Gould of the Office of Labor Production of the War Production Board, in RG 179—NA, Box 203, Folder: "035.606 Service Trades Division, WPB Functions."

32. "Women's Bureau, *Changes in Women's Employment*, p. 18.

33. "Report of Mrs. Betty Sturges Finan on Cleveland Detroit Trip, February 9–17 (1943) Inclusive," pp. 3–4, in Records of the War Manpower Commission—Record Group 211, National Archives, Box 977, Series 137, Folder: "Consultants—Betty Sturges Finan." . . .

34. Gene Minshall to Mauro Garcia, 29 July 1943; Mauro Garcia to DeWitt Patterson, 9 August 1943, in UAW Ford Department Collection, WSUA, Box 13, Folder: "Patterson, DeWitt, Ford Motor (Rouge)."

35. "Transcript of 7 February 1942, Women's Conference, Detroit, Michigan, p. 27, in UAW War Policy Division—Victor Reuther Collection, WSUA, Box 2, Folder: "Conferences."

36. Ibid., p. 26.

37. Ibid., p. 23.

38. Ibid.

39. *Manpower Problems in Detroit*, Hearings, p. 13595. See also Example No. 29, pp. 13594–95, for another example of this type of controversy.

40. "Work and Wage Experience of Willow Run Workers," *Monthly Labor Review* 61 (December 1945): 1086.

41. "Strike is Threatened at Kelsey Hayes Plant," *Detroit News*, 28 October 1941;

"Workers Reject Plea for Truce," *Detroit News*, 29 October 1941, both in Joe Brown Collection, WSUA, Scrapbook No. 21, p. 85.

42. "Clarification of Female Work," 5 November 1941, enclosed in letter from Caroline Manning, Industrial Supervisor with the U.S. Department of Labor, Women's Bureau to J. H. Wishart, Research Director, UAW-CIO, 17 November 1941, in UAW War Policy Division—Victor Reuther Collection, WSUA Box 11, Folder: "U.S. Dept. of Labor."

43. "Kelsey Hayes-Plymouth Plant, Productive Rates," 5 November 1941, UAW Research Department Collection, WSUA, Box 9, Folder: "Dept. of Labor, U.S., 1940–2."

44. "Sample handbill announcing arrival of company employment representatives to interview recruits for Willow Run," in *Willow Run Bomber Plant: Record of War Effort* 2, Notebook 2, p. 8, La Croix Collection, Acc. 435, Ford Archives, Box 15; "History of the Support of the Equal Pay Principle by Official Federal, State, and International Action, and by Unions and Management," Exhibit A submitted by Frieda Miller of the Women's Bureau, in U.S. Congress, Senate, *Equal Pay for Equal Work for Women*, Hearings on S. 1178, Senate Subcommittee of a Committee of Education and Labor, 79th Congress, 1st Session, October 29, 30, and 31, 1945, p. 34.

45. Bureau of National Affairs, *War Labor Reports* 3, pp. 355–56. . . .

46. "Arbitrator's Decision—Women's Rates at Buick Division—Melrose Park, Ill.; Buick Division—Flint, Mich.; Chevrolet Division—Bay City, Mich." In the Matter of General Motors Corporation and United Automobile, Aircraft and Agricultural Implement Workers of America—C.I.O., Case No. 125, 31 July 1943, pp. 5–6, in UAW Research Department Collection, WSUA, Box 32, Folder: "Women—Statistics and NWLB Cases 1943–5."

47. "Summary Brief Submitted by Buick Motor Division, Melrose Park, General Motors Corporation," In the Matter of General Motors Corporation, Buick Motor Division, Melrose Park, Ill., and International Union, United Automobile, Aircraft and Agricultural Implement Workers of America, C.I.O., 14 June 1943, pp. 7, 8, and 12, in Walter Reuther Collection, WSUA, Box 20, Folder: "WLB, GM Women's Rates," and "Summary Brief Submitted by Buick Motor Division, Flint, Michigan, General Motors Corporation," In the Matter of General Motors Corporation, Buick Motor Division, Flint, Mich., and In-

ternational Union, United Automobile, Aircraft and Agricultural Implement Workers of America, C.I.O., 17 June 1943, pp. 11, 14, in Walter Reuther Collection, WSUA, Box 47, Folder: "WLB, GM Women's Rates." . . .

48. "Opinion Explaining Directive Order," NWLB Region XI, Case 125, stamped 9 October 1943, in Walter Reuther Collection, WSUA, Box 47, Folder: "WLB—GM Women's Rates" (emphasis added).

49. This more radical formulation of the equal pay issue did emerge in the 1940s, but not in the auto industry. The United Electrical Workers Union did bring a case to the War Labor Board against General Electric and Westinghouse in 1945, which foreshadowed the "comparable worth" strategy being pursued by feminists in the labor movement today. The case may be found in *War Labor Reports* 28, pp. 666–92. For discussion, see Milkman, "Reproduction of Job Segregation," pp. 192–201.

DOCUMENTS: *Minority Women—Work and Politics*

ROBERT HAMBURGER
"My first job in New York"

As race relations deteriorated in the South at the turn of the century, blacks sought to escape racism, poverty, and the servitude of tenant farming by migrating north. When World Wars I and II created temporary jobs in industry, the migration increased. Between 1910 and 1920, for example, the number of southern-born blacks in the North jumped from 415,000 to 737,000. Women came north in even greater numbers than men, for employment agents traveled throughout the South recruiting black women for domestic work as immigrant women and their daughters moved on to other jobs. Statistics tell the story. In New York State alone black women made up 6 percent of the domestic workers in 1890, 21 percent in 1930, and 50 percent in 1970. Only in the last decade has this flow northward reversed as economic opportunities and race relations in the South improved.

As Robert Hamburger has pointed out, the decision of these women to migrate was a bold one, for the transition from the rural, small-town South to northern cities was not easy. Interviewing two of the more recent of these "new immigrants," Hamburger demonstrates through the stories of Roena Bethune and Rose Marie Hairston the lure of "the promised land," the discrepancy between promise and reality, and the capacity for survival that has distinguished generations of black women. Although some of these black domestics found work in homes pervaded by warmth and generosity, note how barriers of race and class could override the "bonds of womanhood" that black houseworkers presumably shared with the well-to-do white women for whom they often worked. To what extent has the job of domestic workers improved since the period described by David M. Katzman (part IIB)?

ROENA BETHUNE

I was born the 14th of December, 1936, in a little small town called Fayetteville, North Carolina. Coming up as a child, I can remember us living in about a seven-room, white house on Merkson Road. My mother, she was a domestic worker. She

Excerpted from "A Stranger in the House" by Robert Hamburger, in *Southern Exposure 5* (1977):22–31. Copyright © 1977 by Robert Hamburger. Reprinted by permission of the author. An extended version of these narratives appears in Robert Hamburger, *A Stranger in the House* (New York: Macmillan, 1978).

worked in people's homes taking care of children and housekeeping. She could only do so much for us because she had to take care of all the bills and everything because our father had separated from us. My mother, she never received welfare checks. She always believed in going out and working and trying to take care of us herself. And I remembered the time that she would often tell us, "I don't know how I am going to make it, children, but by the help of the Lord we will make it."

She would earn something like $10 to $12 weekly, and we had to live off of this. She had very bad days and she had some good days. As for raising us, a daughter and a son, she would have to go out to work and leave us—and as me being the oldest child at home, I had a lot of work to do in the house. My mother would always tell me that I had to clean, and I had to cook if necessary. I was only about the age of nine years old when I started to learn about housekeeping. My mother had nobody to help her take care of us, but only herself.

Ever since I can remember, my mother worked for white families, but she never discussed with me about the hard times or nothing going on with the jobs. I was only a little girl; I can't remember so much about those times. The only thing that I know—she used to come in the house, and she'd be telling us, "Oh, my day was so hard. I had so much work to do, and I have to come home, and I have to do lots of things. You children have to help me out." That's about as much as I knew. I think my mother really didn't want us to know how hard times was. But, you know, by looking on and observing you could see the expression on her face, you could tell when times come that wasn't so good.

I never went on the job with my mother. She used to work for this family—they had children growing up like me and my brother—and they would give my mother shoes and clothing for me and

such things as that. When I was quite small, I didn't know no difference, but as I became to be a teenager I didn't like it because I wanted new clothes. My mother would bring things home, and I knew that she'd gotten them from someplace that she was working. I didn't want to wear them, cause in school the kids would laugh at you and say, "Ugh, your mother let you wear hand-me-down clothes." . . .

. . . After I was 15, things was better. And at 16, going on close to the age of 17, I was married. So that's about as much as I can say about coming up.

I met my husband in Fayetteville. We had an army base there which is called Fort Bragg. A lot of GIs was there, and my husband was a serviceman. We met each other downtown and we started talking. I was walking down the street and he was standing with some GIs at the corner. Myself and a couple of girlfriends was walking, and so the guys started talking, and so we just made a conversation, and he asked me if he could make a date with me. I hesitated, and we gossiped for a while. So I told him he could come back at Saturday afternoon. My mother didn't really approve of it. I started thinking about growing up and how you don't get things that you want, and I said, "Well I met this boy, a GI, and I know he have money, and he can maybe give you money sometimes and help out with, you know, if it might be something I wanted, he would get it for me." So we dated for about four months, and then we got married.

For five years we was very happy together, but then my husband—I really hate to say this—we started having trouble in the home. He started going outside, and he found something outside better than what he had in his home—or he thought he did. After that we separated and I came up to New York.

Believe me, I was here one week and I was ready to go back. I had heard a lot about the big city, and I had heard a lot about the bright lights. And when I came and I saw all the tall buildings and saw all the people moving in the streets, I said, "Who in the world could live in a place like this with the people in the street; they's pushing each other, it's overcrowded, and everybody's in a hurry, nobody have time to even speak to each other. How in the world can people live in a place like this?" And I was ready to go back home.

I was living with my brother and his wife. They had been living here already, about five years before I came to New York. So, my sister-in-law, she used to tell me, "Roena, you realize you never been in the city before, and the city is much different from just where you come from. You come from the South and you never seen a lot of people all in one place together like this. But if you stay here a while, you will like it. . . .

My first job in New York, I was a chambermaid doing household work at the Saint George Hotel in Brooklyn. As long as I worked in the hotel, the management was great. Dealing with the guests, that's where the little run-ins would come in. I would go in to make up the bed. As a routine, the customer occupying the room is supposed to be out of the room to let the maid make the room up. A couple of times when I'd go to the room the door would be unlocked —I'd go in the room and the man would be in the bathroom closed up, and he would say, "Come in, don't you like to make some fast money?" He'd be nude. I got very angry, very angry, and I would run out of the room and go to the nearest telephone that was on the floor. I would call the desk and say, "The man in such-and-such a room, he's in the nude in the hotel, he's giving me a hard time, and I refuse to make this room up because he's not supposed to be in the room. He's offering me money, and I don't like to be going through stages like this because it's very terrible and embarrassing."

So the manager would say, "Well, just stand outside in the hallway, somebody'll be up in a few minutes and we'll get him out." So they'd come up and they'd talk to the guy and they'd get him to leave the room. Then I'd go in and make it up. Several times this happened.

There is a lot of things you go through working in a hotel. It was a very terrible embarrassment—some of the things, you wouldn't even want to approach nobody telling them about it. You try to get out of the room as fast as you can; you go down and make complaints. What can you do? These things happen living in a hotel.

I think it made a difference I was black —the way they would approach you, you know. You could read them, what they think, "Well, how much money can you be making for a job like this? I know that you will like to make extra money. You can't be making but so much, and nobody would ever know about this but me and you. I can get over fast with you."

Now the way I feel about white people, I don't hate them or nothing, but I do have a little discrimination against them because, you know, it seems like they only class all the black people as one way. As far as I'm concerned with the white man or the white woman, when I go out there and I do a day's work for them, I just do my work. As far as I am concerned they don't love me and I cannot love them because I know that there is a space difference in between; there is a racial gap, because that white women or white man that you go and work for in their house, when the time comes for them to serve dinner, they will not let you sit down at that dinner table and eat with them. They will tell you, "Serve us Roena, and then after you serve us you can have your dinner in the kitchen" where you do the cooking, not in the dining room where they sit down and eat their dinner themselves. So you know when things like this happen, there is a complex racial gap somewhere.

ROSE MARIE HAIRSTON

I was born in Martinsville, Virginia, 38 years ago. There's mostly furniture factories, farming, tobacco there. My family had their own house, but we didn't live there all the time. My parents moved to West Virginia, and my father was a coal miner. He was a motorman in the coal mine and a brakeman. A motorman drives down in the mine to bring the coal out. Sometimes he was a brakeman, and he would ride on the back of the little car, which was very dangerous. I forget what it's called, but from working in the mine he got fluid in his knees and elbows and up in his shoulder. And from getting his back hurt and his hip hurt six or seven times, it caused him to have a type of arthritis. My father started working at the coal mine at age 14, and he was retired about the time he got 40. He had been hurt a lot of times, you know; he was all broken up. . . .

In West Virginia we never knew anything about racial prejudice. Really, we never heard anything about that until we went back to the state of Virginia. Where we lived around the coal mine there was Jews, Italians, Hungarians, Poles and just about any race you could name. Everybody mingled together. When I was about 10, my brother Maurice and me went back to Virginia on the farm for a summer. We didn't know what they were talking about when they used to say "colored people." In West Virginia we didn't use the words. Everybody there was together. But when we were going to Virginia, we got off the bus to go to the bathroom, and we wanted something to eat, and we saw a sign said "Colored in the Rear." We went in there —it was a little, dirty, greasy room about the size of a good chicken house. It was so dirty in there. And then we wondered why all the white people were sitting up

in the best part of the bus. Even the bathrooms said "No Colored." Even the telephones had big signs that said "No Colored." . . .

The schools was all black. We would get up at four o'clock and have breakfast and do some chores like milk the cows and feed the dogs and different little things like that. Then we would walk seven miles to catch a bus, and the bus would take us into town, and then after we got into town we would have about another mile to walk to school. . . .

When I was a little girl, I always had hopes of being a nurse or a doctor. I always wanted my husband to look like my father. I wanted my husband to be his height, his complexion. My daddy was not a big guy, but he was a handsome guy. I said if I ever married I wanted a big farm and a lot of children. One of my sisters, she wanted to be a doctor. Another one wanted to be a nurse, and one wanted to be a schoolteacher. We'd say that one day we'd be the Hairston clinic. We always wanted something that would help others. One time we said we'd work and make a lot of money, and then we'd go back to West Virginia and have an orphanage. Unfortunately, it never happened.

I was about sixteen-and-a-half, and I was reading a newspaper. It said, "Ladies and Girls 18 and over: Jobs in New York." And you didn't even have to pay to come to New York. And this ad said it paid $125 a week. I said, "Oh boy, that's good! I think I'll go up there and talk to this man." He was a preacher, too, and that's what made me mad. It was just another old gimmick. Anyway, I went up there and he interviewed me. He said, "How old are you?" I told him I was 18, and he kept looking at me.

He said, "I don't know, Rose, you look very young. Matter of fact, you look like you're no more than 12."

I said, "No, eighteen." So he told me to bring him proof that I was 18, or bring my mother. I told him all right. I caught the bus and went back home and got my cousin to come back with me. She was a much older lady than I was. She told them that she was my mother. She gave her consent for me to come to New York. So he said all right. He told me to come the next day and that he would meet me at the bus station. Then he described the persons that were to meet me in New York on 50th Street. So I met him the next day, and he gave me the bus ticket and he said, "Good luck, Rose." I said, "Yeah."

And he said, "When you make all that money, put it in the bank." I wasn't scared, I was determined because I thought $125 a week was a long ways from getting $7.50 a week.

I didn't tell my mother I was going. . . .

I went over to the bus station and met the preacher, Brother Plow. He was there with my bus ticket. I jumped on the bus. I was so excited. I was looking out the window, and I was listening good for the man to say New York. I was so excited. I said to myself, "Oooh, now I get to see the movie stars." I thought you'd probably see them on the streets. I had read a book about Harlem, and I was dying to see Harlem—125th Street, the Apollo Theater, and I was dying to see 42nd Street. I didn't understand what Wall Street was, you know. I thought it was somewhere all the rich people and celebrities be—that they'd be there just for you to look at.

When I got off in New York, I saw the people walking—it looked like everybody was walking fast and the cars was whizzing. I said, "Golly, if I get out there on this street, I'm gonna get hit by one of them cars. It's too crowded in New York." Then I saw there was two fellas, two Jewish fellas, there to meet me. I had a photograph of them. They told me that I should come with them, that they were there to meet me. While we were walking down the street, I would look up at the buildings and I ran into a stop-sign. After that I had a stiff neck from looking up at the buildings.

I got in their car and went out to the agency in Long Island. Leaving the city, I got disappointed. I said, "Oh my god, I just left the country and thought I was coming to the big city, and the man was trying to send me back to the country." The man in the agency would tell the people, "I have this nice girl here, she's very attractive, she's 18, and she's good with children." You know, they didn't know a thing about you. So they would say, "We'll bring her over in an hour, and when we get there, you have to give us $150." I said to myself, "He's selling the girls. I come all this way just to be bought and sold."

They took me out to this lady. I remember her well—Mrs. Burke at 250 Central Avenue in Cedarhurst. I got there and looked at this big old apartment building and I said, "It sure is a big old place." I had the idea that she lived there in that big old building all alone, and she expected me to clean it all by myself. I got in there in this little apartment, and she showed me through the rooms. I asked her, "Where do your children live?"

She said, "Here with me."

"Where would I live?"

"Here with me."

"Well, where?"

"You will live and sleep in this room with my children."

"I have to share this room with your children?"

I didn't like it because the little girl slept in a cradle and I slept in one bed and the little boy slept in one bed with me. I never liked to sleep with anybody. Then I had to get used to when the lady would get up early and leave, and you didn't see them no more til five or six or seven o'clock. Then she would come in and have something to eat. She didn't spend time with the children. I would think she don't love her children; she don't stay home. I wondered why.

I worked there about a month, and I kept asking her. "When is payday, when you going to pay me?" She said, "Oh, you'll get paid. Do you want me to give you money until you get paid?" So I said, "Yeah." So she gave me money. Her husband took me to Robert Hall's, and I think I bought a coat and two dresses and shoes. Anyway, I ran out of money, and he came over to the counter, and he asked me did I get everything I wanted, did I have enough money, and did I want anything else. I said no. The lady behind the counter said. "Gee, you have a good boss."

I said, "Boss?"

And she said, "Do you work for him? Is that your husband?"

"No, I work for him."

"Well, that's your boss."

I said, "Well, I just say it's somebody I work for."

When it came time to get paid, they didn't owe me, I owed them. It came up a big argument. I told her I was supposed to get $125 a week. She said, "No, I'll show you on the contract." So she went and got this contract, and she showed it to me. We was only supposed to get $100 a month.

I told her to get in touch with this agency. I told her, "I'm from the country, but I got sense enough not to work for $100 a month. I could stay at home and work for $100 a month." We called the agency, and the agency had went out of business.

She told me that she couldn't afford to pay $125 a week. She said, "You don't do a lot of cooking." I said, "Yeah, I understand that, but I sits here day and night taking care of your children, taking them to parks. I had to spend my money, cause when I take them to the store they be hollering about what they want. I didn't want to be embarrassed, so I used my money to buy them things."

She offered me $40 a week, and I told her I'd try it for awhile till I found something better.

After that she began to get very nasty and prejudiced. When her company came, she said she didn't want me to sit in the other room and watch TV. I would have to go back into my room until her company left. One day she asked me, "You wasn't used to eating steak and pork chops in West Virginia, were you?"

I told her, "Yes, I was used to good food in West Virginia."

So she said, "Well, the maids don't get treated like the family."

I said, "Well, I don't know what you mean by 'maid.' A maid is somebody who works in a hotel, right?"

"No, all of you that came up here are maids to us."

So I said, "Oh, you mean that this will be something like slavery time?"

She was from Georgia, and people were still treated like slaves in the Deep South till about 1960. I began to get very angry when she told me her parents had a lot of slaves. Then she said, "I wish it was slavery time, "I'd make a good slave out of you." I got real mad and cursed her. One word followed another word, and then I got so mad that I slapped her. I slapped her hard as I could. I went into the bathroom, and the little boy came into the bathroom and bit me on the leg. I looked at him a long time and then I grabbed him. I started to throw him in the bathtub, but then I thought better of it. So I grabbed him and picked him up, and I turned him upside down by his feet and started to shake him. Then I just got so mad that I took his head and I put it in the commode.

She asked me was I crazy. I told her no. She said, "Well, you had better go back to West Virginia where they allow you to do that."

I told her that I was going to get me another job. I got my clothes and I went to a friend's house. Later, I called Mrs.

Burke and asked her to pay me, and she said she would pay me when I stopped by. I felt a little uneasy going back, so I asked this boy, one of my friends to go with me. He went and got his two brothers and said, "Come on, go with me back to get the rest of Rose's things." They were great big guys, six foot four.

So I rang the doorbell, and she said, "Who is it?"

I said it was Rose.

She said, "Well come on in."

I started to open the door, and my boyfriend said, "Let me open it." So he opened the door, and when he opened the door, he looked behind the door, and Mr. Burke was standing behind it with a car jack. I guess he was going to hit me. And her mother, father and brother was standing there waiting for me.

I got my money and the rest of my things, and she tried to talk me into staying, but I didn't fall for it. I just laughed a lot. I guess it runs in my family, my mother laughs a lot too. So I got me another job.

ANNE MOODY
"Involved in the Movement"

For Afro-American women the politics of reform and the politics of inclusion merged. For most southern black women, the passage of the Equal Suffrage Amendment was meaningless because most blacks, especially in the deep South, were not permitted to vote whether male or female. Without political power they were unable to fight segregation laws, which consigned blacks to second-class citizenship and economic privation. The National Association for the Advancement of Colored People (NAACP), however, could do so. Founded in 1909, during the progressive era, by blacks and whites—many of the latter women associated with the settlement house movement—and based in New York, the NAACP established a Legal Defense Fund administered by a small staff of highly skilled lawyers who chipped away at *de jure* segregation in a series of important court cases. The 1954 Supreme Court decision, *Brown* v. *Board of Education*, which rejected as unconstitutional the doctrine of "separate but equal" in the field of public education, marked the culmination of decades of litigation. By the mid-1950s blacks had reason to believe that the era of segregation and disfranchisement was coming to an end and that Afro-Americans could regain the political and civil rights that in the South especially had been so long denied.

When expectations aroused by the *Brown* decision were frustrated by white

Excerpted from "The Movement," pt. 4 of *Coming of Age in Mississippi* by Anne Moody (New York: Dial Press, 1968). Copyright © 1968 by Anne Moody. Reprinted by permission of The Dial Press.

recalcitrance, blacks opted for a new strategy through which to attack segregation. That strategy was one of nonviolent direct action. Although the Montgomery bus boycott in 1956 marked the first such action involving thousands of protesters, the sit-ins that took place at a Woolworth lunch counter in Greensboro, North Carolina, in 1960 inaugurated a new stage in the struggle for equal rights. In the months that followed, thousands of young blacks and their white supporters engaged in sit-ins in restaurants, pray-ins at white churches, wade-ins at segregated beaches, and finally "freedom rides" and voter registration drives. Such massive protests prodded the conscience of the nation and resulted in passage of the Civil Rights Act of 1964 and a subsequent Voting Rights Act.

Anne Moody, the daughter of an impoverished black farm family in Mississippi, had worked as a domestic as a teen-ager. A student at Tougaloo College during the early 1960s, she became immersed in the struggle for racial justice. For her, as for many other women, white as well as black, participation in civil rights demonstrations meant risking family disapproval, physical violence, and the possibility of death. Her courage and her commitment to political change ultimately had economic overtones as well. Without gains brought about by the black revolution of the 1960s, Moody and countless women of her generation would have had little opportunity to escape the poverty and racism that had constrained the lives of their mothers and grandmothers. This struggle for freedom, equality, and autonomy on the part of black women in the civil rights movement would not be lost on their white counterparts, as birth of a new feminist movement would ultimately demonstrate.

I had counted on graduating in the spring of 1963, but as it turned out, I couldn't because some of my credits still had to be cleared with Natchez College. A year before, this would have seemed like a terrible disaster, but now I hardly even felt disappointed. I had a good excuse to stay on campus for the summer and work with the Movement, and this was what I really wanted to do. I couldn't go home again anyway, and I couldn't go to New Orleans—I didn't have money enough for bus fare.

During my senior year at Tougaloo, my family hadn't sent me one penny. I had only the small amount of money I had earned at Maple Hill. I couldn't afford to eat at school or live in the dorms, so I had gotten permission to move off

campus. I had to prove that I could finish school, even if I had to go hungry every day. I knew Raymond and Miss Pearl were just waiting to see me drop out. But something happened to me as I got more and more involved in the Movement. It no longer seemed important to prove anything. I had found something outside myself that gave meaning to my life.

I had become very friendly with my social science professor, John Salter, who was in charge of NAACP activities on campus. All during the year, while the NAACP conducted a boycott of the downtown stores in Jackson, I had been one of Salter's most faithful canvassers and church speakers. During the last week of school, he told me that sit-in demonstrations were about to start in Jackson and that he wanted me to be the spokesman for a team that would sit-in at Woolworth's lunch counter. The two other demonstrators would be classmates of mine, Memphis and Pearlena. Pearlena was a dedicated NAACP worker, but Memphis had not been very involved in the Movement on campus. It seemed that the organization had had a rough time finding students who were in a position to go to jail. I had nothing to lose one way or the other. Around ten o'clock the morning of the demonstrations, NAACP headquarters alerted the news services. As a result, the police department was also informed, but neither the policemen nor the newsmen knew exactly where or when the demonstrations would start. They stationed themselves along Capitol Street and waited.

To divert attention from the sit-in at Woolworth's, the picketing started at J. C. Penney's a good fifteen minutes before. The pickets were allowed to walk up and down in front of the store three or four times before they were arrested. At exactly 11 A.M., Pearlena, Memphis, and I entered Woolworth's from the rear entrance. We separated as soon as we stepped into the store, and made small purchases from various counters. Pearlena had given Memphis her watch. He was to let us know when it was 11:14. At 11:14 we were to join him near the lunch counter and at exactly 11:15 we were to take seats at it.

Seconds before 11:15 we were occupying three seats at the previously segregated Woolworth's lunch counter. In the beginning the waitresses seemed to ignore us, as if they really didn't know what was going on. Our waitress walked past us a couple of times before she noticed we had started to write our own orders down and realized we wanted service. She asked us what we wanted. We began to read to her from our order slips. She told

us that we would be served at the back counter, which was for Negroes.

"We would like to be served here," I said.

The waitress started to repeat what she had said, then stopped in the middle of the sentence. She turned the lights out behind the counter, and she and the other waitresses almost ran to the back of the store, deserting all their white customers. I guess they thought that violence would start immediately after the whites at the counter realized what was going on. There were five or six other people at the counter. A couple of them just got up and walked away. A girl sitting next to me finished her banana split before leaving. A middle-aged white woman who had not yet been served rose from her seat and came over to us. "I'd like to stay here with you," she said, "but my husband is waiting."

The newsmen came in just as she was leaving. They must have discovered what was going on shortly after some of the people began to leave the store. One of the newsmen ran behind the woman who spoke to us and asked her to identify herself. She refused to give her name, but said she was a native of Vicksburg and a former resident of California. When asked why she had said what she had said to us, she replied, "I am in sympathy with the Negro movement." By this time a crowd of cameramen and reporters had gathered around us taking pictures and asking questions, such as Where were we from? Why did we sit-in? What organization sponsored it? Were we students? From what school? How were we classified?

I told them that we were students at Tougaloo College, that we were represented by no particular organization, and that we planned to stay there even after the store closed. "All we want is service," was my reply to one of them. After they had finished probing for about twenty minutes, they were almost ready to leave.

At noon, students from a nearby white high school started pouring in to Woolworth's. When they first saw us they were sort of surprised. They didn't know how to react. A few started to heckle and the newsmen became interested again. Then the white students started chanting all kinds of anti-Negro slogans. We were called a little bit of everything. The rest of the seats except the three we were occupying had been roped off to prevent others from sitting down. A couple of the boys took one end of the rope and made it into a hangman's noose. Several attempts were made to put it around our necks. The crowds grew as more students and adults came in for lunch.

We kept our eyes straight forward and did not look at the crowd except for occasional glances to see what was going on. All of a sudden I saw a face I remembered—the drunkard from the bus station sit-in. My eyes lingered on him just long enough for us to recognize each other. Today he was drunk too, so I don't think he remembered where he had seen me before. He took out a knife, opened it, put it in his pocket, and then began to pace the floor. At this point, I told Memphis and Pearlena what was going on. Memphis suggested that we pray. We bowed our heads, and all hell broke loose. A man rushed forward, threw Memphis from his seat, and slapped my face. Then another man who worked in the store threw me against an adjoining counter.

Down on my knees on the floor, I saw Memphis lying near the lunch counter with blood running out of the corners of his mouth. As he tried to protect his face, the man who'd thrown him down kept kicking him against the head. If he had worn hard-soled shoes instead of sneakers, the first kick probably would have killed Memphis. Finally a man dressed in plain clothes identified himself as a police officer and arrested Memphis and his attacker.

Pearlena had been thrown to the floor. She and I got back on our stools after Memphis was arrested. There were some white Tougaloo teachers in the crowd. They asked Pearlena and me if we wanted to leave. They said that things were getting too rough. We didn't know what to do. While we were trying to make up our minds, we were joined by Joan Trumpauer. Now there were three of us and we were integrated. The crowd began to chant, "Communists, Communists, Communists." Some old man in the crowd ordered the students to take us off the stools.

"Which one should I get first?" a big husky boy said.

"That white nigger," the old man said.

The boy lifted Joan from the counter by her waist and carried her out of the store. Simultaneously, I was snatched from my stool by two high school students. I was dragged about thirty feet toward the door by my hair when someone made them turn me loose. As I was getting up off the floor, I saw Joan coming back inside. We started back to the center of the counter to join Pearlena. Lois Chaffee, a white Tougaloo faculty member, was now sitting next to her. So Joan and I just climbed across the rope at the front end of the counter and sat down. There were now four of us, two whites and two Negroes, all women. The mob started smearing us with ketchup, mustard, sugar, pies, and everything on the counter. Soon Joan and I were joined by John Salter, but the moment he sat down he was hit on the jaw with what appeared to be brass knuckles. Blood gushed from his face and someone threw salt into the open wound. Ed King, Tougaloo's chaplain, rushed to him.

At the other end of the counter, Lois and Pearlena were joined by George Raymond, a CORE field worker and a student from Jackson State College. Then a Negro high school boy sat down next to me. The mob took spray paint from the counter and sprayed it on the new demonstrators. The high school student had on a white shirt; the word "nigger" was written on his back with red spray paint.

We sat there for three hours taking a beating when the manager decided to close the store because the mob had begun to go wild with stuff from other counters. He begged and begged everyone to leave. But even after fifteen minutes of begging, no one budged. They would not leave until we did. Then Dr. Beittel, the president of Tougaloo College, came running in. He said he had just heard what was happening.

About ninety policemen were standing outside the store; they had been watching the whole thing through the windows, but had not come in to stop the mob or do anything. President Beittel went outside and asked Captain Ray to come and escort us out. The captain refused, stating the manager had to invite him in before he could enter the premises, so Dr. Beittel himself brought us out. He had told the police that they had better protect us after we were outside the store. When we got outside, the policemen formed a single line that blocked the mob from us. However, they were allowed to throw at us everything they had collected. Within ten minutes, we were picked up by Reverend King in his station wagon and taken to the NAACP headquarters on Lynch Street.

After the sit-in, all I could think of was how sick Mississippi whites were. They believed so much in the segregated Southern way of life, they would kill to preserve it. I sat there in the NAACP office and thought of how many times they had killed when this way of life was threatened. I knew that the killing had just begun. "Many more will die before it is over with," I thought. Before the sit-in, I had always hated the whites in Mississippi. Now I knew it was impossible for me to hate sickness. The whites had a disease, an incurable disease in its final

stage. What were our chances against such a disease? I thought of the students, the young Negroes who had just begun to protest, as young interns. When these young interns got older, I thought, they would be the best doctors in the world for social problems.

Before we were taken back to campus, I wanted to get my hair washed. It was stiff with dried mustard, ketchup and sugar. I stopped in at a beauty shop across the street from the NAACP office. I didn't have on any shoes because I had lost them when I was dragged across the floor at Woolworth's. My stockings were sticking to my legs from the mustard that had dried on them. The hairdresser took one look at me and said, "My land, you were in the sit-in, huh?"

"Yes," I answered. "Do you have time to wash and style it?"

"Right away," she said, and she meant right away. There were three other ladies already waiting, but they seemed glad to let me go ahead of them. The hairdresser was real nice. She even took my stockings off and washed my legs while my hair was drying.

There was a mass rally that night at the Pearl Street Church in Jackson, and the place was packed. People were standing two abreast in the aisles. Before the speakers began, all the sit-inners walked out on the stage and were introduced by Medgar Evers. People stood and applauded for what seemed like thirty minutes or more. Medgar told the audience that this was just the beginning of such demonstrations. He asked them to pledge themselves to unite in a massive offensive against segregation in Jackson, and throughout the state. The rally ended with "We shall Overcome" and sent home hundreds of determined people. It seemed as though Mississippi Negroes were about to get together at last.

Before I demonstrated, I had written Mama. She wrote me back a letter, begging me not to take part in the sit-in. She even sent ten dollars for bus fare to New Orleans. I didn't have one penny, so I kept the money. Mama's letter made me mad. I had to live my life as I saw fit. I had made that decision when I left home. But it hurt to have my family prove to me how scared they were. It hurt me more than anything else—I knew the whites had already started the threats and intimidations. I was the first Negro from my hometown who had openly demonstrated, worked with the NAACP, or anything.

When Negroes threatened to do anything in Centerville, they were either shot like Samuel O'Quinn or run out of town, like Reverend Dupree.

I didn't answer Mama's letter. Even if I had written one, she wouldn't have received it before she saw the news on TV or heard it on the radio. I waited to hear from her again. And I waited to hear in the news that someone in Centreville had been murdered. If so, I knew it would be a member of my family.

JESSIE LOPEZ de la CRUZ
"The first woman farmworker organizer out in the fields"

The tobacco and cotton fields of the rural Southeast were a continent away from the prune and apricot fields of San Jose, California; the ethnic and religious background of Mollie Goodwin equally distant from that of Jessie Lopez de la Cruz. Yet these two women had much in common during their early years: a strict upbringing, early marriage, and a constant struggle with poverty, pregnancy, and illness. That their lives subsequently diverged had much to do with the organizing activities of Cesar Chavez, whose drive to unionize farm workers received national attention in the 1960s. Note the similarities involved in the response to unionization by women workers described by Lopez de la Cruz and by Alice Kessler-Harris (part IIB) and the critical difference made by the contrasting attitudes of Gompers and Chavez. Note, too, the persistent opposition of employers to unionization, whether in 1900 or 1960. The movement of Jessie Lopez de la Cruz from farm worker to union organizer to community leader and Chicano spokeswoman to membership on the California Commission on the Status of Women makes her story not only a part of the long struggle of workers to organize but also of a more recent struggle of minorities and women to improve

Excerpted from *Moving the Mountain: Women Working for Social Change* by Ellen Cantarow with Susan Gushee O'Malley and Sharon Hartman Strom (Old Westbury, N.Y.: The Feminist Press, 1980). Copyright © 1980 by The Feminist Press. Reprinted with permission of The Feminist Press.

their position in American society. If Jessie Lopez de la Cruz shared much in terms of her early life with Mollie Goodwin, she also shared with Anne Moody a determination to change the conditions that had left her and so many women like her impoverished and powerless.

CHILDHOOD

My grandmother was born in Mexico in Aguas Calientes, near Guadalajara. She was raised by a very strict father and she married at thirteen. That was the custom. The girls, as soon as they were old enough to learn cooking and sewing, would get married. She had my mother and my oldest brother when she and my grandfather came across. My grandfather worked for the railroad laying the ties and tracks. Then he worked for a mining company. And after that we moved to Anaheim. We lived in a big four-bedroom house my grandfather built. With my grandparents and their children, three children of my mother's sister who had died, and the three of us, that made a big crowd.

My grandfather would get up Sunday mornings and start the fire in a great big wood-burning stove. He would wrap us up in blankets and seat us around that stove on chairs and say, "Now, don't get too close to the stove. Take care of the younger children." Then he would go out to the store and get bananas and oranges and cereal that he'd cook for us to eat, and milk, and he would feed us Sunday mornings. . . .

Then my grandfather had an accident. The middle fingers of his right hand was crushed and he couldn't work for about two weeks. When he went back he was told that he'd already been replaced by another worker. So he was out of a job. He decided we'd better go on and pick the crops. We had done that before, during the summer. But this time we went for good.

We came North. The families got together; the women would start cooking at night, boiling eggs and potatoes and making piles of tortillas and tacos, and these lunches would be packed in pails and boxes. There was as much fruit as they could get together, and roasted pumpkin seeds. My uncle had a factory where he made Mexican candy in East Los Angeles. And he used to give us a lot of pumpkin seeds. So my mother dried these, and she roasted and salted them for the trip to keep the drivers awake. We'd start in a car caravan, six or seven families together, one car watching for the other, and when it got a little dark they'd pull onto the roadside and build a fire and start some cooking to feed us. Then they'd spread blankets and quilts on the ground and we would sleep there that night. The next morning the women and older children would get up first and start the breakfast. And we smaller children, it was our job to fold the blankets and put them back in the cars and trucks. Then my brothers and the men would check the cars over again, and after breakfast all the women would wash the dishes and pack them, get 'em in the cars, and we'd start again.

We'd finally get to Delano and we would work there a little. If work was scarce we would keep on going till San Jose. I did the same thing my mother and my grandfather and my uncles did, picking prunes on our hands and knees off the ground, and putting them in the buckets. We were paid four dollars a ton and we had to fill forty boxes to make it a ton. They made us sign a contract that we would stay there until all the prunes were picked. When we would finish the prunes, in early September, we would start back. And stop on the way to Mendota to pick cotton.

When I was about 13, I used to lift a 12-foot sack of cotton with 104 or 112 pounds. When you're doing this work, you get to be an expert. I could get that sack and put it on my shoulder, and walk with that sack for about a city block or maybe a little less, to where the scale was. I could hook this sack up on the scale, have it weighed, take it off the hook and put it back on my shoulder and walk up a ladder about eight feet high and dump all that cotton in the trailer.

My brothers taught me how to do it. When I first started picking cotton, they had to untie their sack and go on my side of the row and help me put this sack on my shoulder, so they taught me how to do it when it was full. It's stiff. My brother said, "Just walk over it, pick up one end, and sort of pull it up, up, and then bend down, and when the middle of the sack hits your shoulder, you just stand up slowly. Then put your arm on your waist and the sack will sit on your shoulder and you can just walk with it." At 13, 14 I was lifting 104 and 112 pounds. I weighed 97, I guess!

As a child I remember we had tents without any floors. I think it was Giffen's Camp Number Nine. I remember the water coming from under the tent at night to where we were sleeping. My brothers would get up with shovels and put mud around the tent to keep the water out. But our blankets and our clothes were always damp during the winter. . . .

In thirty-three we came up North to follow the crops because my brothers couldn't find any work in Los Angeles during the Depression. I remember going hungry to school. I didn't have a sweater. I had nothing. I'd come to school and they'd want to know, "What did you have for breakfast?" They gave us a paper, to write down what we had! I *invented* things! We had eggs and milk, I'd say, and the same things the other kids would write, I'd write. There weren't many Mexican people at school, mostly whites,

and I'd watch to see what they were writing or the pictures that they'd show. You know: glasses of milk, and toast, and oranges and bananas and cereal. I'd never had *anything*. . . .

COURTSHIP AND MARRIAGE

When I was a girl, boys were allowed to go out and have friends and visit there in camp, and even go to town. But the girls —my mother was always watching them. We couldn't talk to nobody. If I had a boyfriend he had to send me letters, drop notes on his way or send them along with somebody. We did no dating. If girls came to visit at my house, my grandmother sat right there to listen to what we were talking about. We weren't allowed to speak English because she couldn't understand. . . . We were allowed nowhere except out to the field, and then we always worked between my two older brothers. The only one they trusted was Arnold. He's the one I married! I was fourteen when I met Arnold, in 1933. We lived next door to his family, which was a big one. . . .

Arnold and I got married in 1938 in Firebaugh, where we'd all moved. We had a big party with an orchestra: some of Arnold's friends played the violin and guitar. But we had no honeymoon. On the second day after our wedding, he went back to his job—irrigating. I'd get up at four o'clock in the morning to fix his breakfast and his lunch. He'd start the fire for me. I did the cooking in his mother's kitchen. In the morning I'd get up and run across and I'd fix his breakfast and his lunch and he'd go off and I'd go back to bed. There was no women's liberation at the time! I felt I was overworked in the house. . . . But I felt, "What can she (her mother-in-law) do without the help I'm giving her?" I felt sorry for her. She'd worked very hard and she had so many children, and had to wash her clothes in a tub with a rock board and do the ironing by heating the irons on top of the stove. All of us had to do this, but not many families had eight or nine little children.

I cooked with her until May. But I kept after Arnold: "I want my own kitchen!" So in May we drove all the way into Fresno. We got a few spoons and plates and pots and skillets and I started my own housekeeping. I still went to his mother's to help her during the day when Arnold was working. But I cooked in my own stove.

After I was married, sometime in May, my husband was chopping cotton and I said, "I want to go with you."

"You can't. You have to stay at home!"

"I just feel like going outside somewhere. I haven't gone anyplace. I want to at least go out to the fields. Take another hoe and I'll help you." I went, but only for one or two days. Then he refused to take me. He said, "You have to stay home and raise children." I was pregnant with my first one. "I want you to rest," he said. "You're not supposed to work. You worked ever since I can remember. Now that you're married, you are going to rest." So I stayed home but I didn't call it rest doing all the cooking for his mother.

Arnold was raised in the old Mexican custom—men on the one side, women on the other. Women couldn't do anything. Your husband would say, "Go here," you'd do it. You didn't dare go out without your husband saying you could. . . .

After a time I said, "I have really had it. Why do you have to go with your friends all the time when I'm being left alone?"

"Well, what's wrong with that? You can go visit my mother," I said, "Big deal, you want me to visit your mother and help make some tortillas." So he finally started giving me money, five or six dollars. He'd say, "My mother's going to Fresno. If you want to go with them you can go." Or he would say, "Donna Genoveva," a friend

of ours, "is going to Fresno and she said you can come along." I'd get my two kids ready early in the morning and we'd go to Fresno or to visit her husband, who was up in the mountains in the hospital for TB. One day I just said, "Why do I have to depend on other people to take me out somewhere? I'm married, I have a husband—who should be taking me out." The next time he was home and said, "Here's the money," I said, "I don't want to go." He let it go at that and I did too, I didn't say another word. The following weekend he said, "Do you want to go to a show? My mother's going. They're going to Fresno." I said, "No." Then about the third time this happened he said, "Why don't you want to go anymore?"

"I do, I do want to go. I want to go somewhere, but not with anyone else. I want to go with you." So then he started staying home and he'd say, "Get ready, we're going into Fresno." And both of us would come in, bring the children, go to a show and eat, or just go to the park.

Arnold would never teach me how to drive. One day I asked him to. We were on a ditch bank about eight feet wide. He says, "Get on the driver's side. Now turn around and go back." I got out. I said, "*You* do it! Just tell me you don't want me to learn if that's what you want." Then in 1947 I asked my sister, Margaret, and she showed me. We practiced in a field. After a few times she said, "Hey! You know how to drive! Let's go into town so you can buy your groceries."

So one day I said to Arnold, "I'm going out to get the groceries."

"Who's going to take you?"

"Me. I'm going to do the buying from now on."

I stopped working toward the last months of my pregnancies, but I would start again after they were born. When I was working and I couldn't find somebody I would take them with me. I started taking Ray with me when he wasn't a year old yet. I'd carry one of those big washtubs and put it under the vine and sit him there. I knew he was safe; he couldn't climb out. Arnold and I would move the tub along with us as we worked. I hated to leave him with somebody that probably wouldn't take care of him the way I could.

In 1944 we moved to a labor camp in Huron and we stayed there til 1956. But before that we had a single-room cabin. I used to separate the bed section from the kitchen by nailing blankets or pieces of canvas to divide. We had our bed and another bed for the children. All the boys slept in the bed and the girl slept with us in our bed. During the night Bobby being the youngest of the boys would wake up and be scared and he always ended up in our bed! It was pretty crowded, but what could you do? I was always nailing orange crates on the walls to use as cupboards for dishes. . . .

There was a lot of sickness. I remember when my kids got whooping cough. Arnold was sick, too, he was burning hot. During this time instead of staying in my own cabin at night I'd go to my mother-in-law's. The children would wake up at night coughing and there was blood coming out of their noses. I cried and cried, I was afraid they'd choke. I went to the clinic and they told me the children had whooping cough. That cough lasted six months.

It was like that for all of us. I would see babies who died. It was claimed if you lifted a young baby up fast, the soft spot would cave in and it would get diarrhea and dehydrate and die. After all these years, I know it wasn't that that killed them. It was hunger, malnutrition, no money to pay the doctors. When the union came, this was one of the things we fought against.

FIELD WORK

From 1939 until 1944 we stayed at Giffen's Camp Number Three. We were still following the crops. We would go out to pick cotton or apricots or grapes here near Fresno or we would go farther north to Tracey to pick peas. When there was no work chopping or picking cotton we'd go to Patterson or San Jose to pick apricots. Arnold did the picking and I did cutting for the drying-out in the sheds. . . .

We always went where we wanted to make sure the women and men were going to work because if it were just the men working it wasn't worth going out there because we wouldn't earn enough, to support a family. We would start early, around 6:30 A.M. and work for four or five hours, then walk home and eat and rest until about three-thirty in the afternoon when it cooled off. We would go back and work until we couldn't see. Then we'd get home and rest, visit, talk, then I'd clean up the kitchen. I was doing the housework and working out in the fields, and taking care of the kids. I had two children by this time. . . .

The hardest work we did was thinning beets. You were required to use a short-handled hoe. The cutting edge is about seven to eight inches wide and the handle is about a foot long. Then you have to be bent over with the hoe in one hand. You walk down the rows stooped over. You have to work hard, fast, as fast as you can because you were paid by the row, not by the hour. . . .

I used a short-handled hoe in the lettuce fields. The lettuce grows in a bed. You work in little furrows between two rows. First you thin them with the hoe, then you pick off the tops. My brothers-in-law and Arnold and I and some other friends worked there picking the tops off the lettuce. By the time they had taken up one row I had taken up two. The men would go between the two beds and take one row and break the little balls off. But I took two rows at a time, one with each hand. By the time I finished my two rows at the other end, it was close to a mile long, and my brother-in-law had only taken one row part-way. He said, "I'm quitting! If Jessie can beat me at this kind of work, I'm no good at it." So he never came back. About three or four other men wouldn't go back to work because they were beaten by a woman. They said, "I'm ashamed to have a woman even older than I am work faster than I can. This is women's job." I said, "Hey! What do you mean? You mean the men's job is washing dishes and baking tortillas?" They said working out in the fields was women's work because we were faster at it!

Out in the fields there were never any restrooms. We had to go eight or ten hours without relief. If there wasn't brush or a little ditch we were forced to wait until we got home! Just the women. The men didn't need to pull their clothes down. Later, when I worked for the Farmworkers, in a hearing, I said, "I was working for Russell Giffen, the biggest grower in Huron. These big growers have a lot of money because we earned all that money for them. Because of our sweat and our labor that we put on the land. What they do instead of supplying restrooms and clean water where we can wash our hands, is put posts on the ground with a piece of gunny sack wound around them." That's where we went. And that thing was moved along with us. It was just four stakes stuck in the ground, and then there was canvas or a piece of gunny sack around it. You would be working and this restroom would be right there. The canvas didn't come up high enough in front for privacy. We made it a practice to go two at a time. One would stand outdoors and watch outside that nobody came along. And then the other would do the same for the one inside.

LA CAUSA

One night in 1962 there was a knock at the door and there were three men. One of them was Cesar Chavez. And the next thing I knew, they were sitting around our table talking about a union. I made

coffee. Arnold had already told me about a union for the farmworkers. He was attending their meetings in Fresno, but I didn't. I'd either stay home or stay outside in the car. But then Cesar said, "The women have to be involved. They're the ones working out in the fields with their husbands. If you can take the women out to the fields, you can certainly take them to meetings." So I sat up straight and said to myself, "That's what I want!"

When I became involved with the union, I felt I had to get other women involved. Women have been behind men all the time, always. In my sister-in-law and brother-in-law's families the women do a lot of shouting and cussing and they get slapped around. But that's not standing up for what you believe in. It's just trying to boss and not knowing how. I'd hear them scolding their kids and fighting their husbands and I'd say, "Gosh! Why don't you go after the people that have you living like this? Why don't you go after the growers that have you tired from working out in the fields at low wages and keep us poor all the time? . . . Then I would say we had to take a part in the things going on around us. "Women can no longer be taken for granted—that we're just going to stay home and do the cooking and cleaning. It's way past the time when our husbands could say, 'You stay home! You have to take care of the children. You have to do as I say.'"

Then some women I spoke to started attending the union meetings, and later they were out on the picket lines.

I was well-known in the small towns around Fresno. Wherever I went to speak to them, they listened. I told them about how we were excluded from the NLRB in 1935, how we had no benefits, no minimum wage, nothing out in the fields—no restrooms, nothing. I'd ask people how they felt about all these many years they had been working out in the fields, how they had been treated. And then we'd all talk about it. They would say, "I was working for so-and-so, and when I complained about something that happened there, I was fired." I said, "Well! Do you think we should be putting up with this in this modern age? You know, we're not back in the 20s. We can stand up! We can talk back! It's not like when I was a little kid and my grandmother used to say, 'You have to especially respect the Anglos, "Yessir," "Yes, Ma'am!"' That's over. This country is very rich, and we want a share of the money those growers make of our sweat and our work by exploiting us and our children!" I'd have my sign-up book and I'd say, "If anyone wants to become a member of the union, I can make you a member right now." And they'd agree!

So I found out that I could organize them and make members of them. Then I offered to help them, like taking them to the doctor's and translating for them, filling out papers that they needed to fill out, writing their letters for those that couldn't write. A lot of people confided in me. Through the letter-writing, I knew a lot of the problems they were having back home, and they knew they could trust me, that I wouldn't tell anyone else about what I had written or read. So that's why they came to me.

I guess when the union found out how I was able to talk to people, I was called into Delano to one of the meetings, and they gave me my card as an organizer. I am very proud to say I was the first woman organizer out in the fields organizing the people. There have been Dolores Huerta and others, but they were in cities organizing the people, and I was the first woman farmworker organizer out in the fields. . . .

It was very hard being a woman organizer. Many of our people my age and older were raised with the old customs in Mexico: where the husband rules, he is the king of his house. The wife obeys, and the children, too. So when we first started it was very, very hard. Men gave us the most trouble—neighbors there in Parlier! They were for the union, but they were not taking orders from women, they said. When they formed the ranch committee at Christian Brothers—that's a big wine company, part of it is in Parlier—the ranch committee was all men. We were working under our first contract in Fresno County. The ranch committee had to enforce the contract. If there are any grievances they meet with us and the supervisors. But there were no women on that first committee.

That year, we'd have a union meeting every week. Men, women, and children would come. Women would ask questions and the men would just stand back. I guess they'd say to themselves, "I'll wait for someone to say something before I do." The women were more aggressive than the men.

When the first contract was up, we talked about there being no women on the ranch committee. I suggested they be on it, and the men went along with this. And so women were elected.

The women took the lead in calling for picketing and we would talk to the people. It got to the point that we would have to find them, because the men just wouldn't go and they wouldn't take their wives. So we would say, "We're having our picket line at the Safeway in Fresno, and those that don't show up are going to have to pay a five dollar fine." We couldn't have four or five come to a picket line and have the rest stay home and watch T.V. In the end, we had everybody out there. . . .

At White River Farms one morning very early, we were out there by the hundreds by the road, and these people got down and started working out there in the grapes. We were asking them not to work, telling them that there was a strike going on. The grower had two guards at the entrance and there was a helicopter above us. At other White River Farm ranches they had the sheriff, the county police, *everybody.* But there were pickets at three different ranches and where we were picketing there wasn't anybody except these two guards. So I said, "Hey! What about the women getting together and let's rush 'em!" And they said, "Do you think we could do that?" And I said, "Of course we can! Let's go in there. Let's get 'em out of there any way we can." So about fifty of us rushed. We went under the vines. We had our banners and you could see them bobbing up and down, up and down, and we'd go under those rows on our knees and roll over. When the scabs saw us coming they took off. All of them went and they got on the bus. The guards had guns that they would shoot, and something black like smoke or teargas would come out. That scared us, but we still kept on. After we saw all those workers get back on the busses, we went back. Instead of running this time, we rolled over and over all the way out. The vines are about four feet tall, and they have wire where you string up the vines. So you can't walk or run across one of these fences. You have to keep going under these wires. When I got out there on the road they were getting these big, hard dirty clods and throwing them at us. And then the pickets started doing the same thing. When the first police car came, somebody broke the windshield. We don't know if it was the scabs or someone on the picket lines, but the picketers were blamed.

When we women ran into the fields we knew we'd be arrested if they caught us. But we went in and we told the scabs, "If you're not coming out we're gonna pull you out!"

In Kern County we were sprayed with pesticides. They would come out there with their sprayers and spray us on the picket lines. They have these big tanks that are pulled by a tractor with hoses attached and they spray the trees with this. They are strong like a water hose, but wider. When we were picketing they came

out there to spray the pickets. They had goons with these big police dogs on leashes.

One of the things the growers did to break our strikes was to bring in "illegal aliens." I would get a list of names of the scabs and give them to the border patrol. At that time, you see, we were pitted against each other, us and the people from Mexico, so it was either us or them. When I went to the border patrol office I'd go in and say, "Can I come in?" They'd say, "You can't come in. This is a very small office." They kept telling us they were short of men. But every time I went there, there were all of them with their feet up on the desks in their air-conditioned office. They told me they were under orders not to interfere with labor disputes. So I called Bernie Sisk's office and talked to them about it. Then I came home and called a lot of students who'd been helping us, and other people, and the next morning there we were at the border patrol. I said, "We're paying our tax money, but not for you to sit here while the illegal aliens are being used to break our strike."

While we were in Parlier, I was put in charge of the hiring hall. My house was right next to the office, and I had an extension to the office phone in my house. I could do the housework and take care of the children, but I could take care of the office, too. Before the contract, the hiring hall was just a union office where people came to learn about the union. When they got the first contracts we began dispatching people out to work. The hiring hall was also a place where people could meet and talk. A lot of people were migrants who needed to get to know each other. The people who were there all the time were against the migrants. I said, "We have to get these people together. We can't be divided." I was at the hall all day. People would drop by and I'd introduce them.

The second year we had a contract I

started working for Christian Brothers. The men were doing the pruning on the grape vines. After they did the pruning the women's crew would come and tie the vines. (That was something we got changed; we made them give pruning jobs to women.) I was made a steward on the women's crew. . . . the first time we were paid when I started working, during the break the supervisor would come out there with our checks. It was our fifteen minute break, which the contract gave us the right to. We had to walk to the other end of the row; it took us about five minutes to get there, the rest of the fifteen to get our checks, and walk back, and we'd start working. This happened twice. The third time I said, "We're not going to go after our check this time. They always come during our break and we don't get to rest." So when we saw the pickup coming with the men who had the checks I said, "Nobody move. You just sit here." I walked over to the pickup. I said to the man inside. "Mr. Rager, these women refuse to come out here on their break time. It's their time to rest. So we're asking you, if you must come during our rest period, you take the checks to these ladies." From that day on, every payday he would come to us. That was the sort of thing you had to do to enforce the contract.

I became involved in many of the activities in the community—school board meetings, city council meetings, everything that I could get into. For example I went to fighting for bilingual education at Parlier, went to a lot of meetings about it and spoke about it. Parlier is over 85 percent Chicano, yet during that time there were no Chicanos on the school board, on the police force, nowhere. Now it's changed: we fought to get a Chicano mayor and officials. But then I was asking people, "Why are we always asked to go to the public school for our meetings? Why can't they come over to our side of town in Parlier?" So we began having meetings in *la colonia* at the Headstart Center, and there we pushed for bilingual education.

Fresno County didn't give food stamps to the people—only surplus food. There were no vegetables, no meat, just staples like whole powdered milk, cheese, butter. At the migrant camp in Parlier the people were there a month and a half before work started, and since they'd borrowed money to get to California they didn't have any food. I'd drive them into Fresno to the welfare department and translate for them and they'd get food, but half of it they didn't eat. We heard about other counties where they had food stamps to go to the store and buy meat and milk and fresh vegetables for the children. So we began talking about getting that in Fresno. Finally we had Senate hearings at the Convention Center in Fresno. There were hundreds of people listening. I started in Spanish, and the Senators were looking at each other, you know, saying, "What's going on?" So then I said, "Now, for the benefit of those who can't speak Spanish, I'll translate. If there is money enough to fight a war in Vietnam, and if there is money enough for Governor Reagan's wife to buy a $3000 dress for the Inauguration Ball, there should be money enough to feed these people. The nutrition experts say surplus food is full of vitamins. I've taken a look at that food, this corn meal, and I've seen them come up and down, but you know, we don't call them vitamins, we call them weevils!" Everybody began laughing and whistling and shouting. In the end, we finally got food stamps.

AMY SWERDLOW
Ladies' Day at the Capitol:
Women Strike for Peace versus HUAC

In the years surrounding World War I, women played a significant role in the peace movement. Justifying their involvement in the language of "Reformist Motherhood," Crystal Eastman wrote to Jane Addams in 1915 that, as mothers or potential mothers, women "have a more intimate sense of the value of human life"; therefore, "there can be more meaning and passion in the determination of a woman's organization to end war than in an organization of men and women with the same aim."*

Nearly half a century later, American women would again invoke their role as mothers to urge the end of nuclear testing on behalf of the world's children. The women's peace movement, which Swerdlow explores in the following article, coalesced at a time when the Cuban Missile Crisis had brought the United States and the Soviet Union to the brink of war. It also occurred during a period when virtually any form of political protest was automatically labeled by its critics as "communist inspired." Although the most virulent phase of McCarthyism had subsided by 1962, the machinery of repression was still intact; the women's peace movement was promptly investigated by the House Un-American Activities Committee.

Note how participants in the peace strike countered committee tactics by manipulating traditional gender stereotypes. Who were these women? How can their emergence as political activists be explained?

In mid December of 1962 in the Old House Office Building of the United States Congress, a confrontation took place between a recently formed women's peace movement called Women Strike for Peace (WSP) and the House Committee on Un-American Activities (HUAC). The confrontation took place at a HUAC hearing to determine the extent of Communist party infiltration into "the so-called 'peace movement' in a manner and to a degree affecting the national security."[1] This three-day battle of political and sexual adversaries, which resulted in a rhetorical

"Ladies' Day at the Capitol: Women Strike for Peace versus HUAC" by Amy Swerdlow, in Feminist Studies 8 (1982):493–520. Copyright © 1982 by Feminist Studies, Inc. Reprinted by permission of the publisher, Feminist Studies, Inc., c/o Women's Studies Program, University of Maryland, College Park, Maryland 20742.

* Crystal Eastman to Jane Addams, January 16, 1915, Woman's Peace Party Papers, Swarthmore College Peace Collection, Swarthmore, Pa.

victory for the women of WSP and a deadly blow to the committee, occurred only twenty-five years ago.[2] It is a moment in the history of peace movements in the United States in which women led the way by taking a more courageous and principled stand in opposition to cold war ideology and political repression than that of their male counterparts.[3] However, in keeping with the historical amnesia which besets both the history of women and radical movements in America, the WSP-HUAC struggle is largely forgotten.[4]

This article seeks to reconstruct the WSP-HUAC confrontation and the reasons it took the form it did. By analyzing the ideology, consciousness, political style, and public demeanor of the WSP women as they defended their right as mothers "to influence the course of government," we can learn a great deal about the strengths and weaknesses of women's movements for social change that build on traditional sex role ideology and on female culture.[5]

WSP burst upon the American political scene on November 1st, 1961, when an estimated fifty thousand women in over sixty cities across the United States walked out of their kitchens and off their jobs in a one-day women's strike for peace. As a radioactive cloud from a Russian nuclear test hung over the American landscape, these women strikers staged the largest female peace action in the nation's history.[6] In small towns and large cities from New York to California, the women visited government officials demanding that they take immediate steps to "End the Arms Race—Not the Human Race."[7] Coming on the heels of a decade noted for cold war consensus, political conformity, and the celebration of female domesticity, this spontaneous women's initiative baffled both the press and the politicians. The women seemed to have emerged from nowhere. They belonged to no unifying organizations, and their leaders were totally unknown as public figures.

The women strikers were actually responding to a call from a handful of Washington, D.C., women who had become alarmed by the acceleration of the nuclear arms race. So disheartened were they by the passivity of traditional peace groups, that they had sent a call to women friends and contacts all over the country urging them to suspend their regular routine of home, family, and job to join with friends and neighbors in a one-day strike to end the nuclear arms race.[8]

The call to strike spread rapidly from Washington through typical female networks: word of mouth and chain letter fashion from woman to woman, from coast to coast, through personal telephone calls, and Christmas card lists. Contacts in Parent Teacher Associations (PTAs), the League of Women Voters, church and temple groups, as well as the established peace organizations such as the Women's International League for Peace and Freedom (WILPF) and the Committee for a Sane Nuclear Policy (SANE), also spread the word.

The nature of the strike in each community depended entirely on what the local women were willing, and able, to do. Some marched, others lobbied local officials, a few groups took ads in local newspapers. Thousands sent telegrams to the White House and to the Soviet embassy, calling upon the two first ladies of the nuclear superpowers, Jacqueline Kennedy and Nina Khrushchev, to urge their husbands on behalf of all the world's children to "stop all nuclear tests—east and west." Amazed by the numbers and composition of the turnout on November 1st, *Newsweek* commented:

> They were perfectly ordinary looking women, with their share of good looks; they looked like the women you would see driving ranch wagons, or shopping at the village market, or attending PTA meetings. It was these women by the thousands, who staged demonstrations in a score of cities across the nation last week,

protesting atomic testing. A "strike for peace," they called it and—carrying placards, many wheeling baby buggies or strollers—they marched on city halls and Federal buildings to show their concern about nuclear fallout.[9]

The strikers' concern about the nuclear arms race did not end with the November 1st actions. Within only one year, the one-day strike for peace was transformed by its founders and participants into a national women's movement with local groups in sixty communities and offices in ten cities. With no paid staff and no designated leaders, thousands of women in different parts of the country, most of them previously unknown to each other, managed to establish a loosely structured communications network capable of swift and effective direct action on both a national and international scale.

From its inception, the WSP movement was a non-hierarchical participatory network of activists opposed both to rigid ideologies and formal organizational structure. The WSP women called their format simply "our un-organization." It is interesting to note that the young men of Students for a Democratic Society (SDS), a movement founded in the same year as WSP, more aware of their place in the radical political tradition, more aware of the power of naming, and more confident of their power to do so, named their loose structure "participatory democracy." Eleanor Garst, one of the Washington founders, explained the attractions of the un-organizational format:

No one must wait for orders from headquarters—there aren't any headquarters. No one's idea must wait for clearance through the national board. No one waits for the president or the director to tell her what to do—and there is no president or director. Any woman who has an idea can propose it through an informal memo system; if enough women think it's good, it's done. Those who don't like a particular action don't have to drop out of the movement; they just sit out that action and wait for one they like. Sound "crazy"?—it is, but it also brings forth and utilizes the creativity of thousands of women who could never be heard from through ordinary channels.[10]

The choice of a loose structure and local autonomy was a reaction to hierarchical and bureaucratic structures of traditional peace groups like WILPF and SANE to which some of the early leaders belonged. These women perceived the WILPF structure, which required that all programmatic and action proposals be cleared with state and national offices, as a roadblock to spontaneous and direct responses to the urgent international crisis.[11] The willingness of the Washington founders to allow each group to act in the way that suited its particular constituency was WSP's greatest strength and the source of the confidence and admiration that women across the country bestowed on the Washington founders. Washington came to be considered the WSP national office not only because it was located in the nation's capital, but also because the Washington group was trusted by all.

There was also another factor militating against a traditional membership organization. Only the year before the WSP strike, Linus Pauling, the Nobel Laureate in physics and opponent of nuclear testing, had been directed by the Senate Internal Security Subcommittee to turn over the names of those who had helped him gather signatures on a scientists' antinuclear petition. The commandeering of membership lists was not an uncommon tactic of political intimidation in the 1950s. Membership lists of radical organizations could therefore be a burden and responsibility. As they served no purpose in the WSP format, it was a sensible strategy to eliminate them. Another benefit was that WSP never had to assess accurately its numerical strength, thus allowing its legend to grow even when its numbers did not.

From its first day onward, WSP tapped

a vast reservoir of moral outrage, energy, organizational talent, and sisterhood— female capacities that had been submerged and silenced for more than a decade by McCarthyism and the "feminine mystique." Using standard pressure group tactics, such as lobbying and petitioning, coupled with direct demonstrative action and civil disobedience, executed with imagination and "feminine flair," the WSP women succeeded in putting women's political demands on the front pages of the nation's newspapers, from which they had largely disappeared since the days of the suffrage campaign. WSP also managed to influence public officials and public policy. At a time when peace marchers were ignored, or viewed as "commies" or "kooks," President John F. Kennedy gave public recognition to the women strikers. Commenting on WSP's first antinuclear march at the White House, on January 15, 1962, the president told the nation that he thought the WSP women were "extremely earnest."

> I saw the ladies myself. I recognized why they were here. There were a great number of them, it was in the rain. I understand what they were attempting to say, therefore, I consider their message was received.[12]

In 1970, *Science* reported that "Wiesner (Jerome Wiesner, Pres. Kennedy's Science Advisor) gave the major credit for moving President Kennedy toward the limited Test Ban Treaty of 1963, not to arms controllers inside the government but to the Women Strike for Peace and to SANE and Linus Pauling."[13]

Although WSP, in its first year, was well received by liberal politicians and journalists, the surveillance establishment and the right-wing press were wary. They recognized early what the Rand Corporation described obliquely as the WSP potential "to impact on military policies."[14] Jack Lotto, a Hearst columnist, charged that although the women described themselves as a "group of unsophisticated wives and mothers who are loosely organized in a spontaneous movement for peace, there is nothing spontaneous about the way the pro-Reds have moved in on our mothers and are using them for their own purposes."[15] On the West Coast, the *San Francisco Examiner* claimed to have proof that "scores of well-intentioned, dedicated women . . . were being made dupes of by known Communists . . . operating openly in the much publicized Women Strike for Peace demonstrations."[16]

That WSP was under Federal Bureau of Investigation (FBI) surveillance from its first public planning meeting in Washington in October 1961, is abundantly evidenced in the forty-three volumes of FBI records on WSP which have been made available to the movement's attorneys under the provisions of the Freedom of Information Act. The records show that FBI offices in major cities, North, East, South, and West—and even in such places as Mobile, Alabama; Phoenix, Arizona; and San Antonio, Texas; not known for WSP activities—were sending and receiving reports on the women, often prepared in cooperation with local "red squads."[17]

Having just lived through the Cuban Missile Crisis of October 1962, WSP celebrated its first anniversary in November with a deep sense of urgency and of heightened political efficacy. But, as the women were making plans to escalate their commitment and their protests, they were stopped in their tracks in the first week of December by HUAC subpoenas to thirteen women peace activists from the New York metropolitan area, as well as Dagmar Wilson of Washington, D.C., the WSP national spokesperson.[18]

It is difficult today to comprehend the emotions and fears such a summons could invoke in individuals and organizations. Lillian Hellman's *Scoundrel Time* gives a picture of the tension, isolation, and near hysteria felt by an articulate and prominent public figure, as she prepared her defense against the committee in 1953.[19] By 1962, cold war hysteria had abated somewhat, as the United States and the USSR were engaged in test ban negotiations, but HUAC represented those forces and those voices in American politics that opposed such negotiations. As a congressional committee, it still possessed the awesome power of an agency of the state to command headlines; cast suspicion; and by labeling individuals as subversives, to destroy careers, lives, and organizations.

The HUAC subpoenas gave no indication of the subject of the hearings, or of their scope. So there was, at first, some confusion about whether it was the WSP connection or other aspects of the subpoenaed women's political lives that were suspect. To add to the confusion, it was soon discovered that three of the women called were not even active in WSP. They were members of the Conference of Greater New York Peace Groups, an organization founded by New Yorkers who had either been expelled from, or who had willingly left, SANE because of its internal red hunt. Of these three women, two had already been named by the committee informers as communists in previous HUAC hearings. One of these women, Elizabeth Moss, had achieved considerable notoriety when she was identified by accused Russian spy William Remington as his mother-in-law and a card-carrying communist. Given these circumstances it was clear that the WSP leadership had some important decisions to make regarding their response to the HUAC hearings. There were two important questions to be faced. First, as WSP had no official membership list, would the movement embrace any woman working for peace even if she were not directly involved in WSP activity? Second, would WSP disavow its members who had past or present communist affiliations, and if WSP did not disavow them, would the movement lose its following and its effectiveness?

The key to WSP unity in the face of the "communist issue" which had divided and disrupted peace, labor, and even civil liberties organizations in the previous decade, was the fact that WSP had previously decided to handle forthrightly and in advance of any attack, the issue of communist inclusion. WSP had, even before the HUAC hearings, decided to reject political screening of its members, deeming it a manifestation of outdated cold war thinking. This decision, the women claimed, was based not on fear or expediency, but on principle. The issue of accepting communists in the movement was brought to the floor of the first national WSP conference in June 1962 by the Los Angeles coordinating council. A prepared statement by the Los Angeles group declared: "Unlike SANE and Turn Toward Peace, WSP must not make the error of initiating its own purges." Treating the issue of communist membership as a question of personal conscience, the Los Angeles group asked, "If there are communists or former communists working in WSP, what difference does that make? We do not question one another about our religious beliefs or other matters of personal conscience. How can we justify political interrogation?" The Los Angeles statement continued, "If fear, mistrust and hatred are ever to be lessened, it will be by courageous individuals who do not hate and fear and can get together to work out tolerable compromises."[20] The argument that "this is a role women would be particularly equipped to play," won over the conference and resulted in the inclusion of a section in the WSP national policy statement which affirmed, "we are women of all races, creeds and political persuasions who are dedicated to the achievement of general and complete disarmament under effective international control."[21]

An emergency meeting of about fifty New York area "key women," along with Dagmar Wilson and other representatives from Washington, was called a few days after the HUAC summonses began to arrive.[22] The first decision made at this meeting was that WSP would live up to the national policy statement that had been arrived at six months earlier and make a reality of the phrase, "We are women of all . . . political persuasions." Following from this decision it was clear that WSP would support and embrace every woman summoned before HUAC, regardless of her past or present affiliations, as long as she supported the movement's campaign against both Russian and American nuclear policies. This meant that in addition to supporting its own women, the three women not active in WSP would also come under the movement's protection if they so desired. They would be given access to the same lawyers as the WSP activists. They would not be isolated or attacked either for their affiliations or for the way they chose to conduct themselves at the hearing. This decision was in sharp contrast to the action taken by SANE in 1960 when it expelled a leading member of its New York chapter after he invoked the Fifth Amendment at a Senate Internal Security Subcommittee hearing, and then refused to tell Norman Cousins, a cochairman of SANE, whether or not he had ever been a communist.[23]

The decision made by the New York and Washington women not "to cower" before the committee, to conduct no internal purges, to acknowledge each woman's right to act for peace and to conduct herself according to the dictates of her conscience was bold for its day. It was arrived at within the movement, by the women themselves, without consultation with the male leaders of traditional peace and civil liberties groups, many of whom disagreed with this WSP policy.[24] It was based not only on the decision to resist the demonology of the cold war, but also on a sense of sisterhood, on feelings of identification with and empathy for the women singled out for attack. Even the subpoenaed women themselves turned for counsel and support more to each other and the WSP leadership than to their families and lawyers. Working together at a feverish pace, night and day for three weeks, writing, phoning, speaking at rallies, the key women seemed to be acting as if they were a family under attack, for which all personal resources, passions, and energies had to be marshaled. But the family, this time, was "the movement" and it was the sisters, not the fathers, who were in charge.

In response to the subpoenas, a massive campaign was organized for the cancellation of the hearings and for support of WSP from national organizations and public figures. An anti-HUAC statement was composed in New York and Washington which spoke so well to the concerns and the consciousness of "the women" that it succeeded in unifying a movement in shock. The WSP statement on the HUAC inquisition was quoted widely by the press, used by local groups in ads and flyers, in letters to editors, and in speeches. "With the fate of humanity resting on a push button," the statement declared, "the quest for peace has become the highest form of patriotism."[25] In this first sentence, the women set the ground rules for their confrontation with the committee: it was going to be a contest over which group was more patriotic. But the test of "Americanism" according to the WSP rules, was the extent of one's dedication to saving America's children from nuclear extinction. Addressing the issue of communism in the movement, WSP declared: "Differences of politics, economics or social belief disappear when we recognize man's common peril . . . we do not ask an oath of loyalty to any set of beliefs. Instead we ask loyalty to the race of man. The time is long past when a small group of censors can silence the voice of peace." These words would be the WSP *leitmotif* in the Washington hearings. The women were saying, once again, as they had throughout their first year, that for them, the arms race, cold war ideology, and cold war politics, were obsolete in the nuclear age, as was the committee itself. This is the spirit Eric Bentley caught and referred to when he wrote: "In the 1960s a new generation came to life. As far as HUAC is concerned, it began with Women Strike for Peace."[26]

The WSP strategy against HUAC was innovative. An organizing memorandum from the Washington office declared, "the usual response of protest and public statements is too traditional and ineffectual. . . . Let's Turn the Tables! Let's meet the HUAC challenge in the Good New WSP way!"[27] The "new way" suggested by women all over the country was to insist that WSP had nothing to hide. Instead of refusing to testify, as radicals and civil libertarians had done in the 1950s, large numbers of WSP participants volunteered to "talk." Approximately one hundred women sent wires to Representative Francis Walter, chairman of HUAC, offering to come to Washington to tell all about their movement. The offers were refused by HUAC. But this new WSP tactic pointed up the fact that the committee was less interested in securing information than in exposing and smearing those it chose to investigate. Some WSP groups objected to the free testimony strategy on the grounds that there was a contradiction between denying the right of the committee to exist, and at the same time offering to cooperate with it. But these groups were in a minority. Carol Urner of Portland, Oregon, spoke for all those who volunteered to testify, making it clear that she would not be a "friendly witness." "I could not, of course, divulge the names of others in the movement," she wrote to Representative Walter. "I suppose such a refusal could lead one to 'contempt' and prison and things like that . . . and no

mother can accept lightly even the remote possibility of separation from the family which needs her. But mankind needs us too. . . ."[28]

Only three weeks' time elapsed between the arrival of the first subpoenas from HUAC and the date of the Washington hearings. In this short period, the WSP key women managed to develop a legal defense, a national support system for those subpoenaed, and a broad national campaign of public protest against the committee. The women's performance at the hearings was so original, so winning, and so "feminine" in the traditional sense, that it succeeded in capturing the sympathy and the support of large sections of the national media and in strengthening the movement instead of destroying it.

The hearings opened on December 11, 1962, at 10:00 A.M. in the caucus room of the Old House Office Building of the United States Congress in Washington, D.C. Fear, excitement, and exhilaration were in the air as each WSP woman in the audience looked around to see every seat in the room occupied by sisters who had come from eleven states, some from as far as California, in response to a call for their presence from the national leadership. Clyde Doyle, chairman of the subcommittee of HUAC conducting the WSP hearings, opened with a statement of their purpose. Quoting from Lenin, Stalin, Khrushchev, and Gus Hall, he explained:

Communists believe that there can be no real peace until they have conquered the world. . . . The intitiated Communist, understanding his Marxist-Leninist doctrine, knows that a Moscow call to intensify the "fight for peace" means that he should intensify his fight to destroy capitalism and its major bastion, the United States of America.[29]

The WSP women in the audience rose as one as the committee called its first witness, Blanche Posner, a retired schoolteacher who was the volunteer office manager for New York WSP. The decision to rise with the first witness, to stand *with* her, was spontaneous. It was proposed only a few minutes before Posner was called, as a note from an unknown source was circulated around the room. Posner refused to answer any questions about the structure or personnel of WSP. She resorted to the Fifth Amendment forty-four times, as the press pointed out in dozens of news stories covering the first day of the hearings. They also reported the way in which Posner took matters into her own hands, lecturing the committee members as though they were recalcitrant boys at DeWitt Clinton High School in the Bronx, where she had taught. Talking right through the interruptions and objections raised by the chairman and by committee counsel, Alfred Nittle, Posner declared:

> I don't know, sir, why I am here, but I do know why you are here, I think . . . because you don't quite understand the nature of this movement. This movement was inspired and motivated by mothers' love for children. . . . When they were putting their breakfast on the table, they saw not only the wheaties and milk, but they also saw strontium 90 and iodine 131. . . . They feared for the health and life of their children. That is the only motivation.[30]

Each time Posner resorted to the Fifth Amendment, she did it with a pointed criticism of the committee or a quip that endeared her to the women in the hearing room who needed to keep their spirits up in the face of charges that Posner had been identified by an FBI informer as a Communist party member while working in New York City as a schoolteacher. One prize exchange between Nittle and Posner led to particularly enthusiastic applause and laughter from WSP women. Nittle asked, "Did you wear a colored paper daisy to identify yourself as a member of the Women Strike for Peace?" Posner answered, "It sounds like such a far cry from communism it is impossible not to be amused. I still invoke the Fifth Amendment."[31]

Most of the witnesses were called because the committee believed it had evidence to link them with the Communist party through identification by FBI informers or the signing of party nominating petitions. But the strategy backfired with Ruth Meyers, of Roslyn, Long Island. She stepped forward, according to Mary McGrory's report in the *Washington* (D.C.) *Evening Star*, "swathed in red and brown jersey, topped by a steeple crowned red velvet hat," and "she was just as much of a headache to the committee as Posner had been."[32] There was much sparring between Meyers and the committee about the nature and structure of WSP. "Are you presently a member of a group known as Women Strike for Peace?" Nittle asked. "No, sir, Women Strike for Peace has no membership," Meyers answered. Nittle then asked, "You are familiar, I understand, with the structural organization of Women Strike for Peace as evidenced by this plan?" Meyers replied, "I am familiar to the extent of the role that I play in it. I must say that I was not particularly interested in the structure of Women Strike for Peace. I was more involved in my own community activities. . . . I felt that structure, other than the old telephone, has not much of what I was interested in." Nittle then proceeded to deliver what he believed would be the coup de grâce for Meyers. "Mrs. Meyers," he barked, "it appears from the public records that a Ruth Meyers, residing at 1751 East 10th Street, Brooklyn, New York, on July 27, 1948, signed a Communist Party nominating petition. . . . Are you the Ruth Meyers who executed that petition?" Meyers shot back, "No, sir." She then examined the petition carefully, and announced, "I never lived in Brooklyn, and this is not my signature."[33] Although the official transcript does not contain this statement, many, including the author, remember that she added, "My husband could never get me to move there." This female remark brought an explosion of laughter and applause. Meyers also invoked the Fifth Amendment. As she left the witness stand, Meyers received a one-minute ovation for humor, grace, and mistaken identity. In the corridor outside the caucus room in front of the TV cameras, she told reporters that she had never been a Communist. "But I'll never acknowledge the Committee's right to ask me that question."[34]

Another witness, Lyla Hoffman, chose to tell the committee of her past communist affiliation, asserting that she had left the Communist party, but would not cooperate in naming names or in citing the cause of her resignation. In a statement written after the hearings Hoffman explained, "I felt that it was high time to say, 'What difference does it make what anyone did or believed many years ago? That's not the problem facing humanity today.' But I had to say this in legal terms." She found it very difficult to do so, as the committee was interested only in whether she was a genuine anticommunist or a secret fellow-traveler.[35] Hoffman invoked the Fifth Amendment.

The witnesses that followed Posner, Meyers, and Hoffman, each in her own style, invoked whatever legal and rhetorical strategy her conscience and her situation dictated. They lectured the committee eloquently and courageously on the danger of nuclear holocaust, on women's rights and responsibility to work for peace. In attempting to explain the nonstructured format of WSP, several witnesses suggested that the movement was too fluid and too unpredictable to be comprehended by the masculine mind.

In their most optimistic projections, the WSP women could not have predicted the overwhelmingly favorable press and public response they would receive, and the support and growth for the movement

that would result from the HUAC episode. From the outset, the WSP leadership understood that HUAC needed the press to make its tactics of intimidation and punishment work. So, WSP played for the press—as it had done from its founding—and won! The Washington and New York leadership knew that it had two stories; both were developed to the hilt. The first was "motherhood under attack" and the second was the age-old "battle of the sexes." The contest between the sexes, according to the WSP version, involved female common sense, openness, humor, hope, and naiveté versus male rigidity, solemnity, suspicion, and dark theories of conspiracy and subversion. The WSP women, in their middle-class, feminine, political style turned the hearings into an episode of the familiar and funny "I Love Lucy," rather than the tragic and scary inquisition of Alger Hiss.

For the first time, HUAC was belittled with humor and treated to a dose of its own moral superiority. Headlines critical of the committee and supportive of WSP were featured on the front pages of prominent newspapers from coast to coast. The *Chicago Daily News* declared: "It's Ladies' Day at Capitol: Hoots, Howls—and Charm; Congressmen Meet Match." Russell Baker's column was headed "Peace March Gals Make Red Hunters Look Silly" and a *Detroit Free Press* story was entitled, "Headhunters Decapitated." A cartoon by Herblock in the *Washington (D.C.) Post* of December 13th showed three aging and baffled committee members: One is seated at the hearing table. One is holding a gavel. Another turns to him and says, "I Came in Late, Which Was It That Was Un-American—Women or Peace?"[36] A story in the *Vancouver (B.C.) Sun* of December 14 was typical of many other reports:

The dreaded House Un-American Activities Committee met its Waterloo this week. It tangled with 500 irate women. They laughed at it. Klieg lights glared, television cameras whirred, and 50 reporters scribbled notes while babies cried and cooed during the fantastic inquisition.

Bill Galt, author of the *Vancouver Sun* story, gave a blow-by-blow description of WSP civil disobedience in the Old House Office Building:

> When the first woman headed to the witness table, the crowd rose silently to its feet. The irritated Chairman Clyde Doyle of California outlawed standing. They applauded the next witness and Doyle outlawed clapping. Then they took to running out to kiss the witness. . . . Finally, each woman as she was called was met and handed a huge bouquet. By then Doyle was a beaten man. By the third day the crowd was giving standing ovations to the heroines with impunity.[37]

The hearings were a perfect foil for the humor of Russell Baker, syndicated columnist of the *New York Times*.

> If the House Un-American Activities Committee knew its Greek as well as it knows its Lenin, it would have left the women peace strikers alone. . . . Instead with typical male arrogance it has subpoenaed 15 of the ladies, . . . spent several days trying to show them that women's place is not on the peace march route, and has come out of it covered with foolishness.

Baker, a liberal columnist, understood the committee's purpose and also the "drama of the absurd" that WSP had staged to defeat that purpose. "The Committee's aim was simple enough," Baker pointed out,

> their sleuths studying an organization known as Women Strike for Peace had learned that some of the strikers seemed to have past associations with the Communist Party or its front groups. Presumably if these were exposed, right thinking housewives would give up peace agitation and go back to the kitchen.

The committee had reckoned without female logic, according to Baker:

> How could WSP be infiltrated, witness after witness demanded, when it was not

an organization at all? . . . Try as he might, Alfred Nittle, the committee counsel, never managed to break through against this defense.[38]

The *Detroit Free Press* commented: "The House Committee can get away with attacking college students in California, government flunkies who are forced to shrive their souls to save their jobs, and assorted misguided do-gooders. But when it decides to smear an estimated half-million angry women, it's in deep trouble. We wish them nothing but the worst."[39]

Mary McGrory in the *Washington* (D.C.) *Evening Star* played up the difference between the male, HUAC perceptions and those of the female, WSP:

> "Why can't a woman be like a man?" sings Henry Higgins in *My Fair Lady*. That is precisely the question the House Committee on Un-American Activities is asking itself today. . . . The committee is trying to find out if the ladies' group is subversive. All it found out was that their conduct in the caucus room certainly was.

"The leader of the group kept protesting that she was not really the leader at all," McGrory observed. Pointing out that few men would deny being leaders, or admit they didn't know what was going on, Mary McGrory reported that:

> Dagmar Wilson of Washington, when asked if she exercised control over the New York chapter merely giggled and said, "Nobody controls anybody in the Women Strike for Peace. We're all leaders."

Characterizing Wilson's appearance as the "coup de grâce in the battle of the sexes," McGrory noted that the ladies had been using the Congress as a babysitter, while their young crawled in the aisles and noisily sucked their bottles during the whole proceedings. With a mixture of awe and wonder McGrory described how the ladies themselves, as wayward as their babies, hissed, gasped, clapped entirely at will. When several of their number took the Fifth Amendment, to McGrory's surprise, the women applauded, and

> when Mrs. Wilson, trim and beguiling in red wool, stepped up to take the stand, a mother with a baby on one hip worked her way through the crowd and handed her a bouquet of purple and white flowers, exactly as if she were the principal speaker at a ladies' luncheon.

McGrory caught the flavor of Wilson's testimony which was directed not only at the committee, but also at her sisters in the audience. She reported that when Mr. Nittle asked whether the New York chapter had played a dominant role in the group, Wilson replied, "Other cities would be mortified if you said that."

> "Was it," Mr. Nittle wanted to know, "Mrs. Wilson's idea to send delegates to a Moscow peace conference?" "No," said Mrs. Wilson regretfully, "I wish I'd thought of that." When Mr. Nittle pursued the question of whose idea it was to send observers to Moscow, Dagmar Wilson replied, "This is something I find very difficult to explain to the masculine mind."

And, in a sense, it was. "Mr. Nittle pressed forward to the clutch question," one, according to McGrory, "that would bring a man to his knees with patriotic protest: 'I would like to ask you whether you would knowingly permit or encourage a Communist Party member to occupy a leadership position in Women Strike for Peace.' " Wilson replied:

> Well, my dear sir, I have absolutely no way of controlling, do not desire to control, who wishes to join in the demonstrations and the efforts that women strikers have made for peace. In fact, I would also like to go even further. I would like to say that unless everybody in the whole world joins us in this fight, then God help us.

"Would you knowingly permit or welcome Nazis or Fascists?" asked Mr. Nittle. Mrs. Wilson replied, "if we could only get them on our side."[40] Mr. Doyle then thanked Wilson for appearing and being so helpful. "I want to emphasize," he said,

> that the Committee recognizes that there are many, many, many women, in fact a great great majority of women, in this peace movement who are absolutely patriotic and absolutely adverse to everything the Communist Party stands for. We recognize that you are one of them. We compliment you on your leadership and on your helpfulness to us this morning.

Dagmar Wilson tried to get the last word: "I do hope you live to thank us when we have achieved our goal." But Doyle replied, "Well, we will."[41]

The way in which WSP, a movement of middle-class, middle-aged, white women mobilized to meet the attack by a feared congressional committee was energetic and bold, politically nontraditional, pragmatic rather than ideological, moralistic and maternal. It was entirely consistent with the already established program, tactics, rhetoric, and image of this one-year-old movement, labeled by the University of Wisconsin's student newspaper as "the bourgeois mother's underground."[42]

Were these courageous women who bowed to traditional notions of female behavior merely using the politics of motherhood for political advantage? Or had they internalized the feminine mystique? It is useful to examine the backgrounds of the WSP women in seeking to understand their use of their own female culture to legitimate a radical critique of national, foreign, and military policies. The WSP key women were mostly in their late thirties to mid forties at the inception of the movement in 1961. Most of them, then, had come into adulthood in the late 1930s and early 1940s. They were students or workers in the years of political ferment preceding World War II. Many had married just before, during, or right after the war. The majority of these women participated in the postwar baby boom, the rise of middle-class affluence, and the privatism and consumerism connected with suburban life. It was during the 1950s that they made their adjustment to family, parenting, community, and consensus politics.

As a movement born out of, and responding to, the consciousness of the 1950s, WSP projected a middle-class and politically moderate image. In an article celebrating WSP's first anniversary, Eleanor Garst, one of WSP's early image makers, proclaimed:

> Breaking all the rules and behaving with incredible disorder and naivete, "the women" continue to attract recruits until the movement now numbers hundreds of thousands. . . . Furthermore, many of the women behaving in these unaccustomed ways are no odd-ball types, but pillars of the community long courted by civic organizations. Others—perhaps the most numerous—are apolitical housewives who have never before lifted a finger to work for peace or any other social concern.[43]

Although the movement projected an image of political innocence and inexperience, WSP was actually initiated by five women who were already active members of SANE. The women—Dagmar Wilson, Jeanne Bagby, Folly Fodor, Eleanor Garst, and Margaret Russell—had gravitated toward each other because of their mutual distaste for SANE's internal red hunt, which they felt contributed to an escalation, rather than an end to cold war hysteria. Perhaps, more important, they share a frustration over the slow pace with which the highly structured SANE reacted to international crises. They also resented the reluctance of SANE's male leadership to deal with "mother's issues" such as the contamination of milk by radioactive fallout from nuclear tests.

Dagmar Wilson was forty-five years old, and a political novice when she was moved to call a few friends to her home in the late summer of 1961 to discuss what could be done about the nuclear

crisis. At this meeting WSP was born. Wilson was at that time a successful free-lance children's book illustrator, the mother of three daughters and wife of Christopher Wilson, a commercial attaché at the British embassy. Wilson had been born in New York City, had moved to Germany as a very young child, and had spent most of her adult years in England where her father, Cesar Searchinger, was a well-known broadcast correspondent for the Columbia Broadcasting System and the National Broadcasting Company.

Wilson came to the United States prior to World War II, held a variety of professional jobs as an artist and teacher, and finally became a free-lance illustrator. She worked in a studio at home, so as to be available to her children and to insure a smooth-running household. Despite the fact that Wilson was so successful an artist that one of her children's books had become a best-seller, she nevertheless identified herself as a housewife.

> My idea in emphasizing the housewife rather than the professional was that I thought the housewife was a downgraded person, and that we, as housewives, had as much right to an opinion and that we deserved as much consideration as anyone else, and I wanted to emphasize . . . this was an important role and that it was time we were heard.[44]

A gifted artist, an intelligent person of good sense, good grace, and charm, Wilson possessed the charisma of those who accurately represent the feelings and the perceptions of their constituency, but excel them in passion and the capacity for creative articulation. Having been most of her life a "nonjoiner" Wilson was, as the *New York Times Magazine* reported in a feature story in May 1962, a "political neophyte."[45] Because Wilson had not been involved in U.S. radical politics of the 1940s, she was free from the self-conscious timidity that plagued those who had been involved in leftist organizations and who feared either exposure or a repetition of the persecution and the political isolation they had experienced in the 1950s.

Among the women who met at Wilson's house to plan the emergency peace action was Eleanor Garst, whose direct, friendly, practical, yet passionate political prose played a powerful role in energizing and unifying the WSP women in their first year. It was she who drafted the call for November 1st, and later helped create most of the anti-HUAC rhetoric.

Garst came from a conservative Baptist background. She recalls that everything in her upbringing told her that the only thing a woman should do was to marry, have babies, care for her husband and babies, and "never mind your own needs." Despite this, Garst was the only one of the inner circle of Washington founders, who in 1961 was a completely self-supporting professional woman, living on her own. She was the mother of two grown children. At the time of the founding of WSP, Garst was employed as a community organizer for the Adams Morgan Demonstration project, administered by American University, working to maintain integrated neighborhoods in Washington, D.C. She had become a pacifist in her early childhood after reading about war in novels and poems. Her husband, a merchant seaman, refused to be drafted prior to World War II, a decision that he and Eleanor made together without consulting any other pacifists because they knew none. They spent their honeymoon composing an eighty-page brief against peacetime conscription.

After the war, Garst became a professional political worker, writer, and peace activist on the West Coast before coming to Washington. She had been a founder of the Los Angeles SANE and editor of its newsletter. A forceful and easy writer, Garst had already been published in the *Saturday Evening Post, Reporter, Ladies' Home Journal,* and other national publications when she was asked to draft the letter that initiated the successful November 1st strike.

Folly Fodor, a leading figure in the founding group, had come to Washington in 1960 to follow her husband's job with the U.S. Labor Department. She joined SANE on her arrival in Washington and had been elected to the board. Thirty-seven years old at the time of the founding of WSP, Fodor was the mother of two. Folly Fodor was not new to politics. She was the daughter of parents who had been involved in liberal-to-communist political causes and had herself been a leader in political organizations since her youth. As an undergraduate at Antioch College, in Yellow Springs, Ohio, Folly Fodor had become active in the Young People's Socialist League, eventually becoming "head of it," as she put it. In retrospect she believes she spent too much time fighting the communists on campus, and "never did a goddamn thing." Fodor had been chairperson of the Young Democrats of California and as a Democrat she had clandestinely supported Henry Wallace in 1948. During the mid 1950s, after the birth of her second child, Fodor organized a mother's group to oppose nuclear testing. So Fodor, like Garst, was not new to radical causes, to peace activity, or to women's groups. She was ready and eager for a separate women's peace action in the fall of 1961.

Two other women who founded WSP, Jeanne Bagby and Margaret Russell, were also already active in the peace cause at the time of the founding of WSP. Bagby was a frequent contributor to *Liberation* magazine. Together the founders possessed research, writing, organizing, and speaking talents that were not unusual for women active in a variety of community, civic, and church groups in the 1950s. All the founders shared a conviction that the men in the peace movement and the government had failed them and that women had to take things into their own hands.

But what of the thousands of women who joined the founders? What was their social and political background and their motivation to take to the streets in peace protest? Elise Boulding, a sociologist and long-time pacifist activist, who became involved in the WSP communications network right after November 1st, decided to try to find out. During the six months in which Boulding edited the *Women's Peace Movement Bulletin,* an information exchange for WSP groups, she kept asking herself whether the WSP women were really political neophytes as they claimed, or "old pros with a well defined idea of some kind of world social order?" Using the resources of the Institute for Conflict Resolution in Ann Arbor, Michigan, where she was working, and with the help of WSP colleagues in Ann Arbor, she composed a questionnaire that was sent to every eighth name on the mailing lists of forty-five local groups. By the fall of 1962, shortly before the summonses from HUAC, 279 questionnaires had been returned from thirty-seven localities in twenty-two states. According to Boulding, the respondents represented a cross-section of the movement—not only leaders.[46]

Boulding found that the overwhelming majority of the WSP women were well-educated mothers, and that 61 percent were not employed outside the home. But she concluded that the women who went out on strike for peace on November 1, 1961, and stayed on in the movement in the following months, appeared to be a more complex and sophisticated group than the "buggy-pushing housewife" image the movement conveyed. She characterized the early WSP participants as "largely intellectual and civic-minded people, mostly of the middle class"—very much like the Washington founders themselves.[47]

Most of the women strikers had been liberals, radicals, or pacifists in the 1940s. Although few had been political leaders of any kind, they shared the 1940s belief that society could be restructured on humanistic lines through the direct political action of ordinary people. Dorothy Dinnerstein described the psychological process of depoliticization and privatization that many politically active people experienced in the 1950s. Many radicals, according to Dinnerstein, spent the 1950s in a state of moral shock, induced by the twin catastrophes of Stalinism and McCarthyism. They lost their capacity for social connectedness and, "in this condition they withdrew from history—more or less totally, more or less gradually, more or less blindly into intensely personalistic, inward-turning, magically thing-and-place-oriented life." According to Dinnerstein they withdrew their passion from the larger human scene and sought to invest in something less nightmarish, more coherent and mentally manageable.[48] What the WSP women withdrew into, with society's blessing and encouragement, was the domestic sphere, the management of family, children, home, and local community. Many, when their school-aged children no longer required fulltime care, were propelled into the PTAs, League of Women Voters, Democratic party politics, church, synagogue, or cultural activities by their earlier social, political, and humanitarian concerns.

It took the acceleration of nuclear testing by both the capitalist United States and the socialist USSR to convince the WSP women of something they already suspected: that there was no political force in the world acting morally and humanely in the interest of the preservation of life. It took a series of international crises, the example of the civil rights sit-ins, and the Aldermarston antibomb marches in Britain to give the WSP women both the sense of urgency, and of possibility, that are the necessary ingredients for a political movement. Once out in the political arena, the women found that their moral outrage, their real fear for their children's future, and their determination never to be pushed back into the non-political domestic sphere, made them unafraid of a mere congressional committee before which others had quaked.

The women who were drawn to WSP certainly took the job of motherhood seriously. They had willingly chosen to sacrifice careers and personal projects to raise society's children because they had been convinced by the post-Freudians that the making of human beings is a far more important vocation than anything else; and that the making of human beings was a sex-specific vocation requiring the full-time duties of a resident mother.[49] But where the WSP women differed from the majority of their middle-class cohorts was that they saw motherhood not only as a private function, but also as a contribution to society in general and to the future. When they built on their rights and responsibilities to act politically in defense of the world's children, they were invoking not only their maternal consciousness, but their social conscience as well. They were women of heart, emotion, ingenuity, wit, and guile, but they were also serious political thinkers and activists. They chose to rely on their femininity, as most women did in the fifties and early sixties, to create whatever space and power they could carve out for themselves.

The Birmingham (England) Feminist History Group in an article, "Feminism as Femininity in the Nineteen Fifties?" suggests that feminism of the fifties seemed to be more concerned wtih integrating and foregrounding feminity than in transforming it in a fundamental way.[50] The conduct of WSP before the House Committee on Un-American Activities follows this pattern. The WSP women were not concerned with transforming the ideology of femininity, but rather with using it to enhance women's political power. But in so doing they were transforming that ideology and foreshadowing the feminism that emerged later in the decade.

Very much in the way that the concept of Republican motherhood was used in the late eighteenth century to justify the demand for women's education, and the cult of true womanhood was built upon to project women into the ante-bellum reform movements, WSP used the feminine mystique of the 1950s to legitimize women's right to radical dissent from foreign and military policies. In the repressive political climate of the early 1960s, WSP relied heavily upon sex role stereotypes to legitimize its opposition to cold war policies. But by emphasizing the fact that the men in power could no longer be counted on for protection in the nuclear age, WSP implied that the traditional sex-gender contract no longer worked. And by stressing global issues and international sisterhood, rather than domestic responsibilities, WSP challenged the privatization and isolation of women which was a key element of the feminine mystique. Most important, by performing in relation to HUAC with more courage, candor, and wit than most men had done in a decade of inquisitions, WSP raised women's sense of political power and self-esteem. One of the negative effects for WSP of relying so heavily on the politics of motherhood to project its political message was that it alienated a new generation of younger women who admired the movement's stand for peace, but saw its acquiescence to sex roles stereotypes as regressive. In the late 1960s these younger women insisted upon working for peace not as wives, mothers, and sisters, but as autonomous persons.

Sara Evans in *Personal Politics* points out that those few young women in the civil rights movement who first raised feminist issues within the movement had to step *outside* the sex role assumptions on which they were raised in order to articulate a radical critique of women's position.[51] For WSP it was obviously different. The founders and leaders of WSP certainly did not step outside the traditional sex role assumptions; rather, they stood squarely upon them, with all their contradictions. By using these contradictions to present a radical critique of man's world, WSP began the transformation of woman's consciousness and woman's role.

NOTES

I wish to thank my sisters in WSP, particularly Barbara Bick, Eleanor Garst, Ruth Meyers, Ethel Taylor, and Dagmar Wilson for their helpful comments regarding an earlier version of this paper delivered at the "Fifth Berkshire Conference on the History of Women," Vassar College, 16 June 1981. I am indebted also to Alice Kessler-Harris, Joan Kelly, Gerda Lerner, Ruth Milkman, Melanie Gustafson, and Warren Susman for their valuable insights, advice, and criticism. Research for this article was funded in part by a Woodrow Wilson Women's Studies Dissertation Fellowship, 1980.

1. U.S. Congress, House, Committee on Un-American Activities, *Communist Activities in the Peace Movement (Women Strike for Peace and Certain Other Groups), Hearings before the Committee on Un-American Activities on H.R. 9944.* 87th Cong., 2d. sess., 1962, p. 2057.

2. Historians and political opponents of HUAC agree that the WSP hearing marked the beginning of the end of the committee's power. Eric Bentley called the WSP-HUAC confrontation, "the fall of HUAC's Bastille." See Eric Bentley, *Thirty Years of Treason* (New York: Viking Press, 1971), p. 951. Frank Wilkerson of the National Committee to abolish HUAC wrote to the Washington office after the hearing, "magnificent women. . . . You have dealt HUAC its greatest setback." Frank Wilkerson to Eleanor Garst, et al., 14 December 1962. WSP Document Collection in custody of the author. Peace historian Charles De Benedetti said of the HUAC investigation of WSP, "WSP activists challenged for the first time the House Un-American Activities Committee's practice of identifying citizen peace seeking with Communist subversion. . . . The open disdain of the WSP for HUAC did not end the Congress's preference for treating private peace actions as subversive. But it did help break the petrified anti-Communism of Cold War American politics and gave heart to those reformers who conceived peace as more than military preparedness."

See Charles De Benedetti, *The Peace Reform in American History* (Bloomington, Ind.: Indiana University Press, 1980), pp. 167–78.

3. In May 1960, Senator Thomas Dodd, vice-chairman of the Senate International Security Subcommittee, threatened SANE with congressional investigation if it did not take steps to rid itself of communist infiltrators. SANE responded by voting to exclude all those with communist sympathies. Whole chapters that did not go along with internal red hunts were expelled, as was Henry Abrams, a leading New York activist who refused to tell the Senate committee whether or not he was a communist. Turn Toward Peace also rejected communists or former communists. See Milton S. Katz, "Peace, Politics, and Protest: SANE and the American Peace Movement, 1957–1972" (Ph.D. dissertation, Saint Louis University, 1973), pp. 109–130. Homer Jack, executive director of national SANE, criticized WSP's "welcome everybody" stand. He claimed that it would call into question the political sagacity of groups like his own. See Homer A. Jack, "The Will of the WISP versus the Humiliation of HUAC," transcript of a talk on Radio Station WBAI, New York, 28 December 1962 (WSP Document Collection). After January 15, 1962, many WSP groups and the Washington office referred to themselves as Women's International Strike for Peace (WISP).

4. The way in which WSP's militant role in the peace movement has been either ignored or trivialized by journalists, peace movement leaders, and historians is illustrated by the following examples. Mary McGrory in her syndicated column described a WSP visit to the White House in the following manner: "This week's Cinderella story has to do with Women Strike for Peace, which after 15 years of drudgery in the skullery of anti-war activity has been invited to the White House" (*New York Post*, 8 March 1977, p. 27). Dace Dellinger, one of the most prominent of the male leaders of the 1960s peace movement devoted about 10 lines to

WSP in a 317-page book on the history of the civil rights and peace movements from 1965 to 1973. He described WSP as a group fearful of engaging in civil disobedience in the 1967 "Mobilization March on the Pentagon." Nowhere in the book did Dellinger mention that nine months earlier 2,500 WSP women broke through police barricades to bang their shoes on the Pentagon doors which had been shut in their faces. See Dave Dellinger, *More Power Than We Know* (Garden City, N.Y.: Anchor Press, 1975). Lawrence Wittner, in a critical survey of American politics from 1945 to 1974 that focuses on movements of dissent, devoted only four words to WSP. He included the movement in a list of early critics of radioactive fallout. See Lawrence Wittner, *Cold War America from Hiroshima to Watergate* (New York: Praeger Publishers, 1974), p. 232.

5. For a symposium on the relationship of feminism, women's culture, and women's politics, see Ellen DuBois, Mari Jo Buhle, Temma Kaplan, Gerda Lerner, and Carroll Smith-Rosenberg, "Politics and Culture in Women's History: A Symposium," *Feminist Studies* 6 (Spring 1980):26–64. Also see Temma Kaplan, "Female Consciousness and Collective Action: The Case of Barcelona, 1910–1918," *Signs* 7 (Spring 1982):54–66. Kaplan points out that women's defense of traditional rights, while fundamentally conservative, can have revolutionary consequences.

6. The figure of fifty thousand claimed by the Washington founders after November 1st was accepted in most press accounts and became part of the WSP legend. It was based on reports from women in sixty cities and from newspapers across the country. Often the women's reports and that of the newspapers differed, but even in using the highest figures available I can substantiate only a count of approximately twelve thousand women who struck on November 1st. Nevertheless, this was still the largest women's peace demonstration on record.

7. "End the Arms Race—Not the Human Race" was the central slogan of the November 1st "strike": "Help Wanted" flyer, 25 October 1961, Washington, D.C. See WSP Document Collection. (Mimeographed.)

8. "Dear—, Last night I sat with a few friends in a comfortable living room talking of atomic war." Draft of call to strike by Eleanor Garst, Washington, D.C., 22 September 1961. WSP Document Collection. (Mimeographed.)

9. *Newsweek*, 13 November 1961, p. 21.

10. Eleanor Garst, "Women: Middle-Class Masses," *Fellowship* 28 (1 November 1962), pp. 10–12.

11. Minutes of the WILPF National Executive Committee stated: "Each branch taking direct action should clear with the National Action Projects Committee. The committee should have, and send out to branches, a list of approved action and a list of the organizations with which we formally cooperate." Women's International League for Peace and Freedom, Minutes of the National Executive Committee meeting of 28–29 September 1961. Swarthmore College Peace Collection, DG 43, Series A–2, Box 18, p. 5.

12. "Transcript of the President's News Conference on World and Domestic Affairs," *New York Times*, 16 January 1962, p. 18.

13. *Science* 167 (13 March 1970), p. 1476.

14. A. E. Wessel, *The American Peace Movement: A Study of Its Themes and Political Potential* (Santa Monica: Rand Corporation, 1962), p. 3.

15. *New York Journal American*, 4 April 1962, p. 10.

16. *San Francisco Examiner*, 21 May 1962, p. 10.

17. The FBI files on WSP are located in the offices of the Washington, D.C. law firm of Gaffney, Anspach, Shember, Klimasi, and Marx. These contain hundreds of documents from security officers in major cities to the director of the FBI and from the directors to the security officers. For instance, as early as 23 October 1961, one week before the November 1st strike, the Cleveland office of the FBI already identified one of the WSP planning groups as communist. (FBI Document 100–39566–8). When WSP sent a delegation to lobby the Geneva Disarmament Conference, 2–7 April 1962, the FBI involved Swiss federal police and covert Central Intelligence Agency agents in the American embassy to spy on the women (Legat Bern to Director, FBI 4 April 1962, FBI Document 100–39574–187). An internal security memorandum on 24 July 1962 stated that an informant who had furnished reliable information in the past, made available a list of women "who will be guests of the Soviet Women's Committee in the USSR, 12–26 July 1962." The list which had been circulated to the press by WSP included the names of twelve women from various parts of the country (FBI Document 100–39566–222).

18. Those subpoenaed were (in order of appearance) Blanche Posner, Ruth Meyers, Lyla Hoffman, Elsie Neidenberg, Sylvia Contente, Rose Clinton, Iris Freed, Anna Mac-

kenzie, Elizabeth Moss, Ceil Gross, Jean Brancato, Miriam Chesman, Norma Spector, and Dagmar Wilson. Spector never testified; she was excused due to illness. *Hearings before Committee on Un–American Activities,* p. iii.

19. Lillian Hellman, *Scoundrel Time* (Boston: Little, Brown & Co., 1976), p. 99.

20. Los Angeles WISP, Statement I, Ann Arbor Conference, June 9–10, 1962 (WSP Document Collection); *Women Strike for Peace Newsletter,* New York, New Jersey, Connecticut, Summer 1962, pp. 1–2.

21. "WSP National Policy Statement," *Women Strike for Peace Newsletter,* New York, New Jersey, Connecticut, Summer 1962, pp. 1–2.

22. "Key women" was the name used by WSP for those women who were part of the national and local communications network. They were the ones who were called upon to initiate actions or who called upon others to do so.

23. Katz, "Peace, Politics, and Protest," pp. 122–26.

24. Jack, "The Will of the WISP versus the Humiliation of HUAC."

25. The anti-HUAC statement by WSP was composed by the New York and Washington leadership in their usual collaborative fashion, with no pride or claim of authorship, so it is difficult to know which group wrote what part. It was distributed through official WSP channels via the national office in Washington.

26. Bentley, *Thirty Years of Treason,* p. 951.

27. Women Strike for Peace, Washington, D.C. to "Dear WISP's," 6 December 1962 (WSP Document Collection).

28. Carol Urner, to Representative Francis Walter reprinted in the *Women's Peace Movement Bulletin* 1 (20 December 1962):5.

29. *Hearings before Committee on Un–American Activities,* pp. 2064–2065.

30. Ibid., p. 2074.

31. Ibid., p. 2085.

32. Mary McGrory, "Prober Finds 'Peacemakers' More Than a Match," *Washington* (D.C.) *Evening Star,* 12 December 1962, p. A–1.

33. *Hearings before Committee on Un–American Activities,* pp. 2095, 2101.

34. McGrory, "Prober Finds 'Peacemakers' More Than a Match," p. A–1.

35. Lyla Hoffman, undated typewritten statement (WSP Document Collection).

36. Thirty-seven favorable news stories, columns and editorials were reprinted in a hastily prepared WSP booklet, published less than two weeks after the hearings. Facsimile copies of Russell Baker's column, "Peace March Gals Make Red Hunters Look Silly," appeared on page 2; the *Detroit Free Press* story declaring "Headhunters Decapitated," appeared on page 4; "It's Ladies' Day at Capitol" from the *Chicago Daily News* appeared on page 9; and the Herblock cartoon appeared on page 5. *So Many Great Things Have Been Said* (Washington, D.C.: Women Strike for Peace, 1963).

37. *Vancouver* (B.C.) *Sun,* 14 December 1962, p. 2.

38. "The Ladies Turn Peace Quiz into Greek Comedy," *Detroit Free Press,* 16 December 1962, p. 1.

39. *Detroit Free Press,* 13 December 1962, p. 8–A.

40. Mary McGrory, "Nobody Controls Anybody," *Washington* (D.C.) *Evening Star,* 14 December 1962, pp. A–1, A–9.

41. *Hearings before Committee on Un–American Activities,* p. 2201.

42. *Madison* (Wis.) *Daily Cardinal,* 14 December 1962, p. 2.

43. Garst, "Women: Middle-Class Masses," pp. 10–11.

44. Interview with Dagmar Wilson, Leesburg, Virginia, September 1977.

45. *New York Times Magazine,* 6 May 1962, p. 32.

46. On a WSP activity measure, 38 percent rated themselves as "very active," 10 percent as "active," and 42 percent rated themselves as "not active," or only "slightly active." The profile of the majority of the WSP participants that emerged was indeed that of middle-class, well-educated housewives. Sixty-five percent of the women had either a B.A. or a higher degree, at a time when only 6 percent of the female population over age 25 had a B.A. or more. Seventy-one percent of the WSP women were suburb or city dwellers, with the highest concentrations in the East Central states, the West Coast, and the Midwest, and with low participation in the Mountain states and the South. The WSPers were concentrated in the twenty-five-to-forty-four age bracket. Only 5 percent of the group were "never marrieds." Of the married women 43 percent had from one to four children under six; 49 percent had from one to four or more children over eighteen. Sixty-one percent of the women involved in WSP were not, at the time of the questionnaire, employed outside the home.

Nearly 70 percent of the husbands of the WSP women who responded to the survey were professionals.

Thirty-eight percent of the women who responded claimed to belong to no other organizations, or at least did not record the names of any organizations in response to questions concerning other community activities. Forty percent of the women were active in a combination of civic, race relations, civil liberties, peace, and electoral political activity. Only 11 percent were members of professional organizations. Boulding concluded that many of the WSP women were nonjoiners. As for their goals in joining WSP activities, the Boulding questionnaire revealed that 55 percent gave abolition of war or multilateral disarmament as their primary goals, and 22 percent gave nonviolent solution of all conflict, political and social. The remainder chose as their goals a variety of proposals for world government or limited international controls such as a test ban treaty. As to their reasons for participating in WSP activities: 28 percent of the women said they had joined the movement over concern about fallout, testing, and civil defense, another 4 percent because of the Berlin Wall crisis; but 41 percent listed no specific event, just an increasing sense of urgency about the total world situation and a feeling of the need to make a declaration of personal responsibility. See Elise Boulding, *Who Are These Women?* (Ann Arbor, Mich.: Institute for Conflict Resolution, 1962).

47. Ibid., p. 15.

48. Dorothy Dinnerstein, *The Mermaid and the Minotaur: Sexual Arrangements and Human Malaise* (New York: Harper Colophon Books, 1976), pp. 259–62.

49. Ashley Montagu, "The Triumph and Tragedy of the American Woman," *Saturday Review*, 27 September 1958, p. 14; Dr. Benjamin Spock, *The Common Sense Book of Baby and Child Care* (New York: Duell, Sloan & Pearce, 1945), p. 484.

50. "Feminism as Femininity in the Nineteen Fifties?" Birmingham (England) Feminist History Group, *Feminist Review* no. 3 (1979), pp. 48–65.

51. Sara Evans, *Personal Politics: The Roots of Women's Liberation in the Civil Rights Movement and the New Left* (New York: Alfred A. Knopf, 1979), p. 23.

BETTY FRIEDAN
The Feminine Mystique

If the lives of working-class women were still dominated by the struggle for economic survival, the same cannot be said of middle-class women who enjoyed unprecedented prosperity, especially in the years after World War II. Ensconced in their well-equipped homes in the suburbs, they flourished in an atmosphere of domesticity and affluence that characterized the new consumer culture. Such, at least, was the message of the women's magazines with their advertisements of the latest household appliances and advice columns on marriage and child care. Although there were rumblings of discontent in the 1950s, it was 1963 when Betty Friedan, a suburban housewife herself, exposed the triviality and frustra-

Excerpted from "The Problem That Has No Name," chap. 1 of *The Feminine Mystique* by Betty Friedan (New York: W. W. Norton, 1963). Copyright © 1974, 1963 by Betty Friedan. Reprinted by permission of W. W. Norton & Company, Inc.

tions of a resurgent domesticity. Friedan's indictment, a brief portion of which appears here, was the subject of much controversy. Women who found the gratification associated with child care and housework vastly overemphasized applauded Friedan's forceful articulation of their own dissatisfactions. Other women objected vehemently, insisting that, as wives and mothers and perhaps community activists, they enjoyed a life style that not only benefited both their families and communities but provided them personally with freedom, pleasure, and a sense of self-worth. How are we to explain such different responses? Is the housewife described by Friedan foreshadowed in Ruth Schwartz Cowan's article on housework? In what sense is the role of housewife a product of the fusing of biology, economics, and ideology?

The problem lay buried, unspoken, for many years in the minds of American women. It was a strange stirring, a sense of dissatisfaction, a yearning that women suffered in the middle of the twentieth century in the United States. Each suburban wife struggled with it alone. As she made the beds, shopped for groceries, matched slipcover material, ate peanut butter sandwiches with her children, chauffeured Cub Scouts and Brownies, lay beside her husband at night—she was afraid to ask even of herself the silent question—"Is this all?"

For over fifteen years there was no word of this yearning in the millions of words written about women, for women, in all the columns, books and articles by experts telling women their role was to seek fulfillment as wives and mothers. Over and over women heard in voices of tradition and of Freudian sophistication that they could desire no greater destiny than to glory in their own femininity. Experts told them how to catch a man and keep him, how to breastfeed children and handle their toilet training, how to cope with sibling rivalry and adolescent rebellion; how to buy a dishwasher, bake bread, cook gourmet snails, and build a swimming pool with their own hands; how to dress, look, and act more feminine and make marriage more exciting; how to keep their husbands from dying young

and their sons from growing into delinquents. They were taught to pity the neurotic, unfeminine, unhappy women who wanted to be poets or physicists or presidents. They learned that truly feminine women do not want careers, higher education, political rights—the independence and the opportunities that the old-fashioned feminists fought for. Some women, in their forties and fifties, still remembered painfully giving up those dreams, but most of the younger women no longer even thought about them. A thousand expert voices applauded their femininity, their adjustment, their new maturity. All they had to do was devote their lives from earliest girlhood to finding a husband and bearing children.

By the end of the nineteen-fifties, the average marriage age of women in America dropped to 20, and was still dropping, into the teens. Fourteen million girls were engaged by 17. The proportion of women attending college in comparison with men dropped from 47 per cent in 1920 to 35 per cent in 1958. A century earlier, women had fought for higher education; now girls went to college to get a husband. By the mid-fifties, 60 per cent dropped out of college to marry, or because they were afraid too much education would be a marriage bar. Colleges built dormitories for "married students," but the students were almost always the husbands. A new degree was instituted for the wives—"Ph.T." (Putting Husband Through).

Then American girls began getting married in high school. And the women's magazines, deploring the unhappy statistics about these young marriages, urged that courses on marriage, and marriage counselors, be installed in the high schools. Girls started going steady at twelve and thirteen, in junior high. Manufacturers put out brassieres with false bosoms of foam rubber for little girls of ten. And an advertisement for a child's dress, size 3–6x, in the New York Times in the fall of 1960, said: "She Too Can Join the Man-Trap Set."

By the end of the fifties, the United States birthrate was overtaking India's. The birth-control movement, renamed Planned Parenthood, was asked to find a method whereby women who had been advised that a third or fourth baby would be born dead or defective might have it anyhow. Statisticians were especially astounded at the fantastic increase in the number of babies among college women. Where once they had two children, now they had four, five, six. Women who had once wanted careers were now making careers out of having babies. So rejoiced Life magazine in a 1956 paean to the movement of American women back to the home.

In a New York hospital, a woman had a nervous breakdown when she found she could not breastfeed her baby. In other hospitals, women dying of cancer refused a drug which research had proved might save their lives: its side effects were said to be unfeminine. "If I have only one life, let me live it as a blonde," a larger-than-life-sized picture of a pretty, vacuous woman proclaimed from newspaper, magazine, and drugstore ads. And across America, three out of every ten women dyed their hair blonde. They ate a chalk called Metrecal, instead of food, to shrink to the size of the thin young models.

Department-store buyers reported that American women, since 1939, had become three and four sizes smaller. "Women are out to fit the clothes, instead of vice-versa," one buyer said.

Interior decorators were designing kitchens with mosaic murals and original paintings, for kitchens were once again the center of women's lives. Home sewing became a million-dollar industry. Many women no longer left their homes, except to shop, chauffeur their children, or attend a social engagement with their husbands. Girls were growing up in America without ever having jobs outside the home. In the late fifties, a sociological phenomenon was suddenly remarked: a third of American women now worked, but most were no longer young and very few were pursuing careers. They were married women who held part-time jobs, selling or secretarial, to put their husbands through school, their sons through college, or to help pay the mortgage. Or they were widows supporting families. Fewer and fewer women were entering professional work. The shortages in the nursing, social work, and teaching professions caused crises in almost every American city. Concerned over the Soviet Union's lead in the space race, scientists noted that America's greatest source of unused brainpower was women. But girls would not study physics: it was "unfeminine." A girl refused a science fellowship at Johns Hopkins to take a job in a real-estate office. All she wanted, she said, was what every other American girl wanted—to get married, have four children and live in a nice house in a nice suburb.

The suburban housewife—she was the dream image of the young American women and the envy, it was said, of women all over the world. The American housewife—freed by science and labor-saving appliances from the drudgery, the dangers of childbirth and the illnesses of her grandmother. She was healthy, beautiful, educated, concerned only about her husband, her children, her home. She had found true feminine fulfillment. As a housewife and mother, she was respected as a full and equal partner to man in his world. She was free to choose automobiles, clothes, appliances, supermarkets; she had everything that women ever dreamed of.

In the fifteen years after World War II, this mystique of feminine fulfillment became the cherished and self-perpetuating core of contemporary American culture. Millions of women lived their lives in the image of those pretty pictures of the American suburban housewife, kissing their husbands goodbye in front of the picture window, depositing their station-wagonsful of children at school, and smiling as they ran the new electric waxer over the spotless kitchen floor. They baked their own bread, sewed their own and their children's clothes, kept their new washing machines and dryers running all day. They changed the sheets on the beds twice a week instead of once, took the rug-hooking class in adult education, and pitied their poor frustrated mothers, who had dreamed of having a career. Their only dream was to be perfect wives and mothers; their highest ambition to have five children and a beautiful house, their only fight to get and keep their husbands. They had no thought for the unfeminine problems of the world outside the home; they wanted the men to make the major decisions. They gloried in their role as women, and wrote proudly on the census blank: "Occupation: housewife."

For over fifteen years, the words written for women, and the words women used when they talked to each other, while their husbands sat on the other side of the room and talked shop or politics or septic tanks, were about problems with their children, or how to keep their husbands happy, or improve their children's school, or cook chicken or make slipcovers. Nobody argued whether women were inferior or superior to men; they were simply different. Words like "emancipation" and "career" sounded strange and embarrassing; no one had used them for years. When a Frenchwoman named Simone de Beauvoir wrote a book called *The Second Sex*, an American critic commented that she obviously "didn't know what life was all about," and besides, she was talking about French women. The "woman problem" in America no longer existed.

If a woman had a problem in the 1950's and 1960's she knew that something must be wrong with her marriage, or with herself. Other women were satisfied with their lives, she thought. What kind of a woman was she if she did not feel this mysterious fulfillment waxing the kitchen floor? She was so ashamed to admit her dissatisfaction that she never knew how many other women shared it. If she tried to tell her husband, he didn't understand what she was talking about. She did not really understand it herself. For over fifteen years women in America found it harder to talk about this problem than about sex. Even the psychoanalysts had no name for it. When a woman went to a psychiatrist for help, as many women did, she would say, "I'm so ashamed," or "I must be hopelessly neurotic." "I don't know what's wrong with women today," a suburban psychiatrist said uneasily. "I only know something is wrong because most of my patients happen to be women. And their problem isn't sexual." Most women with this problem did not go to see a psychoanalyst, however. "There's nothing wrong really," they kept telling themselves. "There isn't any problem."

JANE DE HART-MATHEWS
The New Feminism and the Dynamics of Social Change

The resurgence of feminism in the late 1960s drew upon many sources. Some have been encountered in previous material in this part: the civil rights movement that enlisted Anne Moody and her white counterparts, the recognition of the inferior economic status of wage-earning women, and the attack on middle-class domesticity that Betty Friedan articulated with such force. There were other sources as well, among them issues left unresolved by an earlier generation of feminists. The following essay explores the origins of the new feminism, the growth and development of the movement, the ideas it generated and the opposition it incurred. Note in this essay how the four categories appearing throughout this book interact. Observe how *biology* (greater reproductive control and longevity), *economics* (increasing numbers of wage-earning women and their marginality within the labor force), and *politics* (participation in various political efforts to obtain change) contributed in part to the development of a new *ideology* (feminism). Note, too, how the categories continued to interact as a new feminist ideology generated political goals designed to achieve sexual equality—goals that involved, among other things, greater reproductive freedom, economic parity, and a new ideological formulation of what it means for women and men to become equal and autonomous persons in contemporary society.

Present-day feminists are separated by more than a century from their predecessors at Seneca Falls, while more than a half century separates them from their early twentieth-century counterparts. Yet in what sense is the opposition to the enlargement of women's sphere and the creation of a public role for women that was encountered by these earlier generations of feminists paralleled in the opposition that came to focus on ratification of the Equal Rights Amendment during the 1970s and early 1980s? What is at issue?

Fifty years after gaining the right to vote, women who had been suffragists and women young enough to be their great-granddaughters embarked on a new quest. Their motive: to change not only laws and institutions, but values, patterns of behavior, personal relationships, and ultimately themselves. Their goal: equality. This new feminist movement was vigorous, diffuse, and highly controversial. In order to understand its origins and goals, its opponents, and, most important, its potential for changing society, it is necessary to examine the long-term economic and social changes that created an environment within which the movement could emerge. It is important also to appreciate the ferment of the 1960s that provided feminism with its ideological core, vitality, and impetus. To explore such origins is also to explore the sense in which contemporary feminists confronted issues an earlier generation had left unresolved.

UNFULFILLED EXPECTATIONS

By winning the vote in 1920, many women believed that the decisive battle in the long struggle for sexual equality had been won. The atmosphere was electric with a sense of achievement and expectation generated by the euphoria of the moment. The fact that enfranchisement had come on the heels of other reforms identified with women seemed evidence of their growing influence. Congress had passed legislation to protect women in industry, outlaw child labor, and enact prohibition—measures important to those who believed that women and children were the primary victims of exploitative employment and alcohol-related abuse. Champions of women's rights also celebrated gains in education and employment. Since 1900 female enrollment had shot up 100 percent in public colleges and universities and nearly 500 percent in private ones. As ambitious graduates gained access to advanced training, the proportion of women in the professions climbed by 1920 to an unprecedented 11.9 percent.[1] During World War I women in record numbers had moved into skilled jobs and administrative positions formerly held by men.

These very real achievements had been won by a movement that was successful only so long as large numbers of women remained committed to each other and to common goals. This collective commitment had secured the vote and corrected some of the wrongs associated with women's exclusion from full participation in the public sphere of ballot box and marketplace. Few suffragists and reformers, however, were prepared to confront the barriers to equality in the domestic sphere of family. Most women as well as men still accepted as one of the few unchanging facts of life the conviction that woman's primary duty was to be "the helpmeet, the housewife, and the mother."[2] Feminists who hoped to provide additional, complementary, or alternative possibilities gradually found themselves a diminishing minority. Since their understanding of the many kinds of change yet required to ensure full emancipation was shared by so few women, enfranchisement failed to create a bloc of female voters prepared to use the ballot to remove additional barriers to equality. Like their male counterparts, they found issues of class, race, and ethnicity more compelling than the need to improve women's status. The collective power of the "woman's vote" through which suffragists had hoped to achieve further gains never fully materialized in the decade ahead.

Part of the reason for this failure lay in the physical and emotional fatigue of the suffragists themselves. The fight for the ballot, compounded by the stress of World War I, had taken its toll. As one suffragist explained: "After we [got] the vote, the crusade was over. It was peacetime and we went back to a hundred different causes and tasks that we'd been putting off all those years. We just demobilized."[3] For those who still had the energy, there were new causes. Pacifism and disarmament acquired an added urgency not only for pre-war pacifists such as Crystal Eastman and Jane Addams but also for more recent enthusiasts such as suffragist leader Carrie Chapman Catt, who established the

National Conference on the Cause and Cure of War. Other women, whose feminist sympathies and political activism had been tenuous even in the yeasty reformist milieu of the progressive era, gradually yielded to the political conservatism of the 1920s. They could not be effectively mobilized for protest even when the Supreme Court in 1922 and 1923 invalidated two of the major legislative gains of the prewar women's movement—minimum wages for women and the abolition of child labor. Younger women who might have become new recruits found old visions of female equality less exciting than the personal gratification associated with the relaxed social and sexual mores and affluence of the new consumer culture.

As these and other disappointments mounted, divisions developed within the movement itself. The organizations most responsible for winning the vote, the National American Woman Suffrage Association (NAWSA) and its militant offshoot, the Congressional Union, had regrouped under new names. The Congressional Union, under Alice Paul's leadership, became the National Woman's Party. It enrolled between four and five thousand members, many of them professional women, whose first priority was improvement of women's status. Many NAWSA members moved in a different direction, finding their way into the new League of Women Voters created in 1919 to educate women for citizenship. The league represented the persistence of a broad progressive impulse along with the commitment to the advancement of women. Its bipartisan concern for "good government" and legislation protecting women and children made it the more broadly reformist of the two organizations. Disagreement over tactics during the suffrage campaign continued in the debate over the next tactic in the struggle for equality. The Woman's Party advocated a constitutional amendment to guarantee equality before the law.

The league and other organizations—such as the General Federation of Women's Clubs, the Women's Trade Union League, the Young Women's Christian Association, and the American Association of Universty Women—preferred to deal with the many discriminatory aspects of the law through a state-by-state effort to change specific statutes.

The league's preference derived in part from fears that an equal rights amendment would jeopardize legislation regulating hours, wages, and working conditions for thousands of unskilled, nonunionized female workers. Their health and safety, insisted the league, required the special protection of government. The courts, having denied this legislation to men on the ground that such laws interfered with their "freedom of contract," permitted it to women workers only because of their traditional role as mothers. Women workers, opponents of the amendment argued, could ill afford to surrender their concrete gains for the abstract principle of equality.

By the end of the 1920s the league and its allies could point to a few transitory gains in the area of maternal and infant health care and to the easing of legal strictures affecting marriage, divorce, property holding, and contracts. But they failed to shake the unswerving conviction of Woman's Party loyalists that the key to equality lay in amending the Constitution. As a result of these disagreements, intense and acrimonious debate persisted throughout years of fragmentation and frustration. Feminism as an organized mass movement virtually disappeared. To be sure, a loose network of individuals and organizations continued to work to improve the status of women; however, only the Woman's Party, unwavering in its single-minded advocacy of an equal rights amendment, persistently wore the feminist label as a badge of honor. Modest gains in the postsuffrage decades could not obscure the fact that the fundamental circumstances of most women's lives remained little changed.

For working-class women, especially women of color, life was still one of constant toil—on farms, in factories and mills, or in other women's homes. The factory job that had promised escape from poverty or the drudgery of farm work or the servility of domestic service often carried with it new problems. To be sure, increases in productivity during the 1920s allowed a handful of companies to initiate a five-day workweek, the eight-hour day, or a two-week annual vacation with pay. But low wages, long hours, frequent layoffs, monotony, noise, dirt, and danger still characterized many industrial jobs, especially in the nonunionized South. Moreover, wage work brought no escape from domestic duties.

For married women with children, the burden was especially heavy, as Grace Elliott's experience graphically demonstrates. An ambitious young textile worker, she worked as a weaver at the East Marion Manufacturing Company in Marion, North Carolina, during the 1920s. Earning $16 a week, she paid $5 for a cook and $2 for laundry. Because the $9 remaining seemed "such a slow path to home and furniture," she decided to do her own housework, getting up at 4:00 A.M., preparing breakfast and dinner, milking the cow, getting the children's clothes ready for them to wear to school before rushing to the mill for the 5:40 shift. Breaking at noon, she walked home for a cold lunch and then rushed back to the mill where she worked until 6:00 P.M. Returning home, she cooked supper, sometimes sewing after the children had gone to bed. Her schedule was "very hard" but, she insisted, "I had to keep the children in school." For all of her determination, the physical strain was too much. Like so many of her fellow workers, Grace Elliott was exhausted and ill at the end of four years. Struggling with wage labor, housework, illness, pregnancy, and poverty,

such women seemed as powerless to control the conditions in which they lived and worked as did their voteless predecessors.[4]

Middle-class women fared better than their working-class counterparts. More advantaged economically, they had easier access to birth control devices and to the educational and professional opportunities that would equip them to function in the world outside the home. Yet if progress is measured by achievements in business, professional, and political life, middle-class women made few gains in the post-suffrage decades. The proportion of women attending colleges and universities actually declined between 1920 and 1960, as did the proportion of women on college faculties. In 1920, one out of every seven doctoral degrees was awarded to a woman; in 1956, only one in ten. By 1960 only 4 percent of the lawyers and judges in this nation were women, only 6 percent of the medical doctors, and less than 1 percent of the architects. Percentages, of course, can be misleading in that they indicate a share rather than absolute numbers. For example, although the percentage of women awarded the Ph.D. in 1920 was 15 percent as opposed to 10.5 percent in 1960, indicating a decline of one-third, the actual number of women receiving the doctorate had increased from 90 in 1920 to 1,090 in 1960. In certain areas of business, notably real estate, women had increased in both numbers and percentage.[5] In the final analysis, however, there was no escaping the fact that women were still excluded from the higher echelons of business, government, and the professions. The number of women elected to Congress throughout this entire forty-year period totaled a mere three in the Senate and forty-four in the House.[6] The number of female cabinet members was a scant two. A seat on the stock exchange was as difficult to come by as a seat on the president's cabinet. Boards of directors of major corporations were also a male preserve. Veteran champions of equality of the sexes had to admit a certain element of truth in the phrase that is the despair of radicals and the hope of conservatives: *plus ça change, plus c'est la même chose.*

UNRESOLVED ISSUES

The discrepancy between feminists' expectations and the actual accomplishments of women in the postsuffrage decades is a measure of how effectively internal and external barriers interacted to bind women to the traditional pattern of domesticity. That so many women rejected the new possibilities of public life for the old expectations of a private one when the former *seemingly* offered more challenging and potentially rewarding options is testimony both to the power of cultural constraints that undermined real freedom of choice and to the reality of external barriers that denied women equality in the workplace. Although women themselves may have thought they chose "freely," few were actually in a position to do so. Most had grown up in an atmosphere of profound conditioning that from infancy through adulthood assigned individuals of each sex social roles defined essentially by gender.

The cumulative impact of this socialization shaped young women's sense of themselves as females and the options open to them by the time they reached college. There, as in high school, the curriculum reinforced established patterns. Students taking home economics courses learned about the tasks that awaited them as consumer, homemaker, and mother. By the 1940s and 1950s many sociology courses portrayed the "normal" family as one based on a sexual division of labor and "sex-determined" behavioral characteristics. If the campus served as an environment within which to pursue a husband rather than an independent intellectual life or preprofessional training, that acknowledged a basic reality. Getting

a man, especially one with bright prospects, was itself a vocational objective, one preferable to others.

The reason was that in a sexually segregated labor force positions filled predominantly by women carried little pay and prestige—to the financial detriment of the few males involved as well as the many females. Fields such as business, engineering, architecture, law, medicine, and university teaching were only slightly open to women. Female applicants to professional schools were usually confronted with admission quotas limiting the number of women, often to 5 percent. University faculties frequently assumed that female students would marry, get pregnant, and drop out, or, if they did graduate, never practice the profession for which they had been trained. Those young women who persisted, ultimately receiving the Ph.D. or the M.D., could expect continued discrimination in hiring, pay, or promotion once their active work life began.

They also had to face the problem of combining work and family in a society governed by traditional assumptions relating to both. Many business and professional women in the early years of the twentieth century solved the problem by staying single. Successive generations, less attracted to that option, had to find husbands willing to have a spouse pursue an active work life outside the home in an era in which a working wife was thought to reflect poorly on a man's ability to provide for his family. Even if husbands consented, those holding management positions in major corporations or in the military or diplomatic corps were expected to relocate frequently if they wished to be upwardly mobile. Wives of such men often found it difficult to establish their own vocational roots. Those who were able to do so had to contend with still other problems. Nagging fears that successful careers were inconsistent with marital happiness—at least for women—found reinforcement in Hollywood movies, women's magazines, and scholarly studies. The conventional assumption that an achieving woman would lose "her chance for the kind of love she wants" was criticized by the anthropologist Margaret Mead in 1935 to no avail.[7] Twelve years later the sociologist Ferdinand Lundberg and the psychiatrist Marynia Farnham were adamant in their insistence that "the 'successful woman' is only occasionally successful as a woman."[8] In this context, women whose personal and professional lives provided refutation of such assertions were simply too few to make a difference. For those younger women who did persist, the self-doubt and confusion that are a part of role conflict sometimes remained long after the conflict had been resolved.

Parenting complicated the situation even further, creating practical problems and compounding internal anxieties. To be a lawyer and a father in America was to be "normal"; to be a lawyer and a mother was to be "deviant" because motherhood was assumed to be a full-time occupation, especially in middle-class circles. How to cope with the physical and psychological demands of family while simultaneously meeting the performance criteria and competitive pressures of work challenged even the most dedicated and resourceful woman. Pregnancy and child care leaves, tax benefits for child care expenses, public day care centers with strong programs to encourage physical and intellectual growth: these measures had become well established in advanced European nations such as Sweden. But they were never fully incorporated into the structure of American society during the first three-quarters of this century.

Families, too, were ill prepared to accommodate the special needs of women who worked outside the home. With kin networks often scattered about in distant cities and towns, it was difficult to find a grandparent or aunt who could take care of children during an emergency. Husbands, even when supportive in principle, often proved reluctant in practice to assume additional responsibilities at home. The assumption that family responsibilities would not interfere with work efficiency was built into the very structure of their jobs, as was the expectation that the corporate manager, for example, would have at his disposal a wife who could devote significant time and energy to the needs of *his* career. Given the extent to which the lives of both spouses were swallowed up by the institution employing him, wives with careers of their own were understandably a rarity. Yet energetic women somehow managed. They devised suitable child care arrangements, revised household priorities, and balanced work demands and personal needs. That in the process they often acquired a reputation for being "superwomen" was itself indication of the inequities inherent in a sex role system that allowed men the option of combining career and family while denying it to women.

For the vast majority of middle-class women the problems of combining work and family were simply too great. Moreover, their social position was such that most of the working women they knew—clerks, beauticians, domestics— were lower-middle and working-class people. *Not* working for pay outside the home indicated the high status so important to millions of Americans. As internal constraints and external constraints reinforced each other, most middle-class women concluded that they would have a better chance for security and status as wives and mothers than as workers. Economic dependency seemed a small price to pay for the pleasures of domesticity and the rewards of community activism so integral to suburban life. Paying this price was not a conscious decision so much as the unconscious transaction of investing in roles patterned after those of their mothers. The little girls who donned women's clothes on rainy afternoons while "playing house" were also donning attitudes and habits. In doing so, they indicated their "agreement" to contracts yet to be made with little boys who were learning how to be aggressive, independent, and successful. The sentimental myths surrounding middle-class family life created an almost sacred place within which children could take an idyllic apprenticeship in adulthood. This inviolability protected the family from widespread criticism. Champions of women's rights, concentrating on legal and political disabilities that deprived women of a full public life, never effectively challenged the pervasive cultural constraints binding women to dependency. To have raised such issues in the suffrage crusade would have been to play directly into the hands of opponents who were already predicting that giving women the vote would be the undoing of the family.[9]

There were, to be sure, achieving women whose lives were not defined only by domesticity—Helen Keller, Amelia Earhart, Mary McLeod Bethune, and Eleanor Roosevelt. But this was a culture that, while celebrating the "exceptional woman," endlessly romanticized domesticity, extolling the joys of the housewife-mother who lovingly tended her garden and a bumper crop of children. Even the heroines hawked by Hollywood fell into two categories: sex objects and wives. The former wore voluptuous if vacuous—the sexually alluring blonde whom "gentlemen preferred," as Marilyn Monroe so sensationally demonstrated during what one film critic dubbed the "mammary madness" of the 1950s.[10] The latter, invariably played by Doris Day or Debbie Reynolds, were bland, childish, but amusing in a peppy, well-scrubbed, but unmistakably feminine way that projected them from girl-next-door to suburban wife. The message of the culture was clear. To be a woman in this society was to be "feminine"; to be a feminist was to be "neurotic."[11]

THE GROWING GAP BETWEEN IDEOLOGY AND REALITY

The apparent retreat from feminism into domesticity after 1920 hid a more complex reality. Impersonal economic, scientific, and demographic forces were subtly undermining old patterns and assumptions. Although in themselves these new developments did not produce a resurgence of feminism, they did add impetus to the growing gap between conventional attitudes and changing conditions. This in turn lent credibility to a feminist critique of society.

One of the economic realities of modern America has been that many women were never fully in their "place"—the home. They have long been part of a paid labor force. Their numbers increased significantly throughout the twentieth century. Even during the Depression the proportion of women in the work force remained constant. This occurred despite the fact that many employers, including local school boards and the federal civil service, sought to deny employment to married women, assuming, often mistakenly, that their husband's earnings were adequate to support the family and that, as working women, they took jobs away from other men with families to support. But if hard times forced some women back into the home, others were forced out. Many mothers desperately needed even meager wages to keep the family afloat at a time when one out of every five children in this country was not getting enough nourishing food to eat.

As the nation shifted from fighting economic depression to waging global war, women responded by the millions to patriotic appeals to get a war job so as to bring their men home sooner. Between 1940 and 1945 the proportion of women in the work force rose from 25 percent to 37 percent. Money as well as patriotism was involved. The women who flocked to factories were beneficiaries of New Deal legislation governing wages and hours for both sexes. They also benefited from the Congress of Industrial Organizations' (CIO) successful unionization effort during the 1930s and became the first generation of female industrial employees to receive good wages. Not surprisingly many were reluctant to return home when "Rosie, the Riveter," that symbol of women war workers, was told to put down her riveting machine at the return of peace. Forced out of well-paying "male" jobs, many women returned to low-paying "female" jobs in restaurants, laundries, shops, and offices.[12] Moreover, their wartime experience seemingly had little impact on public attitudes. When asked whether married women whose husbands made enough to support them should be allowed to hold jobs if they wanted to, the majority of Americans responded with a resounding no.[13] Yet as white-collar and clerical jobs expanded rapidly in the postwar years, so did the number of working women.[14]

By 1960 some 40 percent of American women were employed in full- or part-time jobs. Moreover, those who worked outside the home were no longer predominantly young, single, or poor. Nearly half were mothers of school-age children; many of them were middle class. When asked why they worked most responded that they regarded their jobs as an extension of family responsibilities as well as a matter of economic need. A second salary made possible a family vacation, a large home better suited to the children's needs, savings for college tuition, or simply a color television set for the family room. During the period when all America seemed about to become one great shopping mall, the definition of economic need was clearly changing. But even if one allows for a rising level of expectations consistent with the consumer culture of the 1950s, the fact remains that, while rhetoric still conformed to the old domestic ideology, the presence of women in the work force did not.[15]

The gap between the old ideology of home and family and the new reality of office and work widened still further as medical advances resulted in improved birth control devices and longer life expectancy. Referring to the extent to which women's lives had been determined by their reproductive role, Sigmund Freud had observed that "anatomy is destiny." But as women gained the ability to control "destiny"—to decide whether to have children, when and how many—they were no longer victims of biological processes. Use of condoms and diaphragms, widespread especially among middle-class couples, made birth control a reality even before the introduction in 1960 of an oral contraceptive—"the pill." As medical science also devised new weapons against disease, the years during which one could expect to function as a healthy, active adult increased accordingly. For example, the average woman in 1900, marrying at twenty-two years of age and having her last child at the age of thirty-two, could expect to live to fifty-one, which was about the time her youngest reached maturity. By 1960, however, the average woman, marrying at the age of twenty, could expect to live until she was sixty-five. If she completed childbearing by the age of thirty, staying home while her children were small, she faced by the age of thirty-five nearly half of her life ahead of her in a house empty of children—empty at first during school hours; empty untimately for many years after the last child had moved out.

The implications were enormous. That they were not immediately grasped is not surprising for a generation seeking in the private world of home and family the security unavailable in a public world wracked successively by economic depression, world war, and the threat of global annihilation. Throughout the 1950s, family experts emphasized the importance of early marriage and motherhood if the "atomic age" family were to be a bulwark of morality and stability. Specialists in marketing techniques continued to fuse the role of homemaker and mother with that of consumer, stressing that true feminine fulfillment lay in maternity, domesticity, and purchase of the "right" products. Yet by glorifying women as homemakers and mothers at precisely the same time important changes were occurring that served to undermine those roles, advertisers, like the family experts, were unwittingly helping to sharpen the discrepancy between the domestic myth and the new reality of many women's lives. The gap between reality (change) and ideology (popular notions) was not yet great enough in the early 1960s for large numbers of women to be shocked into recognition of it. But it was there.

The gap could be ignored initially because it was at first a "bad fit." It was an oval peg in a round hole, a size six foot in a five-and-one-half shoe—a small discomfort with which people thought they could live. Social scientists did report slight deviations in the domestic image: daughters tended to regard working mothers as positive role models; husbands were more likely to accord them a greater voice in financial decisions; and families provided more help with household chores.[16] But new developments were incorporated into old patterns even as women felt the pinch and stress. They still had difficulty seeing themselves as permanent members of the work force. Many seemed reluctant to join unions or press for equal pay, perhaps because they saw themselves as supplementary breadwinners or as housewives whom misfortune had trapped in monotonous, low-paying jobs.[17] That so many women continued to see themselves

and their work primarily as serving family needs is hardly surprising in a culture in which homemaking was described as "the most important and difficult profession any woman can have."[18] But the bad fit was there: the unfairness of unequal pay for the same work, the low value placed on jobs women performed, the double burden of housework and wage work. Those women who sensed the growing discrepancy between the traditional private world of domesticity and new realities in the public world of work needed a new way of looking at things that would allow them to examine afresh the condition of their lives, moving from grudging acceptance to confrontation and change. They needed, in short, a feminist consciousness.

THE CREATION OF A FEMINIST CONSCIOUSNESS

Revolutions are seldom started by the powerless. The feminist revolution of the 1960s was no exception. It was begun largely by educated, middle-class women whose diverse experiences had sharpened their sensitivity to the fundamental inequality between the sexes at a time when America had been thrust into the throes of self-examination by a movement for racial equality. Some were young veterans of the civil rights movement and the New Left, steeped in a commitment to equality and the techniques of protest. Others were young professionals increasingly aware of their secondary status or older women with distinguished careers as professionals or as activists. Still others were women whose outwardly conformist lives belied an intense awareness of the malaise of domesticity and the untenably narrow boundaries of their prescribed roles. To explore how they came self-consciously to appraise women's condition as one demanding collective action is to explore the process of radicalization that helped to create a new feminist movement.

In its early state that movement consisted of two different groups—women's rights advocates and women's liberationists. Although the differences between the two groups began to blur as the movement matured, initial distinctions were sharp. Women's rights advocates were likely to have been older, to have had professional training or work experience, to have been more inclined to form or join organized feminist groups. Reform oriented, these organizations used traditional pressure group tactics to achieve changes in laws and public policy that would guarantee women equal rights. Emphasis on "rights" meant extending to women in life outside the home the same "rights" men had, granting them the same options, privileges, and responsibilities that men enjoyed. There was little suggestion initially of personal or cultural transformation.

Women's liberationists were younger women, less highly educated, whose ideology and political style, shaped in the dissent and violence of the 1960s, led them to look at women's predicament differently. Instead of relying upon traditional organizational structure and lobbying techniques, they developed a new style of politics. Instead of limiting their goals to changes in public policy, they embraced a transformation in private, domestic life as well. They sought liberation from ways of thinking and behaving that they believed stunted or distorted women's growth and kept them subordinate to men. Through the extension of their own personal liberation they hoped to remake the male world, changing it as they had changed themselves. For women's liberationists as for women's rights advocates, however, the first step toward becoming feminists demanded a clear statement of women's position in society, one that called attention to the gap between the egalitarian ideal and the actual position of women in American culture. There also

had to be a call to action from women themselves, *for* women, *with* women, *through* women. Redefining themselves, they had to make being a woman a polical fact; and, as they did so, they had to live with the radical implications of what could only be called a rebirth.

THE MAKING OF FEMINISTS: WOMEN'S RIGHTS ADVOCATES

For some women, the process of radicalization began with the appointment of a Presidential Commission on the Status of Women in 1961. Presidents, Democrat and Republican, customarily discharged their political debt to female members of the electorate, especially to those who had loyally served the party, by appointing a few token women, usually party stalwarts, to highly visible posts. John Kennedy was no exception. He was, however, convinced by Esther Petersen that the vast majority of women would be better served if he also appointed a commission charged with investigating obstacles to the full participation of women in society. Assistant secretary of labor and head of the Women's Bureau, Petersen believed that the report of such a commission could sensitize the public to barriers to equality just as her own experience as a labor organizer had sensitized her to the particular problems confronting women workers. Citizens thus informed could then be mobilized on behalf of governmental efforts at reform.[19] Accordingly, the commisssion was appointed with Eleanor Roosevelt serving as chair until her death a year later. Its report, *American Women* (1963), was conservative in tone, acknowledging the importance of women's traditional roles within the home and the progress they had made in a "free democratic society." It also provided extensive documentation of discriminatory practices in government, education, and employment, along with substantial recommendations for change.[20] Governors, replicating Kennedy's move, appointed state commissions on the status of women. In these commissisons hundreds of men and women encountered further evidence of the economic, social, and legal disabilities that encumbered the nation's "second sex." For some, the statistics were old news; for others, they were a revelation.

Although there were variations from state to state, the pattern documented by the North Carolina Commission soon became increasingly familiar to a small but growing number of women throughout the nation. According to that commission's report, women workers, who made up over one-third of the state's labor force, suffered economically from job segregation and pay inequities. Of the 600,000 women employed outside the home in 1960, most (68 percent) were concentrated in blue-collar jobs or in traditionally low-paying "female" professions such as teaching and nursing. Whatever their occupational level, women earned significantly less than their male counterparts with comparable skills, experience, and responsibilities. They also had fewer opportunities for advancement. (Female mill operatives, for example, earned nearly 30 percent less than male operatives.)

Educational experience, seemingly more equitable, actually foreshadowed economic inequities. At the graduate level, women constituted only a tiny fraction of those enrolled in schools training future members of high-paying professions such as medicine. At the undergraduate level, female students clustered in the humanities, avoiding the math and science courses necessary for providing greater career choice. Whatever their educational level, most women lacked access to diversified vocational training, enlightened career guidance, and the kind of role models provided by women, especially minority women, holding important nontraditional jobs. Worse still, they lacked expert,

readily available child care. (Licensed day care facilities had only one space available for every seventeen preschool children of working mothers.)

Legally women in North Carolina, as elsewhere, were handicapped not only by hundreds of discriminatory federal statutes but also by state laws denying them equal treatment under the law. For example, married women still lacked complete control over their own property; state law required the written assent of the husband before a wife could convey her real property to someone else. Nor did women function as political equals. In North Carolina, as in other states, women were less likely to vote than men and far less likely to hold elective office or significant policymaking jobs. Especially disturbing to the commission was the failure of most women to understand "the direct connection between their own active and informed participation in politics . . . and the solution to many of their most pressing problems."[21]

Some women, however, could make that connection. Aroused by growing evidence of "the enormity of our problem," members of state commissions gathered in Washington in 1966 for the Third National Conference of the Commissions on the Status of Women. Individuals who were coming to know and rely on one another as they pooled their growing knowledge of widespread inequities, they were a network in the making. They were also women who wanted something done. This time they encountered a situation that transformed at least some of those present into activists in a new movement for women's equality. The catalyst proved to be a struggle involving Representative Martha Griffiths and the Equal Employment Opportunity Commission (EEOC), the federal agency in charge of implementing the Civil Rights Act of 1964.

Despite the fact that the law proscribed discrimination on the basis of sex as well as race, the commission refused to take seriously the problem of sexual discrimination. The first executive director of EEOC, knowing that "sex" had been injected into the bill by opponents seeking to block its passage, regarded the sex provision as a "fluke" best ignored. Representative Griffiths from Michigan thought otherwise. While the bill was still in Congress she encouraged a small group of women in the House to become part of an unlikely alliance with legislative opponents of a federal civil rights act in order to keep the sex provision in the bill. Liberals objected, fearing that so encumbering a bill would prevent passage of much-needed legislation on behalf of racial equality. But despite such objections—and the ridicule of many of her male colleagues—Griffiths persisted. Once the bill passed she was determined to see the new law enforced in its entirety. When EEOC failed to do so, she lambasted the agency for its inaction in a biting speech delivered on the House floor only days before the Conference of the Commissions on the Status of Women met.

Griffiths's concern was shared by a group of women working within EEOC. They argued that the agency could be made to take gender-related discrimination more seriously if women had a civil rights organization as adept at applying pressure on their behalf as was the National Association for the Advancement of Colored People (NAACP) on behalf of blacks. Initially the idea was rejected. Conference participants most upset by EEOC's inaction decided instead to propose a resolution urging the agency to treat sexual discrimination with the same seriousness it applied to racial discrimination. When the resolution was ruled inappropriate by conference leaders, they were forced to reconsider. After a whispered conversation over lunch they concluded the time for discussion of the status of women was over. It was time for action. Before the day was out twenty-eight women had paid five dollars each to join the National Organization for Women (NOW), including author Betty Friedan who happened to be in Washington at the time of the conference.[22]

Friedan's presence in Washington was auspicious; her involvement in NOW, virtually inevitable. The author of a brilliant polemic published in 1963, she not only labeled the resurgent domestic ideology of recent decades but exposed the groups perpetuating it. Editors of women's magazines, advertising experts, Freudian psychologists, social scientists, and educators—all, according to Friedan, contributed to a romanticization of domesticity she termed "the feminine mystique." The result, she charged, was the infantilization of intelligent women and the transformation of the suburban home into a "comfortable concentration camp."[23] Harsh words, they rang true to those who found the creativity of homemaking and the joys of motherhood vastly exaggerated. Sales of the book ultimately zoomed past the million mark.

By articulating heretofore inarticulated grievances, The Feminine Mystique had advanced a process initiated by more dispassionate investigations of women's status and the discriminatory practices which made that status inferior. That process was the collective expression of discontent. It is not surprising that those who best expressed that discontent initially were overwhelmingly white, educated, and middle or upper middle class. College women who regarded themselves the equals of male classmates by virtue of intellect and training were, as Jo Freeman points out, more likely to develop expectations they saw realized by their male peers but not, in most cases, by themselves. The frustrations were even greater for women with professional training. The very fact that many had sought advanced training in fields not traditionally "female" meant that they were less likely to find in traditional sex roles the identity and self-esteem such roles provided other women. Moreover, when measuring themselves against fellow professionals who happened to be men, the greater rewards enjoyed by their male counterparts seemed especially galling. Privileged though they were, such women *felt* more deprived in many cases than did those women who were in reality less privileged. By 1966 this sense of deprivation had been sufficiently articulated and shared and the networks of like-minded women sufficiently developed so that collective discontent could be translated into collective action. The formation of NOW signaled the birth of a new feminist movement.[24]

The three hundred men and women who gathered in October for the organizational meeting of NOW were in the main professionals, some of them veterans of commissions on the status of women. Adopting bylaws and a statement of purpose, they elected officers, naming Friedan president. Her conviction that intelligent women needed purposeful, generative work of their own was reflected in NOW's statement of purpose, which attacked "the traditional assumption that a woman has to choose between marriage and motherhood on the one hand and serious participation in industry or the professions on the other." Determined that women should be allowed to develop their full potential as human beings, the organization's goal was to bring them into "full participation in the mainstream of American society NOW, exercising all the privileges and responsibilities thereof in truly equal partnership with men." To that end NOW developed a Bill of Rights, adopted at its 1967 meeting, that exhorted Congress to pass an equal rights amendment to the Constitution, called on EEOC to enforce antidiscrimination legislation, and urged federal and state legislators to guarantee equal and unsegregated education. To ensure women control over their reproductive lives, these new feminists called for removal of penal codes denying

women contraceptive information and devices as well as safe, legal abortions. To ease the double burden of working mothers, they urged legislation that would ensure maternity leaves without jeopardizing job security or seniority, permit tax deductions for child care expenses, and create public, inexpensive day care centers. To improve the lot of poor women, they urged reform of the welfare system and equality with respect to benefits, including job-training programs.[25]

Not content simply to call for change, NOW leaders worked to make it happen. Using persuasion, pressure, and even litigation, they, with other newly formed women's rights groups such as the Women's Equity Action League (WEAL), launched a massive attack on sex discrimination. By the end of the 1960s NOW members had filed legal suits against newspapers listing jobs under the headings "Help Wanted: Male" and "Help Wanted: Female," successfully arguing that such headings discouraged women from applying for jobs they were perfectly capable of doing. Building on efforts begun in the Kennedy administration such as the passage of the Equal Pay Act, they pressured the federal government to intensify its commitment to equal opportunity. They urged congressmen and labor leaders to persuade the Department of Labor to include women in its guidelines designed to encourage the hiring and promotion of blacks in firms holding contracts with the federal government. They persuaded the Federal Communications Commission to open up new opportunities for women in broadcasting. Tackling the campus as well as the marketplace, WEAL filed suit against more than three hundred colleges and universities, ultimately securing millions of dollars in salary raises for women faculty members who had been victims of discrimination. To ensure that women receive the same pay men received for doing the same work, these new feminists lobbied for passage of a new Equal Employment Opportunity Act that would enable EEOC to fight discrimination more effectively.

NOW also scrutinized the discriminatory practices of financial institutions, persuading them to issue credit to single women and to married women in their own—not their husband's—name. WEAL, in turn, filed charges against banks and other lending institutions that refused to grant mortgages to single women, or in the case of married couples, refused to take into account the wife's earnings in evaluating the couple's eligibility for a mortgage. Colleges and universities that discriminated against female students in their sports programs came under fire, as did fellowship programs that failed to give adequate consideration to female applicants.

While NOW and WEAL attacked barriers in industry and education, the National Women's Political Caucus (NWPC) focused on government and politics. Formed in 1971, the caucus was initiated by Friedan, New York congresswomen Bella Abzug and Shirley Chisholm—both outspoken champions of women's rights— and Gloria Steinem, soon to become founding editor of the new mass-circulation feminist magazine *Ms.* Especially concerned about the small numbers of women in government, the caucus concentrated on getting women elected and appointed to public office while also rallying support for issues such as the Equal Rights Amendment (see document 12 in Essential Documents). Meanwhile women in the professions, aware of their small numbers and inferior status, began to organize as well. Physicians, lawyers, and university professors fought for equal opportunity in the meetings of such overwhelmingly male groups as the American Medical Association, the American Association of University Professors, and the American Historical Association.[26]

Collectively such protests served notice that more women were becoming feminists. The particular combination of events that transformed women into feminists varied with the individual. A southern legislator, describing the process that brought home the reality of her own second-class citizenship, wrote:

> As a State Senator, I succeeded in getting Mississippi women the right to sit on juries (1968); the opposition's arguments were appalling. When women began hiring me in order to get credit, I became upset at the discrimination I saw. After I was divorced in 1970, I was initially denied a home loan. The effect was one of the worst traumas I've suffered. Denial of a home loan to one who was both a professional and a member of the legislature brought things to a head.[27]

Although the number of women who understood what it meant to be the "second sex" were still only a tiny minority, they were nonetheless a minority whose energy, talents, and experience enabled them to work for changes necessary to ensure equal rights.

THE MAKING OF FEMINISTS: WOMEN'S LIBERATION

The process of radicalization that transformed some individuals into women's rights advocates occurred simultaneously—but in different fashion and with somewhat different results—among a younger generation of women. Many of them veterans of either the civil rights movement or of the New Left, these were the activists who would become identified with the women's liberation branch of the women's movement. Differing in perspective as well as style, they would ultimately push many of their older counterparts beyond the demand for equal rights to recognition that true emancipation would require a far-reaching transformation of society and culture.

The experiences awakening in this 1960s generation a feminist consciousness have been superbly described by Sara Evans in her book, *Personal Politics*.[28]

"Freedom, equality, love and hope," the possibility of new human relationships, the importance of participatory democracy—letting the people decide—were, as Evans points out, part of an egalitarian ideology shared by both the southern-based Student Nonviolent Coordinating Committee (SNCC) in its struggle for racial equality and the Students for Democratic Society (SDS) in its efforts to mobilize an interracial organization of the urban poor in northern ghettos. Membership in both organizations—"the movement"—thus reinforced commitment to these ideals among the women who joined. In order to translate ideals into reality, however, young, college-age women who had left the shelter of middle-class families for the hard and dangerous work of transforming society found themselves doing things that they would never have thought possible. Amidst the racial strife of the South, they joined picket lines, created freedom schools, and canvassed for voter registration among blacks, often enduring arrest and jailing. SDS women from affluent suburbs entered decaying tenements and were surrounded by the grim realities of the ghetto. They trudged door-to-door in an effort to reach women whose struggle to survive made many understandably suspicious of intruding strangers. Summing up the feelings of hundreds, one young woman wrote: "I learned a lot of respect for myself for having gone through all that." A heightened sense of self-worth and autonomy, Evans argues, was not all they acquired. They also learned the skills of movement building and the nuts and bolts of organizing.

Particularly important was the problem of getting people, long passive, to act on their own behalf. SDS women began by encouraging ghetto women to come together to talk about their problems. This sharing of experiences, they believed, would lead these women to recognize not only that their problems were common but that so-lutions required changes in the system. In the process of organizing, the organizers also learned. They began to understand the meaning of oppression and the valor required of those who fought it. They found new role models, Evans suggests, in extraordinary southern black women whose courage never waivered in the face of violence and in those welfare mothers of the North who confronted welfare bureaucrat and slum lord after years of passivity.

But if being in the movement brought a new understanding of equality, it also brought new problems. Men who were committed to equality for one group were not necessarily committed to equality for another group. Women in SNCC, as in SDS, found themselves frequently relegated to domestic chores and refused a key voice in the formulation of policy. Moreover, the sexual freedom that had been theirs as part of the cultural revolution taking place in the 1960s soon began to feel more like sexual exploitation as they saw their role in the movement spelled out in the draft resister's slogan: "Girls Say Yes to Guys Who Say No." Efforts to change the situation were firmly rebuffed. When SNCC leader Stokely Carmichael announced, "The only position for women in SNCC is prone," he spoke for white males in the New Left as well. Evans concludes: "The same movement that permitted women to grow and to develop self-esteem, energy, and skills generally kept women out of leadership roles and reinforced expectations that women would conform to tradition as houseworkers, nurturers, and sex objects." By 1967 the tensions had become so intense that women left the movement to organize on behalf of their own "liberation."

They did not leave empty handed. As radicals, they were accustomed to challenging prevailing ideas and practices. As movement veterans, they had acquired a language of protest, an organizing tactic, and a deep-seated conviction that the personal was political. How that legacy would shape this burgeoning new feminist movement became evident as small women's liberation groups began springing up spontaneously in major cities and university communities across the nation.

STRUCTURE, LEADERSHIP, AND CONSCIOUSNESS-RAISING

Initially, at least, the two branches of the new feminism seemed almost to be two different movements, so unlike were they in structure and style. Linked only by newsletters, notices in underground newspapers, and networks of friends, women's liberation groups rejected both traditional organizational structure and leadership. Unlike NOW and other women's rights groups, they had no central headquarters, no elected officers, no bylaws. There was no legislative agenda and little of the activism that transformed the more politically astute women's rights leaders into skilled lobbyists and tacticians. Instead this younger generation of feminists, organizing new groups wherever they found themselves, concentrated on a kind of personal politics rooted in movement days. Looking back on male-dominated meetings in which, however informal the gathering, a few highly verbal, aggressive men invariably controlled debate and dictated strategy and left less articulate and assertive women effectively excluded, they recalled the technique they had used in organizing the poor. They remembered how they had encouraged those women to talk among themselves until the personal became political, that is, until problems which, at first glance, seemed to be personal were finally understood to be social in cause—rooted in society rather than in the individual—and political in solution. Applying this same process in their own informal "rap groups," women's liberationists developed the technique of "consciousness-raising." Adopted by women's rights groups such as local chapters of NOW, consciousness-raising sessions became one of the most important innovations of the entire feminist movement.[29]

The immediate task of the consciousness-raising session was to bring together in a caring, supportive, noncompetitive setting women accustomed to relating most intimately not with other women but with men—husbands, lovers, "friends." As these women talked among themselves, exchanging confidences, reassessing old options, and mentally exploring new ones, a sense of shared problems began to emerge. The women themselves gradually gained greater understanding of how profoundly their lives had been shaped by the constraints of culture. Personal experience with those constraints merged with intellectual awareness of women's inferior status and the factors that made it so. By the same token, new understanding of problems generated new determination to resolve them. Anger, aggression, and frustration formerly turned inward in unconscious self-hatred began to be directed outward, becoming transformed into new energy directed toward constructive goals. If society and culture had defined who women were through their unconscious internalization of tradition, they could reverse the process, and, by redefining themselves, redefine society and culture. Or, to put it another way, if woman was a *social construct*—the product not so much of biology, but of what people in a particular society and culture believed to be the implications of biology—then women themselves would recreate the construct. At work was a process of discovery so radicalizing that the individuals undergoing it ultimately emerged in a very real sense as different people. Now feminists, these were women with a different understanding of reality—a new "consciousness," a new sense of "sisterhood," and a new commitment to change.

Consciousness-raising was an invigorating and sometimes frightening experience. As one young woman wrote, "This whole movement is the most exhilarating thing of my life. The last eight months have been a personal revolution. Nonetheless, I recognize there is dynamite in this and I'm scared shitless."[30] "Scared" or not, such women could no longer be contained. Veterans of one rap group fanned out, creating others. For the feminist movement, this mushrooming of groups meant increased numbers and added momentum. For some of the women involved, it meant confronting and articulating theoretically as well as personally what "oppression," "sexism," and "liberation" really meant: in short, developing a feminist ideology.

TOWARD A FEMINIST IDEOLOGY: OPPRESSION, SEXISM, AND CHANGE

To explain the significance of the discovery that woman is a *social construct* and that subordination was built into that construct was no simple process. The concept itself was complex. Moreover, women's rights advocates who were essentially pragmatic were more interested in practical results than in theoretical explanations. Even among feminists who were more theoretically oriented, intellectual perspectives reflected differences in experience, temperament, style, and politics.[31] Manifestos, position papers, and books began to pile up as feminists searched for the historical origins of female oppression. Socialist feminists debated nonsocialist feminists as to whether socialism was a prerequisite for women's liberation. Lesbian feminists argued that the ultimate rejection of male domination required the rejection of sexual intimacy with men; others argued that sexual behavior was less important than being woman identified. Still other feminists

insisted that rigid sex role differentiation oppressed men as well as women and that their goal should be restructuring male-female relations in ways that would encourage greater mutuality and fulfillment for both sexes in all aspects of life. Given such a variety of perspectives, it is almost impossible to talk about *a* feminist ideology in the sense of a unified theory to which all members of the women's movement subscribe. It is possible to say, however, that feminists share a common conceptual framework deriving from the shared belief that *gender* is a primary, if not necessarily exclusive, explanatory factor essential to any understanding of why women *as a group* suffer from an unequal distribution of power and resources in a society.

Although feminists differ as to the historical roots of oppression, they agree that men have been the dominant sex and that women as a group are subordinate. Explanations for the perpetuation of that subordination also vary. Feminists whose socialism was forged in the New Left of the 1960s see oppression as the inevitable result of a capitalist system that keeps women economically dependent on men. Employers benefit inasmuch as they get two workers for the price of one (men being paid wages with their unpaid wives performing the services necessary to enable them to perform their jobs) or, if the women themselves work, the wages received are too meager to ensure economic self-sufficiency. In either case, the men they live with also benefit for they are ensured cheap domestic labor at home. Other feminists, including members of women's rights groups such as NOW, WEAL, and NWPC, point the finger not at the economic system but at culture. They belive the continuation of male domination and female oppression is perpetuated by sex role socialization and cultural values that continue to confer on males higher status, greater options, and greater power, by virtue of their sex. This preference, conscious and unconscious, for whatever is "masculine," feminists term *sexism*. Not surprisingly, they reject the traditional assumption that biology—sexual dichotomy—dictates distinct spheres, status, roles, or personality types. To put the matter most simply, feminists reject the notion that the bearing of children creates for women "natural" roles as wives and mothers, a rightful "place" limited to the home, a subordinate status, and behavior patterns of self-denying submissiveness and service to others. The persistence of gender-based determinism, they believe, continues to limit options resulting in female dependency and the vapid, trivialized image of femininity associated with such dependency—the femininity of the "Total Woman" with its mixture of sexuality and submissiveness. The fact that so many women continue to rely on men not only for financial support but also for social status and even self-esteem, feminists argue, deprives such women of the economic and psychological freedom to determine their own lives, to make real choices, to be judged as individuals on the basis of their own merit and accomplishments, not those of fathers or husbands.

Just as traditional male roles provide access to power and independence in a sexist society, whereas female roles do not, so masculine values define what attributes are admired and rewarded. Thus masculine qualities are associated with strength, competence, independence, and rationality, while female qualities are associated with fragility, dependence, passivity, and emotionalism. These qualities, however, are not intrinsically "male" or "female" in the sense that they are biologically inherent. Rather, feminists argue, they are an extension of the training that is part of sex role socialization. The very fact that masculine values are those Americans of both sexes regard more highly and also constitute the standard by which

mental health is judged has implications feminists find distressing. Women, internalizing these sexist judgments and feeling themselves lacking in competence, tend to undervalue themselves (and women in general) and therefore lack self-esteem. Moreover, society also undervalues the female qualities that are positive, such as nurturing, supportiveness, and empathy. *All* of these qualities—those considered "male" and those considered "female"—feminists insist are shared human qualities. Those that are desirable, such as competence, independence, supportiveness, and nurturing, should be encouraged in both men and women.

Such changes, however, demand the eradication of sexism. And sexism, feminists believe, is persistent, pervasive, and powerful. It is internalized by women as well as men. It is most dramatically evident in the programmed-to-please women who search for happiness through submissiveness to men and in the men who use their power to limit women's options and keep them dependent. It is also evident in a more subtle fashion among women who emulate male models and values, refusing to see those aspects of women's lives that are positive and life affirming, and among men who are unaware of the unconscious sexism permeating their attitudes and actions. Internalized in individuals, sexism is also embedded in institutions—the family, the educational system, the media, politics, the law, and even organized religion.

Given the pervasiveness of sexism, many feminists see no possibility for real equality short of transformation not only of individuals but also of social institutions and cultural values. Even what was once seen as the relatively simple demand of women's rights advocates for equal pay for equal work no longer seems so simple. What seemed to be a matter of obtaining equal rights *within* the existing system in reality demands changes that *transform* the system. Involved is:

a reevaluation of women as workers, of women as mothers, of mothers as workers, of work as suitable for one gender and not for the other. The demand implies equal opportunity and thus equal responsibilities. It implies a childhood in which girls are rewarded for competence, risk taking, achievement, competitiveness and independence—just like boys. Equal pay for equal work means a revision in our expectations about women as equal workers and it involves the institutional arrangements to make them so.

"There is nothing small here," observes a noted feminist scholar.[32] And indeed there is not.

FEMINISM IN ACTION

While the contemporary women's movement contains under its broad umbrella women who differ significantly in the degree of their radicalism, the changes implied in achieving sexual equality are of such scope as to make radical by definition those who genuinely understand what is involved in equality and, beyond that, emancipation.[33] Feminism is not for the fainthearted. To clarify frustration and rage so as to understand problems accurately and then to use that understanding in ways that permit growth and change in one's self are to engage in a process requiring considerable courage and energy. To reform society so that women can achieve legal, economic, and social parity requires even greater commitment—commitment that has to be sustained over time and through defeat. To work for cultural transformation of a patriarchal world in such a way as to benefit both men and women requires extraordinary breadth of vision as well as sustained energy and dedication. Yet despite the obstacles, millions of women during the past decades have participated in the process.

For some the changes have consisted largely of private actions—relationships renegotiated, careers resumed. Others,

preferring to make public statements of new commitments, used flamboyant methods to dramatize the subtle ways in which society so defined woman's place as to deny not only her full participation but also her full humanity. As part of the confrontational politics of the 1960s, feminists picketed the 1968 Miss America contest, protesting our national preoccupation with bust size and "congeniality" rather than brain power and character. (In the process they were dubbed "bra burners," despite the fact that no bras were burned.) Activists pushed their way into all-male bars and restaurants as a way of forcing recognition of how these bastions of male exclusivity were themselves statements about "man's world/woman's place." They sat in at the offices of *Ladies' Home Journal* and *Newsweek* protesting the ways in which the media's depiction of women perpetuated old stereotypes at the expense of new realities.

Still other feminists chose to work for social change in a different fashion. They created nonsexist day care centers, wrote and published nonsexist children's books, monitored sex stereotyping in textbooks, lobbied for women's studies programs in high schools and colleges, and founded women's health clinics. They worked for reform of abortion laws so that women would not be forced to continue pregnancies that were physically or psychologically hazardous but could instead have the option of a safe, legal abortion. They formed rape crisis centers so that rape victims could be treated by caring females; they agitated for more informed, sympathetic treatment on the part of hospital staffs, the police, and the courts. Feminists also lobbied for programs to retrain displaced homemakers so that such women could move from economic dependency to self-support. Feminist scholars used their talents to recover and interpret women's experience, opening new areas for research and in the process furthering change. Feminist legislators sponsored bills, not always successful, to help housewives to secure some form of economic recognition for work performed, to enable women workers to obtain insurance that would give them the same degree of economic security afforded male coworkers, and to secure for battered women protection from the physical violence that is the most blatant form of male oppression. Black feminists, speaking out on the "double jeopardy" of being black and female—"the most pressed down of us all"—lent their support to feminist measures of especial importance to minority women.[34] Actions, like voices, differed. Such diversity, however, was basic to the movement.

FEMINISM: THE PUBLIC IMPACT

In a society in which the media create instant awareness of social change, feminism burst upon the public consciousness with all the understated visibility of a fireworks display on the Fourth of July. The more radical elements of the movement, with their talk of test tube conception, the slavery of marriage, and the downfall of capitalism might be dismissed out of hand. But it was hard to ignore the presence of *Ms.* magazine on newsstands, feminist books on the best-seller lists, women in hard hats on construction jobs or the government-mandated affirmative action programs that put them there. It was harder still to ignore the publicity that accompanied the appointment of women to the Carter cabinet, the enrollment of coeds in the nation's military academies, and the ordination of women to the ministry. A Harris poll of December 1975 reported that 63 percent of the women interviewed favored most changes designed to improve the status of women, although some were quick to insist that they were not "women's libbers."[35]

Evidence of changing views was everywhere. The list of organizations lined up in support of ratification of the Equal Rights Amendment included not only such avowedly feminist groups as NOW, WEAL, and NWPC as well as longtime supporters such as the National Woman's Party and the National Federation of Business and Professional Women's Clubs, but also "mainstream" women's organizations such as the General Federation of Women's Clubs, the American Association of University Women, the League of Women Voters, the National Council of Jewish Women, the National Council of Negro Women, and the YWCA. Included, too, were the Girl Scouts of America, along with a host of churches and labor organizations. Even more potent evidence that feminism had "arrived" was the 1977 National Women's Conference in Houston. Before more than two thousand delegates from every state and territory in the United States and twenty thousand guests, three First Ladies—Lady Bird Johnson, Betty Ford, and Rosalynn Carter—endorsed the Equal Rights Amendment and the goals of the Houston Conference, their hands holding a lighted torch carried by women runners from Seneca Falls where, in 1848, the famous Declaration of Sentiments had been adopted. Confessing that she once thought the women's movement belonged more to her daughters than to herself, Lady Bird Johnson added, "I have come to know that it belongs to women of all ages." Such an admission, like the presence of these three women on the platform, proclaimed a message about feminists that was boldly printed on balloons throughout the convention hall: "We Are Everywhere!"[36]

OPPOSITION TO FEMINISM

For some women the slogan was not a sign of achievement but of threat. Gathered at a counter-convention in Houston and proudly wearing "Stop ERA" buttons were women who shared neither the critique nor the goals of the women's movement. They were an impressive reminder that social change generates opposition and that opposition to feminism had crystalized in the struggle for ratification of the Equal Rights Amendment. ERA—as the amendment is called—is a simple statement: "Equality of rights under the law shall not be denied or abridged by the United States or by any State on account of sex." It was first suggested in 1923 as the logical extension of suffrage. Not all feminists embraced the amendment, however. Some, fearing it would be used to strike down laws to protect women in the workplace, preferred to look for constitutional guarantees of equality through the extension of judicial interpretation of the Fifth and Fourteenth Amendments. By the 1960s sentiments had shifted. NOW called for passage of the amendment as part of its legislative agenda. The President's Task Force on the Status of Women and the Citizen's Advisory Council on the Status of Women endorsed the amendment, as did Presidents Johnson and Nixon. Persuasive feminists helped to bring aboard such historic opponents as the League of Women Voters and the Women's Bureau and organized labor. Arguing in support of the amendment, they pointed out that New Deal legislation provided a basis for protection of both sexes that had not existed in the 1920s. They also pointed out that many state laws granting protection only to women had already been voided by Title VII of the Civil Rights Act of 1964. With unions and many women's organizations thus persuaded, NOW turned its attention to Congress itself, asking legislators to pass a constitutional amendment removing sexual bias from common, statutory, and constitutional law. In the spring of 1972 the Senate finally joined the House and sent ERA to the states for ratification by a lopsided vote of eighty-four to eight. Almost immediately twenty-one states rushed to ratify. By the spring of 1973, however, opponents of ratification had begun a counterattack that ultimately stalled the number of ratified states at thirty-five, three short of the needed three-fourths majority when the deadline for ratification expired on June 30, 1982. Opponents even induced some ratifying states to rescind their approval. Early successes indicated that a majority of Americans favored ERA—but not a large enough majority.

Opposition to ERA is starkly paradoxical. A constitutional amendment proposed especially to benefit women was opposed by many of them. The dimensions of paradox are suggested by the reasons sometimes given for taking a position on the issue. Women opposed the amendment because they wanted to protect the family; other women supported it because they, too, wanted to protect the family. Women resisted ERA because some could not trust men to treat women fairly; and others supported it, giving precisely the same reason.

The paradox is resolved in part by remembering that conservatives of both sexes are often suspicious of the principle of equality, especially when identified with specific controversial federal policies. This is especially true of programs to bus school children in order to achieve equality through "racial balance" in the public schools. The policy was believed by some parents to be a denial of their right to educate their children how and where they pleased. Proponents of busing saw it as an issue of public policy, having nothing to do with private relationships. But opponents believed that education was an extension of the private relationships between parents and children. The moving of children literally from their parents' door to a faraway school was an act reinforcing the sense of losing one's children. Busing, therefore, was seen as an intrusion into the private domain of family, subverting the influence and values of parents. Other federal policies seemed to do the same thing. Attempts to break up segregated housing, for example, were seen as an assault on the right to live in neighborhoods that reflected the private, family lives of the people who lived there. Since ERA was perceived both as a continuation of previous governmental commitment to equality *and* as a symbol of feminism, it was attacked for attempting to give the federal bureaucracy power to change relationships within the family. Opposition to ERA expressed a diffuse anger with federal intervention in "private" relationships. As one woman wrote her U.S. senator: "Forced busing, forced mixing, forced housing. Now forced women! No thank you!"[37]

Opposition to ERA also expressed an elemental response to what many people believe to be a threat to cherished values. "The drug revolution, the sexual revolution, gay liberation, students' rights, children's rights, and the civil rights and the Native American and Latino movements"—to borrow the list of one observer—all challenged basic middle-class values.[38] Above all, there was the women's movement. Feminists believed that theirs was a struggle for justice and liberation—liberation from social roles and cultural values that denied rights and limited autonomy. To require *all* women to conform to patterns of behavior dictated not by biology but by culture was, from the standpoint of feminists, to deny freedom and self-determination to half the population simply because they were born female. To women who did not believe they were oppressed, however, feminists' efforts at liberation appeared *not* as an attack on unjust constraints but rather as an attack on familiar patterns that provide security. To women who had internalized traditional female roles, feminism, with its demands to rethink what it means to be a man or a woman, was perceived not just as an assault upon them personally but as symbolic of every other threat to their identity and traditions. Because ERA has been seen as the instrument through which feminists could achieve goals regarded by antifeminists as Utopian and threatening, the amendment itself has come to symbolize to its opponents both the danger and absurdity inherent in this latest drive for equality of the sexes. Indeed the very idea of oppression seems preposterous to women who believe that they have benefited from being treated as "the fairer sex" and "the better half." Their experience, even if not the ideal of wedded bliss, nevertheless seems to them to be at odds with that of feminists who seem to antifeminists to be attacking women for behaving like women.

From this point of view feminists appear silly for wanting to use *Ms.* instead of the traditional *Mrs.* or *Miss*, tasteless for intruding where men do not want them to be, eccentric for celebrating a filly who won the Kentucky Derby. Worse still, feminists, in the eyes of antifeminists, appear to be women-who-want-to-be-men. The accusation that ERA would require men and women to use the same public toilets is not therefore to be taken literally so much as symbolically. It represents the intrusion of men and of women-who-want-to-be-men into the privacy of women-who-are-proud-to-be-women. The accusation that ERA would destroy the family should also be understood as a way of defending the social significance and indispensability of traditional female roles. Underlying everything is the theme of purity (traditional female roles) against danger and corruption (social disintegration). The result of this formulation of the issue of equality has been to enable antifeminist women to develop a consciousness of their own. The free-floating anxiety aroused by the enormity of the social change inherent in feminism thus acquired a concrete focus. ERA became an issue in which what seemed to be at stake for opponents was their very identity as women—and the fate of society.

Predictions of the terrible consequences that would result from ratification of the amendment were not so important as was the function such statements seemed to serve—that is, the reaffirmation of traditional sex roles identified with social stability. The indictment of feminism and of ERA is an indictment of what Phyllis Schlafly, the chief female opponent of ratification, persistently calls the "unisex society." By rallying women to this danger, Schlafly has revealed that the issue was not whether women should stay at home minding the children and cooking the food—Schlafly herself did not do that. The issue was the *meaning* of sexual differences between men and women.

Many feminists minimize those differences, believing that traditional roles are not only oppressive but outmoded because reproductive control and work in the public sector have made women's lives more like men's. Antifeminists inflate those differences. Their response is a measure both of their belief that women are "eternal in their attributes and unchanged by events" and their anger and distress at changes that have already occurred.[39] It is a reminder, too, of how far the feminist movement has still to go to achieve the political and legal reforms it seeks, much less its more far-reaching goals.[40]

NEW PROGRESS AND OLD PROBLEMS

There were gains to be sure. New reproductive freedom came with the Supreme Court's liberalization of abortion laws that removed the danger of the illegal, back alley abortions so long the recourse of desperate women. Sexual preference and practice became less an occasion for denial of civil rights and more a matter of individual choice. Evidence of expanding educational and employment opportunities seemed to be everywhere. Women assumed high level posts in government, the judiciary, the military, business, and labor. In a new batch of female "firsts," Sandra Day O'Connor assumed a seat on the Supreme Court, NASA's Sally Ride zoomed into space, and Geraldine Ferraro

won the vice-presidential slot on the 1984 Democratic ticket. From an expanding population of female college graduates, younger women moved in record numbers into professional schools, dramatically changing enrollment patterns in such fields as law, medicine, and business. Their blue-collar counterparts, completing job training programs, trickled into the construction industry and other trades, finding in those jobs the decent wage that had eluded them as waitresses, hairdressers, sales clerks, or domestics. Political participation also increased. Women emerged from years of lobbying for ERA with a new understanding of the political process. (So, too, did their opponents.) More female candidates filed for office and more female politicians worked themselves into positions of power. Revision of discriminatory statutes, while by no means completed, brought a greater measure of legal equality. A heightened public consciousness of sexism ushered in other changes. School officials began admitting boys to home economics classes, girls to shop. Some employers transformed maternity leaves into child care leaves, making them available to fathers as well as mothers. Liberal religious leaders talked of removing gender-related references from prayer books.[41]

Such gains, while in some cases smacking of tokenism, are not to be minimized. Most required persistent pressure from feminists, from government officials, and often from both. They were by no means comprehensive, however. As in the case of the civil rights movement, the initial beneficiaries of the feminist movement were predominantly middle-class, often highly educated, and relatively young. The increase in the number of single women, the older age at which women married for the first time, the declining birth rate—changes characteristic of the entire female population during the 1970s—were especially characteristic of a younger generation of career-oriented women.[42] But even for these women and their partners, financial as well as personal costs were sometimes high: couples living apart for some portion of the week or year in order to take advantage of career opportunities; married women devoting virtually all of their salaries to domestic and child care costs, especially during their children's preschool years. Perhaps the personal recognition, independence, and sense of fulfillment associated with career success made the costs "affordable"—especially given the alternatives.

The women who stand to gain most from the implementation of feminists' efforts to change the nation's economic and social structure are not those who are young, talented, and educated but those who are less advantaged. Yet the latter could with good reason argue that more than a decade of feminist activity had left their lives little changed in ways that really count. While the number of women in the work force continues to rise from less than 20 percent in 1920 to a projected 54 to 60 percent by 1990, working women in the 1970s and 1980s saw the gap between male and female income remain virtually unchanged. By 1983 female workers earned 64 cents for every dollar earned by males. College graduates are no exception, their earnings averaging $14,679 as compared to $12,117 earned by men *without* even a high school diploma.[43] A study of alumni of such prestigious graduate business schools as Stanford, Harvard, and the University of Pennsylvania indicated that women graduating in 1977 and 1978 were earning on the average $4,000 less a year than their male classmates.[44] Part of the explanation for this persistent gap lies in pay inequities. More fundamental, however, is the continuation of occupational segregation and the undervaluation of work done by women.[45] Around 80 percent of all working women still cluster in gender-segregated occupations in which wages are artificially low. At American Telephone and Telegraph,

for example, a 1976 court case revealed that 97 percent of the middle management jobs were held by men, while 98 percent of all telephone operators and 94 percent of all clerical workers were women. Moreover, as inflationary pressures drove more women into the work force, competition for jobs in traditionally "female" fields enabled employers to keep wages low.

With the dramatic rise in the number of female-headed households, the continuation of this occupational ghetto has disturbing implications not only for women workers but also for their children. Female heads of households, often lacking both child care facilities and skills that would equip them for better-paying jobs if such jobs were available, earn enough to enable only one in three to stay above the poverty level. Their struggle for economic survival is shared by other women, especially older women—widows or divorcées whose years of housework have left them without employable skills. Indeed divorce often contributes to the problem, for with the breaking up of a marriage, the standard of living for the woman falls by a dramatic 73 percent, while rising 42 percent for the man. The fact that child support, if awarded, is frequently inadequate, unpaid, and uncollectible further exacerbates the economic plight of those women who have custody of their children. Thus ironic as it may seem, the decade that witnessed the revival of the feminist movement also saw the feminization of poverty. By the end of the 1970s, two out of every three poor persons in the United States were female. If this trend continues at the present rate, it is estimated that by the year 2000 the poverty population will be composed entirely of women and their children.[46]

Ironic, too, given the feminist insistence that child care and household responsibilities should be shared by working spouses, is the persistence of the double burden borne by women working outside the home. Working women continue to do 80 to 90 percent of the chores related to running a household, with husbands and children "helping out." For all the talk about the changing structure of family roles, major shifts occurred slowly, even in households in which women were informed and engaged enough to be familiar with current feminist views.[47] Although some fathers, especially among the middle class, have become more involved in parenting, the primary responsibility for children still remains the mother's. And working mothers still receive little institutional help despite the fact that by 1980 nearly half of all mothers with children under six worked outside the home. Without a fundamental rethinking of both work and family, women will continue to participate in the labor force in increasing numbers while, at the same time, remaining in its lower echelons as marginal members.[48]

In sum, economic and demographic change has been the basis of important changes in attitudes and behavior. As a result, life is more challenging for many women, but the feminization of poverty reminds the nation of its failures. We have yet to see the new social policies necessary to create the egalitarian and humane society envisioned by feminists. Indeed, in the climate of political conservatism of the 1980s feminists have had to fight hard to maintain gains already won. The reproductive freedom of poor women had already been eroded by limitations on federal funding of abortions, and the reproductive freedom of all women had been threatened by congressional opponents of legalized abortion. Legislation mandating equal opportunity in education and employment has been weakened by the courts and assaulted by the Reagan administration, which now seeks to weaken further affirmative action. There have been cuts in funds for Title IX, which seeks to ensure sex equity on campus; cuts in grants for traditionally female programs such as nursing; cuts in Small Business Adminis-

tration funding for programs benefiting women. Also under attack is comparable worth, a policy designed to reduce pay inequities by evaluating skills, effort, and responsibilities associated with jobs traditionally held by men and those traditionally held by women so that pay can be equalized for jobs that are indeed comparable. Social programs benefiting women have been curtailed by lack of funding, including day care centers, battered women's shelters, and legal aid centers. Legal equality has also suffered for, without an equal rights amendment requiring legislators to revise the discriminatory statutes that remain, the impetus will have to come not from the governments—state and local—but from individual women and men genuinely committed to equality before the law. Thus the need for collective action on the part of feminists is as great in the 1980s as it was in the 1970s.

Social change is complex and results from the interplay of many factors. Nowhere is this truer than in the women's movement. The swiftness with which a resurgent feminism captured the imagination of millions of American women dramatized the need for change. The inability of feminists to win ratification of ERA dramatized the limits of change. The irony of the polarization, however, was that the failure of ERA did not and could not stop feminism in its tracks and that antifeminist women, in mobilizing to fight the amendment, were themselves assuming a new role whether they acknowledged that fact or not. They organized lobbies, political action committees, and conventions; they also ran for and won public office. Where feminists have led, antifeminists would not be too far behind, defining themselves within the context of change they could not stop. But the rhetoric of liberation that had been so important to the awakening and maturation of women in the 1970s seemed by 1980 to be less appealing. Women could happily benefit from the achievements of feminism without understanding or embracing its critique of style. Transformational politics seemed to have given way to a bevy of career women armed with a copy of *Savvy* or *Working Woman*, "dressed for success," and busily playing "games their mothers never taught them" with scant realization, as one observer noted, that "only a decade ago they would never have been allowed to play."[49] Contrary to appearances, however, feminism has not been co-opted. Always a diverse, decentralized, and structurally amorphous movement, its membership grows even in the midst of antifeminist backlash as millions of women continue to make the connection between the personal and political as they confront in their own lives or the lives of others the trauma of sexual harassment, job discrimination, inequitable divorce settlements, rape, and other forms of sexual violence. Moreover, the challenge of the New Right has made abundantly clear that old patterns of gender-based discrimination have not lost their force. Those patterns had hindered efforts of women to establish a public role in the nineteenth century; they had restricted that public role once it was won. The same patterns, so indelible even under attack, continue to obstruct contemporary efforts to redefine social roles in the drive for equality. The tension between past position and future possibility, however, demands of all women—not merely feminists—a definition of self that extends beyond the definitions of the past.

Notes

I am especially indebted to William H. Chafe, Jacquelyn Dowd Hall, Linda K. Kerber, and Donald G. Mathews for their generous and helpful criticism of earlier drafts of this essay.

1. William H. Chafe, *The American Woman: Her Changing Social, Economic, and Political Roles, 1920–1970* (New York, 1972), p. 58.

2. Theodore Roosevelt, "The American Woman as Mother," in *The Journal of the Century* (New York, 1976), pp. 32–33.

3. Marion K. Sanders, *The Lady and the Vote* (Boston, 1956), p. 142.

4. For Elliott's account, see Marion W. Roydhouse, "The 'Universal Sisterhood of Women': Women and Labor Reform in North Carolina, 1900–1932" (Ph.D. dissertation, Duke University, 1980), pp. 91–92.

5. For a discussion of statistics relating to women in the professions as well as attitudes of college-educated women to careers, see Frank Stricker, "Cookbooks and Law Books: The Hidden History of Career Women in Twentieth Century America," *Journal of Social History* 10 (1976):1–19.

6. Excluded from this list are women who were appointed to congressional office simply to finish out the term of a deceased husband. Among these forty-seven, however, are women who were initially appointed or elected in a special election to fill the seat of a deceased incumbent, often a husband, and who went on to win election to a subsequent term—or terms—on their own. Figures were compiled from Rudolf Engelbart, *Women in the United States Congress, 1917–1972* (Littleton, Colo., 1974).

7. Margaret Mead, "Sex and Achievement," *Forum* 94 (1935):303.

8. Marynia F. Farnham and Ferdinand Lundberg, *Modern Woman: The Lost Sex* (New York, 1947), p. 202.

9. For an example of antisuffrage criticism on the dangers of suffrage to the family, see Anne F. Scott and Andrew M. Scott, *One Half the People: The Fight for Woman Suffrage* (Philadelphia, 1975), pp. 106–11.

10. Marjorie Rosen, *Popcorn Venus: Women, Movies, and the American Dream* (New York, 1973). Rosen uses the phrase as part of her title to chapter 18.

11. An excellent example of the antifeminist stance of many Freudian psychiatrists of the 1940s and 1950s is Helene Deutsch's *Psychology of Women* (New York, 1944). Typical is the statement: "Whenever the young girl exchanges a rich emotional life for scientific thinking, it is to be expected that later in her life sterility will take the place of motherliness even if she has given birth to many children" (2:67). Sports

activities, greater intellectualization, and the one-child syndrome, according to Deutsch, were "visible forms in which the turning away from femininity manifested itself" (1: 303).

12. *Statistical Abstract of the United States, 1949* (Washington, D.C., 1949), p. 296; Sheila Tobias and Lisa Anderson, "What Really Happened to Rosie the Riveter? Demobilization and the Female Labor Force, 1944–47" MSS Modular Publications, Module 9 (1973), p. 3. Chafe argues in *The American Woman* (part 2) that World War II, nonetheless, represented a decisive break with traditional sex roles in that changes in women's economic roles provided a foundation for subsequent challenges to conventional definitions of woman's place inasmuch as it helped to create a constituency for the contemporary women's movement.

13. According to a Gallup Poll, 86 percent of the American people objected to married women working; according to a *Fortune* poll, 67 percent. See Hadley Cantril, *Public Opinion, 1935–46* (Princeton, 1951), p. 1047, and "The *Fortune* Survey: Women in America," *Fortune* 34 (1946):8.

14. For a much more detailed analysis, see Valerie Kincade Oppenheimer, *The Female Labor Force in the United States: Demographic and Economic Factors Governing Its Growth and Changing Composition* (Berkeley, 1970).

15. For a fuller discussion of the way Americans and women in particular responded to this influx of married women in the work force, see Chafe, *The American Woman*, pp. 182–95, 218–19.

16. Lois Wladis Hoffman and F. Ivan Nye, *Working Mothers* (San Francisco, 1974), chaps. 6–7.

17. For a perceptive discussion of this issue, see Leslie Woodcock Tentler, *Wage-Earning Women: Industrial Work and Family Life in the United States, 1900–1930* (New York, 1979), pp. 180–85.

18. Quoted in Marguerite Wykoff Zapoleon, *The College Girl Looks Ahead to Her Career Opportunities* (New York, 1956), p. 9. See also Ashley Montagu, "The Triumph and Tragedy of the American Woman," *Saturday Review* 41 (1958):14.

19. Cynthia E. Harrison, "A 'New Frontier' for Women: The Public Policy of the Kennedy Administration," *Journal of American History* 67 (1980):630–46.

20. U.S. President's Commission on the Status of Women, *American Women* (Washington, D.C., 1963).

21. N.C., Governor's Commission on the Status of Women, *The Many Lives of North Carolina Women* (n.p., 1964). The report benefited from the fact that the study was funded—some state commissions were not—and from the expertise of some of its members among whom were then U.S. commissioner of welfare, Ellen Winston, and economist and later secretary of commerce, Juanita Kreps. The phrase quoted is that of Anne Firor Scott, who chaired the commission. Although none of these three found their involvement with the commission a "consciousness-raising" experience in that the data were already familiar, the findings were new to other members. Scott speculates that the many regional and national meetings attended by chairs of state commissions were important both for developing among those women involved a growing concern with women's issues and for network building. Interviews with Ellen Winston and Anne Firor Scott, December 7 and 8, 1980.

22. For events leading to the founding of NOW, see Jo Freeman, *The Politics of Women's Liberation: A Case Study of an Emerging Social Movement and Its Relation to the Social Policy Process* (New York, 1975), pp. 53–55. For a more detailed study of Title VII of the Civil Rights Act and its implementation, see Donald Allen Robinson, "Two Movements in Pursuit of Equal Employment Opportunity," *Signs: Journal of Women in Culture and Society* 4 (1979): 413–33.

23. Betty Friedan, *The Feminine Mystique* (New York, 1963).

24. Freeman, *Politics of Women's Liberation*, pp. 35–37.

25. National Organization for Women, Statement of Purpose, 1966, reprinted in *Up from the Pedestal*, ed. Aileen S. Kraditor (Chicago, 1968), pp. 363–64; National Organization for Women, Bill of Rights, 1967, reprinted in *Sisterhood Is Powerful: An Anthology of Writings on the Women's Liberation Movement*, ed. Robin Morgan (New York, 1970), pp. 512–14.

26. Freeman, *Politics of Women's Liberation*, chap. 3; Maren Lockwood Carden, *The New Feminist Movement* (New York, 1974), chaps. 8–10; also Gayle Graham Yates, *What Women Want: The Ideas of the Movement* (Cambridge, Mass., 1975), chap. 2.

27. Quoted in Carolyn Hadley, "Feminist Women in the Southeast," *Bulletin of the Center for the Study of Southern Culture and Religion* 3 (1979):10.

28. Sara Evans, *Personal Politics: The*

Roots of Women's Liberation in the Civil Rights Movement and the New Left (New York, 1979); see also Evans, "Tomorrow's Yesterday: Feminist Consciousness and the Future of Women," in *Women of America: A History*, ed. Carol Ruth Berkin and Mary Beth Norton (Boston, 1979), pp. 390–415. The following paragraphs rely heavily on this essay and Evans's *Personal Politics*.

29. For a discussion of women's liberation activities and ideas, see Carden, *New Feminist Movement*, chaps. 5–7, and Yates, *What Women Want*, chap. 3.

30. Quoted in Evans, "Tomorrow's Yesterday," p. 407.

31. The literature is extensive, beginning with Simone de Beauvoir, *The Second Sex*, trans. and ed. H. M. Parshley (New York, 1961). Alice Rossi's "Equality between the Sexes: An Immodest Proposal," in *The Woman in America*, ed. Robert Jay Lifton, *Daedalus* 93 (1964):607–52, was especially important as an early statement by a feminist sociologist. Key works generated by the movement include Caroline Bird, *Born Female* (New York, 1969); Kate Millett, *Sexual Politics* (Garden City, N.Y., 1970); Shulamith Firestone, *The Dialectic of Sex: The Case for a Feminist Revolution* (New York, 1970); Judith Hole and Ellen Levine, *Rebirth of Feminism* (New York, 1971); Elizabeth Janeway, *Man's World/Woman's Place: A Study in Social Mythology* (New York, 1971); Juliet Mitchell, *Women's Estate* (New York, 1971); Evelyn Reed, *Problems of Women's Liberation: A Marxist Approach* (New York, 1971). Anthologies include Morgan, ed., *Sisterhood Is Powerful*; Toni Cade, ed. *The Black Woman: An Anthology* (New York, 1970); Deborah Babcox and Madeline Belkin, eds., *Liberation Now: Writings from the Women's Liberation Movement* (New York, 1971).

32. Judith M. Bardwick, *In Transition: How Feminism, Sexual Liberation and the Search for Self-Fulfillment Have Altered America* (New York, 1979), p. 26.

33. For a fuller discussion of what is meant by the term *emancipation*, see Gerda Lerner's statement in "Politics and Culture in Women's History," *Feminist Studies* 6 (1980): 50.

34. The phrases are those of Frances Beale in "Double Jeopardy: To Be Black and Female," in *The Black Woman*, ed. Cade, pp. 90–100, and of Patricia Haden, Donna Middleton, and Patricia Robinson in "A Historical and Critical Essay for Black Women," in *Voices from Women's Liberation*, ed. Leslie B. Tanner (New York, 1971), pp. 316–24.

According to the 1972 Louis Harris Virginia Slims poll, a higher percentage of black women than white supported efforts to improve women's condition. Black feminists such as Pauli Murray, Elizabeth Koontz, Shirley Chisholm, and Florynce Kennedy have been important to the movement, and black feminist groups have developed; the initial response of many black women, however, was to regard the women's movement as a white woman's movement. Freeman explores some of the factors accounting for this initial reaction in *Politics of Women's Liberation*, pp. 37–43.

35. Louis Harris, "Changing Views on the Role of Women," *The Harris Survey*, December 11, 1975.

36. Caroline Bird and the Members and Staff of the National Commission on the Observance of International Woman's Year, *What Women Want: From the Official Report to the President, the Congress, and the People of the United States* (New York, 1979), p. 68 for Johnson's statement.

37. Violet S. Devieux to Senator Sam J. Ervin Jr., March 23, 1972, Samuel J. Ervin Papers, #3847 Southern Historical Collection, Library of the University of North Carolina at Chapel Hill.

38. Bardwick, *In Transition*, p. 9. For a discussion of the impact of change involving values and the psychological resistance engendered, see pp. 9–20.

39. This apt characterization is William Chafe's; see *The American Woman*, p. 209. Chafe's *Women and Equality: Changing Patterns in American Culture* (New York, 1977) provides the most analytically sophisticated study thus far of the issue of women and equality. It explores the interrelation of economic, demographic, and legal changes that make possible the resonance of a feminist critique and hence the creation of a viable protest movement. Also useful is his exploration of the analogy between race and sex, particularly the patterns of control applied to both blacks and women.

40. For a fuller analysis of the significance of the struggle over ERA and the debate over feminism, see Donald G. Mathews and Jane De Hart-Mathews, *The Equal Rights Amendment and the Politics of Cultural Conflict* (New York, forthcoming).

41. The percentage of female lawyers and judges has risen from 3.3 percent in 1960 to 16.2 percent in 1984. For those same years, the percentage of female physicians rose from 6.8 percent to 16 percent, the greatest gains occurring in the 1970s and 1980s.

Women entering engineering, although still only a tiny minority, increased their representation from less than 1 percent in 1960 to 6.2 percent in 1984, bringing the number of women in that profession to 1,627,000. The number of female bank officials and financial managers also rose dramatically, from 17.6 percent in 1970 to 36.8 percent in 1984. The number of female college and university teachers rose more slowly due to constricting job opportunities. By 1984, however, women made up about 36 percent of college and university faculties and were receiving more than a fourth of all Ph.D.s awarded. The number of female college graduates also increased; by the mid-1980s more than half of the graduating seniors were women.

Women moving into traditionally "male" jobs at the blue-collar level showed greatest gains as transport equipment operatives; they numbered 9.6 percent by 1984. Women also made gains in the military, where by 1984 they made up more than 9.5 percent of the enlisted persons and officers. See U.S. Bureau of the Census, *Statistical Abstract of the United States: 1979* (Washington, D.C., 1979), pp. 373, 639; U.S. Bureau of Labor Statistics, *Perspectives on Working Women: A Databook* (Washington, D.C., 1980), pp. 10–11; U.S. Bureau of the Census, *Statistical Abstract of the United States: 1986* (Washington, D.C., 1985), p. 456; Lois Weis, "Progress But No Parity: Women in Higher Education," *Academe* 71 (1985):29–33.

The number of women elected to office rose throughout the 1970s and 1980s, with substantial gains between 1975 and 1985 at the state and local level, where female officeholders numbered around 17,000. In the 1984 elections women captured the governorship of two states and the secretary of state position in eighteen states. They also held the mayor's office in eighty cities, including San Francisco and Houston. At the federal level their number, although still small, reached an all-time high of twenty-four in Congress (twenty-two representatives and two senators). With respect to high-level appointive positions in the federal government, the first female Supreme Court Justice was appointed in 1981 by President Ronald Reagan, while under the Carter administration the number of women sitting in the cabinet reached an all-time high of three. For additional details, see the National Information Bank on Women in Public Office, a Project of the Center for the American Woman and Politics, the Eagleton Institute for Politics, New Brunswick, N.J.

42. The number of single women, especially between the age of twenty and twenty-four, has risen substantially—from 28.4 percent in 1960 to 57 percent by 1984—while the birth rate has dropped from an average of over three children per family in 1960 to less than one in 1984. See U.S. Bureau of the Census, *Statistical Abstract of the United States: 1986*, p. 36; U.S. Bureau of the Census, *Current Population Reports, Household and Family Characteristics: March 1984* (Washington, D.C., 1985), p. 103.

43. Despite the dramatic narrowing of the gap between the numbers of men and women in the labor force that had occurred by 1985 (53.6 percent of all women age sixteen and over as compared to 76.4 percent of all men) and the minimal differences in educational level (18.5 percent of females had four or more years of college as compared with 22.7 percent of all males), the median earnings for workers fourteen years old and over, working fifty to fifty-two weeks per year, indicate a sex-based earnings gap that has changed relatively little. A Rand Corporation study estimates that in 1920 the average earnings of women were 43 percent of those of men; in 1950, 48 percent; in 1980, 54 percent; and in 1984, 65 percent, with significant increases coming in the 1980s. The study projects women's earnings in the year 2000 to be about 74 percent. See U.S. Bureau of the Census, *Statistical Abstract of the United States: 1986*, pp. 392, 397; and James P. Smith, *The Wage Gap and Comparable Worth*, Rand Paper Series (Santa Monica, 1985), pp. 4, 6.

44. Results of the Stanford survey appeared in the *Raleigh News and Observer*, February 1, 1981.

45. As late as 1986 a vast majority of wage-earning women continue to work in a small number of sex-typed jobs—as clerical workers, semiskilled assembly line workers, waitresses, beauticians, and child care workers. Of those holding professional or managerial jobs, most are teachers, nurses, social workers, and librarians. For a fuller discussion see, Barbara F. Reskin and Heidi I. Hartmann, eds., *Women's Work, Men's Work: Sex Segregation on the Job* (Washington, D.C., 1986).

46. Diane Pearce, "The Feminization of Poverty: Women, Work, and Welfare," *Urban and Social Change Review* 11 (1978):28–36; Barbara Ehrenreich and Frances Fox Piven, "The Feminization of Poverty: When the 'Family Wage System' Breaks Down," *Dissent* 31 (1984):162–70; Leonore J. Weitz-

man, *The Divorce Revolution and the Unanticipated Consequences for Women and Children in America* (New York, 1985).

47. Catherine White Berheide, Sarah Fenstermaker Berk, and Richard A. Berk, "Household Work in the Suburbs: The Job and Its Participants," *Pacific Sociological Review* 19 (1976):491–518.

48. For a fuller discussion of these issues, see Carl Degler, *At Odds: Women and the Family in America from the Revolution to the Present* (New York, 1980), chap. 17; and Alice Kessler-Harris, *Women Have Always Worked* (New York, 1981), pp. 157–65.

49. Quoted in Verta Taylor, "The Future of Feminism in the 1980s: A Social Movement Analysis," in *Feminist Frontiers*, ed. Laurel Richardson and Verta Taylor (Reading, Mass., 1983), p. 442. Taylor's essay provides a useful analysis of the movement in the 1980s.

LINDA K. KERBER, Ed.
Essential Documents

The law of the United States affects all inhabitants, but some statutes have had a special significance for women. This section includes the following selection of statutes, constitutional amendments, court decisions and other documents that have had important impact on the status of women in America:

1. Marriage, Divorce, Dower: Examples from Colonial Connecticut (1640, 1667, 1672)
2. Declaration of Sentiments (1848)
3. Married Women's Property Acts: Examples from New York State (1848, 1860)
4. Reconstruction Amendments (1868, 1870)
5. *Bradwell* v. *Illinois* (1873)
6. Comstock Law (1873)
7. *Minor* v. *Happersett* (1875)
8. *Muller* v. *Oregon* (1908)
9. Equal Suffrage Amendment (1920)
10. *Adkins* v. *Children's Hospital* (1923)
11. Civil Rights Act, Title VII (1964)
12. Equal Rights Amendment (1972)
13. *Frontiero* v. *Richardson* (1973)
14. *Roe* v. *Wade* (1973)
15. *Rostker* v. *Goldberg* (1981)

1

Marriage, Divorce, Dower:

Examples from Colonial Connecticut, 1640, 1667, 1672

MARRIAGE

Each American colony developed its own code of laws. There were major variations from colony to colony, but all drew on their memories of English example. All colonies placed in their statutes a law regulating marriage. This reflected a concern that marriage be celebrated publicly in order to guard against bigamy. Laws also guarded against marriages between close relatives; note the wide number of relatives under prohibition. In the course of the nineteenth century the list of prohibited relatives was shortened.

The statutes that follow are from the laws of the colony of Connecticut. The portion requiring the publication of intent to marry is one of the earliest passed in the colony (1640). The original version included the observation that "many persons, by rash and inconsiderate contracts for their future joining in marriage, involve themselves and their friends in great trouble and grief." Although the Connecticut statute listed degrees of kindred in terms of relationships among men, other colonies provided parallel lists for men and women. Connecticut did provide similar punishments for male and female transgressors.

Why might a woman be pleased that her colony had a law like the following one?

An Act for Regulating and Orderly Celebrating of Marriages . . . , 1640, with revisions 1672, 1702

Forasmuch as the ordinance of marriage is honourable amongst all; so it is meet it should be orderly and decently solemnized:

Be it therefore enacted . . . That no persons shall be joined in marriage, before the purpose or intention of the parties proceeding therein, hath been sufficiently published in some public meeting or congregation on the Lord's day, or on some public fast, thanksgiving, or lecture-day, in the town, parish, or society where the parties, or either of them do ordinarily reside; or such purpose or intention be set up in fair writing, upon some post or door of their meeting-house, or near the same, in public view, there to stand so as it may be read, eight days before such marriage.

. . . And in order to prevent incestuous and unlawful marriages, be it further enacted, That no man shall marry . . . his grand-father's wife, wife's grand-mother, father's sister, mother's sister, fa-

The Public Statute Laws of the State of Connecticut (Hartford, 1808), 1:477–79, 236, 239–40.

ther's brother's wife, mother's brother's wife, wife's father's sister, wife's mother's sister, father's wife, wife's mother, daughter, wife's daughter, son's wife, sister, brother's wife, son's daughter, daughter's daughter, son's son's wife, daughter's son's wife, wife's son's daughter, wife's daughter's daughter, brother's daughter, sister's daughter, brother's son's wife, sister's son's wife.

And if any man shall hereafter marry, or have carnal copulation with any woman who is within the degrees before recited in this act, every such marriage shall be . . . null and void; And all children that shall hereafter be born of such incestuous marriage or copulation, shall be forever disabled to inherit by descent, or by being generally named in any deed or will, by father or mother. . . .

And it shall be in the power of the superior court to assign unto any woman so separated, such reasonable part of the estate of her late husband, as in their discretion the circumstances of the estate may admit; not exceeding one third part thereof.

DIVORCE

Early America was a divorceless society. South Carolina boasted that it granted no divorce until 1868. Most colonies followed the British practice of treating marriage as a moral obligation for life. Occasional special dissolutions of a marriage were granted by legislatures in response to individual petitions or by courts of equity, but these were separations from bed and board, which normally did not carry with them freedom to marry again.

Colonial Connecticut was unusual in treating marriage as a civil contract, which might be broken if its terms were not carried out. Connecticut enacted the earliest divorce law in the colonies. It made divorce available after a simple petition to the superior court under certain circumstances. People who did not fit these circumstances were able to present special petitions to the legislature. Normally a divorce in Connecticut implied that the innocent party had the right to marry again.

Most petitioners for divorce in early America were women. On what grounds might Connecticut women petition for divorce?

An Act relating to Bills of Divorce, 1667

Be it enacted . . . that no bill of divorce shall be granted to any man or woman, lawfully married, but in case of adultery, or fraudulent contract, or wilful desertion for three years with total neglect of duty; or in case of seven years absence of one party not heard of: after due enquiry is made, and the matter certified to the superior court, in which case the other party may be deemed and accounted single and unmarried. And in that case, and in all other cases afore-mentioned, a bill of divorce may be granted by the superior court to the aggrieved party; who may then lawfully marry or be married again.

DOWER

Perhaps no statutes were more important to women in the first 250 years after settlement of the American colonies than the laws protecting their claims to dower. The "widow's dower" should be distinguished from the dowry a bride might bring with her into marriage. "The widow's dower" or the "widow's third" was the right of a widow to use one-third of the real estate that her husband held at the time of his death. It was an old English tradition that he might leave her more in his will, but he could not leave her less. If a man died without a will, the courts would ensure that his widow received her "third."

It is important to note that she only had the right to use the land and buildings. She might live on this property, rent it out, farm the land, and sell the produce. But she could not sell or bequeath it. After her death the property reverted to her husband's heirs, who normally would be their children, but in the case of a childless marriage it might go to others whom he identified.

In the Connecticut statute, printed below, note the provisions protecting the widow's interests. Normally colonial courts were scrupulous about assigning the widow's portion. Observe, however, that widows could not claim dower in "movable" property, which might represent a larger share of their husband's wealth than real estate. As time passed and the American economy became more complex, it became increasingly likely that a man's property would not be held in the form of land. If the land were heavily mortgaged, the widow's prior right to her "third" became a barrier to creditors seeking to collect their portion of a husband's debts. By the early nineteenth century courts were losing their enthusiasm for protecting widows' thirds.

By the middle of the century the married women's property acts began to reformulate a definition of the terms by which married women could claim their share of the property of wife and husband. But between 1790 and 1840, when the right to dower was more and more laxly enforced and the new married women's property acts had not yet been devised, married women were in a particularly vulnerable position.

An Act concerning the Dowry of Widows, 1672

That there may be suitable provision made for the maintenance and comfortable support of widows, after the decease of their husbands, Be it enacted . . . that every married woman, living with her husband in this state, or absent elsewhere from him with his consent, or through his mere default, or by inevitable providence; or in case of divorce where she is the innocent party, that shall not before marriage be estated by way of jointure in some houses, lands, tenements or hereditaments for term of life . . . shall immediately upon, and after the death of her husband, have right, title and interest by way of dower, in and unto one third part of the real estate of her said deceased husband, in houses and lands which he stood possessed of in his own right, at the time of his decease, to be to her during her natural life: the remainder of the estate shall be disposed of according to the will of the deceased. . . .

And for the more easy, and speedy ascertaining such rights of dower, It is further enacted, That upon the death of any man possessed of any real estate . . . which his widow . . . hath a right of dower in, if the person, or persons that by law have a right to inherit said estate, do not within sixty days next after the death of such husband, by three sufficient free-holders of the same country; to be appointed by the judge of probate . . . and sworn for that purpose, set out, and ascertain such right of dower, that then such widow may make her complaint to the judge of probate . . . which judge shall decree, and order that such woman's dowry shall be set out, and ascertained by three sufficient freeholders of the county . . . and upon approbation thereof by said judge, such dower shall remain fixed and certain. . . .

And every widow so endowed . . . shall maintain all such houses, buildings, fences, and inclosures as shall be assigned, and set out to her for her dowry; and shall leave the same in good and sufficient repair.

2

Declaration of Sentiments, 1848

The "Convention to discuss the social, civil, and religious condition and rights of women" that was announced by Elizabeth Cady Stanton, Lucretia Mott, and two of their friends in 1848 was simply an open meeting to which the public was invited. It provided an occasion for debating and publicizing a set of reform proposals. The meeting in Seneca Falls, New York, was followed by a series of other public meetings—in Rochester, New York; Akron, Ohio; and Worcester, Massachusetts. But the manifesto of the Seneca Falls Convention, written by Elizabeth Cady Stanton, remained the basic statement of reformers' goals throughout the nineteenth century.

The rhetoric of the Declaration of Sentiments was borrowed from the Declaration of Independence. Through its lines flowed the conviction that the Revolution had made implicit promises to women which had not been kept.

Declaration of Sentiments, in *History of Woman Suffrage*, edited by Elizabeth Cady Stanton, Susan B. Anthony, and Matilda Joslyn Gage, vol. 1 (New York: Fowler & Wells, 1881), pp. 70–71.

Seneca Falls, New York,
July 19–20, 1848

When, in the course of human events, it becomes necessary for one portion of the family of man to assume among the people of the earth a position different from that which they have hitherto occupied, but one to which the laws of nature and of nature's God entitle them, a decent respect to the opinions of mankind requires that they should declare the causes that impel them to such a course.

We hold these truths to be self-evident: that all men and women are created equal; that they are endowed by their Creator with certain inalienable rights; that among these are life, liberty, and the pursuit of happiness; that to secure these rights governments are instituted, deriving their just powers from the consent of the governed. Whenever any form of government becomes destructive of these ends, it is the right of those who suffer from it to refuse allegiance to it, and to insist upon the institution of a new government, laying its foundation on such principles, and organizing its powers in such form, as to them shall seem most likely to effect their safety and happiness. Prudence, indeed, will dictate that governments long established should not be changed for light and transient causes; and accordingly all experience hath shown that mankind are more disposed to suffer, while evils are sufferable, than to right themselves by abolishing the forms to which they were accustomed. But when a long train of abuses and usurpations, pursuing invariably the same object evinces a design to reduce them under absolute despotism, it is their duty to throw off such government, and to provide new guards for their future security. Such has been the patient sufferance of the women under this government, and such is now the necessity which constrains them to demand the equal station to which they are entitled.

The history of mankind is a history of repeated injuries and usurpations on the part of man toward woman, having in direct object the establishment of an absolute tyranny over her. To prove this, let facts be submitted to a candid world.

He has never permitted her to exercise her inalienable right to the elective franchise.

He has compelled her to submit to laws, in the formation of which she had no voice.

He has withheld from her rights which are given to the most ignorant and degraded men—both native and foreigners.

Having deprived her of this first right of a citizen, the elective franchise, thereby leaving her without representation in the halls of legislation, he has oppressed her on all sides.

He has made her, if married, in the eye of the law, civilly dead.

He has taken from her all right in property, even to the wages she earns.

He has made her, morally, an irresponsible being, as she can commit many crimes with impunity, provided they be done in the presence of her husband. In the covenant of marriage, she is compelled to promise obedience to her husband, he becoming, to all intents and purposes, her master—the law giving him power to deprive her of her liberty, and to administer chastisement.

He has so framed the laws of divorce, as to what shall be the proper causes, and in case of separation, to whom the guardianship of the children shall be given, as to be wholly regardless of the happiness of women—the law, in all cases, going upon a false supposition of the supremacy of man, and giving all power into his hands.

After depriving her of all rights as a married woman, if single, and the owner of property, he has taxed her to support a government which recognizes her only when her property can be made profitable to it.

He has monopolized nearly all the

profitable employments, and from those she is permitted to follow, she receives but a scanty remuneration. He closes against her all the avenues to wealth and distinction which he considers most honorable to himself. As a teacher of theology, medicine, or law, she is not known.

He has denied her the facilities for obtaining a thorough education, all colleges being closed against her.

He allows her in Church, as well as State, but a subordinate position, claiming Apostolic authority for her exclusion from the ministry, and, with some exceptions, from any public participation in the affairs of the Church.

He has created a false public sentiment by giving to the world a different code of morals for men and women, by which moral delinquencies which exclude women from society, are not only tolerated, but deemed of little account in man.

He has usurped the prerogative of Jehovah himself, claiming it as his right to assign for her a sphere of action, when that belongs to her conscience and to her God.

He has endeavored, in every way that he could, to destroy her confidence in her own powers, to lessen her self-respect, and to make her willing to lead a dependent and abject life.

Now, in view of this entire disfranchisement of one-half the people of this country, their social and religious degradation—in view of the unjust laws above mentioned, and because women do feel themselves aggrieved, oppressed, and fraudulently deprived of their most sacred rights, we insist that they have immediate admission to all the rights and privileges which belong to them as citizens of the United States.

In entering upon the great work before us, we anticipate no small amount of misconception, misrepresentation, and ridicule; but we shall use every instrumentality within our power to effect our object. We shall employ agents, circulate tracts, petition the State and National legislatures, and endeavor to enlist the pulpit and the press in our behalf. We hope this Convention will be followed by a series of Conventions embracing every part of the country.

3

Married Women's Property Acts:

Examples from New York State, 1848, 1860

Americans inherited the ancient English custom of *coverture*, by which the married woman's civil identity was covered by or absorbed into her husband's. By common law tradition a husband might spend his wife's property, punish her physically, and provide her with only minimal food, clothing, and shelter. The rigor of the common law was in fact substantially eased both in

Laws of the State of New-York, Passed at the Seventy-First Session of the Legislature . . . (Albany, 1848), pp. 307–308; *Laws of the State of New York, Passed at the Eighty-Third Session of the Legislature* . . . (Albany, 1860), pp. 157–59.

England and the colonies by courts of equity, which permitted more judicial discretion. The common law rights of the husband might, for example, be circumvented by premarital contracts or trusteeships.

But these options were most realistic for women who could obtain the benefit of sophisticated legal advice and who had substantial property to protect. They were not readily available to poorer women who needed them most. The Declaration of Sentiments sharply attacked contemporary practice as "civil death" for women. Reformers gave high priority to legislation that would confirm the right of married women to the property they had brought into their marriages and to wages and income they earned after marriage.

Ironically, the first married women's property acts, passed in Mississippi in 1839 and in New York in 1848, were supported by many male legislators out of a desire to preserve the estates of married daughters against spendthrift sons-in-law. Four out of the five sections of the Mississippi act broadened the rights of married women over their own slaves.

Note the limits of the 1848 New York law and the ways in which women's rights were extended by the 1860 revision. In 1860 married women were also confirmed in their guardianship of their children.

New York State Married Women's Property Acts

1848

The real and personal property of any female [now married and] who may hereafter marry, and which she shall own at the time of marriage, and the rents issues and profits thereof shall not be subject to the disposal of her husband, nor be liable for his debts, and shall continue her sole and separate property, as if she were a single female. . . .

It shall be lawful for any married female to receive, by gift, grant, devise or bequest, from any person other than her husband and hold to her sole and separate use, as if she were a single female, real and personal property, and the rents, issues and profits thereof, and the same shall not be subject to the disposal of her husband, nor be liable for his debts. . . .

1860

[The provisions of the law of 1848 were retained, and others were added:]
A married woman may bargain, sell, assign, and transfer her separate personal property, and carry on any trade or business, and perform any labor or services on her sole and separate account, and the

earnings of any married woman from her trade . . . shall be her sole and separate property, and may be used or invested by her in her own name. . . .

Any married woman may, while married, sue and be sued in all matters having relation to her . . . sole and separate property . . . in the same manner as if she were sole. And any married woman may bring and maintain an action in her own name, for damages, against any person or body corporate, for any injury to her person or character, the same as if she were sole; and the money received upon the settlement . . . shall be her sole and separate property.

No bargain or contract made by any married woman, in respect to her sole and separate property . . . shall be binding upon her husband, or render him or his property in any way liable therefor.

Every married woman is hereby constituted and declared to be the joint guardian of her children, with her husband, with equal powers, rights, and duties in regard to them, with the husband. . . .

4

Reconstruction Amendments, 1868, 1870

Until 1868, the United States Constitution made no explicit distinctions on the basis of gender. Of qualifications for voters, it said only that "the electors in each State shall have the qualifications requisite for electors of the most numerous branch of the State legislature" (Article I, section 2). Reformers merely needed to persuade each state legislature to change its own rules in order to enfranchise women in national elections.

The word *male* was introduced into the Constitution in section 2 of the Fourteenth Amendment, as part of a complex provision—never enforced—intended to constrain former Confederates from interfering with the civil rights of newly freed slaves. Suffragists were bitterly disappointed at the failure to include sex as a category in the Fifteenth Amendment. But until the test case of *Minor v. Happersett* (document 9), they clung to the hope that the first article of the Fourteenth Amendment would be interpreted broadly enough to admit women to the polls.

Fourteenth Amendment, 1868

1. All persons born or naturalized in the United States, and subject to the jurisdiction thereof, are citizens of the United States and of the State wherein they reside. No State shall make or enforce any law which shall abridge the privileges or immunities of citizens of the United States; nor shall any State deprive any person of life, liberty, or property, without due process of law; nor deny to any person within its jurisdiction the equal protection of the laws.

2. Representatives shall be apportioned among the several States according to their respective numbers, counting the whole number of persons in each State,

excluding Indians not taxed. But when the right to vote at any election for the choice of electors for President and Vice-President of the United States, Representatives in Congress, the executive and judicial officers of a State, or the members of the legislature thereof, is denied to any of the male inhabitants of such State, being twenty-one years of age and citizens of the United States, or in any way abridged, except for participation in rebellion, or other crime, the basis of representation therein shall be reduced in the proportion which the number of such male citizens shall bear to the whole number of male citizens twenty-one years of age in such State. . . .

Fifteenth Amendment, 1870

The right of citizens of the United States to vote shall not be denied or abridged by the United States or by any State on account of race, color, or previous condition of servitude. . . .

5

Bradwell v. Illinois, *1873*

Although she could not practice in the courts until the end of her career, Myra Bradwell was perhaps the most notable female lawyer of the nineteenth century. She read law in the office of her husband, a prominent Chicago attorney and county judge. In 1868 she began to publish the *Chicago Legal News*, a weekly newspaper covering developments in courts and legislatures throughout the country. Because she had received a special charter from the state legislature under which she was permitted to act without the usual legal disabilities of a married woman, she ran the *News* as her own business. She wrote vigorous editorials, evaluating legal opinions and new laws, assessing proposed state legislation, and supporting progressive developments like prison reform, the establishment of law schools, and women's rights. She drafted bills improving married women's rights to property and child custody.

It was only logical that she should seek admission to the bar. Although she passed the entrance tests in 1869, she was rejected by the Illinois State Supreme Court on the grounds that she was a married woman, and therefore not a fully free agent. Appealing to the United States Supreme Court, her attorney argued that among the "privileges and immunities" guaranteed to each citizen by the Fourteenth Amendment was the right to pursue any honorable professio . "In-

83 U.S. 130.

telligence, integrity and honor are the only qualifications that can be prescribed . . . the broad shield of the Constitution is over all, and protects each in that measure of success which his or her individual merits may secure."

The Court's decision came in two parts. Speaking for the majority and citing the recent decision of the Supreme Court in the slaughterhouse cases, Justice Samuel F. Miller held that the right to practice law in the courts of any particular state was a right that might be granted by the individual state; it was not one of the "privileges and immunities" of citizenship. Then, in a concurring opinion, Justice Joseph P. Bradley offered an ideological justification for the Court's decision that was based on inherent differences between men and women and that was to be widely used thereafter to defend the exclusion of women from professional careers. (It should be added that in 1890, twenty years after her original application, the Illinois Supreme Court relented and admitted Bradwell to the bar.)

Mr. Justice Joseph P. Bradley:

The claim of the plaintiff, who is a married woman, to be admitted to practice as an attorney and counselor at law, is based upon the supposed right of every person, man or woman, to engage in any lawful employment for a livelihood. The supreme court of Illinois denied the application on the ground that, by the common law, which is the basis of the laws of Illinois, only men were admitted to the bar, and the legislature had not made any change in this respect. . . .

The claim that, under the 14th Amendment of the Constitution, which declares that no state shall make or enforce any law which shall abridge the privileges and immunities of citizens of the United States, and the statute law of Illinois, or the common law prevailing in that state, can no longer be set up as a barrier against the right of females to pursue any lawful employment . . . assumes that it is one of the privileges and immunities of women as citizens to engage in any and every profession, occupation or employment in civil life.

It certainly cannot be affirmed, as a

historical fact, that this has ever been established as one of the fundamental privileges and immunities of the sex. On the contrary, the civil law, as well as nature herself, has always recognized a wide difference in the respective spheres and destinies of man and woman. Man is, or should be, woman's protector and defender. The natural and proper timidity and delicacy which belongs to the female sex evidently unfits it for many of the occupations of civil life. The constitution of the family organization, which is founded in the divine ordinance, as well as in the nature of things, indicates the domestic sphere as that which properly belongs to the domain and functions of womanhood. The harmony, not to say identity, of interests and views which belong or should belong to the family institution, is repugnant to the idea of a woman adopting a distinct and independent career from that of her husband. So firmly fixed was this sentiment in the founders of the common law that it became a maxim of that system of jurisprudence that a woman had no legal existence separate from her husband, who was regarded as her head and representative in the social state; and, notwithstanding some recent modifications of this civil status, many of the special rules of law flowing from and dependent upon this cardinal principle still exist in full force in most states. One of these is, that a married woman is incapable, without her husband's consent, of making contracts which shall be binding on her or him. This very incapacity was one circumstance which the supreme court of Illinois deemed important in rendering a married woman incompetent fully to perform the duties and trusts that belong to the office of an attorney and counselor.

It is true that many women are unmarried and not affected by any of the duties, complications, and incapacities arising out of the married state, but these are exceptions to the general rule. The paramount destiny and mission of woman are to fulfill the noble and benign offices of wife and mother. This is the law of the Creator. And the rules of civil society must be adapted to the general constitution of things, and cannot be based upon exceptional cases. . . .

6

Comstock Law, 1873

This "Act for the Suppression of Trade in, and Circulation of Obscene Literature and Articles of Immoral Use" was passed at the urging of Anthony Comstock, the head of the New York Society for the Suppression of Vice. The first section prohibited the sale of the described materials in the District of Columbia and the territories; subsequent sections prohibited the sending of these materials through the mails or their importation into the United States. In the 1870s many states passed their own versions of the federal law.

The law reflected a widespread belief that both contraception and abortion were acts of interference with the natural order and with God's intentions. No distinction was made between drugs used for abortion and materials used for contraception; all were treated in the same terms as pornographic materials. Note the heavy penalties provided.

A century after the Comstock Law, its limitations on birth control information and on pornography had eroded. By 1973 the Supreme Court finally agreed on the definition of obscene material, that is, material unprotected as an exercise of free speech under the First Amendment: "the average person, applying contemporary community standards, would find that the work, taken as a whole, appeals to the prurient interest . . . [describes sexual conduct] in a patently offensive way . . . and . . . lacks serious literary, artistic, political, or scientific value" (*Miller* v. *California*, 413 U.S. 15 [1973]). In the 1980s some

Public Laws of the United States of America, Passed at the Third Session of the Forty-Second Congress (Boston, 1873), p. 598.

feminists began to argue that pornography ought to be defined not merely as obscenity but as "sexually explicit subordination of women"; that is, that pornography was not simply an expression of free speech, protected under the First Amendment, but an actual injury, to be protected against as a civil liberty. "Depictions of subordination tend to perpetuate subordination. The subordinate status of women in turn leads to affront and lower pay at work, insult and injury at home, battery and rape on the streets," observed a federal court in the course of evaluating an Indianapolis ordinance outlawing pornography in 1985 (*American Booksellers Association* v. *Hudnut*, 771 F.2d 323 [1985]). Although the Court refused to uphold the ordinance, the issue continues to be debated.

Be it enacted . . . That whoever, within the District of Columbia or any of the Territories of the United States . . . shall sell . . . or shall offer to sell, or to lend, or to give away, or in any manner to exhibit, or shall otherwise publish or offer to publish in any manner, or shall have in his possession, for any such purpose or purposes, any obscene book, pamphlet, paper, writing, advertisement, circular, print, picture, drawing or other representation, figure, or image on or of paper or other material, or any cast, instrument, or other article of an immoral nature, or any drug or medicine, or any article whatever, for the prevention of conception, or for causing unlawful abortion, or shall advertize the same for sale, or shall write or print, or cause to be written or printed, any card, circular, book, pamphlet, advertisement, or notice of any kind, stating when, where, how, or of whom, or by what means, any of the articles in this section . . . can be purchased or obtained, or shall manufacture, draw, or print, or in any wise make any of such articles, shall be deemed guilty of a misdemeanor, and on conviction thereof in any court of the United States . . . he shall be imprisoned at hard labor in the penitentiary for not less than six months nor more than five years for each offense, or fined not less than one hundred dollars nor more than two thousand dollars, with costs of court. . . .

7

Minor *v.* Happersett, *1875*

In 1872 suffragists in a number of places attempted to test the possibilities of the first section of the Fourteenth Amendment. "The power to regulate is one thing, the power to prevent is an entirely different thing," observed Virginia Minor, president of the Woman Suffrage Association of Missouri, and she presented herself at the polls in St. Louis in 1872. When the registrar refused to permit her to register to vote, she and her husband sued him for denying her

88 U.S. 162.

one of the "privileges and immunities of citizenship"; when they lost the case they appealed to the Supreme Court.

In a unanimous opinion the justices held that if the authors of the Constitution had intended that women should vote, they would have said so explicitly. The decision of the Court meant that woman suffrage could not be developed by way of a quiet reinterpretation of the Constitution but would require an explicit amendment to the Constitution or a series of revisions in the laws of the states.

Mr. Chief Justice Morrison R. Waite delivered the opinion
of the Court:

The question is presented in this case, whether, since the adoption of the fourteenth amendment, a woman, who is a citizen of the United States and of the State of Missouri, is a voter in that State, notwithstanding the provision of the constitution and laws of the State, which confine the right of suffrage to men alone. . . . The argument is, that as a woman, born or naturalized in the United States and subject to the jurisdiction thereof, is a citizen of the United States and of the State in which she resides, she has the right of suffrage as one of the privileges and immunities of her citizenship, which the State cannot by its laws or constitution abridge.

There is no doubt that women may be citizens. They are persons, and by the fourteenth amendment "all persons born or naturalized in the United States and subject to the jurisdiction thereof" are expressly declared to be "citizens of the United States and of the State wherein they reside." But, in our opinion, it did not need this amendment to give them that position . . . sex has never been made one of the elements of citizenship in the United States. In this respect men have never had an advantage over women. The same laws precisely apply to both. The fourteenth amendment did not affect the citizenship of women any more than it did of men. . . . Mrs. Minor . . . has always been a citizen from her birth, and

entitled to all the privileges and immunities of citizenship.

If the right of suffrage is one of the necessary privileges of a citizen of the United States, then the constitution and laws of Missouri confining it to men are in violation of the Constitution of the United States, as amended, and consequently void. The direct question is, therefore, presented whether all citizens are necessarily voters.

The Constitution does not define the privileges and immunities of citizens. For that definition we must look elsewhere. In this case we need not determine what they are, but only whether suffrage is necessarily one of them.

It certainly is nowhere made so in express terms. The United States has no voters in the States of its own creation. The elective officers of the United States are all elected directly or indirectly by state voters. . . . it cannot for a moment be doubted that if it had been intended to make all citizens of the United States voters, the framers of the Constitution would not have left it to implication. . . .

It is true that the United States guarantees to every State a republican form of government. . . . No particular government is designated as republican, neither is the exact form to be guaranteed, in any manner especially designated. . . . When the Constitution was adopted . . . all the citizens of the States were not invested with the right of suffrage. In all, save perhaps New Jersey, this right was only bestowed upon men and not upon all of them. . . . Under these circumstances it is certainly now too late to contend that a government is not republican, within the meaning of this guaranty in the Constitution, because women are not made voters. . . . If suffrage was intended to be included within its obligations, language better adapted to express that intent would most certainly have been employed. . . .

. . . For nearly ninety years the people have acted upon the idea that the Constitution, when it conferred citizenship, did not necessarily confer the right of suffrage. If uniform practice long continued can settle the construction of so important an instrument as the Constitution of the United States confessedly is, most certainly it has been done here. Our province is to decide what the law is, not to declare what it should be.

We have given this case the careful consideration its importance demands. If the law is wrong, it ought to be changed; but the power for that is not with us. . . . No argument as to woman's need of suffrage can be considered. We can only act upon her rights as they exist. . . .

8

Muller *v.* Oregon, *1908*

The farmer's workday was sunrise to sunset. When the first factories were established in the early nineteenth century, they were operated for equally long hours. It was a particular interest of laborers and of progressive reformers to support enactment of limits on the workday. The ten-hour day was on the agenda of early labor unions, and the federal civil service adopted it shortly after the Civil War.

But in 1905 the United States Supreme Court refused to uphold a state law limiting the hours of bakers to ten hours a day. Ruling in *Lochner* v. *New York* (198 U.S. 45 [1905]), the Court held that such a law was not "a legitimate exercise of the police power of the State, but an unreasonable, unnecessary, and arbitrary interference with the right and liberty of the individual to contract in relation to his labor. . . ."

After the *Lochner* decision progressives were forced to conclude that it was impractical to support limitations on hours that applied to *all* workers. But it occurred to some that a special case might be made in defense of a limit on working hours for women.

When the constitutionality of the Oregon ten-hour law for women was challenged, the National Consumers' League undertook the defense of the statute and hired attorney Louis D. Brandeis to present the case before the Supreme Court. The brief he presented to the court in *Muller* v. *Oregon* was startling and

208 U.S. 412.

unprecedented. It consisted of only two pages of legal argument and over one hundred pages describing the "world's experience regarding women's hours of labor." Although the document became known as the Brandeis Brief, it was prepared largely by his sister-in-law Josephine Goldmark, a social worker and a staff member of the Consumers' League. Goldmark wrote a closely reasoned monograph, drawing on reports of factory inspectors, bureaus of labor statistics, commissioners of hygiene, and observations of physicians, and demonstrating that everywhere in the civilized world long hours had been shown to be detrimental to the health, safety, and morals of employed women. The style of argument, drawing as it did on social evidence as much as upon abstract legal reasoning, came to be known as "sociological jurisprudence." The style was widely employed; the government's case in 1954 in *Brown* v. *Board of Education*, on the desegregation of schools, had much in common with the Brandeis Brief.

In 1908 the Supreme Court upheld the constitutionality of the Oregon law, though making it clear that it was swayed primarily by the case made for women's physical vulnerability and couching the decision in terms of traditional sex roles. Fifteen years later, only five states lacked maximum hour legislation of some sort, although provisions varied widely.

Protective legislation for women had complex consequences. Obviously an eight-hour workday was vastly preferable to a longer one. But in the absence of a minimum wage, women living at the margin of subsistence found that limitations on the hours they could work cut their income or speeded up their piecework; some would not have chosen to trade time for money. Maximum hour legislation was often supplemented by restrictions against night work and "heavy" work (the latter often conveniently defined to include well-paying skilled work like iron molding), which further segregated women in the workplace and gave men an advantage in the competition for jobs. There is substantial evidence that male unions understood this when they supported protective legislation.*

Compare the reasoning in *Muller* to that offered in the *Bradwell* case (document 5) more than thirty-five years before. What were the advantages of pressing the argument of female weakness? What were the disadvantages?

Mr. Justice David J. Brewer:

. . . It may not be amiss, in the present case, before examining the constitutional question, to notice the course of legislation, as well as expressions of opinion from other than judicial sources. In the brief filed by Mr. Louis D. Brandeis for the defendant . . . is a very copious collection of all these matters. . . .

* See Alice Kessler-Harris, *Out to Work: A History of Wage-Earning Women in the United States* (New York, 1982), pp. 201–5.

The legislation and opinions referred to . . . may not be, technically speaking, authorities, and in them is little or no discussion of the constitutional question presented to us for determination, yet, they are significant of a widespread belief that woman's physical structure, and the functions she performs in consequence thereof, justify special legislation restricting or qualifying the conditions under which she should be permitted to toil. . . .

That woman's physical structure and the performance of maternal functions place her at a disadvantage in the struggle for subsistence is obvious. This is especially true when the burdens of motherhood are upon her. Even when they are not, by abundant testimony of the medical fraternity continuance for a long time on her feet at work, repeating this from day to day, tends to injurious effects upon the body, and, as healthy mothers are essential to vigorous offspring, the physical well-being of woman becomes an object of public interest and care in order to preserve the strength and vigor of the race. . . . Differentiated by these matters from the other sex, she is properly placed in a class by herself, and legislation designed for her protection may be sustained, even when like legislation is not necessary for men, and could not be sustained. It is impossible to close one's eyes to the fact that she still looks to her brother and depends upon him. . . . her physical structure and a proper discharge of her maternal functions—having in view not merely her own health, but the well-being of the race—justify legislation to protect her

from the greed as well as the passion of man. The limitations which this statute places upon her contractual powers, upon her right to agree with her employer as to the time she shall labor, are not imposed solely for her benefit, but also largely for the benefit of all. Many words cannot make this plainer. The two sexes differ in structure of body, in the functions to be performed by each, in the amount of physical strength, in the capacity for long continued labor, particularly when done standing, the influence of vigorous health upon the future well-being of the race, the self-reliance which enables one to assert full rights, and in the capacity to maintain the struggle for subsistence. This difference justifies a difference in legislation, and upholds that which is designed to compensate for some of the burdens which rest upon her.

We have not referred in this discussion to the denial of the elective franchise in the State of Oregon, for while it may disclose a lack of political equality in all things with her brother, that is not of itself decisive. The reason runs deeper, and rests in the inherent difference between the two sexes.

For these reasons, and without questioning in any respect the decision in *Lochner* v. *New York*, we are of the opinion that it cannot be adjudged that the act in question is in conflict with the Federal Constitution, so far as it respects the work of a female in a laundry, and the judgment of the Supreme Court of Oregon is Affirmed.

9

Equal Suffrage Amendment, 1920

A federal woman suffrage amendment was introduced into the Senate by S. C. Pomeroy of Kansas in 1868 and into the House by George W. Julian of Indiana in March 1869. It seemed to suffragists to be a logical response to the refusal to include the word *sex* in the Fifteenth Amendment. "The same arguments made in this country," observed Elizabeth Cady Stanton, "for extending suffrage from time to time, to white men, native born citizens, without property and education, and to foreigners . . . the same used by the great Republican party to enfranchise a million black men in the South, all these arguments we have to-day to offer for woman. . . . This fundamental principle of our government—the equality of all the citizens of the republic—should be incorporated in the Federal Constitution, there to remain forever."

After several close votes the Nineteenth Amendment to the Constitution was approved by Congress in the spring of 1920 and was ratified by the necessary thirty-six states in August, just in time for women to register to vote in the 1920 presidential election.

If women could vote, it followed that they could hold office and serve on juries. But it was common for states to exclude women from lists of possible jurors unless they specifically asked to have their names entered. The Supreme Court permitted states to treat all women differently from all men for the purpose of jury service and to exclude women unless they volunteered, on the grounds that women were normally most needed at home. Not until 1975, in the case of *Taylor* v. *Louisiana* (419 U.S. 522 [1975]) did the Court rule that "the exclusion of women from jury venires [lists of eligible jurors] deprives a criminal defendant of his Sixth Amendment right to trial by an impartial jury drawn from a fair cross section of the community."

Section 1. The right of the citizens of the United States to vote shall not be denied or abridged by the United States or by any State on account of sex.

Section 2. Congress shall have power to enforce this article by appropriate legislation.

10

Adkins v. Children's Hospital, *1923*

Minimum wage legislation was the counterpart to maximum hour laws. In 1918 Congress authorized the Wage Board of the District of Columbia to fix minimum wages for women and children in order to protect them "from conditions detrimental to their health and morals, resulting from wages which are inadequate to maintain decent standards of living."

261 U.S. 525.

This act was attacked, much as maximum hour legislation had been, as an interference with the right of the employer and employee to contract freely. Suit was brought against it by a hospital that employed many women at lower than minimum wages. Arguing for the Wage Board and on behalf of the Consumers' League was Felix Frankfurter, who used a Brandeis Brief researched by Molly Dewson that was a thousand pages long. He convinced Justices William Howard Taft and Oliver Wendell Holmes, Jr., that low wages and long hours were linked. In their dissenting opinion they stated that if Congress could regulate one it could regulate the other. Holmes also observed that the phrase "liberty of contract" did not appear in the Constitution.

The majority of the Court was not, however, persuaded. The members of the majority distinguished between maximum hours legislation, which they saw as directly allied to health concerns, and minimum wage legislation, which they thought "simply and exclusively a price-fixing law." The majority also observed that the Nineteenth Amendment obviated the need for protective legislation for women.

The *Adkins* decision blocked progress in minimum wage legislation for fifteen years, until there was a new president (Franklin D. Roosevelt) and a new approach in Congress. In 1938 the Fair Labor Standards Act established a federal minimum wage for *both* men and women. However, women continued often to be paid less than men for the same jobs. In 1963 the Equal Pay Act prohibited different pay for men and women when their jobs require "equal skill, effort and responsibility and are performed under similar working conditions." The Court has ruled that jobs meriting equal pay must be substantially equal but not necessarily identical: "Dusting is dusting is dusting" said one court in ruling that the pay of maids and janitors must be equal. More recently, the definition of what constitutes "equal skill, effort and responsibility" has been broadened to a public debate over what constitutes "comparable worth."

Mr. Justice George Sutherland delivered the opinion of the Court:

. . . the ancient inequality of the sexes, otherwise than physical, as suggested in the *Muller Case* has continued "with diminishing intensity." In view of the great—not to say revolutionary—changes which have taken place since that utterance, in the contractual, political and civil status of women, culminating in the Nineteenth Amendment, it is not unreasonable to say that these differences have now come almost, if not quite, to the vanishing point. . . . we cannot accept the doctrine that women of mature age, . . . require or may be subjected to restrictions upon their liberty of contract which could not lawfully be imposed in the case of men under similar circumstances. To do so would be to ignore all the implications to be drawn from the present day trend of legislation, as well as that of common thought and usage, by which woman is accorded emancipation from the old doc-

trine that she must be given special protection or be subjected to special restraint
in her contractual and civil relationships. . . .

   . . . What is sufficient to supply the
necessary cost of living for a woman
worker and maintain her in good health
and protect her morals is obviously not
a precise or unvarying sum. . . . The

amount will depend upon a variety of circumstances: the individual temperament,
habits of thrift, care, ability to buy necessaries intelligently, and whether the
woman live alone or with her family. . . .
It cannot be shown that well paid women
safeguard their morals more carefully than
those who are poorly paid. Morality rests
upon other considerations than wages. . . .

11

Civil Rights Act, Title VII, 1964

The Civil Rights Act of 1964 was a comprehensive law of enormous significance.
It was a complex statute, twenty-eight printed pages long and divided into
eleven major sections, or *Titles*. Title I dealt with voting rights; Title III with
the desegregation of public facilities; Title V established a Commission on
Civil Rights. Title VII defined a long list of practices that would be forbidden
to employers and labor unions, obliged the federal government to undertake an
"affirmative" program of equal employment opportunity for all employees and
job applicants, and created an Equal Employment Opportunity Commission
(EEOC) to monitor compliance with the law.

   Title VII was notable in that it outlawed discrimination on the basis of gender as well as of race. Sex was added to the categories "race, color, religion and
national origin" by Congressman Howard Smith of Virginia, who hoped to
defeat the legislation; he joked that an amendment adding the category "sex"
would guarantee the "right" of every woman to a husband. Representative
Martha Griffiths of Michigan and other congresswomen supported the bill,
ironically receiving support from conservative colleagues who spoke on behalf
of the amendment in the hope that the prospect of sexual equality might cause
the entire bill to fail.

   The Equal Employment Opportunity Commission, which began to operate in
the summer of 1965, anticipated that virtually all its complaints would come
from blacks. They were surprised to discover that 25 percent of the complaints
received during the first year were from women. In the course of responding to
these complaints, both the commission and the courts were driven to a more

U.S. *Statutes at Large*, 78:253–66. For a full discussion of Title VII, see Donald Allen Robinson, "Two Movements in Pursuit of Equal Employment Opportunity," *Signs: Journal of
Women in Culture and Society* 4 (1979): 413–33.

subtle analysis of female job categories and work patterns. Section 703(e)1 required that employers wishing to define a job category by sex had to show that sex was a "bona fide occupational qualification"; it was not enough to say that men or women had traditionally filled any given job.

The act was amended in 1972 and again in 1978; on both occasions the EEOC was given substantial additional powers and responsibilities. The three major areas of EEOC activity are: (1) furnishing assistance to comparable state agencies, (2) furnishing advice to employers and labor unions about compliance, and (3) enforcing compliance by conciliation and by legal action. In 1978 Congress passed the Pregnancy Discrimination Act, which amplified the definition of *sex* to include pregnancy, childbirth, or related medical conditions. EEOC has been willing to view sexual harassment as a form of sex discrimination but has not endorsed the concept of comparable worth.

Sec. 703. (a) It shall be an unlawful employment practice for an employer—

(1) to fail or refuse to hire or to discharge any individual, or otherwise to discriminate against any individual with respect to his compensation, terms, conditions, or privileges of employment, because of such individual's race, color, religion, sex, or national origin; or

(2) to limit, segregate, or classify his employees in any way which would deprive or tend to deprive any individual of employment opportunities or otherwise adversely affect his status as an employee, because of such individual's race, color, religion, sex, or national origin.

(b) It shall be an unlawful employment practice for an employment agency to fail or refuse to refer for employment, or otherwise to discriminate against, any individual because of his race, color, religion, sex, or national origin, or to classify or refer for employment any individual on the basis of his race, color, religion, sex, or national origin.

(c) It shall be an unlawful employment practice for a labor organization—

(1) to exclude or to expel from its membership, or otherwise to discriminate against, any individual because of his race, color, religion, sex, or national origin;

(2) to limit, segregate, or classify its membership, or to classify or fail or refuse to refer for employment any individual, in any way which would deprive or tend to deprive any individual of employment opportunities, or would limit such employment opportunities or otherwise adversely affect his status as an employee or as an applicant for employment, because of such individual's race, color, religion, sex, or national origin; or

(3) to cause or attempt to cause an employer to discriminate against an individual in violation of this section. . . .

(e) Notwithstanding any other provision of this title, (1) it shall not be an unlawful employment practice for an employer to hire and employ employees, for an employment agency to classify, or refer for employment any individual, for a labor organization to classify its membership or to classify or refer for employment any individual, or for an employer, labor organization, or joint labor-management committee controlling apprenticeship or other training or retraining programs to admit or employ any individual in any such program, on the basis of his religion,

sex, or national origin in those certain instances where religion, sex, or national
origin is a bona fide occupational qualification reasonably necessary to the normal operation of that particular business
or enterprise. . . .

Sec. 705. (a) There is hereby created a
Commission to be known as the Equal
Employment Opportunity Commission,
which shall be composed of five members,
not more than three of whom shall be
members of the same political party, who
shall be appointed by the President by
and with the advice and consent of the
Senate. . . .

(g) The Commission shall have power—

(1) to cooperate with and, with their
consent, utilize regional, State, local,
and other agencies, both public and
private, and individuals; . . .

(3) to furnish to persons subject to
this title such technical assistance as
they may request to further their com-

pliance with this title or an order issued thereunder;

(4) upon the request of (i) any employer, whose employees or some of
them, or (ii) any labor organization,
whose members or some of them, refuse or threaten to refuse to cooperate
in effectuating the provisions of this
title, to assist in such effectuation by
conciliation or such other remedial action as is provided by this title;

(5) to make such technical studies as
are appropriate to effectuate the purposes and policies of this title and to
make the results of such studies available to the public;

(6) to refer matters to the Attorney
General with recommendations for intervention in a civil action brought by
an aggrieved party under section 706, or
for the institution of a civil action by
the Attorney General under section 707,
and to advise, consult, and assist the
Attorney General on such matters. . . .

12

Equal Rights Amendment, 1972

An equal rights amendment, with wording slightly different from that passed
by Congress in 1972, was sponsored in 1923 by the National Woman's Party.
It seemed to party members the logical corollary to suffrage. But that amendment was vigorously opposed by the League of Women Voters and other progressive reformers, lest it undermine the protective legislation for which they
had fought so hard.

An equal rights amendment was introduced regularly in Congress virtually
every year thereafter, but it received little attention until after World War II.
In 1950 and 1953 it was passed by the Senate but ignored by the House.

By 1970 much protective legislation had been applied to both men and
women. It was possible to support an equal rights amendment without risking
the undoing of labor law reforms. The hope that the Supreme Court would
apply the Fourteenth Amendment's "equal protection of the laws" clause to

cases involving discrimination on the basis of sex as firmly as it applied the clause to cases involving racial discrimination had not been fulfilled. When the current Equal Rights Amendment was introduced in 1970, it was endorsed by a wide range of organizations, some of which had once opposed it; these organizations included groups as disparate as the United Automobile Workers and the Woman's Christian Temperance Union. Its main sponsor in the House was Martha Griffiths of Michigan; in the Senate, Birch Bayh of Indiana.

The ERA was passed by Congress on March 22, 1972, and sent to the states for ratification. There was much initial enthusiasm; within two days six states had ratified. But the pace of ratification slowed after 1975, and only thirty-five of the needed thirty-eight states had ratified it by 1978. (Four state legislatures voted to rescind ratification, although the legality of that move was open to question.) In October 1978 Congress extended the deadline for ratification to June 30, 1982; the extension expired with no additional ratifications. The amendment was reintroduced in Congress in 1983 but has not been passed.

Section 1. Equality of rights under the law shall not be denied or abridged by the United States or by any State on account of sex.

Section 2. The Congress shall have the power to enforce, by appropriate legislation, the provisions of this article.

Section 3. The amendment shall take effect two years after the date of ratification.

13

Frontiero v. Richardson, 1973

Sharron A. Frontiero was an Air Force officer who was dismayed to discover that she could not claim dependent's benefits for her husband on the same terms that her male colleagues could for their wives. She and her husband brought suit, claiming that statutes requiring spouses of female members of the uniformed services to receive more than half of their support from their wives to be considered dependents, while all spouses of male members were treated as dependents, violated the due process clause of the Fifth Amendment and the equal protection clause of the Fourteenth Amendment.

The Supreme Court ruled in favor of the Frontieros in a complex decision that used statistical information about woman's place in the work force in a manner reminiscent of the Brandeis Brief. Speaking for three of his colleagues Justice William J. Brennan, Jr., prepared a historically based argument, explain-

411 U.S. 677. See also *Craig* v. *Boren* 429 U.S. 190 (1976).

ing the distance American public opinion had traveled since the *Bradwell* case. He drew analogies between discrimination on the basis of race, which the court subjected to strict scrutiny, and discrimination on the basis of sex.

In concurring with Brennan's opinion, three justices observed that although they agreed with the Frontieros in this particular case, they were not yet persuaded that sex ought to be regularly treated as a "suspect category." Only when—or if—the Equal Rights Amendment were passed could the Court be sure that the public agreed that discrimination on the basis of sex ought to be evaluated as critically as discrimination on the basis of race.

Note that the facts in *Frontiero* relate to discrimination against the husband of the wage earner, not directly against a woman. It is the family of a female wage earner that is discriminated against. A similar case is *Weinberger* v. *Weisenfeld* (420 U.S. 636 [1975]), in which the husband of a dead woman demanded survivor's benefits equal to those available to widows. A number of other sex discrimination cases have been brought by men, challenging older laws that were intended to protect women. *Reed* v. *Reed* (404 U.S. 71 [1971]), in which the Supreme Court struck down an explicit preference for males as administrators of a deceased person's estate, is unusual in that it is a straightforward example of an occasion on which a woman brought suit directly against a law that discriminated against her.

Mr. Justice William J. Brennan, Jr., delivered the opinion
of the Court:

The question before us concerns the right of a female member of the uniformed services to claim her spouse as a "dependent." . . .

At the outset, appellants contend that classifications based upon sex, like classifications based upon race, alienage, and national origin, are inherently suspect and must therefore be subjected to close judicial scrutiny. We agree. . . .

There can be no doubt that our Nation has had a long and unfortunate history of sex discrimination. Traditionally, such discrimination was rationalized by an attitude of "romantic paternalism" which, in practical effect, put women, not on a pedestal, but in a cage. Indeed, this paternalistic attitude became so firmly rooted in our national consciousness that, 100 years ago, a distinguished Member of this Court was able to proclaim. . . . "The natural and proper timidity and delicacy which belongs to the female sex evidently unfits it for many of the occupations of civil life." . . .

It is true, of course, that the position of women in America has improved markedly in recent decades. Nevertheless, it can hardly be doubted that, in part because of the high visibility of the sex characteristic, women still face pervasive, although at times more subtle, discrimination in our educational institutions, in the job market, and perhaps most conspicuously, in the political arena. . . .

Moreover, since sex, like race and national origin, is an immutable characteristic determined solely by the accident of birth, the imposition of special disabilities upon the member of a particular sex because of their sex would seem to violate "the basic concept of our system that legal burdens should bear some relationship to individual responsibility. . . ." And what differentiates sex from such non-suspect statuses as intelligence or physical disability, and aligns it with the recognized suspect criteria, is that the sex characteristic frequently bears no relation to ability to perform or contribute to society. . . .

. . . over the past decade, Congress has itself manifested an increasing sensitivity to sex-based classifications. In Tit[le] VII of the Civil Rights Act of 1964, for example, Congress expressly declared that no employer, labor union, or other organization subject to the provisions of the Act shall discriminate against any individual on the basis of "race, color, religion, *sex*, or national origin." Similarly, the Equal Pay Act of 1963 provides that no employer covered by the Act "shall discriminate . . . between employees on the basis of sex." . . .

With these considerations in mind, we can only conclude that classifications based upon sex, like classifications based upon race, alienage, or national origin, are inherently suspect, and must therefore be subjected to strict judicial scrutiny. Applying the analysis mandated by that stricter standard of review, it is clear that the statutory scheme now before us is constitutionally invalid. . . .

Mr. Justice Lewis F. Powell, Jr., with whom the Chief Justice and
Mr. Justice Harry A. Blackmun join, concurring in the opinion:

I agree that the challenged statutes constitute an unconstitutional discrimination against servicewomen . . . but I cannot join the opinion of Mr. Justice Brennan, which would hold that all classifications based upon sex . . . are "inherently suspect and must therefore be subjected to close judicial scrutiny." . . . The Equal Rights Amendment, which if adopted will resolve the substance of this precise question, has been approved by the Congress and submitted for ratification by the States. If this Amendment is duly adopted, it will represent the will of the people accomplished in the manner prescribed by the constitution. . . . It seems to me that this reaching out to pre-empt by judicial action a major political decision which is currently in process of resolution does not reflect appropriate respect for duly prescribed legislative processes.

14

Roe *v.* Wade, *1973*

The Comstock Law had been echoed by a series of anticontraception and antiabortion laws throughout the country. James Mohr observes, "Every state in the

410 U.S. 113

Union had [by 1900] an antiabortion law of some kind on its books . . . except Kentucky, where the state courts outlawed the practice anyway."* In 1962 the ethics of abortion became a pressing problem when it was revealed that thalidomide, a drug extensively used in Europe and occasionally in the United States, resulted in the birth of thousands of babies with phocomelia (deformed or missing arms and legs). Sherry Finkbine, an Arizona woman who had taken the drug, demanded a legal abortion. Although her doctors supported her, the county medical society refused to approve the procedure, and, lacking confidence that she and her doctors would be spared immunity from prosecution, she fled to Sweden, where abortion was legal. Her plight served to shift opinion, particularly within the medical profession, which would subsequently be instrumental in advocating liberalization of abortion legislation.

Texas law prohibited abortion except for the purpose of saving the mother's life. In 1970 a single pregnant woman, known as Jane Roe to protect her privacy, brought a class action suit challenging the constitutionality of that law as a violation of her right to liberty as guaranteed by the due process clause of the Fourteenth Amendment.

The Court's decision in *Roe* v. *Wade* marked a sharp change from long-established practice. As the opening lines of the majority decision make clear, the justices were aware they were making a sensitive decision. The issues that were raised by *Roe* v. *Wade* have not been settled and are not likely to be easily resolved, touching as they do on basic religious and ethical beliefs. Abortion is an issue of concern to men as well as to women. It is an issue on which women and men hold a wide variety of views. Among the questions raised are:

1. What are the limits of a woman's right to control of her own body?
2. Should the unborn be afforded legal rights?
3. What rights does the father have? In 1976 the Supreme Court held that a state could not require a married woman to get her husband's consent before having an abortion (*Planned Parenthood* v. *Danforth*, 428 U.S. 52 [1976]).
4. What rights does the community have to set general policy? What are the appropriate limits of government intervention? The state may not require a woman to conceive a child; can the state require a woman to bear a child? May a government encourage childbirth by paying for it under government insurance programs when the mother is indigent, but discourage abortion by refusing to fund even medically necessary abortions unless the woman's life is in danger? In 1980 the Supreme Court upheld the "Hyde Amendment," by which Congress refused to fund even medically necessary abortion for indigents (*Harris* v. *McRae*, 448 U.S. 297 [1980]).

* James C. Mohr, *Abortion in America: The Origins and Evolution of National Policy, 1800–1900* (New York, 1978), pp. 229–30.

5. Will any of these rights change as improvements are made in the technology for the discovery of birth defects and genetic abnormalities, and for caring for premature infants at earlier ages?

Mr. Justice Harry A. Blackmun delivered the opinion of the Court:

We forthwith acknowledge our awareness of the sensitive and emotional nature of the abortion controversy, of the vigorous opposing views, even among physicians, and of the deep and seemingly absolute convictions that the subject inspires. One's philosophy, one's experiences, one's exposure to the raw edges of human existence, one's religious training, one's attitudes toward life and family and their values, and the moral standards one establishes and seeks to observe, are all likely to influence and to color one's thinking and conclusions about abortion.

In addition, population growth, pollution, poverty, and racial overtones tend to complicate and not to simplify the problem.

Our task, of course, is to resolve the issue by constitutional measurement, free of emotion and of predilection. We seek earnestly to do this. . . .

The principal thrust of the appellant's attack on the Texas statutes is that they improperly invade a right, said to be possessed by the pregnant woman, to choose to terminate her pregnancy. Appellant would discover this right in the concept of personal "liberty" embodied in the Fourteenth Amendment's Due Process Clause; or in personal, marital, familial and sexual privacy said to be protected by the Bill of Rights . . . or among those rights reserved to the people by the Ninth Amendment. . . .

It perhaps is not generally appreciated that the restrictive criminal abortion laws in effect in a majority of States today are of relatively recent vintage. Those laws, generally proscribing abortion or its attempt at any time during pregnancy except when necessary to preserve the pregnant woman's life, are not of ancient or even of common-law origin. Instead, they derive from statutory changes effected, for the most part, in the latter half of the nineteenth century. . . . At common law, at the time of the adoption of our Constitution, and throughout the major portion of the nineteenth century . . . a woman enjoyed a substantially broader right to terminate a pregnancy than she does in most states today. . . .

When most criminal abortion laws were first enacted, the procedure was a hazardous one for the woman. This was particularly true prior to the development of antisepsis. . . . Abortion mortality was high. . . . Modern medical techniques have altered this situation. Appellants . . . refer to medical data indicating that abortion in early pregnancy, that is, prior to the end of the first trimester, although not without its risk, is now relatively safe. Mortality rates for women undergoing early abortions, where the procedure is legal, appear to be as low as or lower than the rates for normal childbirth. Consequently, any interest of the State in protecting the woman from an inherently hazardous procedure . . . has largely disappeared. . . . The State has a legitimate interest in seeing to it that abortion, like any other medical procedure, is performed under circumstances that insure maximum safety for the patient. . . .

The Constitution does not explicitly mention any right of privacy. In a line of decisions, however . . . the Court has recognized that a right of personal privacy, or a guarantee of certain areas or zones of privacy, does exist under the Constitution. . . . This right . . . whether it be founded in the Fourteenth Amendment's concept of personal liberty . . . or . . . in the Ninth Amendment's reservation of rights to the people, is broad enough to encompass a woman's decision whether or not to terminate her pregnancy. . . . We . . . conclude that the right of personal privacy includes the abortion decision, but that this right is not unqualified and must be considered against important state interests in regulation. . . .

. . . the State does have an important and legitimate interest in preserving and protecting the health of the pregnant woman . . . and . . . it has still *another* important and legitimate interest in protecting the potentiality of human life. These interests are separate and distinct. Each grows in substantiality as the woman approaches term, and, at a point during pregnancy, each becomes "compelling."

With respect to the State's important and legitimate interest in the health of the mother, the "compelling" point, in the light of present medical knowledge, is at approximately the end of the first trimester. This is so because of the now-established medical fact . . . that until the end of the first trimester mortality in abortion may be less than mortality in normal childbirth. It follows that . . . for the period of pregnancy prior to this "compelling" point, the attending physician, in consultation with his patient, is free to determine, without regulation by the State, that in his medical judgment, the patient's pregnancy should be terminated.

. . . For the state subsequent to approximately the end of the first trimester, the State, in promoting its interest in the health of the mother, may, if it chooses, regulate the abortion procedure in ways that are reasonably related to maternal health.

For the state subsequent to viability, the State in promoting its interest in the potentiality of human life may, if it chooses, regulate, and even proscribe, abortion except where it is necessary, in appropriate medical judgment, for the preservation of the life or health of the mother.

Our conclusion . . . is . . . that the Texas abortion statutes, as a unit, must fall. . . .

15

Rostker *v.* Goldberg, *1981*

Classical republican tradition linked political identity with property holding and military obligation. In the United States, the obligations of male citizens include military service; the obligations of female citizens do not. Although women had been employed by the army and navy as nurses, not until World War II were they involved in military service in substantial numbers. Women's

101 Sup. Ct. 2646. For extended comment, see Herma Hill Kay et al., *Text, Cases & Materials: Sex-Based Discrimination*, 2d ed., American Casebook Series (St. Paul, Minn., 1981), pp. 14–26.

sections of the army, navy, and air force accepted volunteers under strict regulations, which excluded them from combat duty, limited the numbers who could be accepted and the rank to which they could rise (until 1967 no woman could serve in a command position), and offered fewer fringe benefits than were received by servicemen of the same rank (see *Frontiero* v. *Richardson*, document 13). Partly in response to the Vietnam War, many of these restrictions were eased; in 1976 women were admitted to West Point, Annapolis, and the Air Force Academy.

When President Jimmy Carter recommended the resumption of peacetime selective service registration in 1980, he proposed registering women as well as men. The president and his supporters on the Armed Services Committees of the Senate and the House sought to separate the issues of registration, the actual draft, and the use of women in combat. They argued that decisions on whether women would actually be drafted (and, if so, whether mothers would be exempted) and whether women would be placed in combat positions could be left for future debate. They also argued that registration did not necessarily mean that one would be drafted, for men who planned to request exemption as conscientious objectors were still required to register.

Opponents insisted that the issues were linked: if the sexes were treated equally in registration, it would be impossible to reject equity in future treatment. Since the primary goal of Selective Service was to identify combat-ready men, opponents also argued that, if women were not used in combat, there was no need to register them. In the course of debate contrasting ideas of the role of women in American society were expressed.* This debate overlapped with the debate on the Equal Rights Amendment, taking place at the same time; probably the single most effective argument used by opponents of the ERA was that it would involve women in the draft. In the end, Congress approved registration for men but not for women.

The Military Selective Service Act of 1980 was challenged by a group of men who argued that they had been denied the equal protection of the laws guaranteed by the Fifth Amendment. The Carter administration was now placed in the odd position of having to defend the statute it had opposed.

Note the reasoning of the Supreme Court and its emphasis on the exclusion of women from combat positions. In recent years women have been placed in positions on patrol ships or stations on the fringes of the defense perimeter, making them vulnerable to involvement or even capture in the event of military confrontation. What implications does that have for the reasoning of the Court? Although the argument was not offered in *Rostker*, some men have argued that if women are drafted but not placed in combat positions, the likelihood that any specific man would be assigned to a noncombat job diminishes and men

* See the *Congressional Record*, June 10, 1980.

are therefore placed at greater risk for combat assignments. Moreover, some men in similar situations, such as police or prison guards, have demanded the exclusion of women on the grounds that women could not back men up effectively in physical confrontation; thus giving women equal opportunity to become prison guards actually increases the risks to men. Yet another perspective is offered by the legal historian Leo Kanowitz, who argues that "the equanimity with which men's exclusive liability for military service is regarded by the general population, even during times of violent combat . . . [suggests] the philosophy that a man's life is less precious than that of a woman." Do you agree?

Mr. Justice William H. Rehnquist delivered the opinion of the Court:

The question presented is whether the Military Selective Service Act . . . violates the Fifth Amendment to the United States Constitution in authorizing the President to require the registration of males and not females. Whenever called upon to judge the constitutionality of an Act of Congress—"the gravest and most delicate duty that this Court is called upon to perform," . . . the Court accords "great weight to the decisions of Congress."

. . . This case is quite different from several of the gender-based discrimination cases we have considered in that . . . Congress did not act "unthinkingly" or "reflexively and not for any considered reason." . . . The question of registering women for the draft not only received considerable national attention and was the subject of wide-ranging public debate, but also was extensively considered by Congress in hearings, floor debate, and in committee. Hearings held by both Houses of Congress in response to the President's request for authorization to register women adduced extensive testimony and evidence concerning the issue. . . . the decision to exempt women from registration was not the "accidental by-product of a traditional way of thinking about women. . . ."

Women as a group, however, unlike men as a group, are not eligible for combat. The restrictions on the participation of women in combat in the Navy and Air Force are statutory. . . . The Army and Marine Corps preclude the use of women in combat as a matter of established policy.* . . . The existence of the combat restrictions clearly indicates the basis for Congress' decision to exempt women from registration. The purpose of registration was to prepare for a draft of combat troops. Since women are excluded from combat, Congress concluded that they would not be needed in the event of a draft, and therefore decided not to register them. . . . This is not a case of Congress arbitrarily choosing to burden one of two similarly situated groups, such as would be the case with an all-black or all-white, or an all-Catholic or all-Lutheran, or an all-Republican or all-Democratic registration. Men and women, because of the combat restrictions on women, are simply not similarly situated for purposes of a draft or registration for a draft. . . . The Constitution requires that Congress treat similarly situated persons similarly, not that it engage in gestures of superficial equality.

* No major country has women in combat jobs in its standing army.

Mr. Justice Byron White, dissenting:

I assume . . . that excluding women from combat positions does not offend the Constitution . . . [but] I perceive little, if any, indication that Congress itself concluded that every position in the military, no matter how far removed from combat, must be filled with combat-ready men.

Mr. Justice Thurgood Marshall, dissenting:

The Court today places its imprimatur on one of the most potent remaining public expressions of "ancient canards about the proper role of women." It upholds a statute that requires males but not females to register for the draft, and which thereby categorically excludes women from a fundamental civic obligation.

Further Resources

Part I

Traditional America, 1600–1820

BIOLOGY

James Axtell, ed. *The Indian Peoples of Eastern America: A Documentary History of the Sexes* (New York, 1981), is organized in terms of life cycle and includes sections on birth, puberty, marriage, and death. *Extracts from the Journal of Elizabeth Drinker*, ed. H. D. Biddle (Philadelphia, 1889), includes extensive comments on Drinker's experience of childbearing and motherhood. For patterns of women's lives, see Robert V. Wells, "Demographic Change and the Life Cycle of American Families," *Journal of Interdisciplinary History* 2 (1971):273–82, and Daniel Scott Smith and Michael S. Hindus, "Premarital Pregnancy in America, 1640–1971: An Overview and Interpretation," *Journal of Interdisciplinary History* 5 (1975):537–70. An energetic debate has developed on the timing of the "demographic transition" to smaller families; see Edward Byers, "Fertility Transition in a New England Commercial Center: Nantucket, Mass., 1680–1840," *Journal of Interdisciplinary History* 13 (1982):17–40, and Barbara J. Logue, "The Case for Birth Control before 1850: Nantucket Re-examined," *Journal of Interdisciplinary History* 15 (1985):371–91.

ECONOMICS

Julia Cherry Spruill, *Women's Life and Work in the Southern Colonies* (Chapel Hill, 1938), is rich in descriptive detail and still repays reading. For a thoughtful introduction to work that occupied most women much of the time, see Susan Burrows Swan, *Plain and Fancy: American Women and Their Needlework, 1750–1850* (New York, 1977). Lyle Koehler, *A Search for Power: The "Weaker Sex" in Seventeenth-Century New England* (Urbana, 1980), examines the work options open to women in a single region. A special issues of the *Pennsylvania Magazine of History and Biography* 107 (January 1983), has useful essays on the economic aspects of colonial women's lives; see especially Sharon V. Salinger, " 'Send No More Women': Female Servants in Eighteenth-Century Philadelphia," pp. 29–48. For women's lives in the Chesapeake, see Lois Green Carr and Lorena Walsh, "The Planter's Wife: The Experience of White Women in

Seventeenth-Century Maryland," *William and Mary Quarterly,* 3d ser., 34 (1977):542–71. Carol Shammas, "The Domestic Environment in Early Modern England and America," *Journal of Social History* 31 (1980:3–24, sets American domestic work in transatlantic context. Marylynn Salmon, *Women and the Law of Property in Early America* (Chapel Hill, 1986), is definitive.

POLITICS

The witchcraft trials of seventeenth-century New England were occasions on which religious and political concerns mingled. The fact that the targets of the trials were, with few exceptions, female, makes them an important episode in women's history. Chadwick Hansen, *Witchcraft at Salem* (New York, 1969), and Richard Weisman, *Witchcraft Magic, and Religion in 17th-Century Massachusetts* (Amherst, 1984), treat the theme in the context of religious and folk belief; Paul Boyer and Stephen Nissenbaum, *Salem Possessed: The Social Origins of Witchcraft* (Cambridge, Mass., 1974), treats the trials as an expression of social and economic tension in the community. John Demos, *Entertaining Satan: Witchcraft and the Culture of Early New England* (New York, 1982), is a wide-ranging study that addresses the subject from the perspectives of psychology, history, biography, and political relationships; it should be read along with Carol F. Karlsen, *The Devil in the Shape of a Woman: The Witch in Seventeenth-Century New England* (New York: forthcoming), which stresses the role of gender as well as the political and economic context of witchcraft accusations.

IDEOLOGY

For a diary rich in insight into the rhythms of daily life, see *The Journal of Esther Edwards Burr, 1754–1757,* ed. Carol F. Karlsen and Laurie Crumpacker (New Haven, 1984). For striking examples of the ways in which some representative colonial women interpreted their own lives, see Anne Firor Scott, "Self Portraits: Three Women," in *Uprooted Americans: Essays to Honor Oscar Handlin,* ed. Richard Bushman et al. (Boston, 1979). For the sources on which these portraits are based, see *The Letters of Benjamin Franklin and Jane Mecom,* ed. Carl Van Doren (Princeton, 1950), and *The Letterbook of Eliza Lucas Pinckney,* ed. Elise Pinckney (Chapel Hill, 1972). For the ways in which religious practices affected women's status, see essays in Janet Wilson James, ed., *Women in American Religion* (Philadelphia, 1980), especially Mary Maples Dunn, "Saints and Sinners: Congregational and Quaker Women in the Early Colonial Period."

1980), especially Mary Maples Dunn, "Saints and Sinners: Congregational and Quaker Women in the Early Colonial Period." For the interaction of biology, economics, politics, and ideology in the Revolutionary era, see Linda K. Kerber, *Women of the Republic: Intellect and Ideology in Revolutionary America* (Chapel Hill, 1980), and Mary Beth Norton, *Liberty's Daughters: The Revolutionary Experience of American Women, 1750–1800* (Boston, 1980).

Part IIA

Industrializing America, 1820–80

BIOLOGY

For an important overview, see Carl N. Degler, *At Odds: Women and the Family in America from the Revolution to the Present* (New York, 1980), especially chaps. 2–9. For attempts to improve the general level of female health, see Regina Markell Morantz, "Making Women Modern: Middle-Class Women and Health Reform in 19th-Century America," *Journal of Social History* 10 (1977): 490–507.

ECONOMICS

Jacqueline Jones, *Labor of Love, Labor of Sorrow: Black Women, Work and the Family from Slavery to the Present* (New York, 1985), devotes chaps. 1 and 2 to the period before 1880. Dorothy Sterling, ed., *We Are Your Sisters: Black Women in the Nineteenth Century* (New York, 1984), includes many well-selected documents of the working lives of black women, slave and free (it also includes documents that have much bearing on politics and ideology); as does Gerda Lerner, ed., *Black Women in White America* (New York, 1972). Willie Lee Rose, ed., *A Documentary History of Slavery in North America* (New York, 1976), and John Blassingame, ed., *Slave Testimony: Two Centuries of Letters, Speeches, Interviews and Autobiographies* (Baton Rouge, 1977), should also be consulted. [Linda Brent], *Incidents in the Life of a Slave Girl*, ed. Lydia Maria Child (1860; reprint, New York, 1973), remains a classic memoir elicited by a leading abolitionist. Richard S. Dunn, "A Tale of Two Plantations: Slave Life at Mesopotamia in Jamaica and Mount Airy in Virginia, 1799–1828," *William and Mary Quarterly*, 3d ser., 34 (1977):32–65, is a comparative study that provides a detailed reconstruction of the work lives of slave women and emphasizes the pressures under which they lived. Many elderly women who had been slaves when young were interviewed by the Federal Writers' Project in the 1930s. Selected interviews appear in B. A. Botkin, ed., *Lay My Burden Down: A Folk History of Slavery* (Chicago, 1945), and Norman R. Yetman, ed., *Voices from Slavery* (New York, 1970). Leon Litwack, *Been in the Storm So Long: The Aftermath of Slavery* (New York, 1979), pays substantial attention to the experience of black women during Reconstruction.

For women's work in the domestic economy, see Nancy F. Cott, *The Bonds of Womanhood: "Woman's Sphere" in New England 1780–1835"* (New Haven, 1977), chap. 1. For domestic work in a frontier context, see Lillian Schlissel, *Women's Diaries of the Westward Journey,* (New York, 1982). For the impact of industrialization, see Thomas Dublin, *Women at Work: The Transformation of Work and Community in Lowell, Massachusetts, 1826–1860* (New York, 1979), and Dublin, *Farm to Factory: The Mill Experience and Women's Lives in New England, 1830–1860* (New York, 1981). A classic memoir is Lucy Larcom, *A New England Girlhood* (1889; reprint, New York, 1961). For a review of recent scholarship, see Judith McGaw, "Women and the History of American Technology," *Signs: Journal of Women in Culture and Society* 7 (1982): 798–828; for a classic text, see Helen Sumner, *History of Women in Industry in the United States* (Washington, D.C., 1910).

For the feminization of schooling, see Richard M. Bernard and Maris A. Vinovskis, "The Female School Teacher in Ante-Bellum Massachusetts," *Journal of Social History* 10 (1977):332–45, and Polly Welts Kaufman, *Women Teachers on the Frontier* (New Haven, 1984). See also the important essays on teaching in Anne Firor Scott, *Making the Invisible Woman Visible* (Urbana, 1984).

For entry into the professions, see Mary Roth Walsh, *"Doctors Wanted, No Women Need Apply": Sexual Barriers in the Medical Profession, 1835–1975* (New Haven, 1977), and Regina Morantz-Sanchez, *Sympathy and Science: Women Physicians in America* (New York, 1985).

POLITICS

Estelle Freedman, *Their Sisters' Keepers: Women and Prison Reform in Nineteenth-Century America* (Ann Arbor, 1981), introduces an important reform movement. Gerda Lerner, *The Grimké Sisters from South Carolina: Rebels against Slavery* (Boston, 1967), is a readable biography that suggests the way in which abolitionism could lead to a concern for women's rights. Ellen C. Du Bois, *Feminism and Suffrage: The Emergence of an Independent Women's Movement in America, 1848–1869* (Ithaca, 1978), is an important interpretation that stresses the radicalism of the demand for suffrage. Nancy Hewitt, *Women's Activism and Social Change: Rochester, New York, 1822–1872* (Ithaca, 1984), follows the history of women and reform in a single city. Readable biographies of political women are Celia Morris Eckhardt, *Fanny Wright: Rebel in America*

(Cambridge, Mass., 1984) and Elisabeth Griffith, *In Her Own Right: The Life of Elizabeth Cady Stanton* (New York, 1984). Five massive volumes of the basic sources on the suffrage movement have been conveniently abridged in *A Concise History of Woman Suffrage: Selections from the Classic Work of Stanton, Anthony, Gage and Harper*, ed. Mari Jo Buhle and Paul Buhle (Urbana, 1978). For women's involvement in the Civil War, the basic book remains Mary Elizabeth Massey, *Bonnet Brigades* (New York, 1966), but see also *Mary Chesnut's Civil War*, ed. C. Vann Woodward (New Haven, 1981).

IDEOLOGY

"The Cult of True Womanhood" was given its name in an essay with the same title by Barbara Welter, *American Quarterly* 18 (1966):151–74. A different reading of some of the same sources is offered by Gerda Lerner, *The Majority Finds Its Past: Placing Women in History* (New York, 1979), chap. 2. The relationship of women's roles to a developing economy is brilliantly dissected in Mary P. Ryan, *Cradle of the Middle Class: The Family in Oneida County, New York, 1790–1865* (Cambridge, 1981). The social construction of gender is insightfully explored in Carroll Smith-Rosenberg, *Disorderly Conduct: Visions of Gender in Victorian America* (New York, 1985). For changes in legal construction of gender, see Norma Basch, *In the Eyes of the Law: Women, Marriage and Property in Nineteenth-Century New York* (Ithaca, 1982). Fictional visions of women's lives are analysed in Mary Kelley, *Private Woman, Public Stage: Literary Domesticity in Nineteenth-Century America* (New York, 1984), and Annette Kolodny, *The Land before Her: Fantasy and Experience of the American Frontiers, 1630–1860* (Chapel Hill, 1984). The making of marriages is evaluated in Ellen K. Rothman, *Hands and Hearts: A History of Courtship in America* (New York, 1984). The invention of a distinctive role for single women is described in Lee Chambers-Schiller, *Liberty–A Better Husband: Single Women in America* (New Haven, 1984). For the way in which religious beliefs affected women's roles and behavior, see Joan Jacobs Brumberg, *Mission for Life* (New York, 1980), and Donald G. Mathews, *Religion in the Old South* (Chicago, 1978), chap. 2. The special roles of southern women are evaluated in Catherine Clinton, *The Plantation Mistress: Woman's World in the Old South* (New York, 1983). In *The Free Women of Petersburg: Status and Culture in a Southern Town* (New York, 1984), Suzanne Lebsock examines the interconnection of biology, economics, politics, and ideology in a single city.

Part IIB

Industrializing America, 1880–1920

BIOLOGY

Biology and ideology interacted in the medical treatment of women, a subject much discussed in scholarly articles. See, for example, Carroll Smith-Rosenberg and Charles Rosenberg, "The Female Animal: Medical and Biological Views of Woman and Her Role in Nineteenth-Century America," *Journal of American History* 60 (1973):332–56. Using data from hospital records, Regina Markell Morantz and Sue Zschoche compare the treatment delivered by male and female physicians in "Professionalism, Feminism, and Gender Roles: A Comparative Study of Nineteenth-Century Medical Therapeutics," *Journal of American History* 67 (1980):568–88. For differing interpretations of Margaret Sanger and the birth control movement, see Linda Gordon, *Woman's Body, Woman's Right: A Social History of Birth Control in America* (New York, 1976), James Reed, *From Private Vice to Public Virtue: The Birth Control Movement and American Society since 1830* (New York, 1978), and David M. Kennedy, *Birth Control in America: The Career of Margaret Sanger* (New Haven, 1970). For an overview of women's sexuality during this period, see Degler, *At Odds*, chaps. 11–12. For developments in childbirth, see Richard W. Wertz and Dorothy C. Wertz, *Lying-In: A History of Childbirth in America* (New York, 1979), chaps. 4–5.

ECONOMICS

Family expectations and work options interacted in different ways with different ethnic groups. For a study of that interaction with respect to black and Italian women, see Jones, *Labor of Love, Labor of Sorrow*, chaps. 4–5, and Virginia Yans-McLaughlin, *Family and Community: Italian Immigrants in Buffalo, 1880–1930* (Ithaca, 1977). Articles on other groups are in the *Journal of Urban History* 4 (1978). For a general study of working-class women, see Leslie Woodcock Tentler, *Wage-Earning Women: Industrial Work and Family Life in the United States, 1900–1930* (New York, 1979). Prostitution provided jobs for women whether they entered such work voluntarily or, as many did, involuntarily. See Ruth Rosen, *Lost Sisterhood: Prostitution in America, 1900–1918* (Baltimore, 1982). New employment opportunities for educated women developed in libraries, with librarianship becoming feminized just as had schoolteaching. See Dee Garrison, *Apostles of Culture: The Public Librarian and*

American Society, 1876–1920 (New York, 1979). For comparable developments in clerical work, see Margery W. Davies, *Woman's Place Is at the Typewriter: Office Work and Office Workers, 1870–1930* (Philadelphia, 1982). For an important overview, see Alice Kessler-Harris, *Out to Work: A History of Wage-Earning Women in the United States* (New York, 1982), secs. 2–3, and Lynn Y. Weiner, *From Working Girl to Working Mother: The Female Labor Force in the United States, 1820–1920* (Chapel Hill, 1985), chap. 3.

POLITICS

There is increasing literature on female political activism in the decades before women could vote. The temperance and women's club movements have been studied by Ruth Bordin in *Woman and Temperance: Quest for Power and Liberty, 1873–1900* (Philadelphia, 1980), and Karen Blair, *The Clubwoman as Feminist: True Womanhood Redefined, 1868–1914* (New York, 1980). For the black woman's club movement, see Lerner, *Majority Finds Its Past*, chap. 6. Nancy Schrom Dye explores the alliance of middle- and working-class women to improve the lives of the latter in *As Equals and as Sisters: Feminism, the Labor Movement and the Women's Trade Union League of New York* (Columbia, Mo., 1980). The most famous group of reformers were the settlement house women. See Kathryn Kish Sklar, "Hull House in the 1880s: A Community of Women Reformers," *Signs: Journal of Women in Culture and Society* 10 (1985):658–77. On Jane Addams, see Allen Davis, *American Heroine: The Life and Legend of Jane Addams* (New York, 1973), and *The Social Thought of Jane Addams,* ed. Christopher Lasch (New York, 1965). Note the role of women in social service and in the new profession of social work in Clarke A. Chambers, *Seedtime of Reform: Social Service and Social Action, 1918–1933* (Ann Arbor, 1967). Barbara J. Steinson explores "The Mother Half of Humanity": American Women in the Peace and Preparedness Movements in World War I," in *Women, War and Revolution,* eds. Carol Berkin and Clara Lovett (New York, 1980). See also *Crystal Eastman on Women and Revolution,* ed. Blanche Wiesen Cook (New York, 1978), for Eastman's extensive involvement in the peace movement. Participation in the socialist movement and its politics was also an important part of the process of political socialization for women, as is ably documented by Mari Jo Buhle in *Women and American Socialism, 1870–1920* (Urbana, 1983). The best brief account of reform activities that helped to prepare a prosuffrage constituency in the South remains Anne Firor Scott, *The Southern Lady: From Pedestal to Politics, 1830–1930* (Chicago, 1970), chap. 6. For a firsthand account of many facets of female activism by a pioneer in industrial medicine, see *Alice Hamilton: A Life in Letters,* ed. Barbara Sicherman (Cambridge, Mass., 1984).

The standard history of suffrage remains Eleanor Flexner, *Century of Struggle: The Women's Rights Movement in the United States* (Cambridge, Mass., 1958). For more recent local studies, see Sharon Hartman Strom, "Leadership and Tactics in the American Woman Suffrage Movement: A New Perspective from Massachusetts," *Journal of American History* 62 (1975):262–82, and Carole Nichols, "Votes and More for Women: Suffrage and After in Connecticut," *Women and History* 5 (1983):1–87.

IDEOLOGY

Attitudes about appropriate behavior for men as well as women are discussed by Peter Gabriel Filene, *Him/Her/Self: Sex Roles in Modern America* (Baltimore, 1986), chaps. 1–4. On ideology and education, see Barbara Miller Solomon, *In the Company of Educated Women: A History of Women and Higher Education in America* (New Haven, 1985); Helen L. Horowitz, *Alma Mater: Design and Experience in the Women's Colleges from Their Nineteenth-Century Beginning to the 1930's* (New York, 1984); and Roberta Frankfort, *Collegiate Women: Domesticity and Career in Turn-of-the-Century America* (New York, 1977). The way ideology affected debate on changing divorce laws is evident in William L. O'Neill, *Divorce in the Progressive Era* (New Haven, 1967). The effect of ideology on changing standards of beauty are explored in Lois Banner, *American Beauty* (New York, 1983). For ideology, sex roles, and changing relationships between men and women, see Carroll Smith-Rosenberg, *Disorderly Conduct: Visions of Gender in Victorian America* (New York, 1985).

Part III

Modern America, 1920–1985

BIOLOGY

Sex and sexuality are the focus of two issues of *Signs: Journal of Women in Culture and Society* 5, 6 (1980). See also Paul A. Robinson, *The Modernization of Sex: Havelock Ellis, Alfred Kinzey, William Masters and Virginia Johnson* (New York, 1976). For the natural childbirth movement, see Wertz and Wertz, *Lying-In,* chap. 6. A feminist perspective on various aspects of biology, including fertility control, abortion, and women's health care is provided in the Boston Women's Health Collective, *The New Our Bodies, Ourselves* (New York, 1984). The role of the state in relation to reproductive freedom cuts across biology, ideology, and politics. For a feminist perspective, see Rosalind Pollack Petchevsky, *Abortion and Woman's Choice: The State, Sexuality and Reproductive Freedom* (New York, 1984). An attempt to bring a variety of perspectives to the abortion debate is Sidney Callahan and Daniel Callahan, eds., *Abortion: Understanding Differences* (New York, 1984). Another area in which biology and ideology intersect is aging. See Susan Sontag, "The Double Standard of Aging," *Saturday Review* 55 (1972):29–38, and Alice S. Rossi, "Life-Span Theories and Women's Lives," *Signs: Journal of Women in Culture and Society* 6 (1980):4–32. Other biologically related issues on which there is now a vast literature include physical abuse of women; a classic is Susan Brownmiller's *Against Our Will: Men, Women, and Rape* (New York, 1975).

ECONOMICS

For an overview, see William H. Chafe, *The American Woman: Her Changing Social, Economic, and Political Roles, 1920–1970* (New York, 1972), and the more recent studies of Kessler-Harris, *Out to Work*, and Weiner, *From Working Girl to Working Mother*, chaps. 4–6. More specialized studies for the 1930s include Lois Scharf, *To Work and To Wed: Female Employment, Feminism and the Great Depression* (Westport, Conn., 1980), and Winifred Wandersee, *Women's Work and Family Values, 1920–1940* (Cambridge, Mass., 1981). Karen Anderson and Susan M. Hartmen explore women's work as part of a larger study of women's status during World War II in, respectively, *Wartime Women: Sex Roles, Family Relations and the Status of Women during World War II* (Westport, Conn., 1981), and *The Home Front and Beyond: American Women in the 1940s* (Boston, 1982). An example of new studies on problems facing women working in traditionally "male" professions is Mary Roth Walsh, *Doctors Wanted, No Women Need Apply."* For the particular problems facing black women, see Jones, *Labor of Love, Labor of Sorrow*, chaps. 6–7.

POLITICS

J. Stanley Lemons, *The Woman Citizen: Social Feminism in the 1920's* (Urbana, 1975), follows politically active reformers and feminists after suffrage, while Susan Ware examines careers of former suffragists and social workers who became part of the Roosevelt administration in *Beyond Suffrage: Women in the New Deal* (Cambridge, Mass., 1981). Important biographies of individual activists include Jacquelyn Dowd Hall, *Revolt against Chivalry: Jessie Daniel Ames and the Women's Campaign against Lynching* (New York, 1974), and Joseph P. Lash's biography of Eleanor Roosevelt, *Eleanor and Franklin* (New York, 1971), and *Eleanor: The Years Alone* (New York, 1972), which is supplemented by the essays in Joan Hoff-Wilson and Marjorie Lightman, eds., *Without Precedent: The Life and Career of Eleanor Roosevelt* (Bloomington, 1984). For the feminist activists of the 1960s and 1970s, see Sara Evans, *Personal Politics: The Roots of Women's Liberation in the Civil Rights Movement and the New Left* (New York, 1979), and Jo Freeman, *The Politics of Women's Liberation: A Case Study of an Emerging Social Movement and Its Relation to the Social Policy Process* (New York, 1975). Women activists in Washington who have played an important role in influencing public policy consistent with feminist goals are the focus of a Sage publication, Irene Tinker, ed., *Women in Washington: Advocates for Public Policy* (Beverly Hills, 1983). For an overview of female political activity since the 1920s, see Virginia Sapiro, *The Political Integration of Women: Roles, Socialization and Politics* (Urbana, 1983), and Sandra Baxter and Marjorie Lansing, *Women and Politics: The Visible Majority* (Ann Arbor, 1983). For constitutional issues, see Mary Frances Berry, *Why ERA Failed: Politics, Women's Rights, and the Amending Process of the Constitution* (Bloomington, 1986) and Jane J. Mansbridge, *Why We Lost the ERA* (Chicago, 1986).

IDEOLOGY

For an important discussion of sexual (and racial) equality that examines ideology as well as economics in an analysis of social change, see William H. Chafe, *Women and Equality: Changing Patterns in American Culture* (New York, 1977). See also Filene, *Him/Her/Self*, chaps. 5–7. Another important study is Rosalind Rosenberg, *Beyond Separate Spheres: Intellectual Roots of Modern Feminism* (New Haven, 1984), which focuses on the first female social scientists to challenge Victorian assumptions about distinct sexual identities that buttressed the notion of separate spheres for men and women. Dolores Hayden provides a survey of women who sought to achieve feminist goals in the nineteenth and twentieth centuries by redesigning the man-made environment in *The Grand Domestic Revolution: A History of Feminist Designs for American Homes, Neighborhoods, and Cities* (Cambridge, Mass., 1981). See also her "What Would a Non-Sexist City Be Like? Speculations on Housing, Urban Design, and Human Work," *Signs: Journal of Women in Culture and Society* 5, supp. (1980): s170–87. For feminist ideology and the contemporary movement, see the notes to DeHart-Mathews, "The New Feminism and the Dynamics of Social Change" (part III). The differing world views of pro- and anti-choice women are explored in Kristin Luker, *Abortion and the Politics of Motherhood* (Berkeley, 1984). The ideology and politics of antifeminist women are explored by lesbian activist Andrea Dworkin, who seeks to understand the concerns of women on the Right from a perspective of a radical feminist. See her *Right-Wing Women* (New York, 1983). For the relationship between ideology and law, see Albie Sachs and Joan Hoff-Wilson, *Sexism and the Law: A Study of Male Beliefs and Legal Bias in Britain and the United States* (Oxford, 1978).

An important reference containing excellent short biographies and a brief bibliography on many of the women appearing in this book is Edward T. James, Janet Wilson James, and Paul Boyer, eds., *Notable American Women, 1607–1950: A Biographical Dictionary*, 3 vols. (Cambridge, Mass., 1971), and Barbara Sicherman and Carol Hurd Green, eds., *Notable American Women: The Modern Period* (Cambridge, Mass., 1980).

Documentary Films

A number of recent films both complement and supplement material in *Women's America*. This list is by no means comprehensive.

Never Turn Back: The Life of Fannie Lou Hamer (1983, 58 min., color) is an informative and powerful documentary that follows the career of black activist Fannie Lou Hamer from the early life as a sharecropper in Sunflower County, Mississippi, to national prominence as a civil rights leader and founding member of the Mississippi Freedom Democratic party in the 1960s (Rediscovery Production, 2 Half Mill Common, Westport, Conn., 06880; 203–226–4489). *The Life and Times of Rosie the Riveter* (1980, 65 min., color) presents the powerful and moving reminiscences of five women who welcomed the challenges and higher pay provided by new jobs in industry during World War II and details their loss of wartime opportunities at the war's end, when women were told to return home (Clarity Educational Productions, Box 315, Franklin Lakes, N.J. 07414). A portrayal of the Bryn Mawr Summer School, which flourished between 1921 and 1938, *The Women of Summer* (1975, 55 min., color) documents the effort to expose blue-collar women to humanistic study in such a way as to empower them to go back to their own communities as leaders. Duplicated in the South, these summer schools for women workers were part of the worker's education movement. Their impact on some of the alumnae is conveyed in archival footage, oral histories, and clips of many of the women leaders who served to link progressivism and the New Deal (Film-Makers Library, Inc., 133 E. 58th Street, New York, N.Y. 10022; 212–355–6545). Based on Alice Lynch's account of the labor movement in the 1930s, *Union Maids* (1976, 50 min., black and white) depicts the personal experiences of three women who were labor organizers in Chicago during this period (New Day Films, 22 Riverside Drive, Wayne, N.J. 07470; 201–663–0212). The story of the Women's Emergency Brigade, *With Babies and Banners* (1979, 45 min., color) is an account of women's critical role in the General Motors sit-down strike in Flint, Michigan, in 1937, which was the key to the success of the Congress of Industrial Organizations' drive for industrial unionism (New Day Films, as above).

Index

Abbot, Gorham, 162, 165, *n.* 14
Abolition movement, 94, 98, 211–212; women in, 13, 19, 96, 201, 204, 215
Abortion: in traditional America, 190–194; in industrializing America, 16, 111–112, 194–201, 315, 478; in modern America, 449, 455, 459, 461; feminist view of, 20; *Roe* v. *Wade,* 491–494
Abrams, Henry, 430 *n.* 3
Abstinence, as means of birth control, 7–8, 16
Abzug, Bella, 450
Achievement, as antithetical to femininity, 17
Adams, Abigail, 84, 85, 218
Addams, Jane: female support network of, 274–278, 279, 286, 287, 292; as social reformer, 14, 223, 269, 270, 271, 278, 286, 294, 415, 438; "Women, War and Babies," 278
Addes, George, 385
Adkins v. *Children's Hospital,* 484–486
Advertising, 337–338, 341 *n.* 38, 341 *n.* 43, 342 *n.* 45, 445, 448
Affirmative action programs, 456, 461
Agricola, John, 64 *n.* 9
Agriculture: women in, in traditional America, 28, 29, 329–330; women in, in industrializing America, 116–131, 250 *n.* 3, 330; women in, in modern America, 325, 348–349, 354, 363, 364, 406–414; blacks in, 250 *n.* 3, 402; division of labor by gender, 12, 28, 116–131, 410–411, 414; and industrialization, 221, 222. *See also* Frontier; Gardening; Slaves; *specific crops*
Agriculture, Department of, 125
Akron, Ohio, women's

rights meeting, 213–214, 471
Albany, N.Y., temperance meeting, 215–216
Alcey (slave), 108
Aldermarston antibomb marches, 428
Alger, Horatio, 137
Alternative life styles, 287
Altgeld, John P., 273
Amalgamated Clothing Workers Union, 245, 250 *n.* 2
Amalgamated Street Workers Union, 244
Amalgamated Textile Workers Union, 246
American Anti-Slavery Society, 202
American Association for the United Nations, 373
American Association of University Professors, 450
American Association of University Women, 264, 439, 456
American Birth Control League, 314
American Booksellers Association v. *Hudnut,* 479
American Civil Liberties Union, 275
American Federationist, 240, 241, 242, 245
American Federation of Labor, 237, 240–243, 244–246, 309, 347
American Historical Association, 450
American Home, 330, 342 *n.* 45
Americanization, 144, 247, 261
American Medical Association, 450
American Psychiatric Association, 182
Americans for Democratic Action, 373
American Student Union, 371
American Telephone and Telegraph, 460
American Union Against

Militarism (AUAM), 275, 276, 281, 286
American Youth Congress, 371
Amerindians: in traditional America, 25, 35, 36, 39 *n.* 27, 62, 65 *n.* 40; in industrializing America, 254–257, 270, 476
Anarchism, 275, 285–287, 288, 289
Anderson, Margaret, 282, 288, 292
Anderson, Marian, 371
Anderson, Mary, 244, 249, 368
Andrews, John, 240
Andrews, Steven Pearl, 297
Animism, in nineteenth-century midwest, 118, 129 *n.* 4
Anne, queen of England, 25
Anthony, Susan B., 94, 206, 207, 208, 216–219, 302
Anthropology: and the study of history, 65, 117, 129 *n.* 9, 196; women anthropologists, 17
Antifeminism, 296–297, 456–459; and abortion, 195
Antimilitarist League, 276
Antin, Mary, *The Promised Land,* 258–263
Antinomianism, 52–65
Antislavery movement. *See* Abolition movement
Apprenticeship, 135–136, 138
Architecture, 11, 295, 296, 441
Ariès, Philippe, 329; *Centuries of Childhood,* 134
Aristotle, 12–13
Aristotle's Master Piece, 68, 77 *n.* 18
Armed Services Committees, 495
Arminianism, 54
Arthur, Helen, 282, 284–285
Arthurdale (W.Va.); Resettlement Administration, 370
Ashley, Jessie, 321
Ashworth, Ethel, 353
Ashworth, M.C., 353
Associated Press, 212

511